Designed for students, this detailed analysis of the principal areas of French grammar combines the insights of modern linguistic theory with those of more traditional grammarians. Theory is placed firmly in the service of description and analysis, and students are guided to an understanding of the French language which will complement the information offered by traditional reference grammars. The book includes discussion of verbs and Verb Phrases, voice, tense and mood, the Noun Phrase and pronouns, and variations in sentence-structure. The author pays special attention to those areas of French grammar which pose difficulties for an English-speaking reader. Each chapter is followed by a set of problems and exercises, and by a useful guide to further reading. *Foundations of French Syntax* will appeal to students and teachers of linguistics, French and other Romance languages.

# CAMBRIDGE TEXTBOOKS IN LINGUISTICS

*General Editors*: S. R. ANDERSON, J. BRESNAN, B. COMRIE,
W. DRESSLER, C. EWEN, R. HUDDLESTON, R. LASS, D. LIGHTFOOT,
J. LYONS, P. H. MATTHEWS, R. POSNER, S. ROMAINE, N. V. SMITH,
N. VINCENT

# FOUNDATIONS OF FRENCH SYNTAX

*In this series*

P. H. MATTHEWS *Morphology* Second edition
B. COMRIE *Aspect*
R. M. KEMPSON *Semantic Theory*
T. BYNON *Historical Linguistics*
J. ALLWOOD, L.-G. ANDERSON, Ö. DAHL *Logic in Linguistics*
D. B. FRY *The Physics of Speech*
R. A. HUDSON *Sociolinguistics*
J. K. CHAMBERS and P. TRUDGILL *Dialectology*
A. J. ELLIOT *Child Language*
P. H. MATTHEWS *Syntax*
A. RADFORD *Transformational Syntax*
L. BAUER *English Word-Formation*
S. C. LEVINSON *Pragmatics*
G. BROWN and G. YULE *Discourse Analysis*
R. HUDDLESTON *Introduction to the Grammar of English*
R. LASS *Phonology*
B. COMRIE *Tense*
W. KLEIN *Second Language Acquisition*
A. CRUTTENDEN *Intonation*
A. J. WOODS, P. FLETCHER and A. HUGHES *Statistics in Language Studies*
D. A. CRUSE *Lexical Semantics*
F. R. PALMER *Mood and Modality*
A. RADFORD *Transformational Grammar*
M. GARMAN *Psycholinguistics*
W. CROFT *Typology and Universals*
G. G. CORBETT *Gender*
H. J. GIEGERICH *English Phonology*
R. CANN *Formal Semantics*
P. J. HOPPER and E. C. TRAUGOTT *Grammaticalization*
J. LAVER *Principles of Phonetics*
F. R. PALMER *Grammatical roles and relations*
B. BLAKE *Case*
M. A. JONES *Foundations of French Syntax*

# FOUNDATIONS OF FRENCH SYNTAX

## MICHAEL ALLAN JONES

DEPARTMENT OF LANGUAGE AND LINGUISTICS
UNIVERSITY OF ESSEX

CAMBRIDGE
UNIVERSITY PRESS

Published by the Press Syndicate of the University of Cambridge
The Pitt Building, Trumpington Street, Cambridge CB2 1RP
40 West 20th Street, New York, NY 10011–4211, USA
10 Stamford Road, Oakleigh, Melbourne 3166, Australia

First published 1996

Printed in Great Britain at the University Press, Cambridge

*A catalogue record for this book is available from the British Library*

*Library of Congress cataloging in publication data*

Jones, Michael Allan.
Foundations of French syntax / Michael Allan Jones.
      p.      cm. – (Cambridge textbooks in linguistics)
Includes bibliographical references and index.
ISBN 0 521 38104 5 (hardback). ISBN 0 521 38805 8 (paperback).
1. French language–Syntax. 2. French language–Textbooks for
foreign speakers–English. I. Title. II. Series.
PC2361.J66   1996
448.2′421–dc20   95–44007   CIP

ISBN 0 521 381045 hardback
ISBN 0 521 388058 paperback

SE

*For Enam and Petra*

# CONTENTS

Contents

*Contents*

*Contents*

# PREFACE

This book is an introduction to the study of French grammar intended principally for advanced students (e.g. at university level) and teachers of French. It is particularly appropriate as a textbook for courses which combine the study of French with linguistics, though no prior knowledge of linguistics is assumed. Its main objectives are as follows:

> to give a detailed analysis of the main areas of French grammar, with the aim of explaining facts rather than simply observing them;
>
> to present some of the insights into French syntax which have been brought to light by research in linguistics (particularly within the transformational-generative approach) and to make this research accessible to students of French;
>
> to equip the reader with an analytical framework within which problems of French grammar can be circumscribed and elucidated;
>
> to enable the reader to make more effective use of traditional reference grammars and dictionaries through a clearer understanding of the grammatical system of French;
>
> to promote a view of grammar as an interesting object of inquiry rather than simply a set of rules to be learnt and applied.

This book is not intended as a substitute for reference grammars of a more traditional kind. On the whole, reference grammars are good at compiling detailed, factual information (e.g. conjugation of verbs, plurals of nouns, lists of expressions which take the subjunctive, and so on), assembled under appropriate headings for ease of reference – I have not attempted to duplicate such information here. They are less good at dealing with problems which cannot be solved by direct observation of the facts. In such cases, guidance is often given by means of illustration, which may be helpful at an intuitive level, but which leaves the user to extrapolate from the examples and to work out how the bits of information fit together. It is this aspect of the problem which is addressed in this book. Starting from the assumption that a human language is a system which enables basic meaningful units (e.g. words) to be combined to produce an infinite range of more complex meaningful expressions (e.g. sentences), the objective is to reconstruct the system of French grammar (comparing it with English where appropriate) by taking it apart to see how it works and by investigating the ways in which the different parts of the system interact to produce the patterns observed informally by traditional grammarians.

The analysis presented here follows a transformational-generative approach, roughly along the lines of Chomsky's (1981) 'Government and Binding' model, but with many simplifications. No prior knowledge of this approach is assumed on the part of the reader; the main concepts are explained and illustrated in chapter 1, others are introduced as and when they are relevant. This model is used principally as a way of making sense of the facts and I have adapted it freely to cater for the needs of language students, avoiding issues of a purely theoretical nature. As far as possible the aim is to explain facts, rather than simply describing them, by showing how particular properties of a construction follow from general principles or other aspects of the grammar. Nevertheless, there comes a point where the degree of abstraction required by an explanatory analysis outweighs the usefulness of the explanation itself and in such cases I have settled for a more modest account of the data. It is important to bear in mind that the explanations proposed here (as in all other accounts) do not represent absolute truths; they represent hypotheses (sometimes tentative or controversial ones) about the workings of a system which we cannot observe directly. As such they are open to question in the light of further evidence or advances in our understanding of the nature of human language. It is in this sense that the study of grammar is a continual process of discovery, not only for the language student seeking a clearer understanding at the practical level, but also for linguists and grammarians. Some readers may find this observation disconcerting; others, I hope, will be stimulated by the intellectual challenge which it offers.

A practical difficulty with an approach which treats grammar as an integrated system is that the detailed analysis of one part of the grammar presupposes an understanding of all the other parts. For this reason, there are one or two topics which are dealt with in rather unexpected places (e.g. the syntax of 'body-part' nouns is discussed in the chapter on pronouns, mainly because it involves issues concerning dative and reflexive pronouns). To alleviate this problem, a general outline of some of the main syntactic phenomena of French is presented in chapter 1 as a frame of reference for subsequent discussion of specific topics. This chapter also contains some discussion of wider issues concerning attitudes and approaches to grammar, the limits of regularity and the problem of variation. I have made the core chapters of the book as self-contained as possible (with appropriate cross-references to other chapters) to allow some flexibility over the order in which they are studied. Nevertheless, the sequence of chapters represents a fairly natural progression, working outwards from the verb as the key element in the sentence. The discussion of the verbal system in chapters 2–3 lays the foundations for much of the analysis in subsequent chapters. The analysis of tense, aspect and mood in chapter 4 also concerns the verbal system, though it is less crucial to an understanding of the rest of the book. Chapters 5–6 deal with the principal elements which are linked by the verb (noun phrases and pronouns). The topics discussed in chapters 7–8 relate, in various ways, to both the verbal and nominal systems. The two final chapters are concerned with phenomena which affect the entire clause or sentence: constructions with the infinitive in chapter 9, the syntactic properties of different types of clauses (particularly questions, relative clauses and exclamative sentences) in chapter 10.

At the end of each chapter there is a section consisting of exercises and questions of various sorts, ranging from fairly routine exercises to more open-ended questions and suggestions for project work. Some of these questions relate directly to the content of the chapter whereas others present further data or issues for the reader to investigate or indeed invite the reader to challenge the analyses which have been proposed.

Many of the ideas and analyses put forward in this book have been proposed, in one form or another, by other linguists. What I have tried to do is to synthesise these insights by abstracting away from differences in theoretical approaches, assumptions about structure, etc., and by integrating them with ideas of my own to produce a coherent account of French syntax. Except in a few cases, bibliographical references are not included in the text, but sources are acknowledged with brief comments in the 'Further reading' sections at the end of each chapter, which also give references to other work which may be of interest to the reader. References in these sections are given in author–date format, with full references in the bibliography. In the case of some works which have been published in more than one place (e.g. in translation) I have given cross-references in the bibliography to help readers locate them more easily; however, I have not attempted to do this systematically. References to books which have been re-edited several times (mainly reference grammars) relate to the edition which I consulted, sometimes with further references to more recent editions in the case of books which have been substantially revised.

This book owes a great deal to many people: to Nicolas Ruwet and Richie Kayne who first stimulated my interest in linguistic theory and the syntax of French, and whose inspiring influence has guided this work; to Andrew Radford, Roger Hawkins and John Green for persuading me that this book was worth writing; to numerous French speakers, particularly Corinne Girard and Jacques Durand, who at various stages of this research helped to clarify my understanding of the data; to generations of students at the University of Essex who have worked through earlier versions of this material and who (sometimes unwittingly) have provided valuable feedback. I am particularly grateful to Rebecca Posner for her encouragement and for her detailed comments on successive drafts of this book, especially on matters of presentation where her guidance has been invaluable. I would like to thank the editorial staff at Cambridge University Press for their help and advice through various stages of the production process, particularly Leigh Mueller whose 'eagle eye' at the copy-editing stage saved me from a number of embarrasing errors. I thank all those who have helped me to bring this work to completion, while accepting full responsibility for any errors or shortcomings which remain.

On a more personal note, I would like to thank my parents for their support and their faith in me. One person who deserves a bigger thank-you than I can express in words is my wife Enam, for her encouragement, moral support and, most of all, her love. I would also like to put in a word for our baby daughter Petra just for being there, sometimes for *just* being there, but also for helping me to appreciate that there are more important things in life than writing books on French syntax.

# NOTATIONAL CONVENTIONS

Since this book is intended for advanced students of French, examples are normally given without translations, except for expressions or constructions which may be unfamiliar and other cases where it is useful to highlight the relevant interpretation.

Ungrammatical examples are prefixed by an asterisk (*) whereas fully acceptable examples are given without a prefix. Intermediate degrees of acceptability are signalled by ? (odd), ?? (very odd), *? (even odder) – these judgements are intended as a rough guide and should be taken as relative to other examples within the same discussion. The symbol % is used for examples of Non-standard constructions (usually colloquial) which are not accepted by all speakers, while †indicates constructions which are restricted to an archaic, literary style (e.g. for English: *%I ain't done nothing, †I know not what to do*).

In examples, parentheses are used to indicate elements which are optional: e.g. *John is (very) tall.* When an asterisk (or other symbol) occurs within the parentheses, this means that the example is ungrammatical if the item is included, e.g. *John is (*much) tall.* Conversely, an asterisk outside the parentheses indicates that the example is ungrammatical without this item: e.g. *John loves Mary *(very) much* (i.e. *John loves Mary very much* is fine but *John loves Mary much* is unacceptable). Curved braces are used to indicate possible alternative expressions within an example. When these are displayed horizontally, alternatives are separated by oblique strokes: e.g. *John is {very / rather / *much} tall* indicates that the sentence is acceptable with *very* or *rather*, but not with *much*. Sometimes, for greater clarity, alternatives are displayed vertically:

$$
\text{John is } \begin{Bmatrix} \text{very} \\ \text{rather} \\ \text{*much} \end{Bmatrix} \text{ tall}
$$

The same conventions are used in the formulation of rules which specify what a particular type of phrase can consist of. For example, rule (a) below states that an Adjective Phrase (AP) can consist of an adjective optionally preceded by a degree modifier (like *very*) while rule (b) states that a Noun Phrase can consist of a determiner (a word like *the*) followed by a noun, or of a proper noun (a name such as *John*) on its own:

(a)  $AP \rightarrow (Deg) + A$

(b)  $NP \rightarrow \begin{cases} D+N \\ N_{PROPER} \end{cases}$

The following symbols are used in rules and representations (references in parentheses indicate the sections in which less familiar concepts are introduced).

| | |
|---|---|
| $\rightarrow$ | 'consists of' (1.1.3); also used in representations of tense to indicate 'occurs before' (4.2.2) |
| $\subset$ | 'is included in' (in representations of tense) (4.2.2) |
| $\Rightarrow$ | 'is transformed into' (1.5.7) |
| $\varnothing$ | Empty syntactic position (1.5.3) |
| __ | 'trace' (position from which an element is moved) (1.5.7) |
| A | Adjective |
| ACC | Accusative Case |
| Adv | Adverb |
| Agr | Agreement (1.4.3) |
| Aux | Auxiliary |
| C | Complementiser (1.3.1) |
| CONJ | Conjunction |
| D | Determiner (1.1.2) |
| DAT | Dative Case |
| Deg | Degree item (1.1.3) |
| E | Event-time (4.2.2) |
| I | Inflection (1.4.3) |
| Inf | Infinitive |
| N | Noun |
| NOM | Nominative Case |
| P | Preposition; also Phrase (e.g. NP = Noun Phrase, VP = Verb Phrase, etc.) |
| PRO | Implicit subject of infinitive (9.2.1) |
| R | Reference-time (4.2.2) |
| S | Sentence; also 'moment of speech' in discussions of tense (4.2.2) |
| SC | 'Small clause' (2.5.2) |
| SG | Singular |
| Spec | Specifier position (1.4.2) |
| V | Verb |

# 1
# Introduction

## 1.1 Some basic syntactic patterns

### 1.1.1 Do human languages have a syntax?

The syntax of a language is the system which determines the possible ways in which words can be combined to produce valid sentences. Our task is to investigate, in a methodical way, the syntactic system of French, to discover and make explicit the rules and principles which enable native speakers of French to formulate and comprehend the full range of sentences of their language, a system which we, as non-native speakers, possess only to a partial extent.

But does such a system really exist? As learners of French, we are painfully aware of aspects of the language which seem strange, illogical or unsystematic. Even in our own language, we may be baffled by apparently simple questions. If a learner of English asks us why we must say (1a) and not (1b), our best response may be simply that (1b) 'sounds funny', and the response of a native speaker of French regarding the opposite facts in (2) is likely to be the same:

(1)  a  That boy often watches that programme
     b  *That boy watches often that programme
(2)  a  *Ce garçon souvent regarde cette émission
     b  Ce garçon regarde souvent cette émission

Moreover, rather than admit ignorance about our own language, we may be tempted to conclude that there is nothing to explain: languages are inherently mysterious, our judgements about what we can or cannot say are based on familiarity not on rules, and so on.

This is a very defeatist conclusion. In other fields of inquiry, we do not give up just because solutions to problems are not immediately obvious. Also it is of no help to the language-learner who is anxious to avoid errors like (1b) and (2a). A more constructive response is to conclude that native speakers are not conscious of the system which underlies their language. In order to explain examples like (1) and (2) we must reconstruct this system, by analysing samples of the language and trying to fit them into a coherent general model. Only in this way can

1

we arrive at an informed answer to the general question raised above. Similarly, it is only by searching for regularities that we can identify those aspects of language which are truly idiosyncratic and which must be simply 'learnt'. Nevertheless, there are also some *a priori* reasons for supposing that human languages are fundamentally regular systems. In the following sections, we shall outline some of these reasons as a way of introducing some of the basic properties of the language system.

### 1.1.2 Word classes

You are unlikely to have encountered either of the sequences in (3) below, but you should be able to recognise (3a) as a valid sentence of French, and to interpret it if you know the meanings of all the words (*caribou* is a Canadian reindeer), while (3b) is gibberish:

(3)     a   Le caribou dévorait une pizza
        b   *Pizza caribou le dévorait une

Your ability to make this distinction must be based on something more abstract than mere familiarity with these examples – if you have never encountered them before, they should be equally unfamiliar, therefore equally invalid according to the 'defeatist' view envisaged in 1.1.1.

Here, you might object that, although you have not encountered (3a) before, you have come across similar sentences, like (4a), but you have never heard anything resembling (3b) or (4b):

(4)     a   Le garçon mangeait une pomme
        b   *Pomme garçon le mangeait une

To this extent, (3a) is more familiar than (3b) in that it it conforms to a familiar pattern – it is just the particular combination of words that is novel.

This observation leads us to a language-system of sorts; let us call it the **category-sequence** model. Somehow, we are able to perceive that *caribou* and *garçon*, *pizza* and *pomme* are words of the same type – they belong to the same **word class** (or **lexical category**), traditionally called **nouns**. Similarly, *dévorait* and *mangeait* belong to a different class (**verbs**, or rather forms of verbs) and *la* and *une* belong to a category which will be called **determiners** (sometimes called 'articles'). Thus, on encountering sentences like (4a) we can deduce that the sequence of categories in (5) constitutes a valid sentence pattern in French (and indeed English) which we can use as a template for forming novel sentences like (3a) by inserting different words of the appropriate categories:

(5)         D + N + V + D + N

Obviously the formula in (5) is not a complete grammar of French, but we might suppose that we could arrive at a complete grammar by pursuing the procedure sketched above – each time a new sequence of categories is encountered, it is entered in the grammar as a further formula for constructing sentences until, eventually, all the possible category-sequences which constitute valid sentences have been listed.

This model amounts to little more than a formalisation of the 'defeatist' view envisaged in 1.1.1. For example, the intuition that (2a) above 'sounds funny' in French while (2b) is fine can now be attributed to the fact that category-sequences of the type (6a) are regularly encountered in French (where *souvent* belongs to the class of **adverbs** and *ce(tte)* is a determiner) and are therefore familiar, whereas the sequence in (6b) never occurs:

(6)      a   D + N + V + Adv + D + N

         b   *D + N + Adv + V + D + N

However, this account scarcely constitutes an explanation, it merely states an observation. Moreover, the information encoded in (6) does not predict the contrast in (7), where we have added an **adjective** (*intelligent*) before the first noun:

(7)      a   *Ce garçon intelligent souvent regarde cette émission

         b   Ce garçon intelligent regarde souvent cette émission

According to the category-sequence account, we would need to be familiar with sequences of the type (8a) but not with those of type (8b):

(8)      a   D + N + A + V + Adv + D + N

         b   *D + N + A + Adv + V + D + N

This seems wrong. Intuitively, once we know that (2a) is ungrammatical and (2b) is fine, we ought to be able to deduce the position of the adverb in (7) without direct experience of sentences which conform exactly to the category-sequences in (8).

### 1.1.3 Phrase structure

The main problem with the category-sequence model is that it does not recognise that there are groups of words within a sentence which belong together in some sense. In the sentences considered above, it seems clear that the sequence of a determiner and a noun (e.g. *ce garçon* in (2), *une pizza* in (3)) forms a unit, in contrast to other adjacent pairs such as N + V (*garçon mangeait*) or V + D (*mangeait une*). Let us call this unit a **Noun Phrase** (**NP**). Similarly, if we place a **degree item** like *très* in before the adjective in (7b), as in (9), it seems clear that this item goes with the adjective, forming an **Adjective Phrase** (**AP**):

(9)     Ce garçon très intelligent regarde souvent cette émission

Moreover, in examples like (9) the AP appears to form part of the NP; e.g. *(très) intelligent* goes with *garçon* rather than with the following verb *regarde.*

By postulating **phrasal categories** like NP or AP as well as lexical categories, we can arrive at a partial solution to problems of the sort raised at the end of 1.1.2. Roughly, in French, adverbs cannot be inserted between the first NP and the following verb but they can be inserted between the verb and the NP which follows it (vice versa for English), regardless of the internal composition of the NPs (e.g. whether they contain an adjective or not):

(10)     a   NP + Adv + V + NP  (English, but not French)
         b   NP + V + Adv + NP  (French, but not English)

There are further complications regarding the position of adverbs which will be addressed briefly in 1.4.3 and in greater detail in 7.5.

Having established the existence of phrasal categories, we must define their content. This can be achieved by means of **phrase-structure rules**, like those in (11), where the sequence of elements to the right of the arrow defines what the phrasal category on the left can consist of, elements in parentheses being optional:

(11)     a   NP → D + N + (AP)
         b   AP → (Deg) + A

Similarly, having defined the internal structure of the NP, we can use this phrasal category to define the sentence pattern of the examples given so far (ignoring adverbs for the moment) as in (12), where S = sentence:

(12)     S → NP + V + NP

The rules in (11)–(12) are intended as illustrations rather than accurate descriptions and will be modified as the discussion proceeds.

Rule (12) defines a sentence pattern which can be represented by the **tree structure** (13):

(13)

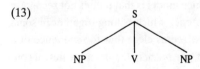

The phrasal category NP can now be expanded by applying rule (11) to give the full structure (14), where dotted branches and parentheses indicate optional elements:

(14)

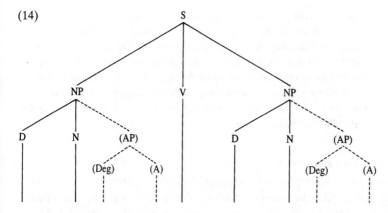

Actual sentences can be created by inserting words of the appropriate category on the branches labelled D, N, V, Deg and A.

The principal difference between the **phrase-structure** model outlined above and the category-sequence model is that the former is modular; each phrasal category is defined independently of the others and independently of the sentence as a whole.

A practical advantage of this model is that the grammar can be modified 'bit-by-bit' to accommodate new patterns. To illustrate, instead of using an NP of the form D + N + (AP) we can often use a **proper noun** (i.e. a name) like *Pierre* or a **pronoun** such as *cela*. To account for these possibilities we can simply modify rule (11a) as in (15), where the curved brace indicate alternative expansions, leaving the rest of the grammar intact:

(15)

$$NP \rightarrow \begin{cases} D + N + (AP) \\ N_{PROPER} \\ Pronoun \end{cases}$$

Since proper nouns and pronouns are defined as possible manifestations of the category NP, a sentence like *Pierre mangeait cela* conforms to the rule in (12). This modular approach also makes the important (and essentially correct) prediction that the possible manifestations of a particular phrasal category (e.g. NP) will be the same regardless of the position of the phrase within the sentence (e.g. before or after the verb in the above examples). Under the linear model, such similarities are purely accidental – e.g. it would be perfectly possible to describe a hypothetical language which allowed sentences of the form $N_{PROPER} + V + D + N$ and $D + N + V + N_{PROPER}$ but not, say, $N_{PROPER} + V + N_{PROPER}$. To this extent, the phrase-structure model goes some way towards explaining a fundamental property of natural languages as well as describing the facts of a particular language.

5

Note that rule (15) analyses items like *Pierre* and *cela* not only as single words but also as phrases (NPs). Similarly, according to rule (11b) an adjective occurring on its own constitutes an AP. This conflicts with the more usual concept of a phrase as an expression consisting of more than one word. In the framework adopted here, a more appropriate way of construing a 'phrase' is as an expression consisting of a key word (e.g. the noun in an NP, the adjective in an AP) and any elements (possibly none at all) which go with it.

### *1.1.4  Verb Phrases*

Most linguists would dispute the analysis of the sentence presented in (12)–(13), claiming instead that the second NP goes with the verb to form a **Verb Phrase (VP)**. Consider the following example containing an **Adverb Phrase (AdvP)** consisting of a manner adverb (*lentement*) optionally preceded by a degree item:

(16)        Ce garçon mangeait une pizza (très) lentement

In (16) the AdvP describes the action denoted by the verb *mangeait* in much the same way as the AP *très intelligent* describes the boy in (9). A natural way of representing this relation is to assume that the AdvP is part of the VP, just as the AP *(très) intelligent* is part of the NP. However, this only makes sense if the intervening NP *(une pizza)* is also part of the VP. Thus, our earlier rule (12) expanding S can be replaced by the rules in (17)–(18):

(17)        S → NP + VP

(18)        VP → V + NP + (AdvP)

The structure of (16) can be represented as in (19):

(19)

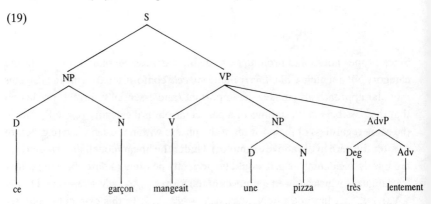

The examples in (20) provide further evidence for the category VP, as well as illustrating an important condition on syntactic structure:

(20)     a   Ce garçon mangeait une pizza lentement hier
         b   ??Ce garçon mangeait une pizza hier lentement

**Time adverbs** like *hier* modify the whole sentence rather than simply the verb and thus form part of the S rather than the VP, as shown in (21) for example (20a):

(21)

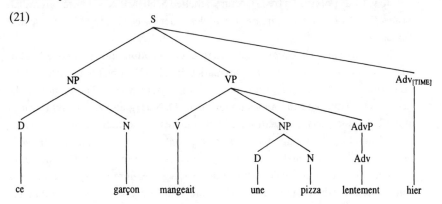

Given our assumption that *hier* forms part of the S whereas *lentement* belongs to the VP, we cannot draw a tree structure for (20b) without making the branches of the tree cross:

(22)

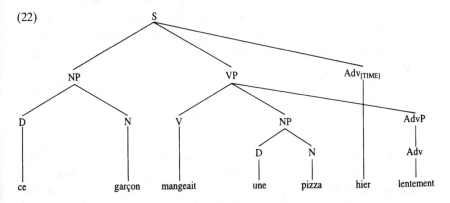

Thus, example (20b) can be excluded by the following condition on syntactic structure:

**The 'no-crossing constraint':** *The branches of a tree cannot cross.*

Note that this account depends crucially on the assumption that *mangeait une pizza lentement* forms a phrasal category VP.

### 1.1.5 Some terminology

Before proceeding further, it may be helpful to introduce some technical terminology and other notational devices which will be used in subsequent discussion.

The various points in a tree structure, labelled S, NP, VP, N, V, D, etc., are called **nodes**. S, NP, VP, AdvP, etc. are **phrasal nodes**, whereas N, V, Adv, D, etc. are **lexical nodes**.

The basic relation between nodes of a tree is that of **dominance**. A node X dominates a node Y if there is a downward path from X to Y along the branches of the tree. Thus, in structure (19), S dominates all the other nodes; VP dominates V, the second NP, AdvP, and the nodes under them (D, N Deg and Adv), and so on. A node X **immediately dominates** Y if X dominates Y and there is no intervening node. Thus, in (19), S immediately dominates only the first NP and the VP while VP immediately dominates only V, the second NP and the AdvP. Kinship terms are sometimes used to describe such relations; e.g. if X immediately dominates Y and Z, then X is the **mother** of Y and Z, while Y and Z are **sisters** of each other and **daughters** of X. Thus, in (19) NP is the mother of D and N, D is a sister of N (and vice versa) and D and N are daughters of NP.

In phrasal categories, the lexical node which determines the category of the phrase is the **head** of the phrase and, conversely, the phrase is a **projection** of the lexical category (e.g. N is the head of NP, and NP is a projection of N – for the purposes of this definition, pronouns and proper nouns introduced by the rule in (15) can be treated as subclasses of nouns). According to the rules we have proposed, S differs from other phrasal categories in that it does not have a clearly identifiable head and is not therefore a projection of any category – we shall return to this matter in 1.3.

A sequence of words is a **constituent** if there is a node which dominates the whole sequence but does not dominate anything else. Thus, in (19) *ce garçon* is a constituent (dominated by NP) as is *mangeait une pizza lentement* (dominated by VP), but *ce garçon mangeait* is not, because the only node which dominates the whole sequence is S, but S also dominates other elements which are not part of this sequence. Similarly, according to (19), *mangeait une pizza* is not a constituent either (though it probably should be, see 1.4.2 below), because the lowest node which dominates this sequence (VP) also dominates *lentement*. A constituent is said to be an **immedient constituent** of X if the node which defines it as a constituent is immediately dominated by X; e.g. the NP *ce garçon* and the VP *mangeait une pizza très lentement* are immediate constituents of S (because the NP and VP nodes are immediately dominated by S), whereas the NP *une pizza* is an immediate constituent of VP.

In example sentences, square brackets will sometimes be used to indicate constituents, with the category label subscripted to the opening bracket. Thus the immediate constituents of S in (19) can be represented as in (23):

(23)    [$_S$ [$_{NP}$ ce garçon] [$_{VP}$ mangeait une pizza très lentement]]

We can use this notation to represent all the constituents in (19), as in (24):

(24)    [$_S$ [$_{NP}$ [$_D$ ce][$_N$ garçon]] [$_{VP}$ [$_V$ mangeait][$_{NP}$ [$_D$ une][$_N$ pizza]] [$_{AdvP}$ [$_{Deg}$ très] [$_{Adv}$ lentement]]]]

The bracketted representation in (24) is equivalent to the tree structure in (19). Bracketted representations are more difficult to read than trees, but they take up less space and are useful when only a partial structural analysis is required (as in (23)). Partial analyses can also be represented in tree diagrams by using a triangle (instead of a branching structure) over the constituent which is left unanalysed; e.g. the tree in (25) is equivalent to the bracketted representation (23):

(25)

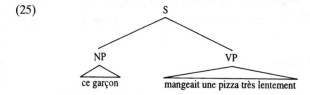

## 1.2    Grammatical relations

### 1.2.1    Subjects and objects

The division of the sentence into its immediate constituents illustrated in (23) and (25) and defined by rule (17) (S → NP + VP) corresponds closely to the traditional partition of the sentence into a **subject** and a **predicate**, as in (26):

(26)    | Ce garçon | mangeait une pizza lentement |
        | SUBJECT | PREDICATE |

The traditional concept 'predicate' can be equated with the phrasal category VP. However, we cannot simply equate 'subject' with NP, since *une pizza* in our example is an NP, but not a subject. Unfortunately, in traditional grammar the term 'subject' is sometimes used rather vaguely to encompass a range of notions which do not always coincide (e.g. 'the performer of the action' or 'the entity about which something is asserted') – more will be said about this in due course. Within the phrase-structure framework we can define the 'core' concept of a subject as the NP which is immediately dominated by S and which is the sister (to the left) of VP.

The category 'subject' is qualitatively different from phrasal categories of the sort presented so far (e.g. NP, AP, VP, . . .). Whereas phrasal categories are defined by their internal composition, principally the word class of the head (e.g. the noun in an NP), a subject is defined in terms of its external relation to other components of the sentence. Consequently, 'subject' will be referred to as a **relational category**.

Another relational category is the **direct object**, represented by *une pizza* in our example. In terms of the structures which have been proposed, the direct object can be defined (provisionally) as the NP which is a sister (to the right) of V and is immediately dominated by VP.

Subjects and direct objects express what linguists sometimes call **argument** relations. The term 'argument' is not widely used in traditional grammar, but is borrowed from formal logic. It denotes a useful and intuitively simple concept, which can best be explained by example. By virtue of its meaning, the verb *manger* involves two participants: an 'eater' and 'something which is eaten', represented respectively by the subject and the direct object. The expressions which identify these participants are the 'arguments' of the verb. Thus, *manger* can be classified as a verb which has two arguments. In contrast, a verb like *dormir* in (27) involves only one participant (the 'sleeper') and thus has only one argument (represented by the subject):

(27)     Le garçon dormait

An example of a verb with three arguments is *donner* in (28), which describes a relation between three participants (the 'giver', the 'gift' and the 'receiver'); the NP *son professeur* represents a further relational category, traditionally called the **indirect object**, which will be discussed in 1.2.2:

(28)     Le garçon donnait une pomme à son professeur

The arguments of a verb can be divided into two types according to their position. Direct objects (and indeed indirect objects) are classified as **internal arguments** in the sense that they occur within the VP, whereas the subject of a sentence is the **external argument** of the verb (occurring outside the VP). A more traditional term for 'internal argument' is **complement.** Thus, direct (and indirect) objects are complements of the verb.

### 1.2.2.  Complements and modifiers
AdvPs like (*très*) *lentement* in (16) and the AP *très intelligent* in *un garçon très intelligent* represent a further relational category of **modifiers**. Unlike complements, they do not identify a participant in the relation but they describe a property of the action denoted by the verb or the entity denoted by the noun. Other phrasal categories can function as modifiers, as in (29) where the modifying expression is a **Preposition Phrase (PP)** consisting of a **preposition** (*à* in (29a) *avec* in (29b)) and an NP:

(29)     a   [$_S$ [$_{NP}$ le garçon [$_{PP}$ aux cheveux longs]] [$_{VP}$ mangeait une pizza]]
         b   [$_S$ [$_{NP}$ ce garçon] [$_{VP}$ mangeait une pizza [$_{PP}$ avec une fourchette]]]

In (29a) the PP describes a property of the boy, in much the same way as an AP, while in (29b) the PP describes the manner of the action denoted by the verb, like the AdvP (*très*) *lentement* in (16).

A problem with PPs is that they can also function as complements, as in (28) above where *à son professeur* is a PP which functions as a complement (indirect object) of *donner*, and in (30) where the PP *sur la table* is a complement of *mettre*:

(30)     Pierre a mis le livre sur la table

The reason for analysing the PPs in (28) and (30) as complements is that they denote entities which are implicit in the meaning of the verb; for example, the meaning of *donner* implies the existence of a receiver and that of *mettre* implies a place to which something is moved. On the other hand, the meaning of *manger* in (29) does not necessarily involve an instrument – the phrase *avec une fourchette* provides extra information about the way in which the action was performed rather than specifying a participant involved in the meaning of the verb. Typically, though not always, PPs which act as complements of verbs are obligatory (e.g. we cannot easily omit the PPs in (28) and (30)) whereas PPs which function as modifiers can be omitted freely without affecting the acceptability of the sentence.

The distinction between modifiers and complements also arises with PPs contained in an NP – these cases will be discussed in 1.2.7.

The rule VP → V + NP + (AdvP) proposed in 1.1.4 needs to be revised to accommodate some of our subsequent examples. For example, we need to include PP as a possible constituent of VP. On the other hand, examples like (27) (*Le garçon dormait*) show that a VP need not contain an NP. Accordingly, let us modify the rule for VP as in (31), where all constituents other than V are specified as optional:

(31)     VP → V + (NP) + (PP) + (AdvP)

This formulation raises a problem which is relevant to the above discussion. AdvPs (and PPs which act as modifiers) are genuinely optional – we can include or omit them freely. However, the presence or absence of an NP (or complement PP) is determined by the choice of verb: *dévorer* requires an NP (\**Le caribou dévorait*) whereas *dormir* does not allow one (\**Le garçon dormait {Pierre / une pizza / la sincérité}*). We can think of phrase-structure rules like (31) as offering a 'menu' of phrasal categories which can potentially accompany the verb (or any other head) but (as far as complements are concerned) particular verbs **select** certain elements, but not others, from this menu. More generally, the grammatical system which defines the set of possible phrases and sentences in a language involves interaction between two components: the syntax proper (e.g. phrase-structure rules) which defines the composition of expressions in terms of categories, and the **lexicon** (or 'mental dictionary') which provides information about the properties of individual words, including their meaning, their form and the types of complement (if any) which they select.

### 1.2.3  Transitivity

In dictionaries and reference grammars, verbs like *dévorer* which require a direct object are classified as **transitive** verbs whereas verbs like *dormir* which do not take a direct object are classified as **intransitive**. In this book, the term 'intransitive' will also be used for verbs like *plaire* which take an indirect object:

(32)      Ce film plaisait à Luc

There is some variation among grammars and dictionaries concerning the use of these terms, and others, to define the syntactic properties of verbs. Consequently, it is important to check how these terms are used when consulting such reference sources.

As long as they are used clearly and consistently, the terms 'transitive' and 'intransitive' are quite handy. However, most linguists prefer a more explicit system of representation which specifies the types of complement which a given verb can take in terms of their category (NP, PP, etc.), whether they are obligatory or optional and, in the case of indirect objects, the appropriate preposition (e.g. *à* with *donner*, *de* with *dépendre*, etc.). A system of this type will be presented in 1.2.5.

### 1.2.4  Theta-roles

Often, terms like 'subject' and '(direct) object' are used rather vaguely to denote both **grammatical relations** (definable in terms of structural positions) and the semantic relations which are typically associated with them (e.g. 'performer of the action', 'entity which undergoes the action'). However, it is sensible to keep these two types of relation separate – only in this way can we investigate any correspondences which may exist between the two – e.g. the extent to which the grammatical relation 'subject' corresponds to the semantic relation 'performer of the action'.

Following the usage of many modern linguists, the term **theta-role** will be used to refer to semantic relations between an argument and the verb (or other item) with which it is associated. Theta-roles are indicated by labels such as **Agent** (the performer of the action), **Experiencer**, **Location**, **Goal** (the place to which something moves), **Source** (the place from which something moves), **Possessor**,

**Receiver**, etc. There is no clear consensus among linguists as to how many theta-roles should be distinguished and there is some variation in the way in which particular labels are used. For present purposes, these labels can be viewed as heuristic characterisations of the ways in which a participant is involved in the situation described by the sentence and the choice of labels will be determined to some extent by the degree of 'fineness' appropriate to the task in hand.

On the whole, these labels should be fairly self-explanatory, at least in context. However, there is one theta-role which requires some comment, namely **Theme**. This term is commonly used for a variety of semantic relations ranging from the entity which undergoes the action or change of state (e.g. the direct object of *manger* or the subject of *tomber*), sometimes called a 'Patient', through to more inert relations such as the object of perception, belief, desire, etc. (e.g. the direct objects of verbs like *voir, admirer, connaître, vouloir*, etc.). To some extent, Theme can be considered as a sort of default label or cover term for semantic relations which do not readily fit into more easily definable categories such as those listed above.

### 1.2.5  Lexical entries

Dictionaries provide information of various sorts about particular words: their meaning, their syntactic category (noun, verb, etc.), other grammatical properties (e.g. transitive vs intransitive verbs, gender of nouns, etc.), morphological peculiarities (e.g. tense forms of irregular verbs), the register in which they are used (e.g. colloquial vs literary), their etymology and so on. For syntactic purposes, a fairly crude characterisation of meaning is sufficient (e.g. in terms of theta-roles) but we need precise information about the grammatical properties of words. To illustrate, there may be subtle semantic differences between the verbs *aimer* and *plaire* in (33), but both verbs express a relation between an Experiencer (Marie) and a Theme (the boy):

(33)     a   Marie aime ce garçon
         b   Ce garçon plaît à Marie

The crucial syntactic difference between these two verbs concerns the way in which these theta-roles are encoded by means of grammatical relations: with *aimer* the Experiencer is expressed by the subject and the Theme by the direct object, while with *plaire* the subject represents the Theme and the Experiencer is expressed as an indirect object. This information can be summarised by **lexical entries** like (34) and (35):

(34)        *aimer*: V      [Experiencer, Theme]
                            Theme = NP

(35)      *plaire*: V      [Theme, Experiencer]

Experiencer = [$_{PP}$ à NP]

The first line of each entry specifies the word-class (verb) and the part in square brackets (the **theta-grid**) identifies the arguments of the verb according to their theta-roles. By convention, the external argument (the subject) is indicated by underlining, while the statements underneath specify the phrasal category of the internal argument (complement) along with further information such as the choice of preposition where appropriate.

### 1.2.6   Complements of adjectives

Verbs are not the only items which can take complements. For example, a relation very similar to that expressed by *aimer* in (33a) above can be described by the adjective *amoureux*, as in (36):

(36)      Marie est amoureuse de ce garçon

This similarity can be captured by formulating the lexical entry for *amoureux* as in (37):

(37)      *amoureux*: A      [Experiencer, Theme]

(Theme = [$_{PP}$ de NP])

In (36), the Experiencer (*Marie*) is the subject of the sentence, immediately dominated by S, and is therefore external to the AP, as specified by the underlining in (37). On the other hand, the Theme appears as a PP complement of the adjective, with *de* as the preposition – the parentheses around this part of the entry indicate that the Theme can remain unspecified (*Marie est amoureuse*), though it cannot be omitted with *aimer*.

The fact that the complement of *amoureux* is a PP, even though the same role is expressed by a direct object with the corresponding verb, reflects a general property of adjectives. There are no adjectives in French (or indeed English) which take an NP as their complement; i.e. adjectives cannot have direct objects. In cases like the above, *de* can be seen as a meaningless preposition which serves to create an acceptable complement type (PP) for adjectives. Accordingly, the phrase-structure rule for AP can be revised to include PP as in (38):

(38)      AP → (Deg) + A + (PP)

A sample of other adjectives which can take PP complements is given in (39):

(39)      a   Jules est {content / fier / soucieux} de son travail
          b   La bouteille est pleine d'eau

   c   Cette voiture est {semblable / identique} à la mienne

   d   Monique est très fâchée contre Patrick

Adjectives which do not describe a relation between entities, but simply describe a property, do not allow complements: e.g. *rouge, long, rond, barbu, imaginaire* and countless others. Adjectives like these can be classified as having only one argument (e.g. a Theme) which is therefore the external argument. Thus, we can formulate the entry (40) for *rouge* in a sentence like *Cette voiture est rouge*:

(40)       *rouge*: A      [<u>Theme</u>]

Entries like (37) and (40) will also work for cases where the AP functions as a modifier within an NP; e.g. *une voiture rouge, une fille amoureuse de Gaston*. In these constructions, the Theme of *rouge* and the Experiencer of *amoureux* is the noun which is modified (or, perhaps more accurately, the whole NP). However, since the N or NP is outside the AP, it qualifies as an external argument.

### 1.2.7 Complements of nouns

Many nouns can take complements. Perhaps the clearest examples are nouns (usually derived from verbs) which denote events, processes or states, like those in (41) where for comparison analogous sentences are given in parentheses:

(41)      a   la démolition de cet immeuble   (On démolit cet immeuble)

          b   la découverte de l'Amérique    (On découvre l'Amérique)

          c   l'évolution de la situation      (La situation évolue)

          d   la réponse à la question       (On répond à la question)

          e   la lutte contre la pollution      (On lutte contre la pollution)

Like adjectives, nouns cannot take direct object NPs. Typically, as in (41a–c), when the complement of the noun corresponds to the direct object or subject of a verb, it is introduced by *de*. Other types of noun which often take complements are **agent nouns** (which define an entity in terms of an activity) like *professeur* or *inventeur*, **kinship nouns** like *frère* and nouns which describe a part–whole relation such as *sommet*:

(42)      a   un professeur de français

          b   l'inventeur de cette machine

          c   le frère de Jules

          d   le sommet de la montagne

Formulating lexical entries for nouns like the above raises some problems which will not be explored here, particularly in cases like (42a, b) where the noun itself stands for one of the arguments in the relevant relation – e.g. an *inventeur* is the

Agent of an 'inventing' relation. The important point here is that the PPs in (41)–(42) correspond to participants in a relation which is implicit in the meaning of the noun, in contrast to PPs which act as modifiers of the noun, as in *le garçon aux cheveux longs* (see 1.2.2) or *l'homme avec un parapluie*.

### 1.2.8 Prepositions and their complements

In the preceding sections, we have discussed PPs as complements or modifiers of other categories. However, PPs have an internal structure (defined by the rule PP → P + NP) consisting of what looks like a head (P) and its complement (NP). In many cases, particularly with prepositions like *de* and *à*, the theta-role of the complement is determined not by the preposition itself, but by the item which selects the PP. For example, in (33b) (*Ce garçon plaît à Marie*), it is the meaning of *plaire* rather than *à* which gives *Marie* an Experiencer interpretation. This situation can be characterised by saying that, in purely structural terms, *Marie* is a complement of the preposition but from a semantic point of view it is an argument of the verb. The semantic interaction between prepositions and other elements in the sentence will be discussed in detail in chapter 8.

In terms of the categories which they can select as complements, prepositions resemble verbs rather than adjectives or nouns. In particular, they can take NPs as in all the examples so far. Indeed, prepositions are often thought of exclusively as items which are placed before NPs. Whether prepositions can also select other categories depends on assumptions about what counts as a preposition. Pending a more detailed discussion of this question in chapter 8, let us suggest that items like *près* and *hors* can be plausibly analysed as prepositions which select a PP complement, with structures like those in (43):

(43)     a    [$_{PP}$ près [$_{PP}$ de [$_{NP}$ Paris]]]
         b    [$_{PP}$ hors [$_{PP}$ de [$_{NP}$ la maison]]]

Similarly, *dessus* in (44) can plausibly be analysed as a preposition which takes no complement at all:

(44)     Pierre est monté dessus

To accommodate such cases, we can revise our phrase-structure rule for PPs as in (45):

(45)     PP → P + (NP) + (PP)

It is not clear whether there are any prepositions which take both an NP and a PP, though (45) allows for this possibility. A plausible case might be *de Londres à Paris* if this is analysed as a single constituent (with the structure [$_{PP}$ de [$_{NP}$ Londres] [$_{PP}$ à Paris]]), but this analysis is debatable. This question will be left open.

## 1.3 Clauses

### *1.3.1 Complement clauses*

In the preceding sections, we concentrated on complements which are projections of lexical categories (principally NPs and PPs). Complete sentences can also occur as complements of verbs, adjectives, nouns and prepositions, as indicated in (46):

(46)     a   Pierre [$_{VP}$ croit que [$_S$ Jean aime Marie]]

          b   Jules est [$_{AP}$ certain que [$_S$ le train arrivera à l'heure]]

          c   [$_{NP}$ Le fait que [$_S$ Luc est parti]] est intéressant

          d   Les élèves dormaient [$_{PP}$ pendant que [$_S$ le professeur parlait]]

When sentences are considered as constituents, they are usually referred to as **clauses**. Thus, each of the sentences in (46) consists of two clauses, one of which is contained (or **embedded**) in the other. The whole sentence is the **main clause** (sometimes called a 'matrix' clause) while the embedded sentences (enclosed in the brackets labelled S) are called **subordinate clauses**.

The subordinate clauses in (46) are quite clearly sentences, since they can be used as sentences in their own right. In some cases, a special form (or **mood**) of the verb is required in the subordinate clause, as in (47) where we have the **subjunctive** form as opposed to the **indicative** in (46) (see 4.9 for discussion):

(47)     a   Pierre [$_{VP}$ veut que [$_S$ Gaston écrive la lettre]]

          b   Jules est [$_{AP}$ content que [$_S$ le train soit arrivé]]

          c   [$_{NP}$ La possibilité que [$_S$ Suzy soit malade]] est inquiétante

          d   Lucien travaille [$_{PP}$ pour que [$_S$ sa famille soit confortable]]

Since the subjunctive cannot normally be used in main clauses, the sequences labelled S in (47) cannot be used as sentences in their own right, but they clearly have the same structure as ordinary sentences (e.g. *Gaston écrit la lettre*, *Le train est arrivé*, etc.) and so can be reasonably analysed as instances of the category S.

All the subordinate clauses in (46) and (47) are introduced by the item *que*. Unlike its English counterpart, *that*, which can often be omitted (e.g. *Peter thinks (that) John loves Mary*), *que* is obligatory (except in a few special cases which will be discussed in 8.3.4; see also 10.5): *\*Pierre croit Jean aime Marie*. Traditionally, *que* is classified as a **subordinating conjunction** (along with various other items which can be more plausibly analysed as prepositions – see 8.3.2), but most modern linguists prefer the term **complementiser** (abbreviated as C or COMP) – i.e. an item which introduces a complement clause. Another example of a complementiser is *si*, used to introduce indirect questions as in (48):

(48)     Gaston demande si [$_S$ le train arrivera à l'heure]

Complementisers form a constituent with the following S. This constituent is labelled as S′ (or S̄, read as 'S-bar') and can be defined by the phrase-structure rule (49) – for an alternative, more recent analysis, see 1.4.3:

(49)      S′ → C + S

### 1.3.2   Infinitival clauses

Subjunctive and indicative forms are referred to as **finite** verb forms, and the clauses which contain them are finite clauses, in contrast to non-finite or **infinitive** forms (with the endings *-er, -ir, -re* or *-oir*). Like finite clauses, expressions with the infinitive can occur as complements of verbs, adjectives, nouns and prepositions:

(50)      a   Nathalie [$_{VP}$ aime [danser avec Paul]]
          b   Jules est [$_{AP}$ capable de [résoudre ce problème]]
          c   Le gouvernement reconnaît [$_{NP}$ la nécessité de [réduire les impôts]]
          d   Robert est parti [$_{PP}$ sans [fermer la porte]]

Infinitives do not normally allow the subject to be expressed, but in other respects they resemble clauses. We therefore assume that the unlabelled bracketted expressions in (50) are dominated by the S node (see chapter 9). This accords with traditional terminology whereby such expressions are referred to as 'infinitival clauses'.

Infinitival clauses are often introduced by the items *de* or *à*, which in most contexts are classified as prepositions. However, there are some cases where it seems appropriate to treat these items as complementisers, analogous to *que* in finite clauses, introduced under S′ by the rule in (49); see 2.3.5 and 9.5.1.

### 1.3.3   Recursion

We saw in 1.3.1 that a sentence can have another sentence (or clause) embedded inside it. By the same token, the subordinate clause can contain another embedded clause, and so on, as in (51) where the S nodes are labelled for convenience:

(51)      [$_S$ Paul croit que [$_S$ Jean a dit que [$_S$ Luc regrette que [$_S$ Suzy suppose que [$_S$ Pierre aime Marie]]]]]

This phenomenon is known as **recursion**.

The recursive pattern illustrated in (51) can be described in terms of successive application of the rules in (52), where irrelevant details are omitted:

(52)      a   S → NP + VP
          b   VP → V + ... + (S′)
          c   S′ → C + S

Rules (a) and (b) define the structure of the main clause, but by selecting the option of S' in (b) and then applying (c), we reintroduce the category S which is defined in (a), so we can apply the rules again, and again, until eventually we break the cycle by selecting an option other than S' under VP. This recursive pattern can be varied by selecting S' as a complement of a noun, adjective or preposition (rather than of the verb) and/or by expanding S as an infinitival rather than finite clause.

Another recursive pattern is formed by the interaction of the rules for expanding NP and PP. As we observed in 1.2.2 and 1.2.7, an NP can contain a PP (as either a modifier or a complement), but PPs typically contain an NP, as indicated in the simplified rules in (53):

(53)     a   NP → ... + N + ... + (PP) + ...
         b   PP → P + (NP)

Because each of these rules introduces (optionally) the category defined in the other, we can apply them successively until we decide to expand NP in a way which does not include a PP, as in (54), where NP and PP nodes are indicated:

(54)     J'admire [$_{NP}$ la sincérité [$_{PP}$ de [$_{NP}$ la femme [$_{PP}$ de [$_{NP}$ l'auteur [$_{PP}$ de [$_{NP}$ ce livre [$_{PP}$ sur [$_{NP}$ la situation économique [$_{PP}$ dans [$_{NP}$ les pays [$_{PP}$ de [$_{NP}$ l'Europe]]]]]]]]]]]]

In principle (if we were immortal and had nothing better to do), we could go on for ever, repeating the recursive patterns defined in (52) and (53), to produce an infinitely long sentence. Similarly, by alternating between them or choosing different options at the points indicated by the dots, we can create an infinite variety of sentence patterns.

### 1.3.4  Some preliminary conclusions

The model which we have developed in the preceding sections has two principal components: a lexicon consisting of words and their properties (as outlined in 1.2.5) supplemented by a set of phrase-structure rules which build phrases and ultimately complete sentences by combining words according to certain patterns. Simplifying somewhat, the lexicon can be construed as a finite list of lexical entries of the sort proposed in 1.2.5, though it is a long list and one which can be extended indefinitely as individuals learn new words and as new words are introduced into the language as a whole. This stock of words and their properties can be taken as the finite set of 'basic units' from which phrases and sentences are formed. The other component of the grammar presented so far, the phrase-structure rules, also consists of a finite set of formulae which define phrases as combinations of lexical categories and phrasal categories. However, as we observed in 1.3.3, the output of this system (the set of sentences or constructions which it defines) is infinite. Thus, this model is consistent with the essential **creativity** of human language – our ability to produce and comprehend an infinite range of novel utterances.

It remains to be seen whether this model is capable of generating all the possible sentence patterns of French without allowing patterns which do not correspond to valid sentences. The short answer to this question is that it cannot. In 1.5, I shall propose further rules and principles of a rather different sort which will remedy this deficiency. These proposals can be viewed as extensions of the present model.

A rather different question concerns the extent to which the rules which have been proposed provide an interesting insight into the way in which the syntax of French (or language in general) works. To the extent that the phrase-structure model is viable, it makes a significant claim about natural languages: namely, that sentences have a hierarchical structure within which recurrent and potentially recursive patterns can be discerned and defined. However, the actual content of the rules which define these patterns is rather banal in the sense that these rules simply record our observations regarding the composition of different types of phrases, expressed in terms of categories. In the following sections a more refined model will be developed which focuses on general properties of phrase structure delegating some of the finer details of description to other principles or components of the grammar.

### 1.4 Refining the model: the 'X-bar' framework

#### 1.4.1 Structure of the NP

One of the problems with the phrase-structure model presented so far is that it does not distinguish between complements and modifiers. This problem is particularly evident in the case of PPs, which, as we have seen, can have either function. For example, an NP like (55) can be defined by the simplified rule in (56), but this rule does not tell us that the complement of *professeur* (i.e. *de français*) must correspond to the first PP, as we can see from the ungrammaticality of (57):

(55)     le professeur de français aux cheveux longs

(56)     NP → D + ... + N + ... + (PP) + ... + (PP) + ...

(57)     *le professeur aux cheveux longs de français

A widely adopted solution to this problem is to postulate that the head of a phrase and its complement(s) form a constituent which does not include modifiers or other elements like determiners. This category is symbolised by the lexical category of the head with a bar over it or (for typographical convenience) with a prime sign after it – the latter notation is adopted here. Thus *professeur de français* is an

N' (read as 'N-bar'). This innovation enables us to distinguish complements from modifiers in purely structural terms:

*The complement of any lexical category X is a sister of X within X', whereas modifiers of X are outside X'.*

Given this hypothesis, the contrast between cases like (55) and (57) is a direct consequence of the 'No crossing constraint' proposed in 1.1.4, which prevents elements which belong to the same constituent from being separated by any element which does not belong to this constituent – in this case, a head and its complement cannot be separated by a modifier.

In the case of NPs, if no modifier is present, the category N' combines with a determiner to give structures like (58):

(58)    $[_{NP} \text{le } [_{N'} \text{professeur } [_{PP} \text{de français}]]]$

Such structures can be defined by the rules in (59)–(60):

(59)    $NP \rightarrow D + N'$

(60)    $N' \rightarrow N + (PP)$

So, where do modifiers fit into this picture? In 1.2.2, we noted that modifiers can occur freely (within certain semantic limits). A natural way of expressing this is to assume that the combination of a modifier and the element which it modifies belongs to the same syntactic category as the modified element. For example, in a case like (56) where *aux cheveux longs* modifies the N' *professeur de français*, the combination of these two expressions is also an N', which can be combined with a determiner according to rule (59), to give the structure in (61):

(61)

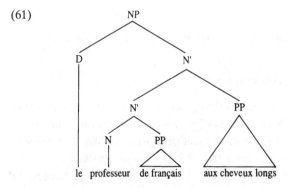

To allow structures like (61), we can add rule (62) to give an alternative expansion of N' from that defined in (60) above:

(62)    $N' \rightarrow N' + PP$

Rules like (62) define a rather special sort of configuration referred to as **adjunction**, defined as follows:

**Adjunction**: *a category X is 'adjoined' to a category Y if X is a sister of Y, and both X and Y are immediately dominated by the node Y.*

Less formally, X is adjoined to Y if the combination of X and Y yields a phrase of the category Y. Thus, in (61), the PP *aux cheveux longs* is adjoined to the N' *professeur de français*. Given that modifiers are always adjoined to the expressions which they modify, they are sometimes referred to as **adjuncts**.

Within certain stylistic limits, we can have as many modifier PPs as we like after the noun, as shown in (63), which is just about within the threshold of acceptability:

(63)        le professeur de français aux cheveux longs d'une intelligence
            extraordinaire avec des lunettes

Such examples can be derived by recursive application of rule (62), giving structures like (64) where each modifier PP is adjoined to an N':

(64)

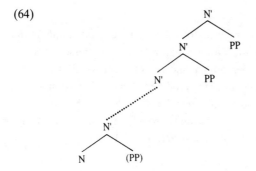

When a noun is not accompanied by a complement, as in (65), the noun constitutes an N' as well as an N:

(65)        le garçon (aux cheveux longs)

One reason for this is that in order for the optional PP to be interpreted as a modifier, it must be a sister of N', not simply of N. This is essentially the same issue as was raised in 1.1.3, where we pointed out that a proper noun like *Pierre* must be analysed as an NP as well as an N, even though it does not occur with a determiner.

In the above discussion, only modifiers and complements of the category PP have been considered. A more complete set of rules allowing APs as modifiers (before or after the noun) and S's as complements is given below:

(66)        NP → (D) + N'

(67)     a   $N' \rightarrow AP + N'$

   b   $N' \rightarrow N' + \begin{Bmatrix} AP \\ \\ PP \end{Bmatrix}$

   c   $N' \rightarrow N + (\begin{Bmatrix} PP \\ \\ S' \end{Bmatrix})$

### 1.4.2   Generalising the 'X-bar' framework

The framework outlined in 1.4.1 in relation to the structure of NPs can be extended to the other phrasal categories in a way which brings out some interesting similarities beween phrases of different categories. In all types of phrases there are some elements which can precede the head (e.g. determiners, degree items and some APs) while others must follow the head. However, complements always follow the head in French. This generalisation can be expressed by the schema in (68), where X stands for any category:

(68)     $X' \rightarrow X + \ldots$

The range of elements which can occur in the position indicated by the dots in (68) depends, to some extent, on the category of X (e.g. NP can only occur if X = V or P).

Within the X-bar framework, our earlier definition of a direct object (in 1.2.1) must be revised slightly as follows:

*A direct object is an NP which is immediately dominated by V' as sister of V.*

In fact, this revision has some empirical advantages. There are some NPs like *plusieurs fois* which can follow the verb (perhaps within VP), but which function as modifiers rather than direct objects, as in (69) where the verb is intransitive:

(69)     Jules a trébuché plusieurs fois

Such NPs can now be distinguished from direct objects by postulating that they are adjoined to V' in the same way as AdvPs and modifier PPs (see below) rather than occurring as sisters of V.

Some linguists have argued that the format of rule (59) above (NP → D + N') can also be generalised to other categories. Although determiners can only occur within NPs, adjectives can be introduced by degree items like *très* or *assez*, which are perhaps analogous to determiners (particularly indefinite determiners like *un*, *quelques* or *plusieurs*, which express different degrees of quantity). Similarly, some prepositions can be introduced by items like *juste* or *droit: juste après la guerre, droit devant la porte.* Consequently, we can postulate a general cross-categorial pattern for **maximal projections** (complete phrasal categories like NP, AP, VP and PP) as in (70), where **Specifier** is a cover term for determiners and other items of the sort just mentioned:

(70)      XP → (Specifier) + X′

> This analysis of degree items is somewhat controversial, and is adopted here tentatively. With categories other than NP, the distinction between specifiers and modifiers which precede the head is rather murky, an issue which will be dealt with as it arises. In more recent versions of X-bar theory, there is a tendency to associate the notion of 'specifier' with functions closer to those of a subject or external argument than to the notions of determination or degree.

Turning now to modifiers, the predominant pattern in French is for modifiers to follow the head, as expressed by the schema in (71):

(71)      X′ → X′ + Modifier

This is always the case, regardless of the category of X, when the modifier is a PP. The alternative pattern in (72) appears to be a more restricted option – available only for certain adjectives, for instance, when X = N:

(72)      X′ → Modifier + X′

Despite appearances to the contrary (see examples (2) in 1.1.1) this pattern can be justified, at an abstract level, for certain adverbs which modify verbs. This matter will be addressed briefly in 1.4.3 and in more detail in 7.5.4.

### 1.4.3   The 'Inflection' node and the structure of clauses

In 1.1.4, the basic structure of the sentence (or clause) was defined by the rule S → NP + VP, and in our examples the finite verb has been represented under the V node in its inflected form. However, within the framework being presented, it is generally assumed that the inflectional features encoded on the verb (e.g. tense and person/number endings) are represented under a separate **Inflection** node (abbreviated as I or Infl) which is outside the VP. Thus, the rule expanding S can be reformulated as in (73), which defines the structure in (74) for the sentence *Pierre mangeait une pizza*:

(73)      S → NP + I + VP

(74)

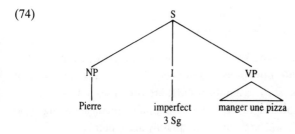

An intuitive basis for this analysis is that, although these inflections are realised on the verb, their semantic content (tense) relates to the sentence as a whole, like time adverbs such as *hier* (see 1.1.4).

The structure in (74) is an abstract representation; in order to derive the actual form of the sentence, the features under I must be amalgamated with the verb. There are at least two ways in which this might be achieved. One way is to transfer the features under I onto the verb; the other is to raise the verb into the I position (under either approach, **morphological** rules will specify the form of the verb which encodes these features, a matter which will not be dealt with here). For various reasons, linguists have argued that the former strategy is adopted in English (except with auxiliary verbs) whereas French adopts the latter approach.

This hypothesis provides a rather neat solution to the problem raised in 1.1.1 concerning the position of adverbs of the *often/souvent* type. Let us assume such adverbs are inserted before the verb in the modifier position defined in (72) in both English and French, as shown in (75):

(75)

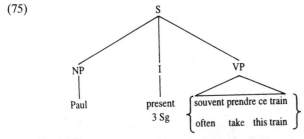

This structure gives the correct order of adverb and verb for the English version, but the wrong order for French. However, this problem is rectified by the assumptions outlined above. In the English version, the verb *take* stays where it is and the features under I are transferred to it whereas in French the verb *prendre* is moved to the I position, crossing the adverb *souvent*, thus giving the correct order. Support for this analysis (as opposed to one which simply stipulated that adverbs are inserted after the verb in French) is provided by examples involving auxiliary verbs, where the adverb occupies the same position in both languages, preceding the main verb:

25

(76)     a   Paul a souvent pris ce train

            b   Paul has often taken this train

In (76a) the order of the adverb and (main) verb reflects the structure in (75). It is not distorted by the **verb-raising** process described above because the element which inflects for tense, person and number (and therefore raises to I) is the auxiliary, not the main verb. Cases of this type and similar phenomena involving negation in French and English will be discussed more fully in chapter 7.

In 1.1.5, we noted that the category S differs from other phrasal categories in that it does not have a clearly identifiable head. A variant of the analysis in (74) treats the inflection element as the head of S, which is accordingly relabelled IP (Inflection Phrase), with the structure in (77):

(77)

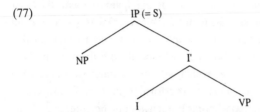

This structure conforms to the general schemata of the X-bar framework discussed in 1.4.2. In structural terms, the VP acts as a complement of I while the subject NP occupies the Specifier position of IP. Apart from the change of labels, the only difference between this structure and the one given in (74) is that I and VP form a constituent I'.

By the same token, some linguists have argued that the complementiser (C) is the head of the constituent which we have labelled S', now relabelled CP, with the structure in (78):

(78)

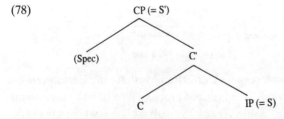

In this framework, the optional Specifier node is the position occupied by items such as *où* or *quand* in questions (see 1.5.2 and, for more detailed discussion, chapter 10).

> More recently (since the late 1980s) some linguists have taken this 'decomposition' of the clause still further, identifying the inflectional elements under I (e.g. 'tense' and 'person–number agreement', and indeed

other features such as 'mood') as separate nodes, each with its own projection (e.g. T (tense) is the head of a TP, Agr (agreement) is the head of an AgrP). This approach will not be developed here, but a simplified version of it will be employed in the discussion of negation in 7.6.

For the most part, the 'traditional' labels S and S' will be retained (since they more clearly evoke the familar notion of 'sentence') and the I node (representing verbs in their inflected form under V) will be omitted except when it is relevant to the discussion. However, the 'X-bar' analysis of clauses in terms of IP and CP will be adopted in chapter 10, where this 'richer' structure permits a clearer description of the phenomena in question.

### 1.5 Movement rules

#### *1.5.1 Underlying and surface structures: the position of pronouns*

In 1.4.3, a rule of a new kind, radically different from those discussed previously was surreptitiously introduced. Unlike phrase-structure rules, which build up structures by defining the content of phrasal categories, the rule which moves the verb from the V position to the I position actually changes one structure into another. Operations of this sort are known as **transformations**, hence the term **transformational grammar** for analytical frameworks which incorporate such rules. This grammar will make extensive use of movement rules of this type. Let us briefly consider some phenomena which lend themselves to an analysis in terms of movement.

Consider first an example like (79) where we have a pronoun, *la*, in front of the verb:

(79)      Pierre la dévorait

Such examples pose a technical problem for the framework established so far. Recall that *dévorer* is a verb which selects a direct object and that a direct object is defined as an NP which follows the verb as a sister to V under the V' node. However, in (79) there is no NP in this position. Moreover, if we substitute a verb like *dormir* which does not select a direct object, the result is ungrammatical:

(80)      *Pierre la dormait

Now, it should be fairly obvious why (79) is grammatical but (80) is not. Both examples contain a direct object, the pronoun *la*, it is just that this item is in the 'wrong' position according to our definition of a direct object. If pronouns in French occurred in the 'right' positions, like normal NPs and indeed pronouns in English, we would expect to find structures of the type in (81):

(81)      $[_S$ Pierre $[_{VP} [_{V'}$ dévorait PRONOUN $]]]$

In fact, the phrase-structure rules proposed so far will generate structures like (81), unless we impose restrictions to prevent certain types of pronouns from occurring in this position. However, we can dispense with any such restrictions by postulating a transformation which moves pronouns to the position immediately to the left of the verb, roughly as in (82):

(82)     $[_S \ldots [_{VP} \quad V \ldots \text{PRONOUN}]]$

The movement rule sketched in (82) will be referred to as **Clitic-placement**. This approach can be extended to cover cases like those in (83) where the pronoun before the verb corresponds to an indirect object (cf. *Pierre a donné cinq francs à Marie, Pierre a mis le livre sur la table*):

(83)     a   Pierre lui a donné cinq francs
         b   Pierre y a mis le livre

> Not all pronouns in French undergo the movement process outlined in (82). For example, demonstrative pronouns like *cela, ceci* and *ça* occur in basically the same positions as normal NPs, just like pronouns in English. Pronouns like those in (79) and (83) are referred to as **clitic** pronouns. The term 'clitic' is used to denote items (not just pronouns) which, as it were, 'cling' to an adjacent word, in this case the verb. (An example of a clitic in English is the contracted negative form *n't*, which can only occur immediately after a verb and, indeed, is written as part of the verb.) In using this term, we assume that the pronouns in (79) and (83) are not simply placed in front of the verb but are attached to it in some way (see chapter 6 for discussion).

The analysis outlined above provides two levels of representation for a sentence like (79). Firstly, the phrase-structure rules define an abstract, **underlying structure** (sometimes called a **deep structure** or 'D-structure'), such as (81), in which all elements occur in the positions appropriate to their interpretation, as determined by structural definitions of relations like direct object and by the lexical entry of the verb. Thus, the underlying structure (81) indicates that the pronoun is a direct object selected by the verb *dévorer*. The movement process sketched in (82) expresses the generalisation that pronouns in French are typically attached to the left of the verb, regardless of their grammatical function (e.g. direct or indirect object). By applying this rule to the underlying structure in (81), we derive the **surface structure** corresponding to the order in which elements actually occur, as in (79).

### *1.5.2   QU- movement and Inversion*
Another type of construction which lends itself to a movement approach is illustrated in (84):

28

(84)        Quel garçon aimait-elle?

Here we have two elements which are in the 'wrong' places; the subject *elle* which occurs after the verb and the direct object *quel garçon* which has been placed at the beginning of the sentence. Let us therefore assume that (84) is derived from the underlying structure (85), which is actually permissible as a surface structure in colloquial French:

(85)        $[_S$ Elle $[_{VP} [_{V'}$ aimait $[_{NP}$ quel garçon]]]]

Simplifying considerably, the surface form in (84) can be derived by applying the following rules:

**QU- movement**: *move the phrase which denotes the questioned element to the beginning of the sentence.*
**Inversion**: *invert the verb with the subject pronoun.*

These two rules are independent of each other. For example, QU- movement occurs without Inversion in indirect questions like (86) whereas Inversion occurs without QU- movement in yes/no questions like (87):

(86)        Je me demande quel garçon elle aimait

(87)        Aimait-elle ce garçon?

Note also that when a direct question is a complex sentence, Inversion applies in the main clause while QU- movement moves the questioned element to the beginning of the whole sentence, extracting it, as it were, from the clause to which it 'belongs', as we can see by comparing (88a) with the colloquial variant in (88b):

(88)        a   Quel garçon crois-tu qu'elle aimait?
            b   Tu crois qu'elle aimait quel garçon?

This account leaves out many important details which will be left for discussion in chapter 10. The present purpose is merely to show how we can simplify our grammar by postulating movement rules to account for systematic variations from the 'normal' or 'canonical' order of elements. If you are not convinced that this amounts to a simplification, you might try to construct a phrase-structure grammar and a set of lexical entries for verbs which will generate the surface forms of the above examples directly and, at the same time, identify which expressions are subjects or objects of which verbs – example (88a) should prove particularly daunting!

### *1.5.3  'Grammatical' and 'logical' subjects: passive constructions*
In 1.2.4, reference was made to a certain confusion on the part of some traditional grammarians concerning the use of terms like 'subject' and 'direct object'. Such

confusion is particularly apparent in the case of **passive** constructions like (89):

(89)     L'immeuble a été démoli

From a syntactic point of view, *l'immeuble* is quite clearly the subject in (89), but in semantic terms it corresponds more closely to a direct object (denoting the 'entity which undergoes the action'). To avoid confusion, some grammarians draw a distinction between 'grammatical' and 'logical' relations. Thus, in (89) *l'immeuble* is the **grammatical subject** but the **logical object** of the sentence, the **logical subject** (the 'performer of the action') being left unspecified, whereas in the active sentence (90) 'logical' and 'grammatical' relations coincide:

(90)     On a démoli l'immeuble

In this way, passive sentences can be characterised as constructions in which the 'logical subject' is suppressed and the 'logical object' is realised as the 'grammatical subject'.

A problem with this terminological approach is that, although 'grammatical' subjects and direct objects can be defined in structural terms, there is no clear definition of what constitutes a 'logical' subject or object. In practice, at least in the clearest cases, the 'logical' status of an expression is determined by comparison with other related constructions in which the 'logical' relations coincide with 'grammatical' relations. Thus, *l'immeuble* in (89) is deemed to be a 'logical object' precisely because it is the 'grammatical (direct) object' in the corresponding active sentence (90).

In a grammar which makes use of movement rules, this approach can be made explicit by equating 'logical' relations with 'grammatical' relations which hold in the underlying structure of the sentence. Thus, what the traditional grammarian calls a 'logical object' will actually occur in the direct object position in the underlying structure. To illustrate, let us assume that active and passive forms of verbs select exactly the same complements – e.g. *démolir* and *être démoli* both select a direct object NP. Secondly, the idea that the 'logical subject' is suppressed in passive constructions can be represented by leaving the subject position empty in the underlying structure. Putting these two proposals together, we can formulate the underlying structure of (89) roughly as in (91), where $\varnothing$ stands for the empty subject:

(91)     $[_S [_{NP} \varnothing ] [_{VP} \text{a été démoli} [_{NP} \text{l'immeuble}]]]$

In this structure, the 'logical' relations coincide exactly with 'grammatical' relations, just as in active sentences – the 'logical object' occurs in the direct object position and the implicit 'logical subject' is represented as a syntactic subject position which has no content. The surface form in (89) can now be derived by a rule which moves the direct object into the empty subject position, as shown in (92):

(92)     $[_S [_{NP}$ l'immeuble $] [_{VP}$ a été démoli $[_{NP}$ ___ $]]]$

### 1.5.4  Extraposition

Contrary to the predictions of X-bar theory, we find examples where a head is separated from its complement by an element which belongs to a higher constituent, as in (93) where the verb and its direct object are separated by a modifier PP *avec sa clé*:

(93)     Pierre a ouvert avec sa clé la porte de l'appartement à côté de chez-lui

This order is possible only when the direct object is particularly 'heavy' (i.e. long or complicated); in other cases the direct object must precede the modifier in accordance with the X-bar principles:

(94)     a    Pierre a ouvert la porte avec sa clé
          b    ??Pierre a ouvert avec sa clé la porte

Examples like (93) can be derived by a stylistic rule which moves the direct object from its normal position (i.e. sister of V under V') rightwards across the PP. For the sake of concreteness, let us assume that the moved NP is adjoined to the VP, as shown in (95), though its exact structural position is not crucial:

(95)

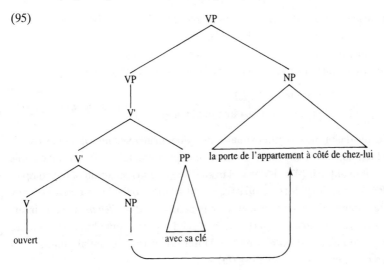

31

This process will be called **Extraposition**:

**Extraposition:** *adjoin a complement of X to the right of XP.*

This rule is optional and appears to apply only when a reordering of elements is motivated by stylistic considerations, in this case the desirability of placing a heavy constituent towards the end of the sentence.

A similar problem arises in constructions with complement clauses, which typically follow all other constituents of the VP including modifiers (like *dans une lettre* in (96)):

(96)    a  Le ministre a proposé dans une lettre que l'on démolisse l'immeuble

         b  ?Le ministre a proposé que l'on démolisse l'immeuble dans une lettre

Example (96a) can be derived from (96b) by Extraposition of the complement clause. One factor which contributes to the oddness of (96b) is that one is tempted to interpret *dans une lettre* as modifying the closest verb *démolir*, even though this gives an absurd meaning. This tendency, stated below, is quite widespread (cf. celebrated examples like *Bathtub for sale by lady with dimpled bottom* where one is tempted to interpret *with dimpled bottom* as applying to the lady rather than the bathtub):

Interpretive strategy: *as a preferred stategy, interpret a modifier expression as modifying the closest element of the appropriate syntactic category.*

Thus, Extraposition in (96) can be seen as a means of making the meaning of the sentence clearer in accordance with this strategy.

The same principle may be at work in cases like (97), where the preferred order is one in which the adjective precedes the complement of the noun:

(97)    a  la démolition illégale de l'immeuble

         b  ?la démolition de l'immeuble illégale

Once again, the preferred order violates the X-bar principles, *illégale* being a modifier which separates the head from its complement in (97a). However, this problem is avoided if (97a) is derived from (97b) by Extraposition of the complement PP. Again, the oddness of (97b) can be attributed to the interpretive strategy proposed above (though other factors may be involved) – *illégale* must be interpreted as modifying *démolition* (because of gender agreement), but in (97b) there is another noun (*immeuble*) which is closer to it; this potential confusion is avoided in the extraposed version (97a).

### 1.5.5 Topicalisation and Dislocation

Another stylistic process, sometimes called **Topicalisation**, involves movement of a constituent to the beginning of the sentence, as in the following examples where the underlying position of the topicalised element is indicated by a dash:

(98) a À son fils, Pierre a donné une voiture __
   b Avec cette clé, on peut ouvrir toutes les portes de l'immeuble __
   c Très doucement, le cambrioleur a monté l'escalier __
   d Sous un rocher, Jules a trouvé une pièce en or __

When the moved expression contains a reference to a specific entity, as in (98a, b), the typical effect is to present this entity as the **topic** of the sentence – the thing that the sentence is about – whereas in other cases the topicalised element has a **scene-setting** function. A concomitant effect is to give greater emphasis to the phrase which occurs in final position, presenting it as new or important information. For example, in (99) the main emphasis would normally fall on *à son fils*, whereas in (98a) this emphasis is shifted onto *une voiture*, perhaps contrasting this entity with other gifts offered to other people:

(99)   Pierre a donné une voiture à son fils

These effects can be seen in terms of a general tendency, sometimes called **Functional Sentence Perspective**, to express old or background information (e.g. related to the previous context) at the beginning of the sentence, leaving new or important information (the **Focus** of the sentence) to the end. This tendency is not absolute, but it holds more strongly in French than in English. In English, we can generally use heavy stress on an item to present it as the Focus of the sentence even though it is not in final position:

(100)   Pierre gave **a car** to his son

This use of **contrastive stress** is not impossible in French, but it is more usual to reorganise the sentence in such a way that the focal element occurs in final position, or to use a special construction (known as a **cleft** contruction, see 10.7.2) in which the Focus is introduced by *c'est*: *C'est une voiture que Pierre a donnée à son fils*.

In French, unlike English, Topicalisation does not normally apply to NPs:

(101) a This book, I have read
   b *Ce livre, j'ai lu

Instead, French resorts to what is known as a **dislocated** construction (marginally possible in English) in which the topic is duplicated within the core of the sentence by means of a pronoun:

(102)     Ce livre, je l'ai lu

The pattern in (102) is known as **left dislocation**, because the element in question is placed to the left of the sentence. Another common pattern is **right dislocation**, illustrated in (103):

(103)     Je l'ai lu, ce livre

It is generally assumed that dislocation does not involve movement of the element in question, because in the underlying structures of (102) and (103), the direct object position is occupied by the pronoun. Rather, the dislocated phrase (*ce livre*) is inserted directly by phrase-structure rules in a position outside the core sentence (perhaps adjoined to S or S', see 10.3.3 for discussion) and its function within the sentence is determined by the **resumptive pronoun.**

Dislocation is particularly common in casual speech, to the extent that some scholars have claimed that it constitutes the normal mode of sentence construction in colloquial French. The effect of left dislocation is similar to that described above for Topicalisation. Right dislocation has the effect of defocalising the element concerned, while sharpening the focus on whatever element occurs finally within the core part of the sentence. Thus, in the 'normal' sentence *J'ai lu ce livre*, the direct object *ce livre* is presented as at least part of the new information, but dislocation in (103) shifts the Focus onto the activity denoted by *lire* (as opposed to some other activity such as photocopying, as in English *I read that book*) or emphasises the truth of the sentence (as when the auxiliary is stressed in English: *I have read that book, I did read that book*).

### 1.5.6  Case

The term **Case** is used to refer to differences in the form of nouns and accompanying elements according to the syntactic function of the NP (subject, direct object, etc.). In many languages (e.g. Latin and German), Case distinctions are found with all types of NP, but in French, as in English, they occur only with certain pronouns; e.g. *he* vs *him*, *il* vs *le*. Nevertheless, as we shall see, Case plays an important role in the syntax of languages like French and English even when it does not affect the form of elements within the NP.

For English, the correct forms of pronouns can be determined by assigning Case features to NPs in the positions indicated in (104)–(106); roughly, [NOM] (**Nominative**) to NPs in the subject position of a finite clause, [ACC] (**Accusative**) to NPs which are complements of verbs or prepositions:

(104)

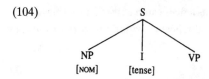

34

(105)

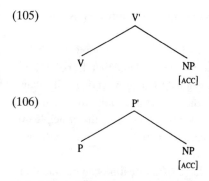

(106)

If the NP consists of a pronoun, the form of the pronoun is determined by the Case feature: e.g. *he* when the feature is [NOM], *him* when the feature is [ACC]. Essentially the same procedure can be adopted for French, provided that we assume that Case features are assigned to pronouns before they undergo the Clitic-placement process described in 1.5.1.

French also has a third Case, **Dative**, represented by the clitic pronouns *lui* and *leur* and by some uses of the preposition *à*. The conditions under which Dative Case is assigned cannot be stated in simple structural terms. Pending a fuller discussion in 6.2.5 and 6.5.1, let us assume that Dative Case is assigned as a lexical property of certain verbs (also some adjectives) to a particular complement, which usually expresses a Possessor or Experiencer role. If this complement is ultimately realised as a clitic pronoun, it is spelt out as a Dative form (e.g. *lui* or *leur*) as in (107a), otherwise Dative Case is expressed by means of the preposition *à* as in (107b):

(107)  a  Ce film lui plaît
       b  Ce film plaît à Pierre

Similarly, *de* in some of its uses can plausibly be regarded as a marker of **Genitive** Case rather than as a genuine preposition – this matter is left for discussion in 5.4.

As well as determining the forms of pronouns, the concept of Case can be exploited, at a more abstract level, as a means of defining the positions in which NPs can occur according to a general principle which requires every overt NP to be assigned a Case feature.

In 1.4.2, we observed that only verbs and prepositions can take an NP complement whereas adjectives and nouns require their complements to be introduced by a preposition, typically *de: la démolition de l'immeuble, Marie est amoureuse de ce garçon* (cf. *On a démoli l'immeuble, Marie aime ce garçon*). This pattern can now be attributed to the fact that adjectives and nouns cannot assign Accusative Case to their complements according to the conditions outlined above. Consequently, the NP which represents the internal argument of the noun or adjective must occur as a complement of a semantically empty preposition whose function is to assign Case to this NP.

In 1.3.2, it was noted that the subject of an infinitive is always implicit in French. This observation can also be explained in terms of Case. Note that the condition in (104) only allows Nominative Case to be assigned to the subject of a finite clause. Assuming that no Case can be assigned to the subject of an infinitival clause, the impossibility of having an overt NP in this position follows from the principle proposed above – see chapter 9 for detailed discussion and further ramifications of this approach.

The principle that every overt NP must have a Case feature can be stated in a slightly different form as follows:

**The Case Principle**: *every overt NP must be assigned a Case feature once, and only once, in the course of a derivation.*

This revised version may explain why, in passive sentences, the underlying direct object must move to the subject position. Let us assume that passive verb forms differ from active verbs in that they cannot assign Accusative Case. Thus, in the underlying structure (108), *ce projet* cannot receive a Case feature:

(108)     $[_S [_{NP} \varnothing ] [_{VP}$ a été proposé $[_{NP}$ ce projet]]]]

However, there is an empty slot in the subject position, to which Nominative Case is assigned, so that *ce projet* can satisfy the Case principle by moving into this position, giving the surface form *Ce projet a été proposé*. This analysis is supported by the fact that when the complement of the passive verb is an element which does not require a Case feature (e.g. a clause, as in (109)), no movement is necessary:

(109)     $[_S [_{NP} \varnothing ] [_{VP}$ a été proposé $[_{S'}$ que l'on démolisse cet immeuble]]]]

Instead, the empty subject position is filled by a dummy pronoun *il* giving *Il a été proposé que l'on démolisse cet immeuble* (see 3.4.11 for further discussion).

With the other movement processes we have presented, the NP is moved from a position where it can receive Case to a position to which no Case is assigned, thus ensuring that the NP does not receive Case more than once in the derivation. For example, in sentence (84) in 1.5.2 (*Quel garçon aimait-elle?*), *quel garçon* is moved from the direct object position (where it gets Accusative Case) to a position at the beginning of the sentence which has not yet been defined, but which does not appear to conform to any of the configurations detailed in (104)–(106) – it is assumed that *quel garçon* is not moved into the subject position.

### *1.5.7 Properties of movement rules*

A fundamental axiom of transformational grammar is that only constituents can be moved. In some cases, this axiom will help to determine the choice between alternative analyses of a particular construction. To take an abstract example, suppose we find surface sequences of the form Y + Z + X which are derived from underlying structures with the order X + Y + Z. In principle, the surface order could be derived either by moving X to the right or by moving Y + Z to the left. However, if we have strong evidence that Y and Z do not form a constituent, our axiom forces us to conclude that X is moved, as in (110):

(110)     X Y Z

On the other hand, if we have clear evidence that the surface order is derived by moving Y + Z, our axiom entails that Y and Z must form a constituent, as shown in (111):

(111)     X [Y + Z]

In practice, the assumptions which lead to one or other conclusion may not be entirely clear and in such cases the matter can only be resolved by looking for further evidence concerning the nature of the movement process or the structural relations between the relevant elements.

Another condition on movement processes which is widely (but not universally) accepted is that elements cannot be moved into a lower structural position. This claim is based partly on the observation that most clear instances of movement involve raising of an element to a higher structural position and that those constructions which appear to involve lowering of some element can often be reanalysed in terms of raising of some other element. For present purposes, this condition will be treated as an interesting hypothesis which, if correct, makes an important claim about the organisation of natural languages. Consequently, all things being equal, analyses which conform to this condition will be favoured over analyses which violate it.

As a general convention, it is assumed that when an element is moved, the node which dominated it is left behind as an **empty category**, sometimes called a **trace**, which has been indicated by means of a dash in the representations so far. Many linguists represent the trace by the symbol *t* (or *e*, for 'empty category'), which is coindexed with the moved element. Thus, the surface structure of example (98a) in 1.5.5 can be represented more explicitly as in (112) below:

(112)     $[_{PP}$ à son fils$]_i$ [Pierre a donné une voiture $[_{PP} t_i]]$

In simple cases, the informal 'dash' notation is an adequate means of indicating the effects of movement but in more complicated cases (e.g. involving movement of more than one element) the more explicit notation illustrated in (112) will be used.

The hypothesis that a trace is left behind when an element is moved entails that movement processes do not destroy any of the underlying structure. In at least some of the cases reviewed so far, movement processes do not add any new structure either. For example, according to the analysis of passive sentences proposed in 1.5.3, the direct object NP is moved into the vacant NP slot in the subject position, leaving an empty trace in the direct object position, as shown in (113):

(113)    $[_S [_{NP} \varnothing]$    $[_{VP}$ a été démoli $[_{NP}$ l'immeuble$]]]$
    $\Rightarrow [_S [_{NP}$ l'immeuble$]_i [_{VP}$ a été démoli $[_{NP} t_i]$    $]]$

On the other hand, some movement processes (e.g. Extraposition) do create extra structure by adjoining the moved element to an existing node; see for instance diagram (95) in 1.5.4, where an extra VP node is introduced to accommodate the extraposed direct object. A currently prevalent view is that all movement processes involve either movement to an empty position (as in (113)) or adjunction to an existing node.

Some movement processes are **bounded** in the sense that they can only apply within a particular part of the sentence. For example, the Clitic-placement rule proposed in 1.5.1 attaches a pronoun to the verb within the clause to which it belongs, not to the verb in a higher clause:

(114)    a    Pierre croit $[_{S'}$ que Marie le connaît __ ]

         b    *Pierre le croit $[_{S'}$ que Marie connaît __ ]

On the other hand, as we saw in 1.5.2, the QU- movement rule can move an element across an indeterminate number of sentence boundaries to attach it to the beginning of the clause which is interpreted as a question:

(115)    Quel homme dis-tu $[_{S'}$ que Pierre croit $[_{S'}$ que Marie connaît __ ]]

In other words, QU- movement appears to be an **unbounded** process.[1]

---

[1] Many linguists have argued that the distinction between bounded and unbounded rules can be eliminated by analysing cases of unbounded movement in terms of successive application of a bounded rule – e.g. in (115) *quel homme* is moved first to the beginning of the lowest clause, then to the beginning of the next clause up and so on until it reaches the beginning of the highest clause. This approach has some theoretical advantages, but, for the sort of problems we shall be concerned with, it represents an unnecessary complication.

Even unbounded rules like QU- movement are subject to certain restrictions. For example, although we can question an element which is conjoined with another element (e.g. by *et*), as in (116a), we cannot move the questioned element to the beginning of the sentence:

(116)    a   Elle connaît [$_{NP}$ [$_{NP}$ Jules] et [$_{NP}$ quel homme]]?

           b   *Quelle homme connaît-elle [$_{NP}$ [$_{NP}$ Jules] et [$_{NP}$ __ ]]?

The same restriction is found with other movement processes such as Clitic-placement: e.g. we cannot replace *cet homme* in (117a) with a pronoun and attach it to the verb:

(117)    a   Elle connaît [$_{NP}$ [$_{NP}$ Jules] et [$_{NP}$ cet homme]]

           b   *Elle le connaît [$_{NP}$ [$_{NP}$ Jules] et [$_{NP}$ __ ]]

A simple way of accounting for such restrictions is to suppose that certain structural configurations, like conjoined structures, are syntactic **islands** – that is constituents out of which nothing can be moved. The 'island' status of conjoined structures is not peculiar to French, but appears to be common to all human languages. However, there are other types of phrases which seem to be islands in some languages but not in others. For example, in English we can move an NP out of a PP, as in (118), but this is not possible in French:

(118)    a   Which question did they talk [$_{PP}$ about __ ]?

           b   This question was talked [$_{PP}$ about __ ]

(119)    a   *Quelle question a-t-on parlé [$_{PP}$ de __ ]?

           b   *Cette question a été parlé [$_{PP}$ de __ ]

The same restriction will explain why we cannot use a clitic pronoun as the complement of a preposition in such cases:

(120)    *On la parlera [$_{PP}$ de __ ]

Let us refer to this restriction as the **PP-Island Constraint**:

**The PP-Island Constraint:** *in French, no item can be extracted from a PP.*

There are more sophisticated ways of explaining restrictions of the type illustrated in (116)–(120), but, for purposes of description, it is sufficient to designate certain configurations as islands. Many of the surface constructions which are ruled out by island constraints (e.g. (116b) and (117b)) are so clearly ungrammatical that it would probably never occur to a language learner that they might be possible. Plausibly, this is because these restrictions are common to all languages and can thus be attributed to the language faculty rather than to the grammar of particular languages. Such cases are of immense interest to theoretical linguists, who are ultimately concerned with defining and explaining the properties of language in general, but they are of limited relevance to language students seeking solutions to grammatical problems which they have experienced. Consequently, in this book, discussion of island constraints will be restricted to cases where they elucidate genuine problems for the student.

### 1.6  Some wider issues

### *1.6.1  Approaches to Grammar*

The model of grammar presented in the preceding sections is a version of the **transformational-generative** approach developed and refined over the last forty years or so by Noam Chomsky and his followers and applied to French by linguists such as Richard Kayne, Nicolas Ruwet, Jean-Claude Milner, Jean-Yves Pollock and many others. In the broadest sense, a **generative** grammar is one which seeks to define the infinite set of possible sentences of a language in terms of a set of explicit rules or principles. However, for many generative linguists, the main objective is not merely to account for the facts of a particular language but rather to develop a theory of the language faculty (sometimes called **Universal Grammar**). Consequently, many generative studies, even when they are based on data from a particular language such as French, are directed towards theoretical issues. In some cases, particularly in more recent work, the level of discussion is quite abstract and remote from the concerns of the student of French. Nevertheless, there is a susbstantial body of work within this framework which is more descriptive in approach and can profitably be read by those who do not have a specialist background in generative theory.

A rather different type of generative approach is pursued by **distributionalists** like Maurice Gross and his associates, who take a more inductive view of linguistic research, characterised by mistrust of theoretical speculation about the nature of language. This approach places a strong emphasis on the classification of words according to the syntactic contexts in which they can occur (i.e. their syntactic **distribution**). Typically, the fruits of this research are presented in the form of tables which list words and their distribution, accompanied by comments on any regular patterns (e.g. words which occur in context X also occur in context Y). Such work constitutes a valuable reference-source, though the mode of presentation is not always 'user-friendly'.

Not all modern linguists subscribe to the generativist view of language which has been presented here. An alternative approach, which can be broadly characterised by the label **functionalist**, is primarily concerned with the ways in which linguistic forms (particular words, expressions or constructions) are used in the act of communication. To some extent this approach can be seen as complementary to the generative approach, though some functionalists would reject this view. For example, the functionalist might be concerned with the attitudes conveyed by expressions like *pourtant, en effet* or *d'ailleurs*, or with the communicative effects of using a dislocated, cleft or passive construction rather than a 'normal' active sentence, whereas the generativist is principally concerned with the positions which these expressions can occupy or the structural conditions which govern these syntactic constructions.

Two other approaches to grammar which have been applied extensively to French data are the **psychomécanique** model pioneered by Gustave Guillaume and the **théorie énonciative** developed by Antoine Culioli and his associates. These two approaches, particularly the former, adopt a very different conceptual framework for the analysis of syntax from that which has been presented here. The references to research within these frameworks will be confined to a few major, influential works, and less technical studies of particular topics.

**Traditional** grammars of French come in many shapes and sizes. Some have a strong **prescriptive** bias – dictating usage rather than describing it. Some are concerned with introducing and illustrating grammatical concepts (e.g. as an introduction to the study of Latin in the case of many nineteenth-century grammars) whereas others are more concerned with documenting or describing French usage. Yet others are destined for non-native learners of French and therefore focus on differences between French and the language of their readers. The main feature which traditional grammars have in common is the lack of a formal system for representing syntactic structure or other properties of sentences. In the main, traditional grammars offer guidance through example and informal observation rather than detailed analysis. Nevertheless, they provide an invaluable source of factual information and examples.

### 1.6.2 Non-structural aspects of syntax

The model which we have outlined defines the class of possible sentences primarily in terms of structural configurations of phrasal and lexical categories. However, there is more to syntax than this. It is not always helpful simply to know whether a sentence is grammatical; we need to know how the sentence is to be interpreted. For example, as well as defining the structural conditions under which pronouns, determiners and finite tense forms can occur, we need to know what elements within the sentence a pronoun can refer back to, what the function of determiners like *le* or *un* is, how particular tense forms situate events in time, etc. Although questions such as these are essentially semantic rather than syntactic, they are important for language students and, for this reason alone, it would be perverse to ignore them. Moreover, there are many syntactic phenomena which are sensitive to semantic factors such as definiteness or indefiniteness of NPs, whether the tense of the verb indicates a punctual or habitual event, and so on. Consequently, this study of the syntax of French will involve some discussion of meaning and the way in which it is represented through syntax. For the most part, the discussion of meaning will be informal, couched in prose (rather than abstract representations) with illustrative examples accompanied by paraphrases where appropriate. Often, the relevant aspects of meaning can be characterised in terms of crude labels (like the theta-roles proposed in 1.2.4) or features which distinguish semantic subtypes within lexical categories. On the other hand, some of the semantic phenomena we shall be dealing with concern functional elements which make a narrow and relatively well-defined contribution to meaning and which are amenable to more formal analysis. A case in point is the system of tense, discussed in chapter 4, whose essential properties can be represented in terms of abstract, but fairly simple, formulae which provide the basis of a systematic analysis of the ways in which particular tense forms can be used.

### 1.6.3 Syntactic variation

A common complaint which is made against grammars is that the rules which they present do not match the way in which people actually speak. One reason for this may be that the grammarian has misinterpreted the facts or has not analysed them carefully enough – an unfortunate deficiency, but understandable in view of the complexity of human languages. Another common reason is that the grammarian is attempting to prescribe usage rather than describing it – sometimes this is done covertly, by adopting a descriptive approach but basing the description on the usage of those whom the grammarian deems to speak the language 'correctly' (e.g. the 'best authors'). Moreover, the concept of 'correctness' is often based on some preconceived notion of logic, clarity or elegance which the grammarian seeks to impose on the language in order to 'improve' it.

As a matter of principle, this prescriptive approach is rejected here. The task of the linguist is to describe and analyse the facts of the language such as they are, not to make value-judgements on these facts. In French, as in all languages, there is some degree of variation, not only in pronunciation and vocabulary, but also in syntax. However, it is important to realise that Non-standard (and so-called 'substandard') varieties of a language are not intrinsically inferior to the standard variety; they are simply different. Investigation of non-standard varieties provides no justification for the popular view that they are degenerate forms of the standard variety, characterised by a failure to observe the 'rules of grammar'. They have their own grammars which are different from the grammar of the standard variety, in much the same way (though to a lesser extent) as the grammar of Standard French differs from that of Standard Italian or Standard Spanish. From this perspective, Standard (Parisian) French can be regarded as a dialect of French which, for social and historical reasons, has gained prestige and acceptance as a norm.

Having recognised the linguistic 'legitimacy' of non-standard varieties, we are faced with a dilemma. Clearly, it would be impractical to try to account for all varieties of French in a book such as this, even if the evidence were available. A more appropriate policy is to concentrate on those varieties which are recognised as standard by a broad cross-section of the French-speaking community, even if this comes close to the type of 'covert prescriptivism' mentioned above. However, this concept of Standard French should not be equated with 'literary' French. In literary usage, we find grammatical constructions which would be out of place, to the point of sounding pretentious, in everyday communication even of a fairly formal nature. By the same token, there are other constructions (sometimes condemned as 'sloppy' or 'incorrect') which are widely used in casual speech even by the highly educated. In so far as such usage is part of the stylistic repertoire of speakers across a wide social and geographical spectrum, there is no objective reason to exclude it from the domain of Standard French. Occasionally, phenomena which are quite clearly Non-standard will be discussed, usually because they provide an interesting comparison with standard usage which may help to elucidate the properties of the standard constructions.

Unless otherwise specified, the examples and the judgements indicated can be taken as representative of 'everyday' Standard French, appropriate in a wide range of communicative situations from casual conversation through to more formal written discourse. Constructions and aspects of usage which are restricted to particular **registers** will be signalled as such by labels such as 'literary', 'formal', 'journalistic', 'colloquial', 'non-standard', etc. The comments on matters of style, register and non-standard usage should be taken only as a rough guide for the reader (to draw attention to constructions which should be used with caution), the main objective being to investigate the linguistic properties of constructions rather than the social factors which govern their use.

### 1.6.4 *The limits of regularity*

In 1.1.1, we noted the widespread view that human languages are fraught with irregularities, to the extent that they may appear inherently chaotic. Against this view, it was argued in 1.1.2 that languages must be governed by a system (a grammar) which enables speakers to create and understand new utterances but which does not allow words to be combined in a random fashion. In subsequent sections, I assumed the essentially regular nature of this system and focused on the task of identifying its properties (as they are manifested in French). A legitimate question is how this approach can be reconciled with the perception of irregularity. To put it another way: How much of language is reducible to a regular system and is it sufficiently important (from the language learner's point of view) to warrant the intellectual investment necessary in order to discover these regularities?

At this point, it is necessary to draw a distinction between the cognitive system which enables a speaker to construct and understand utterances (the speaker's **mental grammar**) and the model of this system which is constructed by the linguist (the **linguist's grammar**). As we have seen, the properties of the mental grammar are not directly accessible but can only be discerned by formulating hypotheses (often at a fairly abstract level) and testing them against the output of the mental grammar (sentences of the language). Now, the question raised above relates to the speaker's mental grammar but it can only be answered in relation to the linguist's grammar. Consequently, discrepancies between the empirical data and the rules of the linguist's grammar do not necessarily reflect irregularities in the speaker's mental grammar, but may well be due to deficiencies in the linguist's model. In other words, apparent irregularity may reflect regularities which linguists have not yet discovered.

Leaving this possibility aside, there are some aspects of language which are quite clearly arbitrary. An obvious case is the relation between the forms of words and their meanings. Generally, we cannot deduce the meaning of a word from its form, nor can we guess the right word for a concept unless we already know it, except perhaps through an awareness of etymology and knowledge of related languages. In some cases, like *injuste* or *pauvreté*, we can distinguish elements within the word (known as **morphemes**) which have an identifiable meaning or function. Thus, the meanings of these words can be derived from the meanings of the **root morphemes** *juste* and *pauvre* and of the affixes *in-* and *-té*. Nevertheless, **derivational morphology** (the process of combining morphemes to create new words) is often subject to rather idiosyncratic restrictions. For example, alongside *injuste* and *incorrect*, we have *mécontent* (but not *\*incontent, \*méjuste*, etc.) and alongside *pauvreté* and *beauté* we have *richesse* and *laideur* (but not *\*richeté, \*laideté, \*pauvresse*, etc.). Moreover, derived words often acquire new meanings which cannot be predicted from their morphological structure: e.g. *décoller* with the meaning 'take off' (of an aeroplane) as opposed to its more transparent meaning 'unstick'. Consequently, although morphological processes of this kind establish connections which may facilitate the acquisition of vocabulary and the creation of new words, the particular combinations of morphemes which constitute actual words and the range of meanings encoded by these words are established by convention rather than by predictive rules.

Sometimes, particular meanings are associated with units larger than individual words, as in the case of **idioms** such as *casser sa pipe* 'to die' (cf. English *kick the bucket*) whose meanings cannot be derived in a predictable fashion from the meanings of the words which they contain.

The above evidence indicates that the human language faculty is capable of storing a very large amount of arbitrary information: associations of meanings with particular forms (morphemes, words or idioms). This observation is consistent with the account of creativity outlined in 1.3.4 as long as the stock of arbitrary information is finite, as seems to be the case in so far as the set of forms can be construed as a finite list. The same approach can be adopted for other properties of words which are arbitrary or partially irregular, such as the gender of nouns, inflectional endings (plural forms of nouns, tense forms of verbs, etc.) or selection of complements (e.g. whether a verb takes a direct or indirect object). In principle, just as we have to learn the meaning of each word, we could learn and store these other properties separately for each word, though in fact this burden is reduced considerably by the existence of tendencies or subregularities.

Observations of this sort have led some linguists to suggest that all irregularities in syntax can be construed as properties of particular words (or similar units such as idioms) while the syntactic rules themselves are totally regular. For example, although there is no reliable way of determining the gender of a noun, the agreement processes which relate to gender appear to be exceptionless. Similarly, although the past-historic form of a verb like *cuire* (*il cuisit*) may be deemed irregular, the conditions which govern the use of this form are the same as for regular past-historic forms.

In answer to the original question, it seems that a substantial portion of language is irregular or at least 'messy', particularly with respect to properties of words. Moreover, some of these properties (e.g. gender) pose considerable difficulties for language learners, presumably because they are so idiosyncratic. Fortunately, most information of this type can be accessed fairly easily by consulting a good dictionary. If we are right in supposing that the rest of syntax is totally regular, the student who has mastered the syntactic system thoroughly ought to be able to produce perfect French consistently with the aid of a dictionary. This is, of course, a highly optimistic prospect, not just because it presupposes an unrealistically high level of dedication on the part of students, but also because there are many aspects of syntax which are poorly understood even by linguists. Moreover, as in other fields of scientific enquiry, as our understanding of the nature of language increases, we discover more problems which are still to be solved.

The hypothesis that the syntactic system itself is totally regular is a very strong one. For this reason, it constitutes a valuable methodological principle. If we come across an example which conforms to the rules of the linguist's grammar but is nevertheless judged to be ungrammatical by native speakers (or vice versa), we are not at liberty to dismiss this example as evidence of the general 'messiness' of language. Rather, we must conclude that, somewhere in the linguist's grammar, a generalisation has been missed or wrongly construed. We should then try to discover the nature of the problem by constructing further examples and by comparing the predictions of our grammar with the judgements of native speakers. If we are successful, the original 'counterexample' will have led us to a fuller understanding of the way in which the language works. If, as often happens, we are not totally successful, we will at least have identified a gap in our understanding and, perhaps, in our attempt to solve the problem, we may have assembled relevant evidence which may provide intuitive clues about what is going on.

The situation described above arises frequently in linguistic research, and we will encounter many instances of it in the course of this book. It is also reminiscent of a situation which we, as non-native speakers of French, may experience when we produce an utterance only to be corrected by a native speaker or teacher. In such cases, we may ignore the error and hope to do better next time or we may despair at our inability to master the language, perhaps subconsciously blaming the language itself for being so complicated. A more constructive reaction is to try and learn from our mistake, by identifying the gap in our knowledge of French and by looking for other examples which might guide us. Like the linguist in our earlier scenario, we may not arrive at any clear solutions, but we will at least be aware of the problem. In this respect, descriptive linguists and language learners share a common cause, though their priorities are rather different. For both, the target language can be seen as a complex puzzle which is there to be solved. For the linguist, the solution must take the form of an explicit model arrived at through conscious analysis, whereas for the language learner the problem-solving process is usually unconscious, culminating (ideally) in a set of intuitions which mirror those of the native speaker's mental grammar. From this perspective, the value of studying grammar does not lie just in the factual information which the grammar provides and which students may be able to assimilate and apply. Perhaps more importantly, it provides a conceptual tool which students can use to supplement the unconscious acquisition process, by learning to identify (and hopefully clarify) 'grey areas' in their intuitive knowledge and by extrapolating from their own errors and the data to which they are exposed.

### Exercises

1  Among English constructions which are condemned by prescriptive grammarians are double negatives (*I didn't do nothing*) and split infinitives (*John tried to quickly leave*). Find examples of constructions in French which are in common use, but are condemned by prescriptivists.

2  In the following examples, try to determine whether the bracketted expressions are modifiers or complements of the verb:

(a) Gaston fumait [dans la salle de bains]

(b) Jacques entrait [dans la salle de bains]

(c) Suzy votera [pour le candidat socialiste]

(d) Luc chantera [pour sa mère]

(e) Jules dansera [avec Marie]

(f) Max téléphonera [à ses parents]

We can continue (a) by ... *et Pierre faisait la même chose dans la cuisine*, where *faisait la même chose* refers back to *fumait*, but such a continuation is not appropriate in (b). Construct similar continuations for the other examples and comment on any generalisations which emerge.

3 In sentence (a), the NP which follows the verb can be replaced by the clitic pronoun *le*, but this is not possible in (b). Suggest reasons for this difference:

(a) Marie prendra le train suivant

(b) Marie partira le jour suivant

(c) Marie le prendra

(d) *Marie le partira

4 Sentence (a) is ambiguous, but the variants in (b)–(g) are not. How can the ambiguity of (a) be represented in structural terms? What structural properties of the processes involved in (b)–(g) might explain the lack of ambiguity in these cases?

(a) Pierre a vu un homme avec un télescope

(b) Un homme avec un télescope a été vu par Pierre

(c) Un homme a été vu par Pierre avec un télescope

(d) Avec un télescope, Pierre a vu un homme

(e) C'est un homme avec un télescope que Pierre a vu

(f) C'est avec un télescope que Pierre a vu un homme

(g) C'est un homme que Pierre a vu avec un télescope.

What happens if we replace *avec un télescope* by *aux cheveux longs*? Why?

5 Draw tree structures for the following sentences in accordance with the principles of X-bar syntax (ignoring the I node and the effects of verb-raising):

(a) Le train partira avant que tu arrives

(b) Ce jeune médecin assez intelligent croit que Marie est très malade

(c)  Le sommet de la montagne est couvert de neige

(d)  La concierge ouvrira la porte de la chambre avec une autre clé

6  A simple way of accounting for the position of adverbs like *souvent* in (a) would be to stipulate that such adverbs immediately follow the verb in French:

(a)  Pierre prend souvent ce train.

What problem would this account pose for the X-bar framework presented in 1.4? How does the relative oddness of (b) bear on this question:

(b)  ?Pierre a pris souvent ce train.

### Further reading

As background to the version of generative grammar adopted in this book, Radford (1981, 1988), both clear and very readable introductions, are particularly recommended. For readers who wish to tackle some of the more abstract theoretical works cited in later chapters, the following provide more detailed introductions: Haegeman (1991), Lasnik & Uriagerika (1988) and Ouhalla (1994). Horrocks (1987) and Sells (1987) give a wider view, comparing different models of generative grammar. Hurford (1994) is a useful reference for grammatical terms.

Ruwet (1967), Dubois & Dubois-Charlier (1970) and Nique (1974) introduce generative grammar in relation to French, but are now outdated. Picabia (1975), Borillo, Tamine & Soublin (1974) and Picabia & Zribi-Hertz (1981) aim to stimulate grammatical awareness through a series of problems and exercises (mainly intended for native speakers). M. Gross (1968, 1975, 1977) discusses many aspects of French from a distributionalist perspective. Dubois (1965, 1967, 1969) applies the generative model in a rather mechanistic way (of limited interest). Influential works on the generative syntax of French include Kayne (1975), Ruwet (1972, 1982, 1991), Milner (1978); also Kayne (1984) which is not specifically devoted to French, but contains significant discussion of aspects of French syntax.

Among reference grammars, Grévisse (1994) is generally regarded as the standard work, though in some respects Le Bidois & Le Bidois (1971) is more thorough. The three volumes by Sandfeld (1965a, 1965b, 1970) represent traditional grammar at its best. Other important reference grammars include Chevalier, Blanche Benveniste, Arrivé & Peytard (1964), Gaiffe, Maille, Breuil, Jahan, Wagner & Marijon (1936), Martinon (1927), Mauger (1968), Wagner & Pinchon (1962), Wartburg & Zumthor (1973). Harmer (1979) gives a detailed discussion of many uncertainties of French usage. Vinay & Darbelnet (1958) and Guillemin-

Flescher (1981) adopt a comparative (French/English) approach. Among grammars intended for English speakers, Judge & Healey (1983) is more detailed and more linguistically informed than most (though information is sometimes difficult to locate); Byrne & Churchill (1986) is a valuable reference (particularly good on syntactic properties of lexical items); Mansion (1952) (available with practical exercises) and Ferrar (1981) are also popular.

More general works on Modern French include Battye & Hintze (1992), Walter (1994), Harmer (1954), Désirat and Hordé (1976). For a historical perspective, see Darmesteter (1922), Harris (1978), G. Price (1971), Lodge (1993), Rickard (1989). Useful information on stylistic and sociolinguistic variation in French can be found in Ager (1990), Sanders (1992) and Offord (1990).

Journals devoted to French linguistics include *Journal of French Language Studies, Le français moderne, Langue française*. Articles on French syntax frequently appear in *Langages, Linguisticae Investigationes, Recherches linguistiques de Vincennes*[2] (Université de Paris VIII), *Cahiers de linguistique de l'UQAM* (Université du Québec à Montréal), *Travaux de linguistique*, and in other journals devoted to Romance linguistics, particularly *Probus, Revue romane* and *Revue de linguistique romane*. (Each issue of *Langue française* and *Langages* is devoted to a particular theme; references to relevant issues are given in the 'Further Reading' sections of the appropriate chapters.)

---

[2] Issues 1–13 of this journal were published under the shorter title *Recherches linguistiques*. In the bibliography the new title is used to refer to all issues, to avoid potential confusion with other journals which bear the earlier title.

# 2
# Verbs and Verb Phrases

## 2.1 Overview

The verb can be considered the key element in the sentence in the sense that it provides the link between all the other major constituents of the sentence. Consequently, the form and interpretation of a given sentence depends to a very large extent on the properties of the verbs which it contains.

2.2 begins with a classification of verbs according to semantic notions such as 'state', 'process', 'action', etc. In 2.3 and 2.4 verbs are investigated according to the types of complements they can take, applying the system of lexical representation introduced in 1.2.4 to explore the ways in which theta-roles are expressed in terms of grammatical relations.

The verbs *être* and *avoir* are atypical in that they do not describe particular types of states or events, but rather provide a syntactic link beween the subject and the complement which together express the basic semantic content of the sentence. The properties of these verbs are discussed in 2.5–2.6 along with other complement constructions which express relations of a similar type without recourse to a verb.

Auxiliary verbs have a rather similar status, supplementing the information conveyed by the main verb. In 2.7 we concentrate on the syntactic properties of verbs which are traditionally classified as auxiliaries (their semantic contribution, particularly as it relates to the concept of time, is analysed in chapter 4). In 2.8 we consider the related questions of the choice of auxiliary (*avoir* vs *être*) in compound tenses and agreement of the past-participle. A large portion of this discussion is devoted to the hypothesis that the surface subject of some intransitive verbs (principally those which select *être*) is a direct object in the underlying structure, a hypothesis which will be evoked quite frequently in discussion of other phenomena in subsequent chapters.

## 2.2 Classification of verbs
### 2.2.1 Are verbs 'doing' words?

Many verbs, like those in (1), fit the popular definition of verbs as 'doing' words, but there are many others, like those in (2), which do not involve 'doing' anything in any obvious sense:

(1)     a   Pierre courait dans le parc
        b   Marie chantait une chanson
        c   Paul a mis des livres sur la table
        d   Jules a donné des fleurs à Suzy
(2)     a   Pierre ressemble à Paul
        b   Marie connaît cette chanson
        c   Ce livre appartient à Paul
        d   Jules aime Suzy

From these examples, we can draw a preliminary distinction between verbs which denote **actions** (as in (1)) and verbs which denote **states** (as in (2)), where a 'state' can be defined as a situation which is stable over time and which does not involve any activity. There is a further class of verbs, illustrated in (3), which do not fit into either of these categories:

(3)     a   Pierre devient riche
        b   Le beurre a fondu
        c   Luc est tombé
        d   Suzy a reçu des fleurs

These verbs, which will be called **process** verbs, describe a change in state, but they do not involve any activity on the part of the subject entity.

This three-way classification can be expressed in terms of the interaction between two sets of semantic features, as shown in figure 2.1, where the **stative/non-stative** distinction relates to stability vs change over time, and the **agentive/non-agentive** relates to the active involvement of the subject entity in causing the change of state:

Figure 2.1  Semantic classification of verbs

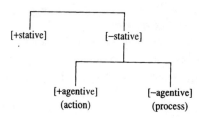

### 2.2.2   More than one category?

Some verbs may belong to more than one of the categories defined in 2.2.1. For example, the verb *savoir* is normally a stative verb (as in (4a)), but it can also be

51

used to describe a change of state ('becoming aware') as in (4b) (see 4.3.1 for discussion of this question in relation to tense):

(4)     a   Pierre sait que Marie est malade
         b   Pierre a su que Marie était malade

Similarly, *apprendre* with the sense 'learn' is always non-stative, but can be interpreted non-agentively as in (5a) or agentively, involving some degree of mental effort, as in (5b):

(5)     a   Pierre a appris que Marie était malade
         b   Pierre a appris ces verbes irréguliers

This problem arises with many non-stative verbs when the subject is human (or, more generally, animate). For example, verbs denoting change of place are clearly non-agentive with an inanimate subject, as in (6a), but favour an agentive reading when the subject is animate, as in (6b):

(6)     a   La poussière est entrée dans la maison
         b   Jacques est entré dans la maison

However, a non-agentive reading for (6b) is not impossible: e.g. if Jacques was pushed by someone else or propelled by some external force. Possibly, verbs like those in (5) and (6) are not actually ambiguous between an agentive and a non-agentive interpretation – they simply assign an Experiencer or Theme role to the subject, the agentive reading being the result of a **pragmatic inference**, based on beliefs about what is likely according to the extent to which the subject entity is in a position to bring about the change of state described by the verb (see 2.8.2 for further discussion). Nevertheless, in many other cases, this distinction is expressed by different verbs: e.g. *tomber* (non-agentive) vs *sauter* (agentive), *recevoir* vs *obtenir*, *voir* vs *regarder*.

### 2.2.3   Causative and non-causative verbs

For the cases in 2.2.2, the question of agentivity hinges on whether a participant in the change of state also causes this change. In examples like (7a), the 'causer' (or Agent) is distinct from the entity which undergoes the change described by the verb *mourir* in (7b):

(7)     a   Luc a tué le chat
         b   Le chat est mort

For verbs like *tuer*, where the relations of cause and effect are fairly distinct, the term **causative** will be used to distinguish them from other agentive verbs like *sauter* and *obtenir* which simply involve the active participation of the entity which undergoes the change in state. The various semantic distinctions which have been proposed are illustrated by the sentences in (8), all of which involve a basic relation of possession:

(8)     a   Marcel {a / possède} plusieurs          (stative)
            livres
        b   Marcel a reçu plusieurs livres          (non-stative, non-agentive)
        c   Marcel a {obtenu / acheté} plusieurs    (agentive)
            livres
        d   Luc a {donné / vendu} plusieurs         (causative)
            livres à Marcel

With causative verbs the entity which undergoes the change of state (the cat in (7a), Marcel in (8d)) is represented by a complement of the verb, whereas the same entity is expressed by the subject with corresponding non-causative verbs, as in (7b), (8a–c).

There are other semantic distinctions which can be superimposed on the classification given in figure 2.1. Within the class of non-stative verbs, we can distinguish between those which describe a transition from one state to another – e.g. alive to dead (*mourir, tuer*), change of location (*descendre, mettre*) or possession (*recevoir, donner*) – and those which describe an activity which can be carried on indefinitely without a final result – e.g. *courir, réfléchir, travailler, secouer*. The terms **accomplishment** and **non-accomplishment** respectively will be used to distinguish these two classes of verbs. One way of checking this distinction is to add a phrase indicating the duration of the event, giving *en . . .* with 'accomplishments', but *pendant . . .* with 'non-accomplishments':

(9)     a   L'arbre est tombé (en trois      (non-agentive, accomplishment)
            secondes)
        b   Luc a gagné le sommet (en cinq   (agentive, accomplishment)
            heures)
        c   Jules a cassé la branche (en trois   (causative, accomplishment)
            minutes)

(10)    a   La maison a tremblé (pendant     (non-agentive, non-accomplishment)
            trois minutes)
        b   Marie a dansé (pendant deux      (agentive, non-accomplishment)
            heures)
        c   Jules a secoué la branche        (causative, non-accomplishment)
            (pendant deux minutes)

Figure 2.2 Semantic classification of verbs (extended)

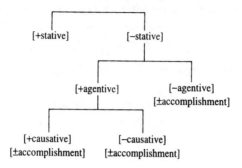

As the examples in (9)–(10) show, this distinction cuts across the non-agentive, agentive and causative division.

To accommodate these further semantic distinctions, the classification proposed in 2.2.1 can be extended as in figure 2.2.

### 2.3 Syntactic classification

#### 2.3.1 Lexical entries of verbs

From a syntactic point of view, the main thing we need to know about any given verb is the types of complement it can take. In 1.2.5, we proposed a system for representing these properties, illustrated in (11) for the verb *mettre*, as used in (12):

(11)     *mettre*: V     [<u>Agent</u>, Theme, Goal]
                         Theme = NP
                         Goal = PP

(12)     Pierre a mis le livre sur la table

Recall that the first line of this entry, the 'theta-grid', identifies the arguments of the verb in terms of their theta-roles, with underlining to indicate the external argument (expressed by the subject), while the subsequent lines specify the syntactic categories of the internal arguments (complements of the verb). Thus, (11) indicates that *mettre* involves three entities: an Agent (who performs the action), a Theme (which undergoes the effect of the action) and a Goal (the place to which something moves), realised respectively as the subject (*Pierre*), the direct object (*le livre*) and the indirect object (*la table*).

An advantage of this system is that it not only indicates the types of complements taken by a verb but also tells us how each complement is interpreted. This advantage can be seen in examples like those in (13):

(13)     a   Pierre a annoncé la nouvelle à Marie
         b   Pierre a informé Marie de la nouvelle

Traditionally, both *annoncer* and *informer* are classified as transitive verbs, but this classification conceals the fact that the direct object of *annoncer* represents the information being conveyed whereas the direct object of *informer* denotes the receiver of the information. This difference is made explicit in the lexical entries in (14)–(15), where the 'information' and the 'receiver' are characterised respectively as Theme and Goal:

(14)  *annoncer*: V  [Agent, Theme, Goal]
  Theme = NP
  Goal = [$_{PP}$ à NP]

(15)  *informer*: V  [Agent, Theme, Goal]
  Goal = NP
  Theme = [$_{PP}$ de NP]

In 1.2.5, we saw how this system can represent the relation between *aimer* and *plaire* in examples like (16a,b), to which we may add *amuser* in (16c):

(16)  a  Paul aime ce jeu
  b  Ce jeu plaît à Paul
  c  Ce jeu amuse Paul

All of these verbs describe a relation between an Experiencer and a Theme, but differ principally with regard to the grammatical relations which express these roles, as shown in (17):

(17)  a  *aimer*: V  [Experiencer, Theme]
    Theme = NP
  b  *plaire*: V  [Theme, Experiencer]
    Experiencer = [$_{PP}$ à NP]
  c  *amuser*: V  [Theme, Experiencer]
    Experiencer = NP

Note in passing that *amuser* also allows an agentive reading, like *apprendre* and *entrer* in 2.2.2, when the subject is animate: *Pierre amusait l'enfant*.

In all the examples we have looked at, if a verb has an Agent as one of its arguments, the Agent is the external argument (i.e. the subject). Indeed, this appears to be an absolute generalisation for verbs in their active form (see 3.2 for discussion of passive constructions), which holds in English and many other languages as well. Note that this does not mean that all subjects are Agents. For verbs which do not involve an Agent role, no firm predictions can be made as to the choice of external argument, as the cases in (17) show.

### 2.3.2 Three-place verbs

In English, many three-place verbs can occur in **double-object** constructions like (18b) in which the Goal is expressed by the first of two NPs, alongside the construction in (18a) where the Goal is a PP:

(18)    a  John {gave / lent / showed} the book to Mary
        b  John {gave / lent / showed} Mary the book

However, in French only the (a) construction is possible:

(19)    a  Jean a {donné / prêté / montré} le livre à Marie
        b  *Jean a {donné / prêté / montré} Marie le livre

This restriction can be stated informally as follows:

*In French, no verb can take more than one direct object.*

It follows from this restriction that, if one complement of a verb is realised as a direct object, any others must have indirect object status. However, this restriction does not tell us which theta-role corresponds to which grammatical relation, nor does it help with verbs like those in (17) which have only one internal argument. With three-place verbs, the general tendency is for the Theme to be realised as the direct object, as with *mettre* in (12), *annoncer* in (14) and with the verbs in (19). However, exceptions to this tendency, like *informer* in (15), are not hard to find – for example, *munir* and *couvrir* can be regarded as causative change of possession or change of location verbs whose direct object denotes the Goal, while the Theme is expressed by a PP:

(20)    a  Jules a muni sa femme d'un revolver
        b  Suzy a couvert la table d'une nappe

A typical property of these 'exceptional' verbs is that they attach a certain importance to the Theme entity which is absent with verbs of the *annoncer, donner, mettre* type. Thus, with *informer* and *munir* the Theme entity is presented as something which the Goal entity needs. With change of location verbs like *couvrir*, a typical implication is that the Theme entity comes to occupy the whole of the space denoted by the Goal; e.g. in (20b) the cloth is placed over the whole of the table. This effect can also be seen with verbs like *charger* which allow both constructions:

(21)    a  Pierre a chargé le blé sur le camion
        b  Pierre a chargé le camion de blé

### 2.3.3 Two-place verbs

With verbs which have only one internal argument, there is a tendency for this argument to be realised as a direct object if it is a Theme, but as an indirect object otherwise. Thus, most verbs which describe an action performed on an entity (the Theme) are transitive (e.g. *casser, manger, frapper, secouer,* etc.) whereas movement verbs typically require the Goal or Source (the place from which something moves) to be expressed by a PP (e.g. *aller, venir, arriver, entrer, sortir, partir,* etc.). Nevertheless, some verbs seem to be quite idiosyncratic in this respect and in order to investigate this matter sensibly we would need a much clearer classification of theta-roles than it is possible to offer here. To give some flavour of the problem, we may note some verbs whose counterparts in English are transitive but which take a PP in French: *abuser (de)* 'abuse', *convenir (à)* 'suit', *douter (de)* 'doubt', *jouer ({à / de})* 'play ({football / the piano})', *hériter (de)* 'inherit', *nuire (à)* 'harm', *obéir (à)* 'obey', *renoncer (à)* 'abandon', *résister (à)* 'resist', *ressembler (à)* 'resemble', *succéder (à)* 'succeed, follow', etc. Verbs which are transitive in French but take a PP in English appear to be much less numerous, the principal examples being activity verbs of perception such as *regarder* 'look at', *écouter* 'listen to', *viser* 'aim at', *chercher* 'look for' – other cases are *approuver* 'approve of', *attendre* 'wait for', *espérer* 'hope for', etc. Of course, in many of these cases the cross-linguistic difference depends on which verb we choose as a translation: e.g. the difference with *chercher* and *attendre* disappears if we compare them with English 'seek' and 'await'.

### 2.3.4 Clauses as direct or indirect objects

In the preceding sections we considered only internal arguments which are realised as NPs or PPs. A further problem arises in cases with complement clauses. In (22) the bracketted clauses have the same theta-role (Theme) as the bracketted NPs in (23):

(22)    a   Pierre a annoncé à Marie [que le Beaujolais nouveau est arrivé]
        b   Pierre a informé Marie [que le Beaujolais nouveau est arrivé]

(23)    a   Pierre a annoncé [l'arrivée du Beaujolais nouveau] à Marie
        b   Pierre a informé Marie de [l'arrivée du Beaujolais nouveau]

An obvious way of capturing this parallel is to treat the complement clause as a direct object in (22a) but as an indirect object in (22b), even though it is not marked as such by a preposition. This approach is implicit in traditional grammars and dictionaries, which classify *annoncer* as a transitive verb even in examples like (22a). It is also supported by the choice of pronouns to replace these clauses when the sentences in (22) are continued as in (24) (given that *le* corresponds to a direct object while *en* typically replaces an indirect object introduced by *de*):

(24)     a   ... et il l'a annoncé à Solange aussi

         b   ... et il en a informé Solange aussi

In order to indicate the indirect object status of the complement clause in (22b), let us suppose that, in the underlying structure, it is introduced by the preposition *de*, which is deleted obligatorily at the surface level. Thus, the sentences in (22) have the underlying structures in (25):

(25)     a   $[_S$ Pierre $[_{VP}$ a annoncé $[_{PP}$ à Marie] $[_{S'}$ que ...]]]

         b   $[_S$ Pierre $[_{VP}$ a informé $[_{NP}$ Marie] $[_{PP}$ de $[_{S'}$ que ...]]]]

To accommodate these structures, our earlier entries for *annoncer* and *informer* can be revised slightly, as follows:

(26)     *annoncer*: V   [Agent, Theme, Goal]

                         Theme = NP/S'

                         Goal = $[_{PP}$ à NP]

(27)     *informer*: V   [Agent, Theme, Goal]

                         Goal = NP

                         Theme = $[_{PP}$ de NP/S']

With some verbs, the complement clause is pronominalised by means of *y*, which usually corresponds to *à* (see 6.5):

(28)     a   Pierre s'attend que le train soit en retard

         b   ... et Paul s'y attend aussi

This can be accounted for by assuming that the *que* clause in (28a) is introduced by *à* in the underlying structure, just like the NP in *Pierre s'attend à cet événement*. In fact, with some verbs, like *s'attendre* (and more marginally *informer*), the 'phantom' preposition actually appears on the surface in alternative constructions in which the clause is introduced by *ce*:

(29)     a   Pierre s'attend à ce que le train soit en retard

         b   ?Pierre a informé Marie de ce que le Beaujolais nouveau est arrivé

Our analysis of finite clauses which function as indirect objects can be summarised as follows:

**Finite indirect object clauses:**

*In the underlying structure, indirect object clauses are introduced by the same*

*preposition (à or de) as introduces an indirect object NP with the same theta-role.*

At the surface level, this preposition must be deleted (or in some cases, *ce* must be inserted before the clause).

### 2.3.5 Infinitival complement clauses

Infinitival complement clauses raise the opposite problem. In (31b, c), the choice of pronoun corresponds to the use of *de* or *à* before the infinitive in (30b, c), but in (31a) we have the pronoun *le* replacing an infinitive introduced by *de*:

(30)     a   Pierre a interdit à Marie de partir
          b   Pierre a empêché Marie de partir
          c   Pierre a incité Marie à partir

(31)     a   Pierre l'a interdit à Marie
          b   Pierre en a empêché Marie
          c   Pierre y a incité Marie

Examples like *Pierre a interdit cette action à Marie* strongly suggest that the infinitive is indeed a direct object, despite the presence of *de*. We also find infinitives with *à* which appear to function as direct objects:

(32)     a   Suzy apprend aux enfants à parler le français
          b   Suzy l'apprend aux enfants
          c   Suzy apprend le français aux enfants

Whereas with finite complement clauses we had to 'invent' an underlying preposition to indicate indirect object status, with infinitives *à* and *de* can occur even when they do not indicate indirect object status.

Given our hypothesis in 1.3.2 that infinitival clauses belong to the category S', this puzzle can be solved by postulating that *à* and *de* before infinitives can function either as prepositions (indicating an indirect object relation) or as complementisers (the equivalent of *que* in finite clauses), as in (33):

(33)     a   $[_{PP} \{à / de\} \, S'_{INF}]$    (30b, c)
          b   $[_{S'} \{à / de\} \, S_{INF}]$    (30a), (32a)

There are various tests which we can use to distinguish between these two structures. One is to substitute an NP or pronoun which has the same interpretation, as in the above discussion. The generalisation in 2.3.2 that a verb cannot take more than one direct object provides a further test: if the verb takes another complement which is clearly a direct object (e.g. *Marie* in (30b, c)), it follows that the infinitive must be an indirect object and that the *à* or *de* which introduces it is a preposition. The converse generalisation also appears to hold: if the other complement is an indirect object, the infinitive functions as a direct object (*à* or *de* being complementisers). However, this test is not always very helpful since, for English students of French, the problem often lies in remembering whether the other complement is a direct or indirect object. In the absence of another complement, it is often difficult to tell whether an infinitive should be classed as a direct or indirect object, either because it cannot be replaced by an NP with exactly the same semantic role or because the use of a pronoun is avoided by simply omitting the infinitive. This problem can be illustrated by the following examples with *essayer*:

(34)     a   Pierre a essayé de nager
         b   Pierre a essayé cette activité
         c   Pierre l'a essayé
         d   Pierre n'a pas réussi à nager, mais il a essayé

Although *l'activité* in (34b) and the pronoun in (34c) are clearly direct objects, their interpretation is rather different from that of the infinitive in (34a) (denoting something which Pierre has actually experienced rather than an aim to be achieved). In contexts where the infinitive is redundant, as in (34d), it is simply omitted. Thus, although *essayer* can take a direct object, we do not have conclusive evidence that the infinitive in (34a) can be classed as such. In practice, it does not seem to matter much how we classify the infinitive in such cases.

The vast majority of verbs which require a preposition before an NP take the same preposition with the infinitive, as in the examples discussed above, but there are some exceptions like *s'efforcer*, which requires *à* with an NP and *y* as a pronoun (*s'efforcer au travail, s'y efforcer*) but usually takes *de* with an infinitive (though *à* is also attested): *s'efforcer de travailler. Forcer* and *obliger* favour *à* with the infinitive in active constructions, but *de* in the passive (*{forcer / obliger} quelqu'un à travailler* vs *être {forcé / obligé} de travailler*) – in corresponding constructions with an NP or pronoun, only *à* and *y* are possible, even in the passive: *{obliger / forcer} quelqu'un à cette démarche, y {obliger / forcer} quelqu'un, être {forcé / obligé} à cette démarche, y être {forcé / obligé}*. This exceptional behaviour is restricted to a small class of verbs which express 'coercion'. Moreover, there do not appear to be any exceptions of the opposite type, i.e. verbs which take *de* with an NP (or *en* as pronoun) but *à* with the infinitive.

Direct object infinitives are usually introduced by *de* or by nothing at all (**bare infinitives**), as in *J'aime nager*, depending on the governing verb. Verbs like *apprendre* which require *à* before the direct object infinitive are rare – other common verbs which favour *à* (though they allow *de*) are *commencer* and *continuer*.

## 2.4 Variations in argument structure

### 2.4.1 *Optional complements*

ʻSome verbs which are normally transitive can be used without a direct object, as in (35), where the NPs in parentheses can be omitted:

(35)  a  Gaston a mangé (le repas)
      b  Jules buvait (un café)
      c  Solange lisait (un journal)
      d  Marie a chanté (cette chanson)

In traditional grammars and dictionaries, this use of verbs without a direct object is termed **absolutive** rather than intransitive – in the absolutive use of a verb, the object-entity is implicit but with genuine intransitives (like *dormir* in *Gaston a dormi*) there is no perception that anything has been missed out.

A technical way of accommodating absolutive uses in our lexical entries is to place parentheses around the instruction specifying the syntactic category which corresponds to the theta-role, as in (36) for *manger*:

(36)  *manger:* V   [Agent, Theme]
                (Theme = NP)

This entry indicates that *manger* always describes a relation between an Agent and a Theme, but expression of the Theme by a direct object is optional. However, this simple notational device obscures a range of complex issues. The option of omitting the object is not a clear-cut property of particular verbs – often it depends on context or tense in ways which vary from one verb to the other (e.g. (35c) is fine in the imperfect, but *?Solange a lu* is odd without a fairly loaded context, whereas there is no clear tense restriction with *manger*). A further problem is that some normally intransitive verbs can be followed by a direct object which serves to specify the nature of the activity in some way:

(37)  a  Jules a sifflé (la Marseillaise)
      b  Suzy a dansé (une gigue)
      c  Marcel a couru (le marathon)

An extreme example of this phenomenon is represented by so-called **cognate objects** whose head noun 'copies' the verb and is typically modified by an expression which is interpreted as if it modified the verb (cf. English *to live a dog's life* 'to live like a dog'):

(38)        Luc vit une vie de chien

Where to draw the line between omission of a complement (as in (35)) and addition of an extra argument (as in (37)) is by no means clear – e.g. there is little difference between (35d) and (37a).

A similar problem arises with optional indirect objects:

(39)      a  Pierre téléphonait (à Marie)
            b  Pierre écrivait (à Marie)
            c  Pierre lisait un poème (à Marie)

In (39a) it seems clear that *à Marie* is a complement (the meaning of *téléphoner* implies a Receiver of the communication), but with *écrire* in (39b) this is less clear (one can write without writing to anybody), whereas in (39c) *à Marie* adds an extra participant to the two-place relation normally described by *lire*.

In short, deciding what complements a verb takes is not always a straightforward matter, and sometimes such decisions may be rather arbitrary. (For further discussion relevant to cases like (39), see 6.8).

### 2.4.2 'Knock-on' effects

Sometimes the presence or absence of one complement may have a 'knock-on' effect on the way in which another argument is realised. For example, we saw in 2.3.5 that *empêcher* can occur with a direct object denoting the affected person and an indirect object infinitive describing the event which is prevented, but if the affected person is omitted, the event is specified by a direct object (NP or subjunctive S'):

(40)      a  Pierre a empêché l'accident
            b  Pierre a empêché que l'accident se produise

Similarly, in *Pierre l'a empêché de partir* the direct object pronoun represents the affected person, but in *Pierre l'a empêché* it typically denotes the event (it could also denote the affected person, the event being left implicit).

A more complicated case of the same type is *payer* in (41), where the direct object can represent the 'payee' (as in (41a)), the 'price' (as in (41b)) or the 'goods' (as in (41c)) depending on what other participants in the relation are specified within the VP[1]:

---

[1] Example (41c) appears to violate the restriction against verbs taking more than one direct object (see 2.3.2), since the verb is followed by two NPs, *le livre* and *cent francs*. Nevertheless, *cent francs* in this case is a rather unusual sort of NP – in (41c) it can be replaced by an adverbial expression such as *très cher*, but not by other NPs like *l'argent* (*Pierre a payé le livre {très cher / *l'argent}*), whereas in (41b) the converse holds: *Pierre a payé {*très cher / l'argent} à Marie*. This evidence suggests that *cent francs* in (41c) functions as a modifier of some sort, indicating quantity, rather than a true direct object.

(41)    a  Pierre a payé Marie
        b  Pierre a payé cent francs à Marie
        c  Pierre a payé ce livre cent francs

Examples like (40) and (41) can perhaps be seen in terms of a tendency to exploit the direct object position wherever possible; e.g. with *empêcher*, if the direct object is not used to express the affected person, the event complement takes over this position. However, the converse phenomenon is observed with *hériter* in (42):

(42)    a  Jules a hérité une fortune de son père
        b  Jules a hérité d'une fortune

In (42a) the Theme (i.e. the inheritance) is represented by the direct object and the Source by an indirect object, but if the Source is not specified, the Theme takes over the indirect object function, as in (42b).

It is difficult to discern a regular pattern in the examples discussed above and no attempt to do so will be made here, though these are by no means isolated examples.

### 2.4.3  Eliminating or adding an Agent

Some verbs can be used transitively (with a causative interpretation) or intransitively (with a process interpretation):

(43)    a  Jules a fondu le beurre
        b  Solange a cuit le poulet
        c  Le gouvernement a changé la situation économique
        d  Le patron a augmenté les prix.

(44)    a  Le beurre a fondu
        b  Le poulet a cuit
        c  La situation économique a changé
        d  Les prix ont augmenté

In (43) the subject expresses the Agent role, but in the absence of an Agent (as in (44)) the Theme occupies the subject position. Note that in (44) it is not the case that the Agent is left unspecified; the meaning of these sentences does not involve an Agent at all – contrast (44a), which simply describes a process, with the passive sentence *Le beurre a été fondu* which describes an action performed by an unspecified Agent (cf. the same contrast in English: *The butter melted* vs *The butter was melted*). Consequently, the uses in (43) and (44) must be represented by different theta-grids, as shown for *fondre* in (45):

63

(45)     *fondre* (1): V  [A̲g̲e̲n̲t̲, Theme]     *fondre* (2): V  [T̲h̲e̲m̲e̲]
                 Theme = NP

The pattern illustrated in (43)–(44) is widespread in English. In French, it extends to certain verbs of movement, where English normally requires the use of different verbs (e.g. *[take / go] down*):

(46)     a   Pierre a descendu les valises du grenier
         b   Marcel a sorti la bière du frigo

(47)     a   Marie est descendue du grenier
         b   Gaston est sorti du bistro

No claims will be made here about whether the intransitive uses in (44) and (47) are derived from the transitive uses by eliminating the Agent or whether the transitive uses in (43) and (46) involve the addition of an Agent. It is merely observed that the verb-forms in question can be used in both ways.

### 2.4.4   Pronominal verbs

With many verbs, the intransitive (process) use is signalled by the obligatory presence of a reflexive pronoun:

(48)     a   Pierre a ouvert la porte
         b   Luc a cassé la branche
         c   Le gouvernement a transformé la situation économique.

(49)     a   La porte s'est ouverte
         b   La branche s'est cassée
         c   La situation économique s'est transformée

The reflexive pronoun in (49) does not indicate that the subject entity performs an action on itself (in contrast to cases like *Pierre s'est frappé*), but serves as a grammatical indicator of the intransitive use of the verb. Intransitive verbs which require the reflexive pronoun in this way are known as **pronominal** verbs. There does not seem to be any clear generalisation which can predict which verbs are pronominal in their intransitive use, distinguishing the cases in (49) from the non-pronominal verbs in (44), though the pattern in (48)–(49) is the more common. Like the cases in (44), the sentences in (49) do not involve an implicit Agent. Thus the relation between *ouvrir* and *s'ouvrir* can be represented in the manner proposed for *fondre* in (45):

(50)     *ouvrir*: V     [A̲g̲e̲n̲t̲, Theme]     *s'ouvrir*: V     [T̲h̲e̲m̲e̲]
                 Theme = NP

There are other constructions with reflexive pronouns, superficially similar to those in (49), which do involve an implicit Agent. These constructions and the criteria for distinguishing them from those in (49) will be discussed in detail in 3.3.

### 2.4.5 *Impersonal verbs*
There are a few verbs, known as **impersonal** verbs, which can only occur with the subject *il*. Clear examples of this type are *falloir* and *s'agir* in (51):

(51)    a   Il faut un marteau
        b   Il s'agit de notre avenir

Impersonal constructions will be discussed in detail in 3.4. In this section, only the basic properties of impersonal verbs and the ways of representing them will be considered.

Intuitively, we know that *il* in (51) does not refer to anything – it does not represent an argument of the verb which can be characterised in terms of a theta-role such as Agent, Experiencer, etc. Rather, its function appears to be purely syntactic, satisfying a requirement that all finite clauses must have a subject. More formally, impersonal verbs can be represented as verbs which lack an external argument, their theta-roles (Themes in the case of (51)) being assigned to complements of the verb, as specified in the lexical entries in (52)[2]:

(52)    a   *falloir*: V    [Theme]
                            Theme = NP
        b   *s'agir*:       [Theme]
                            Theme = [$_{PP}$ de NP]

Because the Theme is not an external argument (it is not underlined in the theta-grid), it cannot be expressed by a subject NP:

(53)    a   *Un marteau faut
        b   *Notre avenir s'agit

Moreover, since no other theta-role is assigned to the subject position, this position cannot be occupied by an expression which must refer to something:

(54)    a   *Pierre faut un marteau
        b   *Ce livre s'agit de notre avenir

        The ungrammaticality of sentences like (54b) with *s'agir* is worth
        emphasising since *s'agir* is often erroneously used in this way by English-

---

[2] For more detailed entries for these verbs, allowing complements other than NP or *de* + NP, see 3.4.1.

speaking students of French to mean something like 'concern' or 'deal with' – this verb can only be used impersonally with the meaning 'it is a matter of ...'.

It is assumed that in (51) the subject position is left empty in the underlying structure, but is filled at some later stage by the **dummy** pronoun *il*:

(55)    a    $[_S \varnothing [_{VP}$ faut un marteau]]
        b    $[_S \varnothing [_{VP}$ s'agit de notre avenir]]

Verbs like *falloir* and *s'agir* which can only occur in impersonal constructions will be referred to as **Intrinsic impersonal** verbs. There are many other verbs which normally take a 'real' subject, but can be used impersonally under certain conditions. For example, impersonal constructions are often used to avoid having a clause in the subject position:

(56)    a    Ce jeu lui plaît
        b    Jouer au bridge lui plaît
        c    Il lui plaît de jouer au bridge

(57)    a    Cette date me convient
        b    Que tu viennes demain me convient
        c    Il me convient que tu viennes demain

The subject clauses in (b) have a similar interpretation to the subject NPs in the (a) examples, but when the subject is a clause, it is more natural to place it within the VP and to use the dummy subject *il*, as in the (c) examples which will be referred to as **derived** impersonal constructions. The 'personal' constructions in (b) are grammatical, if rather clumsy, but corresponding examples with Intrinsic impersonal verbs are completely impossible: *\*Partir faut, \*Que tu reviennes faut* (cf. *Il faut partir, Il faut que tu reviennes*).

Another example of a 'derived' impersonal construction is (58b) which can be used as a stylistic alternative to the 'personal' construction in (58a), with certain verbs when the subject is indefinite:

(58)    a    Trois personnes sont arrivées
        b    Il est arrivé trois personnes

The syntactic properties of 'derived' impersonal constructions will be discussed in detail in 3.4.

### 2.4.6 Weather verbs

**Weather** verbs like *pleuvoir* and *neiger* constitute a rather special class of impersonal verbs:

(59)        Il {pleut / neige}

One approach to weather verbs is to treat them as zero-place verbs, verbs which have no arguments at all. This is plausible in so far as all the essential information about the event is encapsulated in the verb itself: e.g. *pleuvoir* and *neiger* express a process of 'falling from the sky' while specifying the type of 'stuff' which falls. Thus, weather verbs can be represented as in (60):

(60)        *pleuvoir:* V        [ ]

Since there is no theta-role which can be assigned to the subject position, this position is filled by the dummy pronoun *il*, as in the case of *falloir* and *s'agir*.

Some linguists have challenged this analysis, arguing that *il* has a 'pseudo-argumental' status denoting, in a rather vague sense, the ambient situation. No attempt to resolve this issue will be made here, but it may be worth mentioning some of the relevant evidence. Firstly, in colloquial usage, weather verbs allow *ça* as an alternative to *il*, particularly when the verb itself is a colloquial or slang form: *Ça {flotte / caille}* 'it is raining/freezing' – note that *ça* is not available as an alternative to *il* with verbs like *falloir* or *s'agir* in (51). Secondly, weather *il* can function as the understood subject of an infinitive in examples like *Il pleut souvent sans neiger* 'It often rains without snowing', whereas parallel examples with impersonal *il* are impossible: e.g. \**Il s'agit d'enfoncer le clou sans falloir un marteau,* where the intended reading might be something like 'It is a matter of driving home the nail without it being necessary to use a hammer'. Thirdly, weather verbs can occur without the dummy subject as infinitival complements of *faire* in a way that true impersonal verbs cannot: e.g. *Le sorcier a fait pleuvoir* 'the sorcerer made it rain' vs \**Le patron a fait falloir refaire le travail* 'the boss made it be necessary to redo the work'.

Sometimes weather verbs can be followed by an NP:

(61)        a    Il pleuvait une pluie fine
            b    Il pleuvait des balles sur les soldats

Examples like (61a) ('It was drizzling', i.e. raining lightly) are reminiscent of the cognate object construction (38) in 2.4.1. In (61b) ('It was raining bullets on the soldiers'), *pleuvoir* is used metaphorically with the sense of *tomber* (cf. *Il tombait des balles sur les soldats* which is a derived impersonal construction of the same type as (58b) in 2.4.5).

## 2.5   Copular verbs
### 2.5.1   Constructions with 'être'
The term **copular** is often used to designate a small but rather special class of verbs whose principal member in French is *être* (others are *devenir, rester* and some uses

of *sembler* and *paraître* which will be left for discussion in 2.5.3). The special properties of these verbs can be illustrated by comparing the examples in (62):

(62) a Pierre est le mari de Suzy
   b Pierre déteste le mari de Suzy

In (62b), the two NPs denote distinct individuals and the verb describes a certain relation between these individuals. This is not the case in (62a) where the NP *le mari de Suzy* is a description of the individual referred to by the subject *Pierre*. Thus the function of copular verbs like *être* is to associate this description with the subject entity.

In (62a), a definite NP is used to describe a property which is unique to this individual. In other circumstances, the relevant property can be expressed by means of an indefinite NP, a noun without a determiner (e.g. to denote a person's profession, political persuasion, etc.), an AP or a PP (e.g. to describe the location of the person):

(63)  a Pierre est un imbécile
    b Pierre est {plombier / communiste}
    c Pierre est riche
    d Pierre est dans la cuisine

Alongside sentences like (62a), we find mirror image constructions like (64):

(64)  Le mari de Suzy est Pierre

In this case, it is the subject NP which describes a property, while the complement identifies the individual who fits this description. Accordingly, examples like (64) will be referred to as **identificational** constructions whereas examples of the sort in (62a) and (63) will be referred to as **predicational** constructions, the idea being that the complement 'predicates' or asserts something about the subject entity. Schematically, the difference between predicational and identificational constructions can be represented as in (65), where the person or thing which the addressee is expected to identify is labelled as the 'entity' and the description of this entity is labelled as the 'property':

(65)  SUBJECT  COMPLEMENT
    'entity'   'property'  (predicational)
    'property'  'entity'   (identificational)

In all our examples so far we have used a proper noun for the NP which serves to identify the individual concerned, because proper nouns, by their very nature (see 5.2.1), have a purely referential function which does not involve description, thus making it easier to distinguish the 'identifying' part of the sentence from the descriptive part. However, other types of NP (particularly definite NPs) can be used to identify the individual concerned, as in (66):

(66) a Le meilleur ami de Paul est le mari de Suzy
   b Le meilleur ami de Paul est un imbécile
   c Le meilleur ami de Paul est {plombier / communiste}
   d Le meilleur ami de Paul est riche
   e Le meilleur ami de Paul est dans la cuisine

Examples (66b–e) require a predicational reading, expressing a property of the individual identified as Paul's best friend. However, example (66a) is ambiguous between a predicational and an identificational reading, though the difference in meaning is rather subtle. On the predicational reading, (66a) presupposes that the addressee knows who Paul's best friend is and it conveys new information about him (namely, that he is married to Suzy). On the identificational reading, the addressee is presumed not to know who Paul's best friend is and the sentence supplies this information by means of an expression which will enable the addressee to identify him.

The pattern outlined above is basically the same as in English, except for the use of nouns like *plombier* and *communiste* without a determiner. In fact, the distinctions drawn above enable us to define the conditions in which such nouns can occur without a determiner – basically, they can only be used to describe properties in predicational constructions. In particular, they cannot be used as arguments of verbs (*\*Pierre déteste plombier*, *\*Plombier a réparé les robinets*) or as subjects of identificational sentences (*\*Plombier est Pierre*).

In sentences of the identificational type, a dislocated construction (see 1.5.5) is often preferred, with the pronoun *ce* recapitulating the descriptive expression, as in (67) (cf. (64) above):

(67) Le mari de Suzy, c'est Pierre

The use of a dislocated construction is obligatory when the individual is identified by a pronoun (for instance, when pointing at the person concerned):

(68) a Le mari de Suzy, c'est lui
   b \*Le mari de Suzy est lui

Note that *il* cannot be used in place of *ce* in (67) or (68a). Similarly, *ce* must be used as the subject of an identificational sentence when the description is supplied by the previous context, as in (69):

(69) – Qui est le mari de Suzy?
   – C'est Pierre

More generally, *ce* (never *il(s)* or *elle(s)*) is the pronoun used to substitute for the descriptive expression in identificational constructions. To avoid possible misunderstanding, let us quickly add that *ce* can be used in other cases as well. This, and other matters concerning the use of pronouns in copular constructions, will be left for detailed discussion in 6.9.

A further, much more marginal, use of *être* is the **existential** use illustrated in Descartes' famous sentence *Je pense, donc je suis*, where *être* is synonymous with *exister*. A variant of this is the impersonal use of *être* (as a literary alternative to *il y a*): *Il est des personnes qui …* 'There are people who …'.

### 2.5.2 *'Small clauses'*
In many languages such as Arabic and Russian, copular sentences can be formed without recourse to a verb like *être* simply by concatenating the 'entity' and 'property' expressions, e.g. 'Peter Mary's husband', 'Peter rich', etc. This has led some linguists to suggest that in languages like French and English, the copular verb has an essentially syntactic function, satisfying a requirement that every sentence must contain a verb and also acting as a vehicle for the tense features. One way of implementing this idea is to suppose that the 'entity' and 'property' expressions go together to form a constituent, known as a **small clause**, which is analogous to a 'normal' sentence except that the predicate (the phrase which asserts something about the subject) is a category other than VP. The structure of the small clause (**SC**) can be defined roughly as in (70):

(70)     SC → NP + XP (where XP = NP, AP or PP)

Simplifying somewhat, in languages like Arabic and Russian, small clauses can occur as main clauses whereas in French and English they can only be used as complements of certain verbs including *être*. Thus, copular sentences in French have underlying structures of the form (71), where $\emptyset$ represents the empty subject of *être*:

(71)     $[_S \emptyset$ être $[_{SC}$ NP XP]]

An advantage of this approach is that it can capture the relation between predicational and identificational constructions. Consider the underlying structure (72) where the predicate of the SC (corresponding to XP in (71)) is a definite NP:

(72)     $[_S \emptyset$ est $[_{SC} [_{NP}$ Pierre] $[_{NP}$ le mari de Suzy]]]

To derive a valid surface structure, one of the NPs must be moved into the subject position in the main clause, to satisfy the requirement that every sentence needs a subject (perhaps also so that the NP can acquire Case – see 1.5.6 – though this is a complex matter which we shall leave aside). If the subject of the small clause (*Pierre*) is moved, as in (73a), we derive the predicational sentence (62a), but if the predicate NP (*le mari de Suzy*) is moved, as in (73b), we get the identificational sentence (64):

(73)　　a　$[_S [_{NP}$ Pierre] est $[_{SC}$ ___ $[_{NP}$ le mari de Suzy]]]

　　　　　b　$[_S [_{NP}$ le mari de Suzy] est $[_{SC} [_{NP}$ Pierre] ___ ]]]

If XP is represented by a category other than NP (e.g. an AP as in (74)), the second option is not available since APs cannot occur as subjects:

(74)　　$[_S \varnothing$ est $[_{SC} [_{NP}$ Pierre] $[_{AP}$ riche]]]

Thus, from this structure we can only derive the predicational sentence *Pierre est riche*. The same restriction holds when XP is a determinerless NP of the *plombier/communiste* type. With some indefinite NPs, both options are available:

(75)　　a　Pierre est un candidat possible　　(predicational)

　　　　　b　Un candidat possible est Pierre　　(identificational)

### 2.5.3　Other copular verbs

The verbs *devenir, rester, sembler* and *paraître* can be used in a manner similar to *être*, with some restrictions. *Devenir* and *rester* can be considered as aspectual variants of *être*, indicating change or continuation of the state over a period of time, whereas *sembler* and *paraître* incorporate a modal element, presenting the property as apparent (even illusory) rather than real. Unlike *être*, these verbs can only be used in sentences of the predicational type. Thus, these verbs can replace *être* in some or all of the predicational sentences in (62a) and (63), but none of them can substitute for *être* in the identificational example (64):

(76)　　*Le mari de Suzy {devient / reste / semble / paraît} Pierre

(Note that *sembler* and *paraître* can be used with an identificational reading when they are followed by *être*: *Le mari de Suzy {semble / paraît} être Pierre* – for discussion of these verbs with an infinitival complement, see 9.2.4.) There are some differences between these verbs concerning the types of complement they can take. Roughly, *rester* can occur with the full range of complements in (62a) and (63), *devenir* allows all types except PPs, while *sembler* and *paraître* seem to be restricted to APs and NPs with a determiner (though in the latter case the NP must denote a rather subjective quality; e.g. *Pierre {semble / paraît} le meilleur candidat* is decidedly better than *?Pierre {semble / paraît} le mari de Suzy*). All of the verbs in question allow an adjectival complement:

(77)　　Pierre {devient / reste / semble / paraît} riche

The small clause analysis presented in (71) can be adopted for constructions with these verbs. Thus, example (77) can be derived from the structure in (78) (using *devenir* as a representative verb), by raising *Pierre* into the empty subject position in the main clause:

(78)     $[_S \varnothing$ devient $[_{SC} [_{NP}$ Pierre] $[_{AP}$ riche]]]

This analysis provides a simple way of excluding identificational constructions like (76) with these verbs. Consider the underlying structure (79):

(79)     $[_S \varnothing$ devient $[_{SC} [_{NP}$ Pierre] $[_{NP}$ le mari de Suzy]]]

To exclude examples like (76) while allowing *Pierre devient le mari de Suzy*, we can postulate the following restriction:

*With copular verbs other than* être, *only the subject of the small clause can be raised to the subject position in the main clause.*

The small clause analysis captures an interesting similarity between copular constructions with *sembler* and *paraître* and impersonal sentences like (80):

(80)     Il {semble / paraît} que Pierre est riche

According to the analysis presented in 2.4.5, (80) is derived by inserting the dummy pronoun *il* in the subject position in (81a), whereas the small clause analysis derives the copular sentence *Pierre {semble / paraît} riche* from the underlying structure (81b):

(81)     a  $[_S \varnothing$ {semble / paraît} $[_{S'}$ que Pierre est riche]]
         b  $[_S \varnothing$ {semble / paraît} $[_{SC}$ Pierre riche]]

In both constructions *sembler* and *paraître* are impersonal verbs which select a clausal complement (finite clause in (81a), small clause in (81b)). The superficial differences can be attributed to the way in which the empty subject is filled; by inserting *il* in (81a) and by raising *Pierre* to this position in (81b). (A similar analysis can be adopted for infinitival constructions of the type *Pierre semble être riche*; see 9.2.4 for details.)

### 2.5.4   *Other small clause constructions*

A similar parallel can be discerned between the complements of certain verbs of belief, as in (82) and (83):

(82)     a  Je croyais que Pierre était le mari de Suzy
         b  Je considère que Pierre est le meilleur candidat
         c  Je trouve que Pierre est intelligent

(83)    a  Je croyais Pierre le mari de Suzy
          b  Je considère Pierre le meilleur candidat
          c  Je trouve Pierre intelligent

Given the concept of a small clause, the sequences which follow *croire*, etc., in (83) can be analysed as small clauses which function as complements of the main verb in the same way as the finite clauses in (82), as shown in (84):

(84)    a  $[_S$ Je croyais $[_{S'}$ que Pierre était le mari de Suzy]]
          b  $[_S$ Je croyais $[_{SC}$ $[_{NP}$ Pierre] $[_{NP}$ le mari de Suzy]]]

This analysis eliminates an apparent problem with sentences like (83a, b) where, ostensibly, we have two NPs following the verb, contrary to the restriction proposed in 2.3.2 which prevents verbs in French from taking more than one direct object. According to the analysis in (84b) the two NPs are not separate complements (direct objects) of *croire* but parts of a single complement, the small clause.

In early versions of transformational grammar, it was proposed that constructions like (83) could be derived from structures similar to (82) by a rule which deletes *être*. The small clause analysis makes such a rule unnecessary. It also solves a fundamental problem which arose within the *être* deletion approach: namely how to allow sentences like (85a) while excluding (85b):

(85)    a  Je croyais que le mari de Suzy était Pierre
          b  *Je croyais le mari de Suzy Pierre

It is difficult to see how an *être* deletion rule could be prevented from deriving (85b) from (85a). According to the analysis presented in 2.5.2, the subject of a small clause is always the 'entity' expression, whereas the predicate NP describes the 'property'. Thus, a structure like (86) is impossible, since *Pierre* is not a description:

(86)    $*[_S$ Je croyais $[_{SC}$ $[_{NP}$ le mari de Suzy] $[_{NP}$ Pierre]]]

On the other hand, (85a) can be derived in exactly the same way as main clauses of the identificational type, by raising the predicate NP instead of the subject NP to the subject position of *être*:

(87)    $[_S$ Je croyais $[_{S'}$ que $\emptyset$ était $[_{SC}$ $[_{NP}$ Pierre] $[_{NP}$ le mari de Suzy]]]]

Note in passing that, in French, verbs of the type in (82) do not allow infinitival constructions analogous to *I believe Pierre to be the best candidate*:

(88)    *Je crois Pierre être le meilleur candidat

73

This matter will be discussed in detail in 9.2.2.

The small clause analysis extends naturally to examples like (89) with *rendre*:

(89)     Marie a rendu Pierre riche

In (89), *riche* describes a property of Pierre in much the same way as in *Pierre est riche* or *Pierre est devenu riche*. This can be expressed by analysing *Pierre riche* as a small clause which functions as the complement of *rendre*. According to this approach, *rendre* can be characterised as the causative counterpart of *être* in the same way as *devenir* is its 'process' counterpart.

> One of the difficulties with the small clause analysis lies in determining how far it should be extended. Why not, for instance, analyse *le livre sur la table* or *le livre à Marie* in (90) as small clause complements of *mettre* and *donner*?
>
> (90)   a   Pierre a mis le livre sur la table.
>        b   Pierre a donné le livre à Marie.
>
> In fact some linguists have argued in favour of such an analysis. For descriptive purposes, this text will stick to the more traditional view that *mettre* and *donner* are three-place verbs which select two distinct complements, a direct object and an indirect object.

## 2.6 'Have' relations

### 2.6.1 Possessive and 'associative' relations

In sentences expressing a relation of possession or ownership, like (91), *avoir* looks like a straightforward transitive verb, which assigns a Theme role to its direct object and a Possessor role to its subject:

(91)     Pierre a une moto

When the object of *avoir* is an abstract NP denoting a 'quality' of some sort, as in (92), we get an interpretation which is very similar to that of predicational sentences with *être*, such as those in (93):

(92)     Pierre a beaucoup de charme

(93)     a   Pierre est très charmant
         b   Pierre est un homme très charmant

The intuitive difference between (92) and (93) is that in (93) the complement of *être* (an AP or NP) describes the subject entity (Pierre) directly whereas in (92) the relation is more indirect; the object of *avoir* describes a quality which is in turn associated with Pierre by means of the verb *avoir*. Following this characterisation, let us adopt the term **associative** to refer to relations of the type expressed in (92) (though this is not a standard term) to contrast them with copular, predicational constructions of the type in (93).

From the point of view of the student of French, the facts presented above do not pose any problems – we can construct similar examples in English. Also, there is no obvious reason to suppose that sentences like (92) are syntactically different from sentences like (91). At the risk of playing on words, we can say that *beaucoup de charme* in (92) describes an abstract 'property' possessed by Pierre in much the same way as *une moto* in (91) describes something which is literally Pierre's 'property'. The reason for drawing attention to the semantic similarity between the cases in (92) and (93) is that French has some constructions of an associative type (which do not have direct analogues in English) which show a closer syntactic affinity with predicational constructions.

The idea that there is some connection between *avoir* and *être* is also supported by their uses as auxiliaries (forming compound tenses) with different classes of verbs, a matter which will be addressed in 2.8.1.

### 2.6.2 'Avoir soif'

One case of an associative pattern not generally found in English is represented by the use of *avoir* with a 'bare' noun to describe properties which in English would normally be expressed by means of *be* with an adjective, as in (94)–(95):

(94)     Paul a soif

(95)     Paul is thirsty

Other examples of the same type are *avoir faim, avoir peur, avoir raison, avoir envie, . . .* The fact that French favours an associative construction in such cases may be partly due to the fact that French lacks adjectives (in common, idiomatic usage) corresponding to *thirsty, hungry, afraid, right, keen*, etc. (a converse case is *être enrhumé* vs *have a cold*, where English lacks an adjective corresponding to *enrhumé*). Nevertheless, constructions like (94) have certain syntactic peculiarities which cannot be explained solely in terms of 'lexical gaps' (e.g. the lack of an appropriate adjective), the most obvious of which is the absence of a determiner before the noun. Another (perhaps more intriguing) property of these constructions is that the noun can be modified by degree adverbs such as *très* or *absolument* which normally modify adjectives rather than nouns:

(96)     a   Paul a très soif
         b   Paul a absolument raison

This evidence suggests that items like *soif* and *raison* in such constructions have a status intermediate between that of normal nouns and adjectives; they behave like nouns in so far as they describe a 'quality' which is associated with the subject entity by means of *avoir* rather than *être* (like the NP in (92)), but they behave like adjectives (like *charmant* in (93)) with regard to degree modification. No attempt will be made here to explain or formalise this intermediate or hybrid status of words like *soif* and *raison*, but these observations are offered as further evidence of the intuitive similarity between 'associative' and predicational constructions.

### 2.6.3  'Avoir les yeux bleus'

In examples like (97) *les yeux bleus* looks like an NP, functioning as a direct object, just like *les fleurs rouges* in (98):

(97)      Sylvie a les yeux bleus

(98)      Sophie regarde les fleurs rouges

However, this similarity is an illusion, as the following brief observations should make clear.

Normally, adjectives which modify the noun within the NP are 'optional extras' which can be missed out freely without affecting grammaticality (*Sophie regarde les fleurs*), but the adjective is indispensible in (97):

(99)      *Sylvie a les yeux

There are some adjectives, like *joli*, which normally precede the noun which they modify (see 7.3.2), but in the construction (97) they must follow the noun:

(100)     a   Sylvie a {*les jolis yeux / les yeux jolis}
          b   Sophie regarde {les jolies fleurs / ?les fleurs jolies}

Generally, definite NPs can be replaced by a pronoun. In (98) the pronoun *les* must replace the whole NP *les fleurs rouges*, but in (97) *les* can only replace *les yeux*, as the following continuations of (97)–(98) show:

(101)     a   * ... et Nathalie les a aussi
          b   ... mais Nathalie les a verts

(102)     a   ... et Marie les regarde aussi
          b   * ... mais Marie les regarde jaunes

This evidence indicates that in (97) the adjective does not form part of the NP, but has a function similar to that found in the predicational construction (103a), with the underlying structure (103b):

(103)     a   Les yeux de Sylvie sont bleus
          b   $[_S \varnothing$ sont $[_{SC} [_{NP}$ les yeux de Sylvie$] [_{AP}$ bleus$]]]$

In (103) the possessive relation is expressed by means of a PP (*de Sylvie*) within the subject NP whereas in (97) it is expressed by *avoir*. Nevertheless, the predicational relation between the eyes and the property 'blue' is the same in (97) as in (103). This similarity can be captured by postulating a structure for (97) in which the small clause in (103b) occurs as a complement of *avoir*:

(104)    $[_S$ Sylvie a $[_{SC} [_{NP}$ les yeux] $[_{AP}$ bleus]]]

The use of the definite article in (97) can be assimilated to other cases of **inalienable possession** (e.g. possession of body-parts) where the definite article has a possessive interpretation dependent on another NP in the sentence (see 6.8.3–6.8.4 for discussion): *Sylvie a fermé les yeux, On a bandé les yeux à Sylvie.*

The construction in (97) is not restricted to body-part nouns. It can also occur with nouns which denote physical or mental characteristics, dispositions, circumstances, etc.: *avoir l'esprit fin, avoir la mémoire courte, avoir le goût raffiné, avoir la vie facile* (the expression *avoir le vin triste*, said of persons for whom alcohol induces melancholy, can be regarded as an idiomatic extension of this pattern). However, it cannot generally be used with concrete objects which are not intrinsically linked to a person's state of being – e.g. *?Sylvie a la moto rouge* can only mean *La moto rouge appartient à Sylvie* or *Sylvie a pris la moto rouge*, not *La moto de Sylvie est rouge.*

Our observations concerning (97) do not apply to the superficially similar example (105) where the NP is indefinite:

(105)    Sylvie a des yeux bleus

Here our tests show that the adjective forms part of the NP: *Sylvie a des yeux* (banal, but grammatical!), *Sylvie a {de jolis yeux/?des yeux jolis}* (see 5.4.7 for the use of *de* vs *des*). For the pronoun test, the appropriate substitute for the indefinite NP is *en* (see 6.6.4), but the pattern is the same as in (102), not (101): *... et Marie en a aussi, *... mais Marie en a verts.* The English construction *Sylvie has blue eyes* is syntactically parallel to (105) rather than (97); i.e. the construction in (104) does not appear to exist in English, perhaps because English does not generally allow an 'inalienably possessive' interpretation of the definite article (*Sylvie closed the eyes*).

> There are other constructions common to both English and French which are similar to (97) in that the adjective qualifies the noun without forming part of the NP: e.g. *Max aime sa viande bien cuite, Max likes his meat well-cooked*, where the adjective describes the circumstances in which Max likes meat: 'Max likes his meat when it is well cooked'. French examples of this type often show a potential ambiguity which is resolved in English by the position of the adjective: *Jules a acheté les œufs frais* vs *Jules bought the fresh eggs* or *Jules bought the eggs fresh.*

### 2.6.4 Epistemic dative constructions

Many verbs of belief which allow small clause complements of the type discussed in 2.5.4 (corresponding to a finite complement clause with *être*) also allow a construction which we do not find in English, illustrated in (106a, b), which is similar in meaning to a complement clause with *avoir* (106c):

(106)    a  Je trouve beaucoup de charme à Pierre

          b  Je lui trouve beaucoup de charme

          c  Je trouve que Pierre a beaucoup de charme

Following Ruwet (1982), we refer to the construction in (106a, b) as the **epistemic dative** construction ('epistemic' connotes the idea of belief, whereas 'dative' relates to the fact that the person with whom the quality is associated is realised as a dative expression – a Dative pronoun like *lui* or *à* + NP). Often these constructions are more acceptable with the Dative pronoun than with *à* + NP. To facilitate discussion, the NP which immediately follows the verb (*beaucoup de charme* in (106a, b)) will be referred to as the 'Accusative NP'.

Further examples of this construction are given in (107):

(107)    a  Je lui crois beaucoup d'amis

          b  Je lui suppose beaucoup de problèmes

          c  Je prévois un bel avenir à ce jeune auteur

          d  Je lui imagine une vie privée très animée

Generally this construction is possible only when the Accusative NP describes an abstract quality rather than a concrete object which is possessed or owned. This needs to be taken rather loosely in view of examples like (107a) where *beaucoup d'amis* denotes a group of people – nevertheless, this sentence can be construed as indicating the popularity of the person designated by *lui*, in contrast to cases like (108) where the relation is one of literal possession:

(108)      *Je lui crois une moto

In other words, the epistemic dative construction corresponds closely to the 'associative' use of *avoir* discussed in 2.6.1. Note, however, that the epistemic construction is not possible with 'bare' nouns such as *soif* (as in *avoir soif*): *Je lui {crois / trouve / prévois} soif*.

The sentences in (106) are very similar in meaning to those in (109):

(109)    a  Je trouve Pierre très charmant

          b  Je le trouve très charmant

          c  Je trouve que Pierre est très charmant

The similarity between the (c) examples in (106) and (109) reflects the general similarity between associative and predicational constructions noted in 2.6.1. One way of expressing the analogy between the (a) and (b) examples in (106) and (109) is to analyse *beaucoup de charme à Pierre* as a small clause, which associates the quality *beaucoup de charme* with the entity designated by *Pierre*, as in (110):

(110)     [$_S$ Je trouve [$_{SC}$ [$_{NP}$ beaucoup de charme] [$_{PP}$ à Pierre]]]

The correlation between *avoir* and *à* illustrated in (106) shows up in many other cases, including expressions of genuine possession like (111) (though note that in (111c) a Dative clitic pronoun cannot be used: *\*Cette moto lui est*):

(111)     a  Pierre a une moto
          b  Cette moto appartient à Pierre
          c  Cette moto est à Pierre

This correlation could be made explicit by postulating a small clause analysis for sentences with *avoir* as well as *être*:

(112)     [$_S$ ∅ a [$_{SC}$ [$_{NP}$ une moto] [$_{PP}$ à Pierre]]]

The surface sentence (111a) could be derived by raising *Pierre* into the main subject position (deleting *à*). Sentence (111c) could be derived from essentially the same structure by raising *cette moto*:

(113)     [$_S$ ∅ est [$_{SC}$ [$_{NP}$ cette moto] [$_{PP}$ à Pierre]]]

This approach will not be pursued here (some references to work along these lines are given at the end of this chapter). It is presented mainly as a possible way of 'visualising' the intuitive correspondences between *être*, *avoir* and *à* observed above.

A potential problem with the analysis of epistemic dative constructions proposed in (110) is that these constructions fade, almost imperceptibly, into constructions of the 'giving' type:

(114)    a   On attribue beaucoup de charme à Pierre
         b   On attribue ce poème inédit à Mallarmé
         c   On a attribué le prix Nobel à Nelson Mandela

Sentence (114a) is similar to (106a), expressing a belief that Pierre is charming; though note that it cannot be paraphrased by a finite complement (*\*On attribue que Pierre a beaucoup de charme*) and, unlike the other examples we have given, it has a direct counterpart in English (*They attribute a lot of charm to Pierre*). At the opposite extreme, (114c) describes an act of 'giving', whereas (114b) is somewhere in between – it expresses a belief or claim about a relation between Mallarmé and the poem while giving some credit (or blame) to Mallarmé.

79

A possible conclusion is that all constructions of the type [V NP à+NP] have the same syntactic structure and that differences between them are due to the semantic properties of the elements involved. Thus, either the small clause analysis is extended to all cases, including 'giving' sentences (as envisaged at the end of 2.5.4), or the NP and PP are analysed as separate complements of the verb, which are interpreted as forming a semantic unit in cases like (106a,b) and (107) above.

## 2.7 Auxiliary verbs

### 2.7.1 What are auxiliary verbs?

**Auxiliary verbs** can be defined very loosely as verbs which form a close grammatical relation with another verb in the sentence. There is general agreement among grammarians that the verbs *avoir* and *être* (when accompanied by a past participle in compound tenses and passive constructions) belong to this class. There is much less agreement about what other verbs, if any, should be classified as auxiliaries, though favourite candidates are *aller* (in its future use), *venir (de)* (expressing recent past) and the modal verbs *devoir* and *pouvoir* – sometimes these are referred to as 'semi-auxiliaries'.

A special class of auxiliaries is justified only if the verbs assigned to this class behave in a significantly different way from **lexical verbs** (i.e. 'ordinary' verbs) – if no such differences can be found, there would be simply no point in setting up a special class of auxiliaries. Consequently, in order to decide which verbs are auxiliaries, we must look for properties which clearly distinguish these verbs from lexical verbs. The procedure in the following sections is to identify properties of *avoir* and *être* which distinguish them from verbs like *empêcher* which are not recognised as auxiliaries, even though they occur with an infinitival verb, and then to see to what extent these properties are shared by *aller, venir (de), devoir* and *pouvoir*.

A fundamental assumption, which is implicit in traditional accounts, is that generally every verb in a sentence belongs to a clause of its own – thus, if a sentence contains two verbs, as in (115), it must consist of two clauses (as we proposed in 1.3.2):

(115)     Pierre essaie de résoudre ce problème

However, this seems wrong for sentences with auxiliary verbs – there is no obvious reason to suppose that the sentences in (116) consist of two clauses whereas those in (117) consist of a single clause:

(116)     a   Pierre a résolu le problème

          b   Luc est allé à Lyon

          c   La maison sera vendue à Pierre (par Marie)

(117)    a   Pierre résoudra le problème

           b   Luc alla à Lyon

           c   Marie vendra la maison à Pierre

On this basis, lexical and auxiliary verbs can be defined in structural terms as follows:

- *Each* **lexical verb** *in a sentence belongs to a separate clause of its own.*
- **Auxiliary verbs** *belong to the same simple clause as the lexical verbs with which they are linked.*

In itself, this definition is not particularly helpful, because (apart from vague 'gut-feelings' of the sort expressed above in relation to (116) and (117)) we do not have direct, reliable intuitions about whether a sentence consists of one clause or two, which we could apply with confidence to examples like (118):

(118)      Pierre {va / vient de / doit / peut} résoudre le problème

Again we must look for syntactic tests (e.g. processes which can only apply within a clause).

### 2.7.2 Auxiliary verbs and clitic pronouns

One such test is provided by the Clitic-placement process discussed in 1.5.1. If we replace the complements in (116) by clitic pronouns, these pronouns must precede the auxiliary, not the participle:

(119)    a   Pierre l'a résolu. (* ... a le résolu)

           b   Pierre y est arrivé.(* ... est y arrivé)

           c   La maison lui a été vendue par Marie (* ... a lui été vendue ...)

However, a pronoun replacing *le problème* in (115) must be attached to the infinitive,[3] not to *essayer*:

(120)    a   Pierre essayera de le résoudre

           b   *Pierre l'essayera de résoudre

This property can be stated provisionally as follows:

**Clitic pronouns** *are attached to the left of the first verb of the clause to which they belong.*

Note now that the verbs in (118) work like *essayer* in this respect:

---

[3] Attachment of a clitic to the higher verb occurs in certain constructions with *faire, laisser* and some verbs of perception (e.g. *Je le ferai résoudre à Pierre* 'I will make Pierre solve it'). These cases are rather more complicated and they will be left for detailed discussion in 9.4.

(121)   a   Pierre {peut / doit / va / vient de} le résoudre
        b   *Pierre le {peut / doit / va / vient de} résoudre

This evidence suggests that examples like (118) and (121) are complex sentences (consisting of two clauses) and, therefore, that the verbs in question are lexical verbs rather than auxiliaries.

> Examples like (121b) were perfectly acceptable in Old French (up to about the end of the seventeenth century) and are still used occasionally in an archaic literary style (roughly on a par with English †*I doubt not his wisdom* vs *I do not doubt* . . .), but they are no longer standard. This historical development can plausibly be viewed as a change in the status of these verbs from auxiliaries to lexical verbs.

### 2.7.3 Auxiliaries and negation

Within certain semantic limits, it is usually possible to negate either clause in a complex sentence independently of the other by means of *ne . . . pas* (the two elements being placed around the verb if it is finite, but together before the verb if it is infinitival; see 7.6.2):

(122)   a   Pierre n'essaie pas de résoudre le problème
        b   Pierre essaie de ne pas fumer

On the other hand, sentences like (116) can only be negated by placing *ne . . . pas* around the auxiliary:

(123)   a   Pierre n'a pas résolu ce problème
        b   Pierre n'est pas allé à Paris
        c   Le prix ne sera pas donné à Pierre par Marie

We cannot use *ne . . . pas* to negate the past participle on its own: *\*Pierre a ne pas résolu* . . ., *\*Pierre a ne résolu pas* . . ., etc. These facts can be characterised roughly as follows:

*Only the first verb in any clause can be negated by* ne . . . pas.

The modal verbs *devoir* and *pouvoir* pattern like *essayer*, allowing negation of the infinitive, as in (124b, c):

(124)   a   Pierre ne {doit / peut} pas résoudre le problème
        b   Pierre doit ne pas fumer          'Pierre is obliged not to smoke'
        c   Les étudiants peuvent ne          'Students are allowed not to attend class'
            pas assister aux cours

However, negation of the infinitive seems to be impossible with *aller* and *venir (de)*:

(125)  a  Pierre {ne va pas / ne vient pas de} résoudre le problème

   b  *Pierre {va / vient de} ne pas résoudre le problème

The grammaticality of (124b, c) indicates that the infinitive with *devoir* and *pouvoir* must constitute a separate clause according to the restriction proposed above (i.e. these verbs are not auxiliaries according to this criterion). The deviance of (125b) would follow from this restriction if we take *aller* and *venir (de)* to be auxiliaries within the same clause as the infinitive. Nevertheless, these examples might also be excluded on semantic grounds (e.g. the oddness of situating a 'non-event' in time); cf. the similar deviance of *Il est en train de ne pas danser*, *Il est sur le point de ne pas partir*.

### 2.7.4  Auxiliaries and Stylistic-inversion

A rather different repartition of the data emerges in constructions involving a type of inversion known as **Stylistic-inversion**, where a full NP subject is placed after the verb (e.g. in questions introduced by an interrogative item such as *quand*, *où* or *comment*: *Quand arrivera le train?*) – see 10.2.1, 10.3.4. In constructions with the auxiliaries *avoir* and *être*, the inverted subject NP must follow the participle, not the auxiliary:

(126)  a  Quand est arrivé le train?

   b  Où ont dormi les invités?

   c  Comment sera résolu ce problème?

(127)  a  *Quand est le train arrivé?

   b  *Où ont les invités dormi?

   c  *Comment sera ce problème résolu?

In complex infinitival sentences of the *essayer* type, the subject cannot be readily inverted to either position:

(128)  a  *Où essayeront de dormir les invités?

   b  *Où essayeront les invités de dormir?

In this respect, the modal and temporal verbs pattern like the auxiliaries in (126)–(127), though judgements on cases of the type in (129a) are sometimes hesitant:

(129)  a  Où {peuvent / doivent / vont / viennent de} dormir les invités?

   b  *Où {peuvent / doivent / vont / viennent} les invités (de) dormir?

A general problem with Stylistic-inversion is that it is conditioned by various factors which cannot be defined in purely structural terms: e.g. register (the phenomenon is not common in colloquial speech, hence the hesitation mentioned above in more complex examples), the relative length or importance of elements in the sentence and the degree of 'cohesion' between the verb and any elements which follow it (see 10.3.4 for discussion). Consequently, the contrast between (129a) and (128a) may reflect differences in the semantic content of the first verb or in the degree of cohesion between the two verbs rather than fundamental structural differences.

### 2.7.5 Order of auxiliaries

In English, auxiliary verbs occur in the strict order given in (130) and illustrated in (131), where MODAL stands for *can/could*, *may/might*, *must*, *shall/should*, *will/would* and all elements are optional:

(130)     MODAL + *have* + *be*

(131)     a   John may have been lying
          b   John must have left early
          c   John has been singing
          d   *John may must leave
          e   *John has must leave
          f   *John is maying lie

In particular, we can only have one modal verb per clause (see (131d)) and modal verbs cannot follow *have* or *be* (see (131e, f)). In early transformational descriptions of English, this restriction was stipulated by means of a phrase-structure rule which introduced the auxiliaries in the order given in (130).

The French modals *devoir* and *pouvoir* show no restrictions of this sort. They can co-occur with each other and can precede or follow *avoir*:

(132)     a   Pierre doit pouvoir résoudre le problème
          b   Pierre peut devoir passer l'examen
          c   Pierre {doit / peut} avoir menti
          d   Pierre a {dû / pu} partir tôt
          e   Pierre doit avoir pu résoudre le problème

This freedom is consistent with lexical verb status for these verbs. Thus in (132e) *devoir*, *pouvoir* and *résoudre* each belong to their own clause (indicated by brackets in (133)), with *avoir* qualifying *pouvoir* in the middle clause:

(133)     [Pierre doit [avoir pu [résoudre le problème]]]

These verbs can also be followed by *être* if the verb is of the right type: *Pierre {doit / peut} être parti.*

With *aller* and *venir (de)* we must distinguish cases where these verbs denote movement (e.g. to a place, for a purpose in *Pierre est allé acheter du pain*) from their purely temporal use (*Ce livre {va / vient de} paraître*). When no movement is involved, these verbs cannot be preceded by *être* (or *avoir*):

(134)    a  \*Le rideau{est / a} allé tomber.    (cf. *Le rideau allait tomber*)
        b  \*Ce livre {est / a} venu de paraître.  (cf. *Ce livre venait de paraître*)

Both verbs can be followed by *être* in passive sentences, and more marginally by perfective *avoir* and *être*, at least with *aller*:[4]

(135)    a  Ce livre {va / vient d'} être publié
        b  Pierre va être rentré bientôt
        c  Pierre va avoir fini son travail bientôt

As in English, *avoir* can be followed by *être* in passive constructions, as in (136a), but, unlike English *have*, *avoir* can occur twice to form a **double compound-past** 'passé-surcomposé', as in (136b) (see 4.3.5):

(136)    a  Le problème a été résolu par Pierre
        b  Dès que Pierre a eu fini son travail, il est parti

Leaving *pouvoir* and *devoir* aside, the combinatorial possibilities encountered in this section can be summarised as in (137) – items in column I must precede those in column II and no more than one item can be selected from the same column:

(137)    I      II

$$\left\{\begin{array}{c}\text{avoir}\\[6pt]\text{aller}\\[6pt]\text{venir de}\end{array}\right\}\quad\left\{\begin{array}{c}\text{avoir}\\[6pt]\text{être}\end{array}\right\}$$

One way of integrating these restrictions into the grammar would be to formulate a phrase-structure rule which introduces auxiliaries in the order specified in (137) (as in the early accounts of English mentioned above). However, this seems unnecessary.

In their non-movement use, *aller* and *venir (de)* can only occur in the present or imperfect tense: \**Le rideau alla tomber*, \**Ce livre viendra de paraître*. Whatever the reason for this restriction may be, it seems natural to treat cases like (134) as

[4] Examples with *venir (de)* are less acceptable (*?Pierre vient d'être rentré, ?Pierre vient d'avoir fini son travail*), perhaps because *venir (de)* has essentially the same function as perfective auxiliaries, though there is probably more to it than this.

instances of the same restriction (i.e. these items cannot occur in the compound-past either) rather than as part of a structural condition on the order and compat-ibility of auxiliaries. If *aller* and *venir (de)* are taken out of the picture, we are left only with the restriction that *être* cannot precede *avoir*, but this can be accounted for in terms of general conditions on auxiliary selection. Even when *être* is the only auxiliary, it can only occur before verbs of a certain type, which does not include *avoir* (i.e. passives, reflexives and certain intransitives – see 2.8.3), whereas *avoir* is used before all other verbs, including *être*. Thus the order of auxiliaries does not need to be stipulated, but can be deduced from independent properties of auxil-iaries which manifest themselves even when only one auxiliary is present.

### 2.7.6 Relationship of auxiliaries to the lexical verb

There are many structural analyses which are compatible with our working defini-tion of auxiliaries as verbs which occur to the left of the lexical verb within the same clause. The conclusion in 2.7.5 that the rule which introduces auxiliaries does not need to specify the order in which they occur allows the possibility that auxil-iaries are introduced by a recursive rule (see 1.3.3) like (138):

(138)     $VP \rightarrow V_{AUX} + VP$

According to this analysis, in a sentence like *Pierre a vu Marie*, both *vu Marie* and *a vu Marie* constitute VPs:

(139)     $[_S$ Pierre $[_{VP}$ a $[_{VP}$ vu Marie$]]]$

By applying rule (138) over and over again, we can (in principle) introduce as many auxiliaries as we like in any order. In practice, many illicit sequences will be ruled out by the conditions envisaged at the end of 2.7.5. These conditions will not prevent unlimited iteration of *avoir*, giving sentences like (140), though in practice *avoir* never occurs more than twice in the same clause (as in example (136b): *Dès que Pierre a eu fini son travail, il est parti*):

(140)     *Pierre a eu eu eu eu fini son travail

Assuming that the function of the auxiliary *avoir* is to situate an event one stage back in time (see 4.3.5 for a more careful account), we suggest that there is simply no call for a grammatical formula which shifts the event more than two stages back in time.

### 2.7.7 Which are the auxiliary verbs?

The major remaining question is which verbs are introduced under the $V_{AUX}$ posi-tion by the rule (138) and which are lexical verbs introduced as heads of VP?

The three tests presented in 2.7.2–2.7.4 reveal a clear distinction between *avoir* and *être* on the one hand and *essayer* on the other, with the modal and temporal verbs falling somewhere in between (thus giving some credence to the notion of 'semi-auxiliary'). In order to make a binary distinction between auxiliaries and lexical verbs, we must somehow decide which of these tests is to be regarded as determinative.

Of these three tests, the one which most clearly relates to syntactic structure is the Clitic-placement test – recall that only *avoir* and *être* qualify as auxiliaries according to this test. The negation test is conclusive only in one direction. The fact that infinitives with *devoir* and *pouvoir* can be negated indicates that these infinitives are clauses in their own right (i.e. *pouvoir* and *devoir* are not auxiliaries in any structural sense). However, the impossibility of such negation with *aller* and *venir (de)* might be due to semantic properties of these items rather than to their syntactic status. If the conclusion regarding *devoir* and *pouvoir* is correct, it follows that the Stylistic-inversion test in 2.7.4 is not a reliable diagnostic for the relevant structural distinction.

The conclusion is that the only auxiliaries in French (defined now as the class of verbs introduced by rule (138)) are *avoir* and *être*. If the other verbs under consideration were inserted in the same structural position as *avoir* and *être* by rule (138), there would be no obvious explanation for the differences concerning Clitic-placement. This conclusion does not preclude the possibility that all of these verbs (and perhaps some others) form a coherent class of 'semantic' auxiliaries (e.g. verbs which express notions of time or modality rather than describing events or states) and that some syntactic processes are sensitive to these semantic properties.

### 2.7.8 Some differences between auxiliaries in English and French
In English, it is possible to omit the sequence following an auxiliary if its content can be recovered from the preceding context:

(141)     a   Have you solved the problem? Yes, I have
          b   May I leave the table? Yes, you may

This **ellipsis** process is not possible with *avoir* or *être*:

(142)     a   Avez-vous résolu ce problème? *Oui, j'ai
          b   Est-ce que le train est arrivé? *Oui, il est

Among lexical verbs which take an infinitive, some (like *essayer*) allow ellipsis, but others (like *risquer*) do not:

(143)     a   Essayez-vous de dormir? Oui, j'essaie
          b   Risque-t-elle de nous surprendre? *Oui, elle risque

Verbs and Verb Phrases

In this respect, *pouvoir* and *devoir* behave like *essayer*, whereas *aller* and *venir de* show the same pattern as the auxiliaries in (142) and *risquer* in (143b):

(144)    a  Pouvez-vous résoudre ce problème? Oui, je peux
        b  Doit-elle partir? Oui, elle doit

(145)    a  Est-ce que l'echelle va tomber? *Oui, elle va
        b  Venez-vous de manger? *Oui, je viens

The facts in (145) might be taken as evidence of auxiliary-like status for *aller* and *venir de*, but they could equally support the view that these items are lexical verbs like *risquer*. In 9.2.8, an analysis will be presented which offers a natural account of the impossibility of ellipsis in cases like (143b) and (145) and which is based on the assumption that all of the verbs in question are lexical verbs which take a complement clause.

Under certain conditions, the sequence which normally follows an auxiliary in English can be placed at the beginning of the sentence:

(146)    I said that I would solve the problem and ...
        a  ... solved the problem I have
        b  ... solve the problem I will

This process does not occur in French with any of the verbs under consideration:

(147)    J'ai dit que je résoudrai ce problème et ...
        a  ... *résolu le problème j'ai
        b  ... *résoudre le problème je {peux / vais, etc.}

(148)    J'ai dit que j'arriverai à l'heure et ...
        a  ... *arrivé à l'heure je suis
        b  ... *arriver à l'heure je {dois / vais etc.}

### 2.8  Auxiliary choice and past-participle agreement
#### 2.8.1  Auxiliary choice
The factors which determine the choice of auxiliary verb in the formation of compound tenses can be stated informally as follows:

**Choice of auxiliary verb:**
  *I* être *is used when the verb is accompanied by a reflexive clitic.*
  *II* être *is used with a subclass of intransitive verbs (e.g.* mourir, naître, devenir *and most verbs which indicate movement of the subject entity).*
  *III* avoir *is used in all other cases.*

88

In addition, *être* is used with the past participle to form passive constructions (e.g. *Ce problème sera résolu par Pierre*), but when the passive construction is cast in a compound tense, this tense is expressed by *avoir* (e.g. *Ce problème a été résolu par Pierre*).

Let us leave case I aside for the time being since it is reasonably straightforward. From the point of view of the student of French, the main difficulty lies with cases II and III. How do we know which intransitive verbs take *être* and which take *avoir*? Possibly, the safest strategy is to treat this as something which simply has to be learnt. Nevertheless, it is reasonable to ask whether there are any general principles at work.

It might be tempting to suppose that there is a parallel between the use of *être* as a perfective auxiliary and its copular use (see 2.5.1) and that the range of verbs which belong to case II reflects this parallel in some way. At an impressionistic level, there is something to this idea. All of the verbs in this class describe a change of state or the continuation of a state involving the subject entity. As a result, sentences with these verbs allow us to draw inferences regarding the state of the subject entity after the event described. For example, (149a) entails that Luc was rich for some time after the event, (149b) that Pierre was at the office afterwards and so on:

(149)  a  Luc est devenu riche

b  Pierre est arrivé au bureau

c  Marie est {restée / rentrée} chez elle

d  Jules est {mort / né} hier

In other words, these verbs do not simply describe events but they also describe a subsequent property of the subject entity, in much the same way as the complement of *être* in predicational sentences. This is not generally true of verbs, even intransitive verbs, which take *avoir*: e.g. we cannot make any similar deductions in examples like those in (150):

(150)  a  Pierre a pensé à ce problème

b  Jules a dansé

In terms of the theta-roles discussed in 2.3.1, the subjects in (149), and of all non-reflexive verbs which take *être*, can be characterised as Themes whereas those in (150) can be characterised as Agents (or perhaps an Experiencer in the case of (150a)). Thus, all the verbs which belong to class II are intransitive verbs whose subjects are Themes. However, the generalisation does not hold in the opposite direction. There are many verbs which take a Theme as subject, and which carry implications of the sort observed in (149), but which take *avoir* as their auxiliary:

(151)   a   La maison a brûlé
        b   Le beurre a fondu
        c   Les prix ont baissé
        d   Le roi a trépassé

It is hard to see any general semantic difference between the verbs in (149) and (151) which would explain the difference in choice of auxiliary. Indeed, *mourir* in (149d) is virtually synonymous with the literary and rather archaic verb *trépasser* in (151d). On the basis of this evidence, it seems that, within the class of intransitive verbs which take a Theme subject, the choice of auxiliary is a somewhat arbitrary matter.

### 2.8.2   Unaccusative verbs

Some linguists have proposed that the verbs which take *être* belong to a special syntactic class known as **unaccusative** verbs (sometimes called 'ergative' verbs). Essentially, unaccusative verbs are like impersonal verbs (e.g. *falloir*) with regard to the underlying structure – i.e. they lack an external argument and assign all their theta-roles within the VP (see 2.4.5). More specifically, the NP which appears as the subject in the surface form is the direct object in the underlying structure. Thus, according to this approach, the sentence *Pierre arrivera* has the underlying structure (152):

(152)   $[_S \varnothing [_{VP}$ arrivera Pierre]]

However, unaccusative verbs differ from true impersonal verbs like *falloir* in that the underlying object (*Pierre*) must normally move to the empty subject position. In theoretical terms, this movement is triggered by the requirement that every NP must be marked for a Case feature (roughly, Nominative for subjects, Accusative for objects; see 1.5.6). The peculiarity of unaccusative verbs is that, although they select a direct object (i.e. they assign a theta-role to this position), they do not assign Accusative Case (hence the term 'unaccusative'). Consequently, the underlying direct object (*Pierre* in (152)) must move to the subject position where it can be marked as Nominative.

This is all very abstract, and not particularly helpful to the student who is looking for a simple rule which will predict which verbs take which auxiliary. The idea that *être*-taking verbs can be equated with the unaccusative class may be satisfying from a theoretical standpoint, but in practical terms it merely shifts the problem onto a more abstract plane – instead of asking which verbs take *être* we have to decide which verbs are unaccusative. To avoid raising undue expectations on the part of the reader, it should be pointed out that this discussion of the unaccusative hypothesis will not lead to a simple solution to the question of auxiliary selection. The main reasons for considering this hypothesis are: (a) it is adopted in much current research; (b) there will be occasion to refer to it in subsequent discussion of various syntactic phenomena; (c) it raises some interesting questions even if it does not provide clear answers.

One of the attractions of the unaccusative hypothesis is that it reduces the degree of arbitrariness in the correspondence between theta-roles implicit in the meaning of verbs and the grammatical relations (e.g. subject, direct object, etc.) which encode these theta-roles. On the whole, the Theme role is typically expressed by an internal argument (direct object or NP introduced by *de* – see 2.3.2). The unaccusative hypothesis goes some way towards eliminating exceptions to this general tendency in so far as the Theme with unaccusative verbs such as *arriver* in (152) can be analysed as an internal argument (direct object in the underlying structure). However, this approach leads to a dilemma. If we take selection of *être* as the defining criterion for unaccusativity, verbs like those in (151) cannot be unaccusative, which means that the Theme role can be assigned to the underlying subject (external argument), in contradiction to the prevalent tendency. Conversely, if the correlation between Theme and internal argument is taken as absolute (at the underlying level), the verbs in (151) must be unaccusative, which means that not all unaccusative verbs take *être* as their perfective auxiliary. Among linguists who subscribe to the unaccusative hypothesis, the latter solution to the dilemma seems to represent the dominant view: i.e. Theme as surface subject is taken as the diagnostic for unaccusativity whereas the correlation between unaccusativity and selection of *être* is deemed to be rather loose and possibly arbitrary, in the sense that all *être*-taking verbs are unaccusative, but not all unaccusative verbs take *être*. This approach has implications for the question raised in 2.2.2 concerning verbs of movement like *entrer, sortir, aller, venir*, etc. It is suggested that these are essentially change-of-state verbs and that the agentive interpretation of a sentence like *Jacques est entré dans la maison* is a pragmatic inference due to an assumption that human beings are usually in control of their movements. Given that these verbs take *être*, the unaccusative hypothesis entails that the subjects of these verbs are Themes, not Agents.

> Regarding the looseness of the correlation between unaccusativity and selection of *être*, we may note that auxiliary choice with some verbs has changed in the course of history and that there is some variation in Modern French (e.g. Standard *être tombé* vs Non-standard *%avoir tombé*). In fairness to the proponents of the unaccusative hypothesis, it should be mentioned that the convergence between Theme as surface subject and selection of 'be' as perfective auxiliary is much stronger in some languages (e.g. Italian) than it is in French. Consequently, this hypothesis should not be seen as an attempt to impose an artificial

91

structural solution to a problem, but rather as an attempt to investigate the potential relevance to French of an insight which works reasonably well for other, closely related languages such as Italian.

### 2.8.3   A structural approach to auxiliary choice

An interesting aspect of the unaccusative hypothesis is that it may help to unify the cases of *être* selection in I and II. To the extent that choice of *être* correlates with unaccusativity, we may postulate the following generalisation:

**Structural condition on auxiliary choice:**
être *is selected whenever there is a relation of identity between the subject NP and a gap in the VP.*

In a sentence with an unaccusative verb, this relation of identity holds between the subject NP and the position within the VP (indicated by the dash in (153)) from which this NP was moved:

(153)      $[_S$ Pierre $[_{VP}$ est $[_{VP}$ arrivé __ ]]]

In reflexive sentences, this identity relation is indirect. In examples like *Pierre s'est lavé* and *Pierre s'est offert un cadeau*, the reflexive clitic refers to the same person as *Pierre*. At the same time, *se* is the understood direct or indirect object of the verb. This can be represented by assuming that the reflexive pronoun occurs in the normal object position in the underlying structure and is moved in front of the first verb by the general Clitic-placement process outlined in 1.5.1 (see 6.7.3 for detailed discussion), as shown in (154) where the dash represents the position from which *se* is moved and the index *i* indicates that *Pierre* and *se* refer to the same individual:

(154)      a   $[_S$ Pierre$_i$ $[_{VP}$ se$_i$ est $[_{VP}$ lavé __ ]]]
              b   $[_S$ Pierre$_i$ $[_{VP}$ se$_i$ est $[_{VP}$ offert un cadeau (à) __ ]]]

Thus, the condition proposed above is satisfied in two stages: the subject is referentially identical with *se* which is in turn related to the gap in the VP by the Clitic-placement process. Note that if either of these two relations fails to hold, *avoir* must be selected. For example, if we replace *se* by a non-reflexive pronoun, as in (155), this pronoun corresponds to a gap in the VP, but there is no identity between the pronoun and the subject (since the two refer to distinct individuals, as shown by the indices):

(155)      a   $[_S$ Pierre$_i$ $[_{VP}$ le$_j$ a $[_{VP}$ lavé __ ]]]
              b   $[_S$ Pierre$_i$ $[_{VP}$ lui$_j$ a $[_{VP}$ offert un cadeau (à) __ ]]]

Also, if we use a non-clitic reflexive form such as *lui-même*, as in (156), we have the same sort of identity of reference as in (154), but there is no gap within the VP:

(156)     [$_S$ Pierre$_i$ [$_{VP}$ a [$_{VP}$ acheté un cadeau pour lui-même$_i$]]]

The use of *être* in passive constructions (like *Ce problème sera résolu (par Pierre)*) also conforms to our condition in so far as the superficial subject (*ce problème*) corresponds to the direct object of the verb in an active sentence (cf. *Pierre résoudra ce problème*). Given the analysis proposed in 1.5.3, this NP is the direct object of the verb in the underlying structure and is moved into the subject position, leaving a gap behind, as in (157):

(157)     [$_S$ ce problème [$_{VP}$ sera [$_{VP}$ résolu __ (par Pierre)]]]

Note, however, that when a passive sentence is cast in a compound tense, the perfective auxiliary must be *avoir*:

(158)     [$_S$ ce problème [$_{VP}$ a [$_{VP}$ été [$_{VP}$ résolu __ (par Pierre)]]]]

This can be accommodated by refining our condition so that the relevant gap must occur within the minimal VP which follows the auxiliary (i.e. the VP headed by *résolu* in (157) and (158)). This condition is satisfied by *sera* in (157) and *été* in (158) (since these items are immediately followed by the minimal VP containing the gap), but not by *a* in (158), where the following VP (*été . . .*) is not the minimal VP which contains the gap. Further support for this refinement is provided by 'double compound' constructions of the sort which we mentioned in 2.7.5 (e.g. *Quand Pierre a eu fini de manger, nous sommes partis*). This construction is rather rare with *être*-taking (unaccusative) verbs, but when it occurs, only the second auxiliary is *être* and the first is *avoir* (e.g. *Quand Pierre a été arrivé, nous sommes partis*). According to the approach under discussion, the relevant part of this example can be analysed as in (159):

(159)     . . . [$_S$ Pierre [$_{VP}$ a [$_{VP}$ été [$_{VP}$ arrivé __ ]]]] . . .

It is left to the reader to check that the choice of the two perfective auxiliaries in (159) conforms to the refined version of the condition on auxiliary choice outlined above.

### 2.8.4 Agreement of the past participle

Another phenomenon which is closely related to auxiliary choice is agreement of the past participle. The conditions under which a past participle agrees in number and gender with another element are stated informally below:

**Past-participle agreement:**
 *I  in reflexive constructions, the past participle agrees with the reflexive clitic (hence, with the subject), provided that the reflexive clitic is a direct object.*
 *II in non-reflexive constructions with* être *(unaccusative and passive verbs), the past participle agrees with the surface subject.*

*III In constructions with* avoir, *the past participle agrees with the preceding direct object.*

Case I is illustrated by the examples in (160), which are given in an abstract representation indicating coreference and the underlying position of *se*:

(160)  a  [$_S$ Les filles$_i$ [$_{VP}$ se$_i$ sont [$_{VP}$ lavées __ ]]]
       b  [$_S$ Les filles$_i$ [$_{VP}$ se$_i$ sont [$_{VP}$ parlé(*es) (à) __ ]]]
       c  [$_S$ Les filles$_i$ [$_{VP}$ se$_i$ sont [$_{VP}$ offert(*es) des cadeaux (à) __ ]]]

The participle shows the feminine plural endings in (160a) where *se* is the direct object, but not in (160b, c) where *se* corresponds to an indirect object (which has been indicated by *à* in parentheses, though of course this item does not actually appear in the surface form).

Case II is represented in (161), assuming the analysis of unaccusative and passive constructions outlined above:

(161)  a  [$_S$ Les filles [$_{VP}$ sont [$_{VP}$ arrivées __ ]]]
       b  [$_S$ Ces questions [$_{VP}$ ont [$_{VP}$ été [$_{VP}$ résolues __ (par Pierre)]]]]

Note that in (161b) *résolues* agrees with *ces questions*, but *été* does not.

Typical examples of the concept 'preceding direct object' in III are clitic pronouns, interrogative pronouns and nouns modified by a relative clause, as in (162), where these items are interpreted as direct objects of the participle and can thus be treated as corresponding in some way to a gap in the direct object position (see chapter 10 for discussion of cases like (162b, c)):

(162)  a  Pierre les a résolues __
       b  Quelles questions Pierre a-t-il résolues __?
       c  les questions que Pierre a résolues __

Note that there is no agreement in parallel constructions where the preceding element corresponds to an indirect object of the participle:

(163)  a  Pierre leur a parlé(*es)
       b  A quelles questions Pierre a-t-il répondu(*es)?
       c  les questions auxquelles Pierre a répondu(*es)

Also, past participles with *avoir* never agree with their subject or with a direct object which remains in its 'normal' position:

(164)  a  Les filles ont dansé(*es)
       b  Pierre a résolu(*es) ces questions

A common feature of all the cases where past-participle agreement occurs (examples (160a), (161) and (162)) is the presence of a gap in the direct object position. This observation suggests that the three cases of past-participle agreement can be subsumed under a single principle involving agreement of a past participle with its underlying direct object if this direct object has been moved to an earlier position. There are some complications with this approach, particularly in infinitival constructions with verbs like *faire*, *laisser*, *voir*, etc., which will be left for discussion in 9.4.5. Another more general problem is that the rule of past-participle agreement is observed much less strictly in constructions with *avoir* (especially in cases like (162b, c)) than in constructions with *être*. Though prescriptive grammarians may condemn non-agreement in such cases as an error, a more honest approach would be to treat past-participle agreement as optional under condition III but obligatory under conditions I and II.

### Exercises

1   Which of the following verbs can be used both transitively and intransitively?

> accélérer, achever, arrêter, bouger, chauffer, couler, croître, débuter, glisser, grossir, passer, pousser, prendre, remonter, réussir, rouler, secouer, tenir, terminer

For those which can be used in both ways, comment on the correspondence (if any) between the uses (e.g. in terms of the theta-roles of the arguments, semantic restrictions on the arguments, the nature of the process involved, etc.).

2   Verbs expressing transfer of property or movement of an object or substance to a destination appear in two types of construction in French:

> I  $NP^1$ V $NP^2$ (Prep $NP^3$)
> II  $NP^1$ V $NP^3$ (*de* $NP^2$) (sometimes with *en* as an alternative to *de*)

where:

> $NP^1$ = Agent
> $NP^2$ = Theme (object or substance which is transferred)
> $NP^3$ = Goal (receiver or destination)

*donner*, *mettre*, etc. occur only in construction I
*doter*, *remplir*, etc. occur only in construction II
*charger*, *fournir*, etc. occur in both I and II

(a) Check the following verbs in three dictionaries (including one bilingual and one monolingual) and, on the basis of the information in the dictionaries, try to decide which construction(s) they take:

alimenter, emballer, éclabousser, enduire, entourer, farcir, imprimer, pourvoir, semer, surmonter

(b) Comment on the adequacy of the information in the dictionaries consulted. Is this information explicit or do you have to work out for yourself which constructions are possible? Are there any inconsistencies between or within the dictionaries?

3 Discuss the problems involved in formulating a lexical entry for the verb *payer*.

4 Comment on the uses of *faire* illustrated in the following examples:

(a) Jules a fait un beau repas
(b) Max fera un bon avocat
(c) Marie a fait une bonne impression
(d) Deux et deux font quatre
(e) Il fait beau
(f) Pierre fait un mètre quatre-vingts
(g) Marcel fait très professeur
(h) Gaston faisait l'imbécile
(i) Solange faisait les yeux doux

5 In sentences like *Marie a l'air content(e)* agreement of the adjective with the subject is optional. Is this simply a question of indeterminacy of usage, or does it reflect different syntactic structures for this sentence?

6 Comment on the following examples:

(a) Pierre a une grosse voiture
(b) ??Pierre a cette grosse voiture
(c) *Un homme riche a cette grosse voiture
(d) ??Une grosse voiture appartient à Pierre
(e) Cette grosse voiture appartient à Pierre
(f) Cette grosse voiture appartient à un homme riche
(g) *Une grosse voiture est à Pierre
(h) Cette grosse voiture est à Pierre
(i) *Cette grosse voiture est à un homme riche

7    In 2.7.1 it was argued that pronouns are cliticised to the first verb of the clause to which they belong. Suppose we reformulated this rule so that it attaches the clitic to the nearest verb form which is a finite verb or infinitive (but not a past participle). What difference would this make to our conclusions about the verbs which qualify as auxiliaries in French?

In 9.3.2 we argue that the infinitive in (a) is simply a VP (as indicated), not a clause:

(a)  [$_S$ Je ferai [$_{VP}$ réparer les robinets par le plombier]]

What predictions would the two versions of Clitic-placement make regarding the position of a pronoun replacing *les robinets* in (a)?

**Further reading**

The notion of transitivity in relation to French is examined in detail in Blinkenberg (1960). The syntactic properties of verbs are investigated from a distributional perspective in M. Gross (1968, 1975), Boons, Guillet & Ledère (1976), Guillet & Leclère (1992). On dative complements, see Leclère (1978), Barnes (1980), Kayne (1983). The syntactic status of infinitival particles is discussed in Long (1976), Huot (1981). Alternations in the argument structure of verbs are discussed in G. Gross (1989); see also Ruwet (1972, ch. 5), Herschensohn (1992a, 1993) on alternations of the *aimer/plaire/amuser* type and Boons (1974) on cases like *charger le blé sur le wagon* vs *charger le wagon de blé*.

The discussion in 2.5–2.6 owes a great deal to Ruwet (1982), which contains detailed investigation of copular sentences (ch. 6), epistemic datives (ch. 5) and predicational complements of 'belief' verbs (ch. 7), though it has departed from his analysis in certain respects. On various aspects of copular constructions, see Couquaux (1981), Moreau (1976), Pollock (1983), Verheugd-Daatzelaar (1990). The correlation between *avoir* and *être* as main verbs and auxiliaries goes back to Benveniste (1966, ch. 16), and is developed within a generative framework by Guéron (1986) for French, and from a more theoretical, universalist perspective by Kayne (1993); on the historical evolution of these verbs as auxiliaries in Romance, see Vincent (1982). The unaccusative hypothesis is discussed extensively in Burzio (1986), principally in relation to Italian but with some detailed analysis of French data; for discussion with more specific reference to French, see Olié (1984), Herslund (1990), Labelle (1990, 1992), Legendre (1989). This approach is applied to the study of auxiliary choice by non-native speakers of French and Italian in Sorace (1993) and is examined in relation to the properties of weather verbs in Ruwet (1989). The small clause approach is extended along the lines envisaged at the end of 2.5.4 by Kayne (1984, chs. 7 and 9); see also

Guéron (1984), Mouchaweh (1984). Gaatone (1991) makes interesting observations about the construction discussed in 2.6.2. For a rather technical discussion of past-participle agreement, see Kayne (1985).

On the structural properties of French auxiliaries, see Emonds (1978), Spang-Hanssen (1983).

For discussion of other constructions in which the verb acts as a grammatical 'support' for its complement, see Giry-Schneider (1978, 1987), Danlos (1992).

(For references to work on pronominal and impersonal verbs, see 'Further reading' in ch. 3.)

# 3
# Voice

## 3.1 Overview

In traditional grammar, the term 'voice' is used to describe the grammatical devices which allow the participants in an event or state (more precisely, the arguments of the verb – see 1.2.1) to be expressed in different ways.

In 3.2 there is an investigation of passive constructions formed by means of *être* with the past participle, developing the structural analysis proposed in 1.5.3, highlighting differences between French and English.

In 3.3 the use of the clitic *se* to express voice distinctions is discussed. Leaving aside its use as a genuine reflexive pronoun (discussed in 6.7.3), a distinction is drawn between pronominal verbs of the type discussed in 2.4.4 (where *se* signals an intransitive use of a verb) and constructions of a passive-like nature.

The discussion of impersonal constructions in 3.4 is a development of the brief account presented in 2.4.5 and focuses mainly on the properties of 'derived' impersonal constructions which can be seen as variants of sentences with a clause or referential NP in the subject position.

## 3.2 Passive constructions

### 3.2.1. General properties

The relation between **active** and **passive** constructions like those in (1) can be characterised by the informal statements I and II below:

(1)     a   Pierre a mangé le gâteau
        b   Le gâteau a été mangé (par Pierre)

*I  The subject of an active verb is either suppressed in the passive construction or is expressed as a complement of* par *(or* de *with some verbs).*
*II  The direct object of an active verb is expressed as the subject of the passive verb.*

Passive voice is indicated by using *être* with the past participle. Of course, the combination of *être* and the past participle is also used to express various types of

99

compound past tenses (see 4.2.1), in reflexive constructions and with certain intransitive verbs (*Pierre s'est critiqué, Pierre est arrivé*) – see 2.8. Also, as will be seen later in this chapter, there are other constructions which have effects similar to those in I and II above but which do not involve *être* and the past participle. The term 'passive' will be used to refer exclusively to constructions which have the properties I and II and which are constructed by means of *être* and the past participle.

As example (1b) shows, specification of the 'logical subject' by means of *par* is optional. The term **short passive** will be used to distinguish cases where the logical subject is omitted (*Le gâteau a été mangé*) from **long passives** like *Le gâteau a été mangé par Pierre*.

### 3.2.2  A formal analysis

Of the two properties presented in 3.2.1, property I is the more important. In fact, property II can be seen as a consequence of I: suppression or 'demotion' of the logical subject makes the subject position available for the 'logical object'.

In terms of the framework presented in 1.2.4 and 2.3.1, the active verb *manger* can be represented as in (2):

(2)     *manger*:     [Agent, Theme]
        Theme = NP

Recall that the underlining in (2) indicates that the Agent is the external argument (i.e. the subject) whereas the Theme is an internal argument expressed as an NP occurring within the VP (i.e. as a direct object). The passive verb *être mangé* also describes a relation between an Agent and a Theme, but, by virtue of property I, the Agent is treated as an internal argument expressed (optionally) as the complement of *par*. Thus, the effects of property I can be represented as in (3):

(3)     *être mangé*:     [Agent, Theme]
        Theme = NP
        (Agent = $[_{PP}$ *par* NP])

Note that this representation takes no account of property II - the Theme is still identified as an internal argument. Thus, if we map the theta-roles in (3) onto syntactic positions in the manner specified, we obtain structures like (4):

(4)     $[_S \varnothing [_{VP}$ a été mangé le gâteau (par Pierre)]]
                        Theme     (Agent)

In (4), the subject position must be empty (indicated by $\varnothing$) because the lexical entry in (3) does not include a theta-role which is linked to this position (i.e. there is no external argument). Consequently, a sentence like *\*Jules a été mangé le*

*gâteau (par Pierre)* is ruled out because (3) provides no way of interpreting *Jules*.
To derive the correct surface form (1b), the direct object must be moved into the
empty subject position:

(5)      [$_S$ le gâteau [$_{VP}$ a été mangé ___ (par Pierre)]]

The basic idea behind this two-stage analysis of passives is that property I is a
property of passive verb-forms (exemplified by the entry in (3)) whereas property
II (represented by the movement process in (5)) is a reflection of a more general
principle which, roughly, requires every sentence to have a subject. From an
empirical viewpoint, this analysis is supported by the existence of impersonal
passive constructions which manifest property I (suppression of the logical
subject) but do not involve movement of an NP to the subject position (see 3.4.11
for examples and discussion).

In more theoretical terms, the movement process in (5) can be seen as a way of
satisfying the requirement that every NP must bear a Case feature (see 1.5.6). For
present purposes, the relevant conditions under which Case features are assigned
can be summarised as follows:

(6)      a   Nominative Case is assigned to the subject (of a finite clause)
         b   Accusative Case is assigned to the object of a transitive verb or
             preposition

Supposing now that passive verbs do not count as transitive verbs for the purposes
of (6b), the assignment of Case features in a structure like (4) will be as shown in
(7):

(7)      [$_S$  $\varnothing$  [$_{VP}$ a été mangé [$_{NP}$ le gâteau] ([$_{PP}$ par Pierre])]]
         [NOM]                                      [ACC]

Here, we have an NP (*le gâteau*) which lacks a Case feature, but also a Nominative
Case feature which is 'going spare' in the sense that it is assigned to an empty posi-
tion. Consequently, the movement process in (5) enables *le gâteau* to acquire the
Case feature it needs, while also providing a subject for the sentence.

Property I in 3.2.1 can be expressed as a general rule for forming passive forms
of verbs from their active counterparts, as in (8):

(8)      V: [$\underline{\theta}^1, \theta^2, \ldots$]    $\Rightarrow$    *être* + *Vé*:    [$\theta^1, \theta^2, \ldots$]
                                                     ($\theta^1 = [_{PP}$ *par* NP])

This rule is to be interpreted as follows. The symbol $\theta$ stands for any theta-role
(with underlining to indicate the external argument) and *Vé* is shorthand for the
past-participle form. All other specifications in the lexical entry for the active verb

101

are carried over to the entry for the passive form (e.g. the mapping of $\theta^2$ onto a syntactic position, presence of further theta-roles). Thus, (3) can be derived from (2), where V = *manger*, $\theta^1$ = Agent and $\theta^2$ = Theme.

Note that rule (8) does not specify the nature of the theta-roles involved – in principle, $\theta^1$ and $\theta^2$ can stand for any theta-roles. Thus, the sentences in (9), where the external argument is an Experiencer or Goal, can be passivised as in (10):

(9)     a   Pierre a vu l'accident
        b   Marie a reçu la lettre

(10)    a   L'accident a été vu (par Pierre)
        b   La lettre a été reçue (par Marie)

Similarly, sentence (11), where the direct object is arguably a Goal (see 2.3.2), can be passivised as in (12):

(11)    La servante a couvert la table d'une nappe

(12)    La table a été couverte d'une nappe (par la servante)

### 3.2.3 *Lexical restrictions on passives*

Most transitive verbs have passive counterparts, but there are some exceptions. These exceptions tend to be the same in English, so they are unlikely to give rise to practical difficulties. Some of the principal cases are listed below:

> **copular verbs**: *Pierre est {devenu / resté} mon meilleur ami* vs *\*Mon meilleur ami a été {devenu / resté} par Pierre*. In terms of the analysis envisaged in 2.5.2, this restriction might be attributed to the hypothesis that the complement (*mon meilleur ami*) is not an argument of the verb, but the predicate of a 'small clause'. *Avoir* in its normal uses shows the same restriction: *Pierre aura une nouvelle voiture* vs *\*Une nouvelle voiture sera eue par Pierre* (but *Pierre a été eu*, with the sense 'deceive' or 'trick' is fine).
>
> **measure verbs**: (*mesurer, peser, coûter*, etc.) *Cette valise pèse dix kilos* vs *\*Dix kilos sont pesés par cette valise*. These are rather like copular verbs in so far as the complement describes a property of the subject. These verbs can be passivised with the sense 'determine the measurement of': *La valise a été pesée par l'hôtesse de l'air*.
>
> **symmetric verbs**: these are verbs such that a sentence 'X VERB Y' necessarily entails 'Y VERB X': e.g. *Pierre a épousé Marie = Marie a épousé Pierre*, *\*Marie a été épousée par Pierre*. *Rencontrer* shows the same property when it means 'make the acquaintance of'

(*Pierre a déjà rencontré Jules* vs *\*Jules a été déjà rencontré par Pierre*) but allows the passive with the sense 'go to meet': *Jules a été rencontré à l'aéroport (par Pierre)*.

**locative verbs**: (*quitter, traverser*, etc.). These are generally odd in passives when they describe a state or change-of-state: *L'autoroute traverse la ville* vs *??La ville est traversée par l'autoroute*, *Le train a quitté la gare* vs *??La gare a été quittée par le train*. Passives are more acceptable when they describe an action which affects the location in some way: *Paris a été quitté par les Allemands en 1945*.

Possibly some of these exceptions could be accounted for by a modification to the rule in (8). In particular, the passive appears to be deviant in all cases where the external argument of the active verb ($\underline{\theta}^1$ in (8)) is a Theme.

### 3.2.4 Idioms

Some idiomatic expressions can be passivised: e.g. *tirer les marrons du feu* 'defuse a crisis', *promettre monts et merveilles* 'promise the moon':

(13)  a  Les marrons ont été tirés du feu par le Ministre
      b  Monts et merveilles ont été promis par les candidats

However, there are many other idioms which cannot be passivised. For example, in (14) *ramasser une pelle* can mean 'come a cropper', *casser la croûte* 'take a snack':

(14)  a  Jules a ramassé une pelle
      b  La famille a cassé la croûte

The passive counterparts in (15) are ungrammatical with their idiomatic interpretations, though they could be interpreted literally: 'pick up a spade', 'break the crust':

(15)  a  *Une pelle a été ramassée par Jules
      b  *La croûte a été cassée par la famille

The relevant difference between these two types of idiom is not clear. Note that we find similar differences in English: e.g. *let the cat out of the bag* 'divulge a secret' can be passivised, but *kick the bucket* 'die' cannot.

### 3.2.5 Syntactic restrictions on passives

An important restriction on passives in French is that only the **direct** object of a verb can become the subject of a passive sentence. This restriction does not hold in English, where we find examples like *This question was talked about by the* specialists, *The support of the Communists was counted on by the Socialists, This candidate was voted for by most of the electors,* though they are often condemned by prescriptive grammarians. In French, such examples are completely ungrammatical:

(16)    a  *Cette question a été parlée de (par les spécialistes)

          b  *Le soutien des communistes a été compté {sur / dessus} (par les socialistes)

          c  *Ce candidat a été voté pour (par la plupart des électeurs)

This restriction can be explained in terms of the analysis proposed in 3.2.2. If we take an active sentence like *On a parlé de cette question* and suppress the external argument (according to property I), we should obtain the underlying structure in (17):

(17)    $[_S \varnothing [_{VP}$ a été parlé $[_{PP}$ de cette question]]]

Note now that we cannot move *cette question* to the subject position, as in (18), since this would violate the PP-Island Constraint proposed in 1.5.7, a constraint which appears to be absolute in French:

(18)    $[_S$ cette question $[_{VP}$ a été parlé $[_{PP}$ de __ ]]]

A further inhibiting factor may be that *cette question* is not the direct object of the passive verb but the object of a preposition and thus should receive Accusative Case according to (6b) in 3.2.2. Consequently, by moving to the subject position it would end up with two Cases (Nominative and Accusative). In fact, with many verbs, structures of the type in (17) can be 'rescued' simply by spelling out the empty subject as *il,* giving impersonal passives like *Il a été parlé de cette question.* Constructions of this type will be discussed more fully in 3.4.11.

### 3.2.6  Double object constructions

Students of French are unlikely to produce examples like (16) – the impossibility of 'stranding' prepositions in French seems to be quite obvious. A much more widespread problem arises with double object constructions like (19):

(19)    a  This book was given to Paul (by Mary)

          b  Paul was given this book (by Mary)

Example (19a) can be translated word-for-word into French, but the equivalent of (19b) is ungrammatical:

(20)    a  Ce livre a été donné à Paul (par Marie)

          b  *Paul a été donné ce livre (par Marie)

The reason for this difference is quite simple. In English, *give* allows two active constructions (as in (21)), but French allows only the construction in (22a) (see 2.3.2):

(21)  a  Mary gave this book to Paul
      b  Mary gave Paul this book

(22)  a  Marie a donné ce livre à Paul
      b  *Marie a donné Paul ce livre

The English passives in (19) can be derived by suppressing (or 'demoting') the subject *Mary* in (21) and moving the (first) direct object into the subject position (i.e. *this book* in (21a), *Mary* in (21b)). However, since (22b) is ungrammatical in French, we cannot derive (20b) in the same way. Given an underlying structure like (23) (parallel to (22a)), we can move *ce livre* into subject position, but not *Paul*, since this would violate the PP-Island Constraint:

(23)      [$_S$ ∅ [$_{VP}$ a été donné ce livre [$_{PP}$ à Paul] (par Marie)]]

A similar situation is found with pairs like (24):

(24)  a  Paul was asked to leave
      b  *Paul a été demandé de partir

In the active counterparts of (24), *Paul* is a direct object of *ask*, but an indirect object of *demander*:

(25)  a  They asked Paul to leave
      b  On a demandé à Paul de partir

Suppressing the subject and substituting the passive verb form gives the structures in (26):

(26)  a  [$_S$ ∅ [$_{VP}$ was asked Paul [$_{S'}$ to leave]]]
      b  [$_S$ ∅ [$_{VP}$ a été demandé [$_{PP}$ à Paul] [$_{S'}$ de partir]]]

*Paul* can be moved into the subject position in (26a), but not in (26b) since it is part of a PP. Note that if we replace *demander* by *prier*, which takes a direct object, like *ask*, the passive construction is perfectly acceptable:

(27)  a  On a prié Paul de partir
      b  Paul a été prié de partir

### 3.2.7. *Passives vs adjectives*

The following sentences look like 'short' passives:

(28)    a  La porte {est / était} ouverte
         b  Les œufs {sont / étaient} cassés
         c  Les soldats {sont / étaient} blessés

However, it is difficult to interpret them as paraphrases of the active sentences in (29):

(29)    a  On {ouvre / ouvrait} la porte
         b  On {casse / cassait} les œufs
         c  On {blesse / blessait} les soldats

The sentences in (29) describe events, with a habitual or progressive interpretation due to the present or imperfect tense of the verb ('the door {is / used to be} opened', 'the door {is / was} being opened', etc.), but the examples in (28) describe states ('the door {is / was} open'). Moreover, the sentences in (28) do not involve the participation of an Agent, unlike the examples in (30) where the verb appears in a punctual tense form:

(30)    a  La porte a été ouverte
         b  Les œufs ont été cassés
         c  Les soldats furent blessés

Although it is natural to interpret the states in (28) as the result of actions of the type described in (30), this is not part of the meaning of (28) – conceivably, the door might have always been open or the eggs might have been broken from the moment they were laid, and it does not matter how or when the state was brought about. In more technical terms, the passive verbs in (30) denote actions involving an Agent and a Theme (even though the Agent is not mentioned) whereas the items in (28) simply denote stative properties of the Theme. Note that the rule proposed for deriving passive verbs ((8) in 3.2.2) does not allow for differences of this nature.

A plausible reason for this difference is that *ouverte, cassés* and *blessés* in (28) are not passive verb-forms at all, but adjectives – note that *ouverte* translates as 'open' (an adjective) in (28a) but as 'opened' (a passive verb form) in (30a). Like adjectives, but unlike genuine passives, these items can occur (without *être*) as complements of *sembler* (cf. *La porte semble lourde* vs *La porte semble réparée*):

(31)    a  La porte semble ouverte
         b  Les œufs semblent cassés
         c  Les soldats semblent blessés

### 3.2.8 *Passive voice and tense*

The adjectival status of the items in (28) explains why these examples have the stative interpretation noted above, but it does not explain why they cannot easily be interpreted as passive versions of the examples in (29) or as habitual/progressive counterparts of (30) – after all English *broken* can also be an adjective (cf. *a broken egg, The eggs seem broken*) but examples like *The eggs were (being) broken* allow a passive interpretation much more readily than the examples in (28). The relevant generalisation seems to be:–

*In French, passive voice is strongly associated with punctual aspect (describing a completed event rather than a habitual event or event in progress).*

Since the imperfect and the simple-present normally have a non-punctual or durative value (see 4.2.4, 4.4.1), a passive interpretation of the examples in (28) would conflict with the above generalisation.

This generalisation reflects a tendency rather than an absolute restriction, which leads to some degree of oddness or unnaturalness in cases where the tense form requires a non-punctual interpretation but where other features of the sentence impose a passive analysis. If a *par* phrase is added to the examples in (28), the result is somewhat odd:

(32)  a  ?La porte {est / était} ouverte par le concierge
      b  ?Les œufs {sont / étaient} cassés par le marchand
      c  ?Les soldats {sont / étaient} blessés par l'ennemi

Similarly, the addition of an adverbial expression which relates to the event and the Agent rather than the resulting state (e.g. instrumental expressions with *avec* or manner expressions of the type *en V-ant*) is unnatural with the imperfect or simple-present:

(33)  a  ?La porte {est / était} ouverte avec cette clé
      b  ?Les œufs {sont / étaient} cassés avec une cuillère
      c  ?Les soldats {sont / étaient} blessés avec un couteau

(34)  a  ?La porte était ouverte en la poussant
      b  ?Les œufs étaient cassés en les transportant
      c  ?Les soldats étaient blessés en les matraquant

All of the examples in (32)–(34) are perfectly acceptable with a punctual tense form such as the compound-past:

(35)  a  La porte a été ouverte {par le concierge / avec cette clé / en la poussant}

b Les œufs ont été cassés {par le marchand / avec une cuillère / en les transportant}

c Les soldats ont été blessés {par l'ennemi / avec un couteau / en les matraquant}

With items which do not usually function as adjectives, passive sentences with the present or imperfect are likewise rather odd:

(36)  a ?Les fleurs {sont / étaient} données à l'hôtesse (par les invités)

b ?Le livre {est / était} mis sur la table (par Marie)

### 3.2.9 *'Par' or 'de'?*

Some verbs allow or even prefer *de* instead of *par* as a means of introducing the 'logical subject' in what look like passive constructions:

(37)

$$
\text{Pierre est} \left\{ \begin{array}{c} \text{aimé} \\ \text{connu} \\ \text{détesté} \end{array} \right\} \left\{ \begin{array}{c} \text{de} \\ \text{par} \end{array} \right\} \text{tout le monde}
$$

It is not possible to draw up a definite list of verbs which allow *de*, because usage tends to vary. Nevertheless, it seems to be a common property of such verbs that they denote states, usually fairly long-term states.

There is some evidence that, in the constructions with *de*, these items have the status of adjectives. They can be used as complements of *sembler*, in which case *de* is more strongly preferred:

(38)

$$
\text{Pierre semble} \left\{ \begin{array}{c} \text{aimé} \\ \text{connu} \\ \text{détesté} \end{array} \right\} \left\{ \begin{array}{c} \text{de} \\ \text{?par} \end{array} \right\} \text{tout le monde}
$$

In the case of *connu*, we have the negative form *inconnu*, which must be an adjective (not a passive form, since there is no verb *\*inconnaître*). With *inconnu*, only *de* is possible:

(39)  Pierre est inconnu {de / \*par} tout le monde

The hypothesis that the items in (37) are adjectives (at least in the versions with *de*) fits in nicely with our observations in 3.2.8. If they were genuine passives, their stative nature would conflict with the generalisation that passives tend to require a punctual interpretation. On the other hand, in passive-like constructions with *faire* such as (40), *de* (like *par*) clearly specifies the 'logical subject' of a verb, not an adjective (see 3.2.11 and 9.4.4 for discussion of these constructions):

(40)      a   Pierre s'est fait {connaître / détester} de tout le monde
          b   Pierre s'est fait renverser par un taxi

In cases like (37), the putative distinction between adjectives and passive forms of verbs does not make much difference to meaning (in contrast to cases like those in (28), where a state vs event distinction is quite clear) – even the versions with *de* in (37) are reasonably close paraphrases of the active sentences in (41):

(41)      Tout le monde {aime / connaît / déteste} Pierre

### 3.2.10   Functions of the passive construction
The reasons for using a passive construction in preference to the active can be deduced from the structural properties of passive constructions presented in 3.2.1 in conjunction with general principles which relate the order of elements in the sentence to their relative importance within the discourse.

An obvious function of 'short' passives is that they omit all mention of the logical subject. For this reason, the use of a passive construction is particularly appropriate in cases where the speaker does not know, or does not wish to divulge, the identity of the logical subject. For example, an employee might say to his boss:

(42)      Ces documents ont été perdus

By using this sentence, the employee can disclaim any responsibility for the loss of the documents and indeed any knowledge of who might be responsible, whereas the active sentence (43) might incriminate the speaker because of the colloquial use of *on* as a substitute for *nous*:

(43)      On a perdu ces documents

Another motivation for the use of the passive in a case like (42) might be to focus on the meaning of the verb, for instance to contrast (42) with (44):

(44)      Les documents ont été volés

In French, there is a strong tendency for final elements to bear main stress and to be interpreted as conveying the most important information in the sentence (see 1.5.4). Consequently, it is more difficult to emphasise the verb in an active sentence like *On a volé les documents* to express a contrast with (43).

Whereas the 'short' passive construction abstracts away from the identity of the 'logical subject', the 'long' passive has the opposite effect of drawing attention to this entity. Thus, the passive sentence (45a) emphasises the culpability of the boss more strongly than the active version:

(45)  a  Les documents ont été perdus par le patron
      b  Le patron a perdu les documents

Again, this can be attributed to the general tendency for final elements to bear main emphasis. Moreover, since the passive construction allows the 'logical subject' to remain unidentified, the fact that one bothers to mention this entity makes it particularly important.

The above functions of the passive correlate with property I in 3.2.1. We can also discern functions which are attributable to property II. Typically, the subject of a sentence corresponds to the topic of the discourse at the point where the sentence is uttered. Thus, (45a) is a statement about the documents, whereas (45b) is a statement about the boss. Similarly, in a context where one is talking about what happened to Pierre, a passive sentence like (46a) is more appropriate than (46b):

(46)  a  Pierre a été renversé par un taxi
      b  Un taxi a renversé Pierre

The functions of the passive can be summarised as follows:-

*(a)  To avoid mention of the logical subject in 'short' passives*
*(b)  To focus on the logical subject in 'long' passives*
*(c)  To topicalise the syntactic subject (logical object)*

### 3.2.11  Avoidance of the passive: alternative constructions
Reference grammars of French often claim that the passive tends to be avoided in French, particularly in comparison to English. It is difficult to know what to make of this claim. Do the French have an aversion to passive constructions in the same way that they have an aversion to other things which are typically English, such as tea with milk or overcooked vegetables? Or is it simply that passive constructions are less frequent in French than in English?

The latter construal certainly has some justification. As we have seen, the syntactic constraints on passivisation are more restrictive in French than in English. English allows passivisation with many verbs which take a prepositional object, with stranding of the preposition: *Cette question a été parlé de* 'This question was talked about'. Also, many verbs which take a direct object in English take an indirect object in French: *Pierre a été donné un livre*, *Pierre a été demandé de partir*. Moreover, passives in French tend to be restricted to sentences which have a punctual tense form.

A further factor which limits the frequency of passives is the availability of other constructions which fulfil some of the functions of passive constructions. In place of the 'short' passive, an active construction with *on* can be used when the 'logical subject' is assumed to be human: *On a volé mon stylo* (see 6.7.9). In statements of a habitual or modalised type where the logical subject is assumed to be generic, a reflexive 'Middle' construction is used in preference to the passive: *Ce vin se boit chambré* 'This wine should be drunk at room temperature' (see 3.3.4, 3.3.5). Another alternative is an infinitival construction with *se faire* or *se voir*: *Pierre s'est fait renverser par un taxi* 'Pierre got himself run over by a taxi', *Jules s'est vu critiquer par tout le monde* 'Jules found himself criticised by everybody' (see 9.4.4). In these constructions, *faire* and *voir* lose much of their literal meaning, though the construction with *se faire* often has sarcastic overtones, suggesting carelessness. An advantage of the constructions with *se faire* and *se voir* is that the subject can correspond to an indirect (dative) object of the verb (cf. (20b)): *Paul s'est vu donner ce livre par Marie*.

Some of the focusing or topicalising effects of the passive ((b)–(c) in 3.2.10) can be achieved by other means. For example, a strong focus on the subject can be achieved by using a cleft construction (see 1.5.5, 10.7.2): *C'est le patron qui a perdu les documents* (cf. (45a)). Similarly, focus on the verb can be achieved by dislocating the direct object (see 1.5.5): *On les a volés, les documents* (cf. (44)). If the direct object is left-dislocated, this also has the effect of topicalising it: *Les documents, on les a volés*.

For all of the above reasons, a passive sentence may not always be the appropriate construction in cases where one would use a passive in English. However, it is by no means clear that there is a tendency to actually avoid the passive in those cases where the functions of the passive match the needs of the discourse and where no syntactic restriction is violated.

### 3.3 Pronominal voice

#### 3.3.1 Types of pronominal verb constructions

The term **pronominal** is used to describe constructions containing the clitic *se* (also *me, te, nous, vous* when the subject is first or second person), where this clitic does not have a straightforward reflexive or reciprocal interpretation (see 6.7.3). Pronominal verb constructions can be classified into three major types which will be referred to as 'Intrinsic', 'Neutral' and 'Middle'.


*Intrinsic pronominal verbs:*
The clearest cases of this type are verbs like *s'évanouir, se souvenir, s'écrouler*, etc. which can only occur with a reflexive clitic – the clitic being, as it were, an intrinsic part of the verb. Thus, with *s'évanouir*, we cannot replace *se* by a disjunctive reflexive form (*elle-même*), nor do we find constructions where *évanouir* occurs without

*se* (except in infinitival constructions with *faire* – see 9.4.4):

(47)  a  Marie s'est évanouie
      b  *Marie n'a évanoui qu'elle-même
      c  *Marie a évanoui Suzy
      d  *Le choc a évanoui Marie

Within this class, we also include pronominal verbs whose meanings or syntactic properties differ significantly from their non-pronominal counterparts in ways which do not conform to a general pattern. Examples involving semantic differences are *se passer* 'happen' vs *passer* 'pass', *se rendre* 'go' or 'surrender' vs *rendre* 'give back', *se comporter* 'behave' vs *comporter* 'include, contain', *s'attendre* 'expect' vs *attendre* 'wait'. An example of a syntactic difference is the pair *se pouvoir* vs *pouvoir*. Though both these items have a similar meaning they differ syntactically in a manner similar to *falloir* vs *devoir* – *se pouvoir* is an impersonal verb (see 3.4.1) which takes a subjunctive complement clause whereas *pouvoir* allows a 'normal' subject and takes an infinitival complement: *Il se peut que Pierre soit là*, *Pierre peut être là*.

*Neutral pronominal verbs:*
These are intransitive forms of verbs which can also be used transitively, as in (48)–(49):

(48)  a  La porte s'est ouverte
      b  La branche s'est cassée
      c  La situation économique s'est transformée

(49)  a  Pierre a ouvert la porte
      b  Luc a cassé la branche
      c  Le gouvernement a transformé la situation économique

Whereas the transitive verbs in (49) denote events brought about by an Agent (represented by the subject), the pronominal verbs in (48) simply describe processes which do not involve the participation of an Agent. In other words, the examples in (48) are neutral with respect to the way in which the event was brought about, in contrast to short passives like (50) where the participation of an Agent is implicit, even though the Agent is not specified:

(50)  a  La porte a été ouverte
      b  La branche a été cassée
      c  La situation économique a été transformée

*Middle constructions:*

These constructions, illustrated in (51), are superficially similar to Neutral pronominal constructions:

(51)      a  Ce vin se boit chambré

          b  Ce journal se lit en cinq minutes

          c  Les consonnes finales ne se prononcent pas

As in the Neutral construction, the subject corresponds to the direct object (typically a Theme) of the equivalent non-pronominal verb, while the logical subject of the non-pronominal verb is omitted. The crucial difference is that Middle constructions imply the involvement of a human Agent, interpreted in a similar way to generic *on* in (52):

(52)      a  On boit ce vin chambré

          b  On peut lire ce journal en cinq minutes

          c  On ne prononce pas les consonnes finales

This and other important differences between Middle and Neutral constructions will be discussed in 3.3.5.

### 3.3.2  Intrinsic and Neutral cases

A feature which Intrinsic and Neutral pronominal verbs have in common is that they are intransitive verbs which must be accompanied by a reflexive clitic which acts as a kind of a marker of intransitivity. Consequently, we can include both types under a more general class of pronominal intransitive verbs.

The difference between the two types concerns the relation between the pronominal verb and non-pronominal uses of the same verb form. This is largely a matter of degree. At one extreme, we find intransitive verbs like *s'évanouir* which have no non-pronominal counterparts at all. At the other extreme are intransitive verbs like *s'ouvrir* which show a systematic relation to non-pronominal transitive verbs, as illustrated in (48)–(49). Somewhere in the middle, we have intransitive verbs like *s'attendre*, *se comporter* and *se pouvoir* whose semantic or syntactic relation to non-pronominal forms is much more tenuous or idiosyncratic.

There are no clear generalisations which can predict whether an intransitive verb is pronominal or not. For example, it is not obvious why *s'écrouler* is pronominal whereas its near synonym *tomber* is non-pronominal:

(53)      a  Le bâtiment s'est écroulé

          b  Le bâtiment a tombé

*Voice*

Also, as was observed in 2.4.3, there are alternations similar to those in (48)–(49) where the intransitive member of the pair is non-pronominal[1]:

(54)       a  Le beurre a fondu
             b  Le poulet a cuit
             c  La situation économique a changé
             d  Les prix ont augmenté

(55)       a  Jules a fondu le beurre
             b  Solange a cuit le poulet
             c  Le gouvernement a changé la situation économique
             d  Le patron a augmenté les prix

Again, there is no obvious reason why *se transformer* in (48c) is pronominal whereas *changer* in (54c) is non-pronominal. Thus, for both the Intrinsic and Neutral types, the presence or absence of a reflexive clitic with intransitive verbs seems to be an arbitrary property of the verb concerned.

### 3.3.3 Pronominal verbs and 'true' reflexives
In some cases, the distinction between an intransitive pronominal verb and a genuine reflexive construction is not very clear, particularly when the subject is human. Typical cases are verbs of posture, like *s'asseoir* and *se coucher* in (56):

(56)       Pierre s'est {assis / couché} sur le lit

Since these verb forms can be used transitively, we might analyse (56) as a reflexive counterpart of (57), where *se* represents a direct object which is identical with the subject:

(57)       Pierre a {assis / couché} l'enfant sur le lit

Against this analysis, we might object that the action in (56) is fundamentally different from that in (57) – in (57), *Pierre* is not performing an action on himself in the same way as in a sentence like *Pierre s'est frappé*. Consequently, we could argue that *s'asseoir* and *se coucher* are intransitive pronominal verbs, similar to *s'ouvrir* in (48a) except that the subject (being human) is naturally interpreted as an Agent as well as a Theme.

This issue is not particularly important from a practical point of view. We raise it mainly in anticipation of uncertainty on the part of the reader concerning the difference between pronominal verbs and true reflexive constructions.

---

[1] With *changer* the pronominal form is used with the sense 'change into something else' and with the sense 'change one's clothes': *Le plomb s'est changé en or*, *Pour aller au bal, Marie s'est changée*. The pronominal verb *se fondre* also exists as an alternative to *fondre* in (54a).

One consideration which favours the pronominal verb analysis of (56) is that there are other verbs of posture which can be used in the same way as *s'asseoir* and *se coucher* but which do not readily allow a transitive use parallel to (57):

(58)     a   Pierre s'est {agenouillé / prosterné} devant l'autel

          b   Pierre a {?agenouillé / *prosterné} l'enfant devant l'autel

Consequently, it is reasonable to treat (58a) as pronominal verb constructions (with *s'agenouiller* and *se prosterner* as intransitive verbs) rather than as reflexive counterparts of (58b). Since these verbs denote actions of essentially the same type as *s'asseoir* and *se coucher* in (56), it seems appropriate to treat the latter verbs as pronominal intransitive verbs as well. It is perhaps also significant that these verbs translate into English as straightforward intransitives (*{sit / lie} (down)*), as do most other pronominal verbs (e.g. *s'évanouir* = *faint, s'ouvrir* = *open*) whereas true reflexives must be translated by a form with *-self*. For the record, *prostrate oneself* (= *se prosterner*) is a rare example of an Intrinsic pronominal verb in English – another is *behave oneself* (= *se comporter*).

Another problematic case is *se rappeler* 'remember', which looks like a pronominal verb (cf. *se souvenir*). The problem is that *se rappeler* is normally transitive (*Pierre s'est rappelé l'histoire*), in contradiction to the claim that Intrinsic and Neutral pronominal verbs are a subset of intransitive verbs. A possible solution is that *se rappeler* is the reflexive counterpart of transitive *rappeler* 'remind' and that *se* is a reflexive indirect object corresponding to *Luc* in *Pierre a rappelé l'histoire à Luc*. Despite the strictures of prescriptive grammarians, *se rappeler* is often used as an intransitive pronominal verb like *se souvenir* (*%Pierre s'est rappelé de cette histoire*), even by native French speakers, though it is probably best not to imitate this usage.

### 3.3.4  *Middle and passive constructions*

Middle constructions do not show the idiosyncrasy which we observed in 3.3.2 in connection with Intrinsic and Neutral pronominal verbs (e.g. *s'écrouler* vs *tomber, se transformer* vs *changer*). Formation of Middle constructions, like the passive, can be seen as a productive syntactic process. In principle, any transitive verb which takes an Agent as its subject can be used in a Middle construction, though in some cases the availability of a reflexive or reciprocal interpretation may interfere with judgements (see the examples in (64) below). In contrast to Neutral constructions, we do not have to learn which verbs require *se* – *se* is required with all verbs in Middle constructions and can be regarded as the marker of 'Middle voice' in much the same way as the combination of *être* and the past participle indicates passive voice.

The effects of the Middle construction are very similar to those of the passive. The subject (Agent) of the active verb is suppressed in the Middle construction (though it remains implicit) and the direct object of the active verb is promoted to a subject. However, there are two fundamental differences between Middle and passive constructions. Firstly, Middle constructions do not allow the Agent to be specified by means of *par* (or *de*):

(59)     a   *Ce vin se boit par les gourmets
         b   *Ce journal se lit par les ouvriers

Secondly, whereas passive constructions are normally used to report punctual events, Middle constructions can only be used to make general or normative statements regarding habitual or hypothetical events. For this reason, Middle constructions can only be used with non-punctual tense forms such as the simple-present or imperfect (i.e. those forms which tend to be infelicitous with genuine passives, as opposed to adjectival constructions – see 3.2.7, 3.2.8). Thus, the uses of passive and Middle constructions with different tense forms complement each other to a large extent. The punctual event in (60a) cannot be described by a Middle construction, whereas the habitual or normative statement in (61b) cannot be naturally rendered by means of the passive:

(60)     a   Le vin a été bu hier soir
         b   *Le vin s'est bu hier soir

(61)     a   ?Ce vin est bu chambré
         b   Ce vin se boit chambré

With the imperfect, Middle constructions describe situations which were usual in the past:

(62)         En ancien français, les consonnes finales se prononçaient

Note, however, that Middle constructions do not allow a progressive interpretation, a restriction which also applies to passives:

(63)     a   On buvait l'apéritif quand je suis arrivé
         b   *L'apéritif se buvait quand je suis arrivé
         c   *L'apéritif était bu quand je suis arrivé

On the whole, human NPs do not occur readily as syntactic subjects of Middle constructions, perhaps because of possible confusion with a genuine reflexive or reciprocal interpretation, though the restriction seems to hold even in cases where such an interpretation is absurd:

(64)     a   ??Autrefois, les assassins se guillotinaient
         b   ??Un bébé s'embrasse sur le front

This restriction does not apply to passives: *Les assassins ont été guillotinés, Le bébé a été embrassé sur le front*. However, human subjects can occur more readily in Middle constructions if they have generic reference and are dislocated by means of *ça* (see 6.4.3):[2]

(65)  a  Les assassins, ça se guillotinait
      b  Un bébé, ça s'embrasse sur le front

Even with inanimate subjects, dislocation by means of *ça* often makes Middle constructions more acceptable:

(66)  a  ?Les taudis se démolissent
      b  Les taudis, ça se démolit

As in the case of passives, only the direct object of the verb can become the subject of a Middle construction. Consequently, a sentence like (67a) is ungrammatical as a Middle construction with the interpretation in (67b):

(67)  a  *Une jeune fille, ça s'offre des fleurs
      b  On offre des fleurs à une jeune fille

Sentence (67a) can only be interpreted as a genuine reflexive: 'A young girl offers herself flowers.'

### 3.3.5  Middle and Neutral constructions

With verbs which allow the Neutral pronominal construction, there is a potential ambiguity between an intransitive and a Middle interpretation. Consider example (68):

(68)  La porte du château enchanté s'ouvrait

In principle this sentence could mean either 'The door of the magic castle was opening' (Neutral) or 'The door of the magic castle could be opened' (Middle), though in practice the Middle interpretation is difficult to obtain. However, the Middle interpretation comes to the fore if we add an adverbial expression which involves the implicit Agent:

(69)  a  La porte du château enchanté s'ouvrait avec une clé en or
      b  La porte du château enchanté s'ouvrait en disant les paroles
         magiques

Note that in (69b) the understood subject of *disant* must be equated with the implicit Agent of *ouvrir* (assuming that doors, even magic ones, cannot speak); see

---

[2] Note that the use of ça does not preclude a reflexive, reciprocal or Neutral interpretation: e.g. *Les jeunes, ça se couche tard, Les intellectuels, ça se critique tout le temps*.

9.5.2. Conversely, if we choose a verb which is applicable to doors but not to humans, the Neutral interpretation is imposed, as in (70) which can only mean something like 'The door of the magic castle creaked as it opened':

(70)    La porte du château enchanté s'ouvrait en grinçant

Because of the tense restrictions on Middle constructions, the potential ambiguity of (68) disappears entirely in favour of the Neutral intransitive interpretation if we substitute a punctual tense form:

(71)    La porte du château enchanté s'est ouverte

If we embellish (71) with one of the adverbial expressions in (69) the result is deviant, because these expressions impose a Middle interpretation, whereas the use of a punctual tense forces a Neutral interpretation:

(72)    a    ??La porte du château enchanté s'est ouverte avec une clé en or
        b    ??La porte du château enchanté s'est ouverte en disant les
             paroles magiques

However, no such conflict arises in (73):

(73)    La porte du château enchanté s'est ouverte en grinçant

We saw in 3.3.2 that *cuire* is non-pronominal when it is used intransitively. Nevertheless, it can occur with a reflexive clitic when the tense is non-punctual:

(74)    a    Le poulet se cuit dans le four
        b    Le poulet cuit dans le four

However, the presence of *se* makes a difference to the meaning. Sentence (74b) has an intransitive interpretation – 'The chicken is cooking in the oven' – but (74a) must be interpreted as a Middle construction – 'Chicken should be cooked in the oven.' If we add an adverbial expression which relates to the implicit Agent, only the version with *se* is possible:

(75)    a    Le poulet se cuit en le tournant fréquemment
        b    *Le poulet cuit en le tournant fréquemment

The same pattern can be observed with other verbs which are normally non-pronominal in their intransitive use, though it is sometimes necessary to embellish the sentences slightly to bring out the Middle interpretation. Some examples are given with translations in (76) (Middle constructions) and (77) (intransitive constructions):

(76)    a    Le climat, ça se change (facilement)
             'The climate can be changed (easily)'

118

    b  Au moyen âge, les sorcières, ça se brûlait
        'In the Middle Ages, witches used to be burnt'
    c  Les salaires, ça ne s'augmente pas sans améliorer la productivité
        'Wages cannot be increased without improving productivity'

(77)      a  Le climat change
          'The climate is changing'
      b  La maison brûlait
          'The house was burning'
      c  Les salaires n'augmentent pas
          'Wages are not rising'

Intrinsic pronominal verbs like *s'écrouler* do not allow a Middle interpretation even when the tense is non-punctual e.g. they cannot be modified by an adverbial expression which involves an implicit Agent (cf. *Un pont, ça se détruit avec de la dynamite*):

(78)      *Un pont, ça s'écroule avec de la dynamite

The reason for this should be clear. Middle constructions can only be formed with transitive verbs which take an agentive subject, but there is no transitive verb *\*écrouler*; i.e. (78) is ungrammatical for the same reason as *\*On écroule un pont avec de la dynamite* or *\*Le pont a été écroulé avec de la dynamite*.

The fundamental properties of Middle constructions can be summarised as follows:

**Middle constructions:**
- *can only be formed with transitive verbs which take an agentive subject and are possible with all such verbs.*
- *always contain a reflexive clitic.*
- *always imply the participation of a generic Agent, though this Agent cannot be specified by means of* par.
- *can only describe habitual or normative situations and are incompatible with punctual tense forms.*
- *allow (and often require) adverbial expressions which involve an Agent.*

In contrast, intransitive pronominal verbs (Neutral and Intrinsic) have the following properties:

**Pronominal verbs (Neutral/Intrinsic):**
- *may or may not have corresponding transitive forms (Neutral vs Intrinsic).*
- *are restricted to an apparently arbitrary set of verbs (many verbs are non-pronominal in their intransitive use).*

- *do not imply the participation of an implicit Agent and thus cannot be modified by adverbial expressions which involve such an Agent.*
- *can be used with punctual and non-punctual tenses.*

### 3.4   Impersonal constructions

#### 3.4.1   *Intrinsic impersonal verbs*

Impersonal sentences are constructions in which the subject position is occupied by a **dummy** pronoun *il*, which does not refer to anything (see 2.4.5). There are a few verbs which can only occur in such constructions and may therefore be classified as **Intrinsic impersonal** verbs. Clear examples are *falloir* and *s'agir*:

(79)      a   Il me faut un marteau
          b   Il faut que tu viennes
          c   Il faut partir
          d   *Un marteau me faut
          e   *Pierre (me) faut un marteau

(80)      a   Il s'agit de notre avenir
          b   Il s'agit de discuter cette question
          c   *Ce livre s'agit de notre avenir

Other plausible examples of Intrinsic impersonal verbs are weather verbs (*Il pleut, Il neige*, etc.) and the expression *il y a*.

In 2.4.5, we suggested that such verbs can be described by means of lexical entries in which all the theta-roles associated with the verb are assigned to positions within the VP. For example, the entry for *falloir* can be formulated as in (81) (expanded slightly from the entry proposed in 2.4.5 to allow a clausal complement and to accommodate a Dative expression, represented by the pronoun *me* in (79a):

(81)      *falloir*:   [Theme, Experiencer]
                       Theme = NP or S'
                       (Experiencer = $NP_{DAT}$)

Since *falloir* lacks an external argument, the subject position must be filled by the dummy pronoun *il*.

Some verbs show a mixed pattern. For example, *se pouvoir* is impersonal when the 'possible event' is represented by a clause, but it takes the 'personal' construction when the 'possible event' is represented by a pronoun:

(82)      a   Il se peut que le train arrive bientôt
          b   Cela se peut

With *sembler* we find an apparently similar (but actually very different) situation. This verb is impersonal when it takes a finite complement clause but allows a real subject when the complement is an infinitival clause or adjectival expression:

(83)    a  Il semble que Pierre aime Marie
          b  Pierre semble aimer Marie
          c  Pierre semble amoureux de Marie

However, there are strong reasons to suppose that examples like (83b, c) are derived from underlying impersonal constructions similar to (83a), as we saw in 2.5.3 for examples like (83c) (see 9.2.4 for discussion of cases like (83b)).

### 3.4.2  Derived impersonal constructions

With many verbs, an impersonal construction can be used as a stylistic alternative to 'normal' sentences with a referential subject:

(84)    a  Il est arrivé quelqu'un
          b  Il existe beaucoup de problèmes
          c  Il s'est passé une chose bizarre

(85)    a  Quelqu'un est arrivé
          b  Beaucoup de problèmes existent
          c  Une chose bizarre s'est passée

Let us assume provisionally that the impersonal constructions in (84) are derived from the 'personal' constructions in (85) by a rule (**NP-postposing**) which takes the subject NP and places it after the verb, within the VP. The empty subject position is subsequently filled by 'dummy' *il*. This analysis is somewhat problematic, a matter which will be looked at again in 3.4.5, but it provides us with a concrete framework within which to discuss the properties of these constructions.

Constructions like (84) have a rather literary flavour and do not usually occur in casual conversation, though they are more frequent than parallel constructions with *there* in English which are decidedly archaic except with the verb *be* and perhaps *exist* (*?There arrived somebody, There exist many problems*). Note that in cases like (84) the verb is always in the third person singular, agreeing with *il* rather than with the postposed subject (*\*Il existent beaucoup de problèmes*, cf. (84b)), in contrast to corresponding English constructions where agreement with the postposed subject is the norm (*\*?There exists many problems*). Similarly, in compound tenses, the past participle is invariable (*Il est {arrivé / \*arrivées} trois filles*).

121

Impersonal constructions are much more frequent, and indeed strongly preferred over 'personal' constructions, when the subject is a clause (finite or infinitival[3]):

(86)    a    Il me plaît de voyager
        b    Il ne me convient pas que tu viennes à cette heure
        c    Il est important de savoir la vérité

(87)    a    (De) voyager me plaît
        b    Que tu viennes à cette heure ne me convient pas
        c    (De) savoir la vérité est important

With the caveats expressed above, let us assume that sentences like (86) are derived from constructions like (87) by a rule of **Clause-postposing** similar to the 'NP-postposing' rule envisaged for (84).

### 3.4.3   NP-postposing

This process is subject to two major restrictions:

**Restrictions on NP-postposing (derived impersonal constructions):**
*I   the subject NP must be indefinite.*
*II  the verb must be intransitive.*

Condition I will rule out examples like (88):

(88)        *Il est arrivé {Pierre / mon voisin / ce type-là}

It might be objected that examples like (88) are in fact acceptable, with a certain intonation, indicated by a comma in writing:

(89)        Il est arrivé, Pierre

However, (89) is not an impersonal construction but a dislocated construction (see 1.5.5); *il* is not simply a dummy element but a pronoun which refers forward to *Pierre*, as can be seen from the fact that the pronoun changes, as does the inflection of the verb, when the NP is feminine and/or plural: *Elle est arrivée, Marie*; *Elles sont arrivées, ces filles.*

Condition II will rule out examples like (90):

(90)        *Il a gagné la frontière plusieurs réfugiés

For the purposes of II, the notion 'intransitive verb' must be taken to include pronominal verbs (like *se passer* in (84c)) and also passive forms (e.g. *Il a été posé*

---

[3] When an infinitive occurs in subject position, as in (87a, c), the complementiser *de* is optional, though it is more usual to omit it.

*plusieurs questions*; see 3.4.11 for discussion). A more accurate formulation of this condition would be to say that NP-postposing is blocked by the presence of a direct object. A plausible explanation is that the subject is actually placed in the direct object position, so that the process is inapplicable if this position is already occupied. Note that indirect objects do not block this process:

(91)     a   Il est venu quelqu'un dans mon bureau
         b   Il est arrivé un accident terrible à Jules

However, NP-postposing cannot apply when the verb is *être* followed by an adjectival complement (unlike Clause-postposing, see (86c)):

(92)     *Il est important plusieurs questions

There are also semantic conditions on the verb, some of which seem to be related to the indefiniteness condition I; see 3.4.6.

### 3.4.4.  The indefiniteness effect

The indefiniteness restriction must be construed in semantic terms rather than in terms of the determiner which introduces the NP. Sometimes, a singular NP introduced by the indefinite article can have a 'generic' interpretation (referring to the class as a whole) – see 5.3.5. Thus, an example like (93) can be interpreted as a description of a situation involving a particular cat which is being introduced into the discourse for the first time ('A cat is sleeping by the fire') or as a statement about the sleeping habits of cats in general ('Cats sleep by the fire' – this interpretation is clearer when the NP is dislocated: *Un chat, ça dort au coin du feu*):

(93)     Un chat dort au coin du feu

However, only the former interpretation is available for the impersonal sentence (94):

(94)     Il dort un chat au coin du feu

Conversely, the postposed subject can be introduced by the definite article in certain cases:

(95)     Il est arrivé le père d'un de mes amis

Here, the use of the definite article is motivated by the fact that the friend in question can only have one father. However, since *un de mes amis* is an indefinite expression describing an as-yet-unidentified person, it follows that the whole NP which defines an entity in terms of this person is also indefinite.

Derived impersonal constructions are also possible when the subject is a list of definite NPs (e.g. proper nouns):

(96)     Il est arrivé Pierre, Marie, Luc, Gaston, Suzy, . . .

A possible explanation for such cases is that, although the components of the list are definite expressions, the list as a whole functions like an indefinite NP – the particular collection of individuals denotes a new entity.

The indefiniteness restriction applies only to derived impersonal constructions. With Intrinsic impersonal verbs like *falloir* and *s'agir*, the postverbal NP can be genuinely definite:

(97)     a   Il me faut ce marteau-là
         b   Il s'agit de cette question-là

### 3.4.5 Unaccusativity and impersonal constructions

The verbs which occur most readily in derived impersonal constructions with postposed subjects belong to the class of 'unaccusative' verbs discussed in 2.8.2 – i.e. verbs like *arriver* or *venir*, which take *être* as their auxiliary and whose subjects can be characterised as Themes. Indeed, some linguists have claimed that these are the only verbs which can occur in such constructions. In fact, this claim is inaccurate, as we shall see presently, but the putative connection between unaccusativity and derived impersonals is worth exploring.

In 2.8.2, we discussed the hypothesis that syntactic subjects of unaccusative verbs occupy the direct object position in the underlying structure, i.e. a sentence like *Marie est arrivée* is derived from the structure in (98) by moving *Marie* into the vacant subject position:

(98)     $[_S \varnothing [_{VP}$ est arrivée Marie$]]$

Recall that this movement is necessary in order for *Marie* to acquire a Case feature. According to this approach, we will also have underlying structures like (99) with an indefinite NP:

(99)     $[_S \varnothing [_{VP}$ est arrivé quelqu'un$]]$

If *quelqu'un* is moved into the subject position, we derive the 'personal' construction (85a) *Quelqu'un est arrivé*. Suppose, however, that the 'subjectivisation' process is optional with indefinite NPs (e.g. indefinite NPs do not require a Case feature[4]). If *quelqu'un* stays where it is in (99) the impersonal sentence (84a), *Il est arrivé quelqu'un*, can be derived simply by inserting *il* in the subject position.

The difference between intrinsic and derived impersonals regarding the indefi-

---

[4] This proposal is rather controversial, but it will be adopted here for purposes of discussion. An alternative hypothesis is that indefinite NPs can somehow inherit the Nominative Case feature assigned to il.

niteness restriction can be accommodated if we assume that instrinsic impersonal verbs (like *falloir*) can assign Case to the following NP, thus allowing (indeed requiring) this NP to remain in the postverbal position even if it is definite. With unaccusative verbs, which cannot assign Case, a definite NP in this position must move to the subject position in order to acquire a Case feature. An advantage of this approach is that it eliminates the need for the NP-postposing rule envisaged in 3.4.3.

This analysis would also extend naturally to impersonal passives like *Il a été posé beaucoup de questions*. In 3.2.2, we proposed a two-stage analysis of passive constructions. In the argument structure of passive forms, the logical subject (external argument of the active verb) is suppressed or internalised, while subjectivisation of the logical object is effected by a movement rule like that in (98), again to enable this NP to acquire Case. However, if the underlying object is an indefinite NP, as in (100), movement to the subject position would be optional, and the surface form of the impersonal passive could be derived by inserting *il* in the subject position:

(100)     $[_S \varnothing [_{VP}$ a été posé beaucoup de questions]]

If impersonal constructions of this type were restricted to unaccusative and passive verbs, the analysis outlined above would provide a natural explanation for this restriction. Similarly, the 'facts' would provide strong empirical support for the unaccusative hypothesis discussed in 2.8.2 and illustrated in (98). Unfortunately, as has been intimated, the facts are not as simple as this analysis would predict.

Sentence (84b) (*Il existe beaucoup de problèmes*) may be a counterexample to the putative generalisation, since *exister* takes *avoir* as its auxiliary. Nevertheless, *exister* fulfils other criteria for unaccusativity (e.g. its subject is clearly a Theme), so it may be an exception to the generalisation concerning auxiliary choice rather than to the restriction on derived impersonals (see 2.8.2). A more serious problem is posed by examples like (94) above and the sentences in (101):

(101)     a  Il nageait beaucoup de gens dans la piscine
          b  Il travaille deux mille ouvriers dans cette usine
          c  Il mange beaucoup de journalistes dans ce restaurant

These verbs do not satisfy any of the criteria for unaccusativity – they select *avoir* and their subjects are Agents, not Themes. Moreover, *manger* in (101c) is normally a transitive verb, used here in its 'absolute' sense (with suppression of the direct object – see 2.4.1). Thus, these examples show that the generalisation under discussion cannot be maintained at its face-value.

### 3.4.6 The existential function of derived impersonals

Examples like (101) also appear to conflict with a more traditional view: namely, that the verbs in such constructions must assert the existence or 'arrival on the scene' of the indefinite entity. Verbs like *arriver, venir, exister, se passer, être posé* in our earlier examples clearly conform to this characterisation, but *nager, travailler* and *manger* normally describe activities performed by an entity whose existence is presupposed. Nevertheless, if we look at the meanings of the sentences in (101) rather than the meanings of the verbs, it seems that these sentences do assert the existence of the entity in question in the place described by the PP – if we replace the verbs by the existential expression *il y a*, very little of the meaning is lost: *Il y avait beaucoup de gens dans la piscine*, etc.

The presence of the locative PP seems to play an important role in cases like (101). Without such a PP, such examples are much less acceptable (note that this restriction does not apply with verbs like *arriver, se passer*, etc., in our earlier examples):

(102)     a    ??Il nageait beaucoup de gens
          b    ??Il travaille deux mille ouvriers
          c    ??Il mange beaucoup de journalistes

Moreover, the PP must denote a place which is pragmatically appropriate for the activity described by the verb. For example, it is perfectly possible for workers to eat in a factory, and we could describe such a situation by the sentence *Deux mille ouvriers mangeaient dans cette usine*, but a factory is not a 'place for eating in'. Note now that the impersonal sentence (103) is decidedly odd:

(103)     ??Il mangeait deux mille ouvriers dans cette usine

What seems to be going on here is that the PP denotes a location which makes the semantic content of the verb redundant, so that the verb can simply assert the existence of the entities in question. If the PP is absent, as in (102), or pragmatically inappropriate, as in (103), the semantic content of the verb constitutes new information and the purely existential interpretation is precluded.

A further piece of evidence which supports this view is that the addition of a manner adverb drastically reduces the acceptability of examples like (101). In the 'personal' construction we can say *Beaucoup de gens nageaient très bien dans la piscine*, but the corresponding impersonal sentence is odd:

(104)     ??Il nageait très bien beaucoup de gens dans la piscine

Here, the addition of *très bien* focuses on the nature of the activity described by the verb, so that it is no longer redundant.

Possibly this intuitive account can be adapted to the unaccusative analysis presented in 3.4.5. For instance, we might allow the argument which is designated as the external argument (e.g. the Agent with *nager*) to be identified with an NP in the direct object position (if this position is not linked to another theta-role) provided that the semantic content of the verb is redundant. Another way of saying the same thing is to postulate that, when the content of the verb is redundant, the Agent is reinterpreted as a Theme, thus effectively converting the verb into an unaccusative verb which expresses the existence of the Theme entity.

### 3.4.7  Clause-postposing

For expository purposes, I continue to assume that examples like (86) repeated in (105) below are derived by postposing the clause from the subject position:

(105)     a   Il me plaît de voyager
          b   Il ne me convient pas que tu viennes à cette heure
          c   Il est important de savoir la vérité

The conditions on this process are less stringent than those observed for NP-postposing. For example, this process can apply when the verb is *être* followed by an adjectival complement, as in (105c) (cf. example (92) in 3.4.3). However, constructions of this type are more restricted than their English analogues (*It pleases me to travel*, etc.). In particular, like NP-postposing, this process is blocked when the verb is accompanied by a direct object. Note that *me* in (105a, b) is an indirect, dative object (*{plaire / convenir} à quelqu'un*). If we substitute verbs which take direct objects, the corresponding sentences are ungrammatical:

(106)     a   *Il m'amuse de voyager
          b   *Il m'étonne que tu sois venu à cette heure

Similarly, the clause cannot be postposed with *être* followed by an NP complement:

(107)     a   *Il est un vrai plaisir de vous rencontrer
          b   *Il est un véritable scandale que les ministres acceptent des
              pots-de-vin

(cf. English: *It is a real pleasure to meet you, It is an absolute scandal that ministers should accept bribes*).

### 3.4.8.  'Il' vs 'ce/ça'

In examples like (106) and (107) an alternative construction with a demonstrative subject (*ce* with *être*, *ça* (or *cela*) with other verbs) is used:

127

(108)    a  Ça m'amuse de voyager
         b  Ça m'étonne que tu sois venu à cette heure

(109)    a  C'est un vrai plaisir de vous rencontrer
         b  C'est un véritable scandale que les ministres acceptent des pots-de-vin

A demonstrative pronoun can also be used in place of *il* in cases like (105), though this use is rather colloquial and is often considered less 'correct' than the use of *il*:

(110)    a  Ça me plaît de voyager
         b  Ça ne me convient pas que tu viennes à cette heure
         c  C'est important de savoir la vérité

However, demonstratives cannot replace *il* with Intrinsic impersonal verbs:

(111)    a  *Ça faut que tu viennes
         b  *Ça semble que Pierre aime Marie

Nor indeed can a demonstrative be used with postposed NPs:

(112)    a  *Ça est arrivé quelqu'un
         b  *Ça existe plusieurs problèmes

Thus, the demonstrative pronouns are not interchangeable with impersonal *il*.

It is postulated that the constructions with *ce* or *ça* are not impersonal constructions, but dislocated constructions analogous to *Elle est arrivée, Marie*. This entails that the demonstratives are not 'dummy' pronouns, but referential expressions which refer forward to the finite or infinitival clause. As will be seen in 6.4.2, demonstratives are the pronouns which are typically used to refer to propositions. This analysis is supported by the fact that we can have left-dislocated counterparts of the constructions with *ce* or *ça*:

(113)    a  Voyager, ça me plaît
         b  Savoir la vérité, c'est très important

However, such constructions are impossible with *il*:

(114)    a  *Voyager, il me plaît
         b  *Savoir la vérité, il est très important

### 3.4.9  Semantic effects of Clause-postposing

Sentences with clauses in the subject position tend to be rather clumsy. Abstracting away from this stylistic consideration, we can discern a subtle semantic difference between impersonal and 'personal' constructions. In impersonal constructions, the postposed clause can convey new information (as in (115)) or it can recapitulate information which has already been introduced (as in (116)):

(115)     a   Qu'est-ce que tu aimes faire?
             Il me plaît de voyager
         b   Que faut-il que je dise?
             Il est important que tu dises la vérité

(116)     a   Est-ce que tu aimes voyager?
             Oui, il me plaît de voyager
         b   Faut-il que je dise la vérité?
             Oui, il est important que tu dises la vérité

However, the personal constructions in (117) could only be used as answers to the questions in (116):

(117)     a   Voyager me plaît
         b   Que tu dises la vérité est important

In other words, it seems that clauses in subject position can only convey 'given' information.

In this respect, the constructions with demonstratives seem to behave like the examples in (117). Thus, *Ça me plaît de voyager* is an appropriate reply to the question in (116a) but could not be used in a context like (115a). This contrast seems less strong with *ce*; nevertheless, *C'est important de dire la vérité* is more natural in (116b) than in (115b).

### 3.4.10  *Is Clause-postposing necessary?*

Although the description of derived impersonals with clauses has been couched in terms of a postposing analysis, an approach of the type envisaged in 3.4.5 and at the end of 3.4.6 would be applicable to these constructions. Pursuing the suggestion at the end of 3.4.6, let us suppose that an external argument can always be identified with a constituent in the direct object position, provided that no other theta-role is associated with this position. This proviso would automatically exclude examples like (106) (*\*Il m'amuse de voyager, \*Il m'étonne que tu sois venu à cette heure*), where the Experiencer role is associated with the direct object (*me*). Possibly, examples like (107) (with *être* + NP) could be excluded in a similar way, though the issues here are more complicated. Examples with *plaire* and *convenir*, where the Experiencer is a dative object, would allow the external argument to be identified with a clause in the direct object position, since no other theta-role is assigned to this position.

The complications involving indefiniteness and Case do not arise in constructions with clauses. Clauses can remain within the VP, even when they convey given information, since clauses (unlike NPs) do not require a Case feature.

### 3.4.11 Impersonal passives

Impersonal passives like (118) have already been discussed:

(118)    Il a été posé beaucoup de questions

They can be accounted for under either of the approaches which have been envisaged. If we take the view that indefinite NPs do not require a Case feature, *beaucoup de questions* need not move to the subject position. On the other hand, if we assume that all NPs must have Case, and that all direct object NPs must move into the subject position in passives, sentence (118) can be derived by moving *beaucoup de questions* back into the object position by the NP-postposing rule. Either way, the analysis predicts that constructions like (118) are only possible with indefinite NPs:

(119)    *Il a été posé cette question-là

Examples like (120) can be handled in the same way. Either the clause remains in the object position, since it does not require Case, or it moves into the subject position and then back again (by the Clause-postposing rule):

(120)    a    Il a été prouvé qu'Ivan est un espion
         b    Il m'a été demandé de partir

Note, however, that (121) is ungrammatical, in contrast to (120b):

(121)    *Il m'a été prié de partir

The crucial difference is that *me* is an indirect object in (120b) but a direct object in (121). To see the consequences of this difference, consider the underlying structures in (122):

(122)    a    $[_S \varnothing [_{VP}$ a été demandé à PRONOUN $[_{S'}$ de partir]]]
         b    $[_S \varnothing [_{VP}$ a été prié PRONOUN $[_{S'}$ de partir]]]

In (122a) the infinitival clause can be construed as the direct object. Since it is a clause, it can remain in place (or move to the subject position and back again), as discussed above. However, in (122b) the direct object is PRONOUN, which, being a definite NP, must move to the subject position to acquire a Case feature (and cannot move back to the object position, since this would violate the indefiniteness restriction on NP-postposing). Consequently, the valid surface structure corresponding to (122b) is (123):

(123)     J'ai été prié de partir

As we mentioned briefly in 3.2.5, we also find impersonal passives like (124), where the postverbal NP is the object of a preposition:

(124)     a   Il sera parlé de cette question
          b   Il a été procédé à une analyse des données

Sentences of this type are confined to a rather administrative style (e.g. legal documents, minutes of official meetings, etc.). Nevertheless, they do exist, and our grammar must account for them. One thing which these examples show is that the rule for forming passives (rule (8) in 3.2.2) can apply to at least some verbs which do not take a direct object. In a case like *parler* in (124a) suppression of the Agent will yield an entry for the passive form like (125):

(125)     *être parlé*:   [(Agent), Theme]
                          Theme = [$_{PP}$ *de* NP]

If we now project the theta-roles onto syntactic constituents, we obtain the underlying structure in (126):

(126)     [$_S$ ∅ [$_{VP}$ sera parlé [$_{PP}$ de [$_{NP}$ cette question]]]]

*Cette question* cannot move into the subject position, since this would violate the PP-Island Constraint (see 1.5.7). However, this does not matter. Recall that, in the normal situation, movement to the subject position is necessary because passive verbs cannot assign Accusative Case to their objects. However, *cette question* is not the direct object of the passive verb but the complement of the preposition, and will get Case in exactly the same way as in an active sentence like *On parlera de cette question*. Thus, the surface form (124b) can be derived simply by inserting *il* in the subject position.

Note now that the NP in these constructions does not conform to the indefiniteness restriction – *cette question* in (124a) is clearly definite. Again this is explained under either of the analyses we have envisaged. Since *cette question* cannot move into the subject position, it obviously does not get moved back again by NP-postposing, so the indefiniteness restriction (as a condition on this rule) does not come into play. According to the alternative approach envisaged in 3.4.5, the indefiniteness effect is accounted for by the hypothesis that indefinite NPs do not require Case, whereas definite NPs must move to the subject position to acquire a Case feature in passive constructions. However, as we observed above, the NPs in (122) get their Case feature from the preposition, so definite NPs can occur in this position.

One feature of impersonal passives which this analysis does not explain, and which will simply be noted here, is that the logical subject cannot normally be specified by means of *par* (or *de*):

(127)    a   *Il a été posé beaucoup de questions par les étudiants
         b   *Il m'a été demandé de partir par les agents
         c   *Il sera parlé de cette question par le comité

**Exercises**

1   Comment on the following extract from Le Bidois and Le Bidois (1971, vol. I, p. 407), concerning avoidance of the passive in French:

> Voici une phrase prononcée devant nous, dans une université canadienne, par un prince de race anglaise: «Je suis très content *d'être donné* cette canne et ce chapeau» (la canne et le chapeau d'étudiant). Phrase, à coup sûr, des plus anglaises. Le français dit: «Je suis très content *de recevoir* (ou *que vous me donniez*) . . .». En pareil cas, l'anglais va droit au passif, le français à l'actif. Les deux constructions sont en soi également légitimes. Ce qu'il convient de retenir, c'est que le tour passif nous paraît, à nous français, précieux à ménager, qu'il convient de le réserver à peu près exclusivement aux cas où il y a lieu de maintenir au premier plan d'éclairage le sujet du verbe, de lui donner le pas sur l'auteur de l'action. – Fait de langue très important à retenir, et de grande signification, (peut-être va-t-il jusqu'à ouvrir un jour sur la psychologie d'une race. Mais ceci est une autre affaire.)

2   Mansion (1952, p. 52) characterises passive constructions as follows:

> The object of a directly transitive verb becomes subject, and is shown as 'suffering' the action, the agent being then governed by the prepositions *par* or *de*.

> Jean a frappé la petite Louise.
> La petite Louise a été frappé par Jean
> Tout le monde respecte Pierre.
> Pierre est respecté de tout le monde

In the *Lexis* dictionary (Larousse, 1977 edition, p. 1227) the entry for the verb *ordonner* is formulated as follows:

> ORDONNER [ɔrdɔne] v. tr (1352). Donner un ordre: *Je vous ordonne de vous taire* (Giraudoux) (syn. DEMANDER, ENJOINDRE, PRIER). *Faites ce qu'on vous ordonne* (syn. DIRE). *Votre voyage, c'étaient vos maîtres qui vous l'avaient payé et ordonné* (Butor) (syn. DEMANDER, IMPOSER, PRESCRIRE). Fam. et vx. *Monsieur (madame, mademoiselle) j'ordonne*, se dit de personnes qui aiment à donner des ordres impérieux et fréquents.

On the basis of this information, could one deduce that *\*J'ai été ordonné de partir* is ungrammatical? Comment on any respects in which this information is misleading or unhelpful.

3  Most reference grammars cite the verbs *obéir, désobéir* and *pardonner* as exceptions to the normal conditions on French passive constructions. In what respect are these verbs exceptional? Formulate lexical entries for these verbs to clarify the nature of this problem.

4  Collect examples of idioms with transitive verbs in French and English and try to work out which can be passivised. Is there any correspondence between the two languages in this respect?

5  Comment on the possible interpretations of the following sentences (some are ambiguous) and identify the type of pronominal verb construction corresponding to each interpretation (e.g. genuine reflexive/reciprocal, Neutral, Intrinsic or Middle):

  (a)  Cela ne se fait pas
  (b)  Gaston et Sophie s'entendent bien
  (c)  Ce livre se vend dans toutes les librairies
  (d)  Max s'est trouvé dans une situation compromettante
  (e)  Les terroristes se sont rendus en Italie
  (f)  Une fille capricieuse, ça se marie sans hésiter
  (g)  Pierre et Marie se rappellent leurs promesses
  (h)  Un bon professeur, ça s'écoute toujours

6  Discuss the syntactic properties of the following sentences paying particular attention to the properties of voice (e.g. different types of pronominal verbs, impersonal constructions):

  (a)  Il s'est avéré que Paul avait raison
  (b)  Il se boit beaucoup de bière en Belgique
  (c)  Il nous a été proposé de réviser nos projets
  (d)  Il y va de notre avenir
  (e)  Il se peut que la réunion soit reportée
  (f)  Il n'en est pas question
  (g)  Il s'est rassemblé beaucoup de monde
  (h)  Il a été demandé aux voyageurs de ne pas fumer
  (i)  Ça m'a choqué que les étudiants n'aient pas fait leurs devoirs
  (j)  Cette voiture se démarre en tournant la manivelle

7  How do sentences formed by means of *il y a* fit into the classification of impersonal constructions presented in 3.4? Points to bear in mind include the types of phrases which can follow *il y a*, correspondences with other uses of *avoir* (or indeed *être*), and similarities and differences between *il y a* and English *there is/are*.

8  On the basis of examples like (a) and (b), some linguists have claimed that genuine reflexives and reciprocals cannot occur in impersonal constructions:

(a)  ??Il se lavait beaucoup de personnes dans la rivière
(b)  ??Il se contredit beaucoup de linguistes

Are the following sentences counterexamples to this claim?

(c)  Il se baignait beaucoup de touristes dans la mer
(d)  Il se tue beaucoup de personnes sur l'autoroute

Construct further examples of your own which might help to assess the validity of this claim.

### Further reading

As general background to the issues raised in this chapter, see Blinkenberg (1969).

G. Gross (1993) is devoted to passive constructions in French. Otherwise, French passives tend to be discussed in relation to other phenomena rather than as a topic in their own right; see for example various parts of general works such as M. Gross (1968), Kayne (1975), and also Kayne (1984, ch. 9) for a more up-to-date approach. The behaviour of idioms in passives (and other constructions) is investigated by Ruwet (1983b). Péry-Woodley (1991) presents a comparative analysis of the use of passives in French and English texts.

The analysis of pronominal verb constructions is based on Ruwet (1972, ch. 3) which sets the agenda for most subsequent generative studies of this topic. For further discussion see Lyons (1982), Zribi-Hertz (1982, 1987), Lagae (1990), Feigenbaum (1992).

Gaatone (1970) and Martin (1970) discuss impersonal constructions within an early version of transformational grammar, with plenty of interesting examples. Rivière (1981) presents a more extensive study. Ruwet (1982, ch. 1) discusses impersonal constructions in relation to the Subject-raising phenomenon (see 9.2.4); see also Ruwet (1989) for discussion of weather verbs. Some of the more theoretical issues surrounding impersonal constructions are addressed in Herschensohn (1979), Kayne (1979) and Pollock (1979, 1981, 1982). On impersonal passives, see Dobrovie-Sorin (1986).

The passive-like construction with *se faire* is discussed by Kupferman (1995), Tasmowski-De Ryck & van Oevelen (1987). On the syntax and/or pragmatics of other constructions which can be used as alternatives to the passive, see Barnes (1985), Lambrecht (1981, 1988), Dupont (1985), Larsson (1979).

# 4
# Tense, aspect and mood

## 4.1 Overview

This chapter is concerned with aspects of meaning which are conveyed by the inflected forms of verbs and by constructions with auxiliary verbs and similar expressions.

In 4.2 a system is proposed for representing tense, applying it initially to data from English (partly to show how it works, but also to provide a basis for the more detailed analysis of French in 4.3–4.7). In 4.8 there is an examination of the ways in which certain tense-forms can be used to express modality (degrees of probability, potentiality, etc.) rather than to locate events in time. This leads to a discussion of mood, principally the distinction between the indicative and the subjunctive, in 4.9.

## 4.2 Analysing tense and aspect

### 4.2.1 The concept of tense

The concept of **tense** embraces the various grammatical devices which are used to represent notions of time. At the morphological level, the term 'tense' is often used to refer to the inflectional forms of verbs which express notions of time. In this narrow sense, French has five tenses (illustrated in (1) by the third person singular forms of *chanter*, with their conventional labels), whereas English has only two – present (*He sings*) and past (*He sang*):

| (1) | | | |
|---|---|---|---|
| | a | Il chante | 'present' |
| | b | Il chant | 'past-historic' ('simple-past' or 'preterite') |
| | c | Il chantait | 'imperfect' |
| | d | Il chanter | 'future' |
| | e | Il chanterait | 'conditional' |

Some grammarians extend the term 'tense' to include so-called **compound tenses**, constructed by means of an auxiliary verb in an inflected tense form. For example, the auxiliary verbs *avoir* and *être* can be used with the past participle in all the five inflected tense forms to produce the compound tenses in (2):

136

(2)  a  Il a chanté        Il est arrivé     'compound-past' ('(present) perfect')
     b  Il eut chanté      Il fut arrivé     'past anterior'
     c  Il avait chanté    Il était arrivé   'pluperfect'
     d  Il aura chanté     Il sera arrivé    'future-perfect'
     e  Il aurait chanté   Il serait arrivé  'conditional-perfect'

English makes more widespread use of compound tenses than French, compensating for the relative poverty of inflected tense forms. In addition to constructions analogous to those in (2) (e.g. *He has/had sung*), we may note the use of *will* in the present or past (*He will/would sing*) corresponding, roughly, to the future and conditional forms in French, and the use of *be* with the present participle (*He is/was singing*) to characterise an event as being in progress at a particular time.

There are many other phrasal expressions which are not usually recognised as separate tense forms (e.g. they do not have accepted labels of the sort given in (1) and (2)), but which nevertheless convey similar notions of time. These range from fairly grammaticalised constructions such as *aller* + infinitive, expressing future, and *venir de* + infinitive, expressing recent past, through to a more open-ended class of verbs and phrasal expressions such as *commencer, cesser, continuer, être en train, être sur le point, avoir l'habitude.*

### 4.2.2  Representing tense

The notions of past, present and future time can be defined in terms of a relation between the time of the event described, the **event-time**, 'E', and the **moment of speech**, 'S'. Thus, a past event is one which occurs before the moment of speech ('E→S'), a present event is simultaneous with the moment of speech ('E=S') and a future event occurs after the moment of speech ('S→E'). To account for more subtle distinctions within the tense system, we invoke the notion of a **reference-time**, 'R', which is determined by context. The motivation for this third time-index can be illustrated by comparing the English examples in (3):

(3)      a  John read the newspaper (when Mary told him the news)
         b  John had read the newspaper (when Mary told him the news)

Both sentences locate the event in the past (i.e. before 'S'), but the pluperfect in (3b) also indicates that the event occurred before some time which is contextually relevant, specified here by the *when* clause. Assuming that *when* clauses specify the reference-time 'R' for the main clause, the meaning of the pluperfect in (3b) can be characterised by the formula 'E→R, R→S' (the event occurs before the reference-time, which is located in the past), whereas the simple-past in (3a) indicates that the event-time is (roughly) simultaneous with the past reference-time (i.e. 'E=R, R→S'). These formulae can be represented graphically as in (4)[1]:

(4)    (a)  Simple-past:

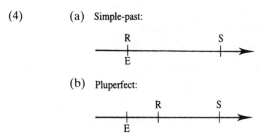

(b)  Pluperfect:

The notion of a reference-time can also be used to explicate certain differences between the simple-past and the present-perfect[2] in English:

(5)    John has read the newspaper (*when Mary told him the news)

The present-perfect is used to report past events from the perspective of the present, often carrying implications which are relevant to the present situation. For example, the sentence *The car has broken down* strongly implies that the car is still out of order, whereas *The car broke down* simply describes a past event, typically as part of a sequence which forms a narrative (e.g. *On my way to work, the car broke down. The mechanic repaired it, but I arrived late*). Also, as (5) shows, the present-perfect is incompatible with expressions which locate the reference-time in the past. These properties of the present-perfect can be represented by the formula 'E→R, R=S' (the reference-time is identified with the moment of speech, and the event-time is located prior to this reference-time):

(6)    Present-perfect (English):

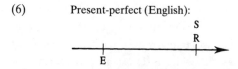

Both the simple-past and the present-perfect locate 'E' before 'S', with no necessary difference concerning the length of time in between, but they differ with respect to the location of 'R' in relation to 'E' and 'S'.

---

[1] In the diagrams, the moment of speech and reference-time are indicated above the time axis, while the event-time is placed below it. There is no significance to this convention, but it will help to simplify representations of more complicated cases where we have several events and reference-times.

[2] The term 'present-perfect' is used to refer to the English form illustrated in (5), but 'compound-past' for the analogous French form (*Jean a lu le journal*). This terminological difference is meant to highlight the fact that the French form frequently lacks the connotations of present-relevance associated with the English present-perfect, but functions in many respects like the English simple-past (see 4.3.3 for discussion).

The English progressive forms, illustrated in (7), can be characterised in a similar way:

(7)      a   John is reading the newspaper (now)

          b   John was reading the newspaper (when Mary told him the news)

The sentences in (7) describe an event which is in progress at a particular point in time, the present in (7a) and a specific moment in the past in (7b), as specified by the *when* clause. This can be captured by representing 'E' as extending beyond 'R', where 'R' is equated with 'S' ('R=S') when the auxiliary *be* is in the present tense, but as preceding 'S' ('R→S') with the past form of *be*, as shown in (8):

(8)      (a)  Present progressive:

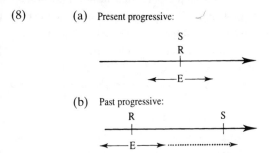

      (b)  Past progressive:

Note that the past-progressive in (7b) does not preclude the possibility that the event is still in progress at the moment of speech, as indicated by the dotted extension of the arrow in (8b); e.g. one can say, without contradiction, *John was reading the newspaper five minutes ago, and he is still reading it.* Thus, the progressive form describes an event which extends across the reference-time, typically beginning before it and continuing indefinitely after it. At the notational level we may represent the progressive by the formula 'R⊂E', where the symbol ⊂ signifies 'is included in', thus entailing that the event extends beyond the reference-time.

### 4.2.3 Aspect

The distinction expressed between simple and progressive forms in English is commonly referred to as an 'aspectual' distinction. Whereas 'tense' relates to the situation of an event in time (past, present or future), **aspect** relates to the way in which the event is distributed over time. Thus, **progressive aspect** indicates an event which is presented as extending beyond a particular point in time ('R'), whereas **punctual aspect** (sometimes called 'perfective aspect') indicates a complete event which is conceived as occupying a point in time. In terms of actual, real-life situations, progressive aspect can be manifested in a variety of ways. For example, it can denote a single event which is protracted in time (9a) or an event which is iterated (9b):

139

(9)      a   John was writing a letter (when I came in)
          b   John was hitting Bill (when I came in)

Both of these situations can be represented by the formula 'RCE'.

Other aspectual distinctions include **habitual aspect** (10a) and **stative aspect** (10b):

(10)     a   John used to sing (when he was young)
         b   John is tall

Habitual aspect involves repetition of an event, but over a long period of time (e.g. 'when he was young') rather than around a particular instant (e.g. 'when I came in' in (9b)). In this case, the event-time ('E') does not correspond to the time of any particular instance of the event, but rather to the period within which the event typically occurred. Moreover, when the clause which specifies the reference-time is one which might normally be interpreted as denoting a single event, it must also have a habitual interpretation: e.g. *When(ever) the juke-box played rock-music, John danced.*

Stative aspect is conditioned by the meaning of the verb (or VP), which must denote a state (as opposed to a process or action – see 2.2.1). By their nature, states are situations which remain constant over a period of time. Stative sentences can have interpretations analogous to progressive or habitual sentences, according to whether the state extends around a particular reference point (as in (11a)) or whether it is coextensive with a long-term period (as in (11b)):

(11)     a   John was happy when I saw him this morning
         b   John was happy when he was a child

Progressive, habitual and stative aspects can be grouped together under a broader category of **durative aspect** (or 'non-punctual' aspect), as in figure 4.1.

Figure 4.1 Aspectual distinctions

| Punctual | Durative (non-punctual) | | |
|---|---|---|---|
| | Stative | Habitual | Progressive |

The term 'durative' conveys the idea of a situation whose beginning and/or end is left unspecified and is presented as extending beyond a salient reference point, whereas punctual aspect presents a single, completed event whose beginning and end are conflated within a time-span which can be perceived as a point. However, this distinction cannot be defined in terms of duration in real time. For example, *John read 'Germinal'* and *John shut the door* are both punctual (describing single completed events), despite their very different durations, whereas *John used to read poetry* (habitual) and *John was shutting the door* (progressive) are both durative.

### 4.2.4 Encoding tense and aspect in English and French

In English, we find a rather neat division of labour between inflectional tenses (also future *will*) and the auxiliaries *have* (with the past participle) and *be* (with the present participle). Essentially, the inflectional tense-forms (and *will*) define a relation between 'S' and 'R', whereas the auxiliaries *have* and *be* express the relationship between 'E' and 'R', as summarised in table 4.1.

Table 4.1. *Representations of tense-forms and auxiliaries in English*

| |
| --- |
| (i) Present: 'R=S' |
|      Past:    'R→S' |
|      *will*:    'S→R' |
| (ii) *have*:   'E→R' |
|     *be*:     'R→E' |
| (iii) In the absence of an auxiliary, 'E=R' |

Some examples showing the interaction between the formulae in table 4.1 are given in (12):

(12)    a  John left                                (R→S, E=R)

        b  John will leave                          (S→R, E=R)

        c  John will have left (when we arrive)    (S→R, E→R)

        d  John will be leaving (when we arrive)    (S→R, R⊂E)

        e  John had left (when we arrived)       (R→S, E→R)

        f  John was leaving (when we arrived)     (R→S, R⊂E)

In French, this division of labour is much less clear. For example, the inflected forms which express past tense (i.e. the past-historic and the imperfect) also convey an aspectual distinction (punctual vs durative). Conversely, the compound-past (formed by *avoir* or *être* and the past participle), which is constructionally analogous to the present-perfect in English, does not necessarily display the implications of present relevance or the incompatibility with expressions of past time which we noted in 4.2.2 with regard to the English present-perfect, and it can often be rendered by the simple-past in English; i.e. it corresponds to both 'E→R, R=S' and 'E=R, R→S' (see 4.3.3).

Both French and English have means of making the aspectual distinctions shown in figure 4.1, but they differ sharply in terms of the aspectual distinctions which must be expressed. Compare typical uses of the simple-past and past-progressive in English with the past-historic and imperfect in French:

(13) a  He arrived yesterday at noon  Il arriva hier à midi  PUNCTUAL
b  He went out every evening  Il sortait tous les soirs  HABITUAL
c  He loved his mother  Il aimait sa mère  STATIVE
d  He was going down the stairs  Il déscendait l'escalier  PROGRESSIVE

In English, the simple-past is essentially non-progressive – it can be used to describe punctual events, habitual events and states (13a–c), but for ongoing events we must use the progressive form (13d). On the other hand, the French past-historic (also the compound-past) is punctual whereas the imperfect is durative (or non-punctual), embracing habitual, stative and progressive aspect. Thus, French makes an obligatory distinction between punctual and durative aspect whereas the obligatory distinction in English is between progressive and non-progressive aspect:

**Aspectual distinctions in past time:**

English                                         French

$$\left.\begin{array}{l} PUNCTUAL \\ HABITUAL \\ STATIVE \\ PROGRESSIVE \end{array}\right\}$$

*simple-past* — { PUNCTUAL / HABITUAL / STATIVE }  *past-historic/compound-past* ; *imperfect*

*past-progressive*  PROGRESSIVE

Of course, when appropriate, French can make a progressive reading explicit by means of *être en train* (e.g. *Il était en train de déscendre l'escalier*, corresponding to (13d)), just as the habitual interpretation of (13b) can be made clear in English by *used to* (*Gaston used to go out every evening*). The important point is that the progressive can be expressed by the simple imperfect (just as habitual aspect can be expressed by the English simple-past) – indeed, over-frequent or unnecessary use of *être en train* will often create a laboured effect.

### 4.3  The expression of past time

#### 4.3.1  *Past-historic vs imperfect*

A major problem for students of French concerns the choice of tense forms in those cases where the simple-past would be appropriate in English. For the moment the past-historic will be used to illustrate punctual aspect in the past (the compound-past is more usual with this interpretation in informal style, but it presents further complications which will be discussed in 4.3.3).

Recall firstly that the punctual vs durative distinction is not based on the actual duration of the event in real time. For example, in (14) the past-historic can be used to describe an event which took place over several millennia:

(14)      Pendant l'époque glaciaire, la géomorphologie de la planète se transforma complètement

At the opposite extreme, an event such as the explosion of a bomb in (15), which would normally be conceived as instantaneous, can be described in the imperfect:

(15)        Le terroriste fut pris de panique: la bombe explosait

In (14), the effect of the past-historic is to present the event as a completed episode in the history of our planet. The effect of the imperfect in the second clause in (15) is to spread out the split-second event, rather like a slow-motion sequence in a film, viewing it as a developing process within which another event (the momentary panic of the terrorist) can be situated.

In 4.2.2, we noted that one of the ways in which an event can be protracted over time is by repetition of the action, either within a short time-span which extends beyond the immediate reference point (giving a progressive reading) or over a much longer period (with a habitual interpretation). However, repetition of the action does not in itself entail use of the durative (imperfect) form, as shown by the following examples with the past-historic:

(16)        a   Le facteur sonna cinq fois
            b   Pierre visita Lyon plusieurs fois

Indeed, when the number of occurrences of the action is specified (even approximately, as in (16b)), the use of the imperfect would force an interpretation where the repeated action constitutes a habitual event (e.g. *Le facteur sonnait cinq fois* = 'the postman used to ring five times (whenever he called)', *Pierre visitait Lyon plusieurs fois chaque année*).

With stative verbs, the choice of tense in French expresses a distinction which is not readily made in English. Often, the past-historic is used to denote a transient state which is contemporary with (and possibly occasioned by) a particular event, such as the watching of the film in (17a) or the entry into the room in (17b):

(17)        a   Marie aima ce film
            b   En entrant dans la salle, Paul eut peur

Compare (17a) with the imperfective version (18):

(18)        Marie aimait ce film

Example (18) can have a 'long-term' interpretation, analogous to a habitual interpretation ('Marie used to like this film'), which is not available for (17a). In the case where a transient state is involved, the past-historic presents the whole experience as completed in the past (e.g. (17a) simply reports Marie's reaction to the past event) whereas the imperfect in (18) presents the experience as ongoing, developing as the film progresses. Often this distinction can be conveyed in English by choosing a non-stative verb which allows the progressive form: e.g.

*Marie enjoyed the film* (= 17a) vs *Marie was enjoying the film* (= 18); similarly (17b) might be rendered by *When he entered the room, Paul (suddenly) felt apprehensive*, whereas the imperfective version *Paul avait peur* could be expressed as *Paul was feeling apprehensive*. In other words, the aspectual distinction made in English with non-stative verbs (simple- vs progressive past) is maintained in French with stative verbs as well, by the use of the past-historic to denote a completed state as opposed to the imperfect to indicate an ongoing state. Note, however, that the progressive expression *être en train de* cannot be used with stative verbs – e.g. *??Elle était en train d'aimer ce film* is as odd as *??She was liking the film*.

Often the use of the past-historic with stative verbs (particularly those denoting cognitive states) has the effect of focusing on the onset of the state rather than its duration, an effect typically achieved in English by using a verb which refers explicitly to a change in state, as shown by the suggested translations in (19) (see 2.2.2):

(19) a Le lendemain, elle sut que son fiancé l'avait désertée
    'The next day she found out that her fiancé had left her'
  b Elle le connut pour la première fois en 1968
    'She first became acquainted with him in 1968'

A similar effect is observed in locative expressions with *être*, particularly in time clauses introduced by *quand, lorsque, dès que*, etc., where the past-historic is used to indicate arrival at a particular point:

(20) a Lorsqu'il fut au sommet, l'alpiniste s'écria de joie
    'When he got to the top, the mountaineer cried out for joy'
  b Dès qu'il fut dans son lit, il s'endormit
    'As soon as he got into bed, he fell asleep'

### 4.3.2 Past tenses in narrative discourse

In a narrative discourse, punctual tense forms (past-historic or compound-past) are used to report the basic sequence of events which can be embellished by background information presented in the imperfect. Consider first the basic narrative in (21) composed entirely of punctual events in the past-historic:

(21) M. Dupont se leva$_{(a)}$ de bonne heure. Il fit$_{(b)}$ sa toilette, s'habilla$_{(c)}$ et prit$_{(d)}$ son petit-déjeuner. Il écouta$_{(e)}$ les informations à la radio. Puis il mit$_{(f)}$ son manteau et sortit$_{(g)}$. Il monta$_{(h)}$ dans l'autobus. Une heure plus tard il arriva$_{(i)}$ à son bureau. Il y travailla$_{(j)}$ toute la journée. Le soir, il rentra$_{(k)}$ chez lui. Il dîna$_{(l)}$, il regarda$_{(m)}$ un peu la télévision et enfin il se coucha$_{(n)}$.

All of the events in this text are presented as single, completed events, and it is this notion of 'completion' which dictates the use of the past-historic, regardless of their relative duration (e.g. event (j) is treated as 'punctual' just like instantaneous events such as (f)). Note also that the order in which the events are reported reflects their chronological sequence (e.g. it would be odd to report events (b) and (c) before (a)). This is a typical property of the past-historic (and of narrative uses of the compound-past) but not necessarily of the imperfect. For example, the use of the past-historic to describe event (e) indicates that this event took place after the sequence of events in (b)–(d), with no significant overlap, but if this event were reported in the imperfect (*Il écoutait les informations à la radio*), this would suggest that this event occurred concurrently with some of the previously reported events (e.g. he listened to the radio while he had breakfast).

Within this skeletal text we can intersperse clauses in the imperfect without affecting the original temporal sequence. For example, an ambient comment such as *Il faisait très froid* might be inserted before or after (f), its textual position being determined by its relevance to the event (f) rather than by its temporal reference. After (g) we could insert a 'descriptive interlude' of ongoing events or states in the imperfect, e.g. *Les magasins s'ouvraient. Les voitures klaxonnaient de partout. Le vent soufflait dans les arbres. M. Dupont avait mal à la tête*, etc. Again, the order of presentation within such an interlude is essentially arbitrary. Descriptions of habitual events or longer-term states can also be intercalated by means of the imperfect: e.g. after (h), *D'habitude il prenait sa voiture* (habitual event), *mais elle était en panne ce jour-là* (temporary state), or after (i) *Son bureau se trouvait à l'autre côté de la ville* (permanent state).

Another function of the imperfect is to elaborate on an event which has been presented in a punctual fashion: e.g. the event (j) might be amplified as in (22):

(22)     Il y travailla toute la journée. Il dictait des lettres. Il rédigeait des rapports. Il négociait avec des clients.

Conversely, the imperfect can be used to 'set a scene' within which a sequence of individual events is situated:

(23)     Pendant toute la journée, il travaillait comme un fou. Pour commencer, il répondit au courrier de la veille. A dix heures, son patron le chargea d'une affaire importante qu'il fallait traiter d'urgence. Ensuite, il reçut un coup de téléphone de la part de l'agent-comptable qui lui demandait de fournir tous les chiffres de vente pour le mois courant.

Note the use of the imperfect in subordinate clauses within this text (*qu'il fallait traiter ...*, *qui lui demandait ...*) with an elaborative function similar to that illus-

145

trated in (22). The past-historic could be used here, but with a subtle difference in meaning which is broadly consistent with our general characterisation. For example, in the former case, *fallut* would suggest that the 'affaire importante' was in fact dealt with urgently, as a subsequent completed event, whereas the imperfect form *fallait* merely describes the nature of this business (as a stative property).

The difference between the past-historic and the imperfect regarding chronological order of presentation can be accounted for by a principle which requires the reference-time to advance (or at least be held constant) with each sentence:

**Temporal Sequence Principle (TSP):**
*for any pair of sentences $\Sigma_{n-1}$, $\Sigma_n$, where $\Sigma_{n-1}$ immediately precedes $\Sigma_n$ in the same discourse,*
*'$R_{n-1} \rightarrow R_n$' (or '$R_{n-1} = R_n$').*

Recall that for the past-historic, the event-time coincides with the reference-time ('E=R, R→S'), so the sequence of reference-times entails chronological ordering of event-times. Thus, the temporal structure of the basic narrative (21) can be represented as in (24):

(24)

$$
\begin{array}{ccccccccc}
R_a & R_b & R_c & R_d & & R_l & R_m & R_n & S \\
\hline
E_a & E_b & E_c & E_d & & E_l & E_m & E_n &
\end{array}
$$

However, for the imperfect, the event-time can extend indefinitely on either side of the reference-time ('R⊂E, R→S'), so no strict ordering of event-times is imposed by the TSP. To illustrate, the revised narrative in (25) can be represented as in (26):

(25)  Il prit$_{(a)}$ son petit-déjeuner pendant qu'il écoutait$_{(b)}$ les informations à la radio. Puis il mit$_{(c)}$ son manteau, parce qu'il faisait froid$_{(d)}$, et il sortit$_{(e)}$.

(26)

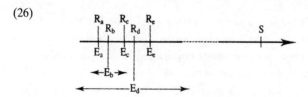

Because the TSP applies to reference-times, rather than event-times, it allows punctual events to be reported out of sequence by the use of tense forms which locate 'E' before or after 'R': e.g. for 'flashbacks', the pluperfect, represented as

146

'E→R, R→S', or to anticipate later events, the conditional, represented as 'R→E, R→S' (see 4.3.5. and 4.5.2 for further discussion). This is illustrated in (27), whose temporal structure is given in (28):

(27)    Il s'habilla$_{(a)}$ et il mangea$_{(b)}$ son petit-déjeuner en vitesse parce qu'il s'était levé$_{(c)}$ un peu tard. Il ferma$_{(d)}$ la radio. Il regarderait$_{(e)}$ les informations à la télévision le soir. Il prit$_{(f)}$ son manteau et il sortit$_{(g)}$.

(28)

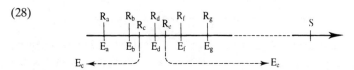

In English, the TSP can be violated in certain cases, such as relative clauses like (29) (cf. . . . *which she had bought* . . . , where the TSP is respected):

(29)    Mary wore the dress which she bought the day before

Such violations are not possible in French:

(30)    a    Marie mit la robe qu'elle avait achetée la veille
        b    *Marie mit la robe qu'elle acheta la veille

It is, however, possible to switch the reference-time from the past to the present and back again, e.g. *M. Dupont était très fatigué ce soir-là. Ce n'est pas étonnant. Il avait travaillé toute la journée.* To accommodate such cases, we must construe the TSP as applying only to reference-times within the time-span of the narrative itself. For reasons which are discussed in the next section, switching between past and present reference-times is more appropriate when past events are reported in the compound-past than when the past-historic is used.

### 4.3.3    Past-historic vs compound-past

The differences between the past-historic and the compound-past are partly stylistic and partly semantic.

The past-historic forms are used only in formal written styles and, sometimes, in prepared speeches. In less formal registers, the compound-past is used to report punctual events in the past in the same way as the past-historic in the cases discussed in 4.3.1–4.3.2. In these registers, the compound-past can have the representation 'E=R, R→S', which has been assumed for the past-historic. However, in all styles, the compound-past can also be used in a similar way to the English present-perfect to report past events in terms of their relevance to the present (see 4.2.2), i.e. with the representation 'E→R, R=S'. In all registers, the imperfect has the

147

Table 4.2. *Functions of past tense forms*

| Function | English | Formal French | Informal French |
|---|---|---|---|
| 'E→R, R=S' | Present-perfect | compound-past | compound-past |
| 'E=R, R→S' | simple-past | past-historic | |
| Stative past | | | imperfect |
| Habitual past | | | |
| Progressive past | past-progressive | | |

durative value discussed in 4.3.1–4.3.2 (but see 4.3.4 below). The cross-linguistic correspondences between these forms can be represented roughly as in table 4.2.

In 4.2.2, we justified the representation 'E→R, R=S' for the English present-perfect on the grounds that this form cannot be used with expressions which refer to past time, e.g. *\*Zola has written that novel in 1881*. This restriction does not apply to the French compound-past, at least not in informal registers, where sentence (31) is perfectly acceptable:

(31)     Zola a écrit ce roman en 1881

Even in more formal registers where the past-historic is used, the compound-past can occur with expressions of past time, particularly when some appeal is made to the interests of the addressee, as in (32):

(32)     Rappelons que Zola a écrit ce roman en 1881

This observation suggests that the concept of 'present relevance' associated with tense forms of the type 'E→R, R=S' is weaker and less clearly defined, even for formal French, than it is in English. Other factors which tend to favour the use of the compound-past in formal French include the use of first-person forms, time expressions which are defined in terms of the present (e.g. *hier, l'année dernière*; see 4.7.1), description of past events whose direct effects endure up to the present and statements about the experiences or achievements of persons who are still alive, though none of these precludes the use of the past-historic.

The stylistic and semantic considerations reviewed above are closely related. In speech, the moment at which a sentence is uttered ('S') usually coincides with the moment at which it is heard, but this is rarely the case with written texts. Consequently, the concept of a present shared by the writer and the addressee, from which past events can be viewed, is much less readily available in written texts, particularly those which are intended for 'posterity' (the sort of texts in which the past-historic is most widely used). Also, the evocation of a 'shared present' may establish a rapport with the addressee which goes hand in hand with some degree of informality. Thus, the use of a sentence like (32) in a formal text can be seen as a combination of these semantic and stylistic effects. The choice of the compound-past rather than the past-historic suggests relevance to the present, but reference to the present in turn marks a shift towards the informal norm in which the compound-past is the 'all-purpose' punctual past form compatible with expressions of past time like *en 1881*.

In the same vein, there are some significant differences between the past-historic and the English simple-past (with punctual reference). According to established convention, the past-historic cannot be used to describe events which occurred on the same day as the moment of speech, a restriction which clearly does not apply to the English simple-past:

(33)     *Paul acheta cette voiture {il y a deux heures / ce matin}
         'Paul bought that car {two hours ago / this morning}'

More generally, the cut-off point at which the notion of 'present relevance' determines the choice between simple and compound tense forms is rather different in the two languages. In English, the use of the present-perfect establishes a clear and explicit link with the present (as shown by the incompatibility with expressions of past time), whereas the simple-past is neutral in this respect (it does not imply present relevance, but does not preclude it either). In French, the emphasis seems to work in the opposite direction: the use of the past-historic has the explicit effect of divorcing the described events from considerations of present relevance, situating them in a self-contained time-span, while the compound-past is neutral. For this reason, the past-historic is particularly appropriate in fictional texts, where the imaginary nature of the events precludes any direct link with the real present. In this connection, we may note that in fiction the past-historic does not necessarily correlate with a formal or 'elevated' style – for example, it is used in novels by authors such as Raymond Queneau or Christiane Rochefort whose language is otherwise highly colloquial.

When the compound-past is used as a narrative tense (with the representation 'E=R, R→S'), it has the same properties as the past-historic with regard to chronological order of presentation and interaction with the imperfect, pluperfect and conditional. Thus, our analyses of the discourses in 4.3.2 apply also to versions with the compound-past instead of the past-historic. Similarly, in cases analogous to (30) in 4.3.2, the pluperfect must be used to refer back to prior events:

(34)     Marie a mis la robe qu'elle {avait / *a} achetée la veille

However, the compound-past can also be used in discourses of a rather different kind, where order of presentation does not necessarily match the chronological order of events.

Consider the discourse in (35), where M. Dupont is summarising his day's work to a colleague, to show how busy he has been:

(35)    Aujourd'hui, j'ai dicté$_{(a)}$ une vingtaine de lettres, j'ai négocié$_{(b)}$ avec plusieurs clients, j'ai rédigé$_{(c)}$ un rapport de trente pages, j'ai répondu$_{(d)}$ au téléphone une centaine de fois ... Bref, j'ai fait$_{(e)}$ le travail de trois personnes

Here, the events are presented as a list of achievements rather than as elements of a story, and we cannot infer anything about the order in which they occurred. Apart from the global statement at the end (which could also be used to introduce the discourse) these activities could be presented in any order, with no difference in meaning.

In this type of discourse, the compound-past corresponds to the English present-perfect and can be represented as 'E→R, R=S' – i.e. each event is presented from the perspective of the present. Here, the compound-past indicates only that each event occurs (and is completed) sometime before the moment of speech (within the relevant time-span) but says nothing about the temporal relations between events. Thus, the discourse in (35) is consistent with a temporal structure like (36), where the individual activities are scattered throughout the day, possibly overlapping with each other or interrupting each other (e.g in the case of answering the phone), as long as the cumulative effect of these activities by the end of the day matches the claims in the discourse:

(36)

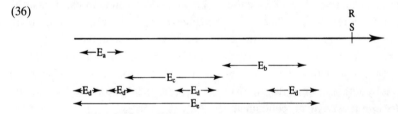

Note that this temporal structure is consistent with the TSP – since the reference-time is kept constant, the 'R' associated with each 'E' is identical with the 'R' for the previously described event ($R_n = R_{n-1}$).

### 4.3.4   The 'dramatic' imperfect
Contrary to our claim in 4.3.1, the imperfect is occasionally used, particularly in journalistic style, to describe punctual, consecutive events in the past, in order to achieve a 'dramatic' effect:

(37)    Au moment de la fermeture, les gangsters entraient dans la banque. Ils obligeaient les employés de leur rendre l'argent de la

caisse. Trente seconds après, ils sortaient et prenaient la fuite en voiture.

Clearly the imperfect in (37) does not convey habitual or stative aspect, and it cannot be rendered by the progressive in English. Nevertheless, this usage can be viewed as a stylistic extension ·of the progressive value of the imperfect rather than as a separate, punctual interpretation of this tense form. Essentially, the presentation of punctual events as being in progress has the effect of placing the addressee in the position of a witness to these events as they unfold. This stylistic device should be used sparingly and with extreme caution. Its success requires considerable skill and sensitivity to style, in the absence of which it is much more likely to be perceived as an error. Above all, the fact that this usage exists should not be taken as an excuse for pretending that the imperfect can be used as an all-purpose past tense.

### 4.3.5 Flashing back and moving forward

The pluperfect (*Il avait chanté, Il était arrivé*) is used in much the same way as its English counterpart, to indicate that an event or state occurs before some other past event or state:

(38)   a   M. Dupont était fatigué, parce qu'il avait travaillé toute la journée

      b   Marie mit la robe qu'elle avait achetée la veille

      c   Quand Luc avait terminé son repas, il s'en est allé

For the pluperfect the representation 'E→R, R→S' has been proposed, where 'R' corresponds to the time of the other event or state (described in the imperfect, past-historic or compound-past in (38)). However, there is a subtle difference between examples (38a, b) and (38c). In (38a), the pluperfect represents a 'flash-back' to a situation which explains the current state and in (38b) the 'flashback' serves to identify an object involved in the current event, as discussed in 4.3.2. However, in (38c) there is no 'flashback'. Rather, the function of the pluperfect is to advance the narrative to a time beyond that of the event described in the *quand* clause. This can be seen more clearly in a contextualised example:

(39)   Luc est entré$_{(a)}$ dans le restaurant et il a commandé$_{(b)}$ un poulet-frites. Quand il avait mangé$_{(c)}$ son repas, il s'en est allé$_{(d)}$.

Common sense tells us that event (c) cannot precede event (b), so we are not flashing back to a period before the previous reference-time established by (b). Rather, the pluperfect exploits our knowledge that the event-time of (c) must be sometime after (b) in order to move the reference-time forward, skipping over the intervening period as it were. In other words, in 'flashback' cases like (38a, b), the 'R' of the pluperfect clauses is given by the context and 'E' is defined as being prior to it, whereas in (39) the 'E' of *avait mangé* is deduced from context and the pluperfect defines a new reference point later than this 'E', from which the subsequent narrative continues. This difference can be represented schematically by annotating the representations of the pluperfect as in (40):

(40)   a   $E_{[NEW]} \rightarrow R_{[GIVEN]}, R \rightarrow S.$   ('flashback' – (38a, b))

       b   $E_{[GIVEN]} \rightarrow R_{[NEW]}, R \rightarrow S$   ('moving forward' – (38c, 39))

In the case of (38c) and (39), the function in (40b) is signalled explicitly by the adverb *quand* (or others like *dès que, après que, à peine*, etc.). However, we also find similar cases where the pluperfect is used in a main clause at the beginning of a discourse in order to set the scene and to establish a reference-time for the ensuing events, as in (41), where the first sentence situates the following discourse at 'the end of a hard day's work':

(41)   M. Dupont avait travaillé toute la journée. Il alluma la télévision et s'installa dans un fauteuil.

The English pluperfect can be used in exactly the same way, so the different functions noted above are unlikely to pose practical problems. However, the distinction represented in (40) is relevant to the use of other French tense forms which are used as alternatives to the pluperfect.

In cases like (38c) and (41), the pluperfect can sometimes be replaced by a form known as the **past-anterior** in which the auxiliary occurs in the past-historic rather than the imperfect:

(42)   a   Quand Luc eut terminé son café, il s'en alla

       b   Aussitôt qu'il eut écrit la lettre, il l'envoya

Like the past-historic, the past-anterior can only denote punctual events and is used only in formal styles of the sort in which the past-historic normally occurs. Whenever the past-anterior is possible, the pluperfect is also possible, but the converse does not always hold. The important restriction on the past-anterior is that it can only have the function represented in (40b) (advancing the narrative) and cannot be used to create a 'flashback' effect. Thus, the pluperfect cannot be replaced by the past-anterior in examples analogous to (38a, b) above:

(43)   a   Pierre était content, parce qu'il {avait / *eut} fini son travail

       b   Georges envoya la lettre qu'il {avait / *eut} écrit

Another difference is that the past-anterior usually implies that one event took place immediately after the other (and therefore typically occurs with expressions like *aussitôt que* or *dès que* rather than *quand*), whereas the pluperfect is unspecific with regard to the time lapse. This property of the past-anterior can be exploited as a stylistic device to create an impression of rapidity, as in the last sentence in (44):

(44)    Le voleur guettait la foule dans le métro. Devant lui il aperçut un portefeuille qui devançait de la pôche d'un voyageur. Il regarda furtivement autour de lui. En un instant il l'eut volé.

If the past-historic (*il le vola*) had been used, the theft would have been presented as being simply part of the sequence of events, on a par with noticing the wallet and looking around, but the past-anterior enhances the rapidity of the action (suggested by *en un instant*) by advancing the reference-time not just to the moment of the theft itself but to a point where the theft has already occurred, thus giving the impression that the event happened so quickly that one did not have time to observe it.

Just as the past-historic is replaced by the compound-past in less formal styles, the past-anterior can be replaced by a **double compound** ('passé surcomposé') construction in which the auxiliary element occurs in the compound-past:

(45)    a  Quand Luc a eu terminé son café, il s'en est allé
        b  Quand Marie a été partie, Paul s'est couché

Note that when the main verb is one which normally requires *être* as its auxiliary, as in (45b), *avoir* is selected as the first auxiliary, and the second auxiliary (*été*) does not show agreement with the subject. This double compound construction is used only in speech and informal writing and, even in these styles, the ordinary pluperfect is more usual.

Another alternative to the pluperfect is the construction formed by the imperfect of *venir* with *de* and the infinitive. In some respects, this construction resembles the past-anterior and the double compound-past, in that it normally describes punctual events which occurred immediately before some other event or a salient reference-time. However, in terms of its function within the discourse and the contexts in which it is appropriate, it is almost the complete opposite of these forms:

(46)    a  Pierre était content parce qu'il venait de finir son travail
        b  Georges envoya la lettre qu'il venait d'écrire
        c  ?Quand Luc venait de terminer son café, il s'en est allé

As the above examples illustrate, *venait de* can be used naturally with a 'flashback' function, as in (46a, b), but it cannot be used readily to advance the reference-time, as in (46c). In other words, *venait de* has the representation in (40a) but not (40b).

**4.4 The present**

*4.4.1 Describing events in the present*

Unlike its English counterpart, the French simple-present tense can be used to describe events which are simultaneous with the moment of speech. For example, (47a) can mean 'Paul is watching TV (right now)', whereas (47b) can only have a habitual interpretation (also available for (47a)):

(47)     a   Paul regarde la télévision
         b   Paul watches television

In practical terms, this difference raises problems for French learners of English rather than the other way round. Nevertheless, a brief discussion of this difference may help to clarify some of the aspectual issues raised in 4.2.4 and to establish a relation between the simple-present and the imperfect which we will develop in 4.4.3.

Let us begin by making two general assumptions. Firstly, present time reference is conceptually incompatible with punctual aspect – for an event to be perceived as punctual, it must be completed, in which case it is already in the past. Secondly, in a present-tense narrative, the moment of speech ('S') is not static, but advances along with the discourse, so that an event which is simultaneous with 'S' when it is described may well be in the past by the time we get to the next sentence.

In 4.3.1, we characterised the imperfect as essentially durative (non-punctual) whereas the English simple-past is non-progressive (see table 4.2, p. 148). Given the conceptual incompatibility between punctual aspect and immediate present reference, the same aspectual ranges can be proposed for the present tense forms, as shown in table 4.3.

On this basis, the French simple-present and imperfect express the same relations between 'E' and 'R' but differ only in terms of the relation between 'R' and 'S' ('R=S' for the simple-present, 'R→S' for the imperfect) – the same correlation can be postulated between the simple-present and simple-past tenses in English.

The relevance of the second observation can be illustrated in terms of a discourse. Consider a situation where a detective is surveying a suspect and reporting events on a radio. In English, the detective would have to use either the present-progressive, as in (48a), or with a momentary delay, the present-perfect, as in (48b) (or indeed a combination of the two), but the simple-present would not be appropriate in this context:

(48)     a   The suspect is getting$_{(a)}$ out of the car ... He is going$_{(b)}$ up to his accomplice ... He is giving$_{(c)}$ him a packet ... He is getting$_{(d)}$ back into his car ...

Table 4.3. *Aspectual properties of present tense forms*

|  | *French* | *English* |
|---|---|---|
| Punctual | Not applicable | |
| Stative | | simple-present |
| Habitual | simple-present | |
| Progressive | | present-progressive |

b The suspect has got$_{(a)}$ out of his car ... He has gone$_{(b)}$ up to his accomplice ... He has given$_{(c)}$ him a packet ... He has got$_{(d)}$ back into his car ...

These two discourses can be represented as in (49):

(49)　(a)

　　(b)

The actual duration of the events is the same in both cases, but the incompatibility between punctual aspect and present reference requires them to be perceived as durative when they are described as they are happening, thus forcing the use of the progressive form in (48a). However, when the events are described with a slight delay (as in (48b)), this incompatibility no longer arises and the punctual present-perfect form can be used.

The same temporal structures can be assumed for the French versions in (50), but since the French simple-present can express progressive aspect this form can be used in the (a) version (with the compound-past as an alternative corresponding to (48b)):

(50)　a Le suspect sort$_{(a)}$ de la voiture ... Il aborde$_{(b)}$ son accomplice ... Il lui donne$_{(c)}$ un paquet ... Il rentre$_{(d)}$ dans sa voiture ...

　　b Le suspect est sorti$_{(a)}$ de la voiture ... Il a abordé$_{(b)}$ son accomplice ... Il lui a donné$_{(c)}$ un paquet ... Il est rentré$_{(d)}$ dans sa voiture ...

To complete the picture, suppose now that the same events are described sometime later in the past tense. In this case, the whole episode precedes the moment of speech which, to all intents, can be considered as static (rather than advancing in time with the actual events as was the case in (49)):

(51)

$$\text{R}_{(a)} \quad \text{R}_{(b)} \quad \text{R}_{(c)} \quad \text{R}_{(d)} \qquad\qquad \text{S}$$
$$\text{E}_{(a)} \quad \text{E}_{(b)} \quad \text{E}_{(c)} \quad \text{E}_{(d)}$$

Again, the incompatibility between punctual aspect and present reference does not arise, so in English the 'non-progressive' simple-past can be used: *The suspect got out of his car ... He went up to his accomplice ...* In French, the corresponding version is identical to (50b) with the compound-past expressing 'E=R, R→S', though in an appropriate register the past-historic could be used.

A generalisation which emerges from this discussion is that, in terms of its semantic representation, the imperfect is the past tense equivalent of the simple-present. In subsequent sections other cases will be examined which reveal further analogies between the imperfect and the simple-present. However, as we have seen, this correlation between the two tense forms does not mean that a sequence of events described contemporaneously by the simple-present can be reported later by means of the imperfect. The reason for this is that when these events are described as they happen, they are necessarily progressive, but when they are reported in the past, they become completed events requiring the use of punctual tense forms such as the past-historic or the compound-past.

### 4.4.2 The 'narrative present'

As well as describing present situations, the simple-present can be used to report events in a real or fictional past. In English, this **narrative present** use is largely confined to jokes or personal anecdotes, but it is more widespread in French and is frequently attested in journalistic, historical and literary prose. In such cases, the simple-present is typically exploited for dramatic effect, particularly when it is used in conjunction with past-tense forms as in the following example, where the imperfect and the past-historic are used to describe fairly low-key events interrupted by a sequence of dramatic events which are highlighted by use of the simple-present:

(52)     L'inspecteur suivait furtivement le suspect. Il s'arrêta un instant et alluma sa pipe. Tout à coup le suspect se retourne, le revolver à la main. L'inspecteur sort vite le sien, il tire sur lui et le descend. Le corps étendu sur le trottoir ne bougeait plus. L'inspecteur s'y approcha lentement.

The effect of the simple-present here is similar to that of the dramatic use of the imperfect discussed in 4.3.4.

### 4.4.3 Describing the immediate past

The simple-present can also be used, with certain verbs which denote 'arrival on the scene' or the onset of an enduring state, to describe events in the immediate past, where English requires the formula *have just...*:

(53)    a    Je sors directement de chez le dentiste
        b    J'apprends à l'instant que ma secrétaire a démissionné

Within a past-tense narrative, the imperfect (but not the past-historic or compound-past) is used in the same way:

(54)    a    Quand j'ai rencontré Pierre, il sortait directement de chez le dentiste
        b    Le patron était de mauvaise humeur parce qu'il apprenait à l'instant que sa secrétaire avait démissionné

The construction with *venir de*, which may be regarded as a grammaticalised manifestation of this use, likewise shows an opposition between the simple-present and the imperfect (and indeed cannot occur with other tense forms; see 2.7.5):

(55)    a    Je {viens / venais} de voir le dentiste
        b    Marie {vient / venait} de démissionner

Note that all the events described by the simple-present or the imperfect in examples (53)–(55) are punctual events, directly contradicting our claim that these tense forms are inherently durative. A further problem with all of these cases is that the event-time does not coincide with the reference-time (i.e. the present in (53) or the past 'R' determined by the context in (54)) but precedes it. These two difficulties appear to be related and can be reconciled by a slight revision to our definition of the aspectual properties of these tense forms. In genuine durative cases (e.g. progressives), the event-time extends beyond the reference-time, as shown in (56):

(56)

Another way of characterising the situation in (56) is to say that part of 'E' is distinct from 'R'. A similar characterisation holds for the cases in (53) and (54) above, except that here the whole of 'E' is distinct from (prior to) 'R', though as we have noted the event itself is connected to 'R' by the fact that it initiates a state which endures until 'R' (and possibly beyond). Thus, we can conflate the durative and immediate past cases by revising the conditions on the simple-present and imperfect roughly as follows:

**Conditions on the simple-present and imperfect:**
 *I  at least some portion of 'E' is distinct from 'R'.*
 *II  the event is connected with 'R' in some way.*

In genuine durative cases, condition (II) is satisfied by the fact that 'E' actually overlaps with 'R' whereas in cases like (53) and (54) the connection is a pragmatic one based on temporal proximity and the onset of a resulting state. According to the formulation proposed above, a durative interpretation is not an inherent part of the meaning of these tense forms, but is induced by condition (I) in just those cases where 'E' partially coincides with 'R' – if some portion of 'E' coincides with 'R' but another portion of 'E' is distinct from 'R', it follows that 'E' must extend beyond 'R'. On the other hand, if there is no overlap between 'E' and 'R', a punctual interpretation is consistent with condition (II).

### 4.5  Looking ahead
### *4.5.1  Describing the future*

Statements about the future can be formulated in a variety of ways. In addition to the inflected-future form (57a), future time reference can be expressed by *aller* with the infinitive (57b) or by use of the simple-present form (57c):

(57)  a  Le train arrivera à minuit
　　　 b  Le train va arriver à minuit
　　　 c  Le train arrive à minuit

Other formulae which can be used to situate events in the future include the expression *être sur le point*, denoting an imminent future event (e.g. *Le train est sur le point de partir*), and constructions with modal verbs such as *devoir* and *pouvoir* which can present future events in terms of a scale of probability (e.g. *Le train {doit / peut} arriver bientôt*).

As we might expect, the formulae which involve the present-tense form ((57b) as well as (57c)) typically imply some connection with the present, whereas the inflected-future form (57a) can be used to make statements about the future which are dissociated from the present situation. In this respect, the inflected-future shows some affinity with the past-historic, whereas the form with *aller* is comparable to the compound-past. There is also a stylistic parallel in that the inflected-future tends to be avoided in colloquial speech in favour of the construction with *aller* – reflecting the demise of the past-historic in favour of the compound-past in informal discourse – though the relevant stylistic factors are much less clear-cut.

When the simple-present is accompanied by a specification of time (e.g. *à minuit* in (57c)) it typically denotes an event which is pre-arranged according to some schedule (e.g. the railway time-table). Note that (57c) would be inappropriate if the train is scheduled to arrive at eleven o'clock but the speaker has reason to believe that it will be an hour late. Conversely, the formulae in (57a, b) relate to the time at which the event is expected actually to occur – it would be misleading to utter (57a) or (57b) if the train is scheduled to arrive at midnight but one expects a significant delay. Similar differences can be observed in English between the simple-present (*The train arrives at midnight*) and constructions with *will* or *be going to*.

In the absence of a specification of time, the simple-present usually denotes an imminent event which would be rendered by the present-progressive in English (*The train is arriving, I am leaving*):

(58)    a   Le train arrive
        b   Je m'en vais

However, the progressive formula *être en train* cannot be used to indicate future time reference (*\*Je suis en train de faire des courses demain* vs *I am going shopping tomorrow*). Note also that the simple-present in (57c) and (58) is used to describe a punctual event. In terms of the proposals in 4.4.3, this is accounted for by the fact that 'E' does not actually overlap with 'R' (the present in this case), but the connection with 'R' is established pragmatically, by a relation of imminence in (58) or by the fact that the event is 'scheduled' in (57c). From this point of view, the impossibility of *être en train* can be accounted for by postulating that this expression requires an overlap between the actual event and the reference-time.

### 4.5.2   *Future tense and predictive modality*
Statements about the future differ from statements about the past in that they are necessarily speculative; they make predictions about states of affairs which are not verifiable at the moment of speech. However, predictions do not necessarily relate to future situations. Indeed, the inflected-future (like *will* in English) can be used to make predictions about states in the present, particularly with the verb *être*, as in (59):

(59)    a   Pierre est parti il y a une heure, donc il sera chez lui maintenant
        b   Ce sera le facteur (e.g. as uttered on hearing the doorbell)

Similarly, the inflected-future can be used in conjunction with the formula *être en train* to express predictions regarding ongoing events in the present:

(60)    Luc sera en train de dîner maintenant

The examples in (59) and (60) differ from their present tense counterparts *Il est chez lui maintenant, C'est le facteur* and *Luc est en train de dîner maintenant* not in terms of time reference but in terms of the degree of certainty on the part of the speaker. Possibly, future time reference is not actually part of the meaning of the future form at all but is simply a potential consequence of a more general predictive value whereby the event itself is projected into a time-span which can only be described in predictive terms.

### 4.5.3 'Aller' vs the inflected-future

The construction with *aller* in (57b) is much more clearly associated with future time reference and typically implies a causal connection with the present, i.e. the described event is presented as emanating in some way from the present situation. However, semantic differences between the *aller* construction and the inflected-future are obscured somewhat by the tendency in colloquial speech to avoid the latter in favour of the former. Consequently, the judgements which will be used to illustrate these differences should be taken as reflecting relative degrees of appropriateness across a range of registers rather than degrees of acceptability on an absolute scale: i.e. the symbol '?' indicates that the form in question is less appropriate (or more restricted in terms of register) than the form which is given without qualification.

The tendency to avoid the inflected-future form appears to be at its strongest when future reference is involved, but is rather weaker in cases where the relevant notion is prediction or conjecture rather than future time. Thus, examples like those in (59) and (60) above are the sorts of cases where the inflected-future tends to be maintained, the corresponding sentences with *aller* being less natural, though not impossible:

(61)    a  ?Pierre va être chez lui maintenant
        b  ?Ça va être le facteur
        c  ?Luc va être en train de dîner maintenant

A more usual way of avoiding the inflected-future in such cases is to use the infinitive construction with *devoir*: *Pierre doit être chez lui maintenant, Ça doit être le facteur, Luc doit être en train de dîner maintenant.*

For the same reason, the inflected-future is favoured in conditional constructions expressing a prediction contingent on the truth of the *si* clause (see 4.8.1):

(62)    a  Si Pierre gagne la loterie, il sera riche
        b  ?Si Pierre gagne la loterie, il va être riche

A case of the opposite type, where the *aller* formula is strongly preferred, is provided by 'urgent warnings' such as (63a), addressed perhaps to someone perched on a shaky ladder:

(63)      a   Attention! Tu vas tomber

           b   ?Attention! Tu tomberas

Here, the causal connection with the present, implied by *aller* in (63a), is entirely appropriate as a way of alerting the hearer to a situation which is already developing. Out of context, example (63b) seems odd, but it might be used to warn of a danger which is not yet imminent, for instance as a warning to someone who has announced an intention to climb up the ladder. Note, however, that in the latter case the utterance is more of a prediction (contingent on an implicit condition) than a warning.

A clearer illustration of the semantic differences between the two formulae is provided by the examples in (64):

(64)      a   Suzy va se marier

           b   Suzy se mariera

Sentence (64a) strongly implies that Suzy is due to get married in the foreseeable future (e.g. she is already engaged) whereas (64b) simply makes the prediction that she will get married at some time in the future (e.g. it would be appropriate even if Suzy is still an infant). On the basis of such examples, some grammarians characterise the construction with *aller* as a 'near future' ('futur proche'). Indeed, in the absence of an adverbial expression of time such as *à minuit* in (57b), the *aller* construction does tend to locate events in the immediate future. However, this can be seen as a natural consequence of the link with the present which we have observed in other examples rather than as an inherent property of this construction.

One way of capturing the above observations formally might be to postulate a representation for the *aller* construction in which 'R' is equated with 'S' (i.e. 'S=R, R→E') whereas for the inflected-future 'R' is equated with 'E' (i.e. 'S→R, R=E', at least for those cases where future time reference is involved). However, in practice, the distinction between these two forms is much less clear than these representations would suggest. It will therefore be assumed that both forms are potentially neutral between these two representations. In particular, the semantic difference between the two formulae is virtually neutralised when the time is specified by an adverbial expression as in (57a, b), the choice being essentially a stylistic one. The interplay between semantics and register can be loosely characterised as follows. In formal styles, the inflected-future is the neutral way of describing events in the future and the *aller* construction is used to emphasise a link with the present whereas in more colloquial registers the implications associated with the *aller* construction are weakened, to the extent that the *aller* construction is adopted as the normal future form, the inflected-future being reserved mainly for cases like (62a) where its function is modal rather than temporal.

### 4.5.4 Future in the past

In past-tense contexts, prospective time reference can be indicated by the so-called 'conditional', the imperfect of *aller* with the infinitive or by the imperfect of the main verb, as in (65):

(65)     Le contrôleur a dit que ...
         a   le train arriverait à minuit
         b   le train allait arriver à minuit
         c   le train arrivait à minuit

In all the examples in (65), the train's arrival is understood to be later than the reference-time (the moment of the ticket-collector's statement) which in turn precedes the moment of speech (i.e. the present): 'R→E, R→S'. Note that no relation is specified between 'E' and 'S' – these sentences could be uttered before or after midnight.

In main clauses, the conditional is used less readily with a future-in-the-past reading than the construction with *aller*. For example, one might begin a discourse by *Suzy allait se marier* (leading perhaps to a description of the preparations for the wedding), but it would be odd to use *Suzy se marierait* in such a context. However, with an appropriate context, the conditional can occur in a main clause:

(66)     a   Suzy allait au mariage de sa sœur pleine de joie. Un jour elle se
             marierait elle aussi
         b   Suzy refusait toute idée de mariage. Pourtant, six mois plus tard
             elle épouserait un jeune officier

There is a subtle difference between the interpretations of the sentences in the conditional in (66). In (66a), this clause is most naturally interpreted as a wish or intention on Suzy's part, which may or may not have been realised. In (66b), the conditional does not describe a situation envisaged from the perspective of the past, but rather reports a subsequent event which is known to the speaker, with the benefit of hindsight. Note that the conditional in (66b) could be replaced by the past-historic or the compound-past, but this would advance the reference-time, requiring the following discourse to proceed from the time of her marriage, in accordance with the TSP, whereas the conditional allows the discourse to revert to the early period as discussed in 4.3.2.

The use of *aller* in the imperfect with an infinitive (as in (65b)) has essentially the same properties as its present-tense counterpart discussed in 4.5.3. It typically connotes a causal connection with the past reference-time and is particularly favoured for the reporting of events which are imminent at that time. Often the imperfect construction with *aller* has a counterfactual interpretation – the event was planned or imminent at the past reference-time, but did not actually occur:

(67)  a  Pierre allait assister à la réunion, mais il a changé d'avis

b  Le verre allait tomber, mais je l'ai attrapé

The conditional is not used in this way, though other expressions with the imperfect are possible (e.g. ... *était sur le point de tomber* in (67b)).

The prospective use of the simple-imperfect, as in (65c), has essentially the same properties as those observed in 4.5.1 for the simple-present. When it is accompanied by an adverbial expression of time, it typically denotes a scheduled event (e.g. in (65c), the train is due to arrive at midnight), but in the absence of such a specification it denotes an imminent event. Moreover, this event is punctual, a fact which can be accommodated in the manner suggested for the future use of the simple-present in 4.5.1.

### 4.5.5  The future-perfect

The **future-perfect** is formed by means of the future tense of *avoir* or *être* with the past participle and is used to locate an event before some reference-time in the future ('E→R, S→R'):

(68)  a  Le train sera déjà parti (quand nous arriverons)

b  Demain j'aurai fini ce travail

Note that the representation of this form does not specify any relation between 'E' and 'S' – in (68a), particularly without the *quand* clause, it is possible that the train has already left at the time when the sentence is uttered ('S'). Thus, just as the simple inflected-future can be used to make conjectures about the present (cf. *Ce sera le facteur*), the future-perfect can be used to make conjectures about past events. In both cases, these forms are appropriate when the truth of the proposition cannot be verified directly at the moment of speech.

In past-tense contexts, the **conditional-perfect** can be used in the same way:

(69)  a  Je pensais que le train serait déjà parti

b  Le plombier pensait qu'il aurait fini ce travail avant minuit

In such cases, a counterfactual interpretation is often favoured (e.g. in (69a), contrary to my expectations the train was still in the station when I arrived).

### 4.6  The tense of infinitives

Infinitives do not provide any direct indication of the relation between the time of the event they describe and the moment of speech. Nevertheless, it is not the case that the time of the event described by an infinitive is totally arbitrary. For example, in (70a) we understand that the event of Pierre's leaving occurs (if at all) sometime after his wish, whereas in (70b) the event of swimming coincides with Pierre's enjoyment, regardless of whether the wish or enjoyment is situated in the present or past:

(70)     a   Pierre {veut / voulait} partir
         b   Pierre {aime / aimait} nager

These judgements can plausibly be deduced from the meanings of the main verbs; e.g. *vouloir* expresses an attitude towards a future event, *aimer* an attitude towards a current situation. However, we do not find cases where a 'simple' infinitive situates an event before the event described in the main clause – in such cases we must use what will be called the **perfective infinitive** (the infinitive of an auxiliary followed by the past participle):

(71)     a   *Paul regrette de voler l'argent hier
         b   Paul regrette d'avoir volé l'argent hier
         c   Paul regrets {stealing / having stolen} the money yesterday

As (71c) shows, this restriction does not hold in English, at least not with gerunds. The same pattern can be seen in time clauses with *après* and *after*:

(72)     a   Marie est partie après {*manger / avoir mangé}
         b   Marie left after {eating / having eaten}

Note that in English constructions which require the infinitive, we must use the perfective form to refer to an earlier event, just as in French:

(73)     a   Jules seems to {*solve / have solved} the problem
         b   Jules semble {*résoudre / avoir résolu} le problème

(74)     a   Sophie claims to {*finish / have finished} the work
         b   Sophie prétend {*finir / avoir fini} le travail

To account for the above examples, let us suppose that infinitives have a reference-time 'R' which is constrained by the 'R' of the higher verb in the following way:

*The 'R' of an infinitive ('$R_{INF}$') cannot be earlier than the 'R' of the main verb ('$R_{MV}$')*

Let us also suppose that with 'simple' infinitives '$E_{INF}$' cannot be earlier than '$R_{INF}$'. Consequently, in order to situate '$E_{INF}$' before the event in the main clause, we must use the 'perfective' form represented as '$E \rightarrow R$'. The temporal structure of (71b) can be represented as '$R_{MV} = S$, $E_{MV} = R_{MV}$, $R_{INF} = R_{MV}$, $E_{INF} \rightarrow R_{INF}$':

(75)

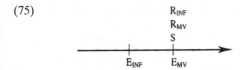

The condition on '$R_{INF}$' proposed above is reminiscent of the Temporal Sequence Principle (TSP) which we proposed in 4.3.2 to deal with cases like (76):

(76)  a  Marie mit la robe qu'elle {*acheta / avait achetée} la veille
      b  Marie wore the dress which she {bought / had bought} the day
         before

Possibly these two conditions can be subsumed under a more general principle which prevents reference-times from being shifted back in time. The evidence above suggests that this principle is observed with all verb forms in French whereas in English it can be relaxed with finite verbs and gerunds.

In cases like (70a) above, it is clear that '$E_{INF}$' is later than '$E_{MV}$', but it is not immediately clear whether '$R_{INF}$' is also shifted forward in time – our account so far allows both of the representations in (77):

(77)  a  '$R_{MV} = R_{INF}, R_{INF} \rightarrow E_{INF}$'
      b  '$R_{MV} \rightarrow R_{INF}, R_{INF} = E_{INF}$'

Examples like (78) provide some evidence for the analysis in (77b):

(78)      Paul veut avoir fini ce travail vendredi

In (78) we can infer that Paul would not be disappointed if he finished the work on, say, Thursday, but this is not the case in (79):

(79)      Paul veut finir le travail vendredi

The meanings of (78) and (79) can be represented as in (80) where '$R_{INF}$' is located at some time on Friday:

(80)  a  '$R_{MV} = S, R_{MV} = E_{MV}, R_{MV} \rightarrow R_{INF}, E_{INF} \rightarrow R_{INF}$'  (= 78)
      b  '$R_{MV} = S, R_{MV} = E_{MV}, R_{MV} \rightarrow R_{INF}, E_{INF} = R_{INF}$'  (= 79)

An alternative, perhaps more natural, way of expressing the proposition in (78) is the sentence (81), where the simple infinitive equates '$E_{INF}$' with '$R_{INF}$' but *avant vendredi* situates '$R_{INF}$' some time before Friday:

(81)      Paul veut finir le travail avant vendredi

It is left to the reader to construct diagrams for the temporal structures of (78), (79) and (81).

This approach enables us to represent the temporal properties of infinitives as follows:

*Simple infinitive:*     $`R_{INF} = E_{INF}`$

*Perfective infinitive:*     $`E_{INF} \rightarrow R_{INF}`$

Verbs which take infinitives can be subclassified according to the way in which they locate the reference-time of the infinitive; e.g. '$R_{MV} \rightarrow R_{INF}$' for *vouloir* (also *ordonner, promettre, persuader,* etc.) but '$R_{MV} = R_{INF}$' for *aimer, regretter, sembler, prétendre,* etc. Within the latter class, there are further distinctions to be made concerning the temporal location of '$E_{INF}$'. For example, *aimer* (unlike *regretter*) does not readily allow '$E_{INF}$' to be shifted back in time by means of the perfective infinitive (*\*?Pierre aime avoir regardé ce film*) whereas this seems to be required by *se souvenir* (*Pierre se souvient d'avoir fermé la porte* vs *\*Pierre se souvient de fermer la porte*), presumably for semantic reasons. Similarly, verbs like *commencer, finir* and *continuer* specify different relations between '$R_{INF}$' and '$E_{INF}$'; *commencer* locates '$R_{INF}$' at the beginning of '$E_{INF}$', *finir* at the end and *continuer* somewhere in between:

(82)        *commencer*        *finir*        *continuer*

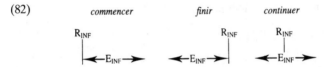

### 4.7   Tense and adverbial expressions of time

#### 4.7.1   *Adverbial expressions of time*

Expressions denoting a specific time or period can be divided into three subclasses:

- **deictic** expressions of time. These are items like *demain, hier, ce matin, l'année dernière, la semaine prochaine,* etc. which define time in relation to 'S'.
- **relative** expressions of time. These are expressions like *le lendemain, la veille, ce matin-là, l'année précédente, la semaine suivante,* etc. which define time in relation to the reference-time 'R' established in the preceding discourse.
- **absolute** expressions of time. These refer to time independently of 'S' or 'R'; e.g. by date (*en 1968, le 22 novembre 1963*) or in relation to an event which the addressee is expected to identify (*pendant la Révolution française, après la réunion, le jour de son mariage,* etc.).

Let us use the symbol '$T_{ADV}$' to represent the time denoted by such expressions. Thus, for *hier* '$T_{ADV}$' is the day before 'S'; for *le lendemain* it is the day after the 'R' of the preceding sentence; for *en 1968* it is the year referred to by that date; for *après la réunion* it is some period which follows the meeting in question, and so on. The relationship between '$T_{ADV}$' and the time of the event described in the sentence is a rather loose one. For example, (83) does not necessarily mean that Pierre was in Paris during the whole of 1968, and yet it allows the possibility that he was there for some time before or after this period (and is perhaps still there):

(83)      Pierre était à Paris en 1968

Similarly, (84) does not imply that the event occurred throughout the day in question, merely that it happened at some point during this day:

(84)      Kennedy fut assassiné le 22 novembre 1963

The time expressions in (83) and (84) designate a period within which the reference-time of the clause is located ('$RCT_{ADV}$'). With a punctual tense form such as the past-historic in (84), where '$E=R$', it follows that the event is also wholly contained within the period '$T_{ADV}$'. However, the durative, imperfect form in (83) indicates that the event-time extends (indefinitely) beyond '$R$', so that '$E$' is defined as '$RCE$' and '$R$' is defined as '$RCT_{ADV}$' but the exact relation between '$E$' and '$T_{ADV}$' is not specified, except in so far as they must overlap, as shown in (85):

(85)
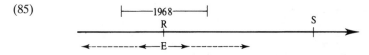

With tenses like the pluperfect which locate '$E$' before '$R$', the situation is more complicated. In some cases, like (86), '$T_{ADV}$' is associated with the reference-time of the pluperfect (i.e. Luc left some time before midday), as shown in the diagram:

(86)      A midi, Luc était (déjà) parti$_{(a)}$. Donc nous avons mangé$_{(b)}$ sans lui.

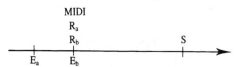

However, more typically '$T_{ADV}$' is associated with '$E$' rather than with '$R$' as in (87) where *à midi* denotes the time of Luc's departure:

(87)      Je suis allé$_{(a)}$ voir Luc à une heure, mais il était parti$_{(b)}$ a midi.

The possibility of the interpretation indicated in (86) depends on a number of factors – in particular, it seems to be facilitated by placing the time adverb before the clause which it modifies and by the presence of an item like *déjà* (see 4.7.3).

With the 'future-in-the-past' use of the conditional (see 4.5.4), '$T_{ADV}$' is also equated with 'E' rather than 'R'; e.g. in (88) Marie's departure takes place during the period denoted by *le lendemain*, not after it:

(88)    Vendredi, Marie a acheté$_{(a)}$ son billet. Le lendemain, elle prendrait$_{(b)}$ l'avion

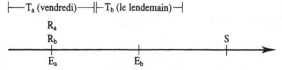

In (88) the reference-time is kept constant, so that the subsequent narrative can continue from the time when Marie bought her ticket (e.g. *Elle est rentrée chez elle et elle a fait ses bagages*). If we used the compound-past in the second sentence, as in (89), the narrative would have to continue from the point where she took the plane:

(89)    Vendredi, Marie a acheté$_{(a)}$ son billet. Le lendemain, elle a pris$_{(b)}$ l'avion

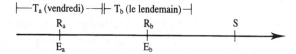

A common feature of the pluperfect and the conditional is that 'E' is totally distinct from 'R'. The evidence suggests that in such cases '$T_{ADV}$' is normally associated with 'E' rather than with 'R', whereas with tenses which locate 'R' within 'E' or which equate 'E' and 'R', '$T_{ADV}$' is associated with 'R'.

### 4.7.2   *'Dans trois jours' vs 'trois jours après'*

Both these types of expression locate the event-time after the previous reference-time ('$R_{n-1} \rightarrow E_n$'). However, they differ with respect to the relation between '$R_n$' and '$R_{n-1}$'. With *dans trois jours* the reference-time must be kept constant ('$R_{n-1} = R_n$'). Consequently, the only way of moving the event-time forward is to use a tense form which contains the specification '$R \rightarrow E$' – e.g. the conditional but not the compound-past in (90), where the diagram represents the grammatical version:

(90)     Samedi, Marie est partie$_{(a)}$. Elle {reviendrait$_{(b)}$ / *est revenue$_{(b)}$}
         dans trois jours.

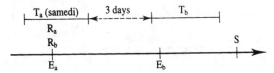

This additional restriction does not apply to *trois jours après*, which allows the reference-time to be kept constant ('$R_{n-1} = R_n$') or to be moved forward:

(91)     Samedi, Marie est partie. Elle {reviendrait / est revenue} trois jours
         après

In this respect, *trois jours après* resembles *le lendemain* in (88) and (89). Also, like
*le lendemain*, *trois jours après* does not allow '$R_{n-1}$' to be equated with 'S' (i.e. these
expressions cannot be used as deictic adverbs), a restriction which does not apply
to *dans trois jours*:

(92)     Marie est partie aujourd'hui. Elle reviendra {dans trois jours / *trois
         jours après / *le lendemain}.

### 4.7.3  'Déjà'

The function of this item is to situate 'E' or some part of 'E' before the prevailing
reference-time. Consequently, *déjà* can only occur with durative tense forms, indicating that the event or state began some time before 'R', or with compound forms
containing the representation 'E→R':

(93)     a   Pierre {travaille / travaillait} déjà
         b   Quand nous sommes arrivés, le train était déjà parti
         c   Quand nous arriverons, le train sera déjà parti
         d   Le train est déjà parti

In particular, *déjà* cannot be used with the past-historic and, with the compound-
past, it forces a 'present-perfect' reading (as in (93d)) which is incompatible with
expressions of past time:

(94)     a   *Pierre travailla déjà
         b   *Hier, le train est déjà parti

### 4.7.4  'Encore' and 'toujours'

*Encore* can be used with all tense forms to indicate repetition of an event-type
(= 'again'): *Pierre est revenu encore, Pierre reviendra encore*, etc. With durative

tenses, it can also have the meaning 'still', indicating that 'E' continues up to (and possibly beyond) 'R':

(95)      Pierre {travaille / travaillait} encore.

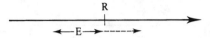

This meaning is also available with negated punctual tenses where 'E→R':

(96)      Pierre {n'est / n'était} pas encore arrivé

Intuitively, negated punctual events can be construed as durative states: e.g. in (96) the state of 'non-arrival' continues up to (or beyond) 'R'. However, this use is not possible with the negated past-historic (where 'E=R'); example (97) can only mean 'Pierre did not arrive again':

(97)      Pierre n'arriva pas encore

*Toujours* can also be used with the meaning 'still' under the same conditions:

(98)      a   Pierre {travaille / travaillait} toujours
          b   Pierre {n'est / n'était} toujours pas arrivé

Note, however, that *toujours* with this meaning must precede *pas*, as in (98b), whereas *encore* must follow *pas*, as in (96). If *toujours* is placed after *pas*, as in (99), it can only mean 'always' ('Pierre has not always liked Mary'):

(99)      Pierre n'a pas toujours aimé Marie

With the 'always' interpretation, there is a subtle difference between durative and compound tense forms:

(100)     a   Gaston posait toujours des questions gênantes
          b   Gaston avait toujours posé des questions gênantes

Roughly, (100a) describes an event which happened regularly during a past period, which could be quite long (e.g. 'Throughout his life, Gaston asked embarrassing questions') or relatively short (e.g. 'During our holiday, Gaston kept asking embarrassing questions'), whereas (100b) describes a habit which lasted up to a relevant reference-point in the past (and possibly beyond) but which began as far back as one can remember.

### 4.7.5   Time clauses

As a working hypothesis, let us assume that time clauses introduced by *quand*, etc., have the same reference-time as the clause which they modify. Thus, in (101) Marie's entrance occurs sometime after Pierre's departure:

(101)    Quand Pierre était parti₍ₐ₎, Marie est entrée₍b₎

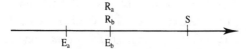

Similarly, in (102) the visit to the Louvre is located sometime during Luc's stay in Paris:

(102)    Quand Luc était₍ₐ₎ à Paris, il a visité₍b₎ le Louvre

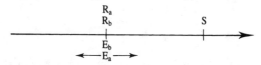

This analysis correctly predicts that when the event in the main clause is projected into the future, the future form must also be used in the time clause:

(103)    Quand Jules reviendra₍ₐ₎, il sera₍b₎ riche

The use of the present tense in the *quand* clause (**Quand Jules revient, il sera riche*) would equate 'R' with 'S', thus preventing the clause from identifying a future reference-time for the main clause. Similarly, we must use the future-perfect in the time clause to situate a main clause event even further in the future:

(104)    Quand j'aurai fini₍ₐ₎ ce livre, je serai₍b₎ content.

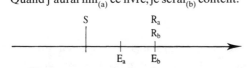

It is not clear why English requires the present or present-perfect in such cases (*When Jules {returns / *will return}, he will be rich*; *When I {have / *will have} finished, I will be happy*).

### 4.7.6 'Depuis'

Phrases of the type *depuis* + NP can be analysed as denoting a '$T_{ADV}$' which endures up to a reference-time determined by the context. When the NP is of the type *trois jours, longtemps, un siècle*, this NP denotes the duration of '$T_{ADV}$', whereas NPs referring to specific times, like *lundi, 1968, la réunion*, etc., denote the onset of '$T_{ADV}$'. Thus, *depuis trois jours* (translated as 'for three days') defines

'T$_{ADV}$' as the period of three days up to 'R' while *depuis lundi* (translated as 'since Monday') defines 'T$_{ADV}$' as the period from Monday until 'R'. The use of a durative tense form (present or imperfect according to whether 'R=S' or 'R→S') indicates that 'E' is coextensive with 'T$_{ADV}$', though possibly continuing beyond 'R':

(105)     (a) Pierre {travaille / travaillait} depuis {trois jours / lundi}
          (b) Pierre {connaît / connaissait} Marie depuis {trois jours / lundi}

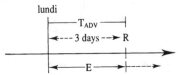

In the corresponding English examples, the present-perfect or pluperfect must be used (in the progressive when the verb is non-stative):

(106)     a   Pierre {has / had} been working {for three days / since Monday}
          b   Pierre {has /had} known Marie {for three days / since Monday}

In French, the compound-past and pluperfect can only be used to situate a punctual event some time within 'T$_{ADV}$'. For some reason, this construction is more acceptable with a phrase specifying the number of times the event occurred or when the sentence is negated (perhaps because of the construal of negated events as states mentioned in connection with (96) in 4.7.4):

(107)     a   Solange {a / avait} téléphoné une fois depuis {trois jours / lundi}
          b   Solange {n'a / n'avait} pas téléphoné depuis {trois jours / lundi}

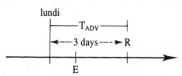

Although the use of tenses in (105) and (107) is different from what we find in English, it is consistent with the representations proposed in earlier sections. In (105), 'E' contains 'R', as is normal for the simple-present and imperfect, while in (107), 'E' precedes 'R'.

Essentially the same analysis applies to constructions with *depuis* followed by a *que* clause. When the tense of the *que* clause is durative, the event-time of the *que* clause defines the duration of 'T$_{ADV}$' in the same way as *trois jours*:

(108)     a   Pierre connaît Marie depuis qu'il est à Paris
          b   Solange avait téléphoné une fois depuis qu'elle était à Paris

When the tense of the *que* clause is punctual, its event-time marks the onset of 'T$_{ADV}$' in the same way as *lundi*:

(109)   a   Pierre est content depuis qu'il a rencontré Marie

   b   Solange avait téléphoné une fois depuis qu'elle était partie

## 4.8   Modal uses of tense forms

### *4.8.1   Conditional constructions*

In conditional constructions, the choice of tense form usually expresses modality rather than location in time. As the adverb *demain* indicates, both the examples in (110) express conjectures about the future:

(110)   a   Si je gagne la loterie demain, j'achèterai une nouvelle voiture

   b   Si je gagnais la loterie demain, j'achèterais une nouvelle voiture

In (110a), the use of the present tense in the **condition** clause (the clause introduced by *si*) suggests that there is some chance of the event happening (albeit a remote one), whereas the use of the imperfect in (110b) presents this event as purely hypothetical or imaginary – e.g. I may not even have bought a ticket.

When the situation described in the condition clause relates to the present, the use of the present tense indicates a potentially real situation, whereas the imperfect has a counterfactual value – sentence (111b) implies that Pierre is not at home:

(111)   a   Si Pierre est chez lui, il répondra au téléphone

   b   Si Pierre était chez lui, il répondrait au téléphone

The same contrast is found between the compound-past and the pluperfect, which are used when the condition clause expresses a conjecture about the past:

(112)   a   Si Luc a pris le train de neuf heures, il sera déjà arrivé

   b   Si Luc avait pris le train de neuf heures, il serait déjà arrivé

In counterfactual conditionals, the 'logical' connection between the condition and the consequence can operate in either direction. For example, in (112b) we might know for a fact that Luc missed the train and we are commenting on a consequence which will not be realised. On the other hand, (112b) might be used to deduce that Luc missed the train from the fact that he has not yet arrived.

In the above examples, the tense form of the finite verb (main verb or auxiliary) in the condition clause expresses a modal distinction, whereas temporal relations are indicated by the use of simple or compound forms, as summarised below:

**Tense forms in condition clauses:**
*present tense* = potential *modality*
*imperfect tense* = hypothetical *modality*
*compound forms* = *past time*
*simple forms* = *'non-past' time (present or future)*

173

A similar pattern is observed in the **consequent** clause (the clause which is modified by the condition clause), where the future-tense form typically correlates with the present tense in the condition clause and the conditional tense form correlates with the imperfect. In cases like (110)–(112), both the future and conditional forms express 'predictions' contingent on some premise, but with the future form this prediction is potentially true, whereas with the conditional it is purely hypothetical or counterfactual. As in the condition clause, the simple forms of these tenses are 'non-past', whereas past time is signalled by using an auxiliary with the past participle, as in (112). Thus, the sequence of tense forms in conditional constructions can be summarised as follows:

**Modality concord:**
*the condition and consequent clauses must agree in modality ('potential' vs 'hypothetical')*

In cases involving potential modality, the predictive nature of the consequent clause can often be indicated by means of a modal verb or similar expression rather than by the future tense form:

(113)   a   Si Luc a pris le train de neuf heures, il doit être déjà arrivé
        b   Si Luc a manqué le train, il risque d'être en retard

In the absence of such indications, the usual 'cause–effect' interpretation of conditional constructions is often suspended, as in (114a) where the content of the condition clause is conceded as a fact, and in (114b) where the consequent clause supplies a reason for this situation:

(114)   a   Si je suis en retard, je m'en excuse
        b   Si je suis en retard, c'est que ma voiture est tombée en panne

Sometimes, the imperfect can occur in the condition clause with the future or present forms in the consequent clause:

(115)   a   Si l'accusé était chez lui à l'heure du vol, il doit être innocent
        b   Si Jules travaillait à cette heure, son patron le confirmera

These examples are consistent with our generalisation concerning modality concord. Note that the imperfect in (115) refers to a past (durative) situation which is presented as potentially real (compare (115a) with (111b) above) – these examples can be paraphrased as *S'il est vrai que l'accusé était chez lui ...*, *Si c'est le cas que Jules travaillait ...* In other words, in condition clauses the imperfect can express either hypothetical modality (in which case past time must be signalled by means of an auxiliary with the past participle) or past time, in which case the modality is 'potential', thus requiring the consequent clause to express potential modality by a future- or present-tense form. To a large extent, this ambiguity of the imperfect is resolved by the form of the consequent clause; e.g. in (115) the use of the present or future imposes a 'potential' reading which in turn entails a temporal (rather than modal) interpretation of the imperfect in the condition clause.

The pattern outlined above is basically the same as that found in English, where the simple-past tense can express hypothetical modality (*If I won the lottery tomorrow, I would buy a new car*) or past time with potential modality (*If the accused was at home, he must be innocent*). Note in particular that the conditional form is not used in the condition clause, just as in (Standard British) English we cannot use *would*:

(116)    a   \*Si je gagnerais la loterie demain, j'achèterais une nouvelle voiture
        b   \*If I would win the lottery tomorrow, I would buy a new car

Note also that only the imperfect form can express hypothetical modality, not the past-historic:

(117)    \*Si Pierre gagna la loterie demain, il achèterait une nouvelle voiture

Conversely, when the imperfect has a temporal interpretation, it must express durative aspect – i.e. we cannot use the imperfect to describe a potentially real punctual event in the past:

(118)    \*Si Pierre gagnait la loterie la semaine dernière, il sera content

In such cases, we must use the compound-past or past-historic:

(119)    Si Pierre {a gagné / gagna} la loterie la semaine dernière, il sera content

There is one type of conditional construction, illustrated in (120), which has no direct counterpart in English:

(120)    Si je faisais un pas de plus, je tombais dans la rivière

This sentence can be paraphrased roughly as in (121), rendered in English as 'If I had gone one step further, I would have fallen in the river.'

(121)    Si j'avais fait un pas de plus, je serais tombé dans la rivière

The imperfect forms in (120) express tense and modality simultaneously, describing counterfactual events in the past. A variant of this construction is illustrated in (122) where again the imperfect describes a past event which did not actually occur (compare similar constructions in English where the conditional perfect is required: *One step further and I would have fallen in the river*):

(122)    a   Un pas de plus et je tombais dans la rivière
         b   Encore un coup de vent et la baraque s'écroulait

The constructions in (120) and (122) can only be used to describe a chain of events which narrowly failed to occur and typically require a phrase such as *un . . . de plus* or *encore un . . .* which indicates just how close the event was to happening.

### 4.8.2   Other modal uses of the conditional

The use of the conditional form to indicate the consequence of a hypothetical or counterfactual situation extends to cases like (123) where the condition is referred to by an adverbial expression rather than by a clause introduced by *si*:

(123)    a   A ta place, j'achèterais une nouvelle voiture
         b   Dans ce cas, il aurait répondu au téléphone

In some cases, the condition may be left totally implicit, as in (124) for which we can reconstruct the general condition *si c'était nécessaire . . .*:

(124)    Luc ferait n'importe quoi pour avoir une moto

Sometimes the complement of an expression may denote the relevant condition, as in (125), which can be paraphrased as *Si on arrivait en retard, ce serait dommage*:

(125)    Ce serait dommage d'arriver en retard

The hypothetical value of the conditional can be exploited for other purposes, such as politeness in (126):

(126)    a   Je voudrais vous parler un instant
         b   Je prendrais bien un café

The use of the conditional here attenuates the request or wish by making it dependent on an implicit condition, e.g. *si cela ne vous dérangeait pas . . .* Similarly, the assertion in (127) is attenuated by an implicit condition of the type *si on demandait mon avis . . .*:

(127)    Je dirais que cette idée est un peu farfelue

Similar uses of the conditional are found in English.

Another use of the conditional which has no direct counterpart in English is illustrated in (128), where a statement is presented as being based on hearsay, often with the intended implication that it is false:

176

(128)  a  Les rues de Paris seraient pavées en or

      b  Les Américains seraient les gardiens de la liberté

Again, we may appeal to a tacit condition in these cases; e.g. *si on croyait ce que disent les gens* . . . or, more idiomatically, *à ce qu'on prétend* . . . The pragmatic effect of the conditional can range from rumour or myth (e.g. 'the streets of Paris are said to be paved with gold') through to sarcasm ('anyone would think that . . .').

### 4.8.3   Modality or 'tense harmony'?

In the complement clauses in (129), the imperfect appears to show modal properties similar to those observed in conditional constructions – indicating that a proposition about the present or future is false:

(129)  a  On m'a dit que Luc partait samedi prochain

      b  Jules croyait que Bruxelles était en Suisse

Use of the present tense in these examples would imply that the proposition is true, hence the oddness of (130b) given the geographical facts:

(130)  a  On m'a dit que Luc part samedi prochain

      b  ?Jules croyait que Bruxelles est en Suisse

However, it would be inaccurate to conclude that the difference between the imperfect and present in such cases is a purely modal one (doubt vs certainty on the part of the speaker), because of examples like (131) where the imperfect in the complement clause expresses a proposition which is assumed to be still valid and the use of the present tense is odd:

(131)  Je savais que Luc {partait / *part} samedi prochain

An alternative approach is to treat examples like (129) as instances of **tense harmony** or what the French call 'concordance des temps':

**Tense harmony** *is respected when the reference-time of the complement matches the reference-time of the main clause.*

In (129) the reference-time of both the main and complement clauses is situated sometime in the past. When tense harmony is observed, the complement clause merely expresses the content of the reported proposition with no indication as to its present validity, the beliefs of the speaker, etc. Thus, (129a) is equivalent to (132):

(132)  On m'a dit «Luc part samedi prochain»

According to this view, (129a) is an instance of the prospective use of the imperfect discussed in 4.5.4, analogous to the prospective use of the present in the direct quotation in (132).

For cases like (130) the following principle is postulated:

**Violating tense harmony:**
*when the reported proposition is presumed to be (still) valid, this can be indicated by using a tense-form which situates the reference-time in the present ('R=S').*

The modal properties of (129) can now be attributed to the speaker's failure to indicate that the proposition is valid, thus inviting the hearer to infer that it is false or at least doubtful.

The observations concerning (131) can be attributed to semantic properties of the verb *savoir*. Unlike *croire* in (129b) and (130b), *savoir* **presupposes** the truth of its complement – even when *savoir* is negated or questioned, and regardless of its tense form, its complement must be interpreted as a true proposition (in the opinion of the speaker); thus all of the following sentences entail that Max did indeed steal the money: *Jules sait que Max a volé l'argent, Savais-tu que Max a volé l'argent?*, *Le patron ne saura jamais que Max a volé l'argent*, etc. Consequently, in (131) there is no need to indicate the truth of the complement by violating tense harmony.

An important aspect of the analysis presented above is that the counterfactual effect of the imperfect in cases like (129) is not an inherent property of the imperfect, but rather a consequence of the speaker's failure to indicate that the proposition is true. Often the need to indicate this will depend on the speaker's reason for reporting the proposition. For example, in (133) a likely reason is that the speaker is passing on information which he has received, so use of the imperfect would be confusing to say the least:

(133)     Le patron a confirmé que tu {pars / *partais} demain

However, the imperfect is perfectly appropriate in (134) where the information *'tu pars demain'* is not part of what is being communicated to the hearer:

(134)     Quand le patron a confirmé que tu partais demain, j'ai fait les
          réservations

There are other more subtle considerations which affect the choice of tense in these constructions, but on the whole they are the same in English.

A final point to note is that in counterfactual cases like (129a), we can use the pluperfect in the main clause (cf. English *I had been told that Max was leaving next Saturday*):

(135)     On m'avait dit que Max partait samedi prochain

Possibly, this use can be interpreted in temporal rather than modal terms. The plu-perfect situates the event described in the main clause before some reference-time which we may construe as 'the moment at which the speaker realised that he was misinformed'.

### 4.9 Mood

#### 4.9.1 The concept of mood

The term **mood** is used to denote verb forms which, very roughly, express the atti-tude of the speaker towards the situation being described. In French we can recog-nise at least three moods: the **indicative** (i.e. the finite verb forms discussed so far in this chapter), the **subjunctive** and the **imperative**. Some grammarians also clas-sify the conditional as a mood rather than a tense, particularly in the uses dis-cussed in 4.8.1–4.8.2.

The main question which will be addressed in the following sections is how to choose between the indicative and the subjunctive.

A very sceptical approach to this question would be to assume that mood is determined as an arbitrary property of the item which introduces the clause. According to this view, we must simply learn that *vouloir* selects the subjunctive whereas *savoir* selects the indicative, and so on for every verb, adjective, etc. that can take a finite complement clause. At the opposite extreme, we might surmise that the choice of mood is predictable on semantic grounds: e.g. the subjunctive and the indicative have different 'meanings' which must be compatible with the semantic properties of the item which selects the clause. It seems reasonable to suppose that the reality lies somewhere between these two extremes – the choice of mood is sensitive to semantic properties of the item which introduces the clause, but not in a way which is entirely predictable.

Most good reference grammars provide a fairly detailed description of the con-texts in which these two moods are used. Rather than reproducing this detailed information, the focus of the attention here will be the more general issues arising from the second hypothesis envisaged above.

#### 4.9.2 Mood and tense

As we have seen, the indicative mood can be realised by a variety of tense forms which specify different relations between 'E', 'R' and 'S'. In Classical French, we also find a tense opposition with the subjunctive, between the present form (*Je veux qu'il vienne*) and the so-called **imperfect subjunctive** (*†Je voulais qu'il vînt*). However, with the exception of a few very common verbs (notably *avoir* and *être*), the imperfect subjunctive forms have become almost obsolete even in formal styles, to the extent that their use is often perceived as pretentious or even ridiculous. Thus, in 'everyday' Modern French, the subjunctive can be regarded as a tenseless form. Our analysis is based on this 'everyday' register which lacks the imperfect subjunctive.

Like the infinitive (see 4.6) and the modal imperfect (see 4.8.1), the simple forms of the subjunctive have a 'non-past' orientation, defining an event concurrent with the reference-time of the higher clause, as in (136a), or situating it sometime later, as in (136b):

(136)    a   Sophie {aime / aimait} qu'on lui fasse des compliments
         b   Je {veux / voulais} qu'il revienne plus tard

In order to refer to a prior event, we must use a compound form (a subjunctive auxiliary with the past participle):

(137)    Je {regrette / regrettais} que Max ait volé l'argent

This pattern is the same as that observed for infinitives in 4.6, and it will be assumed that it can be represented formally in the same way.

The imperative, by its very nature, has a future orientation, though it is occasionally used in a compound form to prescribe an action which must be completed before some time in the future:

(138)    Sois parti avant demain!

### 4.9.3   Mood in main clauses

In main clauses, the indicative forms are used to express **propositions**. A proposition is a mental construct, the representation of an idea within some conceptual system. A sentence is an expression of a proposition in a particular language – thus *Marie est malade* and *Marie is ill* express the same proposition. At the same time, propositions relate in some way to **situations** (events or states) which exist outside the mind of the individual. Very roughly, a proposition is true (as is the sentence which expresses it) if it corresponds to a situation which is real.

In declarative sentences (e.g. *Pierre est arrivé*) the speaker conveys a proposition which is usually meant to be taken as true (even if the speaker is lying). Questions convey a proposition for which the hearer is expected to provide a truth-value (*Est-il arrivé? – Oui / Non*) or which the hearer is expected to complete by supplying information which yields a true statement (*Quand est-il arrivé? – Hier*).

Declarative sentences and questions can be used in an attempt to bring about a situation, as in (139):

(139)    a   Je veux que vous m'aidiez
         b   Pouvez-vous m'aider?

Nevertheless, these sentences express propositions – a statement about the speaker's desire in (139a), a question about the hearer's disposition in (139b). The expectation that the hearer will respond to such sentences by acting in an appropriate way can be attributed to principles of social behaviour (e.g. desire to co-operate) rather than to the semantics of these sentences. For example, although a purely verbal response to (139a) (e.g. *Oui, je sais*) would be uncooperative, it is perfectly legitimate from a strictly linguistic viewpoint. In (139b), the verbal reply *Non* is also a co-operative response if the hearer is genuinely unable to help.

Sentences with the imperative (e.g. *Aidez-moi!*) serve a similar purpose to examples like (139), but they have a different linguistic status; the exchange *Aidez-moi!* – *\*Oui, je sais* is linguistically deviant, and a response *Non* expresses defiance, not the truth value of a proposition. This suggests that imperatives do not express propositions. Similar observations apply to first-person imperatives (e.g. *Allons à la plage!*).

Imperatives can only be used in main clauses. Conversely the subjunctive occurs almost exclusively in subordinate clauses – indeed, etymologically, 'subjunctive' means 'subordinate'. When the subjunctive is used in a main clause, it yields interpretations ranging from 'rhetorical exhortation' as in (140a, b) to commands directed at a third party, as in (140c):

(140)    a   Qu'il pleuve!
           b   Que Dieu vous bénisse!
           c   Qu'ils viennent me voir demain!

The presence of the complementiser *que* in these cases suggests that these may be complements of an implicit higher clause (e.g. *Il faut que . . ., Je souhaite que . . .*). However, like imperatives, subjunctive main clauses do not appear to express propositions: *Qu'il pleuve!* – *\*Oui, je sais* (cf. *Il faut qu'il pleuve.* – *Oui je sais*). Other main-clause constructions with the subjunctive have the same properties: *Vivent le Bretons!*, *Puissent-ils arriver à temps!* 'May they arrive in time!', *À Dieu ne plaise!* 'God forbid!', etc.

> The infinitive can be used in place of the imperative in certain contexts, particularly when addressing a wide, anonymous audience (e.g. in public notices, instruction manuals, recipes, etc.): *Mettre la ceinture de sécurité, Verser le contenu dans un bol*, and so on. There are important syntactic differences between imperatives and infinitives, particularly with regard to negation and the position of clitic pronouns: *Ne fumez pas!* vs *Ne pas fumer*, *Versez-le dans un bol!* vs *Le verser dans un bol* (see 7.6.2 and 6.3.2). Also in pronominal or reflexive constructions, the infinitive requires the third-person form *se*: *Ne pas se pencher au dehors*, *\*Ne pas vous pencher au dehors*.

### 4.9.4   What do complement clauses represent?

The distinction between propositions and situations can be seen in the complements in (141):

(141)     a   Pierre a dit que Marie est malade
          b   Marie veut que le médecin vienne tout de suite

It should be clear that in (141a) what Pierre is communicating is the proposition 'Mary is ill' not the situation to which it relates, whereas in (141b) what Marie desires is a particular situation (a proposition would be no use to her!). Similarly, the complement in (142a) represents a proposition whereas the complement in (142b) represents a situation which Marie is attempting to bring about:

(142)     a   Pierre croit que Marie est malade
          b   Marie exige que le médecin vienne tout de suite

More generally, the complements of verbs (and other items) which describe cognitive states or the communication of information represent propositions, whereas complements of items which describe an emotive attitude or an act of 'manipulation' (causation or prevention) represent situations.

Note now that in (141a) and (142a) the verb of the complement is in the indicative, whereas the (b) examples have the subjunctive form. Moreover, to a large extent, we find the same pattern with the broader classes distinguished above. Thus, as a first approximation we may postulate that indicative complements represent propositions whereas subjunctive complements represent situations. In other words, the indicative has essentially the same value in complement clauses as it does in main clauses. As we shall see, things are more complicated than this, but this hypothesis provides a useful starting point.

In order to test this hypothesis, we must ascertain whether a given clause represents a proposition or a situation. This is not always a straightforward matter:

(143)     a   Max a promis que l'argent sera rendu
          b   Le patron a ordonné que l'argent soit rendu

Both *promettre* and *ordonner* in (143) involve an act of communication, but *promettre* also connotes an attitude (the return of the money is presented as desirable) while *ordonner* expresses an act of manipulation with respect to a situation that the boss desires. The question, then, is whether the complements in (143) represent the proposition which was communicated or the situation which is desired. We cannot know exactly what the protaganists in (143) may have said, but we may infer that their utterances expressed propositions similar to those given in quotes in (144):

(144)    a  Max a déclaré «L'argent sera rendu»

           b  Le patron a déclaré «J'exige que l'argent soit rendu»

On the basis of these paraphrases, we may conclude that the complement in (143a) constitutes a report of what Max said (i.e. a proposition) whereas the complement in (143b) is a description of the situation which the boss wishes to bring about – note that we cannot use the quoted proposition in (144b) as a complement of *ordonner*: *Le patron a ordonné qu'il exige que l'argent soit rendu*. These conclusions are consistent with our hypothesis: the proposition in (143a) is expressed by the indicative, the situation in (143b) by the subjunctive.

### 4.9.5  Complements of cognitive verbs

With verbs which express beliefs, the complement represents a proposition. The choice of mood with such verbs is summarised below:

**Mood in complements of cognitive verbs:**

  *I*  *interrogative complements of these verbs (indirect questions) are always in the indicative.*

  *II*  *verbs which presuppose the truth of their complement (e.g.* savoir*) always take the indicative.*

  *III*  *verbs which deny or cast doubt on the truth of their complement (e.g.* douter*) take the subjunctive, but allow the indicative when questioned or negated.*

  *IV*  *other cognitive verbs (e.g.* croire*) take the indicative in affirmative sentences, but normally take the subjunctive when negated or questioned.*

Cases I and II and the affirmative cases in IV are consistent with our hypothesis that complements which represent propositions are expressed by the indicative. However, the use of the subjunctive in case III and in negative and interrogative constructions in case IV, suggests that choice of the indicative is in some way dependent on the truth of the complement.

The use of the indicative in complements of affirmative clauses is illustrated in (145):

(145)    a  Le médecin croit que Marie est malade

           b  Le médecin sait que Marie est malade

           c  Le médecin se demande si Marie est malade

In (145a) the proposition 'Marie is ill' is true for the doctor, but not necessarily for anybody else (including the speaker). In (145b) this proposition must be true for the doctor and the speaker, and indeed for anybody else who has a view on the matter (more precisely, the speaker assumes that this opinion is shared by others). Sentence (145c) indicates that the truth of this proposition is uncertain for the doctor, the opinions of others being immaterial. Note that in all these cases, the form of the complement correlates with its truth-value for the subject entity – in (145a, b) the positive declarative form expresses a proposition which is true for the subject (and possibly others), while in (145c) the interrogative form reflects the uncertainty of the subject. Let us refer to these formal properties of the clause (positive/negative, declarative/interrogative) by the label **syntactic polarity**. Thus, in (145) the syntactic polarity of the complement matches the truth value of the proposition in the mind of the subject entity.

With verbs of the type in III, this matching does not occur:

(146)     Le médecin doute que Marie soit malade

In (146) the complement is positive-declarative, yet it expresses a proposition which is false or, at best, uncertain in the mind of the subject entity (it could be true or false for the speaker or other relevant people). The use of the subjunctive in (146) appears to reflect this mismatch.

A similar pattern is observed when verbs of the *croire* type are negated (case IV):

(147)     Le médecin ne croit pas que Marie soit malade

Many speakers and grammarians regard the use of the indicative in such cases as 'incorrect' or 'sloppy', though it occurs quite frequently in colloquial style:

(148)     Le médecin ne croit pas que Marie est malade

However, there is a potential semantic contrast between (147) and (148) (obscured to some extent by the 'prescriptive' considerations just mentioned). The indicative can be used as in (148) to underline the speaker's opinion that the proposition is true (i.e. it is obvious to the speaker, and possibly others, that Marie is ill, but the doctor refuses to believe it) whereas (147) is neutral in this respect. Another consideration which may favour the use of the indicative, even in 'careful' usage, is the need to make a tense distinction which cannot be expressed by the subjunctive: e.g. *Je ne pense pas qu'il {pleut / pleuvra}* vs *Je ne pense pas qu'il pleuve* (ambiguous, present or future). Note that the indicative cannot be used with verbs of the *douter* type under such circumstances (*\*Le médecin doute que Marie est malade, \*Je doute qu'il pleuvra*) – it seems to make a difference whether the subject's belief is negated by syntactic means (*ne . . . pas*) or by the use of a 'negative' verb. However, when such verbs are negated they allow the indicative (usually implying assent on the part of the speaker) as well as the subjunctive:

(149)     Le médecin ne doute pas que Marie {est / soit} malade

Questioning of the main clause has a similar effect on mood, favouring the sub-junctive with *croire*-type verbs and allowing the indicative with *douter*: *Croit-il que Marie soit malade?*, *Doute-t-il que Marie {soit / est} malade?*. Interestingly, in negative-interrogative constructions with *croire*-type verbs, the indicative appears to be favoured, though this may depend on what the speaker is trying to convey by the utterance: *Ne croit-il pas que Marie {est / ?soit} malade?* – the effect here seems to be something like 'But surely he believes that Mary is ill, doesn't he?'.

In indirect questions and in constructions with verbs which presuppose the truth of their complements, negation (or questioning) of the main clause has no effect on mood:

(150)    a    Le médecin ne se demande pas si Marie {est / *soit} malade
         b    Le médecin ne sait pas que Marie {est / *soit} malade

The likely interpretation in (150) is that the doctor has no opinion on the truth of the proposition, e.g. the matter has not been brought to his attention or perhaps in the case of (150a) he simply does not care. To this extent, the syntactic polarity of the complement is consistent with (i.e. does not conflict with) the opinion of the subject entity. Moreover, in (150b), negation of the main clause does not cancel the belief of the speaker (or of others) that the proposition is true.

On the basis of the above observations, the following generalisation is postulated:

In complement clauses which represent propositions, the indicative is used:
*I when there is no conflict between the syntactic polarity of the complement and*
   *the beliefs of the subject entity regarding the truth-value of the proposition*
*II (optionally, and more marginally) when the proposition is deemed to be true*
   *by the speaker (and preferably by others whose opinions are relevant).*
*If neither of these conditions is satisfied, the subjunctive must be used.*

Condition I is satisfied in indirect questions and in constructions with verbs of the *savoir* type, which also satisfy II, even when the main clause is negated or questioned. Condition I is also satisfied in affirmative sentences with verbs of the *croire* type. Affirmative sentences with *douter*, etc. and negative/interrogative sentences with *croire*, etc. do not conform to condition I and normally require the subjunctive, but in the latter cases condition II may be evoked to allow use of the indicative.

There are some cognitive verbs which allow the subjunctive or the indicative in affirmative sentences: e.g. *imaginer*:

(151)    a    Pierre imagine qu'il a gagné la loterie
         b    Pierre imagine qu'il ait gagné la loterie

In both these examples, the use of *imaginer* suggests that the speaker does not believe the embedded proposition, but in (151a) we can infer that Pierre believes it (thus satisfying condition I). The use of the subjunctive in (151b) suggests that Pierre does not really believe this proposition either; it relates to a situation in a fantasy world, not in the real world – thus neither condition is satisfied in (151b).

A slightly different case is exemplified by *admettre* 'to concede'[3] in (152):

(152)    a    Marcel admet qu'il y a des contre-exemples à son analyse
         b    Marcel admet qu'il y ait des contre-exemples à son analyse

Even with the subjunctive in (152b), the proposition appears to be true for Marcel (and possibly the speaker). However, in (152b) this truth is conceded somewhat reluctantly, with an implication that it is at variance with other facts – e.g. (152b) might be followed by . . . *mais elle explique bon nombre de faits intéressants*. Sometimes, *admettre* with the subjunctive (particularly in the first-person imperative) introduces a hypothesis which is conceded as true for the purpose of argument: *Admettons que tu aies raison* . . . 'Let's suppose that you are right . . .'. This evidence suggests that the conditions presented above do not apply when the truth of the proposition is presented as a concession.

In this connection, we may note that the subjunctive is often used in complements of the noun *fait* (surprisingly, since facts are true propositions). Nevertheless, the use of the subjunctive tends to correlate with a concessive interpretation, as in (153a) as opposed to (153b):

(153)    a    Le fait que le ministre soit impliqué dans cette affaire ne remet
              pas en cause son intégrité
         b    Le fait que le ministre a démissionné a été rapporté dans tous
              les journaux

### 4.9.6    Complements of declarative verbs

Verbs of 'saying' follow the same pattern as the cognitive verbs discussed in 4.9.5 – e.g. *demander* works like *se demander*, *nier* like *douter*, and *dire* like *croire*. However, intuitions about 'who believes what' are rather more complicated. For example, a sentence of the type *X a dit Y* does not necessarily entail that X believes Y (X might be lying) – nevertheless, the indicative is required (i.e. the choice of mood seems to operate on the premise that X is telling the truth). Negative sentences (*X n'a pas dit Y*) pose a further problem: possibly X does not believe Y, but it could also be the case that X does believe Y, but has not expressed his opinion. Consequently, in addition to the stylistic complications mentioned with regard to (147) in 4.9.5, the semantic effect of using the indicative in a case like (154) is not clear – native-speakers seem to agree that, all things being equal, the indicative version of (154) carries a greater degree of certainty, but it is not clear on whose part:

---

[3] *Admettre* can also be used with the sense 'to tolerate', as in *Le professeur (n') admet (pas) qu'on lui fasse des farces*. In this case the complement represents a situation, not a proposition, and requires the subjunctive.

(154)     Le médecin n'a pas dit que Marie {est / soit} malade

Some verbs of the *dire* class convey presumptions of truth or doubt on the part of the speaker (i.e. the speaker of the whole sentence); e.g. *prétendre* 'claim' suggests scepticism on the part of the speaker whereas *confirmer* strongly suggests that the speaker considers the proposition to be true. This difference does not affect mood in affirmative sentences, the assumption being that the subject entity is telling the truth:

(155)     a   Ce journaliste a prétendu que le ministre a accepté des pots-de-vin
           b   Le Président a confirmé que le ministre a démissionné

However, in negative sentences, the different presumptions associated with these verbs tend to favour the subjunctive with *prétendre* and the indicative with *confirmer* (though this tendency is by no means absolute):

(156)     a   Ce journaliste n'a pas prétendu que le ministre ait accepté des pots-de-vin
           b   Le Président n'a pas (encore) confirmé que le ministre a démissionné

### 4.9.7   Complements of modal expressions

Expressions which indicate different degrees of possibility with respect to their complements can be ranked on a continuum from falsity to truth, as shown in (157):

(157)     faux – peu probable – possible –  |  – probable – certain – vrai
           SUBJUNCTIVE                         |  INDICATIVE

With regard to choice of mood, there is a cut-off point somewhere between *possible* and *probable*, indicated by the line in (157), so that items to the right of this line (expressing a degree of truth equal to or greater than probability) take the indicative in affirmative sentences, while those to the left (expressing a degree of truth no greater than possibility) require the subjunctive. In negative sentences, items to the right of the line often take the subjunctive but the indicative is also possible, particularly with items towards the 'true' end of the spectrum:

(158)     Il n'est pas certain que Marie {est / soit} malade

With the indicative, negation reduces the degree of certainty to a point within the 'probability' range, whereas the subjunctive places it somewhere below the cut-off point. Often this nuance is clarified by modifying expressions:

(159)    a   Il n'est pas tout à fait certain que Marie est malade
         b   Il n'est pas du tout certain que Marie soit malade

Expressions of the type to the left of the line in (157) normally require the subjunctive even when negated or questioned.

The verb *sembler* expresses a degree of probability somewhere around the cut-off point in (157). In affirmative sentences it typically takes the indicative but the subjunctive can be used to express a lesser degree of probability. In negative and interrogative sentences, *sembler* normally requires the subjunctive.

### 4.9.8   Complements of 'emotive' and 'manipulative' expressions

The term 'emotive' is used here in a very broad sense to cover expressions which denote an attitude towards a situation ((dis)pleasure, surprise, desire, need, etc.). Within this class are included verbs such as *aimer, plaire, s'étonner, regretter, souhaiter, vouloir, désirer, craindre, falloir*, and adjectives like *content, fier, agréable, utile, intéressant, nécessaire*. The class of 'manipulative' verbs includes items like *ordonner, permettre, exiger, demander* (followed by a *que* clause, with the meaning 'request'), *empêcher, éviter, interdire*. As was argued in 4.9.4, a semantic property common to both these classes is that the complement must be interpreted as representing a situation, not a proposition. This difference can be seen by comparing *interdire* and *nier*, which some grammarians group together within a class of 'verbs with negative force': in a sentence *X nie que Y*, X denies the truth of the proposition Y, but in *X interdit que Y*, X says something in order to prevent the situation Y from occurring.

With regard to other semantic properties, these two classes are quite heterogeneous. Some manipulative verbs describe the causation of the situation, entailing in some cases that it actually occurred (*Jules a permis que le chien sorte*), whereas others entail that it was prevented (*Jules a empêché que le chat sorte*), while yet others (e.g. *ordonner* and *interdire*) carry no implications as to the occurrence of the event (e.g. the order could have been disobeyed). Within the emotive class, apart from the wide range of attitudes described by different items, there are clear differences concerning the truth-value of the complement. For example, *regretter* presupposes the truth of its complement – in (160) the speaker is committed to the belief that Max stole the money, even when the sentence is negated:

(160)    Jules (ne) regrette (pas) que Max ait volé l'argent

In (161a), *aimer* shows a similar property, implying at least that Suzy has received compliments from time to time, though this implication is cancelled when *aimer* is used in the conditional:

(161)    a   Suzy (n') aime (pas) qu'on lui fasse des compliments
         b   Suzy (n') aimerait (pas) qu'on lui fasse des compliments

On the other hand, with verbs like *souhaiter* in (162) there is no implication whatsoever as to whether the speaker or the subject entity believes that the event will ever occur:

(162)    Suzy souhaite qu'on lui fasse des compliments

As was seen in 4.9.5–4.9.7, implicational differences of this sort are crucial in determining the choice of mood in complements which represent propositions. However, with emotive and manipulative expressions, they have no effect whatsoever. Similarly, negation or questioning of the main clause does not affect the choice of mood. Expressions of these two types invariably select the subjunctive. Thus we can formulate the following generalisation:

*Finite complement clauses which represent situations, as opposed to propositions, systematically occur in the subjunctive, regardless of any considerations of truth.*

> A minor range of exceptions to this generalisation involves verbs (and other items) whose complements are introduced by *de ce que* rather than simply *que*. Some emotive expressions allow or favour the indicative in this construction; e.g. *se plaindre que* and *se réjouir que* require the subjunctive, as expected, but *se plaindre de ce que* normally takes the indicative, while *se réjouir de ce que* allows either mood. There does not seem to be any regular pattern to such cases.

Some problems remain however.

The verb *espérer* looks like an emotive verb, on a par with *souhaiter*, but it takes the indicative:

(163)    a    J'espère que tu viendras à la fête
         b    Je souhaite que tu viennes à la fête

Some grammarians claim that (163a) involves a higher degree of certainty regarding the complement than (163b), but it is hard to see any basis for this judgement – if anything, *souhaiter* seems to impose some element of obligation, which is absent with *espérer*, and to this extent it makes the event more likely to happen. In any case, as we have seen above, considerations of probability do not affect choice of mood with emotive verbs. With regard to choice of mood, *espérer* behaves like a cognitive verb of the *croire* type. In particular, it favours the subjunctive when negated or questioned:

(164)    a    Jules n'espère pas que Solange vienne à la fête
         b    Espères-tu qu'elle vienne à la fête?

It is tentatively concluded that the complement of *espérer* actually represents a proposition: e.g. *espérer* means something like 'believe with optimism'.

The opposite problem arises with *s'attendre*, whose meaning is similar to that of cognitive verbs of the *croire* type. Nevertheless, in Modern French[4] it takes the subjunctive even though it expresses a high degree of probability concerning the complement:

(165)    Je m'attends (à ce) que Solange vienne à la fête

This observation suggests that the complement of *s'attendre* represents a situation rather than a proposition – i.e. *s'attendre* behaves like an emotive verb. This suggestion is supported by the fact that *s'attendre*, unlike most cognitive verbs, can readily take an NP object denoting an event: *Je m'attends à une révolution* (cf. *\*Je crois une révolution*).

### 4.9.9   A syntactic condition on mood

Typically, finite clauses in subject position require the subjunctive (though this generalisation is not absolute), even with expressions which normally take the indicative (e.g. in impersonal constructions):

(166)    a   Que Suzy soit partie en vacances est probable
         b   Que le ministre ait démissionné a été rapporté dans les journaux

(167)    a   Il est probable que Suzy est partie en vacances
         b   Il a été rapporté dans les journaux que le ministre a démissionné

The same pattern is found with left-dislocated clauses:

(168)    a   Que Max ait volé l'argent, c'est certain
         b   Que Marie soit malade, c'est vrai

(169)    a   Il est certain que Max a volé l'argent
         b   Il est vrai que Marie est malade

Possibly this is a purely syntactic condition. However, the use of the subjunctive in (166) and (168) can perhaps be attributed to the fact that at the point where the *que* clauses are introduced, there is no linguistic cue as to their truth-value. Also of possible relevance is our observation in 3.4.9 that postverbal clauses can convey new information (e.g. (167a) can be used to assert that Suzy is (probably) on holiday) whereas subject clauses (and left-dislocated clauses) can only recapitulate propositions which have already been introduced into the discourse. In this respect, the complement clauses in (167) and (169) resemble declarative main clauses in a way that the clauses in (166) and (168) do not.

---

[4] In Classical French, *s'attendre que* favoured the indicative.

#### *4.9.10    Adverbial clauses*

The term 'adverbial clause' is used here to denote clauses which modify the main clause (or possibly the verb in some cases). Most types of adverbial clauses are introduced by prepositions (or so-called 'subordinating conjunctions' – see 8.3.2). To a large extent the choice of mood in adverbial clauses follows the pattern observed for complements of verbs and adjectives outlined in the preceding sections, but there are some differences. Given that the set of prepositions which can introduce adverbial clauses is quite small, it is possible that the choice of mood, in some cases at least, is simply learnt as a property of the preposition in question.

**Time clauses** which describe events prior to or concurrent with the reference-time of the main clause (e.g. with *quand, dès que, lorsque, pendant que, après que*) are expressed by the indicative (though occasionally *après que* is used with the subjunctive, see below). Time clauses of this type are analogous to main clauses: e.g. *Quand Pierre avait fini son travail, il s'est couché* can be paraphrased as *Pierre a fini son travail, puis il s'est couché*. Indeed, sometimes it is the time clause rather than the main clause which conveys the principal assertion of the sentence, as in *J'étais sur le point de partir quand le téléphone a sonné*. Moreover, from the perspective of the reference-time in the main clause, they describe events which are actual rather than merely potential – they have already occurred or are in progress. This is not typically the case with future-oriented time clauses, introduced by *avant que, jusqu'à ce que* or *en attendant que*, which require the subjunctive. In (170a) there is no implication that it will actually rain and in (170b) the action in the main clause prevents the event in the time clause from occurring – these examples cannot be paraphrased as *??Nous devrons rentrer, puis il pleuvra* or *??Pierre a détruit la lettre, puis son père l'a lue*:

(170)    a    Nous devons rentrer avant qu'il pleuve
         b    Pierre a détruit la lettre avant que son père le lise

In these cases, the use of the subjunctive may be attributed to the hypothetical or counterfactual nature of the event which it describes. Nevertheless, the subjunctive must also be used when the event actually occurred, as in (171), which can be paraphrased (roughly) as *Nous avons parlé de cette question, puis le patron s'en est allé*:

(171)        Nous avons parlé de cette question avant que le patron s'en aille

Thus, although the use of the subjunctive is semantically motivated in cases like (170) it appears to have become a purely grammatical feature selected by *avant que*, etc., in all cases. Note in this connection that phrases of the type *avant le moment où, jusqu'à l'instant où*, etc. require the indicative and impose a factual interpretation:

(172)  a  Nous avons parlé de cette question avant le moment où le
          patron s'en est allé
       b  ??Pierre a détruit la lettre avant le moment où son père l'a lue

The use of the subjunctive with *après que* (often condemned by grammarians)
may be attributed to analogy – its grammaticalised use with *avant que* has been
extended to its converse *après que* even though the semantic properties of this
item do not motivate this use.

**Reason clauses**, introduced by *parce que*, *puisque*, etc., require the indicative, as
we might expect since they describe facts and, moreover, can be paraphrased by
main clauses introduced by the conjunction *donc*:

(173)  a  Puisqu'il faisait beau, nous sommes sortis
       b  Il faisait beau, donc nous sommes sortis

The choice of mood in **concessive clauses** (introduced by *bien que, quoique*,
etc.) and **condition clauses** (introduced by *si*) is rather puzzling. Concessive
clauses describe facts, but they require the subjunctive, whereas condition clauses,
which describe potential or hypothetical situations, normally occur in the indicative. The use of the subjunctive in concessive constructions is consistent with our
observations concerning complements of *admettre* and the noun *fait* in 4.9.5,
where the subjunctive signals a concession which is at variance with other facts
presented in the context, as in (174) (compare *Puisque Marie est malade, elle est
restée à la maison*):

(174)     Bien que Marie soit malade, elle est allée au travail

The use of the indicative in condition clauses can perhaps be attributed to the item
*si*, which confers a 'non-factual' value of the sort often associated with the subjunctive; also perhaps to the fact that modal distinctions are expressed by tense
forms (see 4.8.1). In Classical French the imperfect/pluperfect subjunctive was
widely used in *si* clauses of the hypothetical/counterfactual type. In formal registers, this use survives (with the conditional tense as an alternative) in condition
clauses formed by inversion without *si* (see 10.3.5): *{Fût-il / serait-il} arrivé à
l'heure, nous l'aurions vu* (cf. English *Had he arrived on time*). Similarly, when
condition clauses are conjoined, with the second clause introduced by *que*, the *que*
clause usually appears in the subjunctive: *Si vous venez et que je ne sois pas là,
laissez un petit mot*; see 8.3.4. The subjunctive is also used in many other clauses
which have a conditional or concessive function but which are not introduced by
*si*:

(175)  a  Pourvu qu'il fasse beau, nous irons à la plage
       b  À moins qu'il ne pleuve, nous irons à la plage

  c  Qu'il pleuve ou qu'il fasse beau, nous irons à la plage
  d  Quel que soit le temps, nous irons à la plage

Note, however, that *au cas où* and *dans la mesure où* require the indicative (cf. the use of the indicative with *avant le moment où* noted above).

**Purposive clauses**, introduced by *pour que, afin que*, etc., require the subjunctive:

(176)      Je t'écris pour que tu viennes me voir

These cases can be assimilated to complements of emotive verbs such as *vouloir*. They describe situations presented as desirable, but without any implication that they will be realised. Clauses introduced by *de crainte que, de peur que*, describing potential situations which are undesirable, show the same behaviour, though these expressions usually require expletive *ne* (see 7.6.12): *Le voleur s'est caché de peur qu'on ne le voie.*

**Manner clauses** (sometimes called 'consecutive clauses') introduced by *de (telle) façon que, de (telle) manière que*, etc., describe the manner of the action in relation to some consequence which may be realised or merely intended – in the latter case they resemble purposive clauses and take the subjunctive, but in the former they take the indicative:

(177)   a  Jules se comporte de (telle) façon que les gens fassent attention à lui
        b  Jules s'est comporté de (telle) façon que les gens ont fait
           attention à lui

Negative clauses with various functions, introduced by *sans que, loin que* and *non (pas) que*, require the subjunctive:

(178)   a  Le chien est sorti sans qu'on l'aperçoive
        b  Loin qu'elle soit venue à l'heure, elle n'est même pas arrivée
        c  Pierre ne veut pas y entrer; non (pas) qu'il ait peur

### 4.9.11  *Subjunctive relative clauses*
In relative clauses (see 10.5), the subjunctive is normally used when the NP has non-specific reference or to describe entities whose existence is purely hypothetical or explicitly denied:

(179)   a  Jules cherche un fauteuil qui soit vraiment confortable
        b  Solange veut épouser un homme qui n'ait pas de défauts
        c  Il n'y a aucun homme qui puisse m'aider

In (179a) neither Jules nor the speaker has any particular armchair in mind (compare *Jules a acheté un fauteuil qui est vraiment confortable*, where the relative clause describes a property of a specific armchair). In (179b), depending on one's beliefs, there is no person who fits the description, while in (179c) the existence of such a person is denied by the form of the sentence itself. In contexts similar to (179c), the subjunctive is also used with indefinite NPs in negative sentences and with *peu de*:

(180)      a   Il n'y a pas beaucoup d'hommes qui puissent m'aider

           b   Il y a peu d'hommes qui puissent m'aider

Similarly, the subjunctive is used when the existence of the entity is questioned:

(181)      Avez-vous trouvé un livre qui soit intéressant?

The subjunctive is frequently used when the noun is modified by a superlative adjective (e.g. *le meilleur, le plus intéressant*) or a restrictive adjective (e.g. *seul*):

(182)      a   *Germinal* est le meilleur roman que Zola ait écrit

           b   C'est le seul livre qui soit vraiment intéressant

However the indicative seems more appropriate in a case like (183):

(183)      Celui-ci est le livre le moins cher que le professeur {a / ?ait} recommandé

The semantic factors involved here are difficult to pin down. Contrary to the suggestions of some grammarians it does not seem to be a matter of 'doubtfulness' versus 'factuality' concerning the truth of the relative clause, e.g. in (182a) there is no doubt that Zola wrote the novel in question.

A likely interpretation of (183) with the indicative is that it picks out a particular member of a specific set of books recommended by the teacher on a particular occasion, whereas (182a) ranges over the whole class of novels which satisfy the description 'Zola wrote X'. Note that if a definite article is used within the NP to designate a particular set, the indicative must be used even in cases like (182a): *le moins cher des livres que le professeur a recommandés, le meilleur des romans que Zola a écrits*. Often the effect of the subjunctive in (182a) can be rendered in English by inserting *ever* (and indeed by *jamais* in French): *the best novel that Zola ever wrote*. In a case like (183), use of *ever* gives a rather less natural interpretation than the one proposed above: *the cheapest book that the teacher ever recommended* – in fact this is the interpretation which would be imposed by the subjunctive in (183). Thus, one way of deciding whether to use the subjunctive in constructions with superlative or restrictive adjectives is to see whether *ever* would be appropriate in the English translation. This test does not work for all cases because of temporal–aspectual restrictions on this use of *ever* (and *jamais*); e.g. it cannot be used when describing present states as in (182b): *\*the only book* *which is ever interesting.* Nevertheless, in such cases we can often construct a near paraphrase which has the required temporal properties; e.g. *the only book which ever interested me.* A similar test is to insert a phrase containing *any*, which also imposes an interpretation of the sort expressed by the subjunctive: *the only book which is interesting to anybody* (cf. *the cheapest book which the teacher recommended to anybody*, which can only have the 'less natural' interpretation).[5]

The above comments on the subjunctive in relative clauses relate principally to fairly formal styles. In less formal registers the indicative is often extended to all finite relative clauses.

**Exercises**

1  Discuss the temporal structure of the following narrative, showing how the tense forms are used to indicate the order in which events occurred.

> (a) Pierre venait de s'asseoir dans le restaurant
> (b) Il avait mangé un bon repas à midi,
> (c) ... mais il avait faim
> (d) Il a regardé la carte
> (e) ... et il a commandé le plat le plus cher
> (f) Il aurait des problèmes d'argent à la fin du mois,
> (g) ... mais il n'y pensait pas
> (h) À la fin du repas, il a demandé l'addition
> (i) Il allait payer en espèces
> (j) ... mais il s'est aperçu
> (k) ... qu'il avait laissé son portefeuille chez lui
> (l) Pas de problème, il payerait par chèque
> (m) Il a regretté un peu sa gourmandise,
> (n) ... mais il se disait
> (o) ... qu'il avait très bien mangé
> (p) Il a poussé un gros soupir
> (q) ... et il est allé à la caisse

2  Collect samples of newspaper articles and study the use of tense forms to report punctual events in the past. Possible considerations to bear in mind include: degree of formality, dramatic impact of the events, remoteness of the events from the time of writing or publication, subject matter, etc.

---

[5] Items like *ever* and *any* belong to a class of 'negative polarity' expressions. See 7.6.7 for discussion of such expressions in French.

3  Look at the first paragraph or so of a selection of novels or short stories and discuss the strategies used by the authors to situate the reference-time of the first punctual event in the story. Are there any strategies which are typical of particular literary styles or individual authors?

4  Comment on the use of tenses and other time expressions in the following text:

M A I, octobre

J'ai l'impression que je pourrais retrouver avec une exactitude absolue la place qu'occupait mon unique lourde valise dans le filet, et celle où je l'ai laissée tomber, entre les banquettes, au travers de la porte.

C'est qu'alors l'eau de mon regard n'était pas encore obscurcie; depuis, chacun des jours y a jeté sa pincée de cendres.

J'ai posé mes pieds sur le quai presque désert, et je me suis aperçu que les derniers chocs avaient achevé de découdre ma vieille poignée de cuir, qu'il me faudrait soigneusement appuyer le pouce à l'endroit défait, crisper ma main, doubler l'effort.

J'ai attendu; je me suis redressé, les jambes un peu écartées pour bien prendre appui sur ce nouveau sol, regardant autour de moi: à gauche, la tôle rouge du wagon que je venais de quitter, l'épaisse porte qui battait, à droite, d'autres voies, avec quelques éclats de lumière dure sur les rails, et plus loin, d'autres wagons immobiles et éteints, toujours sous l'immense voûte de métal et de verre, dont je devinais les blessures au-delà des brumes; en face de moi enfin, au-dessus de la barrière que l'employé s'apprêtait à fermer juste après mon passage, la grande horloge au cadran lumineux marquant deux heures.

Alors j'ai pris une longue aspiration, et l'air m'a paru amer, acide charbonneux, lourd comme si un grain de limaille lestait chaque gouttelette de son brouillard.

Un peu de vent frôlait les ailes de mon nez et mes joues, un peu de vent au poil âpre et gluant, comme celui d'une couverture de laine humide.

Cet air auquel j'étais désormais condamné pour tout un an, je l'ai interrogé par mes narines et ma langue, et j'ai bien senti qu'elle contenait ces vapeurs sournoises qui depuis sept mois m'asphyxient, qui avaient réussi à me plonger dans le terrible engourdissement dont je viens de me réveiller.

Je m'en souviens, j'ai été soudain pris de peur (et j'étais perspicace: c'était bien ce genre de folie que j'appréhendais, cet obscurcissement de moi-même), j'ai été envahi, toute une longue seconde, de l'absurde envie de reculer, de renoncer, de fuir; mais un immense fossé me séparait des événements de la matinée et des visages qui m'étaient les plus familiers, un fossé qui s'était démesurément agrandi tandis que je le franchissais, de telle sorte que je n'en percevais plus les profondeurs et que son autre rive, incroyablement lointaine, ne m'apparaissait plus que comme une ligne d'horizon très légèrement découpée sur laquelle il n'était plus possible de discerner aucun détail. (Michel Butor, *L'emploi du temps*, Paris, Éditions de Minuit (1956), p. 10.)

(This is an extract from the beginning of a novel about a young Frenchman who goes to spend a year working in England. This passage describes his arrival in the provincial town where he is to live. The novel is written in the form of a 'retrospective diary'. Here the author is writing in May describing events of the previous October, but with occasional comments on the intervening period.)

5   What is the difference in meaning between sentences (a) and (b) and how can it be accounted for?

> Jules a brûlé un feu rouge à cent kilomètres à l'heure.
> (a) Dans dix minutes il serait à l'hôpital
> (b) Dix minutes plus tard il serait à l'hôpital

How can you explain the difference in acceptability between the following examples?

> (c) Pierre s'est pressé parce que le train partait dans trois minutes
> (d) ??Pierre s'est pressé parce que le train partait trois minutes après

6   Expressions of the type *en trois jours*, *pendant trois jours* and *pour trois jours* can be used to specify the duration of an event or state. On the basis of the following examples and others of your own, try to determine the aspectual factors which govern the use of these expressions:

> (a) Pierre a écrit ce roman en trois jours
> (b) *Pierre a travaillé en trois jours
> (c) Autrefois, Pierre écrivait des romans en trois jours
> (d) Pierre a travaillé pendant trois jours
> (e) *Pierre a fini ce roman pendant trois jours
> (f) Pierre a été malade pendant trois jours
> (g) Pierre est venu à Paris pour trois jours

In what ways does *pendant trois jours* differ from *pendant le weekend*?

7   Both *puis* and *alors* can be translated into English as *then*. How do these two items differ with respect to the temporal relation between the sentence which contains them and the preceding context?

8   With the help of a good dictionary, reference grammar or a native speaker, ascertain the choice of mood in complements of the following verbs:

arriver, comprendre, décider, désespérer, ignorer, oublier, se pouvoir, supposer

To what extent are your findings consistent with the account of mood presented in 4.9.4–4.9.8?

9   Typically the problem of mood in complement clauses is construed in terms of the question: 'When do we use the subjunctive?'. Is there anything to be gained by approaching the problem from the opposite direction – i.e. 'When do we use the indicative?'?
Hint: a possible advantage of this approach is that we would not need to look for a coherent set of conditions which determine the use of the subjunctive, they could simply be defined as the set of cases where the indicative is not possible. The crux of this question is whether indicative complements constitute a more homogeneous class than subjunctive complements.

10   In French, as in English, sentences with finite complements can sometimes be transposed, expressing the complement as the main clause and adding the main clause parenthetically or at the end (sometimes with inversion of the subject):

(a)  Je {crois / sais / dis} que Marie est malade
(b)  Marie, je {crois / sais / dis}, est malade
(c)  Marie est malade, je {crois / sais / dis}

To what extent does the class of verbs which allow this transposition (in French or English) coincide with the class of verbs which take the indicative in French?

11   Subordinate clauses with the subjunctive can often be rendered in English by infinitival constructions of the type *for NP to VP*. Invent as many examples of this English construction as you can and try to ascertain whether the main verbs (or adjectives) which allow this construction also take the subjunctive in French. Is there any significant generalisation in the opposite direction – i.e. do (most) items which select the subjunctive allow the *for ... to* construction?

**Further reading**
The framework for representing tense is based on Reichenbach (1947), with some notational modifications. For further background on the concepts of tense and aspect, see Comrie (1976, 1985).

General studies of tense in French include Imbs (1968), Martin (1971), Sten (1952), Korzen & Vikner (1980); also Guillaume (1929), an influential but difficult work within the 'psychomécanique' framework. Vet (1980) presents a detailed study of tense, aspect and adverbial expressions of time within a framework similar to that which has been presented. Verleuten (1979) discusses tense in adverbial clauses. Other articles on various issues of tense and aspect can be found in Moeschler (1993), Vet (1985), Vetters (1993), Wilmet (1976). For discussion of questions relating more specifically to aspect, see David & Martin (1980), Franckel (1989), Fuchs (1978, 1979), Wilmet (1991). Problems relating to use of past-tense forms and the expression of past time are discussed in Benveniste (1966, ch. 19), Ducrot (1979), Engel (1990), Molendijk (1985, 1987, 1990), Tasmowski-De Ryck (1985), Vet & Molendijk (1986), Vetters (1989). On the semantics of conditional constructions, see Ducrot (1972, ch. 6), Haff (1990).

For discussion of mood, see Bysen (1971), Cellard (1978), Cohen (1965), Connors (1978), M. Gross (1978), Nordahl (1969); also, within a general description of subordinate clauses, Sandfeld (1965a). Variation in the use of the subjunctive is studied in Poplack (1992).

The effect of tense and mood on certain syntactic processes is discussed in Pica (1984) and Rouveret (1980); see also Rouveret (1977, 1978).

# 5
# The Noun Phrase

## 5.1 Overview

Most of the questions investigated in this chapter concern the use of determiners.

In 5.2, we look at the classification of nouns according to different semantic and syntactic properties, particularly those which are relevant to the use of determiners.

In 5.3, the determiners themselves are focused upon, their function within the NP and the semantic and syntactic properties of different types of determiner. This discussion is guided by two basic questions: whether the determiner is an obligatory component of the NP and whether an NP can contain more than one determiner. Both of these questions require us to define the class of determiners, as opposed to other items (e.g. adjectives) which can precede the noun. This discussion leads us in 5.3.6–5.3.8 to the structural properties of NPs like *beaucoup de pommes* and *beaucoup de ces pommes* and similar cases where quantity is expressed by a noun (*un kilo de pommes, une bande de voyous*).

Some of the issues raised in 5.3 are taken up in greater detail in 5.4, where various constructions in which a part of the NP is introduced by *de*, are examined, and more particularly the indefinite use of *du, de la* and *des* and the use of *de* in negative sentences. The approach to these constructions is based on the premise that the function of *de* is to assign a Case feature to some element within the NP.

In 5.5, we investigate the syntactic and semantic properties of *tout* and *tous* and other expressions which have a similar function.

## 5.2 Types of noun

### 5.2.1 Common and proper nouns

**Common** nouns, like *chaise, médecin, chien, espoir* or *beauté*, are words which describe classes of entities (persons, things, abstract concepts). In order to refer to specific individuals, the noun must be combined with a determiner which indicates the way in which the individual is to be selected from the general class. Thus, very roughly, *la chaise* refers to a particular chair which the addressee is expected to indentify uniquely, *cette chaise* to a chair which the speaker is perhaps pointing to,

200

whereas *une chaise* denotes an arbitrary member of the class of chairs which the addressee is not expected to identify.

On the other hand, **proper** nouns like *Georges*, *Lyon*, *Belgique* or *Asie* designate particular entities directly. They do not describe classes definable in terms of a shared set of properties, but they are simply names associated with particular persons, places, etc. Consequently, there is no semantic motivation for the use of a determiner with proper nouns. Nevertheless, some types of proper nouns must be accompanied by the definite article (e.g. names of countries or regions). In fact the same is true of some proper nouns in English (e.g. names of rivers, mountain ranges, groups of islands), which also require the definite article in French. In such cases, the presence of the determiner can be seen as a purely syntactic requirement. In the main, the determiner is always the definite article – e.g. we cannot say *Nous avons visité cette Belgique* or *Je connais une Asie*, just as we cannot say *We crossed that Mersey* or *We visited some {Hebrides / Pennines}* in English.

There are some cases where proper nouns can be used as common nouns, denoting the class of entities which bear the name in question, as in (1):

(1)  a Il y a trois Marie dans la classe
    b Il y a plusieurs Villeneuve en France
    c Nous sommes allés voir les Dupont
    d Un certain Jacques Leblanc a téléphoné

Note that proper nouns used in this way do not show any plural inflection (as in (1a–c)).

Sometimes determiners can be used with proper nouns to refer to the entity at some particular time or in some hypothetical situation:

(2)  a Je regrette le Paris de mon enfance
    b Tu n'est plus la Suzanne que j'ai épousée
    c Nous souhaitons {une France plus prospère / un Paris plus propre}

There are other cases where proper nouns can refer to entities other than those which bear the name in question, as when names of famous people are used to evoke certain characteristics associated with the person:

(3)  a Il y a trop d'Hitlers dans ce monde
    b Luc est un véritable Mozart

Another 'derivative' use of proper nouns is illustrated in (4), where *Cézannes* is used to denote instances of the artist's work:

(4)  Il y a trois Cézannes dans ce musée

In such examples, the nouns are tantamount to common nouns or NPs headed by a common noun (e.g. in (3a) *Hitler* is roughly synonymous with *tyran* and in (4) *Cézanne* means *tableau par Cézanne*). Syntactically, they behave like common nouns, allowing the full range of determiners and plural inflection (as in (3a) and (4), though usage is somewhat uncertain on this point), but they are usually written with an initial capital letter.

Brand names used to refer to artefacts show some affinities with proper nouns. They are written with an initial capital and do not normally show plural inflection:

(5)     a   Pierre aime les Renault
        b   J'ai commandé deux Kronenbourg et trois Orangina

In other respects, they can be treated as common nouns – they denote classes of entities and allow the full range of determiners. Indeed, some brand names have become fully assimilated to the class of common nouns, describing types of arte-fects regardless of their brand (e.g. *scotch* 'adhesive tape', *bic* 'ball-point pen') – these are usually written in lowercase and show plural inflection:

(6)     J'ai trois bics dans ma poche

### 5.2.2  Countability

Within the class of common nouns, a fundamental distinction between **countable** and **non-countable** nouns (henceforth [+count] vs [-count]) may be drawn. As these labels suggest, [+count] nouns denote things which can be counted whereas [-count] nouns denote things which cannot; thus, within the physical domain, [+count] nouns designate concrete objects (including animate beings) which have definable boundaries (e.g. *chaise, stylo, arbre, colline, chien, garçon*) whereas [-count] nouns, sometimes called 'mass' nouns, refer to substances (e.g. *acier, beurre, encre, oxygène*). From a syntactic viewpoint, these two classes can be dis-tinguished according to the range of determiners which they allow. Only [+count] nouns can co-occur with numerals (including *un(e)*, with some provisos which will be discussed below) and items such as *plusieurs, quelques*, and the plural forms of determiners like *les, ces, mes, des*. On the other hand, only [-count] nouns can be introduced by *du* or *de la* (unless of course the *de* element functions as a genuine preposition introducing an indirect object). Similarly, in expressions of the type *beaucoup de N*, [+count] nouns are plural, but [-count] nouns are singular – more generally, [-count] nouns lack a plural form.

Many [-count] nouns can also be used as [+count] nouns, to denote a type of the substance (7b) or a unit of the substance (7c):

(7)     a   J'ai acheté {du vin / du café}
        b   J'ai dégusté trois vins     ('three varieties of wine')
        c   J'ai bu trois cafés         ('three cups of coffee')

This pattern is quite productive. The availability of a 'type' or 'unit' interpretation seems to depend on pragmatic factors such as the cultural importance of different varieties of the substance or the existence of an accepted unit of the substance. Although *trois vins* favours a 'type' interpretation and *trois cafés* a 'unit' interpretation, the alternative readings 'three glasses of wine' and 'three types of coffee' are possible in an appropriate context. The range of nouns which allow a 'type' or 'unit' interpretation is similar in French and English, but there are some differences – e.g. *pain* is [±count] (*du pain, trois pains*) but *bread* is only [-count] (*some bread, *three breads*; cf. *cake* which is [±count] like *pain*).

Some [-count] nouns can also be used as [+count] nouns denoting an artefact typically made of the substance: e.g. *du verre* (substance), *trois verres* ('drinking vessel'). Such cases tend to be quite idiosyncratic – e.g. the different types of object which can be denoted by *fer* are not exactly the same as those which can be described by *iron*. Conversely, some [+count] nouns can have a [-count] use, typical examples being words for animals which are consumed as meat: *trois veaux* 'three calves' vs *du veau* 'veal' (note that English usually has separate words, derived from French, for the latter use).

Cross-linguistic differences in countability are much more widespread with abstract nouns, perhaps because the distinction between a 'substance' and an individuable entity is much less tangible with abstract concepts. For example, *conseil* and *renseignement* are [+count] whereas their English counterparts *advice* and *information* are [-count] (**du conseil, quelques conseils* vs *some advice(*s)*), though French *information* is both (*de l'information, quelques informations*). We also find cases where the [±count] distinction with a given noun is associated with a semantic difference which is conveyed by different lexical items in English; for example, *ennui* as a [-count] noun signifies 'boredom' but in its [+count] uses denotes 'something troublesome' (typically rendered in English by a [-count] noun such as *bother*).

By and large, the restrictions on the range of determiners with abstract nouns follow the same pattern as that outlined for concrete nouns, but with some differences which deserve comment. Some abstract [-count] nouns can occur with the indefinite article *un(e)*, usually accompanied by an adjective: e.g. *un courage extraordinaire, une certaine intelligence*. However, in such cases *un(e)* serves to express degree (qualified by the adjective) rather than individuating a particular instance of the phenomenon (cf. the similarity between *avoir un courage extraordinaire* and *être extraordinairement courageux*), and there is no corresponding use of plural quantity expressions: **quelques courages extraordinaires*. Conversely, some abstract nouns which can be classified as [+count] on the grounds that they occur in the plural, do not readily admit the full range of determiners typical of [+count] nouns, particularly numerals. For example, we can say *les charmes de cette fille*, but *?Elle a trois charmes* is odd. Perhaps such restrictions are a reflection of the general 'fuzziness' of abstract concepts as compared with physical objects: e.g. 'charming qualities' are individuable to the extent that one can have many or few of them, or some but not others, but the boundaries between them are too diffuse to allow them to be counted.

### 5.2.3 *'Pluralia tantum' nouns*

The Latin term **'pluralia tantum'** (inherently plural) is sometimes used to denote a range of nouns which can occur only in the plural form. Some of these (e.g. *gens*, *mœurs* and the colloquial item *fringues* 'clothes') are semantically plural – they denote a set of entities – but, unlike genuine [+count] nouns (e.g. *personne*, *coutume, vêtement*), they denote this set in a collective manner and cannot be quantified by items which individuate the members of the set (e.g. we can say *beaucoup de gens*, but not *\*{quelques / plusieurs / cinq} gens*) – note that *gens* differs markedly from English *people* in this respect.

A second class of 'pluralia tantum' nouns is exemplified by items such as *ciseaux* 'scissors', *lunettes* 'spectacles' and *menottes* 'handcuffs' which, though syntactically plural, denote a single object, usually an artefact consisting of two roughly identical parts. Some nouns of this type can be used in the singular, but with a different meaning (e.g. *ciseau* 'chisel', *lunette* 'telescope'). As in English, the objects referred to by 'pluralia tantum' uses of such items can only be individuated by means of a noun like *paire*; e.g. *mes lunettes* (one or more pairs), *beaucoup de lunettes* (a large indeterminate quantity) but *{plusieurs / trois} paires de lunettes*. Note, however, that the French counterparts of many such 'pluralia tantum' nouns in English are straightforward [+count] nouns (e.g. names of garments worn round the legs and torso: *pantalon, caleçon, slip, collant, short*, etc.).

### 5.2.4 *Collective nouns*

**Collective nouns** are items like *foule, groupe, ensemble, bande, troupeau*, etc., which have plural reference even when they are used in the singular form. In English, the semantic plurality of such nouns allows them to trigger plural agreement of the verb, even when the noun is singular in form: *The crowd {has / have} left the main square*. This complication does not arise in French, where such nouns always take the singular form of the verb when they are themselves singular: *La foule {a / \*ont} quitté la place centrale*. In French, these nouns can be classified as straightforward [+count] nouns which denote entities that happen to consist of several members (just as *forêt* denotes an entity consisting of many trees).

Some collective nouns are [-count]: e.g. *police, patronat, vermine, bourgeoisie, canaille, monde* (as used to refer to people). Some of these can be used with *du* or *de la* in the same way as [-count] nouns which denote substances (e.g. *Il y a du monde dans la rue*) whereas others (like *police*) cannot, except perhaps pejoratively. Like the [+count] nouns discussed above, these nouns always take singular inflection of the verb: *La police {arrivera / \*arriveront}* (cf. English *The police {?has / have} arrived*).

### 5.2.5 Quantity nouns

A subset of collective nouns can be used in expressions of the type *une foule de manifestants, une bande de voyous, un troupeau de vaches* in essentially the same way as quantity nouns like *douzaine, kilo*, etc. (e.g. *une douzaine d'œufs, une paire de gants, un kilo de pommes*) – see 5.3.8. In such cases, it is normally the collective or quantity noun which determines the number (and gender) agreement features of other elements in the sentence, as in the examples discussed in 5.2.4: *Une bande de voyous {est arrivée / \*sont arrivés}, Un kilo de pommes {est tombé / \*sont tombées} par terre*. However there are some exceptions to this generalisation. In particular, with *la plupart* and some quantity nouns which are not accompanied by a determiner (e.g. *(bon) nombre*), agreement is determined by the quantified noun: *La plupart des invités {sont arrivés / \*est arrivé}, La plupart de ce fromage est pourri, Bon nombre d'intellectuels ont critiqué cette politique* – note that this pattern still obtains when the quantified element is implicit: *La plupart sont arrivés*. Some quantity nouns are ambivalent in this respect. For example, when phrases of the type *la moitié de N* are used as subjects, the verb must take the singular form if *N* is singular, but may be either singular or plural if *N* is plural: *La moitié de la classe aime le professeur, La moitié des étudiants aime(nt) le professeur*. The exceptional behaviour of such items can be seen as the result of a process of 'grammaticalisation' whereby the quantity noun has lost its status as an independent noun and has become part of a 'fossilised' quantifier expression on a par with *beaucoup*.[1] The effect of grammaticalisation is reflected in restrictions on the choice of determiner with the quantity nouns in question. Whereas nouns such as *paire* or *kilo* allow the full range of determiners, expressions such as *(bon) nombre* occur without the determiner and *plupart* allows only the singular definite article (*\*une plupart, \*cette plupart*) – compare its near synonym *majorité* which conserves its status as an independent noun with respect to both choice of determiner and agreement phenomena: *une majorité, cette majorité, La majorité des électeurs a voté pour Mitterrand*. Similarly, the ambivalent status of *moitié* is restricted to cases where it is accompanied by the definite article *la*; with other determiners it triggers singular agreement regardless of the plurality of the quantified noun: *Cette moitié des étudiants {a / \*ont} réussi aux examens*.

---

[1] Note that *beaucoup* itself is etymologically derived from a combination of the adjective *beau* and the noun *coup* (cf. English *a great deal*), though this etymology is probably not perceived by most French speakers.

### 5.2.6 Compound nouns

Nominal expressions such as *voiture de sport, chemise de nuit, chemin de fer, ceinture de sécurité, chateau d'eau* 'water-tower', *vin d'honneur* 'wine-reception', etc. may be plausibly analysed as compound nouns. This N + *de* + N pattern is extremely common – open a good dictionary at random and you are likely to find dozens of examples on a single page. It is also productive – new expressions are continually being formed to denote novel concepts (e.g. *délit d'initié* 'insider dealing'). Nevertheless, such expressions are fixed in the sense that once a particular locution has been coined and adopted, other (potentially valid) descriptions tend to be excluded – e.g. we do not have *\*auto de sport, \*voie de fer* (cf. *voie ferrée*) or *\*tour d'eau*. Similarly, metaphorical expressions such as *vin d'honneur* cannot be freely extended – e.g. *?cidre d'honneur* or *?pastis d'honneur* could only be used humouristically. Even in examples which are semantically transparent, we find idiosyncratic gaps in the pattern. For example, alongside *chemise de nuit* we have *tenue de soirée* to describe a man's formal evening-dress, but for a woman the appropriate term is *robe du soir* (incorporating a definite article), not *\*robe de soir(ée)*. Thus, even in fairly transparent cases, the appropriate locution must be learnt, which is presumably why they are listed in dictionaries.

Compound nouns differ from constructions in which a noun is accompanied by a complement in that the components of compounds are inseparable. For example, in noun + complement constructions, an adjective which modifies the head noun normally follows the head noun immediately: *l'absence totale de preuves* vs *?l'absence de preuves totale*; see 1.5.4. However, in the locutions under discussion, the adjective must follow the entire expression: *une voiture de sport rouge* vs *\*une voiture rouge de sport*. Similarly, the *de*-complement of a noun can often be extracted or pronominalised, as in (8), but this possibility is absolutely excluded in fixed locutions:

(8)　　a　C'est de documents secrets qu'on a ordonné le vol
　　　　b　Nous en avons constaté l'absence (de preuves)

(9)　　a　*C'est de sport que j'ai acheté une voiture
　　　　b　*Elle en portait une chemise (de nuit)

### 5.2.7 Gender

The subclassification of nouns according to grammatical gender is a problem for English-speaking students of French, perhaps because we are not sensitised to this distinction through our own language, perhaps also even because of a subconscious feeling that the attribution of gender to inanimate entities is fundamentally 'silly' and, therefore, not worth taking seriously. The traditional use of the terms 'masculine' and 'feminine' may have a lot to answer for in this respect, suggesting, as it does, the extension of natural gender to objects or concepts which do not have this biological property. A more appropriate way of looking at this question would be to treat 'gender' as a purely grammatical feature which dictates the form of certain elements which are associated with the noun in question (adjectives, some determiners, past participles and pronouns) and which happens to correlate to some extent with natural gender. Thus, the traditional terms 'masculine' and 'feminine' might profitably be replaced by '*le* nouns' and '*la* nouns', the correspondence between these two categories and the notions 'male' and 'female' being just one of the factors which determines the class to which a noun belongs.

In this connection it may be noted that the gender of nouns denoting animate beings does not always correlate with sex. For some species of animals, particularly types of livestock for which the sex of the animal has practical relevance, the sex distinction is encoded by means of separate lexical items: e.g. *bœuf* vs *vache*, *coq* vs *poule*. For some species, there is a general term which is neutral alongside more specialised terms which are used when sex is practically relevant (e.g. within the class of 'sheep' we have *un mouton* as a general, neutral term, but *un bélier* 'ram' and *une brebis* 'ewe'). For some other species, natural gender is expressed by means of inflection of a common stem: e.g. *un chat* vs *une chatte*, *un loup* vs *une louve*, *un lion* vs *une lionne*, though the masculine form is generally used when sex is immaterial. However, for many nouns denoting animals, the gender and lexical form is fixed regardless of sex: *une souris, un écureuil*.

With nouns denoting human beings, the relation between natural and grammatical gender is a more sensitive issue, since human beings (unlike mice or squirrels) are in a position to express views on how they should be referred to, but a similar pattern can be discerned. Thus we find some nouns which are neutral with regard to sex, but have a fixed grammatical gender (e.g. *personne* (fem.), *bébé* (masc.)), whereas others, like *homme* and *femme* or *oncle* and *tante*, are lexically distinguished with respect to both sex and grammatical gender. In the case of nouns which subclassify human beings according to professional or social status (or other more subjective criteria) the sex difference is often expressed by means of inflection (e.g. *un instituteur* vs *une institutrice, un(e) étudiant(e), un(e) bourgeois(e), un(e) idiot(e)*), the masculine form being used in cases where sex is not significant. In some cases, the form of the noun remains invariable but sex can be indicated by the form of the determiner (*un(e) enfant, un(e) élève*), whereas many other nouns (particularly professional nouns) have a fixed gender, usually masculine (e.g. *un professeur, un médecin, un auteur*). In this connection we may note an increasing tendency, due to social pressures, to express natural gender distinctions with certain professional nouns by means of inflection (e.g. *une avocate* rather than *une femme avocat*) or by the form of the determiner (e.g. in the case of the colloquial abbreviation of *professeur*: *un(e) prof*). On the other hand, there are a few professional nouns whose grammatical gender conflicts with the sex of their typical referents (e.g. *une sentinelle* 'sentry', *un mannequin* 'fashion model').

The above observations support the view that the correlation between grammatical and natural gender is fairly tendentious. In some cases, the form of a noun may provide some clue as to its gender, though such clues amount to little more than tendencies, except with certain derivational suffixes (e.g. *-isme* is systematically a masculine suffix, whereas *-tion* is feminine). These generalisations or tendencies will not be reviewed here since they can be found in most good reference grammars. By and large, grammatical gender is a covert feature in the sense that it manifests itself in the form of elements which accompany the noun rather than in the form of the noun itself. A practical hint for those who have difficulty with grammatical gender is to memorise nouns as part of an expression containing elements which show an overt gender distinction (e.g. certain determiners and adjectives). Since our main concern is syntax, rather than properties of lexical items, the subsequent discussion of gender will be confined to the contexts within which this feature (along with number features) is transmitted to other elements.

### 5.3 The determiner system

#### 5.3.1 Are determiners obligatory?

In English, plural nouns and singular [-count] nouns can occur without a determiner:

(10)      a    Marie likes {vegetables / wine}
          b    Marie bought {vegetables / wine}

In corresponding French examples, we must use either the definite article or *du, de la, des*, which are provisionally taken to be determiners of some sort:

(11)      a    Marie aime {les légumes / le vin}
          b    Marie a acheté {des légumes / du vin}

On the basis of these examples, let us make the following provisional generalisation:

Provisional hypothesis:
*in French, all NPs must contain a determiner.*

This generalisation is clearly wrong in cases like the following:

          I    certain types of proper nouns (names of persons or towns) – see
               5.2.1;

II    nouns denoting professions, etc., in constructions with *être*: *Pierre est professeur*;

III   numerous expressions of a semi-idiomatic nature: e.g. *avoir peur, rendre hommage, faire attention; avec soin, par exemple, à pied.*

Nevertheless, cases I and II are consistent with the characterisation of determiners as items which convert a description of a class into a referential expression. Proper nouns (case I) are referential expressions in their own right and so do not need to be 'converted' by means of a determiner, whereas expressions like *professeur* (case II) seem to function as 'descriptions' of the subject entity rather than as referential expressions; see 2.5.1. Thus the generalisation should be taken as valid only for referential NPs whose head noun is descriptive. Cases of type III are genuine exceptions, but they are essentially idiosyncratic – unlike the English cases in (10) they do not form a regular predictable pattern (see 5.3.3).

In later sections (see 5.4.4–5.4.9) the provisional hypothesis will be revised in ways which make French look rather more like English than the remarks concerning (10) and (11) above would suggest. For the moment, this hypothesis will be taken as a basis for discussion.

### 5.3.2  Appositive NPs

NPs typically lack a determiner when they are used in **apposition** to another NP (typically a proper name) to provide further information about the referent:

(12)      a    Marie Dupont, directrice de l'institut, nous a confirmé que ...
          b    Emile Zola, écrivain célèbre du dix-neuvième siècle, a habité
               dans cette maison

In cases like (12a), where the description applies only to one individual, the definite article can be included (*Marie Dupont, la directrice de l'institut*), though, all things being equal, it is usually omitted. The presence or absence of the article may carry a nuance of meaning. Without the article, as in (12a), the appositive expression states a property of the referent (her professional status in this case), whereas inclusion of the article provides an alternative description whereby the addressee may be able to identify the referent more easily. A clearer example of this type is (13), which would be appropriate in a context where the addressee knows Jean-Luc but does not know his mother's name – omission of the article would be odd in this case:

(13)      Suzanne Legros, la mère de Jean-Luc, est venue à l'école

The definite article is required when the appositive NP contains a superlative expression:

(14)     Frédéric Dubois, le candidat le mieux placé, a déclaré que. . .

In cases like (12b), where the appositive expression could apply to more than one individual, the indefinite article is not normally used (*? Emile Zola, un écrivain du dix-neuvième siècle*, is condemned as an anglicism). By the same token, the determiner is usually absent in the complements of *en tant que* and *comme* as used in the following examples:

(15)     a    En tant que directrice de l'institut, Marie Dupont nous a
              confirmé que. . .
         b    Comme introduction à la discipline, ce livre est excellent

Again, the determinerless expressions in (15) do not have a referential function, but focus on some property or aspect of the entities identified by *Marie Dupont* and *ce livre*. In this respect, the use of *comme* in (15b) can be contrasted with that in (16) where *comme* expresses a comparison between different entities and where a determiner is required:

(16)     a    Jules se comporte comme un tyran
         b    Henri parle comme le patron

The absence of a determiner in appositive NPs is broadly consistent with the pattern outlined in 5.3.1. When these NPs describe a property, as in (12) and (15), they normally lack a determiner (like the complement in examples like *Marie est directrice de l'institut*), but they require a determiner when they serve to identify a particular individual, as in (13).

### 5.3.3   Other determinerless NPs

There are a great many expressions in which a 'bare' noun occurs after a verb (sometimes with another complement): e.g. *rendre hommage (à quelqu'un)*, *porter secours*, *avoir faim*, *mettre fin (à quelque chose)*, *plier bagage*, *donner lieu (à quelque chose)*, etc. There are no overall restrictions on the types of nouns found in such expressions, which can be abstract or concrete (though usually with a metaphorical interpretation in the latter case), [+count] or [-count], though typically the noun occurs in the singular form – *plier bagage* is interesting in both respects since it has a metaphorical interpretation ('pack up and go') and *bagages* is normally a 'pluralia tantum' noun (see 5.2.3). By and large, expressions of this type seem to be fossilised vestiges from a stage in the history of French when nouns could occur more freely without a determiner. In Modern French, a given noun can only be used without a determiner when it occurs with a particular verb, and replacement of either element by a near-synonym results in unacceptability, e.g. we have *porter secours* but *{prêter / donner} assistance*, while no locution of this type is available for the synonym *aide* (*{*porter / *prêter / *donner} aide*). Moreover, in many cases, the noun cannot be modified by an adjective: *\*On a rendu hommage sincère au roi.* These observations suggest that such locutions are fixed idioms and that the absence of the determiner cannot be predicted by general syntactic or semantic principles.

Examples where 'bare' nouns follow a preposition show similar idiosyncracies: *pour cause* (vs *\*pour raison*), *sur mer* (vs *\*sur lac*), *par hasard, sur demande, en retard*, etc. Nevertheless, with some prepositions a regular pattern can be discerned – notably with *de* and *sans* (see 5.4.8–5.4.9). For discussion of cases involving *en*, see 8.6.1–8.6.7.

### 5.3.4 Determiners vs prenominal adjectives

In an example like *la petite chaise*, *la* is clearly a determiner while *petite* is an adjective – *petite* forms part of the description of a class, whereas the addition of *la* converts this description into a referential expression. This difference in function can be represented in terms of the structures proposed in 1.4.1:

(17)

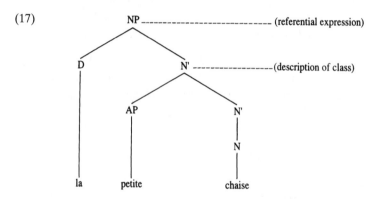

This distinction is also confirmed by the hypothesis presented in 5.3.1. Adding *la* to the noun creates a complete referential NP (*J'ai acheté la chaise*), but merely adding *petite* does not (*\*J'ai acheté petite chaise*). More generally, the hypothesis in 5.3.1 provides the following test which we can use to distinguish determiners from prenominal adjectives in less evident cases:

*If the result of placing an item* x *before a common noun is a complete referential NP (e.g. which can be used freely as a subject or direct object),* x *is a determiner. If the resulting expression is not a complete NP,* x *is an adjective.*

Some traditional grammarians classify demonstratives (*ce, cette, ces*) and possessives (*mon, ton, son*, etc.) as types of adjective, a classification based largely on the syntax of Latin. However, for French (and English), the test above shows clearly that these items are determiners: *J'ai lu {ce / son} livre.* Note also that these items can occur with adjectives like *petit*, but cannot combine with each other or with the definite article: *{ce / son} petit livre*, *\*ce ton livre*, *\*le mon livre*. These facts are consistent with the following generalisation:

*No NP can contain more than one determiner.*

The items *même, autre* and *seul* are semantically similar to determiners – they provide information about how the referent of the expression is to be identified rather than describing a class. Nevertheless, they function as adjectives according to our criteria – they can and must occur with a determiner in order to yield a complete NP:

(18)      a  \*J'ai constaté même(s) problème(s)

         b  J'ai constaté ce(s) même(s) problème(s)

(19)      a  \*J'ai emprunté autre(s) voiture(s)

         b  J'ai emprunté leur(s) autre(s) voiture(s)

(20)      a  \*J'ai lu seul(s) livre(s) (que vous m'avez donné(s))

         b  J'ai lu le(s) seul(s) livre(s) (que vous m'avez donné(s))

The items *un, quelques, plusieurs* and the numerals can be classified as determiners on the grounds that they yield a referential expression, as shown in the following examples, which are ungrammatical if the items in question are omitted:

(21)      a  J'ai lu un livre

         b  J'ai chanté {quelques / plusieurs / trois} chansons

However, some of the items in (21) (*quelques* and the plural numerals) can co-occur with another determiner:

(22)      a  J'ai lu les quelques livres que vous m'avez donnés

         b  J'ai chanté ces trois chansons

This contradiction can be resolved by classifying *quelques* and the plural numerals as both determiners and adjectives, while *un* and *plusieurs* function exclusively as determiners and the items in (18)–(20) are solely adjectives. Another example of categorial ambivalence is the item *certain* which functions exclusively as a determiner in its plural form (*J'ai lu {certains livres / \*les certains livres}*) but only as an adjective in the singular, usually with the determiner *un* (*J'ai lu {\*certain livre / un certain livre}*).

### 5.3.5 Definiteness and generic reference

In the discussion so far, it has been assumed that NPs introduced by definite determiners refer to specific entities which the addressee is expected to identify on the basis of the description provided by the N'. This assumption must be relaxed somewhat to accommodate examples like (23):

(23)     Je suis entré dans un café pour prendre l'apéritif. Ayant faim, j'ai regardé la carte. J'ai appelé le garçon plusieurs fois, mais enfin je suis parti sans payer l'addition.

Here, the addressee is not expected to be able to identify the referents of the definite NPs (*l'apéritif, la carte, le garçon* and *l'addition*) in the 'real world', nor do these NPs refer to entities which have been introduced earlier in the discourse – it would be inappropriate for the hearer to interrupt the story by asking questions like *Quelle carte?* or *Quel garçon?* Rather, the context is such that one can construct appropriate unique referents for these NPs (e.g. 'the menu on the table where I was sitting', 'the waiter who served me'). In English, the definite article can be used in the same way, though not in cases like *l'apéritif* where English would require the indefinite article.

A more radical departure from the earlier characterisation involves **generic** uses of the definite article, where the definite NP does not refer to a particular entity described by the N' but to the whole class of entities which satisfy this description. In French, as in English, the definite article can be used generically with singular [+count] nouns, as in (24):

(24)     a   Le lion est un carnivore
         b   L'article se place devant le nom

This generic use of the definite article is found predominantly in statements of a law-like nature. More commonly, generic reference is expressed in French by the use of the definite article with a plural or [-count] noun, whereas in corresponding English examples, the noun occurs without a determiner:

(25)     a   Pierre aime le vin
         b   Le café m'empêche de dormir
         c   Les femmes apprécient les fleurs
         d   Les Français se méfient des Anglais

In order to obtain a generic interpretation, the verb and tense form must express a protracted state or habitual event. In the following examples, where the verb indicates a single event, the NPs must identify specific entities – e.g. in (a) the glass of wine which was offered, in (b) the cup of coffee which I drank, in (c) particular sets

213

of women and flowers and in (d) perhaps two football teams (or groups of supporters!):

(26)    a   Pierre a bu le vin
           b   Le café m'a empêché de dormir
           c   Les femmes ont arrangé les fleurs
           d   Les Français ont battu les Anglais

One way of construing this evidence is that definiteness or specificity of reference is not an intrinsic semantic property of the so-called 'definite articles' but is rather a pragmatic effect induced by the temporal or aspectual properties of the verb, at least with plural and [-count] nouns. Thus, if the sentence denotes a single event, a definite interpretation is induced, whereas a stative or habitual interpretation of the sentence favours a generic interpretation where the NP refers to the entire class described by the N'.

    As in English, the indefinite article (*un(e)*) can also indicate a generic interpretation when the verb denotes a state or habitual event:

    (27)   a   Un bon étudiant prend toujours des notes
              b   Un caribou ressemble à un cerf

    In colloquial speech, a dislocated construction with *ça* is often used to make the generic interpretation clear: *Un bon étudiant, ça prend toujours des notes* (see 6.4.3).

In French there is a tendency to use a demonstrative to indicate definiteness in some cases where the definite article is permissible in English, particularly when the semantic content of the N' is not precise enough to identify the intended referent explicitly. For example, although (26b) above is grammatical with a definite interpretation for *le café*, it would be more natural to use *ce café* or *le café que j'ai bu avant de me coucher*, though much would depend on the preceding context. The preference for demonstratives is particularly striking in cases where a definite NP is used to refer back to some previously mentioned entity in a manner similar to a pronoun. For example, in a conversation about some unpopular individual, one might remark in English *I detest the man*, but in French one would have to say *Je déteste cet homme* (the use of *l'homme* here would imply hatred of mankind as a whole). Note, however, that demonstratives could not be substituted for the definite articles in (23).

    Demonstrative determiners provide clear cues as to how the referent should be identified, pointing (as it were) either to an antecedent within the discourse (as in our example *Je déteste cet homme*) or to an entity in the physical surroundings (e.g. *Passez-moi ce stylo!*), and tend to be preferred over definite articles when such cues are necessary. On the other hand, definite articles appear to be used most typ-

ically in cases where the descriptive content restricts the range of potential referents to a point where it is virtually coextensive with the intended referent (e.g. *le
café que j'ai bu avant de me coucher, les livres qui sont au programme*) or where
the addressee is invited to construct a suitable referent by pragmatic means (as in
(23)). Thus, even in non-generic uses, the definite article does not provide a strictly
linguistic cue to reference beyond the information expressed in the N' and the
pragmatic resources of the interlocutors.

Possessive determiners are semantically definite in the same way as demonstratives. In a case like *ma chaise*, the particular chair is identified in terms of some
appropriate relation with 'me' (not necessarily strict possession – it could be the
chair that I am sitting on, the chair I made, etc.). The same holds for third-person
forms, with the added requirement that the addressee must be able to identify the
referent of the possessive determiner – e.g. a phrase like *son livre* presupposes
that the addressee knows who *son* refers to and can use this information to identify a particular book through a pragmatically salient relation (possession, author-
ship, etc.). (For possessive uses of the definite article, e.g. with body-part nouns, see
6.8.3–6.8.5).

As a terminological convention, the traditional term 'definite article' will be
used to refer to the forms *le*, *la* and *les* (regardless of their actual interpretation) while 'definite determiner' will be used for items (including demonstratives and possessives as well as definite articles) which have a definite
interpretation.

### 5.3.6 Indefinite quantifiers

The term **indefinite quantifier** is used here to denote a subclass of determiners
exemplified by *un*, *quelques*, *plusieurs*, *aucun* and the cardinal numerals (*deux,
trois*, etc.). These items are indefinite in the sense that they do not presuppose any
ability on the part of the addressee to identify the referents of the NPs which they
introduce. They are called 'quantifiers' because they indicate the quantity of entities referred to (rather vaguely in the case of *quelques* and *plusieurs*). These items
qualify as determiners according to our criteria, though some of them can also
function as adjectives (see 5.3.4).

Alongside the items mentioned above, there are others which have a similar
function except that they require *de* before the following N' (e.g. *beaucoup, peu,
tant, assez, trop, davantage*):

(28)     a   Gaston a bu {beaucoup / peu / tant / . . .} de vin
         b   Marie a lu {beaucoup / peu / tant / . . .} de livres

These items are sometimes classified as adverbs (partly because of examples like
*Pierre travaille {beaucoup / peu / . . .}* where they modify the verb, see 7.5.4).

215

However, there is no obvious reason why these items should not be analysed as determiners in (28), on a par with *un, quelques*, etc., in (29):

(29)    a  Marie a lu un livre

          b  Jules n'a vu aucun film

          c  Henri a acheté {plusieurs / quelques / trois} journaux

The presence or absence of *de* after indefinite quantifiers follows a systematic pattern. All the items which take de can occur with both a singular [-count] noun, as in (28a) and a plural noun, as in (28b), but those which do not take *de* require either a singular noun (*un, aucun*) or a plural noun (*plusieurs, quelques*, etc.).[2] This generalisation can be extended further. Definite articles, demonstratives and possessives can be used with both singular and plural nouns, but since they inflect for number, the individual forms (e.g. *le/la* vs *les*) are restricted in the same way as *un, plusieurs*, etc. Using the term **number concord** to cover both semantic restrictions (as with *plusieurs* and the numerals) and inflectional agreement, the following generalisation can be stated:

**The number concord generalisation:**
*determiners are followed directly by an N' (i.e. without de) if and only if they show 'number concord' with the noun.*

The term **quantitative** will be used to refer to constructions of the types in (28) and (29) where the NP denotes a certain quantity of the entity or substance described by the noun. Quantitative NPs of the type in (29) can be analysed straightforwardly as NPs consisting of a determiner and an N':

(30)    a  $[_{NP} [_D$ un$] [_{N'}$ livre$]]$

          b  $[_{NP} [_D$ plusieurs$] [_{N'}$ journaux$]]$

Let us assume that the constructions in (28) have essentially the same structure except that *de* is adjoined to the N':

(31)    a  $[_{NP} [_D$ beaucoup$] [_{N'}$ de $[_{N'}$ vin$]]]$

          b  $[_{NP} [_D$ tant$] [_{N'}$ de $[_{N'}$ livres$]]]$

This analysis captures the idea that *vin* and *livres* are the head nouns in these NPs, which would be obscured if, for instance, we analysed the *de* phrases as PPs embedded within the NP. The function of *de* in these and other constructions will be reviewed again in 5.4.

---

[2] Possibly the only exception to this generalisation is the literary item *force*, which can quantify a singular or plural noun, but does not take *de*: †*force courage* 'much courage', †*force gens* 'many people'.

### 5.3.7 Partitive constructions

Most of the indefinite quantifiers discussed in 5.3.6. can be used in constructions like (32), where the noun is introduced by a definite determiner:

(32)     a   Pierre a lu {un / trois / plusieurs / beaucoup / ...} de mes livres
         b   Gaston a bu {beaucoup / peu / trop / assez / ...} de ce vin

An exception is *quelques* which assumes the form *quelques-un(e)s* in this construction (see 5.5.5 for a similar alternation between *chaque* and *chacun*):

(33)     Pierre a lu quelques-uns de ces livres

Semantically, these constructions differ from quantitative constructions in that they do not simply refer to a quantity of books or wine, but they designate a part of a specific set of books or instance of wine. For this reason, we refer to these as **partitive** constructions.[3]

In partitive constructions, *de* must be used after all indefinite quantifiers, including those which do not take *de* in quantitative constructions, just as *of* must be used in their English counterparts. Ostensibly, these constructions contradict our claim in 5.3.4 that no NP can contain more than one determiner – in (32) we have a definite determiner in addition to the indefinite quantifier. This problem can be avoided by postulating that partitive NPs consist of two NPs, one embedded inside the other. Thus, in (32a) *mes livres* is a definite NP denoting a specific set of books, which is embedded in the larger NP which describes the part of this set which Pierre read, roughly as in (34):

(34)     Pierre a lu $[_{NP}$ $[_{D}$ {un / beaucoup}] de $[_{NP}$ $[_{D}$ mes] $[_{N'}$ livres]]]]

For present purposes, let us assume that the higher NP is expanded by the rule in (35) and that the head of the embedded NP also acts as the head of the whole expression:

(35)     NP → D + NP

As in the case of quantitative constructions, we assume that *de* does not head a PP but is adjoined to the following NP:

(36)     a   $[_{NP}$ $[_{D}$ un] $[_{NP}$ de $[_{NP}$ $[_{D}$ mes] $[_{N'}$ livres]]]]]
         b   $[_{NP}$ $[_{D}$ beaucoup] $[_{NP}$ de $[_{NP}$ $[_{D}$ ce] $[_{N'}$ vin]]]]]

---

[3] The term 'partitive' is used here only for NPs like (32) and (33) which refer to a part of a specific set. Some grammarians use this term for a wider range of indefinite NPs, particularly those introduced by *du*, *de la* and *des*.

Within this approach, determiners can be subclassified according to whether they select an NP or an N'. Thus, definite determiners and *quelques* select only N', *quelques-uns* selects only NP, whereas most indefinite quantifiers can select either NP or N'.

An important restriction on partitive constructions is that the embedded NP must be definite; phrases like the following are ungrammatical, even though one can imagine plausible interpretations for them:

(37)     a   *plusieurs de cent livres
         b   *beaucoup d'un litre de vin
         c   *trois de plusieurs pommes

Consequently, although phrases like *les étudiants* and *les livres* can refer to students or books in general in some contexts (see 5.3.5), the NPs in (38) can only mean 'many/few of a specific set of students/books':

(38)     a   Beaucoup des étudiants sont intelligents
         b   Peu des livres m'intéressent

To express the meanings 'many students' or 'few books', we must use the quantitative construction: *beaucoup d'étudiants, peu de livres*. For the reasons discussed in 5.3.5, partitive constructions with the definite article are often more acceptable when the descriptive content is sufficiently precise to delimit a well-defined set without recourse to contextual cues – e.g. (39) is rather more natural than (38b):

(39)     Peu des livres que le professeur a recommandés m'intéressent

In English, indefinite quantifiers can often be used without the quantified element when this is given by the context: e.g. when speaking of guests, one can say *Several arrived late, I invited many*, etc. In French, the quantified element must be represented by the clitic *en* when the NP is a direct object, but the quantifier can be used alone in other structural positions (see 6.6.4 for further discussion):

(40)     a   J'en ai invité {plusieurs / beaucoup / quelques-uns}
         b   {Plusieurs / beaucoup / quelques-uns} sont arrivés en retard
         c   J'ai dansé avec {plusieurs / beaucoup / quelques-uns}

### 5.3.8   Constructions with quantity and collective nouns

Expressions with quantity nouns like *un kilo, un litre, une douzaine, un million* can be used to form quantitative and partitive NPs in much the same way as indefinite quantifiers:

(41)     un kilo de pommes, un litre de vin, une douzaine d'œufs, un million
         de francs,...

(42)        un kilo de ces pommes, un litre de ton vin, une douzaine de ces
            œufs, un million des électeurs,...

Although expressions like *un kilo* are NPs, not determiners, they seem to have the same function as indefinite quantifiers. Let us therefore assume that the constructions in (41)–(42) have the same syntactic structures as the quantitative and partitive NPs discussed in 5.3.6–5.3.7, except that the determiner position is occupied by a quantity NP:

(43)        $[_{NP} [_{NP}$ un kilo$] [_{N'}$ de $[_{N'}$ pommes$]]]$

(44)        $[_{NP} [_{NP}$ un kilo$] [_{NP}$ de $[_{NP}$ ces pommes$]]]$

Note, however, that these expressions do not conform to the 'number concord' generalisation proposed in 5.3.6. Although nouns like *kilo* and *litre* can occur with both singular [-count] nouns and plural nouns, items like *douzaine* and *million* (like *plusieurs* and the numerals) can only occur with plural nouns, yet they require *de* in the quantitative construction (in contrast to English: *a dozen (*of) eggs*, *a million (*of) francs*). Similarly, *un peu* can only occur with singular [-count] nouns, but it requires *de*: *un peu de pain*, **un peu de pommes* (cf. English *a little (*of) bread*). This matter will be looked at again in 5.4.1.

In 5.2.4 it was pointed out that some collective nouns can be used in constructions similar to (41):

(45)        un troupeau de vaches, une bande de voyous, une équipe de
            spécialistes,...

Intuitively, however, we know that expressions like *un troupeau* are not analogous to determiners in the manner proposed above for quantity NPs. Rather, a noun like *troupeau* denotes a physical entity whose composition is described by the following *de* phrase. This can be represented syntactically by treating the collective noun as the head of the NP and the *de* phrase as its complement:

(46)        $[_{NP} [_{D}$ un$] [_{N'} [_{N}$ troupeau$] [_{PP}$ de vaches$]]]$

This intuitive difference is supported by syntactic evidence. Alongside cases like (45) we can construct examples which look like partitive constructions: *un troupeau de ces vaches*. However, in sharp contrast to genuine partitive constructions (see 5.3.7, examples in (37)), the embedded NP in such cases can be indefinite:

(47)        un troupeau de quelques vaches, une bande de trente voyous, une
            équipe de plusieurs spécialistes

Also, with collective nouns, we can conjoin *de* phrases with and without determiners:

(48)    un troupeau de moutons et de quelques agneaux, une équipe de
        spécialistes et de leurs assistants

However, partitive and quantitative constructions cannot be conjoined in this
way:

(49)    *beaucoup de pommes et de ces poires, *une douzaine de
        spécialistes et de leurs assistants

The ungrammaticality of (49) follows from the structures which have been proposed along with a general condition which only allows phrases of the same syntactic category to be conjoined. According to the earlier assumptions, the
examples in (49) would involve conjunction of an N' (e.g. *de pommes*) with an NP
(*de ces poires*). However, the examples in (48) are consistent with this condition if
the *de* phrases are PPs functioning as complements of the collective noun, as proposed in (46).[4]

### 5.4    Constructions with 'de'
#### 5.4.1    'De' as a Case marker

In 1.5.6, the function of *de* in phrases like (50) was characterised in terms of a need
to assign Case to the NP *ces documents*:

(50)    [$_{NP}$ la destruction de [$_{NP}$ ces documents]]

In the corresponding sentence (51), the verb *détruire* can assign Accusative Case
to this NP:

(51)    On va détruire ces documents

However, since nouns cannot assign Case features, a preposition (typically *de*)
must be inserted to assign Case to the complement of the noun in (50). Given the
structural analysis proposed in 5.3.8 for constructions with collective nouns, the
same account will hold for *de* in (52):

(52)    J'ai vu [$_{NP}$ un troupeau de [$_{NP}$ (quelques) vaches]]

This account can be adapted for partitive constructions. Suppose that a partitive
NP occurs as the direct object of a verb, as in (53):

(53)    J'ai lu [$_{NP}$ beaucoup de [$_{NP}$ ces livres]]

---

[4] Alternatively, the conjoined complements in (48) might be analysed as NPs with *de* adjoined
to them. The practice here is to treat *de* as a genuine preposition (heading a PP) whenever it
introduces a complement of some item, but as an 'adjoined particle' when it introduces an
expression containing the head of the larger NP.

The entire NP will receive Accusative Case from the verb, in the same way as *ces documents* in (51), but within this NP there is another NP (*ces livres*) which requires a Case feature. Consequently, *de* is inserted to assign Case to the embedded NP.

Suppose now that nouns require a Case feature, as well as NPs (as indeed they do in languages like Latin, German or Old English, where the form of the noun depends on the function of the NP to which it belongs). In an example like (54), we can simply assume that the noun *livre* 'inherits' the Case feature which is assigned to the NP *ces livres* (i.e. Accusative):

(54)      J'ai lu [$_{NP}$ ces livres]

However, suppose that in some types of NP, this **Case-inheritance** process is blocked for some reason. What we might expect to find in such instances is that the noun must get its Case in some other way (e.g. from *de*). This is exactly what we find in quantitative NPs with determiners like *beaucoup*, *trop*, etc. – i.e. with determiners which do not show 'number concord' (see 5.3.6):

(55)      J'ai lu [$_{NP}$ beaucoup de livres]

Thus, the occurrence of *de* in these constructions can be accounted for by postulating the following condition on Case-inheritance:

**Case-inheritance:**
*a noun can inherit the Case of the NP which it heads only if there is number concord between the noun and the determiner.*

This condition is satisfied in (54), where *ces* agrees in number with *livres*, and in (56), where number concord is a semantic property of *trois*, so *livres* can inherit the Accusative Case assigned to the NP:

(56)      J'ai lu [$_{NP}$ trois livres]

However, the absence of number concord in (55) prevents Case-inheritance, so *de* is inserted to assign Case to the noun, just as it assigns Case to the embedded NP in (50), (52) and (53).

In 5.3.8 it was pointed out that quantity nouns like *douzaine* require *de* in quantitative constructions even though they show number concord (of the semantic type):

(57)      J'ai lu [$_{NP}$ une douzaine de livres]

The important difference between (56) and (57) is that *trois* is a determiner, but *douzaine* is a noun and, as such, requires a Case feature of its own. In other words, in (57) the direct object contains two NPs only one of which can inherit the

221

Accusative Case feature. Leaving details aside, it seems that the quantity noun *douzaine* somehow 'usurps' this feature, with the result that *livres* must be case-marked independently by *de*, just as in (55).

### 5.4.2 'Un espèce de cochon'

The bracketted NPs in (58) raise an interesting problem:

(58)      a   Pierre est [un espèce de cochon]
         b   Je ne peux pas lire [ce putain de livre]

Normally, *espèce* and *putain* are feminine, but here they are introduced by a masculine form of the determiner, agreeing with *cochon* and *livre*. Nouns like *espèce* and *putain* in this construction are sometimes called **epithet** nouns – these are nouns which convey an attitude towards the person or thing referred to (usually derogatory, as in (58), but not always: cf. *un ange d'enfant* 'an angel of a child'). A similar effect can be achieved by means of certain adjectives (see 7.2.5), as in (59) (cf. *a real pig, this {dratted / blasted} book*):

(59)      a   Pierre est un {vrai / sale} cochon
         b   Je ne peux pas lire ce maudit livre

The epithet use of *espèce* in (58a) can be contrasted with its literal use ('type of') in (60), where we have normal agreement of the determiner:

(60)      Le sanglier est une espèce de cochon

In (60), *de cochon* can be analysed as a complement of *espèce*, which functions as the head of the whole NP:

(61)      [$_{NP}$ [$_D$ une] [$_{N'}$ espèce [$_{PP}$ de cochon]]]

Given the similarity between (58) and (59), it is proposed that *espèce* and *putain* act as modifiers of the following noun, in the same way as the adjectives in (59). Thus, at an abstract level, the NPs in (58a) and (59a) can be represented as in (62):

(62)

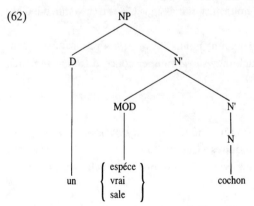

According to (62), *cochon* is the head of the whole NP, thus accounting for the masculine form of the determiner. Note now that *espèce*, being a noun, must bear a Case feature. Let us suppose that it 'usurps' the Case which is assigned to the whole NP in much the same way as *douzaine* in example (57) in 5.4.1. As a result, *de* must be inserted to assign Case to the head noun *cochon*, thus giving the grammatical forms in (58).

As an epithet noun, *espèce* is rather atypical. It can only be used to modify another epithet noun like *cochon* (cf. *?un espèce de professeur*, which is odd unless *professeur* is taken to be a term of abuse). Other epithets can be used to modify 'normal' nouns, like *putain* in (58b): e.g. *un imbécile de professeur, ce fripon de valet* 'that scoundrel of a servant', etc. They can also be used to modify proper nouns: *ce fripon de Jacques* (note that *de* is required; cf. English *that scoundrel Jacques*).

### 5.4.3  *'Quelque-chose d'intéressant'*
Some types of pronouns can be modified by adjectives, but in such cases the adjective must be introduced by *de*:

(63)     a   Marie a lu quelque-chose d'intéressant
         b   Henri a recontré quelqu'un de très intelligent
         c   Je ne fais rien de spécial
         d   Luc n'a vu personne d'autre
         e   Tu vas faire quoi d'autre?

Possibly this use of *de* can be assimilated to those discussed in the preceding sections.

In French, adjectives normally agree in number and gender with the modified noun. However, pronouns of the type in (63) do not have number and gender features in the way that common nouns do – they do not show a singular–plural alternation and there is no gender variation within the class (they are all treated as masculine, even though *quelque-chose* and *personne* are derived from feminine nouns). In so far as number–gender agreement signals the link between adjective and noun, we may think of *de* as an alternative means of indicating this link when the features relevant to agreement are absent. Moreover, in languages with overt Case inflection, adjectives must agree in Case as well as number and gender – i.e. they inherit the Case of the noun. Suppose now that the same is true in French, though the Case features are not overt. Given the suggestion in 5.4.1 that Case-inheritance is dependent on agreement relations (e.g. number concord), the absence of number–gender agreement in (63) would prevent the adjective from inheriting the Case of the pronoun. From this perspective, the 'link-indicating' function of *de* can be seen as an extension of its more general casemarking function.

### *5.4.4   Indefinite 'du', 'de la' and 'des'*

With plural and [-count] nouns, indefiniteness is typically expressed by *du*, *de la* or *des* unless some indication of quantity is required (e.g. by *beaucoup*, *peu*, etc.):

(64)    J'ai acheté {du pain / de la viande / des pommes}

In 5.3.1, these items were provisionally treated as determiners, satisfying the requirement that every NP in French must contain a determiner. A problem with this view is that, in some constructions, *de* and the definite article element appear to be independent of each other – e.g. when the noun is preceded by an adjective and in negative sentences, *de* occurs without the article: *J'ai lu d'autres livres*, *Je n'ai pas acheté de pain*. These and other related constructions will be discussed in 5.4.5–5.4.9. For the moment, they provide prima facie evidence that *du*, *de la* and *des* do not function as single, indivisible words equivalent to English *some*.

For English constructions like *I bought {bread / apples}*, it is widely assumed that the determiner position is not absent, but is simply left empty, as in (65):

(65)    I bought $[_{NP} [_D \varnothing] [_{N'}$ apples]]

At the semantic level, this empty determiner expresses indefiniteness without indicating quantity; i.e. it is neutral with respect to the distinctions expressed by overt quantifiers such as *many* or *few*. From the ungrammaticality of such constructions in French we might conclude that French lacks this empty determiner:

(66)    *J'ai acheté $[_{NP} [_D \varnothing] [_{N'}$ pommes]]

The hypothesis which will be developed in this section is that this conclusion is inaccurate. French does have an empty determiner, but this element takes an NP rather than an N', like *beaucoup*, etc., in partitive constructions. Moreover, for the reasons discussed in 5.4.1, the embedded NP must be casemarked by means of *de*:

(67)    J'ai acheté $[_{NP} [_D \varnothing]$ de $[_{NP}$ les pommes]]

A slight difficulty with this analysis is that while the structure (67) resembles the partitive construction in (68), the sentence which it represents can only have a quantitative interpretation – i.e. *des pommes* is semantically analogous to *beaucoup de pommes* 'many apples', not to *beaucoup des pommes* 'many of the apples':

(68)    J'ai acheté $[_{NP} [_D$ beaucoup] de $[_{NP}$ les pommes]]

This problem is partially overcome by the observation in 5.3.5 that the definite article with [-count] and plural nouns can have a generic interpretation, as in *J'aime les pommes*, whereby *les pommes*: refers to the entire class described by the noun *pommes*. Thus, if *les* in structure (67) has this generic value, we can derive the correct interpretation for *des pommes* 'an unspecified quantity of apples in general'. In order to exclude the partitive reading for (67) ('some of the apples'), the following restriction is postulated:[5]

*[$_D$ Ø] can only quantify over an open-ended class (as opposed to a particular set)*

This pattern is not entirely unique to the empty determiner. The item *bien* can be used with a meaning similar to *beaucoup* in what look like partitive constructions:

(69)     J'ai vu bien {des / *de} choses

However, like the examples in (64), such sentences require a quantitative interpretation 'I have seen many things' (not 'many of the things').

The structural analysis proposed in (67) is supported by some apparently puzzling facts concerning the clitic pronoun *en*. In genuine quantitative and partitive constructions, *en* can replace the quantified expression, which can be specified as a dislocated element[6] (indicated in parentheses in (70)):

(70)     a   J'en ai acheté plusieurs, (de pommes)
         b   J'en ai mangé beaucoup, (de pain)
         c   J'en ai lu un, (de ces livres)

However, *en* cannot replace the entire indefinite NP – i.e. in (71), *en* cannot be interpreted as corresponding to the expression in parentheses:

(71)     a   *J'en ai acheté, (plusieurs pommes)
         b   *J'en ai mangé, (beaucoup de pain)
         c   *J'en ai lu, (un de ces livres)

With *du, de la* and *des*, we find exactly the opposite pattern – *en* cannot replace the sequence following *des*, etc., but it can replace the entire NP:

(72)     a   *J'en ai acheté des, (de pommes)
         b   *J'en ai mangé du, (de pain)

(73)     a   J'en ai acheté, (des pommes)
         b   J'en ai mangé, (du pain)

---

[5] This restriction is not absolute. With certain 'ingestive' verbs (notably *manger* and *boire*) NPs with *de* can have a genuine partitive interpretation: *Je mangerai de ta viande, Ils ont bu de mon vin* (cf. similar constructions in archaic English style: *I will eat of your meat, They drank of my wine*).

[6] Note that a dislocated N' must be introduced by *de* even with determiners like *plusieurs*: *\*J'en ai acheté plusieurs, livres*. This is consistent with the analysis in 5.4.1 if we assume that the head noun cannot inherit the Case of the NP to which it belongs when it is dislocated.

This pattern is puzzling only if we treat *des*, etc., as determiners on a par with *un* or *plusieurs*. According to the analysis in (67), the examples in (73) are structurally identical to (70c), as shown in (74) where the dash indicates the position from which *en* is moved:

(74)    a    J'en ai lu [$_{NP}$ [$_D$ un] [$_{NP}$ — ]]
        b    J'en ai acheté [$_{NP}$ [$_D$ ∅] [$_{NP}$ — ]]

Similarly, the ungrammatical examples in (72) are parallel to *\*J'en ai acheté plusieurs des, (de pommes)* and *\*J'en ai mangé beaucoup du, (de pain)*.

### 5.4.5  'De' in negative sentences
In negative sentences, the direct object is typically introduced by *de* alone when it is indefinite:

(75)    a    Je n'ai pas lu de romans cette semaine
        b    Frank ne mange jamais de viande
        c    L'enfant n'a offert de bonbons à personne

This construction is also possible with singular [+count] nouns:

(76)    a    Je n'ai pas de vélo
        b    Il ne porte jamais de cravate

The evidence in (76) indicates that these constructions cannot be derived simply by deleting the definite article in structures of the type proposed in 5.4.4, since singular [+count] nouns cannot occur in these structures:

(77)    a    *J'ai du vélo
        b    *Il portait de la cravate

From this evidence, we may conclude that the constructions in (75) and (76) consist of an empty determiner followed by an N′, not by an NP; e.g. (75a) has the structure (78):

(78)    Je n'ai pas lu [$_{NP}$ [$_D$ ∅] [$_{N'}$ de romans]] cette semaine

Note that the obligatory presence of *de* before the noun follows directly from the principles presented in 5.3.6 and 5.4.1. Since the empty determiner can occur with both singular and plural nouns, it does not show number concord. Consequently, the noun cannot inherit the Case of the NP and must be casemarked by *de*. In other words, these constructions have the same structural properties as quantitative constructions with *beaucoup*, except that the determiner is not overt:

(79)    J'ai lu [$_{NP}$ [$_D$ beaucoup] [$_{N'}$ de romans]] cette semaine

The structure in (78) invalidates the suggestion in 5.4.4 that the empty determiner in French takes only an NP. We must conclude that $[_D \varnothing]$ can take either an NP or an N', but with different interpretations, summarised roughly below:

*I When $[_D \varnothing]$ takes an NP, it has an indefinite interpretation similar to English* some.

*II When $[_D \varnothing]$ takes an N', it can occur only in negative sentences with an interpretation similar to English* any.

NP structures of the type in (78) have a more restricted distribution than English NPs with *any*. In particular, they cannot occur as objects of prepositions:

(80)    a    *Jules n'a pas dansé avec de filles
        b    Jules did not dance with any girls

These NPs also cannot occur in the surface subject position, but they can occur as postverbal subjects in impersonal constructions:

(81)    a    *D'invités ne sont pas encore arrivés
        b    Il n'est pas encore arrivé d'invités

NPs with *du, de la* and *des* can occur in all structural positions, except as objects of *de* (see 5.4.8).

### 5.4.6   Remote quantification

The phenomenon of **remote quantification** ('quantification à distance') is illustrated in (82), where an indefinite determiner is separated from the NP which it quantifies, occurring in the position normally occupied by adverbs:

(82)    a    Pierre a beaucoup mangé de pommes
        b    Jules a tant chanté de chansons

This phenomenon occurs with all indefinite determiners which can also be used as degree adverbs modifying a verb, as in (83) (see 7.5.4):

(83)    a    Pierre a beaucoup aimé son repas
        b    Jules a tant chanté

A plausible way of analysing the constructions in (82) is to suppose that the determiner has been moved from its normal position within the NP, as in (84):

(84)    [Pierre a  mangé $[_{NP}$ beaucoup de pommes]]

An alternative view is that *beaucoup* or *tant* are inserted directly as adverbs, which have the syntactic function of modifying the verb, but which are interpreted as indicating the 'quantity' of the direct object. According to this view, the direct objects in (82) have an empty determiner, with the same structure as the NPs in negative constructions:

(85)     [Pierre a beaucoup mangé $[_{NP}$ $[_D$ ∅] $[_{N'}$ de pommes]]]

If this analysis is correct, the condition on the use of $[_D$ ∅] with an N' must be revised as follows:

*When $[_D$ ∅] takes an N', its quantity value must be deducible from the context.*

Note that this condition would apply also to the negative examples discussed in 5.4.5. In a sentence like *Je n'ai pas lu de romans*, the quantity of novels involved (i.e. none at all) is deducible from the negative force of the sentence. As in the negative cases, the NP with $[_D$ ∅] can only occur as a direct object or postverbal subject:

(86)     Il est tant arrivé de gens
(87)     a   *De filles ont beaucoup dansé
         b   *Jules a beaucoup dansé avec de filles

### 5.4.7 *'De' with prenominal adjectives*

When a plural noun is preceded by an adjective, indefiniteness is usually expressed by *de*, though *des* is sometimes used in colloquial speech:

(88)     a   J'ai lu {de / ?des} beaux romans
         b   On a trouvé {d'autres / ?des autres} examples

With singular [-count] nouns, use of *de* alone is generally perceived as literary or even archaic, whereas the formula in (89b) is acceptable in all registers:

(89)     a   † Ils vendent de bon vin
         b   Ils vendent du bon vin

It is not clear why the presence of a prenominal adjective should favour or allow the use of *de* without a definite article to indicate indefiniteness. It may be noted that this use is possible in all structural positions in which *du*, *de la* and *des* can occur:

(90)     a   De nouveaux livres sont au programme
         b   Jules a dansé avec d'autres filles

These constructions do not appear to have any of the semantic properties of the constructions discussed in 5.4.5–5.4.6 – i.e. the quantity value of the NP cannot be deduced from other features of the sentence. It is assumed here that these constructions are derived from the structures discussed in 5.4.4, by a stylistic rule which optionally deletes *les* (and marginally *le* or *la*), as in (91):

(91)     $[_{NP} [_D \varnothing] [_{NP}$ de $[_{NP} [_D$ les] beaux romans]]]
     $\Rightarrow [_{NP} [_D \varnothing] [_{NP}$ de $[_{NP} [_D \varnothing]$ beaux romans]]]

### 5.4.8   The 'cacophony' phenomenon

An absolute restriction on indefinite NPs of the types discussed in 5.4.4–5.4.7 is that they cannot occur as complements of the preposition *de*:

(92)     a   *Pierre se méfie de des médecins
     b   *Gaston était content de du vin
     c   *Luc se souvient de de vieilles histoires
     d   *L'espion s'est emparé de des documents secrets

Some grammarians have attributed this restriction to the cacophonous effect of repeating *de*. Though the appeal to an aesthetic notion of this kind is suspect, the term **cacophony** has become widely adopted for the phenomenon illustrated in (92). Moreover, a constraint excluding repetition of the item *de* appears to be generally valid,[7] the only exceptions being cases where the second *de* is part of a proper name (e.g. *les mémoirs de De Gaulle*):

**The cacophony constraint:**
*Sentences containing the sequence . . . de de . . . are ungrammatical.*

In some cases, the complement of *de* can consist of a noun (or N') without a determiner, as in (93):

(93)     a   Cette bouteille est pleine de vin
     b   Le jardin fourmille de moustiques
     c   Nous avons déjeuné de jambon et de légumes
     d   On a privé l'enfant de bonbons
     e   On a ordonné le vol de documents secrets

Note that the item *de* in (93) is not part of the indefinite NP but is the preposition required by the governing adjective, verb or noun.

Some linguists have proposed that examples like those in (93) are derived by a rule which obligatorily deletes *des*, *du*, etc., after the preposition *de*, in order to satisfy the cacophony constraint. Thus, (93a) would be derived from the underlying structure (94) by obligatory deletion of *du*:

---

[7] Constraints of this sort are quite common in natural languages. A similar constraint prevents restrictive *ne . . . que* from modifying finite complement clauses: e.g. *Je dis seulement que . . .* but *\*Je ne dis que que . . .*

(94)    Cette bouteille est pleine [$_{PP}$ de [$_{NP}$ du vin]]

However, a major problem with this approach is that not all violations of the cacophony constraint can be rescued by this deletion process; for example, application of this process to the examples in (92) does not give an acceptable output:

(95)    a  *Pierre se méfie de médecins
        b  *Gaston était content de vin
        c  *Luc se souvient de vieilles histoires
        d  *L'espion s'est emparé de documents secrets

These facts suggest that there is some semantic restriction on the apparent use of a 'bare' N' after the preposition *de*, which cannot be easily built in to a purely mechanical deletion rule of the type envisaged above.

In view of this difficulty, let us assume that the objects of *de* in (93) are generated directly with an internal structure consisting of an empty determiner followed by an N', as shown in (96) for example (93a):

(96)    Cette bouteille est pleine [$_{PP}$ de [$_{NP}$ [$_D$ ∅] [$_{N'}$ vin]]]

Within this perspective, our task is to define the conditions under which structures of this form (where N' does not contain *de*) can occur.

The clearest cases are those where the *de* phrase functions as a complement of a verb or adjective (as in examples (93a–d)). In these cases, the possibility of the construction in (96) appears to conform to a condition of the sort suggested at the end of 5.4.6. In examples like (93a–d) the quantity value of the NP can be deduced to some extent from the semantic properties of the governing verb or adjective. Thus, in (93a) the quantity of wine must be sufficient to occupy the whole of the bottle, in (93b) the verb *fourmiller* 'to swarm' implies a large quantity of mosquitos, in (93c) we can deduce that the quantity of ham and vegetables is sufficient to constitute a meal and in (93d) the verb *priver* induces a 'none at all' interpretation in rather the same way as a negated verb (cf. *On n'a pas donné de bonbons à l'enfant*). In contrast, the verbs and adjectives in (95) provide no indication whatsoever about the quantity of doctors, wine or stories involved. It may be noted that in the acceptable examples cited above, independent quantification of the noun tends to be awkward: e.g. *?La bouteille est pleine de beaucoup de vin*, *?Le jardin fourmille de plusieurs moustiques*, etc. Similarly, whereas *du*, *de la* and *des* can usually be translated by *some* and NPs of the form *de*+noun in negative contexts can be translated by *any*, these examples do not readily allow such translations but are best rendered by a determinerless NP in English.

The situation with complements of nouns is less clear, as indeed are the judgements in some cases. Some nouns do provide clues as to the quantity value of the complement (e.g. *une foule de manifestants, l'absence de preuves, la prolifération d'armements*), but this is not the case in (93e), where the noun *vol* is analogous to the verb *s'emparer* in (95e). Possibly the difference between event-nouns and verbs in such cases can be attributed to a difference in the way in which nouns and verbs (or NPs and sentences) denote events. Whereas sentences express propositions which can be used to report events, NPs simply refer to events as part of a larger proposition. Moreover, an event-NP (unlike a corresponding sentence) has a determiner of its own which may affect the interpretation of the complement in such a way that the quantity-value of the complement is regarded as immaterial. For example, sentence (93e) might be glossed, very artificially, as 'they ordered an event of document-theft', where the reference to 'documents' contributes to the description of the type of event.

The structure proposed in (96) also raises a syntactic problem. Given that $[_D \varnothing]$ in these cases can occur with both singular and plural nouns, it should prevent the noun from inheriting the Case of the whole NP, for the reasons discussed in 5.4.1. Consequently, we might expect the noun to be casemarked by *de* as in (97):

(97)     *Cette bouteille est pleine $[_{PP}$ de $[_{NP} [_D \varnothing] [_{N'}$ de vin]]]

This is presumably ruled out by the cacophony constraint, but we must still explain how the noun gets its Case in the valid structure (96).

The solution to this problem is not clear. What seems to be going on in (96) is that when *de* is inserted as the default casemarker for the whole NP it can simultaneously casemark the head noun without being repeated. One way of implementing this idea is to suppose that *de* assigns a 'special' Case (let us call it 'Genitive') which is transmitted in a different way from Accusative or Nominative Case. Whereas Accusative and Nominative are assigned initially to the whole NP and are then passed down to certain elements under conditions of the sort envis- aged in 5.4.1–5.4.3, we postulate that Genitive Case is assigned directly to what- ever element immediately follows *de* (ignoring empty nodes), i.e. to both the NP and the noun in (96).

### 5.4.9   Complements of 'sans'

As was noted in 5.3.3, *de* is not the only preposition which can take an NP without a determiner. Most examples of this type can be regarded as fixed expressions (e.g. *à pied, par hasard, sous terre, pour cause*), but in some cases a more pro- ductive pattern can be discerned. For example, *avec* can be used with a wide range of abstract nouns to form expressions of manner or attitude (e.g. *avec plaisir, avec* *soin, avec difficulté*, etc.), though it requires a determiner of some sort with concrete nouns: *Je suis sorti {avec des camarades / *avec camarades}, J'ai mangé du pain {avec de la confiture / *avec confiture}, Je l'ai réparé {avec des outils / *avec outils}*. Also, the preposition *en* is often used, as a near-synonym of *dans*, when the following NP lacks a determiner: *Je suis rentré {en voiture / dans une voiture}* (see 8.6.1–8.6.7 for discussion). However, there is one case (that of *sans*) which deserves immediate attention since it exhibits many of the properties which have been highlighted in the discussion of *de* with a determinerless NP.

This preposition can be followed by a wide range of nouns, which do not seem to show any idiomatic restrictions:

(98)    a   Il a réparé la voiture sans outils
        b   J'ai mangé le pain sans confiture
        c   Je l'ai fait sans plaisir
        d   Il est parti sans explications
        e   Il est sorti sans chapeau

As (98a, b) show, this use is possible with concrete as well as abstract nouns – in contrast to *avec* – and with singular [+count] nouns, as in (98e).

The use of *des*, etc., after *sans* tends to be infelicitous, though it is not absolutely excluded:

(99)    ?Il a réparé la voiture sans des outils

Thus, there is no analogue to the cacophony constraint with *sans*, reasonably enough since cases like (99) do not involve repetition of the same item.

For the examples in (98), let us assume that the complement of *sans* is an NP with an empty determiner position, as shown in (100):

(100)    Il a réparé la voiture [$_{PP}$ sans [$_{NP}$ [$_D$ ∅] [$_{N'}$ outils]]]

From a semantic viewpoint, these examples show an obvious affinity with the cases involving sentential negation discussed in 5.4.8. Like *ne . . . pas, sans* clearly induces the quantity-value 'none at all' for [$_D$ ∅], which is therefore licensed semantically according to the condition proposed in 5.4.6.

Syntactically, the constructions with *sans* differ from cases of sentential negation in that the N' is not introduced by *de*:

(101)    a   *Il a réparé la voiture sans d'outils
        b   *Il est parti sans d'explications

In line with the approach which has been adopted throughout, this implies that the noun in (100) does not need to be casemarked independently of the NP. This property can be accommodated by postulating that *sans*, like *de*, assigns Genitive

Case, so that the noun is casemarked simultaneously with the NP in the manner suggested in 5.4.8.

## 5.5 Universal quantifiers

### 5.5.1 *'Tous' and 'tout'*

The items *tous* and *tout* (and their feminine variants) belong to a class of determiners sometimes called **universal quantifiers** – items which indicate that the proposition holds for the whole of a given set or entity (compare (102a) below with *Beaucoup des invités sont arrivés*, where the proposition holds only for a subset of the guests). These items are typically followed by an NP, introduced by a definite article or a demonstrative or possessive determiner:

(102)  a  Tous les invités sont arrivés
        b  Gaston a fumé toutes ces cigarettes
        c  Pierre a bu tout mon vin
        d  J'ai lu tout le livre

It is assumed that these constructions have a structure in which one NP is embedded inside another, as shown in (103):

(103)     $[_{NP}$ tous $[_{NP}$ les invités]]

When the embedded NP is plural and introduced by the definite article, it can have either a definite or generic interpretation – thus (104) can relate to all of a specific set of students (= *all the students*) or to students in general (= *all students*):

(104)     Tous les étudiants sont intelligents

Note that the embedded NP cannot be introduced by *de*, in contrast to English where *of* may occur (*all (of) the guests, all (of) my wine*, etc.): *\*tous des invités, \*toutes de ces cigarettes, \*tout de mon vin, \*tout du livre*. The absence of *de* indicates that the embedded NP does not need to be casemarked separately, but can inherit the Case of the whole NP (in sharp contrast to partitive constructions, see 5.4.1). This property can perhaps be attributed to the universal value of these quantifiers which ensures that the reference of the embedded NP is coextensive with that of the whole NP – whatever set of guests is picked out by *les invités*, *tous les invités* must refer to exactly the same set. Let us assume that this relation of identity allows Case to be inherited by the embedded NP.

In constructions of the type in (102), *tout* and *toute* can be regarded as the singular forms of *tous* and *toutes*. Note that the singular NP quantified by *tout(e)* can be [-count], as in (102c), or [+count], as in (102d), with an interpretation of the type 'the whole of X' in the latter case. Also, *tout(e)* can quantify a singular, collective NP with animate reference:

(105)     a   Tout le personnel s'est mis en grève
          b   Tout le troupeau est entré dans le pré

The singular forms can be followed directly by an N', as in (106):

(106)     a   Toute réclamation doit être addressée à la direction
          b   Tout étudiant qui échoue à l'examen doit redoubler le cours
          c   Tout progrès dans ce domaine est impossible

This use correlates with a hypothetical interpretation (of the sort conveyed by *any* in English). This is particularly apparent in (106c) where the content of the sentence denies the existence of an actual referent, but even in (106a, b) there is no necessary implication that there are, or will be, any complaints or unsuccessful students, an inference which tends to be invited by constructions of the type *toutes les réclamations, tous les étudiants qui échouent à l'examen*. In particular, the construction in (106) cannot be used with specific reference, as shown by the unacceptability of (107a), where the punctual aspect of the verb would impose such an interpretation, as in (107b):

(107)     a   *Tout étudiant a échoué à l'examen
          b   Tous les étudiants ont échoué à l'examen

The plural forms cannot be used in this way (compare English *All complaints should be addressed to the management*):

(108)     a   *Toutes réclamations doivent être addressées à la direction
          b   *Tous étudiants qui échouent à l'examen doivent redoubler le
              cours

The use of *tous* (or *toutes*) with a 'bare' noun occurs only in a few fixed expressions, most of which are introduced by a preposition: e.g. *de tous genres, toutes directions, de tous côtés, à tous égards*, etc.

### 5.5.2 *'Tout' and 'tous' as pronouns*
The singular form *tout* (only in the masculine) can be used as a pronoun (without a following NP or N') to mean 'everything':

(109)     a   Je lui donnerai tout
          b   Tout me plaît
          c   On a pensé à tout

As a pronoun, *tout* can only have inanimate reference, even though as a determiner it can occur with animate NPs or nouns (see examples (105) and (106b) in 5.5.1).

In formal or literary style, *tous* can also be used as a pronoun with the sense 'everybody', though the locution *tout le monde* is far more current:

(110)     a   Cette règle s'applique à tous
          b   Tous sont égaux devant Dieu

This use of *tous* appears to be most natural after prepositions, and is impossible as a direct object (in this respect, *tous* behaves rather like disjunctive personal pronouns – see 6.2.1):

(111)     *Cette règle concerne tous

Note that in (109) and (110) the syntactic singular vs plural distinction is used to express a distinction between inanimate objects (*tout*) and human beings (*tous*). In this use, these items range over an open-ended set of things or people which is not defined by an antecedent in the discourse and they are invariable for gender.

The plural forms *tous* and *toutes* can also be used on their own to quantify over a set which has been mentioned previously; e.g. in (112a), *tous* refers to the set of students who took the exam:

(112)     a   Plusieurs étudiants ont passé l'examen et tous ont réussi
          b   Henri a voulu épouser plusieurs femmes, mais toutes l'ont refusé
          c   Marie a écrit cinq romans et tous ont été publiés
          d   Plusieurs lois ont été proposées et toutes ont été promulguées

As these examples show, the quantifier can have inanimate as well as human reference, and it agrees in gender with its antecedent. Syntactically, the 'restricted' use of *tous/toutes* referring back to an antecedent is even more tightly constrained than the open-ended use in (110) in that it is only possible with subjects, as in (112), in contrast to (113):

(113)     a   * Plusieurs étudiants ont passé l'examen. Le professeur a
                 refoulé tous
          b   *Henri a voulu épouser plusieurs femmes, mais il a été rejeté
                 par toutes
          c   *Marie a écrit cinq romans et elle est fière de tous.
          d   *Plusieurs lois ont éte proposées et le parlement a approuvé
                 toutes

The use of *tous/toutes* in (112) has a distinctly literary flavour. More typically, in such cases, the quantifier is used in addition to a pronoun, as in (114):

(114)     a   Plusieurs étudiants ont passé l'examen et ils ont tous réussi
          b   Marie a écrit cinq romans et ils ont été tous publiés

Note that when *tous* is used as a pronoun or when it is separated from the item which it quantifies, as in (114) and other cases discussed in 5.5.3, the final -*s* is pronounced.

### 5.5.3 *Quantifier floating*

When the plural forms *tous* and *toutes* quantify a subject, they can be **floated** to a position after the verb, as in (116):

(115)     a   Tous les invités sont arrivés
            b   Toutes les filles voulaient danser
            c   Tous les enfants chantaient

(116)     a   Les invités sont tous arrivés
            b   Les filles voulaient toutes danser
            c   Les enfants chantaient tous

We find the same phenomenon in English (*The guests have all arrived*) but the potential positions of the floated quantifier are slightly different. When the verb is in a simple tense form, the quantifier precedes it in English (*The girls all wanted to dance, The children all sang*) but must follow it in French, as in (116b, c) (cf. *\*Les filles toutes voulaient danser*, *\*Les enfants tous chantaient*). These differences reflect differences in the normal positions of adverbs in the two languages (see 7.5.4). With compound tenses, it is also possible (though less natural) to float the quantifier to the end of the VP in French:

(117)      Les invités sont arrivés tous

This construction is more natural in the presence of an expression which specifies the way in which the proposition applies to the members of the set:

(118)      Les invités sont arrivés tous en même temps

Under similar circumstances, the quantifier can be floated rightwards from a direct object:

(119)     a   J'ai mis les chemises toutes dans le même tiroir
            b   J'ai envoyé ces lettres toutes à la même personne.

In the absence of such an expression, floating from the direct object is not possible:

(120)     a   *J'ai repassé les chemises toutes
            b   *J'ai mis les chemises toutes dans l'armoire

Floating of the quantifier from the subject is obligatory when the subject is a clitic pronoun:

(121)       a   Ils sont tous arrivés

               b   Elles voulaient toutes danser

               c   Ils chantaient tous

When *tous* or *toutes* quantifies a direct object clitic pronoun, the quantifier can occur in the normal direct object position:

(122)       a   Je les ai achetés tous

               b   Je veux les lire tous

Alternatively, it can be floated leftwards to a position preceding a non-finite verb (infinitive or past participle):

(123)       a   Je les ai tous achetés

               b   Je veux tous les lire

However, leftward floating is not possible when *tous/toutes* quantifies a full NP (in this respect *tous/toutes* differs from indefinite quantifiers like *beaucoup* in 'remote quantification' constructions like *J'ai beaucoup acheté de livres*; see 5.4.6):

(124)       a   *J'ai tous acheté ces crayons    (cf. *J'ai acheté tous ces crayons*)

               b   *Je veux tous lire ces livres     (cf. *Je veux lire tous ces livres*)

When *tous/toutes* quantifies a disjunctive personal pronoun, it must follow the pronoun (cf. English *I voted for them all*):

(125)       a   J'ai voté pour eux tous

               b   Gaston est sorti avec elles toutes

As with *all* in English, *tous* and *tout* precede demonstrative pronouns: *tout cela*, *toutes celles que j'ai achetées*. Similarly, *tout* can precede *ce* in 'free' relative clauses of the type *tout ce que j'ai vu* (note that the form here is *tout*, not *tous*: *\*tous ce que j'ai vu(s)*).

### 5.5.4  *Floating of 'tout'*

When *tout* is used as a pronoun ('everything') functioning as a direct object, it can be floated to a position before a non-finite verb:

(126)       a   J'ai acheté tout

               b   Je veux manger tout

(127)       a   J'ai tout acheté

               b   Je veux tout manger

In such cases, the floated constructions (127) tend to be preferred (cf. the same phenomenon with the negative item *rien*, where floating is even more strongly preferred: *?Je n'ai acheté rien, Je n'ai rien acheté* (see 7.6.6)).

Whether *tout(e)* as a determiner (quantifying an NP or clitic pronoun) can be floated in the same way as *tous/toutes* is not entirely clear. In apparent cases of this sort, *tout* could just as well be construed as a degree adverb modifying the verb or adjective with the sense 'completely'. For example, (128a) could be analysed either as a syntactic variant of (128b) or as the equivalent of (128c):

(128)    a  Le pain est tout rassis
          b  Tout le pain est rassis
          c  Le pain est complètement rassis

Similarly, it is not clear whether (129a) should be related to (129b) or to (129c):

(129)    a  L'enfant l'a tout dévoré
          b  L'enfant a dévoré tout le pain
          c  L'enfant a dévoré le pain complètement

However, when we try to construct analogous examples with verbs or other elements which do not readily allow degree modification of the 'completely' type, the resulting sentences are odd:

(130)    a  ??Le beurre est tout dans le frigo
          b  ??Je l'ai mis tout dans le frigo
          c  ??Je l'ai toute vue. (cette pièce)

These examples are significantly worse than their perfectly acceptable counterparts involving plural NPs or pronouns:

(131)    a  Les œufs sont tous dans le frigo
          b  Je les ai mis tous dans le frigo
          c  Je les ai toutes vues. (ces pièces)

From this evidence, we can conclude that floating of *tout(e)* as a determiner is not possible and that the examples in (129) and (130) illustrate the use of *tout* as a degree modifier.

### 5.5.5 *'Chaque' and 'chacun'*

The items *chaque* and *chacun* can also be classified as universal quantifiers, but they focus more closely than *tous* on the participation of the individuals within the set. While *tous* indicates that the proposition holds for the whole set, *chaque* and *chacun* indicate further that the proposition holds separately for each individual member of the set. For this reason, the examples in (132) are rendered more natural by adding the phrases in parentheses which qualify the individuals in the set:

(132)  a  Chacun des invités est arrivé (dans une voiture différente)
       b  J'ai acheté chaque livre (séparément)

Conversely, these items cannot be used when the proposition expresses a relation which holds reciprocally within the set (compare (133) with *Tous les délégués se sont réunis à l'hôtel, Tous ces devoirs sont identiques*):

(133)  a  *Chaque délégué s'est réuni à l'hôtel
       b  *Chacun de ces devoirs est identique

The form *chaque* is followed directly by a singular [+count] N′ as in (132b), while *chacun* is either used alone as a pronoun or it quantifies over a definite plural NP introduced by *de* as in (132a). It is assumed that phrases like *chacun des invités* have the same structure as partitive NPs:

(134)  $[_{NP} [_D \text{chacun}] [_{NP} \text{de} [_{NP} \text{les invités}]]]$

Like *tous*, *chacun* is a universal quantifier, so the set of entities referred to by the highest NP is co-extensive with the set denoted by the embedded NP. However, the embedded NP must be casemarked independently by *de*. This appears to be due to the individuating function of *chacun* described above. Note in particular that the embedded NP must be plural but the entire expression (like *chacun* itself) is syntactically singular. Let us assume that this lack of number concord between *chacun* and the embedded NP prevents the Case of the whole NP from being passed down to the embedded NP in this construction.

In circumstances similar to those mentioned for *tous* in 5.5.3 (see examples (118)–(120)) *chacun* can be detached from the NP which it quantifies:

(135)  a  Le voleur a caché les diamants chacun dans un endroit différent
       b  J'ai envoyé les lettres chacune à une personne différente
       c  Les missionaires sont allés chacun à un pays différent

(136)  a  *Le voleur a caché les diamants chacun
       b  *J'ai envoyé les lettres chacune
       c  *Les missionaires sont allés chacun en Afrique

Apparent floating of *chacun* is also shown in examples like the following where the verb is accompanied by a 'measure' NP:

(137)  a  Ces melons pèsent deux kilos chacun
       b  Je les ai payés cinq francs chacun

In such examples, *chacun* can be replaced by *chaque* in colloquial speech (e.g. *Ils pèsent deux kilos chaque*).

The examples in (135) and (137) cannot be derived simply by movement of *chacun* from the subject or object NP since *chacun* requires the quantified NP to be introduced by *de* and, in subject position, requires the singular form of the verb (e.g. the 'non-floated' counterpart of (137a) is *Chacun de ces melons pèse deux kilos*, not *\*Chacun ces melons pèsent deux kilos*) – the problem is still more acute with the colloquial variants of (137) with *chaque*. For these cases at least, it may be postulated that *chacun* does not originate as a part of the quantified NP but recapitulates it in order to indicate how the property expressed by the PP or measure phrase is distributed among the members of the set. Note that a similar function can be served by other expressions which could not plausibly originate within the subject or object NP: e.g. *Les garçons sont allés les uns en Suisse et les autres en Autriche, Ces melons pèsent deux kilos la pièce, Je les ai payés cinq francs le kilo.*

### 5.5.6 *'Tous les deux'*

Apparent cases of floating of expressions like *tous les deux* raise problems similar to those noted with *chacun* in 5.5.5:

(138)    Les filles sont arrivées toutes les deux

To derive (138) simply by movement of *toutes les deux*, we must postulate the underlying structure (139) which is not grammatical as a surface sentence:

(139)    *[Toutes les deux les filles sont arrivées]

Alternatively, if (138) is derived from the grammatical sentence (140), we will need some mechanism to insert an extra determiner – also this derivation entails movement of a non-constituent if the NP has the internal structure in (141):

(140)    Toutes les deux filles sont arrivées

(141)    $[_{NP} [_{D} \text{ toutes}] [_{NP} \text{ les } [_{N'} \text{ deux filles}]]]$

Note also that in literary style, *les* can be omitted in (138) (and in similar constructions with numerals under five), but not in (140):

(142)    a    Les filles sont arrivées toutes deux
         b    *Toutes deux filles sont arrivées

These difficulties suggest that *toutes (les) deux* in (138) and (142a) is not moved from some position within the subject NP, but that the semantic link between this expression and the subject NP is established by a rule of interpretation.

Expressions like *tous les deux* can occur more readily than plain *tous* in sentence-final position after complements of the verb:

(143)    a    Ces garçons ont offert des fleurs à Marie tous les deux
         b    ??Ces garçons ont offert des fleurs à Marie tous

Conversely, *tous* fits more easily between verbs than *tous les deux*:

(144) a ?Les enfants voulaient tous les deux danser
    b Les enfants voulaient tous danser

This contrast seems to be sharper when the quantified element is an object clitic:

(145) a ??Je les ai tous les deux achetés
    b Je les ai tous achetés

The differences between *tous* and *tous les deux* appear to be essentially stylistic, reflecting the general tendency for 'heavy' expressions to occur towards the end of the sentence whereas single words can be intercalated more easily between elements within the sentence. If this view is justified, we may conclude that *tous les deux* can, potentially, occupy the same range of positions as *tous*. Consequently, an interpretive rule of the type envisaged above for *tous les deux* would naturally extend to cases of 'floated' *tous* (and possibly *tout*), thus undermining the motivation for a movement account of 'floating'. However, this matter will not be pursued here.

### Exercises

1 In 5.2.1, the use of the article with names of countries and regions was characterised as an extension of its use with names of rivers, mountain ranges and groups of islands (which we also find in English). To what extent do phrases like *la reine d'Angleterre, le vin d'Alsace, les fromages de France*, etc., compromise this view?

2 In colloquial speech, NPs denoting places are sometimes used without a preposition or determiner as complements of verbs of movement: *Je vais rue de Rivoli*. With the help of a native speaker, try to work out what types of NP allow this construction. To help you get started, here are a few names of places to try out: *la place de la Nation, le boulevard Saint-Michel, le quartier latin, Clichy, Notre Dame, le Louvre, le bois de Vincennes, la porte de Clignancourt*.

3 Comment on the countability and number properties of the following nouns and the English words which can be used to translate them in their different senses:

affaire, bagage, bouchon, commerce, connaissance, dégât, divertissement, épinards, fruit, gazon, liège, malheur, médicament, meuble, œuvre, ordure, pince, soin.

Can you find any clear examples of nouns which are [-count] in French but which are typically translated by a [+count] noun in English?

4  In literary French, the word *maint* is used with a meaning similar to that of *beaucoup*. With the help of a good dictionary or reference grammar, determine the syntactic properties of this item. Are these properties consistent with the generalisation concerning 'number concord' presented in 5.3.6?

5  Account for the interpretation and acceptability of the examples below, paying particular attention to the use of determiners

    (a)  Pierre a mangé le pain
    (b)  Pierre a mangé du pain
    (c)  *Pierre a mangé de pain
    (d)  *Pierre a mangé pain
    (e)  Cette brioche ressemble au gâteau
    (f)  Cette brioche ressemble à du gâteau
    (g)  *Cette brioche ressemble à de gâteau
    (h)  *Cette brioche ressemble à gâteau
    (i)  Solange s'est privée du gâteau
    (j)  Solange s'est privée de gâteau
    (k)  *Solange s'est privée de du gâteau
    (l)  Henri a rencontré les ambassadeurs
    (m)  Henri a rencontré des ambassadeurs
    (n)  *Henri a rencontré d'ambassadeurs
    (o)  *Henri a rencontré ambassadeurs
    (p)  Henri n'a pas rencontré d'ambassadeurs
    (q)  Robert pense à des filles
    (r)  Robert pense aux filles
    (s)  *Robert pense à de filles
    (t)  *Robert pense à filles
    (u)  *Robert ne pense pas à de filles
    (v)  Sophie rêve des enfants
    (w)  Sophie rêve d'enfants
    (x)  *Sophie rêve de des enfants

6  The contrast between the following examples can be attributed to the PP-Island Constraint (see 1.5.7) which prevents anything from being extracted from a PP (the dash indicates the position from which *de cet auteur* has been extracted:

C'est de cet auteur que j'ai lu plusieurs romans __

*C'est de cet auteur que je me souviens de plusieurs romans __

To what extent can the following data be explained by this restriction and the structures which have been proposed in this chapter?

    (a)  *C'est de cet auteur que j'ai lu le compte-rendu de plusieurs livres __

    (b)  C'est en phonétique que l'on a engagé une douzaine de spécialistes __

    (c)  *C'est en phonétique que l'on a engagé un groupe de spécialistes __

    (d)  *C'est en phonétique que l'on a engagé plusieurs de ces spécialistes __

    (e)  C'est en phonétique que l'on a engagé des spécialistes __

7   Milner (1973) uses the term 'dislocation qualitative' to refer to constructions like the following:

    (a)  Il a cassé le verre, l'imbécile

    (b)  Pierre, l'imbécile, a cassé le verre

In view of the following data, discuss the similarities and differences between this process and cases of Dislocation and apposition of the types discussed in 1.5.5, 3.2.11 and 5.3.2.

    (c)  Pierre a cassé le verre, l'imbécile

    (d)  *Pierre, imbécile, a cassé le verre

    (e)  Pierre, il a cassé le verre, l'imbécile

    (f)  Il a cassé le verre, Pierre, l'imbécile

    (g)  *L'imbécile, Pierre a cassé le verre

    (h)  L'imbécile, il a cassé le verre

    (i)  *J'ai vu Pierre, l'imbécile

    (j)  Je l'ai vu, l'imbécile

What types of nouns can participate in these constructions?

**Further reading**

For general background to the syntax of NPs, with some reference to French, see Giorgi & Longobardi (1991).

   An early structuralist analysis of the syntax of NPs in French is presented in Dubois (1965). M. Gross (1977) gives a general account from a distributionalist perspective. Within a framework closer to that adopted in this chapter, Milner (1978) discusses many aspects of the syntax of NPs (particularly quantitative and partitive constructions and the properties of 'epithet' nouns – see also Milner (1973, ch. 2)), while Milner (1982, chs. 1–2) addresses various questions relating to reference and the argument structure of NPs. Detailed analysis of NPs as complements of *faire* and other 'support' verbs is presented in Giry-Schneider (1978, 1987). Godard (1992) investigates constraints on the extraction of elements from within NPs.

Proper nouns and their relation to definite descriptions are discussed extensively in Kleiber (1981) and Gary-Prieur (1994); see also Kleiber (1992b) on uses of proper nouns as common nouns.

Various papers on countable and non-countable nouns are presented in David & Kleiber (1989).

On compound nouns, see Noailly (1990), Picone (1992), and Barbaud (1992), which also deals briefly with verbal expressions containing determinerless nouns. Tucker, Lambert & Rigault (1977) present interesting experimental evidence to assess the predictability of the gender of nouns in French.

General works on determiners and determination include Guillaume (1919) (highly esoteric), Wilmet (1986) and Karolak (1989); see also Picabia (1986). On the syntax and use of indefinite and definite determiners, see Corblin (1987); also, on more specific topics, Azoulay (1978), Corblin (1983), Ducrot (1970, 1972), Galmiche (1989), Kleiber (1984, 1992a), Van de Velde (1994). Kleiber (1990) presents a detailed study of generic uses of the definite article while Kleiber (1984) discusses the semantics of demonstratives. Anscombre (1991b) presents a collection of papers on NPs which lack a determiner; see also Anscombre (1991a) on determinerless NPs after prepositions, Huot (1978) on appositive NPs and Kupferman (1979b) on constructions of the type *il est médecin*.

The discussion of quantitative and partitive constructions is strongly influenced by Milner's (1978) account, incorporating some of the insights of Battye (1991), though within a different structural framework (Battye adopts the so-called 'DP hypothesis' whereby the determiner rather than the noun acts as the head of the noun phrase). For further discussion of the status of *du*, *de la* and *des*, see Attal (1976), Kupferman (1979a), Muller (1977), Skårup (1994). The 'cacophony' phenomenon and related issues are discussed in M. Gross (1967), Gaatone (1971a, 1992). On 'remote quantification' see Obenauer (1983) and Azoulay-Vicente (1989). Gaatone (1971c) discusses the use of *bien* as a quantifier. Constructions in which adjectives are introduced by *de* are studied in detail in Azoulay-Vicente (1985); see also Kupferman (1980). Constructions of the type *un espèce de cochon* and others with 'epithet' nouns are discussed extensively in Ruwet (1982, ch. 7).

The syntax of *tous* and *tout* is examined in detail in Kayne (1975); see also Quicoli (1976) and Sportiche (1988). For a traditional survey of the use of *tout* see Andersson (1954, 1960).

# 6
# Pronouns

## 6.1  Overview

In this chapter we will look at pronouns which, informally speaking, act as substitutes for NPs and other phrases in cases where a full description or use of a proper noun would be unnecessary or inappropriate. Other types of pronoun which have more specialised functions will be discussed in other chapters: negative pronouns in chapter 7, interrogative and relative pronouns in chapter 10.

A dominant theme of this chapter is that the Clitic-placement process outlined in 1.5.1 serves not only to account for constructions in which pronouns are attached to the verb but also to explain the conditions in which disjunctive pronouns (i.e. pronouns which are not attached to the verb) can be used.

In 6.2 and 6.3, this hypothesis is investigated in relation to structural conditions on the Clitic-placement rule, while 6.4 focuses on the semantic properties of different types of pronouns. In 6.5 and 6.6, we study in greater detail the properties of the so-called 'adverbial' clitics *y* and *en*, looking at questions such as the difference between *y* and Dative clitics as substitutes for expressions introduced by *à*, the choice between *en* and possessive determiners as substitutes for phrases introduced by *de* within NPs and the various uses of *en* to replace indefinite NPs.

In 6.7, the structural relations between pronouns and their antecedents are studied, and the ways in which these relations determine the form of pronouns (e.g. reflexive vs non-reflexive forms), focusing particularly on differences between French and English.

6.8 is principally concerned with a range of cases where Dative clitics do not appear to correspond to phrases of the type *à* + NP. In the course of this discussion, detailed consideration will be given to the syntax of constructions in which possession of a body-part is expressed without recourse to a possessive determiner.

Finally, in 6.9, we look at the use of pronouns in sentences with *être* and related constructions, pursuing the analyses proposed in 2.5.

## 6.2 Clitic-placement

### *6.2.1 Clitic and disjunctive pronouns*

In 1.5.1 it was suggested that in underlying structures pronouns occupy the same positions as NPs according to their grammatical relation and are attached to the verb by a **Clitic-placement** transformation, stated provisionally below:

**Clitic-placement:**

*attach the pronoun to the first verb of the clause.*

When this process applies, the pronoun is realised as a **clitic** form. However, there are other pronouns, called **disjunctive** pronouns,[1] which occur in the same positions as NPs at the surface level (with certain restrictions which will be discussed as we proceed). To illustrate, the underlying structures of the French sentences corresponding to *Max {supported / voted for} them* are represented as in (1) (ignoring the finer details of structure):

(1)     a   [$_S$ Max [$_{VP}$ a soutenu PRONOUN]]
        b   [$_S$ Max [$_{VP}$ a voté [$_{PP}$ pour PRONOUN]]]

In (1a) Clitic-placement attaches the element PRONOUN to the verb where it is realised as the clitic form *les*, but (for reasons discussed in 6.2.2) Clitic-placement cannot apply in (1b) so PRONOUN remains in its underlying position and is realised as the disjunctive form *eux*:

(2)     a   [$_S$ Max [$_{VP}$ les a soutenus __ ]]
        b   [$_S$ Max [$_{VP}$ a voté [$_{PP}$ pour eux]]]

In the representations the symbol PRONOUN will be used to stand for whatever is being referred to; thus the sentences in (2) are the surface realisations of (1) when PRONOUN is third person, masculine plural (e.g. referring to a set of male individuals not including the speaker or hearer).

In (1a) we do not have the option of leaving the pronoun where it is and realising it as a disjunctive form:

(3)     *Max a soutenu eux

To exclude examples like (3) the following informal principle is proposed:

---

[1] The term 'clitic' (from a Greek word meaning 'to lean') conveys the idea of attachment to another word, whereas 'disjunctive' suggests syntactic independence. Other common terms for the disjunctive vs clitic distinction are 'stressed' vs 'unstressed', 'strong' vs 'weak', or in French 'tonique' vs 'atone'. A problem with these terms is that they connote phonological properties which do not always correlate with the relevant syntactic distinction. In the distributionalist literature, clitics are sometimes referred to as 'particules préverbales' (or 'ppv' for short).

**The 'favour clitic' principle:**
*apply Clitic-placement whenever you can.*
**Corollary:**
*disjunctive pronouns can only occur when Clitic-placement is inapplicable or when the properties of clitic pronouns are not sufficient to identify the intended referent.*

The general idea behind this hypothesis is that the Clitic-placement rule serves not only to account for sentences in which a pronoun precedes the verb, but also (to some extent) to define the conditions under which disjunctive pronouns can be used.

#### 6.2.2 *Structural conditions on Clitic-placement*

In (1b) Clitic-placement is blocked by a general condition proposed in 1.5.7, repeated below:

**The PP-Island Constraint:**
*in French, no item can be extracted from a PP.*

Another case where Clitic-placement cannot apply is when the utterance contains no verb for the pronoun to be attached to, as in short answers to questions:

(4)     Qui as-tu vu?
        – Eux

Clitic-placement is also blocked when a pronoun is conjoined with another NP:

(5)     *Je l'ai vu [$_{NP}$ __ et sa mère]

Also clitic pronouns cannot be conjoined with each other:

(6)     *Je le et la verrai

Modification of the pronoun by *ne ... que* also blocks Clitic-placement (cf. *Je n'ai vu que Pierre*):

(7)     *Je ne l'ai vu que

In all of these cases, disjunctive pronouns must be used (though in a case like (6) it would be more natural to use the plural clitic form: *Je les verrai*):

(8)     a   J'ai vu lui et sa mère
        b   Je verrai lui et elle
        c   Je n'ai vu que lui

The restriction in (6) can perhaps be attributed to the 'affix-like' properties of clitics (elements which must be attached to another word). The other restrictions seem to reflect general island constraints; see 1.5.7 for discussion of cases like (5). No attempt will be made from here to define the restriction involved in (7) but it will merely be noted that phrases modified by *ne . . . que* function as islands with respect to other movement processes: e.g. QU- movement in questions (*\*Quel livre n'as-tu lu que?*; cf. *Tu n'as lu que quel livre?* ) and movement of the underlying object in passives (*\*Le premier chapitre n'a été écrit que*; cf. *On n'a écrit que le premier chapitre*). For further discussion of *ne . . . que*, see 7.6.10.

In 2.7.2, it was argued that Clitic-placement can only apply within a simple clause, a hypothesis which was used to distinguish genuine auxiliary verbs from other verbs which take an infinitival complement clause:

(9)      a  Je l'ai fait
          b  Je vais le faire
          c  *Je le vais faire

The restriction to application within a simple clause is not a general condition on movement rules, but some linguists have argued, on the basis of data from a variety of languages, that the subject position plays a significant role in determining the domains within which certain types of movement processes can apply. For present purposes, the relevant generalisation can be expressed as follows:

**Specified Subject Condition (SSC):**
*no item may be moved out of a clause across a subject position (by movement rules of certain types).*

Assuming the underlying structures in (10), where ∅ represents the implicit subject of the infinitive (see 9.2 for detailed discussion), the data in (9) can be accounted for in terms of the SSC:

(10)     a  $[_S$ Je $[_{VP}$ ai $[_{VP}$ fait PRONOUN$]]]$
         b  $[_S$ Je $[_{VP}$ vais $[_{S'}$ ∅ $[_{VP}$ faire PRONOUN$]]]]$

In (10b) PRONOUN cannot be attached to the higher verb without crossing the subject ∅, but in (10a) there is no intervening subject position to block attachment of PRONOUN to the auxiliary. Given the SSC and the other island conditions mentioned above, the formulation of the Clitic-placement rule can be simplified as follows:

**Clitic-placement:**
*cliticise PRONOUN to the leftmost V (within general conditions on movement processes).*

For the data in (9) this analysis gives the same results as one which stipulates that Clitic-placement can only apply within the simple clause. However, in later sections other cases will be discussed, which provide empirical motivation for this revised analysis (see 6.6.2, 6.9.3 and 9.4).

### 6.2.3 Properties of clitic and disjunctive pronouns

The basic properties of clitic and disjunctive pronouns are summarised below:

**Clitic pronouns:**

I  *Clitic pronouns are always attached to the verb (preceding the verb, except in positive imperative sentences – see 6.3.2).*

II  *Clitic pronouns cannot be separated from the verb except by another clitic.*

III  *Clitic pronouns occur in a fixed order (see 6.3).*

IV  *The grammatical function of clitic pronouns (subject, direct object, etc.) is indicated by their form, not by their position (i.e. clitics inflect for Case).*

V  *Clitic pronouns cannot be conjoined.*

**Disjunctive pronouns:**

VI  *Disjunctive pronouns occur in the same positions as normal NPs.*

VII  *Disjunctive pronouns can be used in isolation (e.g. short answers to questions).*

VIII  *Disjunctive pronouns do not vary in form according to their grammatical function (i.e. they do not inflect for Case).*

> When applying these conditions it must be borne in mind that some pronoun forms can have more than one function. For example, first- and second-person clitics do not show the full range of Case distinctions: *me* and *te* are both Accusative and Dative, while *nous* and *vous* are Nominative as well, showing no overt Case distinction at all. Moreover, *nous* and *vous* are disjunctive forms as well as clitics (e.g. they can be used in isolation). Similarly, *elle* and *elles* are subject clitics, but also function as disjunctive pronouns, while the form *lui* is used both as a Dative clitic (for both genders) and as a masculine singular disjunctive pronoun. Such ambiguities raise presentational problems which will be avoided as far as possible by using unambiguous forms to illustrate the properties of different types of pronoun.

### 6.2.4 Subject pronouns

According to the definitions in 6.2.3, subject pronouns (*je, tu, il*, etc.) qualify as clitics, even though they appear to occupy the same position as ordinary NP subjects. For example, *ils* is a Nominative Case form (used only for subjects) contrasting with *les* (Accusative) and *leur* (Dative, used for certain types of indirect object – see 6.2.5). Also, *ils* cannot be used in isolation (cf. conditions (I) and (VII)):

(11)       Qui a fait cela? – {*Ils / Eux}

Similarly, they cannot be conjoined (condition (V)):

(12)     *Il et elle sont arrivés

Moreover, unlike NP subjects, subject clitics cannot be separated from the verb:

(13)     a   Luc, je crois, est déjà arrivé
         b   *Il, je crois, est déjà arrivé

Example (13b) illustrates condition (II), exemplified for object clitics in (14):

(14)     a   *Max le, je crois, fera bientôt
         b   Je le lui donnerai

Although *le* (and *je*) is separated from the verb in (14b), the intervening element *lui* is another clitic, so condition II is satisfied. For the purposes of this condition, the negative particle *ne* counts as a clitic (though it is not a pronoun): *Je ne viendrai pas*. To account for these properties, it must be assumed that subject clitics are attached to the verb in the same way as object clitics, even though this usually makes no difference to the linear order.

A further property of subject clitics is that, unlike NP subjects, they can be inverted with the (first) verb, e.g. in yes/no questions (see 10.2.1):

(15)     a   Est-il arrivé?
         b   *Est Luc arrivé?

Under certain conditions of emphasis (e.g. to express contrast) third-person disjunctive pronouns can be used in subject position, in which case they can be separated from the verb:

(16)     a   Lui a fait cela (pas moi)
         b   Lui, je crois, a fait cela

However, Inversion with the verb is impossible:

(17)     *A-lui fait cela?

Note that *elle* (and *elles*) can be used in both (16b) and (17), thus confirming its ambivalent status: *Elle, je crois, a fait cela, A-t-elle fait cela?* First- and second-person forms cannot be used in subject position – e.g. we do not have *\*Toi as fait cela* or *\*Nous, je crois, devons partir*. A more usual way of emphasising a subject pronoun is to place the disjunctive form in dislocated position, with the clitic in the normal subject position: *Lui, il a fait cela; Toi, tu as fait cela.*

The acceptability of examples like (16) suggests that one of the factors which allows the 'favour clitic' principle to be violated is the need for emphatic stress, which clitic forms cannot generally express. However, for some reason, disjunctive pronouns cannot be used in the direct object position (see 6.2.1 example (3)) even when emphasised.

### 6.2.5 Dative clitics

Very roughly, the Dative clitics *lui* and *leur* correspond to NPs introduced by *à*; e.g. the sentences in (18) could correspond to *Pierre parlait à Marie* and *Max a donné un cadeau à ses parents*:

(18)    a   Pierre lui parlait
        b   Max leur a donné un cadeau

One way of capturing this correspondence would be to derive a sentence like (18a) from the underlying structure (19):

(19)    [$_S$ Pierre [$_{VP}$ parlait [$_{PP}$ à PRONOUN]]]

However, this analysis raises a number of problems. Firstly, application of Clitic-placement to PRONOUN in (19) would violate the PP-Island Constraint proposed in 6.2.1. Secondly, we would need some mechanism to delete the preposition *à*. Now one might argue that in some sense these two problems cancel each other out, but there is a further problem, namely that not all complements of *à* can be replaced by a Dative clitic: e.g. we do not have (20) corresponding to *Pierre pensait à Marie*:

(20)    *Pierre lui pensait

In this respect *à* with *penser* behaves just like any other preposition (e.g. *pour* in example (2b) in 6.2.1) in blocking Clitic-placement. Similarly, it allows the use of a disjunctive form, whereas with *parler* a disjunctive pronoun is odd except under conditions of emphasis of the sort mentioned for disjunctive pronouns in subject position in 6.2.3:

(21)    a   Pierre pensait à elle
        b   Pierre parlait à elle (pas à toi)

To account for this difference, it is proposed that, with verbs of the *penser* type, the complement is a genuine PP headed by *à*, whereas with verbs like *parler* and *donner*, *à* is a marker of Dative Case. In structural terms, the two cases can be distinguished as in (22):

(22)    a   [$_S$ Pierre [$_{VP}$ pensait [$_{PP}$ à NP]]]
        b   [$_S$ Pierre [$_{VP}$ parlait NP$_{[DAT]}$]]

In (22b) if the NP is realised as a pronoun which is cliticised to the verb, the Dative feature determines the form of the pronoun (e.g. as *lui* in (18a)), otherwise it is realised as the preposition *à* by application of the following rule:

### À insertion:

$$NP_{[DAT]} \Rightarrow [_{PP} \; à \; NP]$$

The effect of this rule is to make the complement of *parler* identical with that of *penser* at the surface level. However, the underlying difference between the two constructions ensures that the complement of *penser* cannot be expressed by a Dative clitic, assuming that Dative clitics can only replace Dative NPs, not genuine PPs introduced by *à*. Given that a pronoun corresponding to the NP in (22a) cannot be cliticised to the verb (because of the PP-Island Constraint), the 'favour clitic' principle does not come into play (thus allowing a disjunctive pronoun without any particular emphasis as in (21a)) but in (22b) failure to apply Clitic-placement must be motivated by considerations of contrastive emphasis.

### 6.3   Order and compatibility of clitic pronouns

### *6.3.1   Declarative sentences*

In declarative sentences, clitic pronouns must occur before the verb in the order shown in table 6.1.

Table 6.1. *Order of clitics in declarative sentences*

| I | II | III | IV | Va | Vb |
|---|---|---|---|---|---|
| NOM | ACC/DAT | ACC | DAT | *Pro-PP* | |
| je | | | | | |
| tu | me | | | | |
| il | | le | lui | | |
| elle | te | | | | |
| nous | | la | | y | en |
| vous | se | | | | |
| ils | | les | leur | | |
| elles | nous | | | | |
| ce | | | | | |
| on | vous | | | | |

With respect to the third person, non-reflexive forms, this order reflects the normal order of full NPs in a sentence: subjects (column I) come first, followed by direct objects (column III) followed by indirect objects (columns IV and V[2]). Thus the participants in (23) are presented in the same order as in (24):

---

[2]   *En* can also represent an indefinite indirect object (see (26a, b) below and 6.6.4). On the characterisation of *y* and *en* as pro-PPs, see 6.4.6.

(23)    a   Il la lui donnera

          b   Elle les y a mis

(24)    a   Pierre donnera la fleur à Marie

          b   Suzy a mis les livres sur la table

However, this pattern breaks down with the items in column II (clitics which can represent direct objects or dative complements), which must precede direct object clitics:

(25)    a   Il nous la donnera    (Subj > Ind Obj > Dir Obj)

          b   Elle se l'offrira      (Subj > Ind Obj > Dir Obj)

It also breaks down in cases where *en* represents an indefinite direct object:

(26)    a   Je leur en donnerai       (Subj > Ind Obj > Dir Obj)

          b   Elle s'en offrira         (Subj > Ind Obj > Dir Obj)

          c   Marie donnera du vin aux invités   (Subj > Dir Obj > Ind Obj)

Thus, the order of clitics cannot be defined entirely in terms of their grammatical functions.

There are also some restrictions on the possible combinations of clitics:

- *No two clitics from the same column can be combined.*
- *Clitics in column II cannot be combined with those in IV.*
- Lui *and* y *cannot be combined.*
- *Sequences of* y *and* en *are rare (except in* Il y en a*).*

The first restriction is fairly straightforward for columns I, III and IV in so far as no simple sentence can contain more than one subject, direct object or dative complement. However, there is no obvious reason why clitics in column II cannot be combined with each other or with those in IV. The following examples would make perfect sense (with the interpretations indicated), but they are ungrammatical[3]:

(27)    a   *Il me vous a déjà présenté     'He has already introduced me to you'

          b   *Elle se nous présentera       'She will introduce herself to us'

(28)    a   *Vous me lui avez déjà présenté   'You have already introduced me to him'

          b   *Elle se leur présentera       'She will introduce herself to them'

---

[3] There is one rather special case, that of so-called 'ethic datives', where such combinations are possible; see 6.8.7 for examples and discussion.

Clitics in II and IV can be combined with the Accusative clitics in III:

(29)      a  Il me les a présentés    'He introduced them to me'

            b  Il la leur présentera    'He will introduce her to them'

In cases of conflict (e.g. (27)–(28)), the problem is resolved by using a disjunctive pronoun for the dative complement:

(30)      a  Il m'a déjà présenté {à vous / à eux}

            b  Elle se présentera {à nous / à eux}

The disjunctive pronouns in (30) are perfectly natural without a contrastive, emphatic interpretation, unlike those in (31) which are odd unless they bear contrastive stress:

(31)      a  ?Il a présenté Pierre {à vous / à eux}

            b  ?Elle présentera son mari {à vous / à eux}

This difference follows from the 'favour clitic' principle. In (30) the use of a clitic form is excluded by syntactic restrictions on combinations of clitics, but in (31) there is nothing to stop us using a clitic instead of the disjunctive pronouns: e.g. *Elle {vous / leur} présentera son mari.* Consequently, the use of disjunctive forms in (31) must be motivated by special considerations such as contrastive stress. (For further discussion of cases like (30) see 6.5.2.)

The incompatibility between *lui* and *y* is traditionally explained on phonetic grounds. Basically, in a case like (32) we would either have an awkward hiatus between *lui* and *y* or *y* would be 'swallowed up' in the vowel of *lui*:

(32)        *Pierre lui y a parlé    (e.g. Pierre a parlé à Marie dans la cuisine)

Whatever the merits of this explanation may be, we may note that the restriction applies only to these two items and does not extend to *leur* (i.e. it is not a general restriction on Dative and prepositional clitics): *Pierre leur y a parlé* 'Pierre spoke to them there'.

The restriction concerning *y* and *en* is most clearly illustrated in cases where both clitics have a locative value:

(33)        *Pierre y en est allé    (e.g. Pierre est allé de Paris à Lyon)

In literary style we occasionally find examples where *en* represents an indefinite direct object (*Je n'y en ai pas vu, Pierre y en a mis*), but such cases are not typical of modern usage, except as noted above in expressions of the type *il y en a.* To all intents and purposes, we can treat *y* and *en* as belonging to the same column in table 6.1.

### 6.3.2 Clitics in imperative sentences

In positive imperative sentences, clitic pronouns follow the verb: *Mangez-le!, Vas-y!, Regarde-le!, Parlez-lui-en!*, etc. This pattern is also found with first-person-plural imperatives, translatable as 'Let us . . .': *Allons-y!, Buvons-le!, Parlons-en!*, etc. On the other hand, clitic pronouns precede the verb in negative imperatives just as in declarative sentences, at least in Standard French[4]: *N'y va pas!, Ne le fais pas!, Ne me le dites pas!*, etc. Other constructions which have imperative force but lack the imperative form (e.g. infinitives used for instructions and finite clauses with a subject pronoun) also follow the declarative pattern: *Les mettre dans une casserole et y ajouter du sel, Vous me le rendrez tout de suite, On y va!*, etc.

In positive imperatives, the order of clitic pronouns with respect to each other is also different from that found in declaratives, with some variation according to register.

In Standard French, the normal order in imperatives can be defined in terms of the grammatical functions of the clitics. Essentially, direct objects precede indirect objects, except that *en* always occurs last even when it represents an indefinite direct object. This pattern can be represented as in table 6.2.

Column I consists of the clitics which are unambiguously Accusative (corresponding to column III in table 6.1). Column II is composed of clitics which are potentially Dative, but includes first- and second-person forms which can also be

Table 6.2. *Order of Clitics in Positive Imperatives (Standard French)*

| I<br>ACC | II<br>DAT | III<br>*Pro-PP* |
|-----|------|--------|
| le | lui | y |
| la | leur | en |
| les | ACC/DAT | |
| | m' (moi) | |
| | t' (toi) | |
| | nous | |
| | vous | |

[4] In colloquial French, clitics may follow the verb when *ne* is omitted: *Vas-y pas!, Fais-le pas!* However, even without *ne*, clitic pronouns may precede the verb: *Y va pas!, Le fais pas!* It is perhaps worth noting that *ne* is itself a clitic (though not a pronoun) – it can occur between a subject clitic and the verb and it cannot be separated from the verb by anything other than a clitic pronoun (except *pas* with the infinitive; see 7.6.4). Since *ne* always precedes the verb, we may postulate that its presence in Standard French has the effect of attracting all the other clitics to the preverbal position, whereas its absence in colloquial French allows clitic pronouns to follow the verb in line with the pattern for positive imperatives.

used as Accusatives (subsuming columns II and IV in table 6.1, except for *se* which can never occur since the understood subject of an imperative is always first- or second-person). The items *y* and *en* are placed in the same column since the cases where they can readily be combined (e.g. *Il y en a*) do not arise in imperatives. Subject clitics are not listed since they do not occur in genuine imperatives.

This pattern is illustrated in (34):

(34)      a  Donnez-le-moi!

           b  Donnez-m'en!

           c  Donnez-lui-en!

           d  Donnez-les-lui!

           e  Mettez-les-y!

           f  Parlez-leur-en!

           g  Occupe-t'en!

In written French and fairly formal speech, the variants *moi* and *toi* are used only in final position, as in (34a) and cases like *Embrasse-moi!*, *Tais-toi*, whereas the elided forms *m'* and *t'* are used before another clitic, usually *en* as in (34b, g). However, in more colloquial styles, the forms *moi* and *toi* are used in all positions (with an intrusive *-z-* to avoid hiatus with a following vowel), though apparently not in *Va-t'en!* (cf. *\*Va-toi-z-en!*):

(35)      a  Donnez-moi-z-en!

           b  Occupe-toi-z-en!

Despite appearances, it seems clear that these forms function as clitics rather than as disjunctive pronouns. In writing, they are always joined to the verb or another clitic by a hyphen (a clear symptom of a close syntactic relation). In colloquial French, they can occur between the verb and another clitic, e.g. *en* in (35). Conversely, they cannot be separated from the verb by anything except another clitic: *\*Donnez cela moi!*, *\*Embrasse encore moi!*, *\*Dépêche vite toi!* Moreover, they can be used as dative complements without recourse to *à*, as in (34a), a property which is exclusive to clitic pronouns.

The use of *y* is fairly restricted in imperatives. The most natural cases are those where this item occurs without another clitic (*Vas-y!*, *Pensez-y!*). Its use is systematically avoided, in favour of *là*, after elided clitic forms: *??Mets-t'y!*, *??Menez-m'y!* vs *Menez-moi là!*, *Mets-toi là!*. This is reminiscent of the restriction against combinations of *lui* and *y* noted in 6.3.1, which also holds in imperatives: *\*Parlez-lui-y!*. In colloquial styles which allow examples like (35), *y* can be used after *moi* and *toi*: *Mets-toi-z-y!*, *Menez-moi-z-y!*

As in declaratives, no two clitics from the same column can be combined:

(36)      a  *\*Présentez-vous-moi!* 'Introduce yourself to me!'

b   *Présentez-moi-leur!   'Introduce me to them!'
c   *Présentez-nous-lui!   'Introduce us to him/her!'

Recall that in 6.3.1 we had to invoke a special restriction against combinations of clitics from columns II and IV in table 6.1 to exclude the declarative counterparts of examples like (36b, c) (e.g. *Il me leur présentera*). However, no additional restriction is necessary to exclude (36b, c) since *moi, nous,* and *leur, lui* belong to the same column.

In colloquial speech, the first- and second-person clitics (functioning as Datives) are often placed before the third-person Accusative forms (*le, la* and *les*), giving the same order as we find in declarative sentences:

(37)     a   Donnez-moi-le!
         b   Rendez-nous-les!

Examples like (37) can be derived by a rule which operates on the standard configuration given in table 6.2 and which optionally places ACC/DAT clitics before Accusative clitics in colloquial French, as shown in (38):

(38)

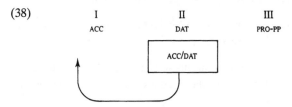

A similar approach might be envisaged for clitics in declarative sentences. In the first instance, Clitic-placement would attach object clitics to the left of the verb in the order given in table 6.2 (corresponding roughly to the underlying Direct Object > Indirect Object order). At this stage, combinations of *me, te, se, nous, vous* and *lui, leur* would be excluded since all of these clitics occupy the same structural position, thus eliminating the need for the special restriction proposed in 6.3.1. Obligatory application of the rule in (38) would then give the correct surface order. In fact, there is some historical justification for this approach. Up until the early seventeenth century we find attested examples of the type *On le me dit, Je les vous montre*. In other words, in Old French the rule in (38) was optional in declarative sentences just as in imperatives in modern colloquial French.

## 6.4   Personal, demonstrative and 'adverbial' pronouns

### 6.4.1   Referential properties of personal pronouns

The term **personal pronoun** is used here for pronouns which designate entities by means of features such as person, number and gender – i.e. disjunctive and clitic

257

pronouns of the type considered so far. Clitic forms of personal pronouns do not necessarily refer to human beings: for example, *il* and *le* in (39) could refer to an inanimate entity (such as a film) which is denoted by a masculine noun (the same is true even of the Dative clitics – see 6.5.1):

(39)     a   Il m'amuse
         b   Je le regarderai

However, the disjunctive forms of personal pronouns are used almost exclusively to refer to animate beings; e.g. it is difficult to interpret *lui* in (40) as referring to a film:

(40)     a   Je pense à lui
         b   Je n'ai vu que lui

Nominative and Accusative clitics inflect for gender; for example, if we were referring to a TV programme (*une émission*) in (39) we would use the forms *elle* and *la*. However, *le* can also be used as a *neuter* form to refer to things whose gender has not been established, as in (41a), or to refer back to a sentence, as in (41b):

(41)     a   Je ne sais pas ce que c'est, mais je le mangerai
         b   J'ai menti, et je le regrette

The Nominative form *il* cannot be used in this way (though it can be used as a dummy subject in impersonal sentences, where it does not refer to anything – see 3.4):

(42)     a   *Je ne sais pas ce que c'est, mais il me plaît
         b   *J'ai menti, et il me fait de la peine

### 6.4.2   *Demonstrative pronouns*

A question which arises from examples like (40) is what pronoun we can use to refer to an inanimate object, given that the use of a clitic is precluded for syntactic reasons and a personal disjunctive form can only have animate reference. Similarly, what pronoun can be used in cases like (42), given that subject clitics cannot function as neuter forms?

A possible solution in both cases is to use a **demonstrative pronoun**, *cela* or *ça* (or, with a different effect, *ceci*):

(43)     a   Je pense à {cela / ça}
         b   Je n'ai vu que {cela / ça}

(44)     a   Je ne sais pas ce que c'est, mais {cela / ça} me plaît
         b   J'ai menti, et {cela / ça} me fait de la peine

These items are called 'demonstratives' because they often have the effect of 'pointing' at the thing in question (an effect known as **deixis**). This deictic or 'pointing' effect can be quite literal (e.g. when one utters *Je veux manger ça* while pointing at a particular dish), sometimes it is rather vaguer, indicating something which is the focus of attention but not necessarily present in the immediate linguistic context. Unlike the personal pronouns, these items do not vary according to person, number or gender, and, in sharp contrast to personal disjunctive forms, they almost always have inanimate reference (except in one rather special case discussed in 6.4.3); consequently, they are appropriate as neuter pronouns. These items are disjunctive forms: e.g. they can be used in isolation and when used as subjects they do not allow Inversion: *\*A-ça plu à Pierre?* (thus, although *ça* can be considered a reduced form of *cela*, it is not a clitic). There is a demonstrative clitic, *ce*, but this item can only be used as the subject of the verb *être*, with additional restrictions (see 6.9.1–6.9.2 for discussion).

Unlike personal disjunctive pronouns, demonstratives can occur readily as direct objects:

(45)     J'ai lu {cela / ça}

This appears to conflict with the 'favour clitic' principle, since a clitic form is available: *Je l'ai lu*. Nevertheless, there are some subtle differences in the interpretation of demonstratives which are broadly consistent with the 'favour clitic' principle. Generally, when *cela* and *ça* occur as direct objects, they tend to have a deictic interpretation, referring to something in the extralinguistic context. It is odd to use these forms to refer back to something just mentioned:

(46)     ?J'ai acheté un livre et j'ai lu ça

Similarly, a demonstrative is rather odd in place of *le* in cases like (41) – the examples in (47) are much less natural than those in (44) where the demonstrative is in subject position:

(47)     a   ?Je ne sais pas ce que c'est, mais je mangerai ça
         b   ?J'ai menti, et je regrette ça

This difference is not simply a matter of the position of the pronoun (direct object in (47) vs subject in (44)); the following example is also odd, with the subject *ça* referring back to *le verre*:

(48)     ?Le verre est tombé par terre et ça s'est cassé

The general pattern seems to be that, in order to refer back to something just mentioned, the deictic cue provided by *cela* or *ça* is unnecessary – a personal clitic form agreeing in gender with the antecedent (e.g. ... *et je l'ai lu*, ... *et il s'est cassé*) or

259

neuter *le* in (41) will do just as well and is therefore preferred according to the 'favour clitic' principle. However, in (44) there is no clitic form which can refer back to the antecedent, so the 'favour clitic' principle does not come into play, thus allowing the use of *cela/ça* even though no deictic cue is needed.

### 6.4.3   Generic 'ce' and 'ça'

Despite the general tendency for demonstratives to function as neuter forms, *ce* and *ça* (more rarely *cela*) can be used, even though gender is evident, when a generic interpretation is intended (i.e. when the statement applies to an entire class of entities). This is particularly apparent in dislocated constructions, where the pronoun is used in addition to an appropriate NP designating the class:

(49)   a   La bière d'Alsace, c'est délicieux
       b   Le café, ça empêche de dormir

Note that in (49a) the adjective is in the masculine form (agreeing with *ce* rather than *la bière*). In parallel examples where a specific instance of the substance is referred to, the appropriate personal pronoun is used:

(50)   a   Cette bière, elle est délicieuse
       b   Le café que j'ai bu hier soir, il m'a empêché de dormir

The same pattern is observed with plural expressions:

(51)   a   Les films d'épouvante, c'est comique
       b   Les livres de linguistique, ça m'intéresse

(52)   a   Ces deux films, ils sont amusants
       b   Les livres que tu m'as prêtés, ils m'ont plu beaucoup

In colloquial style, the generic use of *ce* and *ça* extends to human beings:

(53)   a   Les enfants, c'est mignon
       b   Les étudiants, ça ne travaille pas

This construction often conveys a pejorative attitude towards the persons concerned and may be perceived as patronising or sarcastic even when the comment is complimentary.

### 6.4.4   Objects of prepositions

The acceptability of demonstrative pronouns as objects of prepositions depends to some extent on the preposition concerned. Consider the following examples:

(54)   a   ?Marie est descendue dans cela
       b   J'ai pensé à cela

    c   Je me souviens de cela

    d   Pierre a travaillé pour cela

Where the preposition denotes a spatial relation, as in (54a), the use of *cela* (or *ça*) is decidedly odd unless one is actually pointing at the thing referred to (cf. *??Marie a ouvert la porte de la cave et elle est descendu dans cela*). If one is referring back to some previously mentioned entity, the use of a special form of the preposition, *dedans* optionally prefixed by *là-*, is highly preferred:

(55)       Marie est descendue (là-)dedans

The item *là-* can be regarded as a clitic on a par with *le* in (39b) except that it is attached to a preposition rather than to a verb. Thus, ignoring the form of the preposition, the version of (55) with *là* can be derived as in (56):

(56)       [$_S$ Marie [$_{VP}$ est descendue [$_{PP}$ dedans PRONOUN]]]

Note that this derivation does not violate the PP-Island Constraint, since the pronoun is not extracted from the PP but is moved within it. (For further discussion of forms like *dedans* and their use without any complement, *Elle est descendu dedans*, see 8.3.6.) The item *ci-* in *ci-dessus*, etc., can likewise be analysed as a clitic, though it has a much clearer deictic orientation than *là-* (see 6.4.8).

    Given the availability of a clitic in (55), its use is preferred unless there is some motivation in the structure of the discourse to exploit the potential deictic properties of disjunctive demonstrative pronouns. This accords with our observation concerning the interpretation of (54a). In cases like (54b–d) there is no alternative construction with the clitic *là-* (and the PP-Island Constraint prevents the pronoun from being cliticised to the verb). Consequently, the use of the disjunctive demonstrative form does not need to be motivated by any special deictic effect.

### 6.4.5  *'Adverbial' clitics*

In examples (54a–c), but not (54d), an alternative possibility is to use the **adverbial clitics** *y* or *en* (so called because they appear to replace the whole PP rather than the NP; see 6.4.6):

(57)       a   Marie y est descendue

            b   J'y ai pensé

            c   Je m'en souviens

In cases like (57a), the use of *y* is only possible when the particular spatial relation (specified by *dans*) is not particularly important, but in (57b, c) where the clitic replaces a preposition with an essentially grammatical function, no meaning is lost. True, the disjunctive pronoun in (54b, c) allows emphasis on the entity in question, which is not possible with *y* or *en*, but this is not a necessary condition for the use of the disjunctive form, any more than it is in (54d) where the alternative with *y* or *en* is not possible.

In appropriate contexts, the clitics in (57b, c) allow a human interpretation, referring back to Marie in (58):

(58)    a   Max adore Marie; il y pense tout le temps
        b   Luc a rencontré Marie une seule fois, mais il s'en souvient

Nevertheless, the alternatives with *à elle* or *d'elle* are possible (and even preferred) in the same contexts, and do not convey any element of contrast of the sort found with disjunctive pronouns in Dative complements or in subject position (cf. examples (16) in 6.2.4 and (21b) in 6.2.5).

In other words, it seems that the availability of the clitics *y* or *en* does not induce effects of the sort indicated in the corollary of the 'favour clitic' principle when a disjunctive pronoun is used.

### 6.4.6  'Y' and 'en' as pro-PPs

The observation in 6.4.5 that the availability of *en* or *y* does not preclude the normal, non-emphatic use of alternative constructions with a preposition + disjunctive pronoun can be accommodated by assuming that *en* and *y* are not realisations of the element which we have designated as PRONOUN but rather act as substitutes for the entire PP, as implied by the traditional term 'adverbial' pronoun. This analysis allows us to maintain the corollary of the 'favour clitic' principle with the proviso that it holds only when the competing clitic and disjunctive forms are realisations of the same element – i.e. the element designated as PRONOUN.

The idea that *en* and *y* are not pronouns in the strict sense (i.e. not 'pro-NPs' but **pro-PPs**) is supported by the fact that, unlike genuine pronouns, they do not encode features of person, number or gender, but they do encode a distinction which is roughly parallel to that between the prepositions *de* and *à*. More generally, these items do not seem to be sensitive to the content of the phrase introduced by *à* or *de*. Not only can they be used with animate or inanimate reference, as we saw in 6.4.5, but in appropriate contexts they can substitute for first- or second-person forms:

(59)    a   Je pense à toi, et j'y penserai toujours
        b   Il a parlé de moi, et il en parlera encore

Similarly, as we saw in 2.3.4–2.3.5, these items can replace clauses introduced by the prepositions *à* or *de* (at the underlying level in the case of finite clauses).

262

These observations do not demonstrate beyond doubt that *y* and *en* must be regarded as substitutes for the entire PP, but in conjunction with the observations in 6.4.5, they constitute a reasonable case for entertaining this hypothesis. Further evidence will be given in subsequent sections where these items are discussed in detail.

According to this approach, the analysis of *J'y pense* is different from that proposed for cases like *Je lui parle* in 6.2.5. For reasons already discussed, PRONOUN in (60) cannot be cliticised either to the verb or to the preposition:

(60)     [$_S$ Je [$_{VP}$ pense [$_{PP}$ à [$_{NP}$ PRONOUN]]]]

Consequently, PRONOUN can be realised as a disjunctive form without emphasis. However, in so far as *y* corresponds to PPs introduced by *à* (an oversimplification), we have the alternative option of replacing the whole PP by *y* and cliticising it to the verb, giving *J'y pense*. Note that this operation does not violate the PP-Island Constraint, since *y* represents the whole PP not some element within it. The same analysis can be applied to cases where *en* corresponds to a complement PP introduced by *de*.

### 6.4.7  Disjunctive pro-PPs

The items *là* (used as an independent word) and *ici* can be analysed as disjunctive pro-PPs, since they occur in the same positions as PPs: *J'ai mis le livre {là / ici}*. Like the demonstratives, these items have deictic properties and must be used instead of *y* when actually pointing at the place in question. Conversely, *y* is preferred when referring back to a place which has just been mentioned: *J'ai apporté une boîte pour y mettre les livres* (vs *?? ... pour mettre les livres là*). Nevertheless, in many cases *là* and *y* are more or less interchangeable: *Max a mangé dans ce restaurant et Luc {y a mangé / a mangé là} aussi* (see also the remarks on *là* and *y* in imperatives in 6.3.2). Note, however, that *là* can only be used to refer to places and cannot replace *y* in cases like *J'y pense*. (See 8.3.7 for further discussion of *là* and *ici*.)

### 6.4.8  A note on deixis

In English, distinctions such as *this* vs *that* or *here* vs *there* can be characterised fairly accurately in terms of distance – 'near to speaker' vs 'far from speaker'. In French, the distinction between forms in *-ci* and *-là* is less clear-cut.

This difference can be seen most clearly in the case of locative expressions. In English, one can say *Come here!* but not *\*Come there!*, because *come* indicates movement towards the speaker which conflicts with the meaning of *there*, but in French *Viens là!* is acceptable as well as *Viens ici!*. In French, *ici* implies proximity to the speaker, but *là* is more neutral with respect to distance, meaning something more like 'the place in question'.

With the demonstrative pronouns there is a closer correspondence between *cela* and *that* and *ceci* and *this* in terms of distance from the speaker. However, we do find a subtle difference with regard to the use of these items within a discourse. In English, we tend to use *this* to refer to something which has just been said: e.g. *This shows that*... rather than *That shows that*... In French, *cela* is generally preferred in such cases (*Cela démontre que*...) whereas *ceci* tends to anticipate something which follows: *Je te propose ceci: on parlera de cette question demain.*

With items like *celui* (and *celle(s)*, *ceux*), the suffix -*ci* picks out the nearest antecedent in the discourse whereas -*là* picks out the more remote antecedent (corresponding to *the latter* and *the former* respectively): *J'ai deux frères, Pierre$_p$ et Luc$_t$, Celui-ci$_t$ est médecin et celui-là$_p$ est avocat.*

### 6.5 The pro-PP 'y'

#### 6.5.1 Dative clitics and 'y'

In traditional grammars, the difference between Dative clitics and *y* is often presented in terms of the sorts of entities which they can refer to, *lui* and *leur* being used for human or at least animate beings, whereas *y* is used for inanimate objects or abstract concepts. There is perhaps something to this generalisation, but it is wrong to assume that *lui* and *leur* are simply the animate (or human) counterparts of *y*. As has already been observed, *y* can be used with *penser* to denote a human being, and (more significantly) *lui* and *leur* cannot be used with this verb – similarly with *réfléchir*, *songer*, *habituer*, *renoncer* and a few other verbs. Conversely, we find cases where a Dative clitic is used with inanimate reference:

(61)  a   Pour vendre cette vieille voiture, le garagiste lui a donné un coup de peinture

  b   Cette machine est une encyclopédie électronique. On lui pose une question et elle vous donne la réponse

  c   Je suis heureux de mes malheurs, puisque je leur dois mon amitié

In these examples, *y* could not be used in place of *lui/leur*.[5] A traditional response to such examples is to suggest that the entity is being personified in some way (see for example Byrne & Churchill, 1986, p. 134, from which example (61c) is taken). However, it is difficult to see how this notion of personification can be made precise or how it can explain the impossibility of *y* in these cases.

[5] This is not true of all varieties of French. There are some non-standard dialects is which *y* is used systematically in place of *lui* and *leur* (and sometimes other clitics as well). It is likely that *y* in these dialects has a very different status from that assumed here. The analysis presented here is based on Standard French. Possibly even in Standard French, *y* might be used in some of the examples in (61) but with a different interpretation (denoting a place) – e.g in (61b) with a reading 'pose the question on the keyboard' rather than 'ask it a question' which is the meaning conveyed here by the use of *lui*.

The analyses proposed in 6.2.5 and 6.4.6 represent a radically different approach which makes no direct appeal to the referential properties of the items in question, but treats the choice between Dative clitics and *y* as a selectional property of the verb. In practical terms, this analysis does not help us to decide whether a given instance of *à* + NP should be pronominalised by *y* or by *lui/leur*, whereas the traditional account at least enables us to make a 'good guess' on the basis of what the NP refers to. Nevertheless, the distinction beween Dative complements and PPs introduced by *à* provides a framework within which possible semantic generalisations can be investigated. Generally, it seems that verbs which select a Dative complement ($NP_{DAT}$) express semantic relations which typically involve human or animate beings in the role of Experiencer (*plaire*), Possessor/Receiver (*appartenir*, *donner*), Perceiver (*parler, dire, montrer*), etc. Thus, the tendency for *lui/leur* to have animate reference can be seen as a reflection of the semantic roles encoded by dative complements rather than as an intrinsic property of these items. Similarly, to the extent that any 'personification' is involved in examples like (61), this can be attributed to the use of verbs such as *donner, poser* (in the sense of 'ask') or *devoir*, rather than directly to the pronouns.[6]

On the other hand, the PP complements of verbs like *penser, songer, habituer*, etc., denote entities towards which a mental activity or attitude is directed, in a way which does not typically presuppose any human-like characteristics on the part of these entities. For example, the complements in *Pierre pense à sa femme* and *Ce professeur est habitué aux mauvais élèves* can be thought of as expressing a 'Phenomenon' role in the same way as the inanimate complements in *Pierre pense à ce film, Ce professeur est habitué aux mauvais résultats*.

Alongside verbs like *parler* which select $NP_{DAT}$ and verbs like *penser* which select [$_{PP}$ *à* NP], there are many verbs which appear to support the traditional view, in so far as they take Dative clitics when referring to animate beings but *y* for inanimate entities. In some of these cases, it seems quite clear that a difference in the meaning of the verb is involved rather than simply the referential properties of the complement. For example, the verbs in (62) denote movement of some entity to a place represented by *y*, whereas the same verbs in (63) express an experiential relation affecting the Dative entity:

(62)    a  Le train y est arrivé
          b  Pierre y a posé son manteau
          c  Jules y va souvent
          d  Marie y est venue

---

[6] To take an extreme example, in a sentence like *Max leur parle, à ces arbres*, it is Max who is attributing human-like qualities to the trees (by the act of talking to them) not the speaker of the sentence (by using the pronoun *leur*).

(63)     a  Un accident lui est arrivé
           b  L'étudiant lui a posé une question
           c  Cette robe lui va très bien
           d  Cette idée lui est venue dans son bain

In many other cases the semantic difference is more subtle. Consider the following examples, where the phrases in angled brackets indicate possible interpretations for the clitics:

(64)     a  Marie y a envoyé une lettre <à cette maison>
           b  Marie leur a envoyé une lettre <à ses parents>

(65)     a  Le professeur y a répondu <à la question>
           b  Le professeur lui a répondu <à l'étudiant>

It seems wrong to suggest that the verbs in (a) have a different meaning from those in (b). Nevertheless, there is a perceptible difference in the semantic roles of the complements, which is broadly in line with what has been observed in clearer examples. In (64a), *y* denotes a Location or destination on a par with the examples in (62), whereas *leur* in (64b) denotes a Receiver in the same way as the indirect object of a verb like *donner*. In (65b), *lui* has a Perceiver role parallel to the object of *parler*, whereas *y* in (65a) is analogous to the Phenomenon role with verbs like *penser* or *réfléchir*. However, there are other cases where it is difficult to discern any clear difference between the semantic roles of the complements other than those which can be attributed to the human vs non-human distinction:

(66)     a  Luc y a consacré sa vie <à son travail>
           b  Luc leur a consacré sa vie <à ses enfants>

(67)     a  Luc y est fidèle <à ses principes>
           b  Luc lui est fidèle <à sa femme>

At best, the entities in the (b) examples are affected by Luc's attitude in a way that the entities in (a) are not, but this inference amounts to little more than the fact that human beings can experience emotions whereas the inanimate referents of *y* in the (a) examples cannot. Finally, with verbs which express similarity or comparison, the choice between *y* and a Dative clitic seems to be determined entirely on the basis of animacy:

(68)     a  Jules y ressemble <à cette statue>
           b  Jules lui ressemble <à son père>

Examples like (66)–(68) provide the strongest evidence in favour of the traditional view which equates Dative clitics with animate reference and *y* with inanimate reference. Within this account we must stipulate in the lexical entries for *consacrer, fidèle, ressembler* and other similar items that the complement is expressed as $NP_{DAT}$ when NP is animate but as [$_{PP}$ *à* NP] otherwise. This may look like an *ad hoc* strategy which would be unnecessary within the traditional approach. However, there is some empirical support for this analysis. In (68b), *lui* must not only have an animate interpretation, it must also refer to a specific individual – sentence (68b) cannot be a paraphrase of *Jules ressemble à un soldat*, meaning that he has a military appearance. This reflects a general property of personal pronouns – namely that they must have specific reference. However, sentence (68a) can mean *Jules ressemble à une statue* describing statue-like appearance rather than similarity to a particular statue. Moreover, in an appropriate context, *y* in (68a) can have non-specific human reference: *Pierre ressemble à un soldat, et Jules y ressemble aussi*. This evidence indicates that even with *ressembler*, the choice between *lui/leur* and *y* is not solely a matter of animacy; moreover, it supports the claim that *y*, as a pro-PP replacing [$_{PP}$ *à* NP], is 'blind' to the properties of the NP (e.g. it can be definite or indefinite).

### 6.5.2 Suppletive 'y'

In 6.3.1 we saw that Dative clitics cannot be used to represent the indirect object if the direct object is realised as *me, te, se, nous* or *vous*, because of a general restriction on compatibility of clitics. Thus, we must use disjunctive pronouns in cases like (69):

(69)  a  Je vous présenterai à elle
      b  Luc s'est consacré à eux

However, for some speakers, an alternative possibility is to use the clitic *y*, even though with the verbs in (69) *y* can normally only be used to denote an inanimate entity (e.g. *Je les y présenterai* can only mean 'I will introduce/present them there' and *Luc y a consacré sa vie* can only mean 'Luc dedicated his life to it'). Thus, for these speakers, examples like (70) are acceptable with interpretations of the sort indicated in angle brackets, even though the same speakers would require *lui* or *leur* in (71):

(70)  a  %Je vous y présenterai <à cette actrice>
      b  %Luc s'y est consacré <à ses enfants>

(71)  a  Je lui présenterai mes amis
      b  Luc leur a consacré sa vie

This usage is generally deemed non-standard, but it may help to clarify the approach developed in 6.2.5, 6.4.6 and 6.5.1.

To account for the choice of clitic in (71) we must assume that the indirect object of these verbs is $NP_{DAT}$ when it refers to a human being; thus (69a), (70a) and (71a) are derived from (72):

(72)     $[_S$ Je $[_{VP}$ présenterai $NP_{ACC}$ $NP_{DAT}]]$

If $NP_{ACC}$ is realised as a third-person clitic or as an ordinary NP, $NP_{DAT}$ must be realised as a Dative clitic if it is pronominalised, as in (71a). However, if $NP_{ACC}$ is realised as a second-person clitic, as in (69a) and (70a), the use of a Dative clitic for the indirect object is excluded because of the incompatibility restriction mentioned above, so the $\hat{A}$-insertion rule proposed in 6.2.5 will apply, giving (69a), with the structure (73):

(73)     $[_S$ Je $[_{VP}$ vous présenterai $[_{PP}$ à PRONOUN$]]]$

At this point, for the speakers in question, there is the option of replacing the entire PP by *y*, giving (70a). Example (70b) can be accounted for in essentially the same way.

The important point about the examples in (70) is that they show that the *lui/leur* vs *y* distinction cannot be stated simply in terms of animacy, even if we allow for 'exceptional' verbs like *penser* which always require *y*. Whereas *lui* and *leur* are realisations of a special type of indirect object represented as $NP_{DAT}$, which is expressed by the preposition *à* when the element cannot be cliticised, *y* can be used to replace all phrases of the type $[_{PP}$ *à* PRONOUN$]$ (and PPs with other prepositions which denote places) where the element PRONOUN cannot be cliticised directly to the verb. Note that this account would not allow the use of *y* instead of the Dative clitics in examples like (71). In such cases, the only valid reason for not using a Dative clitic would be to give contrastive stress to the pronoun, but this consideration would also preclude the use of *y*.

This analysis can also derive examples like *Pierre y ressemble <à un soldat>* from the underlying structure (74), assuming that *ressembler* selects $NP_{DAT}$ when the referent is human:

(74)        $[_S$ Pierre $[_{VP}$ ressemble $NP_{DAT}]]$

In this case, the complement cannot be realised as a Dative clitic, because Dative clitics can only have definite reference. Consequently, the $\hat{A}$-insertion rule will apply, giving (75), at which point the whole PP can be relaced by *y*:

(75)        $[_S$ Pierre $[_{VP}$ ressemble $[_{PP}$ à NP$]]]$

## 6.6 The pro-PP 'en'

### *6.6.1 'En' and 'de'*

In examples like the following, *en* can plausibly be analysed as a pro-PP which replaces phrases introduced by *de* in much the same way as *y* replaces PPs introduced by *à*:

(76)  a  Pierre s'en souvient <de son enfance / de son grand-père>
      b  Jacques en est sorti <de la maison>
      c  Jules en est amoureux <de Marie>
      d  Solange en est fière <de son travail>

As the suggested interpretations indicate, *en* can be used with human reference, though a construction with a disjunctive pronoun is often preferred: *Pierre se souvient de lui, Jules est amoureux d'elle.* In cases involving movement from a place (e.g. (76b)), an alternative construction with *de* and a disjunctive pro-PP, *là* or *ici*, can be used: *Jacques est sorti de {là / ici}.*

### *6.6.2 'En' or 'son'?*

*En* can also be used to represent the complement of a noun in the direct object position, as in (77a) which has the underlying structure (77b):

(77)  a  J'en ai lu la préface. <de ce livre>
      b  [$_S$ Je [$_{VP}$ ai lu [$_{NP}$ la préface [$_{PP}$ de PRONOUN]]]]

A less natural alternative in such cases is to use the so-called 'possessive' determiner:

(78)  J'ai lu sa préface

However, the construction with the possessive determiner is strongly preferred when human reference is involved:

(79)  a  J'ai trouvé son stylo
      b  ?J'en ai trouvé le stylo

Nevertheless, the choice between *en* and a possessive determiner is not simply a matter of human or non-human reference. Sentence (80) is perfectly acceptable on a reading where *en* denotes the person depicted (i.e. the complement of *portrait*), but is harder to interpret if *en* is meant to denote the artist or the owner:

(80)  J'en ai vu le portrait

This evidence suggests that *en* with human reference can only be used readily to represent a complement of the noun, as opposed to an Agent or a Possessor. In

269

fact, this restriction also seems to hold for *de* + disjunctive pronoun within an NP. Sentence (81a) is reasonably acceptable with a 'depicted person' reading, but (81b) is even worse than (79b):

(81)     a   J'ai vu le portrait de lui
         b   *J'ai trouvé le stylo de lui

In cases requiring emphasis on the Possessor, the usual strategy is to use a possessive determiner 'reinforced' by *à* + pronoun: *J'ai trouvé son stylo à lui.*

This restriction on *en* and *de* + pronoun does not hold for possessive determiners. Thus *son* in (82) can be readily interpreted as denoting the artist, the owner or the depicted person:

(82)       J'ai vu son portrait

However, if more than one of these participants is expressed, there is a 'pecking order' which gives the Agent or Possessor priority over the complement for realisation as a possessive determiner; thus, in *son portrait de Pierre, Pierre* must be interpreted as the depicted person while *son* can denote either the artist or the owner. Note now that if *Pierre* in this construction is replaced by a pronoun, a disjunctive form must be used, not *en*:

(83)     a   J'ai vu son portrait de lui
         b   *J'en ai vu son portrait

Some linguists have argued that possessive determiners (and phrases like *John's* in English) qualify as subjects of the NP in which they occur (this is particularly plausible in cases where the noun denotes an action: e.g. *ma discussion de la question* vs *J'ai discuté la question*). Adopting this assumption, the ungrammaticality of examples like (83b) can be accounted for by extending the Specified Subject Condition proposed in 6.2.2, to subjects of constituents other than clauses:

**Specified Subject Condition (extended version):**
*no item can be extracted from a phrase across the subject of that phrase.*

Thus, the derivation of (83b) from the structure in (84) is ruled out, since this would entail moving the PP out of the NP across the subject of that NP, *son*:

(84)      [$_S$ Je [$_{VP}$ ai vu [$_{NP}$ son portrait [$_{PP}$ de PRONOUN]]]]
                                  *

The use of *en* to represent part of an NP is not possible when the NP in question is the complement of a preposition:

(85)     a   *J'en pensais à la préface
         b   *Je m'en souviens du portrait

c  *Ce personnage en apparaît dans le premier acte <de cette pièce>

These examples have underlying structures of the form in (86):

(86)  $[_S$ NP $[_{VP}$ V $[_{PP}$ Prep $[_{NP}$ Det N $[_{PP}$ de PRONOUN$]]]]]$

To derive the examples in (85) we would have to replace *de* + PRONOUN by *en* and cliticise it to the verb, as shown by the arrow. However, this movement violates the PP-Island Constraint which prohibits movement out of a PP in French (see 6.2.2).

### 6.6.3 'En-avant'

In some cases, *en* can represent the complement of a noun in subject position:

(87)  a  La préface n'en est pas intéressante
      b  La préface en devient ennuyeuse vers la fin
      c  La préface en a été critiquée par beaucoup de gens

Examples of this type are restricted to a fairly erudite style and, indeed, not all speakers find them acceptable. Consequently, the subtleties of these constructions may be of limited relevance to the practical concerns of students of French. Nevertheless, such constructions raise some interesting questions which have been discussed extensively by linguists because of their relevance to other aspects of French syntax.

Note, firstly, that *en* does not remain within the subject NP, but is cliticised to the verb, as shown by the fact that it follows the negative particle *ne* in (87a). This suggests the derivation in (88):

(88)  $[_S$ $[_{NP}$ la préface $[_{PP}$ de PRONOUN$]]$ $[_{VP}$ ne est pas intéressante$]]$

This process (called **En-avant** by Ruwet 1972) is rather odd in two respects. Firstly, it appears to involve a lowering operation. Secondly, it can only occur with a restricted class of verbs: essentially copular verbs (e.g. *être, devenir, rester*, etc.) and passive forms. In the case of passives, it has been argued (see 1.5.3 and 3.2.2) that the surface subject occupies the direct object position in the underlying structure. Thus (87c) is derived from the structure (89):

(89)  $[_S$ $\emptyset$ $[_{VP}$ a été critiqué $[_{NP}$ la préface $[_{PP}$ de PRONOUN$]]$ $[_{PP}$ par beaucoup de gens$]]]$

Note now that *en* (= *de* + PRONOUN) can be cliticised to the verb by the general process illustrated in (77b), provided that Clitic-placement applies before the direct object is moved into the subject position. Examples like (87a, b) can be treated in a similar way, if we adopt the analysis suggested in 2.5.2, where the subject of *être, devenir*, etc., is represented as the subject of a 'small clause' in the underlying structure, as in (90):

(90)     $[_S \varnothing [_{VP}$ ne est pas $[_{SC} [_{NP}$ la préface $[_{PP}$ de PRONOUN$]] [_{AP}$ intéressante$]]]]$

Again, the surface structure (87a) can be derived by first cliticising *de* + PRONOUN to the verb as *en* and then moving *la préface* into the main subject position.

In so far as the analyses in (89) and (90) enable us to eliminate the rather odd operation in (88) by reducing apparent cases of 'En-avant' to the more general Clitic-placement process, examples like those in (87) provide evidence in support of the abstract underlying structures proposed for passive and copular constructions.

### 6.6.4  Indefinite 'en'

As well as representing *de*-type complements of verbs, adjectives and nouns, *en* can be used as a substitute for the nominal element in certain types of indefinite NP:

(91)     a   Henri en a lu beaucoup <de (ces) livres>
         b   Gaston en a acheté assez <de (ce) vin>

As the suggested interpretations show, *en* can have either a partitive interpretation (denoting a specific set of books or a specific sample of wine) or a quantitative interpretation (expressing a certain quantity of books or wine); see 5.3.6–5.3.7 for detailed discussion of partitive and quantitative constructions. These examples conform to the general pattern established for *en* in so far as *en* replaces an expression introduced by the preposition *de*. However, this parallel appears to break down in cases like (92) whose counterparts in (93) do not contain *de*:

(92)     a   Henri en a lu plusieurs
         b   Marie en a acheté une
         c   Luc en a mangé trois

(93)     a   Henri a lu plusieurs livres
         b   Marie a acheté une moto
         c   Luc a mangé trois gâteaux

In 5.3.6, items like *un(e)*, *plusieurs* and numerals were analysed as determiners which occur in the structure $[_{NP}$ Det N'$]$ in cases like (93). On this basis, it would

seem that *en* can act as a substitute for an N' introduced by an indefinite determiner, as well as for an expression introduced by *de* in the other examples discussed so far. Nevertheless, it may be noted that the determiners in (92) can also
be used in partitive constructions like (94) where they are followed by *de*:

(94)  a  Henri a lu plusieurs de ces livres
      b  Marie a acheté une de ces motos
      c  Luc a mangé trois de ces gâteaux

Moreover, the sentences in (92) can be interpreted in the same way as those in (94).

To cut a long story short, we can simplify our characterisation of *en* by supposing that examples like (92) are syntactically parallel to partitive constructions like
(94) even though they can have the quantitative interpretation illustrated in (93) –
i.e. we assume that *en* always replaces expressions of the form [*de* [NP
PRONOUN]][7], not an N'. Some justification for this view is provided by examples
with *quelques* which must have the form *quelques-uns* in partitive constructions,
as shown in (95):

(95)  a  Henri a lu [$_{NP}$ quelques [$_{N'}$ livres]]
      b  Henri a lu [$_{NP}$ quelques-uns [$_{NP}$ de [$_{NP}$ ces livres]]]

Corresponding examples with *en* also require *quelques-uns*, even though they can
have the quantitative interpretation of (95a):

(96)      Henri en a lu {quelques-uns / *quelques}

In examples like (91), (92) and (96), *en* cannot be omitted, in contrast to English
where the determiner can be used on its own: *Gaston bought enough, Henry read
several/some, Luc ate one/three*, etc.:

(97)  a  *Gaston a acheté assez
      b  *Henri a lu plusieurs/quelques-uns
      c  *Marie a acheté une
      d  *Luc a mangé trois

Similarly, *en* is obligatory with quantity expressions like *un kilo, une douzaine*:
*J'en ai acheté un kilo / une douzaine*. Some items of the type in (91) can be used on
their own, as in *Gaston boit {beaucoup / trop}*, but in these cases they act as modifiers of the verb rather than determiners of the direct object.

---

[7] In 5.3.7 and 5.4.1 *de* in partitive constructions was analysed as a Case-marker adjoined to a
NP rather than the head of a PP. For the sake of consistency, this analysis will be maintained.
However, the syntax of *en* does not appear to be sensitive to this distinction. For purposes of
presentation, the characterisation of *en* as a pro-PP should be taken as meaning that it can
replace either a genuine PP or an NP to which *de* is adjoined.

The indefinite use of *en* is not possible with complements of prepositions:

(98)    a    *Pierre en a pensé à beaucoup <de (ces) problèmes>
        b    *Jules en a voté pour trois <candidats>

Such examples are ruled out by the PP-Island Constraint, since *en* would have to be moved out of a PP:

(99)    [Pierre    a pensé [$_{PP}$ à [$_{NP}$ beaucoup [$_{NP}$ de PRONOUN]]]]

Also, *en* cannot represent a subject quantified by an indefinite expression; i.e. we do not have counterparts of the 'En-avant' cases in (87) with the indefinite use of *en*:

(100)   a    *Plusieurs en sont pourries <(de ces) pommes>
        b    *Un kilo en a été perdu <de plutonium>

In cases like (98) and (100) the quantity expression can be used without *en*, as in (101), though it is generally preferable to reformulate the sentence so that the indefinite NP is in the direct object position (e.g. *Il y en a plusieurs qui sont pourries*):

(101)   a    Jules a voté pour trois
        b    Plusieurs sont pourries

The generalisation seems to be that *en* must be used with an indefinite expression whenever this is syntactically possible.

In examples like (102b), *en* appears to replace the whole of the direct object NP:

(102)   a    Pierre a mangé {du pain / des carottes}
        b    Pierre en a mangé

Such examples bear out the general correspondence between *en* and phrases introduced by *de*, but they appear to conflict with the claim that *en* is a pro-PP since *du pain* and *des carottes* in (102a) are quite clearly direct objects of *manger*, therefore Accusative NPs rather than PPs or Genitive NPs. However, this paradox is resolved if we adopt the analysis proposed in 5.4.4, whereby NPs like *du pain* contain a null determiner which resembles *beaucoup, peu, assez*, etc., in that it requires the quantified expression to be introduced by *de*, roughly as in (103):

(103)   [$_{NP}$ ∅ [$_{NP}$ de [$_{NP}$ le pain]]]

Given this analysis, (102b) can be derived as in (104), cliticising *de* + PRONOUN to the verb as *en* leaving behind the null determiner and the NP structure which contains it:

(104)     [$_S$ Pierre [$_{VP}$ a mangé [$_{NP}$ $\varnothing$ [$_{NP}$ de PRONOUN]]]]

The impression that *en* replaces the whole NP in (102) simply reflects the fact that the remainder of the NP which is left behind does not contain any overt material, in contrast to analogous cases like (91) and (92) where this NP contains a 'real' determiner like *beaucoup* or *plusieurs*.

Note that *en* in (102b) can only have a plural or non-countable interpretation; e.g. (102b) cannot mean *Pierre a mangé un sandwich*. When a singular, countable interpretation is required, the overt determiner *un* must be used: *Pierre en a mangé un*.

## 6.7 Pronouns and their antecedents

### 6.7.1 Coreference across sentences

Often, though not always, pronouns are used to refer back to an earlier expression (known as the **antecedent**), their function being to avoid unnecessary repetition of a full NP. The relation between a pronoun and its antecedent is a particular case of **coreference**, the semantic relation between two expressions which designate the same entity. As was seen in 6.4.1, personal pronouns with inanimate reference typically depend on an antecedent to provide the appropriate gender feature, whereas pronouns with animate reference and demonstratives can be used more readily to refer directly to entities in the 'real world'. This is particularly true of the first- and second-person forms, which refer to participants in the act of communication.

In cases where the pronoun and its antecedent occur in different sentences, the appropriate use of the pronoun is largely a matter of common-sense. Essentially, the antecedent must occur before the pronoun and it must be sufficiently prominent in the discourse to enable the addressee to make the connection between the two. For example, in (105) *il* can readily refer back to *Pierre* or *ce livre* (as indicated by the subscripts) and repetition of the full NP would be clumsy, though possible:

(105)     a   J'ai vu Pierre$_p$ hier ... Il$_p$ portait un chapeau
          b   J'ai lu ce livre$_l$ ... Il$_l$ est très intéressant

In normal discourse, we cannot use the pronoun first and then identify the referent in a later sentence: e.g. *Pierre* and *le* cannot be coreferential in *Je l'ai vu hier ... Pierre portait un chapeau*, unless Pierre has been mentioned previously.[8] Also, the use of *il* in (105) might be inappropriate or confusing if the intervening discourse

---

[8] Cases of this sort are found in novels by authors like Robbe-Grillet who often introduce characters 'anonymously' by means of a pronoun and reveal their identity later in the narrative. However, this is not typical of normal discourse.

(indicated by the dots) changed the topic or introduced other potential antecedents for the pronoun.

### 6.7.2 *Structural conditions on coreference*

When the pronoun and its antecedent both occur in the same sentence, principles of a rather different sort come into play. Note firstly that in some cases the pronoun can precede its antecedent[9]:

(106)　　a　Lorsque je l$_p$'ai vu, Pierre$_p$ portait un chapeau
　　　　　b　Bien que je ne l$_l$'ai pas lu, ce livre$_l$ me paraît intéressant

In (106), the pronoun forms part of a subordinate clause which modifies the main clause containing the antecedent, as shown roughly in (107):

(107)

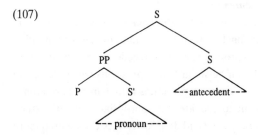

It is also possible to construct examples in which the two clauses are conjoined by a co-ordinating conjunction such as *mais* or even *et* as in the following examples which have the structure in (109):

(108)　　a　Je ne l$_l$'ai pas lu mais ce livre$_l$ me paraît très intéressant
　　　　　b　Je l$_l$'ai lu très soigneusement et ce livre$_l$ me paraît effectivement très intéressant

(109)

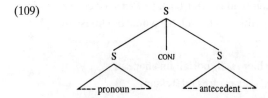

Although the clauses in (108) are structurally on an equal footing, the use of the pronoun requires us to interpret the first clause as presenting the background to the main assertion expressed by the second clause (e.g. (108a) involves a concessive relation similar to that signalled by *bien que* in (106b)). When the conjoined clauses

---

[9] There is perhaps a terminological contradiction here in so far as 'antecedent' literally means 'coming before'. However, let us ignore etymology and use this term simply to designate the phrase which supplies the referent for the pronoun regardless of linear order.

express independent propositions of equal importance, as in (110), coreference between the pronoun and a following NP is much more difficult to obtain:

(110)     ??Je l$_1$'ai acheté hier et je lirai ce livre$_1$ ce soir

This evidence suggests that the conditions governing the **cataphoric** use of pronouns (where the pronoun precedes its antecedent) are pragmatic rather than structural in nature, involving the relative importance of different parts of the sentence to the message conveyed by the sentence as a whole. However, examples like the following show that structural principles are also at work:

(111)     a   *Il$_p$ pense que Pierre$_p$ est intelligent
          b   Sa$_p$ femme pense que Pierre$_p$ est intelligent

In (111a), coreference between *il* and *Pierre* is totally impossible, whereas in (111b) the possessive determiner *sa* (a pronoun in the determiner position) can easily refer to *Pierre*.

To account for the difference in (111) we appeal to a structural relation known as **c-command**:

**C-command:**
*X c-commands Y if the lowest branching node which dominates X also ultimately dominates Y.*

A simple way of checking whether one item c-commands another is to look at the relevant tree structure and follow the upward branch from one item (X) until you reach the first branching node. If there is a downward path from this node to the other item (Y), then X c-commands Y. Applying this procedure to the structures in (112), we can see that the subject of the main clause *il* c-commands *Pierre* in (112a), but *sa* in (112b) does not (the arrows against branches indicate the relevant paths):

(112)     (a)

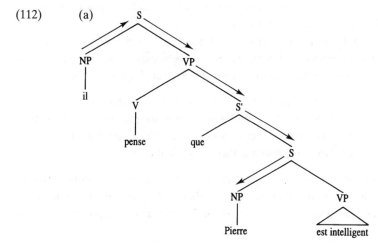

*Pronouns*

(112)    (b)

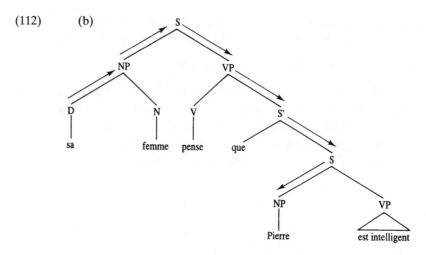

In (112a) we can trace a path from *il* up to the first branching category S and then downwards to *Pierre*, but in (112b) working upwards from *sa*, the first branching node we come to is NP, which does not dominate *Pierre* – there is no downward path from this NP to *Pierre*. In fact, in (112a) *il* c-commands everything else in the structure whereas *sa* in (112b) only c-commands *femme*.

This notion of c-command may appear very technical and abstract, but it plays a crucial role in determining the possibilities of coreference between expressions, and indeed in many other syntactic processes. In particular, the contrast between (111a) and (111b) can be explained by the following condition:

*A pronoun cannot c-command its antecedent.*

Note that the examples in (106) and (108) are consistent with this condition since the pronoun forms part of a clause (and indeed a lower branching category, VP) which does not contain the antecedent.

This condition can be strengthened further. Note that in cases like (106), (108) and (111b) it is possible (though perhaps cumbersome) to use the full NP twice with the same referent, but this is not possible in examples like (111a):

(113)    a    Lorsque j'ai vu Pierre$_p$, Pierre$_p$ portait un chapeau
         b    Je n'ai pas lu ce livre$_l$, mais ce livre$_l$ me paraît très intéressant
         c    La femme de Pierre$_p$ pense que Pierre$_p$ est intelligent
         d    *Pierre$_p$ pense que Pierre$_p$ est intelligent

The crucial difference here is that in (113d) the first *Pierre* c-commands the second whereas in the other examples neither of the relevant NPs c-commands the other. Thus, examples like (113d) can be excluded by a general condition

278

which prevents any full NP from being coreferential with another item (either a pronoun or a full NP) which c-commands it. To facilitate this presentation, let us introduce a new relation, known as **binding**, which involves both coreference and the c-command relation:

**Binding:**
*if two expressions X and Y are coreferential and X c-commands Y, then X binds Y.*

Given this concept, the condition just proposed can be formulated as follows:

*A full NP (i.e. not a pronoun) cannot be bound.*

A consequence of this condition is that when two expressions refer to the same thing and a c-command relation holds between them, the lower expression must be realised as a pronoun (as in (114) below), whereas if no c-command relation obtains, the use of a pronoun for either expression is optional within the pragmatic limitations suggested above.

(114)      Pierre$_p$ pense qu'il$_p$ est intelligent

The facts reviewed above are identical to those found in English and are thus unlikely to cause practical problems. However, the concepts of binding and c-command shed some light on other more problematic cases.

### 6.7.3  Reflexive and reciprocal pronouns

When a direct object or dative complement refers back to the subject of the clause, we cannot use the ordinary Accusative or Dative clitics (in the third person):

(115)      a   *Paul$_p$ l$_p$'admire
          b   *Paul$_p$ lui$_p$ parle

In such cases, the reflexive clitic *se* must be used:

(116)      a   Paul s'admire
          b   Paul se parle

Similarly, in English we must use *himself* rather than *him*:

(117)      a   Paul$_p$ admires {himself$_p$ / *him$_p$}
          b   Paul$_p$ talks to {himself$_p$ / *him$_p$}

When *se* has a plural antecedent, it can express a *reciprocal* relation (= 'each other') as well as a strictly **reflexive** one (= 'themselves'); e.g. (118) can mean either 'They admire each other' or 'They admire themselves':

(118)     Ils s'admirent

Even under the reciprocal interpretation it seems reasonable to suppose that *se* is coreferential with *ils*, in so far as the set of 'admirers' is identical to the set of 'admirees'. In English, we are forced to specify whether this relation holds reflexively for each individual or whether it holds between distinct individuals within the same set, whereas French looks only at identity at the level of the set.

### 6.7.4  Anaphors

To avoid possible confusion over the term 'reflexive', let us use the term **anaphor** to denote items like *se, himself, themselves* and *each other.*[10] More generally, anaphors are items which must have an antecedent, whereas non-anaphors ('ordinary pronouns') do not need an antecedent. The conditions governing the use of these two types of pronouns can be stated provisionally as follows:

*I  Anaphors must be bound within the simple clause.*
*II  Non-anaphors cannot be bound within the simple clause.*

The examples in (116) above satisfy (I), but *le* and *lui* in (115) cannot refer back to *Paul* since, if they did, they would be bound by *Paul* within the simple clause. In (119) below, *Paul* binds the clitic, but the two elements are in different clauses, so only the non-anaphor can be used:

(119)     a   Paul croit que je {le / *se} déteste
          b   Paul croit que je {lui / *se} parlerai

Similarly, a non-anaphor must be used in (120) to refer back to *Paul* (though the versions with *se* are fine if the antecedent is *la femme de Paul*):

(120)     a   La femme de Paul {le / *se} déteste
          b   La femme de Paul {lui / *se} parlera

Although *Paul* and the clitic are in the same simple clause, *Paul* does not c-command the clitic (*Paul* is part of an NP which does not contain the clitic) and therefore cannot bind it.

In English, anaphors like *each other* can refer back to a direct object NP, but *se* cannot be used in this way, nor indeed can a non-anaphor such as *leur*:

(121)     a   The hostess will introduce the guests to each other
          b   *L'hôtesse se$_i$ présentera les invités$_i$
          c   *L'hôtesse leur$_i$ présentera les invités$_i$

---

[10] The term 'anaphor' is often used in a much wider sense to denote any expression which refers back to some other expression in the sentence or discourse. The technical use of this term adopted here is based on Chomsky (1981).

A simple way of describing this difference would be to stipulate that *se* (unlike English anaphors) can only refer back to a subject, though this would not explain the ungrammaticality of (121c). However, a more obvious difference between *se* and *each other* is that *se* is a clitic whereas *each other* is not. Leaving aside the fine details of structure, let us assume that when a pronoun is cliticised to the verb, it c-commands everything else within the VP. Thus both *se* and *leur* can be ruled out by the condition proposed in 6.7.2 which prevents a pronoun from c-commanding its antecedent. Example (121a) does not violate this condition since *each other* remains within the PP and therefore does not c-command the antecedent, which is outside this PP.

### 6.7.5 *Derived subjects*

The differences observed in (121) also show up in the corresponding passive sentences:

(122)  a  The guests will be introduced to each other (by the hostess)
      b  *Les invités$_i$ se$_i$ seront présentés (par l'hôtesse)
      c  *Les invités$_i$ leur$_i$ seront présentés (par l'hôtesse)

The judgements of (122a) and (122c) are unsurprising since the subject c-commands (and binds) the pronoun within the clause, as is required for an anaphor like *each other* but prohibited for a non-anaphor like *leur*, but (122b) ought to be grammatical according to the principles proposed so far. A clue to this mystery lies in the assumption that the subject of a passive sentence is the underlying direct object of the verb. Thus, (122b) is derived as in (123) (ignoring the *par* phrase):

(123)  a  [  ∅  [$_{VP}$  seront présenté les invités P R O N O U N$_{DAT}$]]
      b  [ les invités [$_{VP}$  se seront présentés ___  ___  ]]

After the movement processes in (123b) have applied, *se* is bound by its antecedent (*les invités*) within the clause, as required by condition (I) in 6.7.4, but *se* c-commands the trace of the antecedent (the position from which the antecedent is moved). Consequently, a natural way of excluding (122b) is to modify the condition invoked with regard to (121b) as follows:

*A pronoun cannot c-command its antecedent or the trace of its antecedent.*

This condition may explain another puzzling restriction on *se*. Some adjectives, like *fidèle*, can take a dative complement (with human reference) as in (124):

(124)  a  Paul est fidèle à sa femme
      b  Paul lui est fidèle

In (124b), *lui* must refer to someone other than Paul, as expected. However, we might also expect to to find *se* (parallel to *each other*) in a case like (125) where there is a reciprocal relation between the subject and the complement:

(125) a Those lovers are faithful to each other
   b *Ces amants se sont fidèles

The ungrammaticality of (125b) can be explained by appealing to the 'small clause' analysis of copular constructions proposed in 2.5.2. According to this analysis, (125b) is derived as follows:

(126) a [ $\emptyset$ [$_{VP}$ sont [$_{SC}$ ces amants [$_{AP}$ fidèles PRONOUN$_{DAT}$]]]]
   b [ces amants [$_{VP}$ se sont [$_{SC}$ ___ [$_{AP}$ fidèles ___ ]]]]

As (126b) shows, once *se* is cliticised to the verb, it c-commands the trace of its antecedent, violating the condition proposed above. Of course, if the pronoun is not coreferential with the subject, as in (124b), it will also c-command the trace of the subject, but in this case the subject is not the antecedent, so there is no violation of this condition.

### 6.7.6 First- and second-person clitics

The items *me, te, nous* and *vous* can function as both anaphors and non-anaphors. They can thus be used in exactly the same way as *se* and *le/lui* in the examples discussed above, and with the same restrictions:

(127) a Vous vous admirez
   b Nous croyons que Jules nous déteste
   c Vos parents vous admirent
   d *Vous vous serez présentés par l'hôtesse
   e *Nous nous sommes fidèles

Note that when these items function as anaphors they require *être* as the perfective auxiliary (like *se*), but *avoir* is used when they have non-anaphor status:

(128) a Nous nous sommes regardés
   b Vous vous êtes téléphoné

(129) a Pierre nous a regardés
   b Pierre nous a téléphoné

In the (a) examples, the past participle normally agrees with the clitic, since the clitic represents the direct object. Similarly, the lack of agreement in the (b) examples can be attributed to the Dative status of the clitic (*téléphoner* takes an indirect object). Moreover, examples like (128b) suggest that past participles in reflexive constructions agree with the preceding direct object rather than with the subject.

### 6.7.7 Pronouns with '-même'

Adding *-même* to a disjunctive personal pronoun (or *-mêmes* if the pronoun is plural) converts it into a reflexive anaphor, as can be seen in (130):

(130)      a    Paul pense toujours à lui-même
           b    *Paul veut que je pense à lui-même
           c    *La mère de Paul pense à lui-même

In (130a), the antecedent *Paul* c-commands *lui-même* within the simple clause, as required, but in (130b) *Paul* is in a different clause, whereas, in (130c), although *Paul* is in the same clause, it does not c-command *lui-même* and therefore cannot bind it. This situation is the same for *himself* in English.

Like ordinary disjunctive pronouns, forms with *-même(s)* can only occur in certain structural positions. For example, they can occur readily as the object of a preposition, as in (130a), but not as a direct object unless they are modified by *ne ... que* or conjoined with another NP:

(131)      a    *Paul admire lui-même
           b    Paul n'admire que lui-même
           c    Paul admire lui-même et sa famille

Similarly, it is rather odd to use a form with *-même(s)* as a dative complement in cases like (132):

(132)      a    ?Paul parlait à lui-même
           b    ?Paul a offert une nouvelle voiture à lui-même

In cases like (131a) and (132), the clitic anaphor *se* would be used. In 6.7.4 and 6.7.5, it was pointed out that *se* cannot be used when its antecedent is a direct object or the subject of a passive construction, nor can it be used as the dative complement of an adjective like *fidèle*. Relevant examples with a true reflexive (rather than reciprocal) interpretation tend to describe rather unusual situations. Nevertheless, the appropriate way of describing reflexive relations of this sort is by means of a form with *-même(s)*:

(133)      a    La psychanalyse a révélé Paul à lui-même
           b    Paul a été révélé à lui-même
           c    Paul est fidèle à lui-même

These examples bear out the generalisation that disjunctive forms are used in just those cases where the corresponding clitic cannot be used. Apart from this restriction, forms like *lui-même* can be used in essentially the same way as *himself* in English.

Although it has been established that forms with *-même(s)* are anaphors, like English reflexive pronouns, it is by no means clear that forms without *-même(s)* are non-anaphors. In this respect, French is rather different from English. In the English counterpart of (130a) we must use *himself* to refer back to *Paul* (*him* in (134a) must refer to someone else), but in French we can use an ordinary disjunctive pronoun:

(134)    a    *$Paul_p$ is always thinking of $him_p$
         b    $Paul_p$ pense toujours à $lui_p$

Similarly, in (135) we can use *lui* as an alternative to *lui-même*, whereas English requires *himself*:

(135)    a    $Paul_p$ n'admire que lui(-même)$_p$
         b    $Paul_p$ est fier de lui(-même)$_p$

The English example (134a) is ruled out by condition (I) in 6.7.4 which prevents a non-anaphor like *him* from being bound within the simple clause. A possible way of accounting for the French examples in (134b) and (135) is to suppose that disjunctive personal pronouns (without *-même(s)*) are neutral with respect to the anaphor/non-anaphor distinction – that is, they can be bound within the simple clause, though they do not need to be.

The choice between forms with or without *-même(s)* in cases like (134b) and (135) seems to be determined by pragmatic factors. Essentially, if the relation described is one which can naturally apply reflexively (like 'admiring oneself', 'thinking of oneself' or 'being proud of oneself') and if there is no other, more plausible, antecedent for the pronoun, there is no need to use *-même(s)*. Thus, in (136a), we have no difficulty in interpreting *lui* as referring back to *Paul*, whereas in (136b) *son père* is a more natural antecedent and we would need to add *-même* if a reflexive interpretation were intended:

(136)    a    Etant égoiste, Paul pense toujours à lui
         b    Depuis le départ de son père, Paul pense toujours à lui

Similarly, in cases like (133) above and (137) below, where the reflexive interpretation is somewhat contrived or unexpected, it must be signalled by *-même(s)*:

(137)    a    Paul a voté pour lui-même
         b    Paul ne méprise que lui-même

Conversely, there are some cases where the explicit reflexive form is excluded, notably as a complement of *chez* and *entre*:

(138)    a   Marie est rentrée chez elle(\*-même)

           b   Les étudiants parlaient entre eux(\*-mêmes)

In (138b), *entre eux* denotes a loosely reciprocal relation and, for this reason, it is difficult to interpret *eux* as referring to anyone other than *les étudiants* (cf. the oddness of *\*Nous parlions entre eux*); thus the exclusion of *-mêmes* in this case might be attributed to the fact that it is superfluous. However, this reasoning does not help with (138a) since we cannot use *-même* to signal a reflexive interpretation even in cases like (139) where the context provides an alternative antecedent (*sa mère*) for the pronoun (here *elle* can refer to either *Marie* or *sa mère*, though the former interpretation is the more likely):

(139)        Après avoir quitté sa mère ce matin, Marie est rentrée chez elle ce soir

This appears to be a peculiarity of *chez*, for which I have no explanation.

Like English reflexive pronouns, forms with *-même(s)* can be used to 'reinforce' another NP (typically a subject) to indicate that the person(s) concerned performed the action directly, rather than through some intermediary:

(140)    a   Le Président répondra lui-même à cette question

           b   Marie a réparé la voiture elle-même

           c   Les enfants ont écrit cette histoire eux-mêmes

Also, forms with *-même(s)* can be used in addition to a clitic anaphor such as *se*, particularly when the antecedent is plural in order to indicate that *se* is to be interpreted reflexively rather than reciprocally:

(141)    a   Les étudiants se critiquaient eux-mêmes

           b   Les filles se sont offert des fleurs à elles-mêmes

(For ways of disambiguating *se* in favour of a reciprocal interpretation, see 6.7.11.)

### 6.7.8  Possessive determiners

Like disjunctive personal pronouns, possessive determiners appear to be neutral with regard to the anaphor/non-anaphor distinction. In (142a), *sa* can refer back to *Paul*, which c-commands it within the simple clause, or to some other person such as *Jules* in (142b):

(142)      a   Paul a réparé sa voiture

            b   Jules pense que Paul a réparé sa voiture

Similarly, in (143), *sa* can refer back to the NP which c-commands it (*le père de Marcel*) or to the lower NP (*Marcel*), which does not c-command it, or indeed to some other party:

(143)     Le père de Marcel a réparé sa voiture

We find the same situation in English (*his* has the same range of potential referents in the counterparts of (142) and (143)), though the potential for ambiguity is more widespread in French, because possessive determiners agree in gender with the 'possessee' rather than the 'possessor':

(144)     a  Marie pense que Paul a réparé sa voiture
              Mary thinks that Paul has repaired {his / her} car
          b  Le père de Marie a réparé sa voiture
              Mary's father has repaired {his / her} car

Just as *-même(s)* can be used to impose a reflexive (anaphor) interpretation on a disjunctive personal pronoun, we can specify a reflexive interpretation for a possessive determiner by means of the adjective *propre(s)*. Thus, *sa* must refer back to *Paul* in (145a) and to *le père de Marie* in (145b) – i.e. to the NP which c-commands it in the simple clause:

(145)     a  Marie pense que Paul a réparé sa propre voiture
          b  Le père de Marie a réparé sa propre voiture

In English, the use of *own* after the possessive has the same effect, as readers can verify for themselves.

Apart from the matter of gender, the referential properties of possessives (with or without *propre(s)* or *own*) are the same in English and French and are unlikely to pose practical problems (but see 6.8.3–6.8.5 below for cases where French can express possession without recourse to a possessive determiner, as in *Pierre a levé le bras*, *Je lui ai brossé les dents*). Nevertheless, this discussion of the status of possessives may help the reader to gain an intuitive grasp of the situation regarding *-même(s)* with disjunctive pronouns. By and large, *-même(s)* is used to specify a reflexive relation in the same sort of contexts as *own* or *propre(s)* with possessive determiners.

### 6.7.9 *'On'*

The subject clitic *on* can be used in a variety of ways. We may distinguish three basic uses, illustrated in (146) – (a) generic, referring to people in general, (b) as a colloquial alternative to *nous*, (c) indefinite, roughly equivalent to *quelqu'un* or the understood subject of a passive (e.g. *mon stylo a été volé*):

(146)     a  En France, on mange les escargots
          b  On a passé les vacances dans le Midi
          c  On a volé mon stylo

The generic interpretation (a) is only available when the verb has a non-punctual tense (e.g. the present or imperfect, denoting a state or habitual event – see 5.3.5 for similar restrictions on the generic use of the definite article). Thus, *On a mangé les escargots* can only have the interpretations (b) and (c). To the extent that generic *on* has a disjunctive counterpart, it is *soi* (see 6.7.10). Since *on* has no Accusative or Dative counterpart, the second-person clitics are used with generic reference, as in (147) where *te* or *vous* refers back to *on*:

(147)      Quand on est pauvre, les gens {te / vous} méprisent

Note that when *on* occurs more than once in the same sentence, it can refer to different classes of people (as in *Quand on est pauvre, on {te / vous} méprise* with the same interpretation as (147)) or to the same class (as in *Quand on est pauvre, on méprise les riches*).

The colloquial use of *on* as an alternative to *nous* (b) tends to imply some degree of familiarity (roughly, *on* = the speaker and other persons whom one would address as *tu*). In this use, *on* has some rather peculiar agreement properties. It is treated as third-person singular with regard to the inflection of the finite verb and the choice of reflexive clitic: *On s'est acheté une nouvelle voiture.* However, it is normally treated as first-person plural (and feminine if all the referents are female) with regard to agreement of adjectives and past participles and the choice of other pronouns or possessives:

(148)      a   On est arrivé(e)s
           b   On est prêt(e)s
           c   On est rentré(e)s chez nous
           d   On a réclamé nos bagages

Also, in dislocated constructions, *on* can act as the resumptive clitic for *nous*:

(149)      a   Nous, on s'en va
           b   On s'en va, nous

Although indefinite *on* (c) is similar in meaning to *quelqu'un*, it behaves more like the implicit Agent of passive constructions from a syntactic point of view. In particular, it cannot act as the antecedent of another pronoun (except a reflexive) or possessive:

(150)      a   *On$_i$ a volé mon stylo. Il$_i$ s'appelle Jules
           b   *On$_i$ a garé sa$_i$ voiture devant ma porte

Parallel examples with *quelqu'un* are fine, but *il* and *sa* cannot refer to the implicit Agent in *Mon stylo a été volé. Il s'appelle Jules* or *Sa voiture a été garée devant ma porte*.

### 6.7.10 *'Soi'*

In traditional grammars, *soi* is sometimes presented as the disjunctive form of *se*. From a morphological point of view, this makes sense in so far as *se/soi* follows the same pattern as *me/moi* and *te/toi* (also *que/quoi* as interrogative pronouns, see 10.4.1). However, with regard to the ways in which these pronouns can be used, the parallel between *soi* and *se* is very tenuous. As we saw in 6.7.7, the usual disjunctive counterparts of *se* are *lui, elle, eux* and *elles* accompanied by *-même(s)* when the reflexive relation needs to be made clear. To the extent that *soi* is parallel to any other pronoun, the most plausible candidate is *on* when it has generic reference (referring to people in general). Thus, in (151), *soi* (optionally accompanied by *-même*) has generic *on* as its antecedent:

(151)     On doit être fier de soi(-même)

Without *-même*, *soi* can be bound by *on* outside the simple sentence, as in (152):

(152)     On imagine souvent que les autres se moquent de soi

Other potential antecedents of *soi* are *chacun, tout le monde, personne* and similar expressions which range over an indeterminate set:

(153)     a   Chacun doit penser à soi
          b   Tout le monde travaille pour soi
          c   Personne n'est maître de soi

However, when such expressions designate a specific set of individuals, the normal disjunctive pronoun is *lui* (or *elle* if the referents are female):

(154)     Chacun (des candidats) a pensé à lui(-même)

The use of *soi* is also dependent on a tense form which is capable of expressing general statements (e.g. the simple present in (151)–(153)). In examples like (154) the punctual tense form (e.g. the compound-past) requires the sentence to be interpreted as describing a particular event involving a particular set of people, thus precluding the use of *soi*.

*Soi* can also be used to refer back to the implicit subject of an infinitive in complements of impersonal verbs such as *falloir*:

(155)     a   Il faut être fier de soi
          b   Il est important d'être maître de soi

These examples conform to the pattern outlined above in so far as the implicit subject of the infinitive is construed as referring to people in general. (On the syntactic status of the implicit subject in such constructions, see 9.2.3.)

In a rather archaic literary style, one sometimes finds examples where *soi* has an antecedent with specific human reference, including proper nouns and personal pronouns: †*Pierre est fier de soi*, †*Il a toute sa vie devant soi*. In this style, *soi* is sometimes exploited instead of a form with *-même* to eliminate potential ambiguity as in *Jules veut que Paul soit fier de {lui /* †*soi}*, where *lui* could refer to either *Jules* or *Paul*, but *soi* imposes the latter interpretation. In so far as *soi* picks out the closest antecedent, and typically one which binds it within the simple clause, it shows some affinities with the anaphor *se*. However, this usage is not typical of Modern French.

There are also a few expressions, notably *aller de soi* 'be self-evident' and *en soi* 'in itself', in which *soi* has inanimate reference: *Cette conclusion ne va pas de soi*, *Cet événement n'est pas très important en soi*.

### 6.7.11 *'Les uns . . . les autres'*

Expressions of this type correspond roughly to *each other* in English. The form of these expressions varies as follows:

* *When the reciprocal relation holds between just two entities, both elements of the expression appear in the singular form:* l'un(e) . . . l'autre.
* *If all the participants in the relation are female or are referred to by a feminine noun, the feminine form is used:* l'une . . . l'autre, les unes . . . les autres.
* *In cases involving a preposition, the preposition occurs between the two elements:* l'un à l'autre, les unes avec les autres, *etc.*

When the relation involves the subject of an active verb and either a direct object or a dative complement, the reciprocal expression is used in addition to a clitic anaphor (*se, nous* or *vous*):

(156)   a   Ces étudiants s'admirent les uns les autres

        b   Les amants se parlaient l'un (à) l'autre

        c   Les filles s'écrivaient des lettres les unes {aux / les} autres

When *se* functions as a dative complement, as in (156b, c), the use of *à* within the reciprocal expression is optional, though generally preferred.

In cases where a clitic anaphor cannot be used (for the reasons discussed in 6.7.4 and 6.7.5) the reciprocal expression is used on its own and the appropriate preposition must be inserted between the two elements:

(157)   a   Les étudiants parlent souvent les uns des autres

        b   Les candidats ont voté les uns pour les autres

        c   Marie et Suzy pensent l'une à l'autre

        d   L'hôtesse a présenté les invités les uns aux autres

    e  Les invités ont été présentés les uns aux autres
    f  Les amants sont fidèles l'un à l'autre

In (157a–c), the reciprocal relation between the subject and the complement cannot be expressed by *se* because the complement is neither a direct object nor a dative complement, whereas in (157d–f) it is the status of the antecedent which precludes the use of *se* (direct object in (d), subject of a passive or copular construction in (e)–(f)).

Note that *à* is obligatory in (157d–f), in contrast to (156b, c), even though the complement is Dative. This difference can be attributed to a more fundamental distinction concerning the function of the reciprocal expression in (156) and (157). Consider first the underlying structures of (157a) and (157d) represented roughly in (158):

(158)    a  $[_S$ les étudiants$_e$ $[_{VP}$ parlent $[_{PP}$ de PRONOUN$_e]]]$
          b  $[_S$ l'hôtesse $[_{VP}$ a présenté les invités$_i$ PRONOUN$_{DATi}]]$

The element PRONOUN cannot be realised as *se* because it is the object of a preposition in (158a), and, in (158b), its antecedent is not the subject. As in other cases where Clitic-placement is blocked, we would expect PRONOUN to be realised as an appropriate disjunctive form, with the [DAT] Case-feature spelt out by *à*. Thus, it seems reasonable to treat *les uns ... les autres* in these examples as a disjunctive reciprocal pronoun (on a par with disjunctive reflexive forms in *-même(s)*), its only peculiarity being that the relevant preposition must appear in the middle.

The situation in (156) is rather different. The basic propositions expressed by these examples can be represented as in (159):

(159)    a  $[_S$ ces étudiants$_e$ $[_{VP}$ admirent PRONOUN$_e]]$
          b  $[_S$ les amants$_a$ $[_{VP}$ parlaient PRONOUN$_{DATa}]]$
          c  $[_S$ ces filles$_f$ $[_{VP}$ écrivaient des lettres PRONOUN$_{DATf}]]$

In all three cases, PRONOUN can (and usually must) be realised as *se*, giving potentially ambiguous sentences (allowing a reflexive interpretation) like *Ces étudiants s'admirent*. Thus, *les uns ... les autres*, etc., can be seen as an optional element which indicates that a reciprocal interpretation is intended, in much the same way as an adverb like *mutuellement* in *Ces étudiants s'admirent mutuellement*.

The crucial difference between the two cases is that in (157) the reciprocal expression is itself the complement of the verb or adjective (corresponding to PRONOUN in (158)), whereas in (156) PRONOUN is realised as *se* and the reciprocal expression simply tells us how this pronoun is to be interpreted. The difference concerning the presence of *à* in (156b, c) and (157d–f) can now be stated as follows:

- *When* les uns . . . les autres *corresponds directly to* $PRONOUN_{DAT}$ *(examples (157d–f)), Dative Case must be indicated by* à, *as in all other instances where the dative complement is a disjunctive pronoun or a full NP.*
- *When* les uns . . . les autres *merely specifies a reciprocal interpretation for Dative* se *(or* nous/vous*) in the manner of* mutuellement, à *is optional (examples (156b, c).*

A final point to note is that reciprocal expressions of the *les uns . . . les autres* type are anaphors, i.e. they must be c-commanded by an appropriate antecedent within the same simple clause. Thus, we do not have examples like (160), with the meaning 'Paul thinks that Mary loves Pierre and Pierre thinks that Mary loves Paul':

(160)       *Paul et Pierre pensent que Marie est amoureuse l'un de l'autre

The same is true of *each other* in English.

### 6.7.12   *Other constructions with 'les uns' and 'les autres'*

The items *les uns* and *les autres* (and their feminine or singular forms) can be used as separate NPs, as in (161):

(161)       a   Les uns admirent les autres
            b   Les uns voteront pour les autres
            c   Les uns espèrent que le syndicat soutiendra les autres
            d   Si les uns sont renvoyés, les autres se mettront en grève

Such examples can have a variety of interpretations, according to context. At one extreme, the two expressions may denote distinct sets defined by previous context, with a 'one-way' relation between them: e.g. (161b) might mean 'the communists will vote for the socialists' in a situation where the communists are not standing for election. A reciprocal relation between the two sets is not excluded however – e.g. (161b) might describe an electoral pact between the two parties. On the other hand, the two expressions may range over members of the same set with a potentially reciprocal relation between them; e.g. (161c, d) could mean 'each of the workers hopes that the union will support the others', 'if any of them are sacked, the others will go on strike'.

Note that there are no restrictions on the structural relation between the two expressions – *les uns* can c-command *les autres* in the same simple clause (as in (161a, b)), or in separate clauses (as in (161c)), or there may be no c-command relation between them (as in (161d)).

These items can be conjoined by means of *et, ou* or *ni ... ni,* with interpretations of the type 'both/either/neither of them'. The singular forms are used when referring to two individuals, the plural forms when referring to two sets; e.g. appropriate referents might be Pierre and Paul in (162) or the communists and the socialists in (163):

(162)  a  L'un et l'autre sont partis
       b  Marie épousera l'un ou l'autre
       c  Suzy n'aime ni l'un ni l'autre

(163)  a  Les uns et les autres ont voté contre le gouvernement
       b  Marie votera pour les uns ou pour les autres
       c  Ce journal ne soutient ni les uns ni les autres

Expressions of the type *l'un(e) et l'autre* can also be used in apposition to a pronoun or full NP, as an alternative to *tou(te)s les deux* (see 5.5.6): *Ils sont allés l'un et l'autre à Paris, Mes frères sont devenus riches l'un et l'autre.* Expressions of this type should not be confused with the reciprocal expressions discussed in 6.7.11; compare *Ils sont amoureux l'un et l'autre* 'Both of them are in love' with *Ils sont amoureux l'un de l'autre* 'They are in love with each other.'

### 6.8   Incidental datives
### *6.8.1. Dative clitics and 'à'+NP*
Throughout the discussion so far, it has been assumed that whenever a Dative clitic can be used we can also use a non-pronominal expression of the type *à* + NP (though not necessarily vice versa, with verbs like *penser*). This generalisation is fairly robust in cases where the Dative element is a complement of the verb or adjective, i.e. it expresses a theta-role which is part of the meaning of the verb or adjective (e.g. the indirect objects of *donner, plaire, parler, téléphoner, ressembler, agréable, fidèle,* etc.). However, there are many contexts where a Dative clitic is fine, but a corresponding phrase of the type *à* + NP is deviant to some extent. Generally, these appear to be cases where the Dative entity fulfils an additional relation which does not form part of the meaning of the verb itself, hence the term **incidental dative**.

By way of illustration, consider the examples in (164):

(164)  a  Je lui ai donné une tranche de pain
       b  Je lui ai coupé une tranche de pain

In both examples, *lui* is interpreted as the Receiver of the slice of bread. However, the involvement of a Receiver is clearly part of the meaning of *donner*, but not of *couper*, which simply describes an action performed on a physical object. It is in this sense that the Receiver role in (164b) can be characterised as 'incidental'. Note now that the use of *à Pierre* to denote the Receiver is perfectly natural in (165a), but much less so in (165b):

(165)     a   J'ai donné une tranche de pain à Pierre

            b   ?J'ai coupé une tranche de pain à Pierre

Acceptability judgements for examples like (165b) are not very clear-cut – some speakers may be quite happy with this sentence, whereas others may find it decidedly odd. The use of asterisks and question marks with such examples should be taken as indicating relative degrees of oddness or unacceptability in comparison to parallel examples with a Dative clitic. One factor which may interfere with judgements in these cases is that corresponding dislocated constructions, where *à* + NP is used in addition to the Dative clitic, are generally deemed to be fully acceptable: *Je lui ai coupé une tranche de pain, à Pierre.*

### 6.8.2   Datives of interest

Incidental datives of the type in (164b) above are sometimes referred to as **datives of interest**. Further examples of this type are given below:

(166)     a   L'hôtesse nous a versé du vin

            b   Son père lui a construit une maison

            c   Je lui ai lavé la vaisselle

            d   Ces voyous lui ont cassé sa voiture

            e   Les invités lui ont mangé tout ce qu'il y avait dans le frigo

            f   La servante lui a mis de l'arsenic dans son café

In some of these examples, the Dative entity can be construed as a Receiver (e.g. in (166a, b) and possibly (166f)). More generally, the Dative clitic denotes someone who is affected by the action (beneficially or adversely, depending on one's point of view), but the involvement of this entity is not given by the meaning of the verb. Corresponding examples with *à* + NP are deviant to some extent: *?L'hôtesse a versé du vin aux invités, ??J'ai fait la vaisselle à ma mère, ??La servante a mis de l'arsenic dans son café au marquis.*

For some of these examples an approximate paraphrase with *pour* is possible: *L'hôtesse a versé du vin pour les invités, Son pére a construit une maison pour Jules, J'ai lavé la vaisselle pour ma mère.* This might suggest that Dative clitics can act as replacements for phrases introduced by *pour* as well as *à*. However, there are some significant differences between datives of interest and phrases with *pour* which argue against such an approach. Most obviously, *pour* always indicates a benefactive relation whereas datives of interest can be interpreted adversatively – e.g. a paraphrase with *pour* would not be appropriate in (166d–f) under normal assumptions. Even when a benefactive interpretation is intended, the dative of interest suggests a more immediate effect than *pour* + NP. For instance, sentence (167a) could be uttered appropriately by someone whose grandfather was dead and whose grandchildren were still unborn, but (167b) would be odd in these circumstances:

(167)  a  Mon grand-père a construit une maison pour mes petits-enfants
       b  Mon grand-père leur a construit une maison (à mes petits-enfants)

Also, *pour* + NP can occur more freely than datives of interest: *Pierre est allé au supermarché pour sa mère, Jules a fait un effort pour ses étudiants* vs *\*Pierre lui est allé au supermarché, \*Jules leur a fait un effort.*

The circumstances under which a dative of interest can occur are rather hard to pin down. In the clearest cases, the verb describes an action which can be construed as affecting the dative entity in a fairly direct way and is accompanied by a complement (usually a direct object) which can be 'associated' with the dative entity. Often this 'association' involves possession of some sort, signalled by a possessive determiner (as in (166d)) or construed as a result of the event (as in (166a, b)).

### 6.8.3 Possessive datives

A well-known difference between French and English concerns the expression of **inalienable possession** – principally the relation between body-parts and the persons to whom they belong. In French, under certain conditions, NPs denoting body-parts can be used without a possessive determiner, the possessor being identified by another constituent in the sentence.[11] Among the elements which can identify this possessor are Dative clitics, as in (168):

(168)  a  La mère lui a lavé les mains
       b  Jules lui a tiré les cheveux
       c  Le dentiste lui a plombé trois dents
       d  Je te casserai la gueule

The clitics in (168) resemble datives of interest in that they denote persons who are clearly affected by the event, yet their participation in the event is not part of the meaning of the verb (like *couper* in (164) above, these verbs express two-place relations involving an Agent and a physical object). However, in these cases, paraphrases with *à* + NP in place of the clitic are perfectly acceptable:

---

[11] Actually, this phenomenon is not entirely unknown in English. We find it in cases like *I hit him on the head*, where *him* is clearly the possessor of the head.

(169)    a   La mère a lavé les mains à l'enfant
           b   Jules a tiré les cheveux à sa sœur
           c   Le dentist a plombé trois dents à son client
           d   Je casserai la gueule à Jean-Luc

One might argue that the *à* phrase in cases like (169) forms part of the body-part NP, like the *de* phrase in (170):

(170)       La mère a lavé [$_{NP}$ les mains de l'enfant]

An advantage of this analysis is that it would eliminate examples like (169) from the range of cases where the possessor is identified by an expression outside the body-part NP, since the relevant structure would be [$_{NP}$ les mains [$_{PP}$ à l'enfant]]. Furthermore, we might extend this analysis to the cases in (168) by allowing the *à* phrase to be replaced by a Dative clitic, roughly as in (171):

(171)       [$_S$ la mère [$_{VP}$ lui a lavé [$_{NP}$ les mains à PRONOUN]]]

This analysis is basically the same as that proposed in 6.6.2 for cases where *en* corresponds to a *de* complement of the object NP, as in (172):

(172)       a   Pierre a trouvé [$_{NP}$ la solution du problème]
           b   Pierre en a trouvé [$_{NP}$ la solution ___ ]

However, despite its apparent attractions, there are a number of compelling objections to this approach.

Firstly, if sequences like *les mains à l'enfant* were analysed as single constituents (NPs), we would expect them to occur in all NP positions, just like the superficially similar sequences with *de*. However, this is not the case (at least not in Standard French), as we can see when we try to place the relevant expressions in subject position:

(173)       a   Les mains {de / *à} l'enfant ont été lavés
           b   Les mains {de / *à} l'enfant étaient sales

Moreover, even in the direct object position, the versions with *à* are acceptable only when the verb denotes an action which can be construed as affecting the possessor (and the body-part) in some way:

(174)       a   Pierre a reconnu les mains {de / *à} sa femme
           b   Jules a vu le visage {de / *à} l'assassin

Note that the variants with a Dative clitic are scarcely any better:

(175)       a   ??Pierre lui a reconnu les mains
           b   ??Jules lui a vu le visage

When a body-part NP is the object of a preposition, its possessor can be specified by a Dative clitic, but not by *à* + NP:

(176)　a　Pierre lui a marché sur les pieds
　　　　b　Le gangster lui a tiré dans le ventre
　　　　c　Un pot de fleurs lui est tombé sur la tête

(177)　a　*Pierre a marché sur les pieds à Marie
　　　　b　*Le gangster a tiré dans le ventre à l'agent
　　　　c　*Un pot de fleurs est tombé sur la tête à Luc

The acceptability of examples like (176) poses a further problem for the analysis under consideration. If the Dative pronoun formed part of the body-part NP, cliticisation of this pronoun to the verb would violate the PP-Island Constraint:

(178)　　　... $V [_{PP}$ sur $[_{NP}$ les pieds à P R O N O U N $]]$
　　　　　　　　　　　　　　　　　　　　　*

Recall that parallel examples with *en* are ungrammatical: *\*Pierre en a pensé à la solution*.

The evidence in (173)–(177) strongly suggests that possessive datives do not form part of the body-part NP in the underlying structure, unlike possessive uses of *de* + NP and *en*. Instead, it is proposed that these possessive datives are essentially datives of interest, denoting persons who are affected by the event, but they can have a secondary function of specifying the possessor of a body-part NP. When the dative expression is *à* + NP, it must have both of these functions to be fully acceptable. Moreover, the body-part NP must be a direct object (cf. (169) and (177)). For Dative clitics, the availability of an 'affected entity' interpretation is sufficient. As the examples in 6.8.2 illustrate, Dative clitics do not need to be linked to a body-part NP, but if a body-part NP is present (in any syntactic position), the Dative clitic can denote its possessor. However, for both types of dative, the availability of an 'affected entity' interpretation is a a prerequisite for the possessive function, as shown by the oddness of (174)–(175) where the meanings of the verbs are not conducive to such an interpretation.

The same pattern can be seen when a body-part NP occurs in subject position. In (179) the Dative clitic denotes the person who is affected and the possessor of the body-part:

(179)　a　La tête lui tourne
　　　　b　Les mains lui brûlent
　　　　c　Les pieds lui font mal

Parallel examples with *à* + NP are significantly less acceptable (e.g. *??La tête tourne à Jean*), in line with the condition that *à* + NP must be linked to a direct object. In some cases, even the construction with a Dative clitic is deviant:

(180)     a   *Le visage lui pâlissait
          b   *Les mains lui sont sales
          c   ??Le bras lui a enflé

The difference seems to be that the verbal expressions in (179) imply an effect on the person concerned in a way that those in (180) do not, thus confirming the hypothesis that the possessive use of Dative clitics is contingent on a dative of interest interpretation.

### 6.8.4   'Il lève les mains' vs 'Il se lave les mains'

With some verbs, the possessor of a body-part can be identified directly by the subject NP:

(181)     a   Pierre a levé la main
          b   Jules a ouvert la bouche
          c   Marie a hoché la tête
          d   Luc a mis la main dans le feu

With many other verbs, a reflexive clitic must be used:

(182)     a   Pierre s'est lavé les mains
          b   Jules s'est brossé les dents
          c   Marie s'est peigné les cheveux
          d   Suzy s'est coupé les ongles

The construction in (181) can only be used to describe 'internal actions': that is, an action or gesture which involves only the body-part itself.

> Some verbs can only be used to describe internal actions (e.g. *hocher la tête* in (181c), *froncer les sourcils*, etc.), whereas others like *ouvrir* in (181b) can also describe 'external actions' (e.g. *J'ai ouvert la porte*). With verbs of the latter type, the addition of a Dative clitic (dative of interest) may lead to ambiguity concerning the 'possessor' of the body-part. Thus, *Je lui ai ouvert la bouche* can mean either 'I opened his mouth' (analogous to *Je lui ai brossé les dents*) or 'I opened my mouth for him', where *ouvrir la bouche* describes an 'internal action' and *lui* is a dative of interest which lacks a possessive function (as in *Je lui ai ouvert la porte*).

This construction is also used to describe 'internal experiences' (see also the construction discussed in 2.6.3):

(183)     a   Henri a mal au ventre
          b   Il faisait si froid que l'on ne sentait plus les pieds

The reflexive construction in (182) is used for actions which are performed on a part of the body, usually with the intervention of some other body-part. The clitic in this construction can be analysed as a dative of interest in the same way as the non-reflexive clitics discussed in 6.8.3, except that (being an anaphor) it must refer back to the subject NP. Note that when the subject is plural, the relation can be reciprocal as well as reflexive: *Elles se sont peigné les cheveux* 'They combed {their / each other's} hair'. The hypothesis that the clitic in (182) is primarily a dative of interest is supported by the fact that this construction cannot be used with verbs which do not imply an effect on the person concerned (cf. examples in (175) in 6.8.3):

(184)  a  *Marie s'est reconnu le visage
       b  *Henri s'est vu le nez

In (182) the subject NP is interpreted as the Agent of the action. However, such constructions can often have an interpretation where the subject is merely an Experiencer (as in comparable English examples like *Paul burnt his fingers*):

(185)  a  Paul s'est brûlé les doigts
       b  Jules s'est cassé la jambe
       c  Henri s'est fait mal au dos

### 6.8.5 *'On l'a poignardé dans le dos'*

With some verbs, mainly verbs of 'hitting', the direct object can be interpreted as the possessor of a body-part expressed by means of a PP:

(186)  a  L'assassin l'a poignardé dans le dos
       b  Marie a giflé Luc au visage
       c  Jules l'a blessé au genou

This construction presents the action as being performed on the person as a whole while the body-part PP serves to localise the action, in contrast to cases like *Jules lui a cassé la jambe* where the action is performed directly on the body-part. Note that the possessor can be expressed as a full NP, even though the body-part NP is the object of a preposition (in contrast to cases like *\*Le gangster a tiré dans le ventre à l'agent* discussed in 6.8.3, see examples in (177)). This is because the restriction involved in cases like *tirer dans le ventre* applies only to incidental datives, whereas the possessor in (186) is clearly a complement of the verb. Note now that this restriction does not apply in examples like (187):

(187)  a  Le gangster lui a donné un coup de pied dans le ventre
       b  Le gangster a donné un coup de pied dans le ventre à l'agent

Although *à l'agent* is a dative expression, it is plausibly a complement of the verb (*donner* normally takes an indirect object) and is thus not subject to the restriction which applies to incidental datives.

In constructions like (186) the direct object can be a clitic anaphor (interpreted reflexively or reciprocally):

(188)   a   Ils se sont poignardés dans le dos
        b   Marie et Luc se sont giflés au visage
        c   Jules s'est blessé au genou

With verbs like *blesser* which can describe an involuntary action, the subject can be interpreted as an Experiencer rather than an Agent, just as in cases like *Jules s'est cassé la jambe* (see 6.8.4, examples in (185)).

### 6.8.6   *'On leur a tiré dessus' vs 'On a tiré sur eux'*

In fairly colloquial styles, a Dative clitic can be used to represent the understood object of certain prepositions, as in examples (189) which are similar in meaning to (190):

(189)   a   Les soldats leur ont tiré dessus
        b   Le chien m'a sauté dessus
        c   Marie lui court après
        d   Les enfants lui tournaient autour

(190)   a   Les soldats ont tiré sur eux
        b   Le chien a sauté sur moi
        c   Marie court après lui
        d   Les enfants tournaient autour d'elle

One might be tempted to capture this similarity by treating the pronouns in (189) as underlying objects of the preposition which are optionally cliticised to the verb (in the Dative form), with a change in the form of the preposition in cases like (189a, b), roughly as in (191):

(191)        $[_S$ NP $[_{VP}$ V $[_{PP}$ P PRONOUN$]]]$

This, of course, would violate the PP-Island Constraint. Moreover, the process in (191) would have to be restricted to certain uses of these prepositions:

(192)   a   *Jules lui compte dessus
        b   *Marie lui est arrivée après

(193)   a   Jules compte sur lui
        b   Marie est arrivée après lui

Conversely, there are some expressions like *rentrer dedans* (in the sense of 'collide with') for which this process appears to be obligatory:

(194)    a   Un taxi lui est rentré dedans
         b   ??Un taxi est rentré dans lui

A general property of the pronouns in cases like (189) and (194a) is that they denote persons who are affected in a fairly obvious way by the action (examples (189c, d) carry strong connotations of 'chasing' or 'pestering' which are not necessarily present in (190c, d)). However, the verbs in (192)–(193) do not evoke an effect of this sort. This observation suggests that the clitics in (189) and (194a) are datives of interest similar to the 'possessive datives' discussed in 6.8.3, except that they are linked to the implicit object of a preposition rather than to a body-part NP. Note that in these cases the use of *à* + NP instead of a clitic is generally infelicitous:

(195)    a   *Les soldats ont tiré dessus aux manifestants
         b   *Le chien a sauté dessus à Pierre
         c   *Marie court après à Gaston
         d   *Les enfants tournaient autour à l'institutrice
         e   *Un taxi est rentré dedans à Paul

This ties up with the observation that incidental datives of the *à* + NP type must be linked to an NP in the direct object position (see the discussion of examples in (177) in 6.8.3: e.g. *Le gangster a tiré dans le ventre à l'agent*).

### 6.8.7   Ethic datives

The second-person clitics in (196) illustrate a rather special type of incidental dative, often referred to as **ethic dative:**

(196)    a   Un type comme ça, il te tue son père sans hésiter
         b   Cet ivrogne vous boit un litre de vin en dix secondes
         c   Au Mont St Michel la mer te monte à une de ces vitesses
         d   A ta place, je te le mettrais à la porte

The effect of these pronouns is not to present the addressee as someone who is immediately affected by the event but rather to make the assertion more dramatic by calling on the addressee as an imaginary witness to the event. Thus, (196a) does not mean 'He would kill his father for you' but something more like 'He would kill his father before your very eyes'.

This use is generally possible only with second persons (usually *te* rather than *vous*, occasionally also with *me*, though it is difficult to distinguish such cases from datives of interest). It occurs predominantly in assertions about typical or hypothetical events rather than in reports of actual events. For example, (197a) might be uttered by a husband to draw his wife's attention to his mother's devotion to housekeeping (with *te* as an ethic dative) whereas *te* in (197b) is more naturally interpreted as a dative of interest ('for you'):

(197)    a   Ma mère te nettoyait l'escalier tous les matins
          b   Ma mère t'a nettoyé l'escalier ce matin

A peculiarity of ethic datives is that they can violate the normal constraints on compatibility of clitics (see 6.3.1):

(198)    a   A ta place, je te lui donnerais une belle paire de claques
          b   Ce pleurnicheur, il te se met en larmes pour un rien
          c   Ce jaloux, il te me tuera

Note that the ethic dative precedes all other object clitics.

### 6.9   Pronouns in copular constructions

#### 6.9.1  *Identificational sentences*

In identificational constructions (see 2.5.1), only *ce* (and more marginally the other demonstrative pronouns *cela* and *ceci*) can occur in subject position, and as complements only disjunctive pronouns are possible:

(199)    a   C'est lui
          b   C'est nous
          c   Ce sont eux

Note that when the complement is pronominalised, but the subject is a full NP, a dislocated construction must be used: *Le vainqueur, c'est lui.*

When the complement is third-person plural, *être* normally takes the plural form (as in (199c)), though the singular inflection is quite common in colloquial speech: *C'est eux.*

#### 6.9.2  *Predicational sentences*

In predicational sentences with *être, devenir, sembler*, etc. (see 2.5.1), an adjectival complement is replaced by *le*:

(200)    a   Marie était contente ce matin et elle le sera ce soir
          b   Les oranges sont fraiches, mais les pommes ne le sont pas
          c   Jules est riche et son frère le deviendra aussi

Note that the clitic is obligatory (in contrast to English where the adjective is simply omitted) and must occur in the masculine singular form regardless of the number or gender of the NP which it qualifies. The same holds for PPs which describe properties (for locative PPs we would of course use *y* or *là*):

(201)      a   Les jupes-culottes étaient à la mode l'année dernière et elles le sont toujours

            b   La patronne était en colère hier et elle le sera demain

Similarly, we find invariable *le* replacing 'bare' nouns which denote professions, etc.:

(202)      Solange est institutrice et sa fille le sera aussi

However, with definite NPs, number and gender agreement is the norm:

(203)      a   Je suis sa femme et je la serai toujours

            b   Êtes-vous les nouveaux voisins? Oui, nous les sommes

Nevertheless, usage is often uncertain, and in cases which focus on the status of the individuals rather than their identity, invariable *le* is used:

(204)      Nous sommes les parents de Jean-Luc et nous sommes fiers de {l' / *les} être

All of the constructions in (200)–(204) have a rather formal, literary flavour. In more conversational style, they are typically avoided by repeating the relevant expression or in examples like (203b) by using an identificational sentence: *Oui, c'est nous*.

In subject position, the choice between *ce* and an appropriate personal pronoun depends partly on the nature of the referent and partly on the type of complement. Consider example (205), uttered while pointing at a strange object in the sky:

(205)      C'est une soucoupe volante

Here, *ce* is the only possible pronoun since the object in question has not been previously identified in such a way as to provide the natural gender for a personal pronoun (cf. the neuter use of *cela/ça* discussed in 6.4.2). However, with an NP complement, *ce* is generally preferred even when the gender can be determined:

(206)      a   Je viens de lire ce livre. C'est une autobiographie

            b   Aimez-vous ce film? Oui, c'est mon film préféré

In these constructions, *ce* is preferred even with human reference:

(207)      a   J'ai rencontré le Président. C'est un homme charmant

            b   Au début je n'aimais pas Pierre, mais maintenant c'est mon meilleur ami

When the complement is a bare noun, the personal pronoun must be used as subject:

(208)     {Il / *c'} est professeur

Similarly, personal pronouns are used for human subjects of *être* when the complement is an AP or PP:

(209)     a   J'ai rencontré le Président. Il est charmant
          b   Où est Marie? Elle est dans le jardin

When referring to inanimate entities as subjects of *être, ce* tends to be overused by English students of French. When the complement is an AP or PP, the use of *ce* is restricted to cases where the gender of the subject cannot be determined, like *cela* or *ça* with verbs other than *être*. Typical cases are those where the subject refers to an idea expressed by a clause, a place, or something previously described by a headless relative clause (*ce que*...) or an expression like *quelque chose*:

(210)     a   Pierre n'est pas là. C'est bizarre
          b   Je suis allé à Knokke-le-Zout. C'est en Belgique
          c   Regarde ce qu'il a dessiné. C'est joli
          d   Je t'ai fait quelque chose à manger. C'est dans le frigo

However, if the gender of the referent can be determined, an appropriate personal pronoun is normally used:

(211)     a   On m'a déjà parlé de cette idée. Elle est absurde
          b   Je connais cette ville. Elle est en Belgique
          c   Regarde son dessin. Il est joli
          d   Je t'ai fait un sandwich. Il est dans le frigo

Similarly, in the context proposed for (205) above, one might offer the comment *Elle est magnifique!* if one agreed that the 'thing' was a flying-saucer whereas *C'est magnifique!* would suggest dissent from this claim.

### 6.9.3   *Predicational complements*
In 6.9.2 we saw that APs and other property expressions can be pronominalised by *le* when they occur as complements of *être, devenir*, etc. However, this is not possible with small-clause complements of verbs like *trouver* or *rendre* (see 2.5.4) – e.g. we do not have examples like (212) corresponding to *Je trouve Sylvie jolie* or *J'ai rendu Jules malade*:

(212)     a   *Je le trouve Sylvie
          b   *Je l'ai rendu Jules

Given the analysis proposed in 2.5.4, this restriction follows from the revised version of the SSC presented in 6.6.2. In the structure (213) we cannot replace *jolie* by a pronoun and attach it to the verb without extracting it from the small clause across the subject (*Sylvie*):

(213)     $[_S$ Je $[_{VP}$ trouve $[_{SC}$ $[_{NP}$ Sylvie] $[_{AP}$ jolie]]]]

The same condition will prevent the complement of the adjective (*à son mari*) in (214) from being cliticised as a Dative pronoun to the verb, as in (215):

(214)     $[_S$ Je $[_{VP}$ croyais $[_{SC}$ $[_{NP}$ Nathalie] $[_{AP}$ fidèle à son mari]]]]

(215)     *Je lui croyais Nathalie fidèle

Note, however, that the subjects of the small clauses in (213) and (214) can be realised as clitics attached to the verb:

(216)     a   Je la trouve jolie
          b   Je la croyais fidèle à son mari

This is consistent with the SSC, since the cliticised elements are the subjects of the small clause and thus are not extracted across the subject position.

This evidence provides strong support for the small clause analysis of these constructions and for the hypothesis that Clitic-placement is restricted by the SSC rather than by a stipulation to the effect that it can only apply within a simple clause. If we analysed the NP and the AP as separate complements of the verb, there would be no obvious reason why only pronouns corresponding to the former can be cliticised to the verb. Under the 'within the simple clause' formulation, if small clauses count as simple clauses, examples like (216) should be excluded as well as (212) and (215), but if they do not all of these examples should be grammatical.

Before we rub our hands with glee, it should be pointed out that the same considerations ought to exclude perfectly acceptable sentences like *Suzy l'est* and *Suzy lui reste fidèle* if we adopt the small clause analysis of copular constructions proposed in 2.5.2 and 2.5.3. Given the structures in (217), where the dash indicates the trace of the subject NP *Suzy* (i.e. the position from which it has been moved), the presence of this trace should prevent a pronoun corresponding to *jolie* or *à son mari* from being cliticised to the verb according to the SSC:

(217)     a   $[_S$ Suzy est $[_{SC}$ ___ $[_{AP}$ jolie]]]
          b   $[_S$ Suzy reste $[_{SC}$ ___ $[_{PP}$ fidèle à son mari]]]

Since these predictions are false, we might draw either of the following conclusions: (i) the small clause analysis of copular sentences is simply wrong, or (ii) the trace in the subject position of the small clause does not qualify as a subject for the purposes of the SSC. Before we jump to conclusion (a), we should recall that our explanation of examples like *\*Les amants se sont fidèles* in 6.7.5 depended on the small clause analysis of copular constructions. On the other hand, the account in 6.2.2 of the position of the clitic in examples like *Je vais le faire* rests on the assumption that implicit subjects of infinitival clauses count as subjects for the purposes of the SSC. No attempt will be made to solve this dilemma here. This situation is an example of the sort envisaged in 1.6.4 – although our analysis does not account for the whole range of data, it does at least enable us to identify the nature of the problem in a way that would not be possible simply by observing the facts in a superficial manner.

### 6.9.4 Impersonal small clauses

In English we find impersonal small clause constructions like *Max considers it strange that Jules left* and *Suzy finds it pleasant to go swimming*, where *it* acts as a dummy subject of the small clause in much the same way as in main clauses like *It is strange that Jules left*. However, *le* cannot be used in this way: *\*Max l'estime étrange que Jules soit parti*, *\*Suzy le trouve agréable de se baigner*. Instead French uses a construction without a pronoun:

(218)　　a　Max estime étrange que Jules soit parti  
　　　　　b　Suzy trouve agréable de se baigner

Unlike its Nominative counterpart, *le* cannot be used impersonally – i.e. *le* must always refer to something.

For the English examples a structure like (219) is assumed, where the empty subject of the small clause is spelt out by *it*:

(219)　　[$_S$ Suzy finds [$_{SC}$ ∅ pleasant to go swimming]]

Such structures are not possible in French, because there is no pronoun which can be used to spell out the empty node. For the French examples, a structure like (220) is assumed, where the clause occurs as subject of the small clause, but is moved to the end of the construction in line with the generalisation that complement clauses normally follow all other constituents of the sentence (see 1.5.4):

(220)　　[$_S$ Suzy trouve [$_{SC}$ [$_{S'}$ (de) se baigner] [$_{AP}$ agréable]]]

An alternative possibility in French is to use a dislocated construction in which the clause is represented by *cela* or *ça*:

(221)　　a　Max trouve cela étrange, que Jules soit parti  
　　　　　b　Suzy trouve ça agréable, de se baigner

**Exercises**

1  In 1.5.5, we saw that one way of giving contrastive focus to an element is to use a cleft construction, as in (ii) and (iii) corresponding to (i):

(i)  Elle m'a téléphoné
(ii)  C'est elle qui m'a téléphoné
(iii)  C'est à moi qu'elle a téléphoné

Try to construct similar cleft constructions to focus on each of the italicised pronouns in the following examples, commenting particularly on cases where no cleft construction is possible or where the clitic in the example can be represented by more than one form in the cleft construction:

(a)  *Je lui* parlerai
(b)  *Il* s'agit d'une question importante
(c)  Pierre *en* a parlé
(d)  *On* est arrivés à l'heure
(e)  Pierre *y* est arrivé
(f)  Jules *leur* a posé une question
(g)  Max *en* est sorti
(h)  *Ils y* consentiront
(i)  Les enfants *se* sont donné des cadeaux
(j)  Les étudiants *se* sont réunis dans l'amphithéâtre
(k)  Marcel *l'*admire beaucoup
(l)  Gaston *leur en* a donné plusieurs

(For discussion of the syntax of cleft constructions, see 10.7.2.)

2  In what ways do expressions like *celui-là, celle-ci*, etc., differ from *cela* and *ceci*?

3  Which of the italicised phrases in the following examples can be replaced by the clitic *en*?

(a)  Max a écrit plusieurs *livres*
(b)  Marie a lu ces trois *livres*
(c)  Sophie a des centaines *d'amies*
(d)  Jules est amoureux de beaucoup *de filles*
(e)  Beaucoup *de vin* a été consommé
(f)  Suzy a lu quelques livres *de Zola*
(g)  La porte *de la grange* était ouverte

(h) Marcel a réparé le bout du pied *de la table*

(i) Ernestine est revenu *de Lyon*

(j) Jacques a acheté une voiture *de sport*

Comment on your findings, with particular reference to the types of phrase which can be replaced by *en* and to syntactic conditions on Clitic-placement.

4   In 6.4.5, it was pointed out that *en* and *y* can be used instead of *de* or *à* with a disjunctive pronoun to refer to human beings, as in the following examples where the items in question refer back to *Pierre*:

(a) Marie aime Pierre et elle pense toujours à lui

... et elle y pense toujours

(b) Depuis que Marie a rencontré Pierre, elle est amoureuse de lui

... elle en est amoureuse

(c) La femme de Pierre soupçonne que Marie est amoureuse de lui

... Marie en est amoureuse

However, *en* and *y* cannot refer back to *Pierre* in (d)–(e):

(d) Pierre$_p$ veut que Marie pense à lui$_p$

*Pierre$_p$ veut que Marie y$_p$ pense

(e) Pierre$_p$ regrette que Marie soit amoureuse de lui$_p$

*Pierre$_p$ regrette que Marie en$_p$ soit amoureuse

Examples analogous to (a)–(e) but with an inanimate antecedent (e.g. *ce film*) are all grammatical:

(f) Marie a vu ce film en 1958 et elle s'en souvient toujours

(g) Depuis que Marie a vu ce film, elle y pense tout le temps

(h) Le directeur de ce film croit que le public en sera ravi

(i) Ce film exige qu'on y prête attention

(j) Ce film mérite qu'on en parle davantage

How can these differences between human and inanimate uses of the pro-PP clitics be accounted for in terms of the concept of Binding introduced in 6.7.2?

5   Discuss the possibilities of coreference in examples like the following, paying particular attention to the conditions under which 'epithet' nouns can refer back to an antecedent.

    (a)  J'ai invité Pierre$_p$, mais l'imbécile$_p$ n'est pas venu

    (b)  J'ai invité Pierre$_p$, mais il$_p$ n'est pas venu

    (c)  J'ai invité Pierre$_p$, mais Pierre$_p$ n'est pas venu

    (d)  *J'ai invité Pierre$_p$, mais l'étudiant$_p$ n'est pas venu

    (e)  Pierre$_p$ n'est pas venu parce que l'imbécile$_p$ a oublié la date

    (f)  Quand Pierre$_p$ est sorti, l'imbécile$_p$ a laissé la porte ouverte

    (g)  *Pierre$_p$ avoue que l'imbécile$_p$ a laissé la porte ouverte

Construct further examples (by replacing *l'imbécile* by *il*, *l'étudiant* and *Pierre* in (e)–(g) and by reversing the order of the clauses and/or the coreferential expressions) and comment on the effects of these changes.

6   Comment on the possible interpretations of the following sentences in terms of which body-part belongs to which participant:

    (a)  Pierre lui a mis la main sur l'épaule

    (b)  Pierre a mis la main sur l'épaule à Marie

7   In 6.8.3 it was argued that the following sentences have fundamentally different structures:

    (a)  J'ai lavé les mains à l'enfant

    (b)  J'ai trouvé la solution de ce problème

To what extent do the following facts support this conclusion (judgements are based on the acceptability of these examples as paraphrases of (a) and (b))?

    (c)  Je les lui ai lavées

    (d)  *Je l'en ai trouvée

    (e)  *Je les ai lavées

    (f)  Je l'ai trouvée

8   Corresponding to the English sentence (a), French has (b), but not (d) corresponding to (c):

    (a)  I consider it necessary to leave

    (b)  J'estime nécessaire de partir

    (c)  I consider it time to leave

    (d)  *J'estime temps de partir

How does this observation bear on the analyses proposed in 6.9.4 for these constructions?

**Further reading**
For a very solid traditional description of French pronouns, see Sandfeld (1970). The syntax of clitic pronouns is discussed extensively and in detail in Kayne (1975); see also Emonds (1975), Fiengo & Gitterman (1978), Herschensohn (1980) and Kayne (1984, ch. 4). The adverbial clitics *y* and *en* are studied from a fairly traditional perspective in Pinchon (1972) and from a generative perspective in Ruwet (1990). On the constructions with *en* discussed in 6.6.2–6.6.4, see particularly Ruwet (1972, ch. 2), also Y.-C. Morin (1974), Couquaux (1981), Tasmowski-De Ryck (1990) and Kupferman (1991). Couquaux (1976) discusses the relation between *y* and Dative clitics with particular reference to the suppletive use of *y*. On possessive datives and the syntax of inalienable possession, see Herslund (1983), Guéron (1983, 1984), Authier (1992), Authier & Reed (1992) and Herschensohn (1992b); also on ethic datives, Leclère (1976). Possessive determiners and related isues are discussed in Milner (1982, ch. 2). Various aspects of reflexive constructions are studied in Wehrli (1986), Gaatone (1975) and Zribi-Hertz (1978, 1980). Dannell (1973) presents a detailed survey of cases where disjunctive pronouns can have inanimate reference. Ronat (1979) discusses constructions in which disjunctive pronouns co-occur with clitic forms. On the pronoun *ce*, see Rosenberg (1970) and Moreau (1976). Couquaux (1981) discusses many aspects of pronouns in copular constructions; see also Ruwet (1982, chs. 1 & 7) for relevant discussion.

Cornish (1986) presents a detailed study of pronouns and other devices for expressing coreference in French and English, from a discourse perspective. Other works dealing with general matters of coreference in French are Fauconnier (1974, 1980), M. Gross (1983) and Milner (1982, ch.1); see also Cadiot & Zribi-Hertz (1990).

# 7

# Adjectives, adverbs and negation

## 7.1 Overview

The three main topics discussed in this chapter are related in the following ways. Adjectives and adverbs have similar functions – while adjectives are used to modify nouns, adverbs act as modifiers of other categories (principally verbs). The link with negation is provided by items like *pas* and *jamais* which behave like other adverbs in many respects, but which share other properties with non-adverbial items like *personne, rien* and *aucun*.

In 7.2 a semantic classification of adjectives is presented, and then applied in 7.3 to various problems concerning the position of adjectives: e.g. before or after the noun, order of adjectives, etc. In 7.4, we look at some adjectival constructions involving complements and the degree modifiers *trop* and *assez*.

The discussion of adverbs in 7.5 develops the 'Verb-raising' hypothesis outlined in 1.4.3, as a means of accounting for the various positions which different types of adverbs can occupy, highlighting differences between French and English and also drawing attention to syntactic similarities between adverbs and adjectives.

This approach is extended in 7.6 to the study of negation, particularly in 7.6.1–7.6.5 where we investigate the syntactic properties of *pas* and other negative adverbs (*jamais, plus*, etc.). In 7.6.6–7.6.8 our attention turns to negative pronouns and determiners (*personne, rien, aucun*, etc.), focusing particularly on the semantic and syntactic relations between these items and the particle *ne*. The remaining sections (7.6.9–7.6.13) deal with other constructions involving the use of *ne* and *non*.

7.7 deals with various issues concerning comparative and superlative constructions.

## 7.2 Types of adjectives
### 7.2.1 Adnominal and predicative uses
Adjectives can be used in two basic ways: as modifiers of a noun, as in (1), or as complements of copular verbs (see 2.5), as in (2):

310

(1)  a  un livre intéressant
     b  le petit chat

(2)  a  Ce livre est intéressant
     b  Ce chat est petit

The term **adnominal** (i.e. 'occurring with the noun') will be used to refer to the uses illustrated in (1) and **predicative** (i.e. 'forming part of the predicate (or VP)') for the cases in (2).[1] Where necessary, the uses in (1a) and (1b) will be distinguished as **postnominal** ('after the noun') and **prenominal** ('before the noun'). Adjectives in 'small clause' constructions of the type in (3) (see 2.5.4) are also classified as predicative[2]:

(3)  a  Je trouve cela intéressant
     b  Ce vin a rendu Gaston malade

When an adjective is used adnominally, it usually provides information which helps the hearer to identify the particular entity which the speaker has in mind, whereas adjectives used predicatively say something about an entity which has already been identified. For example, in a context involving more than one cat, the adjective *petit* in (1b) describes a property which may serve to distinguish the cat in question from all the others. In the corresponding predicative construction (2b), the NP *ce chat* provides sufficient information to identify the particular cat, and the adjective *petit* says something new about this cat.

The terms 'predicative' and 'adnominal' refer to the different ways in which adjectives can be used rather than to distinct classes of adjectives, though not all adjectives can be used in both ways. In the following sections, a semantic classification of adjectives is outlined as background to discussion in 7.3 of the ways in which adjectives can be used and the positions which they can occupy.

### 7.2.2  Gradability

Most adjectives are **gradable**: they describe properties which can be possessed to varying degrees, and they can be accompanied by **degree modifiers** such as *très*, *assez*, *trop*, and by the comparative items *plus*, *moins*, *aussi* (see 7.7). Thus, *intéressant*, *intelligent*, *petit*, *riche*, *content*, *joli*, *facile*, etc., are all gradable, whereas *hexag-*

---

[1] Traditional terms for this distinction can be very confusing. Many grammarians use the term 'attributive' for (1) in contrast to 'predicative' for (2), but others use 'attributive' for the use in (2) in contrast to 'epithet' for (1). Some grammarians restrict the term 'epithet' to a class of adjectives (like *dratted*, *blasted*, in English) which lack an identifiable meaning but convey an attitude to the thing in question – the term 'attitudinal' is used here for these (see 7.2.5).

[2] Some examples of this type are potentially ambiguous between a predicative and an adnominal interpretation: e.g. *J'ai trouvé ce livre intéressant* can mean 'I found this book interesting' (predicative) or 'I found (discovered) this interesting book' (adnominal).

*onal, légal, possible, identique*, etc., are **non-gradable**, or at least not easily gradable.

Adjectives like *petit, grand, gros, lourd, léger, long, court*, etc., represent a subclass of gradable adjectives which are here referred to as **relative**, since they express a property relative to some norm which varies according to the noun that they modify – e.g. the degree of 'smallness' implied in *petit chat* is different from that in *petit éléphant* or *petit bâtiment*, and a *petit éléphant* is likely to be much larger than a *gros chat*. Possibly all gradable adjectives are 'relative' to some degree (e.g. the norm for *intelligent* may be different for human beings than for other animals), but the effect is clearest with adjectives which denote measurable properties.

Adjectives like *excellent, atroce, énorme, minuscule*, which will be referred to here as **intrinsically superlative** adjectives, describe extremes of a gradable property. Although the properties which they describe are gradable, the fact that they denote extremes of the scale normally precludes the use of degree modifiers such as *très, assez*, and the comparative items: *\*?un livre très excellent, \*?Ce livre est plus excellent que l'autre*.

### 7.2.3 Classificatory and argumental adjectives

Many non-gradable adjectives belong to a class which will be termed **classificatory**, illustrated in (4).

(4)  a un problème (\*assez) financier
    b un phénomène (\*très) social

These adjectives are typically derived from nouns by suffixes such as *-ique* or *-al* and are defined in dictionaries by formulae of the type 'pertaining to' (e.g. *financier* 'pertaining to money/finance', *social* 'pertaining to society', etc.). Indeed, they can often be replaced by nouns introduced by the preposition *de*: *un problème d'argent, un phénomène de société*. Another class of adjectives which have a rather similar noun-like status is illustrated in (5), where the adjectives have an **argumental** function, denoting participants in the action or event:

(5)  a la victoire gaulliste
    b le bombardement américain de Hanoï
    c un décret ministériel

The interpretation of the adjectives in (5) is similar to that of the subject NPs in *Les Gaullistes ont gagné, Les Américains ont bombardé Hanoï, Le ministre a décrété quelque-chose* or the complements of the noun in *la victoire des Gaullistes, le bombardement de Hanoï par les Américains* and *un décret du ministre*. We may assume that the adjectives in (5) are assigned a theta-role by the head noun.

### 7.2.4 *'Intensional' adjectives*

The adjectives in (6) represent a rather special class, which will be termed **intensional** adjectives (for an explanation of this term, see 7.2.7):

(6)     a   un ancien étudiant
        b   un problème éventuel
        c   un bon menteur
        d   un gros buveur

These adjectives do not describe properties of the person or thing denoted by the noun, but they modify the meaning of the noun in some way: e.g. if *étudiant* means 'someone who studies', *ancien étudiant* means 'someone who used to study'; similarly *problème éventuel* means 'something which might be a problem'. In (6c, d) the adjectives describe the manner of an activity which forms part of the definition of the noun – e.g. 'someone who lies well', 'someone who drinks heavily'. Examples of this type are more widespread in English than in French: e.g. *a slow writer* cannot be translated as *\*un écrivain lent*, but must be rendered by an expression like *quelqu'un qui écrit lentement*.

### 7.2.5 *'Attitudinal' adjectives*

In English, there are quite a few adjectives, like *dratted, blasted, blooming* (and others more offensive) which do not describe definable properties, but convey an attitude towards the thing referred to (e.g. irritation in *these dratted mosquitos*) – these will be referred to as **attitudinal** adjectives. French appears to lack adjectives which can only be used in this way, but instead makes widespread use of constructions with epithet nouns (e.g. *ces putains de moustiques, cet espèce de menteur*, see 5.4.2 for discussion). Nevertheless, there are a few French adjectives which can be used in this way, in addition to their literal 'property' uses, as in (7) where the remarks in parentheses indicate, roughly, the type of attitude involved:

(7)     a   un sacré mensonge   (outrage)
        b   ma petite amie     (affection)[3]
        c   la pauvre victime   (pity)

In their attitudinal use, these adjectives are non-gradable: *\*un assez sacré mensonge, \*la très pauvre victime* (*ma très petite amie* can only mean 'my very small friend') – cf. English, *\*these very dratted mosquitos*.

---

[3] Possibly *petite amie* 'girlfriend' should be analysed as a fixed expression. Nevertheless, *petit* is often used as a term of endearment, particularly when addressing children, like *little* in English (though not *small*): *un petit chat* (a little cat, but not necessarily a small one), *ta petite maman*, etc.

### 7.2.6 Specificational adjectives

In 5.3.4, we looked briefly at a class of adjectives which have similar functions to determiners (and indeed many of them can also be used as determiners) – these will be termed **specificational** adjectives. They can be divided into two major subtypes: those which express quantity, as in (8), and those which help to identify which member of the class described by the noun is being referred to, as in (9):

(8)     a   les quelques exemples qu'il a donnés
        b   une seule question
        c   de nombreux étudiants
        d   les trois mousquetaires

(9)     a   la même question
        b   une autre question
        c   son propre stylo
        d   un certain auteur
        e   le deuxième chapitre
        f   la prochaine fois

The 'quantity' class includes all the **cardinal numerals**, except for *un* and items which are nouns (*million, milliard*, also *douzaine*, etc.). The 'identifying' class includes **ordinal numerals** (*premier, deuxième*, etc.) and other items like *prochain* which define an entity in terms of an ordered sequence.

### 7.2.7 How adjectives modify nouns

In the study of meaning, a distinction is drawn between the **extension** of an expression and its **intension**. To illustrate, the extension of a noun like *table* is the class of things which this noun can refer to (the class of tables) whereas its intension is the set of properties which define or characterise this class (e.g. 'artefact with a flat upper surface suitable for eating/working on', etc.). Similarly, the extension of the adjective *hexagonal* is the class of hexagonal objects whereas its intension is the property of having six sides.

The meaning of an expression like *table hexagonale*, can be characterised in purely extensional terms: the extension of the whole expression is the intersection of the classes of 'tables' and 'hexagonal objects', indicated by the shaded zone in figure 1:

Figure 7.1

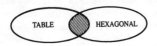

This approach will also work for gradable examples such as *livre intéressant*, as long as we bear in mind that the class of 'interesting things' is a 'fuzzy' class, with 'very interesting things' at its core and 'less interesting things' at the periphery. However, this approach does not work for gradable adjectives of the 'relative' type, for the reasons discussed in 7.2.2: e.g. *petite maison* cannot be represented as the intersection of 'houses' and 'small things'. Adjectives of the *petit, grand* type do not have extensions which can be defined independently of those of the nouns which they modify. Rather, they provide a scale according to which the members of a particular class can be ranked (e.g. in terms of size). Thus, *petite maison* denotes members of the class of houses which are at the lower end of this scale (i.e. 'smaller than the typical house'). Similarly, intrinsically superlative adjectives like *minuscule* and *énorme* designate members of the particular class which are ranked at the extreme ends of this scale.

In all the cases reviewed above, the addition of an adjective has the effect of restricting the extension of the noun. Moreover, the adjective describes a property of the entity referred to by the NP. This is not the case with expressions of the type in (6) (*ancien étudiant, problème éventuel, gros buveur*, etc.). Here, the adjective does not operate on the extension of the noun, but modifies part of the intension of the noun – hence the use of the term 'intensional'. Thus, *gros* in *gros buveur* does not describe the person, but the way he drinks. Moreover, in some cases, the addition of the adjective does not merely restrict the extension of the noun, but yields a different extension: e.g. an *ancien étudiant* is not a member of the class of 'students'.

The extensional approach illustrated in figure 7.1 is also inappropriate for the other types of adjectives which we have distinguished, since they do not describe properties which define classes of entities. Specificational adjectives indicate the way in which the referent of the NP is to be picked out from the class described by the noun, while argumental adjectives fulfil a theta-role which is selected by the noun.

### 7.3    Positions of adjectives

#### 7.3.1    *Restrictions on predicative use*

Not all adjectives can be used predicatively. The adjectives which allow a predicative use most readily are those which partition the extension of the noun in terms of a property (gradable or non-gradable):

(10)     a   Cette table est hexagonale
         b   Ce livre est intéressant
         c   Ce repas est excellent

Gradable adjectives of the relative type can also be used predicatively:

315

(11)  a  Cette table est grande
      b  Cette maison est petite
      c  Ce piano est (très) lourd

In cases like (11), the adjective still expresses a property relative to some norm (e.g. *petit* indicates a greater size in (11b) than *grand* in (11a)), but this norm appears to be determined pragmatically rather than by the subject noun. For example, (11c) could be asserted of a piano which is quite light as pianos go, the norm being established relative to a wider class (e.g. items of furniture) or in relation to some action (e.g. if (11c) is uttered while carrying the piano up a flight of stairs). Note that such an interpretation is not readily available in the adnominal construction *C'est un piano (très) lourd*.

The other types of adjective discussed in 7.2.3–7.2.6 cannot be used predicatively. However, many adjectives which belong to these classes also have other meanings which are compatible with predicative use. Moreover, as we shall see in 7.3.2, these differences in meaning are also relevant to the position of the adjective relative to the noun in adnominal position.

With adjectives of the 'intensional' type, we do not have predicative constructions corresponding to the examples in (6), though some of these adjectives can be used to describe independent properties – e.g. 'fat' in (12a), 'ancient' in (12c):

(12)  a  *Ce buveur est gros
      b  *Ce menteur est bon
      c  *Ce président est ancien
      d  *Ce problème est éventuel

Similarly, the adjectives in (13) cannot have an attitudinal interpretation, but are grammatical only if the adjective describes a property ('sacred', 'small', 'destitute'):

(13)  a  *Ce mensonge est sacré
      b  *Mon amie est petite
      c  *La victime est pauvre

The same is true of 'argumental' adjectives (cf. 7.2.3, examples in (5)):

(14)  a  *Cette victoire est gaulliste
      b  *Le bombardement de Hanoï était américain
      c  *Ce décret est ministériel

Again, many adjectives like those in (14) can occur in predicate position, but with a 'property' interpretation, e.g. indicating origin (*Cette voiture est américaine*) or a quality which is associated with a particular group (*Cette attitude est très {améri-*

*caine / gaulliste}*). With 'classificatory' adjectives, the degree of deviance is less strong than with the other classes discussed above; although the examples in (15) are odd, they are improved when the adjectives are emphasised or contrasted, as in (16):

(15)      a  ??Ce problème est financier

         b  ??Ce phénomène est social

(16)      a  Cette crise est plutôt sociale qu'économique

         b  Cette crise est à la fois sociale et économique

It is not clear why examples like (15) are deviant. Perhaps these adjectives do not describe independent properties but rather define the referent in terms of a relation with something else (e.g. 'money', 'society'). This would bring classificatory adjectives into line with argumental adjectives, where the relation is defined by a theta-role assigned by the noun. Note that PPs corresponding to argumental or classificatory adjectives are also deviant in predicative position: *?\*Cette victoire est des Gaullistes, ?\*Ce phénomène est de société*. Some classificatory adjectives can also be used to describe properties, in which case they can occur naturally in predicative position: e.g. *une voiture économique* 'an economical car', *Cette voiture est (très) économique*.

When specificational adjectives of the 'identifying' type occur after *être*, they are always introduced by a determiner, which strongly suggests that they are part of an NP, the missing noun being supplied by an antecedent (e.g. *candidate* in (17a)):

(17)      a  Cette candidate est la seule

         b  Pierre est un des candidats. Marie est l'autre

         c  Ma réaction est la même

         d  Cette réunion sera la dernière

Note in particular that the English construction *Robert is {first / last}*, where an ordinal expression occurs without a determiner, is not possible in French; instead French uses expressions like *en {première / dernière} place, en tête, au {premier / dernier} rang*.

Cases where specificational adjectives appear to be used predicatively actually involve a 'quality' use: e.g. *seul* in (18a) does not have the restrictive function illustrated in (8b) or indeed (17a) but describes a property, 'alone'; similarly, *autre* can be used predicatively (usually preceded by *tout*), as in (18b), but here it means 'different in nature', whereas in examples like *J'ai posé une autre question* it indicates that the question being referred to is not the same as some other question mentioned earlier:

(18)      a   Cette femme est (toute) seule
          b   Cette question est (tout) autre.

Some quantity items can occur in predicate position, the clearest case being *nombreux*:

(19)      Les problèmes sont nombreux

We find similar constructions with cardinal numerals, as in (20a), but since this construction is also possible with some indefinite determiners which cannot function as adjectives (cf. *\*ces {beaucoup / plusieurs} questions*), it seems reasonable to treat *trois* in (20a) as a determiner (e.g. as an elliptical version of *trois personnes*):

(20)      a   Nous sommes trois
          b   Nous sommes {beaucoup / plusieurs}

Note that constructions like (20) do not occur readily in English, but they are perfectly natural in French as translations of *There are {three / many} of us*.

### 7.3.2   *Prenominal and postnominal adjectives*
The factors which determine whether an adjective (or AP) precedes or follows the noun are rather complicated. As a guiding principle, let us assume that adjectives normally follow the noun and that occurrence in the prenominal position is indicative of a rather 'special' use.

Typically, phrases of the form D + N + AP can be paraphrased by expressions of the type D + N *qui est* AP (where the AP occurs predicatively within a relative clause). If this paraphrase relation were absolute, it would predict that the class of postnominal adjectives should coincide exactly with the range of adjectives which can be used predicatively. This prediction is inaccurate, but it is sufficiently near the mark to serve as a useful starting point. The following working hypothesis is therefore advanced as a basis for discussion:

*On the whole, an adjective can follow the noun in an adnominal construction only if it can be used predicatively with the same meaning.*

The correlation between postnominal and predicative uses can be seen most clearly with adjectives whose meaning differs according to whether they precede or follow the noun. In all the (a) examples below, the postnominal adjectives describe properties which can also be expressed by the adjective in predicative position, whereas the prenominal adjectives in (b) have other functions (indicated in parentheses) which are incompatible with the predicative use:

(21)      a   un document ancien
          b   l'ancien président      'the former president'      (intensional)

318

(22)    a   une preuve certaine

          b   un certain individu     'a particular individual' (specificational)

(23)    a   un mouchoir propre

          b   mon propre mouchoir  'my own handkerchief' (specificational)

(24)    a   les mains sales

          b   un sale type         'a rotten fellow'      (attitudinal)

(25)    a   une question simple

          b   une simple formalité   'a mere formality'     (intensional)

In accordance with our working assumption, specificational adjectives normally precede the noun. Many apparent counterexamples actually involve a 'property' use. Thus, *seul* must precede the noun when it has a restrictive function (meaning 'only') but follows the noun with the meaning 'alone, unaccompanied': e.g. *Une seule femme s'est présentée aux élections* 'Only one woman stood for election' vs *Ce quartier est dangereux pour une femme seule* 'This district is dangerous for a woman on her own.' With *nombreux* there is a subtle difference according to its position relative to the noun. When it occurs prenominally, the noun must be plural and *nombreux* is more or less synonymous with *beaucoup*: *de nombreux étudiants* = *beaucoup d'étudiants*. In postnominal position it modifies a collective noun (*une foule nombreuse*) and expresses quantity as a property of the set (i.e. 'large, consisting of many members'). This difference is clearer when the noun is both plural and collective: *de nombreuses familles* 'many families' vs *des familles nombreuses* 'large families'.

Some constructions with the 'ordinal' adjectives *prochain* and *dernier* constitute genuine counterexamples to our generalisation. These adjectives follow the noun when referring to time in relation to the present: *la semaine {dernière / prochaine}* '{last / next} week', *jeudi {dernier / prochain}* '{last / next} Thursday'. Similarly, *suivant* and *précédent* follow the noun in expressions of time (usually relative to a contextually determined reference time – see 4.7.1): *la semaine {précédente / suivante}*. These seem to be genuine specificational uses, and therefore exceptions to our working assumption. Nevertheless, with nouns denoting other types of sequentially ordered entities (e.g. events), *prochain* and *dernier* normally precede the noun: *la {prochaine / dernière} réunion*. Similarly, *dernier* always precedes the noun, even in expressions of time, when it means the last in a finite sequence: e.g. *la dernière semaine du mois*. Note that *prochain* follows the noun with the sense 'imminent', as in *une victoire prochaine* 'an imminent victory', but here it describes a property of the event rather than identifying it by its position in a sequence (cf. *la prochaine victoire* 'the next victory').

As far as we can ascertain, all 'attitudinal' adjectives precede the noun, though it is sometimes hard to distinguish genuine 'attitudinal' uses from cases where an adjective suggests a certain attitude by virtue of the property which it describes. For instance, *un film terrible* ('a terrific film') looks like a counterexample to our claim – *terrible* follows the noun, but it seems to convey an attitude. However, *terrible* behaves more like an 'intrinsically superlative' adjective (like *excellent*) than a genuine 'attitudinal' adjective. In particular, it can occur predicatively with the same meaning (*Ce film est terrible*) – cf. *ce sacré film ≠ ce film sacré*; N.B. *Ce film est sacré* can only mean 'This film is sacred'.

With intensional adjectives, there are some genuine counterexamples to the proposed generalisation. For instance, *éventuel* and *actuel* normally follow the noun: *un problème éventuel, le président actuel*.

Among adjectives which describe properties and which can be used predicatively, there are a few which almost always precede the noun, principally those listed in (26):

(26) beau, bon, grand, gros, haut, jeune, joli, mauvais, meilleur, petit, vaste, vieux

These adjectives appear to describe fairly basic, gradable properties, often of a rather subjective sort. As we have seen in earlier examples, many of them have figurative uses (e.g. attitudinal or intensional) which are generally associated with the prenominal position. Also, they are relatively short words with a high frequency of use. However, none of these criteria clearly distinguish this particular set of adjectives from others which normally follow the noun (e.g. *laid* as opposed to *beau* or *joli*). Other adjectives which normally precede the noun but can also be used postnominally include *long, court, large* and *bref*.

At the other extreme, adjectives of the types listed below almost always follow the noun in modern usage:

**Adjectives which systematically follow the noun:**
- *classificatory adjectives*
- *adjectives derived from proper nouns, regardless of their function (*anglais, parisien, marxiste, *etc.)*
- *past participles which function as adjectives:* une porte ouverte, les feuilles mortes, . . . *(Exceptions are all 'non-property' adjectives:* le prétendu assassin *'the alleged murderer' (intensional),* ce {sacré / maudit} garçon *'that {blessed / damned} boy' (attitudinal))*
- *Colour adjectives (except as a stylistic device, in poetry)*
- *Adjectives of shape:* rond, carré, hexagonal, . . .

Between these two extremes there are many adjectives which can occur in either position. Sometimes this difference of position correlates with a subtle difference in meaning. For example, when *long, court* and *large* precede the noun, they tend to emphasise extent along a particular dimension (e.g. *un {long / court} chemin, une large éspace*) and in this sense are analogous to *grand* or *petit*, but after the noun they have an interpretation closer to that of adjectives of shape (e.g. *une jupe {longue / courte / large}*).

Often the prenominal use of an adjective correlates with a figurative meaning, describing an abstract property rather than a physical one: *l'eau froide (*la froide eau)* vs *une froide réponse* (or *une réponse froide*).This correlation is not absolute, however – e.g. with *lourd* we have *une valise lourde* vs *une lourde responsabilité*, but the opposite order is possible in both cases. Adjectives which describe emotional states normally follow the noun when the noun denotes the Experiencer (*un enfant heureux, une femme triste*) but the prenominal position is possible, and often preferred, when the noun denotes the source or cause of an emotion (*une heureuse occasion, une triste affaire*).

There are many adjectives which normally follow the noun but can be used prenominally without any appreciable difference in meaning.These are mainly adjectives which describe subjective, gradable properties (including inherently superlative items like *excellent* and *énorme*):

(27)     une agréable soirée, une charmante femme, une étrange histoire, un excellent repas, un énorme éléphant, un extraordinaire résultat, etc.

Placing such adjectives before the noun is largely a stylistic device (common in literary and journalistic usage) and may be perceived as pretentious when taken to excess, particularly with long adjectives such as *extraordinaire*. One effect of this device is that the adjective no longer occupies the intonationally prominent position at the end of the NP, an effect which sometimes has a semantic correlate. A typical function of an adnominal adjective is to restrict the class denoted by the noun in terms of a distinctive property.Thus, in (28a), the proposition applies only to a subset of actors (those who are famous):

(28)     a   Les acteurs célèbres gagnent beaucoup d'argent
         b   Les célèbres acteurs gagnent beaucoup d'argent

However, in (28b), the distinguishing function of the adjective is much less evident – rather *célèbre* seems to make a passing comment on the whole class of actors. Similarly, in (29), *excellent* does not distinguish the meal in question from other less noteworthy meals but acts as a way of paying a compliment:

(29)     Je vous remercie de cet excellent repas

This pattern should not be taken as absolute.The choice of determiner plays an important role in the actual interpretation of an adjective, regardless of its position. Generally, indefinite determiners favour a restrictive interpretation for the adjective whereas demonstratives tend to favour a 'passing comment' interpretation, presumably because demonstratives indicate reference to something which can be identified by context: e.g. *Le Président a fait [une déclaration importante / une importante déclaration]* (restrictive) vs *Le Président a fait [cette déclaration importante / cette importante déclaration]* (passing comment). The relative length and 'specificity' of the noun and adjective can also affect acceptability, as shown in (30):

(30)      a   un extraordinaire résultat
          b   ?une extraordinaire chose

The oddness of (30b) can be attributed to the general tendency to place long or informative expressions in phrase-final position, *chose* being a short word with little semantic content in contrast to *résultat* and *extraordinaire* which are comparable in terms of length and specificity.

The trends outlined above are broadly in line with our earlier observations concerning adjectives which regularly precede the noun. Like the items in (26), the adjectives in (27) express subjective, gradable qualities, often implying a value-judgement. On the whole, properties of this sort do not provide a very reliable way of distinguishing between members of a class (in so far as the hearer's subjective judgements may differ from the speaker's), but they are highly appropriate for 'passing comments', in contrast to objective, concrete properties such as colour, size, nationality or the classificatory properties conveyed by *financier, social*, etc. Moreover, the 'value-judgement' function is similar to the 'attitudinal' function of adjectives like *sacré*. On the other hand, whereas the adjectives in (27) describe fairly narrow, specific properties and in many cases are quite long, those in (26) are short words which describe basic, wide-ranging properties. Thus, the restriction illustrated in (30) does not come into play with the adjectives in (26) in so far as these adjectives are unlikely to be significantly longer or more specific than the nouns which they modify.

Figure 7.2. Characteristics of prenominal and postnominal adjectives

| *Prenominal* | *Postnominal* |
|---|---|
| 'non-property' interpretation | 'independent property' interpretation |
| subjective property | objective property |
| abstract/figurative property | concrete property |
| gradable property | non-gradable property |
| basic/wide-ranging property | specific property |
| 'passing comment' | distinctive property |
| short adjectives | long adjectives |
| literary/affected style | 'normal' style |

The various factors which determine the position of the adjective relative to the noun are summarised roughly in figure 7.2. The features listed under each column, many of which are related, should be taken as favouring one position or the other, but none of them is decisive in itself. The general idea is that the more features an adjective shares with those listed in a given column, the more likely the adjective is to occur in the position indicated for that column.

### 7.3.3 Syntactic restrictions on the position of adnominal adjectives

Adjectives which normally precede the noun (e.g. those in (26)) can occur after the noun when they are modified by degree items like *très, assez, plus, si*, etc.:

(31)  a  un très bon résultat       un résultat très bon
      b  un assez beau tableau      un tableau assez beau
      c  une plus grande maison     une maison plus grande
      d  une si jolie fille         une fille si jolie

This can be attributed to the fact that the addition of a degree item lengthens the AP as well as increasing its semantic content (e.g. *très bon* is comparable to *excellent* in both respects). With *très* and *assez* (in the sense of 'rather'), there is no strong preference for either position. However, the postnominal position tends to be preferred with items like *plus, moins* and *si*, perhaps because these items are semantically more complex – they express degree in comparison with some other entity, in the case of *plus* and *moins* (see 7.7.3), or in relation to some effect in the case of *si* (e.g. 'so pretty (that I can't take my eyes off her)' in (31d)). The preference for the postnominal position seems to be stronger still with *assez* in the sense of 'sufficiently' and *trop*, which also express degree in relation to some circumstance (e.g. a purpose of the type suggested in parentheses in (32)), see 7.4.2:

(32)  a  ?une assez grande maison  une maison assez grande  (for us to live in)
      b  ?un trop gros paquet      un paquet trop gros      (to send by post)

With longer degree items (mainly forms in *-ment*), the postnominal position is obligatory, even with adjectives which normally precede the noun:

(33)  a  *un extrèmement bon résultat      un résultat extrèmement bon
      b  *un drôlement beau tableau        un tableau drôlement beau
      c  *une suffisamment grande maison   une maison suffisamment grande
      d  *une vachement jolie fille        une fille vachement jolie

The postnominal position is likewise obligatory when the adjective is immediately followed by a complement or modifying expression:

(34) a  *une jolie à regarder fille      une fille jolie à regarder

     b  *une plus grande que la tienne maison    une maison plus grande que
                                                 la tienne

     c  *un trop vieux pour elle mari       un mari trop vieux pour elle

This restriction also applies in English, but whereas English often gets round it by splitting up the AP (e.g. *a pretty girl to look at, a larger house than yours*), this is not generally possible in French: *?une jolie fille à regarder*, *?une plus grande maison que tienne*, *?un trop vieux mari pour elle*.

### 7.3.4  Order of adjectives

The order of adjectives before the noun is shown in table 7.1.[4] Note that the order of 'quantity' and 'identifying' adjectives is the opposite to that found in English: *\*les autres trois questions* vs *the other three questions*, *\*les derniers quelques mois* vs *the last few months*. However, *propre* and *même* follow the English pattern, preceding 'quantity' adjectives: *mes propres deux mains* 'my own two hands', *les mêmes trois questions* 'the same three questions'.

Table 7.1. *Order of prenominal adjectives*

| D | Specificational | | Attitudinal | Property | Noun |
|---|---|---|---|---|---|
| | *'quantity'* | *'identifying'* | | | |
| les | trois | autres | | bonnes | questions |
| ces | quelques | derniers | | | mois |
| le | | deuxième | sacré | | livre |
| ce | | | pauvre | jeune | garçon |
| un | seul | autre | | grand | problème |
| ses | nombreux | autres | | | intérêts |

'Intensional' adjectives follow specificational or attitudinal adjectives, but their position relative to property adjectives depends on the sense: *une ancienne belle actrice* 'someone who used to be a beautiful actress' vs *une belle ancienne actrice* 'a beautiful woman who used to be an actress'.

In cases where more than one 'property' adjective precedes the noun, the general tendency seems to be that adjectives which denote basic, concrete proper-

---

[4] The examples in table 7.1 are to be read horizontally as phrases (e.g. *les trois autres bonnes questions*). In principle, one could construct examples instantiating all the classes of prenominal adjectives, but, in practice, phrases containing more than two or three adjectives before the noun tend to be too cumbersome (e.g. *?les quelques autres pauvres jeunes garçons*).

Table 7.2. *Order of postnominal adjectives*

| D | Noun | Classificatory | Argumental | Property | | Intensional |
|---|------|----------------|------------|----------|---|-------------|
| | | | | *objective* | *subjective* | |
| une | situation | économique | | | difficile | |
| une | intervention | militaire | américaine | | décisive | éventuelle |
| une | émeute | | | | violente | éventuelle |
| une | victoire | | gaulliste | | spectaculaire | imminente |
| une | maison | | | blanche | pittoresque | |
| une | table | | | ronde | élégante | |

ties occur closest to the noun, whereas those which describe more distinctive or subjective qualities occupy a more peripheral position. Some manifestations of this tendency are listed below.

**Order of 'property' adjectives before the noun:**
- meilleur *precedes other 'property' adjectives:* le meilleur jeune acteur
- *adjectives modified by* très, *etc., precede other 'property' adjectives:* un très gros vieux chat
- *adjectives which typically follow the noun (e.g. those in (27) above) precede adjectives which regularly precede the noun:* un excellent jeune acteur, un énorme vieux chat
- *within the provisos above, adjectives of 'size' usually occur closest to the noun:* un joli petit enfant, un vieux gros chat

The usual order of postnominal adjectives is shown roughly in table 7.2 (some of these combinations are rather contrived – see below for discussion). In certain respects, this order is the mirror-image of that presented above for prenominal adjectives. For example, adjectives which denote subjective properties are more peripheral than those which describe more concrete objective properties. Intensional adjectives are normally more peripheral than 'property' adjectives, but the order is reversed if the property adjective is modified: *un problème éventuel assez difficile*. Indeed, modified adjectives normally follow unmodified ones: *une table élégante très longue*.

The fact that argumental adjectives precede adjectives which describe properties is consistent with the principles of X-bar structure (see 1.4.2) which define complements (i.e. internal arguments) as sisters of the head word while modifiers are adjoined to the X′ node, as shown by the structure in (35):

(35)

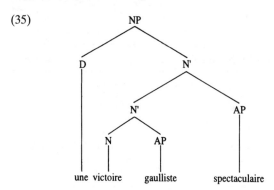

The fact that classificatory adjectives precede all other adjectives suggests that they are in a close syntactic relation with the head noun – e.g. within the minimal N′ like complements or, possibly, adjoined to the N node to create a type of compound noun.

Some of the examples given in table 7.2 are rather cumbersome or contrived. Often, a sequence of postnominal adjectives is avoided by placing one of them before the noun (within the limitations discussed in 7.3.2):

(36)    a  une éventuelle intervention américaine
        b  une spectaculaire victoire gaulliste
        c  une pittoresque maison blanche

In such cases, the adjective which is placed before the noun is the one which would occur in final position according to the order given in table 7.2: e.g. in (37a, b) the intensional adjective *éventuel* is placed before the noun in preference to the 'property' adjective *violent*, though the latter can be preposed in (37c), where the other adjective, *populaire*, is arguably an argumental adjective (cf. *une émeute du peuple*):

(37)    a  une éventuelle émeute violente
        b  ?une violente émeute éventuelle
        c  une violente émeute populaire

Another strategy is to use a phrase of a different category which can be extraposed to the end of the NP (see 1.5.4), e.g. a PP instead of an argumental adjective:

(38)       une intervention éventuelle par les américains

By combining both strategies, the cumbersome phrase *une intervention militaire américaine décisive éventuelle* can be rephrased more elegantly as in (39):

(39)       une éventuelle intervention militaire décisive par les américains

When two or more adjectives have the same function, they are usually conjoined rather than concatenated:

(40)      a   une belle et vieille église
           b   la troisième et dernière question
           c   les trois ou quatre exemples
           d   une table longue et rectangulaire
           e   la politique économique et sociale
           f   l'intervention américaine et britannique
           g   une crise éventuelle ou imminente

However, adjectives with different functions (e.g. 'property', 'argumental', 'intensional', etc.) cannot be conjoined:

(41)      a   *une ancienne et belle église
           b   *le troisième et jeune étudiant
           c   *une intervention militaire et américaine
           d   *la politique économique et britannique
           e   *un problème difficile et éventuel

### 7.3.5 Some problems of agreement

In both adnominal and predicative uses, adjectives agree in number and gender with the noun which they modify (except for some invariable adjectives such as numerals and some colour adjectives derived from nouns – e.g. *marron*, *orange*, also qualified colour adjectives like *bleu clair*). However, there are some complications involving conjoined NPs or adjectives.

Where two (or more) singular NPs are conjoined, an adjective which is construed as modifying all of the NPs takes the plural form (and the feminine if all the NPs are feminine):

(42)        J'ai acheté une voiture et une moto nouvelles

However, if the adjective precedes the noun, it must be repeated (in the singular form, with the appropriate gender) before each noun:

(43)        J'ai acheté une grande voiture et une grande moto

In cases where a plural noun is modified by two (or more) conjoined adjectives which describe different individual members of the set denoted by the noun, each adjective takes the singular form:

(44)        Les partis socialiste et communiste ont signé un pacte électoral

In (44), the subject NP means *le parti socialiste et le parti communiste*, whereas the plural form *les partis socialistes et communistes* would mean *les partis socialistes et les partis communistes.* This construction is also possible with prenominal adjectives:

(45)     Cette ville s'est développée pendant les dix-neuvième et vingtième siècles

Adjectives used as complements of certain verbs (e.g. of measurement) are invariably masculine singular:

(46)     a   Cette valise pèse lourd
         b   Cette femme chante faux

Because of this lack of agreement, some grammarians treat the adjectives in these constructions as adverbs, modifying the verb rather than the subject NP; see 7.5.2. for further examples and discussion.

> In the written language, the item *tout* modifying an adjective shows agreement only when the following adjective begins with a consonant (or '*h* aspirée'):
>
> (47)   a   Elles sont toutes contentes
>        b   Elle est toute honteuse
>        c   Elles sont tout heureuses
>
> This rather peculiar rule (established by prescriptive grammarians in the eighteenth century) seems to reflect confusion between morphological agreement and the phonological effects of liaison (pronunciation of a final consonant before a word beginning with a vowel, as in *mes amis* [mezami]). The result of these two processes in the spoken language is that the item *tout* is pronounced [tut] before all feminine adjectives as well as before all adjectives beginning with a vowel (or 'mute *h*'), while [tu] occurs only before masculine adjectives beginning with a consonant (or '*h* aspirée').

### 7.3.6  Adjectives as nouns

There are many cases where where what looks like an adjective (or AP) can occur with a determiner to form an NP, but without a head noun, as in the following examples where the relevant phrases are enclosed in brackets:

(48)     a   [Ces jeunes] apprennent [le français]
         b   Entre ces deux voitures, j'achèterais [la (plus) petite]
         c   Il faut aider [les pauvres]
         d   La marquise a appelé [la bonne]
         e   Jules a épousé [une Anglaise]

The question is whether these items are adjectives, modifying a 'missing' noun, as in the structures in (49), or whether they are actually nouns, as shown in (50):

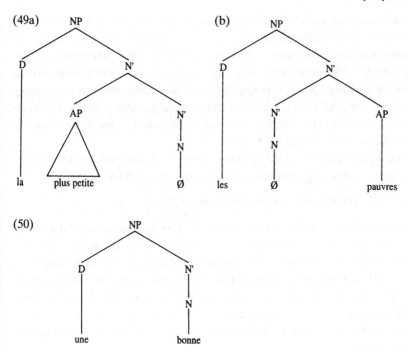

How then can we choose between these two approaches for cases like those in (48)?

For *bonne* 'housemaid' in (48d) the analysis in (50) seems plausible, for the following reasons: (i) there is no obvious semantic connection between this item and the normal meaning of the adjective *bon* (housemaids are not necessarily good people), (ii) there is no corresponding use of the masculine form *bon*, (iii) this item cannot be modified by degree items like *très* or *plus* (nor can it be replaced by the comparative form *meilleure*): *Elle a appelé la (\*tres / \*plus) bonne*. We can therefore conclude that *bonne* in (48d) is a noun which happens to be derived from an adjectival form. Other examples of deadjectival nouns are *un bleu* 'bruise', *du bleu* (non-countable) 'blue cheese' and *une circulaire* 'circular (letter)' – although the meanings of these items are clearly related to those of the corresponding adjectives, their precise meaning is not predictable by rule.

The status of *petite* in (48b) is very different. It conserves its normal adjectival meaning 'small' and can be modified by a degree item (e.g. *plus* in (48b)). Moreover, its interpretation is dependent on an antecedent (*voitures*) which also supplies the appropriate gender feature (if the context had been *entre ces deux jouets...*, we would have had *le (plus) petit*). Thus, in structure (49) the empty noun (Ø) corresponds to the antecedent, typically represented by *one* in English (*I would buy the small(est) one*). In English, the construction with a missing noun is

329

possible only with superlative forms (*I would buy the smallest* vs *\*I would buy the small*) and some specificational adjectives (see below). In French this restriction applies with some adjectives (e.g. in the context of (48b), *j'achèterais {la plus confortable / ??la confortable}*) but others can be used in the non-superlative form: *j'achèterais {la petite / la rouge}*. In French, the restriction seems to be a pragmatic one – the AP must describe a reasonably recognisable property which can identify the referent uniquely – whereas in English it is purely grammatical (superlative vs non-superlative forms).

The status of *pauvres* in (48c) is more complicated. This item can be modified by *plus, très*, etc., thus suggesting that it is an adjective rather than a noun:

(51)     Il faut aider les {plus / très} pauvres

On the other hand, unlike *petite* in (48b), its interpretation is not dependent on an antecedent. In (48c), *les pauvres* has a generic, human interpretation ('poor people in general'), and we do not need an antecedent like *gens* in the context to obtain this interpretation. In English, items like *poor* can only have a generic interpretation in such cases (*We must help the (very) poor* vs *\*I helped {a / that} poor*), but this restriction does not hold in French: *J'ai aidé {un / ce} pauvre*. Note, however, that when *pauvre* is used non-generically, it cannot be modified by degree items:

(52)     *\*J'ai aidé ce {très / plus} pauvre*

This can be explained if *pauvre* is a noun in (52) (corresponding roughly to English *pauper*) but *pauvres* in (51) is an adjective (like English *poor*) modifying an empty noun (as in (49b)) which is interpreted as generic and human. For sentence (48c), either analysis is possible, though both yield essentially the same meaning; cf. English *We must help {paupers / the poor}*.

For structures of the type in (49) two strategies have been proposed for interpreting the empty noun:

*When an empty noun is modified by an AP, the empty noun must be interpreted either*
*(I)  by reference to an antecedent*
*or*
*(II)  as generic and human.*

The situation is essentially the same in English except that strategy (I) is restricted to cases where the AP is a superlative form.

Among 'adjectives' which function as nouns, some items, like *bonne* or *bleu* have highly specialised meanings which must simply be learnt, whereas others, like *pauvre* in (52), have a more generalised meaning – roughly 'person who is

ADJECTIVE'. Another example of the latter type is *jeunes* in (48a), which does not require an antecedent and has a specific rather than generic interpretation (because of the demonstrative determiner). Note that in (48a) this item cannot be modified by *très*, etc., nor can it be translated by the adjective *young* in English (cf. the generic examples *Les très jeunes devraient apprendre le français, The (very) young should learn French*):

(53)  a  *Ces très jeunes apprennent le français
      b  *Those young(s) are learning French

The use of adjectives as nouns is much more widespread in French than in English – e.g. *malade, vieux, aveugle, sourd, fidèle* and many others behave like *pauvre* and *jeune*, whereas their English counterparts can only function as adjectives and allow only a generic interpretation in the absence of a noun.

This difference between the two languages can be seen with items which denote nationality or geographic origin. In English, only a subset of these can be used as nouns denoting specific persons, mainly forms ending in *-an* and a few others like *Greek, Pakistani*: e.g. *He married {an Italian / a Greek}* but not **He married an English* (cf. (48e)). Items like *English* can only be used generically in the same way as *poor* (*He admires the English*), i.e. as adjectives. In French, all adjectives of geographic origin can be used as nouns. Items of this sort also function as nouns denoting languages – e.g. *le français* in (48a).

Some adjectives can be used on their own with an abstract interpretation:

(54)  a  {L'important / Le difficile}, c'est de découvrir la vérité
      b  Marie a fait {le nécessaire / l'impossible}
      c  Le beau est plus séduisant que le réel

Expressions of this type can be paraphrased roughly by expressions of the type *ce qui est* ADJECTIVE. With this interpretation, all items of this sort are masculine and can occur only in the singular with the definite article. The cases in (54a) are the most adjective-like and most amenable to an analysis of the type in (49b) – they can be modified by *plus* and in English we must supply a noun like *thing* which might be taken as the overt counterpart of the empty noun in (49b). Expressions of this sort are restricted to occurring as subjects of *être*, usually left-dislocated by means of *ce*.

The items in (54b, c) are more difficult to classify. The examples in (54b) have a rather idiomatic flavour – restricted to certain adjectives in combination with particular verbs: *faire {*l'inévitable / *l'utile / *l'agréable}* (cf. *joindre l'utile à l'agréable*), *accepter {l'inévitable / le nécessaire}*. The use of adjectives to denote the concept itself, as in (54c), is more productive. Note, however, that for the concepts 'good' and 'evil', French uses the adverb forms *bien* and *mal*:

(55)     Il faut distinguer entre le bien et le mal

Since *bien* and *mal* cannot be analysed as adjectives modifying an empty noun, we must treat them as nouns, an analysis which would extend naturally to items like *beau* and *réel* in (54c).

As well as adjectives which describe properties, many specificational adjectives can be used without a noun, usually with a contextually determined interpretation of the sort observed for *la plus petite* in (48b) (see also examples in (17) in 7.3.1).

(56)     Pierre a pris le premier train. Marie prendra {le deuxième / le prochain / le dernier / l'autre}

Similarly, they assume the gender of the antecedent (e.g. with *voiture* instead of *train*, we would have feminine forms throughout). Consequently, these items can be analysed as adjectives modifying an empty noun, with the structure in (49a) (note that in comparable English examples, *one* is optional, as with superlative forms). Nevertheless, some of these items can be used as nouns with a specialised meaning and fixed gender (comparable to *bonne*, *bleu*, etc.): e.g. *première* 'first showing of a film or play', *prochain* 'neighbour, fellow human-being', feminine forms of ordinal numerals for classes in school, masculine forms for floors of a building, etc.

### 7.4 Complements of adjectives

#### 7.4.1 'Object-gap' constructions

Some adjectives allow an infinitival construction which is reminiscent of passive constructions:

(57)     Ces livres sont difficiles à trouver

Although *ces livres* is the syntactic subject, determining the agreement inflection of the verb and adjective, from a semantic viewpoint, *difficile* describes the action 'finding the books' rather than the books themselves. Thus, (57) is roughly synonymous with the impersonal construction (58):

(58)     Il est difficile de trouver ces livres

In early transformational analyses, this relationship was captured by deriving sentences like (57) from structures underlying sentences like (58) by a rule which raises the direct object of the infinitive to the subject position in the main clause, roughly as in (59):

(59)     $[_S [_{NP} \varnothing]$ est difficile $[_{S'} C [_S$ trouver ces livres$]]]$

The same relationship is found in English: *These books are difficult to find, It is difficult to find these books.* However, French presents an additional complication. In the impersonal construction (58), the infinitive is always introduced by the complementiser *de* (see 3.4.7), but if the **Object-raising**[5] rule is applied, the complementiser is always à. Also, as in the case of passives, only direct objects can undergo this raising rule in French: *\*Paul est difficile à parler (à)* vs *Paul is difficult to talk to.*

The range of adjectives which participate in these constructions seems to be the same as in English; some typical examples are: *facile, impossible, agréable, pénible, douloureux, dangereux,* etc. A common semantic property of these adjectives is that they involve an experiential relation towards the entity described ('effort' with *facile/difficile*, 'pleasure' with *agréable*, 'pain' with *pénible*, etc.). In English, the Experiencer can be expressed by *for* + NP, whereas in French it is realised as a dative element, usually a clitic: *Il lui est difficile de trouver ces livres, Ces livres lui sont difficiles à trouver.* Moreover, in Object-raising constructions, this Experiencer is the understood subject of the infinitive, even if it is not specified. Thus, in (60a), the 'experiencer of displeasure' implied by *désagréable* is also the 'watcher of the film' – this sentence cannot mean that watching the film causes offence to someone else, an interpretation which is possible for (60b):

(60)    a   Ce film est désagréable à regarder
        b   Il est désagréable de regarder ce genre de film

With an adjective like *cruel*, which implies pain on the part of someone other than the Agent (e.g. the foxes in (61)), the object-gap construction is impossible:

(61)    a   Il est cruel de chasser les renards
        b   *Les renards sont cruels à chasser

Many adjectives of this type can be accompanied by *à* + NP (alternatively *de la part de* + NP) which corresponds to *of* + NP and denotes the Agent of the infinitive rather than the Experiencer associated with the adjective:

(62)        C'était cruel à Pierre de punir l'enfant

Unlike the dative phrase which accompanies adjectives of the *facile/agréable* type (*Il est facile à Pierre de résoudre ce problème*), this *à* phrase cannot be realised as a Dative clitic: *\*Ce lui était cruel de punir l'enfant* vs *C'était cruel à lui de punir l'enfant.*

There are some constructions of the type in (57) for which an Object-raising analysis is implausible:

---

[5] This process is sometimes called 'Tough-Movement' (because in English *tough* is one of the adjectives which allows this process) – similarly constructions like (57) are called 'Tough' constructions, even in discussions of French.

(63) a Cette valise est lourde à porter
   b Cette femme est belle à contempler
   c Ce poulet est tendre à manger

Note that the adjectives in (63) do not allow the impersonal construction:

(64) a *Il est lourd de porter cette valise
   b *Il est beau de contempler cette femme
   c *Il est tendre de manger ce poulet

In (63) the adjective describes a property of the subject entity, while the infinitive provides some sort of criterion for judging this property, e.g. in (63a) 'heavy as far as carrying it is concerned'. Nevertheless, the constructions in (63) resemble those in (57) in that the subject of the main clause is also the understood direct object of the infinitive. Moreover, the complementiser in the infinitival clause is always *à*. This correspondence between *à* and a missing direct object is also found in infinitival relative clauses (see 10.5.9): *Je cherche un livre à lire.* This observation leads to the following generalisation:

*When an infinitival clause is incomplete (in the sense that the direct object is missing and is identified outside the clause), the complementiser is always* à.

Note, however, that the generalisation does not hold in the opposite direction. Some verbs and adjectives select complete infinitives introduced by *à*: *Je commence à lire ce livre, Je suis disposé à voir ce film.*

### 7.4.2 Constructions with 'trop' and 'assez'
In English, adjectives modified by *too* or *enough* can be accompanied by infinitival clauses of the following types:

(65) a Paul is {too young / old enough} to go to school
   b Paul is {too young / old enough} to send to school
   c Paul is {too young / old enough} for you to send to school

The corresponding constructions in French are:

(66) a Paul est {trop petit / assez grand} pour aller à l'école
   b Paul est {trop petit / assez grand} pour l'envoyer à l'école
   c Paul est {trop petit / assez grand} pour que vous l'envoyiez à l'école'

The phrases which follow the adjectives in (65) and (66) are not complements of the adjectives themselves (they do not normally occur without the degree items). Their function is to define a criterion by which the degree of the property is judged to be excessive or sufficient; e.g. the meanings of (65a) and (66a) can be glossed as 'Paul is young to such an extent that he should not go to school' and ' Paul is old to such an extent that he should go to school.' Note that a criterion of this sort is always implicit with these degree items, even if it is not specified, except when *assez* means 'quite, rather' (i.e. indicating a moderate degree of the property in question).

In French, these **criterion phrases** are introduced by *pour*. When the entity modified by the adjective corresponds to an object of the 'criterion phrase' it must be represented by a pronoun (examples (66b, c)) whereas English allows it to be simply omitted (examples (65b, c)), though a pronoun can be used: *[too young / old enough] (for you) to send him to school*. If the subject of the 'criterion phrase' is specified, French requires a *que* clause in the subjunctive (example (66c)).

English examples like (65b, c) look like the 'object-gap' constructions discussed in 7.4.1. This construction is not generally possible in French:

(67)     *Paul est {trop petit / assez grand} à envoyer à l'école

We do find superficially similar constructions with adjectives of the type discussed in 7.4.1:

(68)     a   Ce problème est trop difficile à résoudre
         b   Cette valise est assez lourde à porter

However, the infinitives in (68) do not have the same function as the *pour* phrases in (66). For example, (68a) does not mean 'this problem is so difficult that we cannot solve it' but rather 'this problem is so difficult to solve that we cannot ...', where the criterion is left unspecified (indicated by the dots in the gloss). In other words, the infinitives in (68) are complements of the adjective, not 'criterion phrases' associated with the modifier. Indeed, we can have a criterion phrase in addition to the complement:

(69)     Ce problème est trop difficile à résoudre pour le poser aux
         étudiants de première année

A similar situation can be seen with an English example like *Jules is too happy to stay at home*, which has two interpretations corresponding to the French sentences in (70):

(70)     a   Jules est trop content pour rester à la maison
         b   Jules est trop content de rester à la maison

In (70a), the infinitive specifies the criterion relevant to *trop* (i.e. 'Jules is so happy that he should not stay at home') whereas the infinitive in (70b) is simply the complement of *content*, the relevant criterion being implicit, but potentially

335

specifiable as in (71) ('Jules is so happy to stay at home that we should not make him go out'):

(71)     Jules est trop content de rester à la maison pour l'obliger à sortir

As in English, the criterion can be specified by elements other than clauses, as in (72) where the *pour* phrase denotes some entity which is involved in a relevant situation, the nature of this situation being determined pragmatically:

(72)     a   Ce pantalon est trop grand pour Pierre
         b   Ce problème est trop difficile pour les étudiants
         c   Ce tapis n'est pas assez épais pour la salle de bains

## 7.5   Adverbs
### 7.5.1   What are adverbs?

Items traditionally classified as adverbs constitute a very disparate class and, as has been argued in other chapters, some so-called 'adverbs' should perhaps be assigned to other syntactic categories (e.g. determiners, prepositions, nouns). The term 'adverb' itself suggests items which accompany verbs and, indeed, the clearest, least controversial members of this class act as modifiers of the verb in much the same way as adjectives modify nouns. However, to define adverbs strictly in terms of this function would exclude many items which do not clearly belong to any other syntactic category. The terminological issue is complicated further by the widespread use of the term 'adverbial' to refer to expressions of other syntactic categories which have a similar function to adverbs (e.g. PPs like *avec soin* or *d'une manière intelligente* corresponding to *soigneusement* and *intelligemment*). In other words, there is some confusion between the concept of 'adverb' as a lexical category (on a par with noun, verb, adjective, etc.) and the use of 'adverbial' to denote a relational category more or less equivalent to 'modifier' (usually, modifier of a verb but also modifiers of other categories except nouns).

This terminological confusion may be rather disconcerting. However, the important question is not whether a particular word (in a particular use) should be called an 'adverb' or something else. What we really need to know is how the word in question can be used, what sort of phrases it can occur with, what positions it can occupy, and so on. By investigating these questions, we may be able to discern properties which are shared by certain items and which may provide a basis for determining their syntactic category. This is the policy which will be adopted in the following sections, taking a fairly broad view of the class of adverbs.

### 7.5.2  A traditional typology of adverbs

Some of the classes into which adverbs are traditionally divided are outlined below, with brief comments on further subclasses which will be referred to in subsequent discussion.

#### Manner adverbs

This represents the 'core' class of adverbs, items which most clearly modify the verb. Most adverbs of this type are derived from adjectives by adding *-ment* (with minor modifications). Often we can discern a clear parallel between the way these adverbs modify verbs and the way the corresponding adjectives modify nouns: *agir violemment* 'to act violently', *une action violente* 'a violent action'; *demander discrètement* 'to ask discreetly', *une question discrète* 'a discreet question'; *gagner facilement* 'to win easily', *une victoire facile* 'an easy victory', etc. However, the suffix *-ment* (like English *-ly*) is not restricted to manner adverbs (e.g. *probablement* and *actuellement* are not manner adverbs). There are a few manner adverbs which are not derived in this way: e.g. *bien, mal, vite, exprès, volontiers, ainsi, ensemble*. Also some adjectives can be used as adverbs without *-ment*, usually with particular verbs: *travailler dur* 'to work hard', *marcher droit* 'to walk straight', *parler fort* 'to talk loud(ly)', *chanter faux* 'to sing out of tune', etc. In some expressions of this type, the adverb is interpreted in the same way as a predicative adjective – describing the subject entity rather than modifying the verb – though, unlike genuine adjectives, it does not show number or gender agreement: e.g. *Cette valise pèse lourd* 'That case weighs a lot' (cf. *Cette valise est lourde*), *Cette viande sent {bon / mauvais}* 'That meat smells good / bad', *Cette voiture coûte cher* 'That car costs a lot' (also, describing the object entity, *Je l'ai {achetée / vendue} cher* 'I bought / sold it for a lot of money').

Some manner adverbs can modify adjectives: *facilement déchiffrable* 'easily decipherable', *farouchement violent* 'terribly violent', *agréablement léger* 'pleasantly light', etc.

#### Degree adverbs

This class consists of items like *très, trop, assez, tant, peu, presque, si, plus, moins*, etc., referred to elsewhere simply as 'degree items' or 'degree modifiers'. The types of category which such items can modify depends on the item in question. For example, *trop* can modify an adjective (*trop lent*), an adverb (*trop lentement*), a verb (*Il a trop dansé*) and even another degree item (*trop peu*); *très* can only modify adjectives and adverbs (*très lent, très lentement*); *presque* can modify certain prepositions (*presqu'à la fin*), verbs (*Il a presque fini*), adjectives (*presque impossible*) and adverbs (*presque toujours*), and so on for other items. Some items of this type can also function as determiners introducing NPs (see 5.3.6): *{trop / beaucoup / assez} de (ces) pommes*

Whether such items constitute a subclass of adverb or whether they belong to a separate category is a largely terminological question which will be left open. One observation which supports the adverb analysis is that many forms in *-ment* can function in this way, though the distinction between a degree interpretation and a manner interpretation is not always clear: *extrèmement intéressant, complètement pourri, absolument délicieux, drôlement bon, vâchement joli*, etc. Also, some forms in *-ment* and other items which otherwise function as adverbs can act as determiners: *énormément de gens, bien d'autres, pas mal de livres*. On the other hand, *tout* as a degree modifier of adjectives does not appear to be an adverb since, in certain circumstances (see 7.3.5), it shows number and gender agreement (*toute petite, toutes tristes*) whereas genuine adverbs are invariable.

Following the suggestion in 1.4.2, let us tentatively assume that degree items occupy the Specifier position of the phrase which they modify, in contrast to other modifiers which are adjoined to X', but see 7.5.4. This assumption may help to defuse the category question – as specifiers of NP, these items acquire the status of determiners ('completing' the NP) whereas as specifiers of other categories they have a more 'adverb-like' function (modifying elements other than nouns).

### Adverbs of time

This class encompasses items like *hier, aujourd'hui, demain, maintenant, longtemps, alors, souvent, toujours, déjà, parfois*, etc. The main reason for treating these as adverbs is that they act as modifiers of clauses or VPs. However, this is also true of many nouns and NPs which refer to periods of time:

(73)     Pierre est arrivé {lundi / ce matin / la semaine dernière}

Consequently, it might be reasonable to treat items like *hier* or *demain* as nouns which can function as modifiers in the same way as the expressions in (73). Note that these items can also occur as complements of verbs or prepositions which normally take an NP: *Nous avons passé hier à la plage* 'We spent yesterday on the beach', *depuis hier, pour aujourd'hui, avant demain*, etc. The syntactic properties of these items do not appear to be significantly different from those of NPs (or PPs like *pendant la nuit*) which describe periods of time. However, other items do show distinctive syntactic properties which are typical of adverbs in general – these are mainly **aspectual** adverbs, like *toujours* and *souvent*, which express notions such as duration or frequency rather than situating events in time (see 7.5.4 below; also 4.7 for discussion of semantic properties of time expressions).

*Adverbs of place*
Representatives of this class are items like *ici, là, dessus, dedans, ailleurs, partout*. On the whole these behave like PPs which denote places and can be analysed either as intransitive prepositions or pronominal substitutes for PPs – see 6.4.7 and 8.3.6 for detailed discussion.

*Modal adverbs*
These are adverbs which express degrees of certainty, possibility, doubt, etc., regarding the truth of the sentence in which they occur: e.g. *certes, probablement, peut-être, apparemment, évidemment*.

*Speaker-oriented adverbs*
This category is represented by adverbs like *(mal)heureusement, franchement, honnêtement*, etc., when they convey the speaker's attitude to what is being expressed: e.g. *(Mal)heureusement, le train est en retard*; *Franchement, c'est un scandale* (cf. the manner use in *Il vivait (mal)heureusement, Il a parlé franchement*). Possibly these belong with the modal adverbs in so far as modal concepts like certainty, doubt, etc., can also be regarded as attitudes of the speaker towards what is being said. Within this class we may also include sentence-connectives like *cependant, pourtant, néanmoins, ainsi, donc*, etc., which express notions such as contrast or consequence in relation to the preceding discourse.[6]

Cutting across the above classification, we also have interrogative and negative adverbs. Thus *comment, combien, quand* and *où* are interrogative adverbs of manner, degree, time and place respectively (*pourquoi* can be analysed as an adverb of reason) – see 10.4. Negative adverbs include: *guère* (degree or time); *plus, jamais* (time) – see 7.6.5 for discussion.

### 7.5.3 Adverbs modifying adjectives, prepositions or other adverbs
In these cases, the adverb always precedes the head regardless of its interpretation (manner, degree etc.), though adverbs modifying prepositions or other adverbs almost always have a degree interpretation. In terms of the X-bar framework presented in 1.4.2, this situation can be summarised as in (74):

---

[6] These items are traditionally classified as conjunctions rather than adverbs. However, unlike genuine conjunctions such as *et, mais* or *ou*, they do not normally link elements within the same sentence but usually introduce independent sentences. Also, they do not necessarily occur at the beginning of the sentence.

*Adjectives, adverbs and negation*

(74)

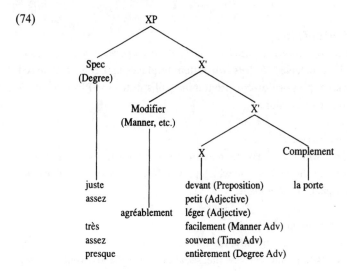

### 7.5.4 VP adverbs

Adverbs which modify the verb normally appear in one of the following positions within the VP:

**Positions of VP adverbs in French:**

*(A) (with simple tense forms) immediately after the verb*
*(B) (with compound tense forms) between the auxiliary and lexical verb*
*(C) (with simple or compound tense forms) at the end of the VP, after any complements*

These possibilities are illustrated in (75):

(75)    a   Jules apprendra vite son rôle
          b   Jules a vite appris son rôle
          c   Jules {apprendra / a appris} son rôle vite

In English, the preferred positions are as follows, illustrated in (76):

**Positions of VP adverbs in English:**

*(A) (with simple tense forms) immediately before the verb*
*(B) (with compound tense forms) between the auxiliary and the lexical verb*
*(C) (with simple or compound tense forms) at the end of the VP, after any complements*

(76)    a   Jules quickly learnt his lines
          b   Jules will quickly learn his lines
          c   Jules {learnt / will learn} his lines quickly

340

Note that the two languages differ only with respect to the positions defined in (A). Swapping the conditions in (A) around leads to ungrammaticality:

(77)     a  *Jules vite apprendra son rôle
          b  *Jules learnt quickly his lines

The positions defined for English conform to the normal X-bar pattern as long as we assume that the adverb occurs within the VP headed by the lexical verb rather than the auxiliary:

(78)

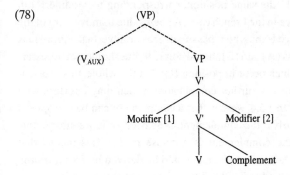

In (76a, b) *quickly* occupies the Modifier[1] position whereas in (76c) it occupies the Modifier[2] position.

In fact, the same analysis can be adopted for French if we adopt the structure of the clause proposed in 1.4.3 where inflectional features of tense and agreement are represented as a constituent of the S node. According to this approach, the verb raises to the I position, moving across an adverb in the Modifier[1] position, as shown in (79) which corresponds to sentence (75a):

(79)

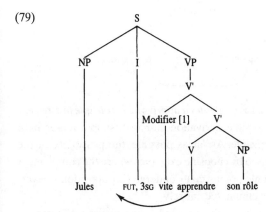

341

Recall that, in English, lexical verbs do not raise to the I position but the inflectional features are simply transferred onto the verb, leaving the order of Modifier[1] and the verb unaffected, as in (76a). Similarly, in the (B) and (C) cases, the linear order of adverbs and the lexical verb is not affected by Verb-raising – in the (B) case it is the auxiliary verb that raises to I, so the lexical verb remains in its underlying position, while in the (C) case, the adverb is in the Modifier[2] position and thus continues to follow the verb regardless of whether the verb is raised to I.

An important feature of this analysis is that the positions of the adverb defined in (A) and (B) are actually the same position, corresponding to Modifier[1] in (78), the apparent difference in the French case (A) being due to movement of the verb. A natural consequence is that the types of adverbs or adverbial expressions which can occur in positions (A) and (B) should coincide, but should not necessarily be the same as those which occur in position (C). On the whole, this expectation is borne out, but there is a further complication which may interfere with judgements in some cases. In 1.5.4, we saw that a complement can be extraposed across a modifier, particularly if the complement is 'heavier' or more informative than the modifier or if the complement is a clause or PP. This means that sequences of the type V – Adv – Complement could be derived by Extraposition of the complement across an adverb in Modifier[2] position (as shown in (80)) as well as by raising the verb across an adverb in Modifier[1] position, as in (79) above:

(80)

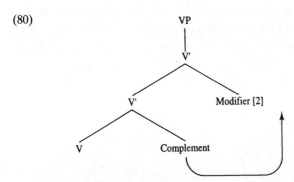

For examples with compound tenses (e.g. *Jules a appris vite le rôle que le directeur lui a donné*), this is the only possible derivation, but with simple tenses both derivations are available in principle. As far as possible, the possibility of the derivation in (80) will be minimised by choosing examples where the complement is a short direct object which would not normally undergo Extraposition – nevertheless, this possibility cannot be eliminated entirely.

The adverbs *bien* and *mal* do not readily occur in VP final position (C), but are fine in positions (A) and (B) (unlike English *well* and *badly*):

(81)     a  Jules apprendra {bien / mal} son rôle

          b  Jules a {bien / mal} appris son rôle

          c  ?Jules apprendra son rôle {bien / mal}

In other words, *bien* and *mal* normally occupy the Modifier[1] position, like the adjectives *bon* and *mauvais*, which normally precede the noun. Just as adjectives of this sort can follow the noun when modified by degree items (see 7.3.3, exs. (31) and (32)), example (81c) is improved by the addition of a degree item:

(82)         Jules apprendra son rôle {assez bien / trop mal}

With longer degree modifiers, the VP-final position is strongly preferred[7] (cf 7.3.3, exs. (33)):

(83)     a  ?Jules apprendra extrèmement {bien / mal} son rôle

          b  ??Jules a extrèmement {bien / mal} appris son rôle

          c  Jules apprendra son rôle extrèmement {bien / mal}

In 7.3.3, it was noted that adjectives followed by a complement or other expression always follow the noun that they modify. The same constraint applies to adverbs:

(84)     a  ??Jules apprendra plus vite que Marie son rôle

          b  *Jules a plus vite que Marie appris son rôle

          c  Jules a appris son rôle plus vite que Marie

In 1.4.2, it was postulated that PPs (unlike Adjective or Adverb Phrases) always follow the element which they modify: i.e. they occur in the Modifier[2] position in (78). The relative deviance of (85a, b) is consistent with this hypothesis, given the analysis under discussion:

(85)     a  ??Jules apprendra avec difficulté son rôle

          b  *Jules a avec difficulté appris son rôle

          c  Jules a appris son rôle avec difficulté

Sometimes the position of an adverb makes a subtle difference to meaning which is similar to that observed in 7.3.2 for prenominal and postnominal uses of adjectives. In (81c) and (82), *bien* means 'well, efficiently' but in (81a, b) it can express certainty: e.g. 'Jules will/did indeed learn his lines'. Similarly, in (75c), *vite* indicates that the action was performed rapidly, whereas (75a, b) suggest immediacy or early completion of the action: e.g. 'Jules soon learnt his lines'. The same

---

[7] Example (83a) seems less deviant than (83b). This may be due to the possibility of an Extraposition derivation, as shown in (80) (cf. *Jules apprendra extrèmement bien le rôle que le directeur lui a proposé*). This complication also arises with other examples given in the text, where position (A) is marginally more acceptable than position (B).

difference can be seen in the English examples (76c) vs (76a, b) – it is perhaps clearer when the verb describes an activity which has no completion point: *Jules a couru vite* vs *?Jules a vite couru*, *Jules ran quickly* vs *?Jules quickly ran*. In (86a), *gentiment* describes the way in which Pierre accepted the invitation ('in a kind fashion'), but in (86b) it expresses the speaker's attitude to the event ('It was kind of Pierre to accept the invitation'):

(86)     a   Pierre a accepté l'invitation gentiment
         b   Pierre a gentiment accepté l'invitation

Generally, manner adverbs in the Modifier[2] position have a strict 'manner' interpretation, but can convey other types of information, often of a rather subjective sort, in the Modifier[1] position. By the same token, many manner adverbs tend to favour the Modifier[2] position: *Marie a résolu le problème facilement*, *?Marie a facilement résolu le problème*. Adjectives which function as adverbs only allow this position:

(87)     a   Pierre a {travaillé dur / marché droit}
         b   *Pierre a {dur travaillé / droit marché}

The positions discussed above are not restricted to manner adverbs. Many adverbs of time (principally aspectual adverbs like *souvent, longtemps, toujours* and *déjà*) show the same pattern, usually with a slight preference for the Modifier[1] position, as in (88b):

(88)     a   Pierre a pris ce train {souvent / toujours / déjà}
         b   Pierre a {souvent / toujours / déjà} pris ce train

With forms ending in *-ment*, particularly longer forms, the VP-final position tends to be preferred, as in (89b):

(89)     a   Pierre a {rarement / ?fréquemment} pris ce train
         b   Pierre a pris ce train {rarement / fréquemment}

However, NPs and PPs with a similar function only allow the VP-final position (as in the case of manner expressions, see (85c) above):

(90)a

                      *Pierre a   { plusieurs fois / pendant un an }   pris ce train

b

                      *Pierre a pris ce train   { plusieurs fois / pendant un an }

Most degree adverbs which modify the verb can occur in the same positions as manner and aspectual adverbs:

(91)    a  Solange a beaucoup dansé
        b  Solange a dansé beaucoup
        c  Pierre admire beaucoup Marie
        d  Pierre admire Marie beaucoup

The position of *beaucoup* in (91a, c) is consistent with the hypothesis envisaged in 7.5.2 that degree items occupy the Specifier position, assuming that the finite verb in (91c) raises across this position to the I node, but adjunction of *beaucoup* to the left of V' would yield the same result. Moreover, to accommodate examples like (91b, d), we must assume that *beaucoup* can be adjoined to the right of V' in the Modifier[2] position. Thus, there is no clear evidence that items like *beaucoup* function as Specifiers of VP rather than modifiers. On the other hand, the degree item *presque* does appear to function solely as a Specifier:

(92)    a  Pierre a presque fini son travail
        b  *Pierre a fini presque son travail
        c  *Pierre a fini son travail presque
        d  *Pierre finit presque son travail

Examples (92b, c) show that *presque* cannot occupy a postverbal position within the VP (example (92c) is only possible with *presque* added as an afterthought: *Il a fini son travail, ... (ou) presque*). In (92a) we cannot tell whether *presque* is in the Specifier position of the VP headed by *finir* or whether it is adjoined to the left of V'. However, the deviance of (92d) suggests that *presque* has a different status from other preverbal modifiers. To exclude (92d) we must assume that the verb cannot raise to I across *presque*, even though verbs can raise freely across other adverbs (see (79) above). If *presque* is a Specifier, as shown in (93), the relevant difference can be expressed by a restriction which prevents a verb from being raised across its Specifier, though not across a modifer adjoined to V':

(93)        [$_S$ Pierre I [$_{VP}$ [$_{SPEC}$ presque] [$_{V'}$ finir son travail]]]

Since finite verbs in French must raise to I to acquire their inflectional features, there is no valid surface form corresponding to (93): *\*Pierre presque finit son travail* (cf. English: *Pierre almost finished his work*).

### 7.5.5 Sentence adverbs

Time expressions like *hier* normally occur at the beginning or the end of the sentence, but not between elements of the VP:

(94)  a  Hier, Pierre a pris ce train
      b  Pierre a pris ce train hier
      c  *Pierre a hier pris le train
      d  *Pierre prendra demain le train

This is consistent with the view that these items modify the sentence rather than the verb, situating the whole event in time. The same restriction holds for NPs and PPs with a similar function (e.g. *ce matin, à neuf heures*). Consequently, if *hier* and *demain* are nouns (as envisaged in 7.5.2) rather than adverbs, the deviance of (94c, d) might be attributed to the restriction noted in 7.5.4 (90). Note that some items with this function (more plausibly adverbs) can occur between elements of the VP:

(95)  a  Marie aimait alors ce film
      b  Pierre a pris ensuite l'avion

On the other hand, *puis* is restricted to the sentence-initial position:

(96)  a  Puis, Pierre a pris l'avion
      b  *Pierre a pris puis l'avion
      c  *Pierre a pris l'avion puis

*Puis* can only be used with a 'scene-setting' function which relates the time of the event to the preceding discourse.

Modal and speaker-oriented adverbs can be construed as modifiers of the sentence rather than of the verb. In colloquial speech, many of these items (except the 'sentence-connectives') can be followed by a sentence introduced by *que*, a fact which suggests that they are attached to S' rather than S:

(97)  a  Peut-être qu'il viendra
      b  Probablement que Marie sera en retard
      c  Heureusement que je suis là

In the absence of *que*, in more formal style, some of these adverbs (notably *peut-être*) trigger Inversion of the subject (see 10.2.3):

(98)      Peut-être viendra-t-il

Others can occur sentence-initially without *que* or Inversion:

(99)  a  Malheureusement, Jacques n'est pas venu
      b  Éventuellement, nous prendrons les mesures nécessaires
      c  Pourtant, elle est belle

Modal adverbs do not readily occur in sentence-final position (except perhaps as an afterthought), though *peut-être* can be used colloquially in this position with a rather special interpretation, often to present a statement as absurd or to issue a challenge:

(100)    a   Les Martiens vont nous envahir peut-être!
         b   Tu veux te battre peut-être!

However, this position is available for most sentence-connectives:

(101)    a   Elle est belle pourtant
         b   Vous avez pris la retraite donc

A notable exception is *ainsi* 'therefore' which can only have a manner interpretation ('like that') in final position.

Most modal and speaker-oriented adverbs can occur between elements of the VP, ostensibly in the (A) and (B) positions defined for VP-adverbs (but see 7.6.3 below):

(102)    a   Luc a peut-être perdu les documents
         b   Pierre a probablement pris le train
         c   Jules a malheureusement oublié son script
         d   Elle est pourtant belle
         e   Vous avez donc pris la retraite

## 7.6  Negation and related phenomena

### 7.6.1  *The status of 'ne'*

In Standard written French, negation of a whole sentence (**total negation**) is expressed by the combination of *ne* with *pas* or, in more formal style and for greater emphasis, *point*. In colloquial speech, *ne* is typically omitted, so that *pas* expresses negation on its own. On the other hand, in literary French, *ne* can express negation without *pas* in certain contexts (see 7.6.11). A further complication is that *ne* can be used in certain constructions where it does not negate the truth-value of the clause (see 7.6.12).

This mixed pattern may lead us to ask which of the items *ne* and *pas* is the negative element. This question has consequences for the analysis of items like *jamais* or *personne* in cases of **partial negation** (where the negation focuses on some particular element of the sentence such as its time reference or a participant in the event) – are they negative in their own right (like English *never* or *nobody*) or positive elements which are negated by *ne* (like English *ever* or *anyone*)? See 7.6.7.

The analysis here will be based on the more formal varieties of French, where *ne* is obligatory in all types of negative sentence. In cases of total negation, it will be assumed that *pas* is the item which actually expresses negation, while *ne* is a redundant particle. Colloquial usage can be described by a rule which deletes *ne* wherever it occurs. Literary constructions in which *ne* can express negation on its own may be seen as vestiges of an earlier stage in the history of French where *ne* was quite clearly the marker of negation.[8] For descriptive purposes, let us assume that *pas* is present in the underlying structure of these constructions and is optionally deleted under certain circumstances.

Syntactically, *pas* can be analysed as an adverb, though of a rather special type. The particle *ne* behaves like a clitic – except in infinitival constructions (see 7.6.2), it appears to cling to the verb and cannot be separated from it by anything except a clitic pronoun.

### 7.6.2 *The syntax of 'pas' and 'not'*

Despite many obvious differences, French *pas* and English *not* behave in fundamentally similar ways. Most of the differences can be attributed not to these items themselves but to other aspects of the syntax of the two languages.

As a first approximation, let us assume that *pas* and *not* are inserted somewhere between the I node and the verb, with *ne* attached to the left of I in French, roughly as in (103):

(103)    $[_S$ NP ne+I pas/not V ... ]

In French, the first verb of the clause (whether an auxiliary or a lexical verb) raises to the I position to acquire its inflectional features, as discussed previously, thus placing this verb between *ne* and *pas*:

(104)    a    $[_S$ Marie ne+$[_I$ regardait] pas ___ ce film]

b    $[_S$ Marie ne+$[_I$ a ] pas ___ regardé ce film]

In English, auxiliary verbs (and the copular verb *be*) also raise to I, giving (105) parallel to (104b):

(105)    $[_S$ Mary $[_I$ has] not ___ watched this film]

As we saw in our discussion of VP adverbs in 7.5.4, lexical verbs in English do not raise to I, so we do not get (106) corresponding to (104a):

---

[8] Historically, *pas* is the noun meaning 'step' which was initially used in Medieval French to reinforce the negation with verbs of motion (e.g. *Il ne marcha pas*, literally 'he did not walk a step') in common with other nouns indicating something small or insignificant with different types of verbs (*ne boire goutte, ne manger mie*, etc. – cf. English *not a fig, not a drop*, etc.). Eventually, *pas* (also *point*) extended its use to all verbs, acquiring the status of a negative particle, to the point where its connection with the noun meaning 'step' is no longer perceived.

(106)      *[$_S$ Mary [$_I$ watched] not ___ this film]

In the normal situation the inflectional features are transferred onto the verb, but it seems that the presence of *not* blocks this process. Instead, in a structure like (107a) the dummy auxiliary *do* is inserted in the I position, where it assumes the appropriate tense features, giving (107b):

(107)     a   [$_S$ Mary [$_I$ PAST ] not watch this film]
          b      Mary   did     not watch this film

In infinitival clauses, *ne* and *pas* normally occur together before the verb, like *not* in English:

(108)     a   Marie semble ne pas aimer ce film
          b   Marie semble ne pas avoir aimé ce film

(109)     a   Mary seems not to like this film
          b   Mary seems not to have liked this film

Note that the order of elements in (108) and (109) is the same as in the underlying structure (103). This order follows if infinitival verb forms do not raise to the I position, perhaps because they do not inflect for agreement or tense. Thus, the infinitival clauses in (108) have the structure in (110):

(110)     a   ... [$_S$ ∅ ne [$_I$ ∅ ] pas [$_{VP}$ aimer ce film]]
          b   ... [$_S$ ∅ ne [$_I$ ∅ ] pas [$_{VP}$ avoir [$_{VP}$ aimé ce film]]]

However, in literary style, the infinitival forms of some verbs (principally *avoir*, in its auxiliary use, *être*, *pouvoir* and *devoir*) can occur between *ne* and *pas* just like finite verbs, but this is not possible with most lexical verbs, except in a highly archaic style:

(111)     a   *Marie semble n'aimer pas ce film
          b   Marie semble n'avoir pas aimé ce film

Thus, with this restricted class of verbs, it seems that Verb-raising is marginally possible in infinitival clauses:

(112)     a   ... *[$_S$ ∅ ne [$_I$ aimer ] pas [$_{VP}$ ___ ce film]]

          b   ... [$_S$ ∅ ne [$_I$ avoir ] pas [$_{VP}$ ___ [$_{VP}$ aimé ce film]]]

It may be significant that the verbs which allow this option express notions of tense or modality and correspond roughly to the class of verbs which undergo Verb-raising in finite clauses in English.

In gerundive clauses, we find a sharp contrast between English and French. In French, the present participle occurs between *ne* and *pas*, like finite verbs, but in English it follows *not*, like infinitives:

(113)    a  N'aimant pas ce genre de film, je ne le regarderai pas

          b  N'ayant pas vu ce film, je ne peux pas en parler

(114)    a  Not liking this sort of film, I will not watch it

          b  Not having seen this film, I cannot talk about it

This difference can be captured by postulating that present participles raise to the I position in French, but remain in the V position in English

### 7.6.3 *'Pas' and other adverbs*

VP-adverbs, such as *souvent*, normally follow *pas* when they occur in the Modifier[1] position (before any complements of the verb):

(115)    a  Pierre ne prend pas souvent ce train

          b  Marie n'a pas toujours aimé ce genre de film

          c  Jules n'apprend pas vite son rôle

If VP-adverbs are adjoined to the V′ node, as assumed in 7.5.4, this order can be accounted for by supposing that *pas* is outside the VP (e.g. immediately dominated by the S node).

In 7.5.5, we saw that many sentence adverbs can occur in what looks like the same position as VP-adverbs (between the auxiliary and lexical verb or, in simple tenses, between the verb and its complement). However, these adverbs usually precede *pas* in negative sentences:

(116)    a  Pierre ne prendra donc pas l'avion

          b  Marie n'a peut-être pas aimé ce film

          c  Jules n'a malheureusement pas appris son rôle

If *pas* is outside the VP, it follows that the adverbs in (116) are also outside the VP. This is consistent with their function as modifiers of the whole sentence rather than of the verb. The fact that they occur between the finite verb and elements which belong to the VP is due to the effect of Verb-raising (i.e. in the surface structure, the finite verb is also outside the VP, under the I node). Thus, the positions of the relevant elements can be represented roughly as in (117):

(117)    $[_S$ NP ne I S-Adv pas $[_{VP}$ $(V_{AUX})$ $[_{VP}$ $[_{V'}$ VP-Adv V ... $]]]]$

Raising of the first verb ($V_{AUX}$ if present, otherwise V) to the I position gives the surface orders in (115) and (116). An example containing all the elements in (117) is *Pierre n'a donc pas souvent pris l'avion.*

There are some complications with the analysis outlined above. Although *toujours* follows *pas* with the meaning 'not always', as in (115b), it precedes *pas* with the meaning 'not yet' (= 'still not'):

(118)     Marie n'a toujours pas vu ce film

A possible solution is to treat *toujours* as a VP-adverb when it mean 'always' but as a sentence adverb when it means 'still'.

The degree adverb *presque* can precede or follow *pas*, again with a difference in meaning:

(119)     a    Henri n'a presque pas fini son travail
               'Henry nearly did not finish his work'
          b    Henri n'a pas presque fini son travail
               'Henry has not nearly finished his work'

Example (119b) represents the expected order, if *presque* modifies the verb and occurs within the VP (e.g. in the Specifier position as argued in 7.5.4). Example (119a) can be accommodated if *presque* modifies *pas*, giving a reading of the type 'It was nearly not the case that Henry finished his work.' A similar pattern can be seen with *absolument* in (120):

(120)     a    Les paramilitaires n'ont absolument pas renoncé au terrorisme
          b    Les paramilitaires n'ont pas absolument renoncé au terrorisme

In (120b) *absolument* modifies the verb indicating 'absolute renunciation' but in (120a) it reinforces *pas* giving the interpretation 'not at all'.

### 7.6.4    The 'split Inflection' hypothesis

The hypothesis that lexical verbs do not raise to I in infinitival clauses (7.6.2) gives the right results for negative constructions, but (on the whole) the wrong result for VP-adverbs. If infinitives do not undergo Verb-raising, we would expect VP-adverbs to precede them freely but not to occur between the infinitive and its complement. In fact, the opposite seems to be the case:

(121)     a    *Jules essaie de vite apprendre son rôle
          b    *Pierre regrette de toujours prendre ce train

(122)     a    Jules essaie d'apprendre vite son rôle
          b    Pierre regrette de prendre toujours ce train

For the examples in (122) we might appeal to the Extraposition analysis envisaged in 7.5.4 (e.g. deriving (122a) from ... *d'apprendre son rôle vite* by moving the direct object to the right). The examples in (121) might also be ruled out by invoking some constraint which prevents adverbs from intervening between the complementiser (*de* in (121)) and the infinitive, rather like the prescriptive constraint against split infinitives in English (% *to quickly learn his lines*).

A more sophisticated solution to this problem is to postulate that the agreement and tense features are represented under separate nodes, Agr and T (rather than under a single I node as we have assumed so far), roughly as in (123):[9]

(123)     $[_S$ NP Agr T $[_{VP}$ V ... ]]

In finite clauses, the verb raises first to T and then to Agr to pick up the relevant features. Suppose now that in infinitival clauses, the infinitive marker occurs under T, but the Agr position is empty. In English, the infinitive marker is a separate word (*to*) but in French it is an inflectional affix (*er, -re, -ir* or *-oir*). Consequently, it is reasonable to suppose that in French the infinitival verb must raise to T to pick up this affix, but does not normally move further to the Agr position. The effect of this operation is to place the infinitive before any VP-adverbs such as those in (121) and (122) above, but after any elements which occur between Agr and T. Thus, if *pas* occurs between Agr and T, the data in (121) and (122) can be accounted for without discrediting the view that only finite verbs (and, marginally, infinitival forms of *être, avoir, pouvoir* and *devoir*, see 7.6.2, example (111b)) are raised to the left of *pas*. The main points of this analysis are summarised in (124) which represents the structure and derivation of the infinitival clause in *Pierre regrette de ne pas prendre toujours l'avion*:

(124)     $[_S \varnothing$ ne $[_{Agr} \varnothing ]$ pas $[_T$ -re $] [_{VP} [_{V'}$ toujours prend- l'avion]]]

### 7.6.5 Negative adverbs

The negative adverbs *jamais, plus* and *guère* typically occur in the same positions as *pas*, between the auxiliary and lexical verb or, in simple tenses, immediately after the verb:

(125)     a   Henri n'a jamais visité Paris
          b   Jean n'admire plus Suzanne
          c   Françoise ne prend guère le métro

They usually precede infinitival verbs, but they can follow the infinitive rather more readily than *pas*:

---

[9] Linguists who advocate this approach also assume that T (tense) and Agr (agreement) project as phrasal categories (as envisaged for I in 1.4.3). For descriptive purposes the simplified representation in (123) is adequate. There is some controversy over whether Agr or T is the highest node. See 'Further reading' at the end of this chapter for references to discussion of these issues.

(126)    a    Jacques essaie de ne {jamais / plus / guère} se tromper
         b    Jacques essaie de ne se tromper {jamais / plus / guère}

This evidence suggests that they can occur in the same structural position as *pas* but can also occupy the Modifier[1] position typical of aspectual adverbs. However, they cannot occur in the VP-final (Modifier[2]) position:

(127)    *Robert ne mange des frites {jamais / plus / guère}

Like aspectual adverbs, *jamais* can also be placed at the beginning of the sentence, though this option is not available with *plus* or *guère* unless *plus* accompanies *jamais*:

(128)    a    Jamais je ne ferais une chose pareille
         b    {Plus jamais / Jamais plus} je ne l'inviterai

Note that the presence of a negative adverb at the beginning of the sentence does not trigger Inversion as it does in English: *Never (again) will I do that.*

Unlike *pas*, these adverbs are compatible with each other and with other negative items such as *rien* or *personne* within the same clause:

(129)    a    Je ne le ferai {jamais plus / plus jamais}
         b    Martine ne danse {plus guère / guère plus}
         c    Jules ne voit plus personne
         d    Henri ne dit jamais rien à personne

(130)    a    *Je ne le ferai pas jamais
         b    *Martine ne danse pas guère
         c    *Jules ne voit pas personne
         d    *Henri ne dit pas rien à personne

### 7.6.6 Negative pronouns and determiners

The items *personne* and *rien* can be analysed as pronouns whereas *aucun(e)* functions as a determiner. They can occur as objects of verbs or prepositions or as subjects, depending on which element of the sentence is negated:

(131)    a    Pierre n'aime {personne / rien / aucun de ses voisins}
         b    Pierre ne pense à {personne / rien / aucune question}
         c    {Personne / Rien / Aucun étudiant} n'est arrivé

Note that *aucun* follows the pattern of *plusieurs* in that it occurs directly before the noun in quantitative constructions (131b, c) but takes *de* in partitive constructions (131a), see 5.3.7.

When *rien* is a direct object of a verb in the past-participle or infinitive form, it can undergo the 'floating' process described in 5.5.4 for *tout*:

(132)    a  Je n'ai rien vu

           b  Je ne veux rien faire

The effect of this process is to place *rien* in the normal position of *pas* and other negative adverbs. *Rien* can remain in the direct object position, though the order in (132) is much preferred:

(133)    a  Je n'ai vu rien

           b  Je ne veux faire rien

This floating process cannot apply to *personne* or *aucun*:

(134)    a  *Je n'ai personne vu

           b  *Je ne veux personne rencontrer

           c  *Je n'ai aucun vu de ces films

           d  *Je ne veux aucun lire de ces livres

### 7.6.7   *Partial negation and negative polarity*

In English, there are two ways of expressing partial negation. We can use a negative adverb, pronoun or determiner for the element which is negated, as in (135):

(135)    a  They have never visited Paris

           b  He saw {nothing / nobody}

           c  I took no photos

Alternatively, we can use the sentence negator *not* and represent the negated element by items such as *ever* or forms with *any*:

(136)    a  They have not ever visited Paris

           b  He did not see {anything / anybody}

           c  I did not take any photos

The question which will now be addressed is whether the French constructions in (137) correspond to (135) or (136):

(137)    a  Ils n'ont jamais visité Paris

           b  Il ne voyait {rien / personne}

           c  Je n'ai pris aucune photo

In other words, are *jamais, personne*, etc., inherently negative elements like *never* or *nobody* or are they indefinite expressions like *ever* or *anybody* which are interpreted negatively through their association with a negative particle (*not* in English, *ne* in French)?

Items like *ever* and *any* are sometimes called **negative polarity** items, because they can only occur in sentences which do not express an affirmative statement (e.g. negative sentences and questions)[10]:

(138)  a  *They have ever visited Paris
      b  *He saw {anything / anybody}
      c  *I took any photos

In French, the class of negative polarity items includes expressions like *grand-chose, la moindre idée, lever le petit doigt*:

(139)  a  Pierre n'a pas fait grand-chose
         *Pierre a fait grand-chose
      b  Luc n'a pas la moindre idée
         *Luc a la moindre idée
      c  Max n'a pas levé le petit doigt pour nous aider
         *Max a levé le petit doigt pour nous aider

Thus, expressions like these provide us with a basis for determining the status of items like those in (137). If *jamais, personne*, etc., are negative polarity items like *ever* or *anybody*, we would expect them to behave like the expressions in (139).

Note now that the presence of *ne* alone is not sufficient to license negative polarity expressions:

(140)  a  *Pierre n'a fait grand-chose
      b  *Luc n'a la moindre idée
      c  *Max n'a levé le petit doigt

Conversely, the items in (137) cannot occur with *pas* in the same clause (except perhaps if the two items negate independently – e.g. for (141b) 'It is not the case that he saw {nothing / nobody}'):

(141)  a  *Ils n'ont pas jamais visité Paris
      b  *Il n'a pas vu {rien / personne}
      c  *Je n'ai pas pris aucune photo

In both French and English, negative polarity items cannot precede the sentence negator:

(142)  a  *Grand-chose n'est pas arrivé
      b  *Anything did not happen
      c  *Ever would I not do such a thing

---

[10] With regard to *any* and its derivatives, this restriction only applies to unstressed forms. With stress on *any* we can have *He will do anything, He will talk to anybody*, etc. This is the use of *any* which is rendered in French by *n'importe quoi, n'importe qui*, etc.

However, the items in (137) can precede *ne*:

(143)    a   {Rien / Personne / Aucun étudiant} n'est arrivé

          b   Jamais je ne ferais une chose pareille

In this respect, these items behave like the English negative elements in (135): *Nothing happened, {Nobody / no student} arrived, Never would I do such a thing.* Furthermore, these items can be used negatively without *ne* in colloquial speech and in elliptical constructions such as short answers to questions: *Qui est venu? Personne; Quand partiras-tu? Jamais.*

The above evidence suggests that the items in (137) are not negative polarity items but genuine negative elements parallel to the English items in (135), the only difference being that in written French, they are normally accompanied by *ne,* just like *pas.* By way of comparison, it may be noted that French has the alternative expressions *qui que ce soit* and *quoi que ce soit* corresponding to *anybody* and *anything.* These expressions behave much more like negative polarity items according to the criteria presented above:

(144)    a   Il n'a pas vu {qui que ce soit / quoi que ce soit}

          b   *{Qui que ce soit / Quoi que ce soit} n'est (pas) arrivé

          c   Qui est venu? *Qui que ce soit

Nevertheless, there are other constructions in which the items in (137) do appear to function as negative polarity items. As we mentioned above, negative polarity items can often occur, without a negative interpretation, in questions:

(145)    a   Did he see {anybody / anything?}

          b   Has he ever visited Paris?

          c   A-t-il vu {qui que ce soit / quoi que ce soit}?

          d   A-t-il fait grand-chose?

They can also occur in subordinate clauses which are not themselves negative but which are interpreted negatively by virtue of the semantic properties of a higher clause:

(146)    a   I do not believe that he saw {anybody / anything}

          b   I refuse to believe that he has ever visited Paris

          c   Je ne crois pas qu'il ait vu {qui que ce soit / quoi que ce soit}

          d   Je refuse de croire qu'il ait fait grand-chose

In a fairly literary style, items like those in (137) can be used in the same way:

(147)    a   A-t-il vu personne?

          b   A-t-il rien vu?

          c   A-t-il jamais visité Paris?

(148)     a   Je ne crois pas qu'il ait vu personne
          b   Je refuse de croire qu'il ait rien vu
          c   Je ne crois pas qu'il ait jamais visité Paris

In colloquial speech, the questions in (147) would be most naturally interpreted as negative, through deletion of *ne* in *N'a-t-il vu personne?* However, in more formal registers where deletion of *ne* is disallowed, *personne* and *rien* function as stylistic variants of *quelqu'un* and *quelque-chose* in *A-t-il vu {quelqu'un / quelque-chose}?* and *Je ne crois pas qu'il ait vu {quelqu'un / quelque-chose}*, while *jamais* corresponds to English *ever*. This type of interpretation seems to be most readily available with *jamais*. Similarly, the relevant interpretation for examples of the type (a) and (b) is easier to obtain if *jamais* is added: *A-t-il jamais embrassé personne?*, *Je ne crois pas qu'il ait jamais embrassé personne*.

The ambivalent status of these items can be characterised by assuming that they can function both as true negatives (like *never, nobody*) and as negative polarity items, with the important restriction that, as negative polarity items, they cannot be licensed by *pas* within the same clause (to rule out cases like (141)). In more formal registers, these items must be accompanied by *ne* when they function as true negatives, just like *pas*. The term **Negative-association** will be used to refer to the rule which links a negative item to the clitic *ne*.

### 7.6.8  Partial negation of complex sentences

With negative pronouns and determiners (*personne, rien, aucun*) and the locative expression *nulle part, ne* can sometimes occur in a higher clause than the negative item itself, as in (149) where the boundaries of the clause containing the negative item are indicated by square brackets:

(149)     a   Tu ne dois [t'occuper de rien]
          b   Luc ne veut [offenser personne]
          c   Pierre n'a envie de [voir personne]
          d   Jules n'a essayé de [aller nulle part]
          e   Marie n'est arrivée à [lire aucun de ces livres]

These constructions look rather like those in (148), except that there is no *pas* in the main clause, but there are some important differences between the two constructions. In particular, the construction in (149) is not possible with negative adverbs like *jamais* or *plus*:

(150)     a   *Pierre n'a envie de [jamais sortir]
          b   *Jules n'a essayé de [plus fumer]

In cases with a 'bare' infinitive, like *Luc ne veut jamais sortir*, it is impossible to tell whether the adverb is part of the main clause or the infinitive. However, the contrast in (151) shows that only the first possibility is available:

(151)  a Pierre n'a jamais voulu sortir

     b *Pierre n'a voulu jamais sortir

In other words, the rule of Negative-association can apply across a clause boundary with negative pronouns and determiners, but not with negative adverbs.

On the whole, Negative-association across clause boundaries is restricted to infinitival constructions, though some speakers admit examples with a subjunctive complement (e.g. *?Je n'ai exigé que tu sortes avec personne*). In (149), the understood subject of the infinitive is also the subject of the main clause, which expresses some sort of 'disposition' towards the event described by the complement. When the main verb indicates awareness of the 'fact' described by the complement, Negative-association is blocked. For example, *savoir* with an infinitive can express either capacity (*Il sait parler plusieurs langues*) or awareness (*Il sait avoir fait plusieurs fautes* 'He knows that he has made many mistakes'), but only the first case allows the construction in (149):

(152)  a Il ne sait parler aucune langue étrangère

     b *Il ne sait avoir fait aucune faute

When the understood subject of the infinitive appears as a direct or indirect object in the main clause, Negative-association is often possible when this understood subject is represented by a clitic pronoun or left unspecified, but not when it is realised as a full NP:

(153)  a Je ne l'ai vu embrasser personne

     b Il ne la laisse parler de rien

     c Je ne te permets de regarder aucun film

     d Je ne l'empêche d'aller nulle part

     e Il n'est permis de consulter aucun dictionnaire

(154)  a *Je n'ai vu Pierre embrasser personne

     b *Il ne laisse sa femme parler de rien

     c *Je ne permets aux enfants de regarder aucun film

     d *Je n'empêche mon fils d'aller nulle part

     e *Il n'est permis aux étudiants de consulter aucun dictionnaire

Note also that the process is blocked when the clause containing the negative element is in subject position (cf. (153e)), or when the negative element is embedded in a subject NP:

(155)  a *Consulter aucun dictionnaire n'est permis

     b *La femme de personne n'est arrivée

There are other restrictions on this process, but they tend to involve rather subtle judgements. The particular restrictions noted above should be taken as symptomatic of more general criteria which determine the domains within which certain syntactic or semantic processes can apply. Defining these domains is a complex issue which linguists have addressed in a variety of ways – see 'Further reading' at the end of this chapter for references to relevant works.

### 7.6.9  'Ni . . . ni'

The item *ni* can be classified as a conjunction. Typically, it precedes each of the conjoined elements (a possibility also available with *et* and *ou*: *Pierre n'a vu ni Marie ni Suzy*; cf. *Pierre a vu et Marie et Suzy, Pierre a vu ou Marie ou Suzy*). *Ni* can conjoin phrases of various categories as shown by the labelled brackets in (156):

(156)  a  Pierre n'a lu ni [$_{NP}$ ma lettre] ni [$_{NP}$ ta réponse]
       b  Il n'est ni [$_{AP}$ riche] ni [$_{AP}$ puissant]
       c  Il ne travaille ni [$_{AdvP}$ régulièrement] ni [$_{AdvP}$ soigneusement]
       d  Il n'a ni [$_{VP}$ lu la lettre] ni [$_{VP}$ envoyé une réponse]
       e  Je ne pense ni [$_{S'}$ que Luc soit intelligent] ni [$_{S'}$ que Max soit riche]
       f  Il n'essaie ni [$_{S'}$ de chanter] ni [$_{S'}$ de danser]

NPs conjoined by *ni . . . ni* can occur in subject position (like *rien, personne, aucun*) – note that the verb shows plural agreement:

(157)  Ni Pierre ni Luc ne sont arrivés

In all of the above cases, each of the conjoined expressions must be introduced by *ni*. Also, *ni . . . ni* is incompatible with *pas*:

(158)  *Pierre n'a pas vu ni Marie ni Suzy

However, it is often possible to negate the whole sentence with *ni* occurring only before the last of the conjoined expressions:

(159)  a  Pierre n'a pas lu ta lettre, ni ma réponse
       b  Il n'est pas riche, ni puissant

In such cases, the *ni* phrase tends to be construed as an afterthought.

In terms of the discussion in 7.6.7, *ni . . . ni* appears to function as a true negative, associated with *ne* as in (156) and (157), while single *ni* functions more like a negative polarity item, licensed by *pas* in (159). As a true negative, *ni . . . ni* can be associated with *ne* in a higher clause under the conditions discussed in 7.6.8:

(160)    a   Pierre ne veut voir ni Marie ni Suzy

             b   Je ne te permets d'aller ni à Paris ni à Lyon

             c   Luc ne sait parler ni l'anglais ni l'allemand

As a negative polarity item, *ni* can occur in clauses whose negative force is inferred from the context:

(161)    a   Je ne crois pas qu'il soit riche, ni puissant

             b   Je refuse de croire que Marie soit sortie avec Paul, ni avec Gaston

In literary style, main clauses can be conjoined by *ni ... ni*, with *ne* in each clause, as in the following example cited by Gaatone (1971b, p.128):

(162)      Mais ni ces images n'invitent au plaisir, ni le plaisir n'évoquait ces images

However, this construction is rare. More typically, if the clauses have the same subject, we find the construction in (163), with single *ni* and the subject omitted in all but the first clause:

(163)      Ils ne parlaient, ne chantaient ni ne dansaient

### 7.6.10  'Ne ... que'

Constructions with *ne ... que* are not strictly speaking negative, but they show many affinities with the constructions discussed above. The item *que* has a restrictive function similar to *seul* or *seulement* and precedes the phrase which it modifies: e.g. *Je n'ai donné que du pain au clochard* 'I gave bread (and nothing else) to the tramp', *Je n'ai donné du pain qu'au clochard* 'I gave bread to the tramp (and to nobody else).' In structural terms, let us assume that *que* is adjoined to the phrase which it modifies:

(164)    a   Je n'ai donné [$_{NP}$ que [$_{NP}$ du pain]] au clochard

             b   Je n'a donné du pain [$_{PP}$ que [$_{PP}$ au clochard]]

Note that when *que* modifies the complement of a preposition, it must be adjoined to the entire PP, even if it is interpreted as modifying the complement (contrast English *I voted for only two candidates*):

(165)    a   Je n'ai voté que pour deux candidats

             b   *Je n'ai voté pour que deux candidats

Also, *que* cannot modify a subject NP:

(166)    a   *Que Marie n'est arrivée à l'heure

             b   *Que deux candidats ne se sont présentés

In this respect, *que* differs sharply from negative pronouns and determiners and from expressions with *ni . . . ni*, see (143) in 7.6.7 and (157) in 7.6.9. In cases like (166), *seul* is used (before or after full NPs, but after pronouns, which must be disjunctive forms):

(167) a Seule Marie est arrivée
    b Marie seule est arrivée
    c Lui seul a répondu à la question

APs and AdvPs can be modified by *que*:

(168) a Ce garçon n'est que tout petit
    b Cette voiture ne roule que très lentement

Finite verbs cannot be modified by *que*:

(169) a *Solange ne que souriait
    b *Solange ne souriait que

In compound tenses, modification of the past participle by *que* is marginally acceptable:

(170) ?Solange n'a que souri

In cases like (169) and (170), the verb can be modified by *seulement*: *Elle souriait seulement*, *Elle a seulement souri*. Alternatively, if the verb denotes an action, a construction with *ne faire que* and the infinitive can be used:

(171) a Solange ne faisait que sourire
    b Solange n'a fait que sourire

When *que* modifies an infinitival complement introduced by *de* or *à*, it must precede the complementiser:

(172) a Henri n'essaie que de travailler
    b Jules n'apprend qu'à danser

This evidence suggests that *que* is adjoined to the infinitival S':

(173) Henri n'essaie [$_{S'}$ que [$_{S'}$ de [$_{S}$ $\varnothing$ travailler]]]

Since *que* cannot readily modify other verb forms (see (169) and (170)), it can be assumed that when *que* precedes a bare infinitive it is also adjoined to the S' rather than to the verb or VP:

(174) a Solange ne faisait [$_{S'}$ que [$_{S'}$ [$_{S}$ $\varnothing$ sourire]]]
    b Henri ne veut [$_{S'}$ que [$_{S'}$ [$_{S}$ $\varnothing$ travailler]]]

Finite declarative complement clauses cannot be modified by *que* (cf. English *I know only that Pierre lied*):

(175)     *Je ne sais [$_{S'}$ que [$_{S'}$ que Pierre a menti]]

This can be plausibly attributed to the repetition of *que*. Note that *que* can modify a finite interrogative S' introduced by the complementiser *si*:

(176)     Je ne demande [$_{S'}$ que [$_{S'}$ si Pierre a menti]]

Except in colloquial speech, restrictive *que* must be associated with *ne*. Within the conditions discussed in 7.6.8, it can be associated with *ne* in a higher clause:

(177)     a   Pierre ne veut parler qu'avec Marie
          b   Jules ne sait parler que le français

Unlike the other items which have been discussed, *que* is compatible with *pas* in the same clause, with a 'not only' interpretation:

(178)     Gaston n'a pas mangé que du gâteau
          'Gaston did not eat only cake'

However, *que* cannot occur alone in contexts where negative polarity items are licensed by a negative inference (except in colloquial speech where *ne* is freely omitted):

(179)     a   *Je ne crois pas que Gaston ait mangé que du gâteau
          b   *Je refuse de croire que Gaston ait mangé que du gâteau

In more formal style, we would need *ne* in the complement clause:... *que Gaston n'ait mangé que du gâteau*.

### 7.6.11   Total negation without 'pas'

In formal registers, *ne* can express total negation on its own in certain contexts. The principal cases are summarised below:

- with *cesser, oser, pouvoir* followed by an infinitive: *Il ne cesse de travailler, Je n'ose lui parler, Il ne pourra résoudre ce problème.*
- with *savoir* followed by an interrogative complement (indirect question): *Je ne sais s'il reviendra, Je ne savais que faire* (cf. *Je ne savais pas quoi faire*, see 10.4.7).
- in hypothetical conditional clauses introduced by *si*, particularly when the main clause is also negated: *Si je n'avais pris la voiture, l'accident ne serait pas arrivé.*
- in sentences modified by time expressions of the type *il y a ... que*,

*voilà . . . que, Cela fait . . . que* (only with compound tenses): *Il y a longtemps que je ne l'ai vu, cela faisait des années qu'il ne l'avait vu.*

- in rhetorical questions or exclamations introduced by QU- items: *Que ne ferait-il pour réussir?*
- in subjunctive relative clauses modifying some entity whose existence is denied: *Il n' y a personne qui ne veuille être riche.*
- after *ce n'est pas que* and *non que*: *Ce n'est pas qu'il n'ait fait un effort* 'It is not that he did not make an effort', *non pas qu'elle ne soit malade* 'not that she is not ill'.

In all of the above cases, *ne . . . pas* is also possible, without any difference in meaning.

In addition there are a number of fixed expressions in which *pas* cannot occur: e.g. *n'empêche que, n'importe quoi*, etc.; *à Dieu ne plaise*; *je ne sais quoi* (as a nominal expression: *un certain je ne sais quoi*).

### 7.6.12 Expletive uses of 'ne'

These are uses of *ne* which do not express negation and where the addition of *pas* leads to ungrammaticality or a change in meaning. The principal cases are as follows:

- in comparative constructions (see 7.7.3): *Il est plus riche qu'il ne l'était, Il est moins intelligent que ne croyais.*
- in complements of *à moins que, avant que* and (more rarely) *sans que*: *Je sortirai, à moins qu'il ne pleuve, Elle a attrapé le verre avant qu'il ne tombe par terre, Je suis entré sans qu'ils ne me voient.*
- in complements of *craindre* and other expressions of fear regarding a possible situation: *Je crains que ce ne soit vrai, Elle est partie de peur qu'il ne revienne.*
- in complements of verbs of doubt or denial when these are negated (sometimes also in questions): *Je ne doute pas qu'elle ne vienne* 'I have no doubt that she will come', *Je ne nie pas qu'elle ne soit belle.*
- in complements of verbs of prevention: *J'ai empêché que cela ne se produise.*

The use of *ne* in the above cases is optional, though preferred in more formal styles. Although expletive *ne* does not express negation, the clauses in which it occurs typically describe hypothetical situations.

### 7.6.13 'Non pas'

These items can be used together or separately to negate a fragment of a sentence which is contrasted with some element in a full sentence, as in (180):

(180)  a  J'ai vu Pierre, non pas Jacques
       b  J'ai vu Pierre, pas Jacques
       c  J'ai vu Pierre, non Jacques

In this construction, *non* can be viewed as the non-clitic counterpart of *ne* in full sentence negation, used when there is no verb for *ne* to be cliticised to. There is a stylistic parallel with *ne ... pas* in that the use of *pas* alone (in (180b)) is typical of less formal registers (though it is not as stigmatised as omission of *ne* in full sentences), while the use of *non* alone (in (180c)) has a more literary flavour. The order of the contrasted elements can be reversed, as in (181):

(181)  J'ai vu non (pas) Jacques, mais Pierre

Here, the use of *pas* on its own is excluded in Standard French, though we could have normal negation in the full sentence, with omission of *ne* in colloquial speech: *Je (n')ai pas vu Jacques, mais Pierre*. Again, the use of *non* alone is the more formal variant.

In disjunctive constructions like (182) there is a choice between *non* and *pas*, but we cannot use both together:

(182)  a  Je ne sais pas si elle est malade ou {non / pas}
       b  Est-ce qu'il est arrivé ou {non / pas}?

In this construction, *non* can be analysed as a substitute for a negative sentence, just as in a reply to a question; e.g. *Est-elle malade? Non* (= *Elle n'est pas malade*). A similar use of *non* can be seen in cases like *Je crois que non*, where *non* replaces the S in the structure (183):[11]

(183)  Je crois [$_{S'}$ que [$_S$ elle n'est pas malade]]

Consequently, the variant of (182a) with *non* can be analysed as in (184):

(184)  Je ne sais pas [$_{S'}$ si [$_S$ [$_S$ elle est malade] ou [$_S$ non]]]

However, this analysis is not plausible for the variants of (182) with *pas*, since *pas* cannot act as a substitute for a sentence in other constructions (e.g. *\*Je crois que pas*). In this case, *pas* appears to modify a redundant adjective or participle, which can be repeated as in (185):

(185)  a  Je ne sais pas si elle est malade ou pas malade
       b  Est-ce qu'il est arrivé ou pas arrivé?

Note that *non* cannot be used in place of *pas* in this construction:

---

[11]  Note that *oui* and *si* are used in the same way: *Je crois que {oui / si}*.

(186)    a  *Je ne sais pas si elle est malade ou non malade
         b  *Est-ce qu'il est arrivé ou non arrivé?

The use of *pas* to negate elements other than complete sentences is attested in many other constructions:

(187)    a  Pierre habite un petit village pas loin de Rouen
         b  C'est un roman très long et pas très intéressant
         c  Jules a l'air pas content du tout

In some cases, *non* can also be used in this way: *Il habite un village non loin de Rouen*. However, this use of *non* is lexically determined whereas the construction with *pas* is fully productive and tends to be preferred even in formal styles. In many cases of this sort, *non* appears to function as an alternative to the negative prefix *in-* – e.g. *une classe non dénombrable, une classe indénombrable*.

## 7.7 Comparative and superlative constructions

### 7.7.1 Types of comparison

Comparative constructions can be divided into three semantic types illustrated in (188):

(188)    a  Pierre est plus riche que Luc    **(comparative of superiority)**
         b  Pierre est moins riche que Luc   **(comparative of inferiority)**
         c  Pierre est aussi riche que Luc   **(comparative of equality)**

The syntactic properties of these three types are essentially the same.

Ostensibly, the sentences in (188) express a comparison between Pierre and Luc. However, it may be more useful to view them as comparing degrees of wealth as they apply to the two individuals: e.g. (188a) may be paraphrased as in (189):

(189)    'The degree to which Pierre is rich is greater than the degree to which Luc is rich'

In other cases the degree of a property may be compared for the same individual with respect to different times:

(190)    Pierre est plus riche maintenant qu'auparavant
         'The degree to which Pierre is rich now is greater than the degree to which he used to be rich.'

To facilitate discussion, the term **parameter of comparison** will be used to refer to the property or concept which is being compared (represented by *riche* in (188) and (190)) and **contrasted elements** to refer to *Pierre* and *Luc* in (188) and *maintenant* and *auparavant* in (190). The term **standard of comparison** will be used to refer to the phrase introduced by *que*. None of these are standard terms.

In the above examples, the parameter of comparison is represented by an adjective, but other categories can fulfil this role, as indicated in (191):

(191)  a  Max va au théâtre plus souvent que Jules  (Aspectual AdvP)
       b  L'avion va plus vite que le train  (Manner AdvP)
       c  Jules a dépensé plus d'argent que Gaston  (NP)
       d  Marie travaille plus que Solange  (VP)

Note that when the degree item (e.g. *plus*) modifies a VP, as in (191d), it normally follows the verb, obligatorily if the verb is finite, as in the case of other degree modifiers like *beaucoup* (see 7.5.4).

In (188)–(191) the expression modified by the degree item represents the parameter of comparison. However, it can also represent one of the contrasted elements – e.g. with the interpretation 'The quantity of apples that Henri bought is greater than the quantity of bananas that he bought' for (192a):

(192)  a  Henri a acheté plus de pommes que de bananes
       b  Pierre est plus malin qu'intelligent
       c  Sophie danse plus énergiquement qu'élégamment
       d  Solange se repose plus qu'elle ne travaille

Note that when the standard of comparison consists of a finite verb, as in (192d), it must be accompanied by a subject, usually with expletive *ne*.

### 7.7.2 Comparative degree items

In comparatives of superiority, *plus* can modify all categories, as shown in the examples in 7.7.1. The alternative item, *davantage*, can only modify NPs and VPs: *davantage d'argent, Elle travaille davantage, *davantage riche, *davantage vite*. For *bon* and *bien*, the comparative forms *meilleur* and *mieux* are used systematically instead of *plus {bon / bien}*, except in cases parallel to (192b, c) above where *bon/bien* represents one of the contrasted elements[12] (e.g. *Il est plus bon que mauvais, Il va plus bien que mal*). The items *mauvais* and *mal* have the comparative forms *pire* and *pis*, but *pis* is obsolete except in a few expressions like *tant pis*, and *pire* tends to be used only with an abstract interpretation: *Ces résultats sont pires que les autres* but *Ce vin est plus mauvais que l'autre*. Generally, *plus mauvais* is preferred in informal registers. Often, the problem is avoided altogether by using the comparative of inferiority *moins {bon / bien}* instead. The adjective

---

[12] In these examples, *plutôt* would be more natural than *plus*, comparing as it were the relative appropriateness of the adjectives or adverbs rather than degrees of different properties.

*moindre* may be regarded as the equivalent of *plus petit* (*or moins grand*), but only with an abstract sense: *Ces résultats sont d'une moindre importance que les autres*. In comparatives of inferiority, *moins* is used with all categories.

In comparatives of equality, *aussi* is used to modify adjectives and adverbs, while *autant* is used with nouns and verbs:

(193)　　a　Pierre est aussi riche que Luc
　　　　　b　Max va au théâtre aussi souvent que Jules
　　　　　c　Gaston a dépensé autant d'argent que Robert
　　　　　d　Marie travaille autant que Solange

In negative sentences, *si* can be used as an alternative to *aussi*:

(194)　　a　Pierre n'est pas {si / aussi} riche que Luc
　　　　　b　Max ne va pas au théâtre {si / aussi} souvent que Jules

Note that *si* can be used in affirmative sentences with a slightly different function, like English *so*:

(195)　　a　Pierre est si riche qu'il n'a pas besoin de travailler
　　　　　b　Max va au théâtre si souvent qu'il a acheté une carte d'abonnement

No comparison of properties is involved here, but *si* expresses a degree which is sufficiently great to motivate the circumstance described in the *que* clause (cf. the constructions with *trop* and *assez* discussed in 7.4.2). Syntactically, this *que* clause differs from 'standard of comparison' clauses in that it does not allow expletive *ne*: *\*Il y va si souvent qu'il n'a acheté une carte d'abonnement*. With verbs and nouns, *tant* is used with a similar function:

(196)　　a　Pierre a tant d'argent qu'il n'a pas besoin de travailler
　　　　　b　Marie a tant travaillé qu'elle est épuisée

Comparative items of degree can be modified by other degree adverbs. For example, *plus* and *moins* (more rarely *davantage*) can be modified by *beaucoup*, *bien*, *même*, *tellement* and *autrement*, while *aussi* can be modified by *tout*:

(197)　　a　Pierre est {beaucoup / bien / autrement} plus riche que Luc
　　　　　b　Pierre est tout aussi riche que Luc

### 7.7.3　Expressing the 'standard of comparison'

In the cases reviewed so far, the phrase which indicates the standard of comparison can be construed as a reduced clause in which redundant elements, shown in angle brackets in the following illustrations, are omitted:

(198)    a   Pierre est plus riche que Luc <est riche>

           b   Pierre est plus riche que <Pierre était riche> auparavant

           c   Henri a acheté plus de pommes que <Henri a acheté> de bananes

In this way, the ambiguity of a sentence like (199), and its English counterpart, can be represented as in (200):

(199)      Jean admire Jacques plus que Paul

(200)    a   Jean admire Jacques plus que <Jean admire> Paul

           b   Jean admire Jacques plus que Paul <admire Jacques>

In English, the interpretation in (200b) can be made explicit by using the dummy verb *do*: *John admires Jack more than Paul does*. However, in French, we must repeat the verb and represent the redundant complement by a pronoun (usually with expletive *ne* – see 7.6.12) :

(201)      Jean admire Jacques plus que Paul ne l'admire

The same situation obtains when the verb in the *que* phrase must be included because its tense or semantic content is one of the contrasted elements. Thus, the propositions *Gaston spends more money than he earns* and *Pierre is richer than he was* must be expressed as in (202), where *en* represents the redundant NP (*d'argent*) and *le* the redundant AP (*riche*):

(202)    a   Gaston dépense plus d'argent qu'il n'en gagne

           b   Pierre est plus riche qu'il ne l'était

Similarly, in English, we can use an auxiliary verb without the participle in the *than* clause (*Harry has danced more than Bob has*), but in French the participle must be repeated if the auxiliary is present, though usually the whole VP is omitted:

(203)      Henri a dansé plus que Robert (n'a dansé)

From the above observations, the following generalisation can be deduced for French:

*When, for any reason, the* que *phrase contains a verb (lexical or auxiliary), the* que *phrase must constitute a complete sentence, with redundant complements represented by appropriate pronouns.*

The general tendency is for redundant elements in the *que* phrase to be omitted as far as possible. However, there are syntactic restrictions which can override this tendency. In English, a redundant preposition can often be omitted (e.g. *Jules talks more often about his family than (about) his career*), but in French the preposition must be repeated:

(204)     Jules parle plus souvent de sa famille que de sa carrière

Similarly, when an infinitive introduced by *à* or *de* is one of the contrasted items, the appropriate preposition or complementiser must be repeated in the *que* phrase:

(205)     a   Solange cherche plus à s'amuser qu'à gagner sa vie
          b   Il me plaît plus de regarder la télévision que de sortir

In cases involving a bare infinitive, the complementiser *de* is optionally inserted in the *que* phrase:

(206)     J'aime mieux regarder la télévision que (de) sortir

The optional use of *de* here is perhaps related to the situation with subject clauses (*(De) sortir me plaît*, see 3.4.7).

There are some types of *que* phrases which cannot be construed as reduced versions of full clauses of the type illustrated in (198) and (200). The clearest case is exemplified in (207) where *cela* refers to an assumption about the degree of Marie's intelligence:

(207)     Marie est plus intelligente que cela

In examples like (208), the pronoun *le* can be construed in the same way as *cela* in (207): i.e. it refers to a previous belief about the degree of Marie's intelligence:

(208)     Marie est plus intelligente que je ne (le) croyais

The optionality of the pronoun in (208) can be related to cases of possible ellipsis of the object of verbs like *croire* when referring back to earlier propositions in the discourse, as in (209):

(209)     Est-ce que Marie est intelligente? Oui, je (le) crois

In appropriate pragmatic situations, the standard of comparison need not be specified:

(210)     a   Luc est assez pauvre, mais Pierre est plus riche
          b   Pierre est devenu plus riche

In all of the cases discussed so far, the standard of comparison is expressed by a phrase introduced by *que*. With numerals and other quantity expressions *plus* and *moins* are followed by a phrase introduced by *de*:

(211)    a  Le patron a renvoyé plus de cinquante ouvriers
           b  Gaston a bu moins de la moitié de la bouteille

However, *que* must be used in cases like the following:

(212)    a  Étienne travaille plus que trois ouvriers
           b  Gaston boit moins que la plupart de ses camarades

In (212) the degree item modifies the verb and the *que* phrase clearly indicates the standard of comparison, as we can see from rather artificial paraphrases such as *Étienne travaille plus que trois ouvriers ne travaillent, Gaston boit moins que la plupart de ces camarades ne boivent.* In (211), the comparative item can be more plausibly construed as modifying the quantity expression – e.g. *plus de cinquante* means any number greater than fifty.

### 7.7.4 Superlative constructions

Superlative degree (rendered by *most, least* or the suffix *-est* in English) is expressed by the same forms as are used in comparatives of superiority or inferiority (except *davantage*) preceded by the definite article:

(213)    a  Cette question est la plus intéressante
           b  Ta réponse était la meilleure
           c  Marie est l'étudiante la plus intelligente
           d  C'est Max qui va le plus souvent au théâtre
           e  C'est Gaston qui travaille le moins

In superlative constructions, the standard of comparison is not expressed, because it is implicit in the meaning of the superlative form – e.g. (213a) means *Cette question est plus intéressante que toutes les autres.* However, a phrase introduced by *de* may be added to indicate the class of entities which are taken into consideration:

(214)    a  Cette question est la plus intéressante de celles que le
               professeur a posées
           b  Marie est l'étudiante la plus intelligente de la classe

When a superlative AP occurs in the postnominal position, the definite article must be repeated: e.g. *l'étudiante la plus intelligente* in (213c). This construction is also possible with adjectives which normally precede the noun: *la maison la plus grande.* Alternatively, the AP can precede the noun, in which case the presence of a definite determiner (or a possessive) induces a superlative interpretation:

(215)    a  Il habite la plus grande maison (de la ville)
           b  Son plus grand problème, c'est de trouver un appartement

This is the preferred construction with *meilleur* and the only option with *pire* and *moindre*: *mon meilleur ami, les {moindres / pires} défauts* vs *?mon ami le meilleur, *les défauts les {moindres / pires}*.

In examples like (216), the definite article must agree in number and gender with the adjective:

(216)      a   Solange est la moins élégante de ces actrices
            b   Ces étudiantes sont les plus heureuses de la classe

However, in (217) the invariable form *le* must be used:

(217)      a   Solange est le moins élégante quand elle se lève le matin
            b   Les étudiantes sont le plus heureuses à la fin du cours

The difference between these two cases is that in (216) the feminine/plural NP is one of the contrasted elements, whereas in (217) the contrast involves the situations described by *quand elle se lève le matin* and *à la fin du cours*. This difference can be seen more clearly in the comparative constructions corresponding to (217a):

(218)      a   Solange est moins élégante que les autres actrices
            b   Solange est moins élégante quand elle se lève que lorsqu'elle
               est sur scène

In English, superlative adjectival expressions can be used with the indefinite determiner to indicate the highest degree of a property: *That is a most interesting question*. This construction is not possible in French – **C'est une question la plus intéressante*. Instead, the superlative expression must be cast in the plural (with the appropriate gender) and introduced by *de*:

(219)      C'est une question des plus intéressantes

The same construction is used in predicative position, where English has the superlative form without a determiner (*That question is most interesting*):

(220)      Cette question est des plus intéressantes

Although *plus* and *moins* can be used as determiners expressing comparative quantity (*Gaston a bu {plus / moins} de vin que Luc*), they cannot be used with the definite article to express superlative quantity (cf. *Gaston drank the most wine*):

(221)      *Gaston a bu le {plus / moins} de vin

In such cases, we must use an appropriate quantity noun modified by a comparative AP (or use a comparative construction like *Gaston a bu {plus / moins} de vin que tous les autres*):

(222)    Gaston a bu la plus grande quantité de vin

Where English uses *most* as a determiner without the definite article, French uses *la plupart*: *Most students are intelligent*, *La plupart des étudiants sont intelligents*.

### 7.7.5 'Plus... plus...'

Comparative adverbs can be used to indicate a proportional correlation of degree between two situations, as in (223):

(223)    a  Plus on rit, (et) plus on s'amuse
         b  Plus on gagne d'argent, (et) moins on est content
         c  Moins je mange de viande, (et) mieux je me sens

Note that the degree item is not preceded by the definite article (cf. English *The more we laugh, ...*) and that the two clauses can be conjoined by *et*. A further difference between the two languages emerges in cases like (223b) (and the first clause in (223c)) where the degree item is interpreted as modifying a noun or adjective (rather than the verb as in (223a)). In English, the degree item and the modified expression normally occur together at the beginning of the clause (*The more money we earn, the less happy we are*), but in French only the degree adverb is placed at the beginning of the clause: *\*Plus d'argent on gagne, (et) plus content on est*. The same phenomenon can be seen with cases involving *meilleur* (= *plus bon*):

(224)    a  Plus on y mettra de sel, (et) plus la soupe sera bonne
         b  *Plus on y mettra de sel, (et) meilleure la soupe sera

With *mieux*, we can have either the construction in (223c) or the construction in (225), parallel to (224a):

(225)    Moins je mange de viande, (et) plus je me sens bien

The relevant generalisation for French seems to be that, in these constructions, the item which introduces each clause must be a comparative degree adverb, not an adjective like *meilleur* or a phrase containing a degree item (e.g. an NP like *plus d'argent* or an AP like *moins content*).

### Exercises

1  The following adjectives can occur before or after the noun, some-times with a difference in meaning: *bref, cher, divers, faible, fameux, franc, honnête, honteux, léger, misérable, nouveau*. Discuss the factors which determine the position of these adjectives, giving illustrative examples.

2 Collect attested examples where a noun is preceded or followed by two or more 'property' adjectives and consider the effects of reversing the order of the adjectives.

3 The following adjectives can be used in constructions like those discussed in 7.3.6 (sometimes in feminine or plural forms): *complet, éternal, faux, fou, maternel, mort, nouveau, petit, plein, savant, serieux, suisse*. Construct relevant examples and try to determine whether these items should be analysed as nouns or as adjectives modifying an empty noun. (N.B. Some items may have more than one use.)

4 In English some adjectives can be used with the progressive form of *to be*, giving an interpretation of the type 'to act in a certain manner': *He is being clever*. In French, a construction with *faire* is used in such cases: *Il fait le malin*. Construct further examples and try to establish whether *malin* and other items used in this way are adjectives or nouns.

5 What types of adjectives can be used to modify body-part nouns in constructions like the following?

   (a) Pierre a levé la main
   (b) Je lui ai cassé le bras

How do these types compare with those which can occur in the construction in (c) (see 2.6.3)?

   (c) Marie a les yeux bleus

Suggest reasons for the differences which you observe

6 Summarise the analyses which have been proposed for constructions like the following in this chapter (see also 1.5.4):

   (a) la *révision immédiate du programme*
   (b) On *révisera immédiatement le programme*

Since both of the italicised expressions in (a)–(b) manifest the surface order head – modifier – complement, do the proposed analyses miss an important generalisation?

7 Comment on the relationship between mood and negative polarity illustrated in the following examples:

   (a) Le professeur ne croit pas que Pierre {ait / ??a} fait le moindre effort
   (b) ?Ne crois-tu pas que le médecin a levé le petit doigt pour nous aider?

8 Bearing in mind the questions discussed in 7.6.7, how can you account for the use of negative items in comparative constructions like the following?

(a) Marie travaille plus que personne
(b) Les livres de linguistique m'intéressent plus que rien
(c) Pierre gagne plus d'argent que Luc n'en a jamais gagné
(d) Suzy est plus belle que jamais

What other negative items can be used in this way?

9 In terms of their meaning, adjectives like *aîné, antérieur, majeur* and *supérieur*, resemble comparative adjectives. Do they behave like comparative forms from a syntactic point of view?

10 To what extent and in what respects do *autrement, autre* and *plutôt* in constructions like the following share the properties of comparative adverbs or adjectives?

(a) Pierre a résolu le problème autrement que Luc
(b) Henri a choisi un autre jouet que Paul
(c) Jean est plutôt malin qu'intelligent

**Further reading**

A detailed study of the syntax of adjectives is presented in Picabia (1978a); see also Riegel (1985) on predicative adjective constructions and Bartning (1980) on adnominal adjectives. Stati (1973) gives a brief overview of adjectives. Properties of object-gap constructions are discussed in Picabia (1976), Ruwet (1982, ch. 2) and Zaring (1992); see also Picabia (1978b) for constructions with adjectives of the *cruel* type.

On the properties of different classes of adverbs, see Schlyter (1974), Sueur (1978), Muller (1975) and Nølke (1983). The Verb-raising account of the position of adverbs and negative items in French and English was first put forward by Emonds (1976) and is developed in Pollock (1989), who advocates the splitting of the Inflection category into separate Tense and Agreement nodes; see Williams (1994) for a critique of this approach.

General descriptions of negation in French are presented in Gaatone (1971b) and Muller (1991); Callebaut (1992) is also devoted to this topic. On negative adverbs, see Rowlett (1993). The phenomenon of Negative-association is discussed in detail in Muller (1984), Milner (1979) and Moritz & Valois (1994); see also Pica (1984) and Kayne (1984, ch. 2) for relevant discussion. Negative polarity is discussed in Fauconnier (1975, 1980). For other aspects of negation in French, see Cornulier (1973, 1974b), Gaatone (1971a, 1992), Heldner (1992). Ashby (1976, 1981, 1991) and Posner (1985) investigate negation without *ne* from a sociolinguistic/historical perspective. Expletive uses of *ne* are studied in Muller (1978).

On comparative constructions, see Pinkham (1985), Muller (1983) and S. Price (1990), who compares French with Spanish in this respect. Barbaud (1974) investigates superlative constructions and related phenomena.

# 8
# Prepositions

## 8.1 Overview

Prepositions are often thought of as grammatical particles which introduce NPs, indicating an indirect object or modifier relation, rather than as fully fledged lexical items on a par with nouns, verbs or adjectives. This issue is addressed in 8.2, with an investigation of the syntactic functions and structural properties of prepositions in comparison with other lexical categories and items of a more grammatical nature. In 8.3, we shall pursue the idea that prepositions (like verbs, adjectives and nouns) can take complements other than NPs, or no complement at all, thus subsuming many items traditionally classified as 'subordinating conjunctions' or adverbs within the category of prepositions. Here, as elsewhere, the important question is not whether one term is more appropriate than another – the issue is raised principally as a way of looking at similarities and differences which cut across the traditional classification of the parts of speech. In 8.4, the syntactic properties of so called 'complex prepositions' are discussed.

One area of meaning in which prepositions play an important role is the expression of spatial relations. In 8.5, there is an investigation of some significant differences between French and English concerning the ways in which prepositions can combine with verbs of movement to indicate the place to or from which an entity moves.

There are many difficulties surrounding the use of particular prepositions. In 8.6, this chapter is concluded by a look at a few cases (principally involving *en* and *avec*) which are amenable to systematic analysis.

## 8.2 Structural properties of prepositions
### 8.2.1 The properties and functions of prepositions

A small sample of items whose status as prepositions is uncontroversial is given in (1), though some of these forms can be used as other parts of speech: e.g. *devant* as a noun 'front', *à* and *de* as infinitival complementisers (see 2.3.5, 9.5.1), *en* as an 'adverbial' clitic (see 6.4.5–6.4.6):

(1)      à, de; avec, contre, dans, devant, en, entre, malgré, par, pour, sans,
         selon, sur, vers

Unlike verbs, adjectives and nouns, prepositions are morphologically invariable
– i.e. they do not inflect for tense, number or gender – this can be taken as a
defining property of prepositions,[1] though it is one which they share with
adverbs.

All of the prepositions in (1) can be followed by an NP. Indeed, many
grammarians take this to be a defining property of prepositions, a matter
which will be addressed in some detail in 8.3. In more technical terms,
prepositions resemble verbs (but not adjectives or nouns) in that they can
assign a Case feature to a following NP (see 1.5.6). In earlier chapters we
have seen many instances where a preposition serves primarily to assign Case
to an NP which is interpreted as a complement of some other item, as in the
expressions in (2):

(2)      hériter d'une fortune, renoncer à la violence, être amoureux de
         quelqu'un, la destruction des documents

In these examples, the prepositions do not make any obvious contribution to
meaning, but have an essentially grammatical function. On the other hand, there
are many cases, like those in (3), where prepositions have a clear semantic function, expressing a relation (such as 'instrument', 'purpose', 'place') which is not
implicit in the meaning of the verb:

(3)      ouvrir la boîte avec un tournevis, voyager pour le plaisir, danser sur
         la table

In other cases, like (4), the preposition elaborates on a semantic relation which is
expressed by the verb:

(4)      mettre les livres {dans / sur / sous / devant / derrière} le placard

Here, *mettre* entails a spatial relation between the books and the cupboard, while
the preposition defines the nature of this spatial relation (see 8.5.1) as well as
assigning Case to *le placard*.

Typically, *de* and *à* have a predominantly grammatical function, whereas other
prepositions have a more clearly identifiable meaning, but this distinction is not
absolute. For example, in (5) *de* and *à* express a semantic contrast (Source vs
Goal), while *pour* and *sur* in (6) do not make any clear contribution to meaning
(e.g. they do not contrast with other prepositions in the same context) but can be

---

[1] It is assumed that *au, aux, du* and *des* are contractions of *à* and *de* with the following definite
article rather than inflected (masculine or plural) forms of *à* and *de*.

regarded as the prepositions which are selected by the verb in order to assign Case to the NP, in much the same way as *de* and *à* in (2):

(5)        Pierre vient {de / à} Paris

(6)        a    J'ai opté pour cette solution
           b    Je compte sur votre coopération

The functions of prepositions can be summarised as follows:

**Functions of Prepositions:**
*Grammatical function:*    to assign Case to an NP
*Semantic functions:*
 *I  (in modifier expressions) to define the nature of the modification
 (e.g. 'instrument', 'purpose', etc.)*
 *II  (in complements) to elaborate on the theta-role assigned to the complement
 (e.g. specifying the spatial relation with Locative complements).*

In examples like (3)–(5), the prepositions have both functions – they assign Case to the following NP as well as defining the semantic relation between this NP and some other element in the sentence. When the semantic contribution of the preposition is non-existent or negligible, as in (2) and (6), the preposition only has a grammatical function. To anticipate later discussion, let us assume that prepositions which introduce elements other than NPs (e.g. finite clauses) have only a semantic function, since the elements in question do not require a Case feature. Thus, *pour* in (7) expresses a 'purpose' relation (similar to that in *voyager pour le plaisir* in (3)), but does not have a grammatical (Case-assigning) function:

(7)        Je travaille pour que ma famille vive dans le confort

### 8.2.2   Structure of the PP
Apart from some uses of *de* discussed in 5.3.6–5.4.8 (where it was proposed that *de* is adjoined to the N′ or NP in quantitative and partitive constructions), it is assumed that prepositions function as heads of their own phrasal category (PP) and that the element introduced by the preposition (e.g. an NP) is its complement. Some prepositions can also be accompanied by degree modifiers of various sorts: *juste derrière la maison, peu après la guerre, droit devant toi, tout près de l'église, absolument contre cette idée*. Following the proposal in 1.4.2, let us assume that these degree items occur in the Specifier position of the PP. Thus, the structure of the PP can be represented as in (8):

(8)

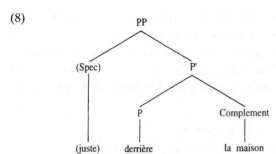

### 8.2.3 Conjoined PPs

In English, it is generally possible to conjoin two prepositional expressions without repeating the preposition:

(9)    a   John went to Paris and to Brussels

       b   John went to Paris and Brussels

It is assumed that examples like (9a) involve conjunction of two PPs whereas (9b) involves conjunction of two NPs governed by the same preposition, as shown in (10):

(10)   a   [$_{PP}$ PP CONJ PP]

      b   [$_{PP}$ P [$_{NP}$ NP CONJ NP]]

In French, constructions of the type in (10b) are much more restricted.

With the prepositions *à*, *de* and *en*, the construction in (10b) is impossible, i.e. the preposition must be repeated in examples like (11):

(11)   a   Jean est allé à Paris et *(à) Bruxelles

      b   Ces légumes viennent de France et *(de) Belgique

      c   Ces voitures sont fabriquées en Angleterre et *(en) Allemagne

The only exceptions to this generalisation are cases where the two elements form a single entity, as in (12) where Paul and Marie are construed as the joint authors or recipients of the letter:

(12)   a   J'ai reçu une lettre de Paul et Marie

      b   J'ai envoyé une lettre à Paul et Marie

This restriction on *à*, *de* and *en* also applies when these items introduce an infinitive or gerund:

(13)   a   Luc apprend à lire et *(à) écrire

      b   Marie a fini de boire et *(de) manger

      c   Jules est entré en chantant et *(en) dansant

*Prepositions*

The facts observed in (9), (11) and (13) reflect a more´general difference between English and French. For example, in English it is often possible to conjoin two nouns introduced by a single determiner or two finite clauses introduced by the same complementiser: *those men and women, I thought that Marie was at work and Paul was at home.* However, in French the determiner or complementiser must be repeated:

(14)      a   ces hommes et *(ces) femmes
          b   Je pensais que Marie travaillait et *(que) Paul était chez lui

In structural terms, it may be postulated that English allows constructions of the types in both (15) and (16) whereas French allows only those in (16):

(15)      a   $[_{NP} D [_{N'} N' \text{ CONJ } N']]$
          b   $[_{S'} C [_{S} S \text{ CONJ } S]]$

(16)      a   $[_{NP} NP \text{ CONJ } NP]$
          b   $[_{S'} S' \text{ CONJ } S']$

In so far as determiners, complementisers and the prepositions *à, de* and *en* can be classified as 'function' words rather than 'content' words, these observations can be subsumed under the following generalisation, leaving aside special cases like those illustrated in (12) above:

*French does not allow structures of the form*
*[Y [$_X$ X CONJ X]]*
*where Y is a function word and X is any category.*

With other prepositions, which have more semantic content than *à, de* and *en*, constructions of the type in (10b) are possible, though less widely used than in English:

(17)      a   Il est interdit de fumer dans les autobus et (dans) les trains
          b   Les livres étaient entassés sur les chaises et (sur) les tables
          c   Pierre est sorti sans son chapeau et (sans) son parapluie
          d   L'autobus s'arrête devant la banque et (devant) l'église

Generally, conjunction without repetition of the preposition is possible only when the two elements are similar in kind, but is excluded when there is a contrast between the two:

(18)      Il faut être courageux dans la misère et *(dans) la richesse

Similarly, discontinuous expressions, such as *aussi bien ... que* and *ou ... ou*, only allow conjunction of the PPs in such cases, with the components preceding the prepositions rather than the NPs:

(19)    a  Il est interdit de fumer aussi bien dans les autobus que dans les
           trains
        b  Marie sortira ou avec Pierre ou avec Paul

(20)    a  *Il est interdit de fumer dans aussi bien les autobus que les trains
        b  *Marie sortira avec ou Pierre ou Paul

### 8.3  Prepositions and their complements

#### 8.3.1  Prepositions which select PPs

Among the items which some grammarians classify as prepositions, there are a
few which cannot be followed directly by an NP but require an intervening
'grammatical' preposition (*de* or *à*) e.g. *près (de)*, *loin (de)*, *lors (de)*, *grâce (à)*,
*quant (à)*. Such cases can be accommodated by subcategorising these items as
prepositions which select a PP as their complement (in much the same way as
verbs like *douter* and *nuire* select PPs headed by *de* and *à* respectively), as in
(21):

(21)

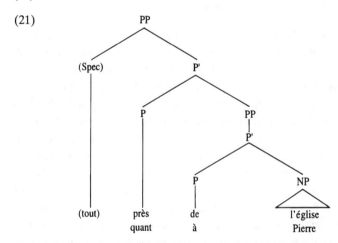

In terms of our discussion in 8.2.1, items like *près* and *quant* can be classified as
prepositions which have a semantic function but which lack the ability to assign
Case to their complement (just like intransitive verbs), thus requiring the use of a
purely 'grammatical' preposition which can fulfil this function.

#### 8.3.2  Prepositions and 'subordinating conjunctions'

There are quite a few items which can be followed either by an NP or by a finite
clause introduced by *que*, like *pendant* in (22):

(22)    a  Pierre regardait la télé pendant le repas
        b  Pierre regardait la télé pendant qu'il mangeait

Other items which show this pattern include *après, avant, depuis, dès, pour* and *sans*. Traditionally, words like *pendant* are classified as prepositions when they take an NP, as in (22a), whereas *pendant que*, in cases like (22b), is classified as a subordinating conjunction. However, this distinction seems rather artificial. A simpler approach is to treat *pendant* and the other items just listed as prepositions which can select either an NP or a finite S′ (i.e. a clause introduced by *que*) as their complement. According to this approach, the phrase *pendant qu'il mangeait* can be analysed as in (23):

(23)

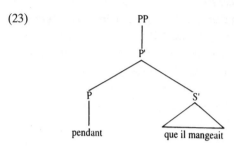

The ability to take an NP or finite clause as complement seems to be a partially arbitrary property of the preposition. For example, *durant*, which is similar in meaning to *pendant*, can only select an NP: *durant le repas, *durant qu'il mangeait*. The converse situation is found with the item *tandis* which, in a rather archaic, literary style, can be used with more or less the same meaning as *pendant* in (22b) (though nowadays it usually means 'whereas'), but can only be used with a finite clause: *tandis qu'il mangeait, *tandis le repas*. Once it is accepted that prepositions can introduce phrases other than NPs (e.g. clauses), it is natural to classify as prepositions items like *tandis* which select other types of phrases even though they cannot introduce NPs. Thus, *tandis* can be classified as a preposition which selects only a finite S′. Other items which introduce a subordinate *que* clause can be analysed in the same way – e.g. *ainsi, afin, alors, aussitôt, bien, pourvu* and, if we ignore the absence of a space in the written language, the items *lors, puis* and *quoi* in *lorsque, puisque* and *quoique*.

### 8.3.3 Prepositions vs complementisers

There are some so-called 'subordinating conjunctions' which introduce a finite clause directly, without *que*: namely, *comme, quand, si* and the item *que* itself.

In 1.3.1, *que* was assigned to a special class of 'complementisers' (words which present the following clause as a complement of some other item). In general, it would not be appropriate to analyse *que* as a preposition, since it can introduce clauses which function as subjects or direct objects (see 2.3.4 and 3.4.7):

(24)      a   Que Pierre soit arrivé est possible

           b   Je reconnais que Pierre est arrivé

The same observation holds for *si* when it introduces indirect questions:

(25)      a   Si Pierre est arrivé n'est pas certain

           b   Je me demande si Pierre est arrivé

Nevertheless, there are other uses of *que* and *si* in which they might plausibly be analysed as prepositions.

In 7.7.1–7.7.3 it was noted that *que* is used to introduce the 'standard of comparison' in comparative constructions: *Pierre est {plus / aussi} grand que Paul.* Although *que Paul* in this example might be regarded as a reduced clause (corresponding to *que Paul est grand*), we saw in 7.7.3 that there are other cases which cannot be analysed in this way: e.g. *Marie est plus intelligente que cela.* Given that *que* in comparative constructions can introduce phrases which are not clauses, we can conclude that here it is not a complementiser but a preposition (as is generally assumed for its English counterparts *than* and *as*), even when it does introduce a finite clause (e.g. in *Pierre est plus riche qu'il ne l'était*).

In conditional constructions like (26) the *si* clause is not a complement of the main verb, but an adjunct expression which modifies the main clause (*je sortirai*):

(26)      S'il fait beau, je sortirai

As we saw in 4.8.2, the *si* clause can be paraphrased by a PP such as *dans ce cas.* Similarly, the reason and time clauses introduced by *comme* and *quand* in (27) are adjunct expressions of the sort which can be rendered by PPs (e.g. *à cause du beau temps, à ce moment-là* and indeed clauses introduced by *puisque* or *lorsque* which were analysed in 8.3.2 as prepositions followed by a complementiser):

(27)      a   Comme il faisait beau, je suis sorti

           b   Quand Pierre est arrivé, nous sommes partis

It therefore seems reasonable to treat *si, comme* and *quand* in such constructions as prepositions which select a finite clause as their complement.

### 8.3.4 'Que' deletion

The absence of *que* in clauses introduced by *comme, quand* and conditional *si* is rather puzzling if these items are prepositions, since *que* appears systematically in most types of finite subordinate clauses – for example, unlike English *that*, it cannot be omitted in the complements of verbs (*\*Je pense il pleut* vs *I think it is raining*) and occurs after most prepositions (*avant qu'il arrive* vs *before he arrives*). One way of capturing this exceptional property is to suppose that *que* is present in the underlying structure (as in other finite subordinate clauses) but is subsequently deleted immediately after the items *si*, *comme* and *quand* (for discussion of other constructions which involve deletion of *que*, see 10.5). Thus, the reason clause in (27a) would be derived as in (28):

(28)  $\qquad$ $[_{PP}$ comme $[_{S'}$ que $[_S$ il faisait beau$]]]$
$\qquad$ $\Rightarrow$ $\quad$ $[_{PP}$ comme $[_{S'}\varnothing$ $\quad$ $[_S$ il faisait beau$]]]$

There is some syntactic evidence in favour of this analysis. When two adjunct clauses are conjoined, it is often possible to omit the preposition before the second clause, leaving only *que* behind (even with cases like *lorsque* where the preposition and *que* are written as a single word):

(29)  $\quad$ a  $\quad$ Bien que Pierre soit malade et qu'il n'ait pas d'argent, il est content
$\qquad$ b  $\quad$ Lorsque je suis sorti et que j'ai fermé la porte, Max est arrivé

Such constructions can be accounted for by assuming that two *que* clauses are conjoined to yield a coordinate S′ which functions as the complement of the preposition, as shown in (30):

(30)  $\qquad$ $[_{PP}$ {bien / lors} $[_{S'}$ $[_{S'}$ que S$]$ et $[_{S'}$ que S$]]]$

Note now that similar constructions are possible with *si*, *comme* and *quand*, as in (31) where *que* in the second clause appears to replace the preposition in the first:[2]

(31)  $\quad$ a  $\quad$ S'il fait beau et que je n'aie rien à faire, je sortirai
$\qquad$ b  $\quad$ Comme il faisait beau et que je n'avais rien à faire, je suis sorti
$\qquad$ c  $\quad$ Quand je suis sorti et que j'ai fermé la porte, Max est arrivé

Given the derivation proposed in (28), underlying structures of the type in (32) can be postulated for the adjunct clauses in (31):

(32)  $\qquad$ $[_{PP}$ {si / comme / quand} $[_{S'}$ $[_{S'}$ que S$]$ et $[_{S'}$ que S$]]]$

If the deletion rule applies only to *que* immediately after *si*, *comme* and *quand*, only the first *que* in (32) will be deleted, thus giving the correct surface forms illustrated in (31).

Note that the apparent substitution of *que* for *si* in (31a) is not possible in indirect questions:

(33)  $\qquad$ Je me demande si Pierre est arrivé et {si / *que} Marie est partie

---

[2] When condition clauses are conjoined as in (31a), the clause introduced by *que* normally requires the subjunctive; see 4.9.10.

This is consistent with the earlier claim that interrogative *si* is a complementiser, not a preposition (i.e. it forms part of the S'). Consequently, (33) has the structure in (34):

(34)     Je me demande [$_S$' [$_S$' si S] et [$_S$' {si / *que} S]]

The ungrammatical version of (33) (with *que*) can be ruled out by a plausible constraint to the effect that S's can only be conjoined if they have the same complementiser in underlying structure (which must be *si* in indirect questions).

### 8.3.5  Prepositions with infinitives

Many prepositions can take an infinitive (in contrast to English, where prepositions select the gerundive (-*ing*) form). Conversely, in French, the only preposition which can be used with the gerundive (-*ant*) form is *en*. The infinitive-taking prepositions can be divided into two classes: those which are followed immediately by the infinitival verb (e.g. *par, pour, sans* and, with the infinitive in the compound past, *après*) and those which require *de* or *à* before the infinitive (e.g. *avant (de), faute (de), près (de), quant (à)*):

(35)     a   Les étudiants ont fini par comprendre

         b   Max a pris un couteau pour couper le pain

         c   Luc est sorti sans fermer la porte

         d   Après avoir mangé, Jules s'est couché

(36)     a   Jules a mangé avant de se coucher

         b   Faute d'avoir mis de l'huile, la voiture est tombée en panne

         c   Nathalie était près de s'évanouir

         d   Quant à dire une chose pareille, je n'y oserais jamais

In 2.3.5 it was argued that *à* and *de* before infinitives can function either as prepositions, indicating an indirect object relation, or as infinitival complementisers analogous to *que* in finite clauses, with the structures in (37):

(37)     a   [$_{PP}$ {à / de} [$_S$' $\varnothing$ S$_{INF}$ ]]
         b   [$_S$' {$\varnothing$ / à / de} S$_{INF}$ ]

The analysis in (37a) is appropriate in examples like (38) where the infinitive corresponds to an indirect object, as can be seen by replacing the infinitival expression by *cela* or some other appropriate NP (e.g. *Luc se souvient de cela, Marie est prête au travail*):

(38)     a   Luc se souvient d'avoir fermé la porte

         b   Jules tient à rester dans son lit

         c   Je suis content de te voir

         d   Marie est prête à travailler

On the other hand, the infinitives in (39) correspond to direct objects (cf. *Luc apprend cela, Jules évite le travail, Marie aime la danse*), with the structure in (37b):

(39)  a  Luc apprend à nager
      b  Jules évite de travailler
      c  Marie aime danser

Returning now to examples of the type in (35)–(36), we can postulate a similar analysis. For example, both *pour* and *avant* can be classified as prepositions which select either an NP or an S' complement, but when the S' is infinitival they differ in that *pour* selects an S' with a zero complementiser (i.e. a 'bare' infinitive), just like *aimer* in (39c), whereas *avant* selects an S' with the complementiser *de*, like *éviter* in (39b), as shown in (40):

(40)  a  $[_{PP}\text{ pour }[_{S'} \varnothing S_{INF}]]$
      b  $[_{PP}\text{ avant }[_{S'}\text{ de }S_{INF}]]$

On the other hand, in (36b–d) *à* and *de* function as prepositions, with structures of the type in (41), as can be seen by replacing the infinitive by an NP: *faute de cela, près de la maison, quant à Pierre*.

(41)  $[_{PP}\text{ faute }[_{PP}\text{ de }[_{S'} \varnothing S_{INF}]]]$

### 8.3.6  Intransitive prepositions

Since there are many verbs, adjectives and nouns which can occur without any complement at all, we might expect the same to be true of prepositions. In English, cases of this type are very common: *John went out, Bill fell down*, etc. Among the items traditionally classified as prepositions in French, there are a few which can occur without a complement in colloquial style:

(42)  a  Luc est sorti avec
      b  Les députés ont voté {pour / contre}
      c  Je ne l'ai pas vu depuis
      d  Après, nous irons au cinéma
      e  Jacques est passé {devant / derrière}

These constructions are highly elliptical. In order to interpret them we must be able to recover an appropriate complement from the context (e.g. a friend in (42a) or a particular proposal in (42b)). Most other prepositions cannot be used in this way. However, alongside the items *sur, sous* and *dans*, we find the related forms (traditionally classified as adverbs) *dessus, dessous* and *dedans* which do occur without a complement:

(43)     a   Pierre est passé dessus/dessous
         b   Luc est entré dedans

Indeed, in Modern French, these items cannot occur with an NP complement (*{dessus / dessous} la table, *dedans la boîte) except in the case of dessus and dessous when governed by par (Pierre est passé par {dessus / dessous} la barrière). In other words, pairs like sur and dessus seem to be in complementary distribution. A natural way of expressing this relationship is to treat the items in question as the intransitive forms of sur, sous and dans.

There is some syntactic evidence to support this analysis. In 6.4.4, we noted that locative prepositions do not readily allow the demonstrative pronouns cela or ceci to occur as their complement (e.g. ?Le livre est {derrière / devant / sur / sous / dans} {cela / ceci}) unless one is actually pointing at the thing referred to by the pronoun. Instead, we find constructions in which là- or ci- is prefixed to the preposition, but in this construction sur, sous and dans must be replaced by their intransitive forms:

(44)     a   Le livre est {là-derrière / ci-devant}
         b   Le livre est {là-dessus / là-dessous / là-dedans}. (*là-sur, *là-dans, etc.)

The forms with ci- and là normally express a deictic orientation, corresponding roughly to 'here' vs 'there' (see 6.4.8). When no such orientation is appropriate, the intransitive preposition is used on its own, as in (45):

(45)     a   Le jardin n'est pas devant la maison, il est derrière
         b   Le chat n'est pas dans le lit, il est {dessus / dessous}
         c   Le livre n'est pas sur le placard, il est dedans

### 8.3.7  Adverbs of place and time

Once the concept of an intransitive preposition is recognised, the next logical step is to see whether other so-called adverbs might be more properly classified in this way. Plausible candidates for such a classification are the 'adverbs of place' là and ici, which might be regarded as the intransitive counterparts of à in its locative uses. Note that the restriction concerning cela and ceci holds even more strongly with locative à (*Le livre est à {cela / ceci}), a gap which is filled by là and ici (Le livre est {là / ici}), though this restriction does not hold with non-locative uses of à (Je pense à {cela / ceci}). Moreover, on the whole, these items seem to have the same distribution as locative PPs such as à cet endroit – for example they can occur as indirect objects of movement verbs and as adjunct expressions:

(46)     a   Max est arrivé {là / ici}

      b   J'ai mis les clés {là / ici}

      c   {Là / Ici}, j'ai vu un renard

Also, like *à* they can be preceded by the item *jusque* (see 8.5.3): *jusqu'à la banque, jusque-là, jusqu'ici.* On the other hand, they cannot be used in place of direct object NPs even when these denote a location:

(47)        a   Les réfugiés ont gagné la frontière

             b   *Les réfugiés ont gagné {là / ici}

However, this parallel breaks down in so far as these items can be used as complements of *de* and *par*, whereas most locative PPs (particularly those with *à*) cannot; thus, in the following examples, *là* and *ici* appear to correspond to NPs (e.g. *la banque*) rather than to a locative PP:

(48)        a   Luc est parti de {là / ici}

             b   Marie est passée par {là / ici}

(49)        a   Luc est parti de (*à) la banque

             b   Marie est passée par (*à) mon bureau

Nevertheless, the hypothesis that *là* and *ici* are locative PPs in (48) cannot be dismissed since there are some locative PPs which can occur as complements of *de* and *par*, notably PPs headed by *chez*: *Luc est parti de chez Pierre, Marie est passée par chez moi.*

    Another item which might be classified as an intransitive preposition is the time adverb *alors*, which shows obvious morphological and semantic affinities with the preposition *lors* (as in *lors de la réunion* and *lorsque je suis parti*, see above). Its syntactic distribution seems to be similar to that of temporal *à*, as in *à ce moment*. In particular, like many other prepositions (especially *à*) this item can be preceded by *jusque*: *Jusqu'alors j'ignorais la situation.*

### 8.4  Complex prepositions

#### 8.4.1  *Two structural approaches*

Alongside prepositions consisting of a single word, there are many phrasal expressions which have a similar function, a selection of which is given in (50):

(50)         à côté de, au-dessus de, par-dessus, étant donné, en face de, par rapport à, à l'instar de, à l'insu de, au lieu de, à moins de, de la part de, à partir de, au sujet de, à titre de, à travers

One approach to such expressions is to ignore the word boundaries within them and to treat them just like simple prepositions. Thus a phrase like *au sujet de Pierre* might be analysed as in (51):

(51)

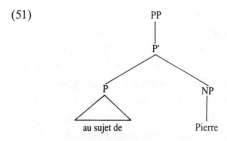

An alternative is to assign an internal structure to such expressions. For example, *au sujet de Pierre* (and the many other complex prepositions composed of P + D + N + P ...) could be analysed in the same way as a phrase like *dans la voiture de Pierre*, as shown in (52):

(52)

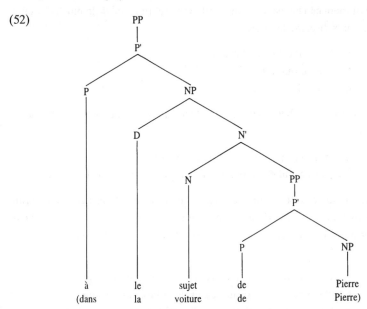

A similar analysis might be proposed for expressions like *à côté de*, except that there is no determiner before the noun.

No attempt will be made here to choose between these two approaches, but they provide a useful basis for discussion of the syntactic properties of such expressions. The essence of the analysis in (51) is that *au sujet de* constitutes a single word for the purposes of syntax and, as such, we would not expect any parts of it to undergo processes which apply to syntactic constituents within phrases like *dans la voiture de*. The fact that these expressions are spelt as several words is not in itself an argument against this approach since this could be simply an arbitrary convention (cf. the analysis of items like *lorsque* as two separate words in 8.3.2). Conversely, the fact that these expressions are grammaticalised to some extent, with meanings which are not always completely transparent (e.g. *au-dessus de* does not actually mean 'at the top of'), does not necessarily invalidate the approach in (52), since this is a property of many idiomatic expressions which are quite clearly phrasal. From a structural point of view, the fundamental difference between the two approaches is that in (51) *Pierre* is a complement of *au sujet de* whereas in (52) *Pierre* is governed by the functional preposition *de* to form a complement of the noun *sujet* within an NP governed by another preposition *à*.

### 8.4.2   The status of 'de' in 'complex prepositions'

With regard to the integrity of these so-called 'complex prepositions' we may note that some of them can be used intransitively without the final *de* in much the same way as the items discussed in 8.3.6:

(53)     a   L'avion est passé au-dessus
         b   La banque est en face
         c   Marie habite à côté

There are also a few of these expressions which can be used before a finite clause, again without *de*:

(54)     a   A moins qu'il (ne) pleuve, je sortirai
         b   Jules est allé à la plage, au lieu que Marie est restée chez elle

This evidence suggests that, in these cases at least, the final *de* is a separate element which occurs only when the following constituent is an NP. This conclusion is supported more generally by cases involving conjunction, where *de* is usually repeated:

(55)     a   L'autobus s'arrête en face de la banque et de l'église
         b   Il y a des tableaux au-dessus de la table et du sofa
         c   Pierre a écrit des articles au sujet de la syntaxe et de la
             phonétique
         d   Luc est parti à l'insu du patron et de ses collègues
         e   J'ai reçu des lettres de la part du Ministre et du Maire

Moreover, although intuitions are not always clear, conjunction without repetition of *de* seems to imply that the two elements constitute a single entity. For example, *L'autobus s'arrête en face de la banque et l'église* strongly implies that the bus stops in only one place, defined in terms of two buildings, whereas (55a) can be interpreted as involving two distinct locations. In the light of the discussion in 8.2.3, this evidence suggests that the governing element is the grammatical preposition *de* rather than the whole 'complex preposition' which has semantic content.

The observations so far indicate that the analysis in (51) is wrong, at least for those expressions which end in *de*. However, they are consistent with a compromise analysis, given in (56), in which *de* is an independent element, but the preceding sequence is treated as a single (genuine) complex preposition:

(56)

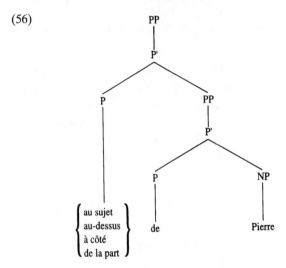

$$\left\{\begin{array}{l} \text{au sujet} \\ \text{au-dessus} \\ \text{à côté} \\ \text{de la part} \end{array}\right\}$$

According to this approach, *au sujet, au-dessus*, etc., have essentially the same status as simple prepositions like *près* or *lors* (*de* NP) which select a PP complement (see 8.3.1). By the same token, expressions like *par-dessus* or *à travers* can be analysed as prepositions which take an NP complement in the same way as *devant* or *derrière*: *par-dessus la barrière, à travers les champs*.

### 8.4.3 'Complex prepositions' with possessive determiners

In order to justify the more radical analysis in (52), we would need to show that 'complex prepositions' are susceptible to internal syntactic processes of the sort found with phrases like *dans la voiture de Pierre*. Note now that most prepositions which allow a human complement can take a personal pronoun in this position (e.g. *devant lui*), but in phrases like *dans la voiture de Pierre* a possessive determiner must be used instead: **dans la voiture de lui, dans sa voiture*. In parallel situations, we find that some 'complex prepositions' require a personal pronoun, some a possessive determiner, while others allow both:

(57)     a   à côté de lui, au-dessus de lui, en face de lui, à l'instar de lui, *à
             l'insu de lui, au lieu de lui, *de la part de lui, par rapport à lui,
             ?au sujet de lui, . . .

      b   à son côté, *à son dessus, *en sa face, *à son instar, à son insu, *à son lieu, de sa part, *par son rapport, à son sujet, ...

A similar contrast can be found with the use of *cela* as opposed to the demonstrative article:

(58)     a   à côté de cela, au-dessus de cela, en face de cela, à moins de cela, ?au sujet de cela, à titre de cela, ...

         b   à ce côté, *à ce dessus, *en cette face, *à ce moins, à ce sujet, à ce titre, ...

Since choice of determiner is a productive syntactic phenomenon, which we would not expect to find within a word, an analysis along the lines of (52) seems appropriate to the expressions which allow the (b) constructions in (57)–(58). Conversely, the expressions which allow the (a) constructions display a degree of 'fossilisation' which is consistent with the analysis in (51), perhaps modified as in (56). For expressions which allow both constructions, we may postulate that both analyses are valid.

From a descriptive point of view, the distinction between 'phrasal' and 'fossilised' expressions does not appear to show any clear pattern. Presence or absence of a determiner in the basic form (e.g. *à côté de* vs *au-dessus de*) does not play a decisive role, nor does the degree of idiomaticity. For example, *à l'insu de* and *à l'instar de* are highly idiomatic in so far as the nouns *insu* and *instar* do not occur outside these expressions, yet, according to the criteria above, the former is phrasal (*à son insu*) whereas the latter is a fossilised expression (*à son instar*).

### 8.4.4 'Complex prepositions' based on verbs

We have focused attention on 'complex prepositions' whose central element is a noun (or at least can be used as a noun), since this seems to be the most common type. Similar issues arise with expressions like *à partir de* whose central element is a verb, the question being whether *partir* retains its status as a verb. Possible evidence that it does not is provided by the fact that the complement cannot be pronominalised by means of *en* (e.g. we have *à partir de là* or *à partir de cela* but not *à en partir*). A rather different problem is posed by the expression *étant donné*, which is composed of two verbs in participle form, with no elements recognisable as prepositions. Although *donné* looks like a passive form, we may note that it shows no agreement with the following noun: *étant donné(*es) les circonstances*. Since lack of inflection is a characteristic property of prepositions, it may tentatively be concluded that this expression has become fossilised as a single preposition, with a structure like that in (51) – in this respect, it behaves like *vu* (as in *vu(*es) ces circonstances*).

## 8.5 Prepositions and the expression of movement

### 8.5.1 Locative prepositions in French and English

One of the most common uses of prepositions is to describe relations of place, situating some entity in the sentence in terms of its spatial relation to another entity. Thus, in *Le livre est {dans / sur} le placard*, the prepositions *dans* and *sur* specify the location of the book in terms of different spatial relations to the cupboard. As well as static relations of the sort just illustrated, prepositions can also be used in sentences which describe a change in location, to specify the Goal (the place to which something moves), as in *Marie a mis le livre {dans / sur} le placard*, or the Source (the place from which something moves), as in *Marie a sorti le livre du placard*.

There are some significant differences between English and French prepositions concerning the ways in which information of a spatial nature (e.g. the distinction between *dans* and *sur*) can be combined with information of a dynamic nature (static Location vs Source or Goal). If we take what are arguably the three simplest spatial relations, *at* (roughly, relation to a point), *on* (relation to a line or surface) and *in* (relation to an area or space), we find that English possesses the full range of Source and Goal counterparts, as shown in table 8.1:

Table 8.1. *Locative prepositions in English*

|  | Static Location | Goal | Source |
|---|---|---|---|
| *Point* | at | to | from |
| *Line/Surface* | on | onto | off |
| *Area/space* | in | into | out of |

Turning now to French, it may be noted that this language makes no distinction between *at* and *to*, but uses *à* for both (e.g. *Pierre est à l'école*, *Pierre va à l'école*). Similarly, there are no counterparts to *onto* and *into* which can be used to specify a Goal interpretation as opposed to a static one (*sur* and *dans* being used for both). On the other hand, French does not have separate Source prepositions to distinguish the different spatial relations expressed by *from*, *off* and *out of*, but uses a single preposition *de* for all cases. These observations are summarised in table 8.2.

Table 8.2. *Locative prepositions in French*

|  | Spatial relation | Source |
|---|---|---|
| *Point* | à | |
| *Line/surface* | sur | de |
| *Area/space* | dans | |

One way of construing the situation described above is in terms of the amount of information which can be expressed by prepositions in the two languages. On the evidence so far, English prepositions can express spatial and dynamic information simultaneously whereas French prepositions can specify either a particular spatial relation (*à, sur, dans*) or a dynamic orientation (*de*), but not both.

### 8.5.2 Specifying the Goal

In many cases, locative prepositions like *à, sur* and *dans* can be used to identify the Goal, as in the following examples where the entity denoted by the direct object moves to the place described by the PP:

(59)  a  Pierre a envoyé le ballon à l'autre bout du terrain
      b  Jean a jeté le livre sur la table
      c  Suzy a mis du fromage sur ses pâtes
      d  Charles a enfoncé le clou dans le mur

However, there are other cases where these prepositions cannot express a Goal relation. The French sentences in (60) are not possible as translations of the English examples, with a meaning similar to those in (59), though some (e.g. (60a)) are perhaps acceptable if the PP is interpreted as simply denoting the place where the event occurred (indicating static Location):

(60)  a  *Pierre a tapé le ballon à l'autre bout du terrain
         Peter hit the ball to the other end of the pitch
      b  *Jean a secoué les dés sur la table
         John shook the dice onto the table
      c  *Suzy a râpé du fromage sur ses pâtes
         Suzy grated cheese onto her pasta
      d  *Charles a {frappé / martelé} le clou dans le mur
         Charles {knocked / hammered} the nail into the wall

The relevant difference between these two sets of examples is that movement from one place to another is an intrinsic part of the meanings of the verbs in (59) whereas the verbs in (60) describe actions which may or may not cause movement of the thing on which the action is performed – e.g. one can hit, shake or grate something without making it move somewhere else.

Putting this observation together with the analysis of the relevant prepositions in 8.5.1, the judgements in (59) and (60) can be accounted for in terms of the following general principle:

*A Goal interpretation for a PP is possible only if movement to a Goal is part of the meaning of some element in the sentence (either the verb or the preposition).*

In (59) the verb contributes the idea of movement to a Goal, while the preposition simply characterises this resulting location in terms of a spatial relation. However, since the verbs in (60) do not express the idea of movement as part of their meaning, the possibility of a Goal interpretation depends on whether this aspect of meaning can be supplied by the preposition. As has been argued, this requirement is satisfied by the English prepositions in (60) but not by *à, sur* or *dans* which merely describe a spatial relation. In other words, the French prepositions can only be used to identify a Goal in conjunction with movement verbs which imply the existence of a Goal.

Intransitive verbs of movement show a similar pattern to that observed in (59) and (60) above, though they raise some additional problems concerning the type of movement which is expressed by the verb. A selection of intransitive verbs which readily allow a Goal interpretation of a locative PP is given in (61), with illustrative sentences in (62):

(61)     aller, venir, arriver, entrer, sortir, monter, descendre, tomber, se rendre, se poser, atterrir, chuter, aboutir

(62)     a   Pierre est arrivé à la gare
         b   Les ouvriers sont montés sur le toit
         c   L'alpiniste a chuté dans une crevasse

Generally, intransitive movement verbs which take *être* as their auxiliary belong to this class, along with a few *avoir*-taking verbs such as *atterrir, chuter* and *aboutir*. In the light of the discussion in 2.8.2, these verbs may be characterised as unaccusative verbs of movement (bearing in mind that the correlation between unaccusativity and selection of *être* is not absolute). Note also that these verbs provide some information about the direction of movement (e.g. 'up' vs 'down', towards vs away from the speaker, into or out of some place, etc.).

Among the intransitive verbs of movement which cannot occur with a Goal complement are those listed in (63), which are divided into subclasses to facilitate discussion:

(63)     a   courir, marcher, danser, se tortiller, conduire, nager, voler, skier, patiner, ramer, . . .
         b   errer, s'égarer, flâner, se balader, se promener, voyager, . . .

Although some of the French sentences in (64) are possible with an interpretation where the PP denotes the place where the event occurred (e.g. for (64b), 'Christine performed a dance on the stage'), they are unacceptable with the Goal interpretation expressed by the English examples:

(64)     a   *Paul a {marché / couru} à la gare
             Paul {walked / ran} to the station

    b   *Christine a dansé sur la scène
         Christine danced onto the stage
    c   *Le ver s'est tortillé dans le trou
         The worm wriggled into the hole
    d   *Max a conduit dans le parking
         Max drove into the car park
    e   *Le poisson a nagé dans le lac
         The fish swam into the lake
    f   *Les touristes ont flâné à Montmartre
         The tourists sauntered to Montmartre
    g   *Claudine s'est égarée sur la scène
         Claudine wandered onto the stage
    h   *Marcel a voyagé dans le Midi
         Marcel travelled to the South of France

The verbs in (63a), illustrated in (64a–e), can be loosely characterised as describing actions which may or may not result in movement of the subject entity from one place to another. This is most evident with verbs like *danser* or *se tortiller* which merely describe bodily motions, but even with the other verbs listed in (63a) one can imagine circumstances in which the action can be performed without actually getting anywhere (e.g. walking or running on an exercise machine, swimming or rowing against the tide, etc.). Moreover, even when there is a strong pragmatic implication of movement, these verbs focus on the manner in which this movement is brought about rather than on the destination.

The verbs in (63b), illustrated in (64f–h) are more problematic since they clearly entail movement from one place to another. Nevertheless, they do not provide information about the direction of movement – some of them (e.g. *errer* and *s'égarer*) indicate movement of a rather aimless sort, while others (like *flâner*, *se promener*, *se balader* and *voyager*) seem to focus on aspects of the journey itself (e.g. a leisurely attitude on the part of the subject entity, the distance covered, etc.).

Although examples with *à*, *sur* and *dans* have been used to illustrate the restrictions on specifying the Goal in French, the same pattern is found with other prepositions which define a spatial relation (e.g. *devant*, *derrière*, *sous*, *près de* and more complex expressions like *à côté de*, *en face de*, etc.).

### 8.5.3 *'Vers' and 'jusque'*

The suggestion in 8.5.1 that French prepositions cannot combine spatial and dynamic information does not preclude the possibility of a preposition which expresses a Goal orientation without defining a spatial relation. Indeed, *vers* is a plausible example of this type – it expresses movement in the general direction of a location but does not define this location in terms of a particular spatial relation. This view is supported by the fact that *vers* can occur with many of the verbs which do not allow a Goal interpretation with spatial prepositions (cf. (60) and (64) above):

(65)  a  Pierre a tapé le ballon vers le filet
      b  Paul a {marché / couru} vers la gare
      c  Le poisson a nagé vers le lac
      d  Les touristes ont flâné vers Montmartre

These examples also support the claim that the unacceptability of the French examples in (60) and (64) (with the relevant interpretation) is due to the inability of spatial prepositions like *à, sur* and *dans* to express the notion of movement to a Goal which is not implied by the verb.

Another way of introducing a Goal orientation in French is to use the item *jusque* in combination with a spatial preposition (most commonly *à*). Again, many of the French examples in (60) and (64) can be rendered acceptable with a Goal interpretation in this way:

(66)  a  Pierre a tapé le ballon jusqu'à l'autre bout du terrain
      b  Henri a marché jusqu'à la gare
      c  Max a conduit jusque dans le parking

However, *jusque* does not only add a dynamic orientation to the following preposition, but it also expresses the concept 'as far as' (drawing attention to the distance covered). For this reason, the use of *jusque* will be inappropriate as a means of expressing movement to a Goal in many cases (e.g. sentence (60c) could not be rephrased as *\*Suzy a râpé du fromage jusque sur ses pâtes*).

### 8.5.4 The expression of 'Source'

In 8.5.1 *de* was characterised as a Source preposition which is neutral with respect to the spatial distinctions expressed in English by *from, off* and *out of*. This preposition can occur with many intransitive movement verbs of the type listed in (61), but not all:

(67)  a  Le train est {arrivé / venu} de Paris
      b  Luc est sorti du café
      c  Max est descendu du toit
      e  Marie est partie du bureau
      f  Jules {est tombé / a chuté} de l'avion

(68)  a  ??Suzy est entrée du jardin

b   *L'avion {s'est posé / a atterri} de Paris
c   *Marie s'est rendue du bureau

With *aller*, specification of the Source tends to be odd unless the Goal is also specified:

(69)     a   ?Marie est allée du bureau
         b   Marie est allée du bureau au restaurant

The verbs in (68) focus attention on the destination in certain ways – e.g. those in (68a, b) characterise the Goal in spatial terms ('in' or 'on') while *se rendre* suggests a particular purpose associated with reaching the destination. Conversely, the verbs in (67b–f) focus attention on movement away from the Source and in some cases (particularly *sortir*) define the Source in spatial terms. The contrast between (67a) and (69a) appears to be related to the different deictic orientations of these verbs (roughly, movement towards the speaker or to a contextually determined location with *venir* and *arriver* vs movement to a place remote from the speaker with *aller*), though the nature of this relation is not entirely clear.

Intransitive verbs which do not allow specification of the Goal by means of a spatial preposition (see (63) and (64) in 8.5.2) do not allow the Source to be specified by means of *de*: *\*Henri a marché de la banque*. The same is true of transitive verbs of the type in (60): *\*Pierre a tapé le ballon de la ligne médiane* ('. . . from the centre-line'). In some cases, *depuis* can be used to indicate the Source, particularly if the Goal is specified by means of *jusque*: *Les touristes ont flâné depuis le Quartier latin jusqu'à Montmartre, Pierre a tapé le ballon depuis la ligne médiane jusqu'au bout du terrain*. Note that this construction can be used even with verbs which do not convey any idea of movement: *L'enfant a {dormi / bavardé} depuis Paris jusqu'à Marseille* – in such cases the phrase *depuis . . . jusqu'à . . .* may be more properly construed as an expression of time, parallel to *pendant tout le trajet*.

With transitive verbs which express movement as an intrinsic part of their meaning, we find a pattern similar to that observed in (67)–(68) above. For convenience, let us divide such verbs into three broad classes:

**'removal' verbs:** e.g. *enlever, ôter, expulser, éjecter, sortir*
**verbs of 'putting':** e.g. *mettre, poser, insérer*
**'transfer' verbs:** e.g. *transférer, transporter, verser*

'Removal' verbs concentrate on the Source part of the movement process (it does not really matter where the object entity ends up and it could even disappear altogether) whereas verbs of 'putting' concentrate on the position which the entity comes to occupy (its previous location, if it has one, being largely immaterial). 'Transfer' verbs give more or less equal weight to the Source and Goal, encompassing the whole of the movement process. Not surprisingly, the Source can be specified, by means of *de*, with 'removal' and 'transfer' verbs, but not with verbs of 'putting', even if the Goal is also specified:

(70)   a   Jules a enlevé le timbre de l'enveloppe
       b   Annie a sorti une robe de l'armoire
       c   Max a transporté quelques meubles de son bureau
       d   Gaston a versé du vin de la carafe
       e   *Pierre a mis le timbre de son portefeuille (sur l'enveloppe)
       f   *Marie a posé un livre de l'étagère (sur la table)

Indeed, the converse generalisation seems to hold in so far as 'removal' verbs cannot occur with a Goal expression, even if the Source is specified, but 'transfer' verbs allow both:

(71)   a   *Jules a enlevé le timbre (de l'enveloppe) dans son album
       b   *Annie a sorti une robe (de l'armoire) sur le lit
       c   Max a transporté quelques meubles (de son bureau) à sa maison
       d   Gaston a versé du vin (de la carafe) dans son verre

### 8.5.5   *Locative prepositions indicating Source*

There is a further class of verbs (**verbs of 'taking'**) which do not allow the use of *de* to indicate the Source, but instead use an appropriate spatial preposition such as *sur* or *dans*:

(72)   a   Luc a pris un couteau {sur / *de} la table
       b   Eve a cueilli une pomme {sur / *de} l'arbre
       c   Le clochard a ramassé un journal {dans / *de} la poubelle

Similarly, *à* is used to indicate the Source with many verbs which involve possession rather than physical location:[3]

(73)   a   Sophie a emprunté dix francs {à / *de} sa mère
       b   Luc a volé un stylo {à / *de} Paul
       c   Jean a acheté une voiture {à / *de} Marcel

Note in this connection that *enlever* and *ôter* (which take *de* with the sense 'remove from a place' – see (70a)) require *à* when used with the sense 'take from a person': *{enlever / ôter} quelque-chose à quelqu'un.*

---

[3] In these cases, as well as *enlever* and *ôter* mentioned below in the text, *à* is the realisation of Dative Case according to the analysis proposed in 6.5.1, since the Source expression can be represented by a Dative clitic. Sentence (73c) is potentially ambiguous, allowing a benefactive interpretation of *à Marcel*: 'Jean bought a car for Marcel.'

A defining property of these verbs of 'taking' is that the Goal is identified with the Agent – for example, in (72a) the result of the action is that Luc has the knife on his person and in (73a) Sophie is the immediate recipient of the money. On the other hand, the 'removal' and 'transfer' verbs which select *de* as the Source preposition do not carry any implications of this sort.

English speakers are sometimes puzzled by constructions like (72) and (73), presumably because English requires a Source preposition (*from, off* or *out of*) in such cases and, perhaps, because of a tendency to perceive *à*, *sur* and *dans* as having a potential Goal orientation. However, the facts in (72) and (73) are consistent with the hypothesis that these prepositions are, in fact, completely neutral with respect to any dynamic orientation. Since these prepositions can be used to describe spatial (or possessive) properties of a Goal which is implied by the meaning of the verb (as in (59)), it is quite natural that they should be used to describe the spatial (or possessive) properties of a Source under analogous conditions.

### 8.5.6 Some lexical gaps in French and English

French does not have any counterparts to the directional prepositions *up* and *down* or the items *away* and *back*, as in sentences like the following: *Max went {up / down} the ladder, Marie moved away from the fire, Paul came back to Paris.* Instead, the relevant information must be encoded in the verb:

(74)  a  Max a {monté / descendu} l'échelle
      b  Marie s'est éloignée du feu
      c  Paul est revenu à Paris

To some extent, this tendency holds in the opposite direction. Although verbs like *ascend*, *descend* and *distance oneself* exist in English, they have a rather artificial, unidiomatic flavour. Similarly, although sentence (74c) could be translated by means of the verb *return*, this verb lacks the deictic orientation ('come back' rather than 'go back') which is associated with *revenir*. Much the same point can be made in connection with the encoding of spatial relations. For example, English has no verbs which correspond to *sortir* in either its transitive or intransitive uses (except for the rather marginal verb *exit*), but makes extensive use of an appropriate verb of movement combined with the preposition *out*. The consequences of this cross-linguistic redistribution of information content among the elements of the sentence will be discussed in the following section.

### 8.5.7 The 'chassé-croisé' phenomenon

The term 'chassé-croisé' is sometimes used to describe the 'criss-cross' translational relation illustrated in (75), where elements of meaning expressed by the preposition in English are encoded by the verb in French and, conversely, aspects of meaning conveyed by the main verb in English are expressed by a separate 'adverbial' expression in French, in this case a gerundive phrase:

(75)     Max ran out of the office
         Max est sorti du bureau en courant

Other examples of this phenomenon are given in (76):

(76)     a   Marie flew to America
             Marie est allée en Amérique en avion
         b   Charles crawled down into the cave
             Charles est descendu dans la grotte à quatre pattes
         c   Suzy walked back to the office
             Suzy est revenue au bureau à pied
         d   Paul kicked the ball into the net
             Paul a envoyé le ballon dans le filet d'un coup de pied

This redistribution of semantic content can be seen as a direct consequence of the restrictions discussed in the previous sections. Since French verbs which describe the manner of motion (or, more properly, denote actions which may or may not induce movement) cannot occur with a Source or Goal PP (except with *vers* or *jusque*), French requires the use of an appropriate verb which does not express the manner of movement, with the result that this information must be conveyed, if at all, by means of a separate phrase. Moreover, since French lacks prepositions corresponding to *out of*, *down*, *back*, etc., this information must be encoded by the verb.

Although the French and English sentences in (76) have essentially the same information content, they are not necessarily appropriate translations of each other. Consider the examples in (76a). In so far as flying is nowadays the usual mode of intercontinental travel, the stipulation *en avion* in the French sentence is rather odd unless this information is particularly important for some reason. Similarly, the French sentence in (76d) would be decidedly strange in a commentary on a football match, where kicking the ball is the norm. Note, however, that when this superfluous information is encoded in the verb, as in the English versions of these sentences, it ceases to be obtrusive, with the result that these sentences are perfectly appropriate in the 'normal' contexts envisaged above. Thus, the differences which were discussed in the previous section do not only affect the way in which information is distributed within the sentence but also force different choices regarding the type of information which can or should be expressed in relation to context. This effect can be seen in other, more subtle ways. For example, the English sentence in (76a) could be uttered equally well by someone in America or by someone in, say, Europe, but the proposed French version would only be possible in the latter case. This is because *fly* (like all verbs which express the manner of motion) is neutral with respect to the deictic contrast which distinguishes *aller* and *go* from *venir* and *come*. French also has movement verbs which are deictically neutral, but these are mainly verbs like *entrer, sortir, descendre* and *monter* which incorporate a particular spatial or directional element. To the extent that such verbs would be inappropriate in this example, the system of French forces a deictic choice which can be avoided in English by the use of a 'manner' verb.

### 8.6 Problems relating to particular prepositions
#### 8.6.1 The problem of 'en'

The use of the preposition *en* is subject to some rather peculiar restrictions which often pose problems for students of French. The principal restriction is stated below:

*En cannot normally occur before definite determiners (definite articles, demonstratives and possessives).*

In cases where this restriction would be violated, *dans* is often used instead (but see 8.6.7):

(77)    a   J'ai confiance en {Pierre / lui}
        b   J'ai confiance dans {les médecins / sa sincérité}

Most prepositions which can take an NP complement can also be followed by nouns without a determiner in semi-idiomatic expressions (e.g. *à tort, avec plaisir, de grâce, sans peine, par exemple, pour compte*, etc.), but there are no such expressions with *dans*. In cases where we might expect to find *dans*, we have *en* instead: e.g. *en prison* (cf. *dans la prison de Nantes*), *en principe, en fait, en réalité*, etc. Thus, *en* and *dans* appear to be in a partially suppletive relation; *dans* before definite determiners (including demonstratives and possessives), *en* before nouns without a determiner. Both prepositions can be used before indefinite determiners, quantifiers and numerals, with certain differences in meaning or acceptability which will be discussed as we proceed.

There are some exceptions to the restriction on *en* stated above, like those in (78), but they can be regarded as fixed, semi-grammaticalised expressions:

(78)    en l'absence de, en l'air, en la matière de, en l'occurrence 'namely',
        en l'honneur de, en ce cas, en ce sens, en ce moment, en son nom, en
        ces termes

Although there are cases of this type where *en* is followed by *la* or *l'*, there are no such expressions where *en* is followed by *le* or *les*. This restriction cannot be stated simply in terms of the number and gender features of the noun since we do find examples with masculine or plural nouns like *nom, moment, air* and *termes*, provided that the determiner is demonstrative or possessive or, indeed, the elided form *l'*. This might be a coincidence, since expressions like those in (78) are not very numerous anyway, but it turns out to be significant. In many examples with masculine or plural nouns, replacement of the demonstrative or possessive determiner gives rise to expressions with *au* or *aux*: *en son nom* vs *au nom de, en ce moment* vs *au moment de, en ces termes* vs *aux termes de*. A similar pattern is found with nouns denoting countries, seasons, etc. (see 8.6.3–8.6.4).

This apparent alternation between *en* and *à* is restricted to just those cases where *à* coalesces with the definite article to give *au* and *aux*: i.e. before masculine nouns beginning with a consonant (including *h* 'aspiré') and plural nouns. We do not find systematic correspondences between *en* + N and *à la* + N or *à l'* + N (or indeed *à* with other types of NP). In other words, the examples with *au(x)* appear to fill the gap created by the absence of expressions of the type *en le(s)*.

### 8.6.2 Prepositions with names of languages

With names of languages, *en* is normally used without a determiner unless the noun is modified, in which case *dans* is used with the definite article:

(79)    a    en français, en breton, etc. (also *en argot, en patois, en dialecte*)
         b    dans le français d'aujourd'hui, dans l'anglais de Shakespeare, etc

> The construction with *en* can be used with some modifiers which form
> part of an accepted name for a language: *en français moderne, en latin
> classique, en vieil anglais*. The distinction between the two types of
> modifiers is not rigid and can sometimes be exploited to enhance the
> status of a language-variety; thus *en français de Montréal* suggests that
> Montreal French is, in some sense, a separate recognised language in a
> way that *dans le français de Montréal* does not.

Before indefinite determiners, both *en* and *dans* can be used in expressions which denote the manner or means of communication, as in (80a), but *dans* must be used when the language is presented as a kind of abstract domain, as in (80b):

(80)    a    Ce professeur s'est exprimé {en / dans} un français très érudit
         b    Cette expression subsiste {*en / dans} un français très érudit

A similar contrast can be seen in *Ce document a été publié en trois langues* vs *Cette construction est attestée dans plusieurs langues*. Note that this nuance disappears, in favour of *dans*, when the definite article is used: *Ce professeur s'exprime {dans / *en} le français des Académiciens, Ce document a été publié {dans / *en} les trois langues officielles*.

### 8.6.3   Prepositions with names of countries

With names of countries, regions and continents, *en* is used (without the article) before singular feminine forms, but also before masculine forms beginning with a vowel (including mute *h*):

(81)        en France, en Bretagne, en Amérique, en Afghanistan (m.), en Hindoustan (m.)

Before singular masculine forms beginning with a consonant and before plural forms, *à* is used with the definite article, giving the contracted forms *au* and *aux*:

(82)        au Canada, aux États-Unis, aux Antilles (f.), aux Maldives (f.)

However, if the noun is modified, *dans* is used with the article:

(83)        dans la France d'aujourd'hui, dans le Canada d'avant la colonisation

Again, some modifiers can be taken as part of the name, in which case *en* is used (e.g. *en Irlande du nord* and, before reunification, *en Allemagne fédérale*).

### 8.6.4   Prepositions with names of seasons and dates

The same pattern can be discerned with names of seasons in that *en* is used before nouns which begin with a vowel (or mute *h*) (*en {été / automne / hiver}*), whereas *printemps*, which is both masculine and consonant-initial, requires *au* (*au printemps*). Again, if the noun is modified, *dans* is used (though other prepositions such as *pendant* or *au cours de* are also possible): *dans l'été de 1789, dans le printemps de 1968.*

With names of months and year-dates, *en* is used systematically: *en juin, en décembre, en 1993.* These forms can be used after some other temporal prepositions (e.g. *{avant / après / depuis} juin, {avant / après / depuis} 1968*), but not after prepositions (other than *en*) which indicate inclusion in the relevant period (*{*à / *dans / *pendant} décembre, {*à / *dans / *pendant} 1968*); instead an expression containing a common noun is used: *au mois de mai, pendant le mois de janvier, pendant l'année 1945.*

### 8.6.5   'En' vs 'dans'

Leaving cases with *au(x)* aside for the moment, the choice between *dans* and *en* is largely conditioned by syntactic factors (presence or absence of a definite determiner). Cases where both prepositions are possible also reveal subtle semantic differences: roughly, *dans* seems to indicate inclusion within a bounded spatial, temporal or abstract domain whereas *en* suggests a vaguer situational relation sometimes involving notions like status, quality or manner (see 8.6.7 for further discussion). At an intuitive level, we can link the syntactic and semantic factors in so far as the presence of a definite determiner or modifying expression creates the type of specificity or boundedness which is appropriate to the use of *dans* whereas the absence of a determiner with an unmodified noun suggests the sort of vagueness associated with *en*.

Nouns of the types discussed in 8.6.2–8.6.4 normally require the definite article in French, even when the article has no obvious semantic function (see the discussion of nouns denoting countries in 5.2.1). For example, in *J'aime {le français / la France / l'été}*, the determiner does not serve to identify a particular member or instantiation of the class described by the noun and is absent in English: *I like {French / France / Summer}*. When these nouns occur as complements of *en*, the semantically redundant determiner is omitted in order to satisfy the restriction given in 8.6.1. However, in just those cases where *dans* is used, the determiner does have an identifying function and usually occurs in English – e.g. *dans l'été de 1789* designates a particular member of the class of 'Summers' while *dans {le français / la France} d'aujourd'hui* refers to a particular instantiation of the language or country (cf. *in the Summer of 1789, in the {French / France} of today*.

Given these observations, the alternation between *en* and *dans* with such nouns can be summarised as follows.

**'En' and 'dans' with names of languages, countries and seasons:**
- *when the definite article has no semantic function, it is omitted and* en *is used.*
- *when a definite determiner is semantically motivated, it cannot be omitted and* dans *is used.*

### 8.6.6 *'En' vs 'à': a historical account*

The alternation between *en* and *à* can be attributed to a historical accident. In Old French, *en* could be used more freely with determiners (i.e. the restriction given in 8.6.1 did not hold). Expressions of the type listed in (78) in 8.6.1 can be seen as vestiges of this earlier stage. Like *à* and *de* in Modern French, *en* contracted with *le* and *les*, giving the forms *ou* and *es* (the latter form survives in academic titles like *docteur ès lettres*). This accounts for the absence of expressions with *en le(s)* – no such expressions could survive into Modern French since they did not exist in the earlier stage. The contracted forms *ou* and *es* did not simply disappear but were assimilated to the phonetically similar forms *au* and *aux*, thus giving rise to the alternations which have been observed. More precisely, the forms which had become assimilated to *au(x)* escaped the later restriction against *en* with definite determiners, which was satisfied in other cases by omitting semantically redundant occurrences of *la* and *l'* after *en*. Thus, from a historical perspective, the apparent alternation between *en* and *à* can be seen more properly as an alternation between *en* and the contracted forms of *en* + *le* and *en* + *les*.

This alternation is restricted to fixed expressions of the type in (78) (e.g. *en son nom* vs *au nom de*) and to cases where the definite article has no distinguishing function (e.g. with names of countries, seasons, etc.). In other cases, as we have seen, combinations of *en* with definite determiners are avoided by substituting its near-synonym *dans*, sometimes with a subtle change in meaning.

### 8.6.7 Further uses of 'en'

There are some cases where the meaning of *en* cannot be expressed by *dans*, as when *en* expresses a relation of quality, composition or change of state: *Jules s'est déguisé en prêtre, Cette maison est bâtie en pierre, J'ai coupé le bois en trois morceaux, L'alchimiste a transformé le plomb en or*. Such constructions are not possible with definite complements because of the incompatibility of *en* with definite determiners and because of the inability of *dans* to express the appropriate semantic relations: *\*Jules s'est déguisé {en / dans}le Pape, \*Cette maison a été bâtie {en / dans} les pierres de l'ancien château, \*J'ai coupé le bois {en / dans} ces trois morceaux, \*Hausmann a transformé Paris {en / dans} la ville que nous connaissons*. Instead, these propositions must be expressed in a more roundabout way: e.g. *Cette maison a été bâtie en utilisant les pierres de l'ancien château, Hausmann a transformé Paris pour créer la ville que nous connaissons* – it is left to the reader to invent appropriate paraphrases for the other examples.

Another case where *en* and *dans* differ in meaning arises in expressions involving quantified expressions of time, where *en* denotes the duration of an event whereas *dans* indicates the interval between the present, or a contextually determined reference time (see 4.7.2), and the occurrence of the event: *J'ai écrit la lettre en dix minutes* 'I wrote the letter in ten minutes' (i.e. 'It took me ten minutes to write the letter') vs *J'écrirai la lettre dans dix minutes* 'I will write the letter in ten minutes' time (from now)' or *J'ai dit que j'écrirais la lettre dans dix minutes* 'I said I would write the letter in ten minutes' time (from then).'

The preposition *en* (unlike all other prepositions) can also take a gerundive complement (e.g. *en chantant*); see 9.5.2 for discussion.

### 8.6.8 'De' vs 'avec'

In 2.3.2 we saw that *de* is used to introduce the Theme with verbs denoting change of location or possession when the Goal is represented as a direct object:

(84)    a   Le fermier a chargé le camion de blé

         b   Jules a muni sa femme d'un revolver

A similar pattern is observed with predicates which denote a locative or possessive state when the Location or Possessor is represented by the subject:

(85)    a  Le camion est chargé de blé    (cf. *Le blé est chargé sur le camion*)

        b  Sa femme est munie d'un revolver

        c  Le jardin fourmille d'abeilles    (cf. *Des abeilles fourmillent dans le jardin*)

A common mistake on the part of English speakers of French is to use *avec* instead of *de* in such cases, by analogy with English *with*. In fact, there are some cases of this type where *avec* is possible:

(86)    a  L'infirmière a couvert le blessé {d'un manteau / avec un manteau}

        b  On a farci les tomates {de riz / avec du riz}

        c  On a lesté le bateau {de sable / avec du sable}

        d  On a revêtu le toit {de toile goudronnée / avec de la toile goudronnée}

        e  On a enduit la barrière {d'huile / avec de l'huile}

On the other hand, *avec* could not replace *de* in (84) or (85). The problem, then, is how to distinguish those cases which allow *avec* from those which do not.

A reasonable hypothesis is that *avec* in examples like (86) expresses an instrumental relation parallel to that illustrated in (87), whereas *de* identifies the Theme which enters into a locative relation with the direct object entity:

(87)    a  Le cambrioleur a ouvert la porte avec un tournevis

        b  Pierre a découpé le poulet avec son canif

This intuition is supported by the observation that examples like (86) and (87) can be paraphrased by means of verbs like *se servir* or *utiliser*:

(88)    a  L'infirmière s'est servie d'un manteau pour couvrir le blessé

        b  On a utilisé du riz pour farcir les tomates

        c  On a utilisé du sable pour lester le bateau

(89)    a  Le cambrioleur s'est servi d'un tournevis pour ouvrir la porte

        b  Pierre a employé son canif pour découper le poulet

Sentences which do not allow *avec* cannot be readily paraphrased in this way:

(90)    a  ??Le fermier a chargé le camion avec du blé

        b  ??Le fermier s'est servi de blé pour charger le camion

The deviance of (90) seems to be pragmatic in nature. In cases like (86) (and indeed (87)) the verb and its direct object can be construed as denoting an objective or purpose (e.g. protecting the injured person, the fence or the roof, giving more substance to the tomatoes, stabilising the boat) which is independent of the means employed in the sense that the desired effect could have been achieved by using something else (e.g. a blanket in (86a)). In the case of (84a) and (90), it is difficult (though perhaps not impossible) to view loading the truck as an objective in its own right, independently of the goods to be carried. Similarly, in (91a) below, it is difficult to construe the wine simply as a means of getting the bottles filled, since presumably the purpose is to contain the wine, while in (91b) 'riddling the wall' is hardly a plausible objective at all:

(91)　　a　On a rempli les bouteilles {de vin / ??avec du vin}

　　　　b　Les policiers ont criblé le mur {de balles / *avec des balles}

The still sharper deviance of the following examples (cf. (85c) above) can be attributed to further constraints on the use of instrumental expressions:

(92)　　a　*Le jardin fourmille avec des abeilles

　　　　b　*Le jardin se sert d'abeilles pour fourmiller

Normally, instrumental expressions can only occur with non-stative verbs which imply the existence of an Agent who manipulates the instrument, as can be seen from the following example where *ouverte* is an adjective denoting a state (see 3.2.7): *La porte est ouverte avec un tournevis* (similarly English *The door is open with a screwdriver*). Clearly, *le jardin* in (92) is not an Agent, nor does the verb *fourmiller* involve any implicit Agent. By the same token, in the stative, adjectival counterparts of (86), the instrumental construction with *avec* is impossible, though *de* is fine:

(93)　　a　Le blessé est couvert {d'un manteau / *avec un manteau}

　　　　b　Les tomates sont farcies {de riz / *avec du riz}

　　　　c　Le bateau est lesté {de sable / *avec du sable}

　　　　d　Le toit est revêtu {de toile goudronnée / *avec de la toile goudronnée}

　　　　e　La barrière est enduite {d'huile / *avec de l'huile}

To summarise, the potential overlap between *avec* and *de* in (86) stems from the fact that in these cases the object of the preposition can be construed either as the Theme which enters into the locative relation implicit in the meaning of the verb or as an instrument, albeit one which exerts its function by participating in this locative relation. If an instrumental interpretation is inappropriate, only *de* can be used. Conversely, if the verb does not express a locative relation or if the entity in question does not participate in this locative relation, only *avec* is possible. A case of the former type is (94) below, since *protéger* (unlike *couvrir* in (86a)) does not in itself involve a 'putting on' relation, whereas (95) illustrates the second type in that the pitchfork is not the object which comes to occupy the truck and can only be construed as an instrument:

(94)    L'infirmière a protégé le blessé {* d' un manteau / avec un manteau}

(95)    Le fermier a chargé le camion {* d'une fourche / avec une fourche}

In English, there is no need to make this distinction between a Theme and an instrument, since the preposition *with* is used in both cases.

Finally, we may note that *de* can also introduce the Theme with certain verbs of 'removal' which express the Source as a direct object: e.g. *débarrasser* in (96a), in contrast to *enlever* in (96b) where the Theme is the direct object and *de* indicates the Source:

(96)    a   Le concierge a débarrassé l'escalier d'objets encombrants
        b   Le concierge a enlevé des objets encombrants de l'escalier

In constructions of the type in (96a), English follows the same pattern as French, using *of* to indicate the Theme (e.g. *{rid / clear} the stairs of debris*), whereas *with* can only express an instrumental relation with such verbs (e.g. *clear the stairs with a broom*).

### Exercises

1   Within certain limitations, it is possible to conjoin prepositions which share the same complement:

   Luc a planté des fleurs devant et derrière sa maison

   Construct examples of this type with other prepositions (including 'complex' prepositions and the 'functional' prepositions *à, de* and *en*) and discuss any generalisations which emerge.

2   The following sentences with *bouger* and *(se) déplacer* are not acceptable with the meanings expressed by the English examples:

   (a)   *Pendant le tremblement de terre, la table a bougé à l'autre côté de la pièce
         During the earthquake, the table moved to the other side of the room
   (b)   *Après le dîner, les invités se sont déplacés dans le salon
         After dinner, the guests moved into the lounge

(c) *Hercule a bougé le rocher au sommet de la montagne

Hercules moved the rock to the top of the mountain

(d) *Jules a déplacé le piano dans la salle à manger

Jules moved the piano into the dining room

To what extent are these observations consistent with the account proposed in 8.5.2? Suggest possible translations for the English examples.

3   The impossibility of conjoined constructions like *du beurre et la confiture* or *aux États-Unis et le Canada* might be related to contraction of the preposition with the determiner (giving *du, aux*, etc.). Could such an approach be extended to cover cases like *en France et (la) Belgique*?

4   Comment on the following data in the light of the alternation between *en* and *au(x)*:

(a)  Je reviens {de France / d'Angleterre / d'Afghanistan}

(b)  *Je reviens {de Canada / d'États-Unis / d'Antilles / de Maldives}

(c)  Je reviens {du Canada / des États-Unis / des Antilles / des Maldives}

5   The preposition *en* cannot occur with indefinite NPs introduced by *du, de la* or *des*. How might this restriction be accounted for in view of data like the following and the discussion of the 'cacophony' phenomenon in 5.4.8?

(a)  Le professeur a créé des groupes de travail

(b)  L'alchimiste a fabriqué de l'or

(c)  Le professeur a divisé la classe en (*des) groupes de travail

(d)  L'alchimiste a transformé le plomb en (*de l') or

6   Investigate the use of prepositions and determiners with names of towns and *départements*, commenting on any similarities or differences between these cases and those discussed in 8.6.3.

7   To what extent do the uses of French *avec* and English *with* coincide? Consult the entries for these items in one or more bilingual dictionaries and discuss the adequacy of the information which they provide.

8   The phrase *a man with black hair* can be translated as *un homme avec*

*des cheveux noirs* or *un homme aux cheveux noirs*. Try to construct similar examples with the French equivalents of the following modifying expressions and comment on any syntactic or semantic differences between the two constructions which emerge: *with a moustache, with a green umbrella, with big feet, with a happy smile, with a comfortable house, with an ugly scar.*

**Further reading**

Articles on various aspects of prepositions in French can be found in Berthonneau & Cadiot (1991, 1993), Leeman (1990), Schwarze (1981) and Vandeloise (1993). Spang-Hanssen (1963) gives a detailed description of prepositions whose function is primarily grammatical. Vandeloise (1986) presents a semantic analysis of locative prepositions; see also Spang-Hanssen (1993). Ruwet (1969) discusses some interesting syntactic properties of locative prepositions (particularly *à* and complex prepositions). For further discussion of some of the issues raised in 8.5, see Boons (1984, 1987), Jones (1983) and Guillet & Leclère (1992). Zribi-Hertz (1983) deals with constructions in which prepositions occur without a complement. Other articles concerned with specific prepositions or constructions include Cadiot (1991b) (on *pour*), Cadiot (1991a) and Eriksson (1979, 1994) (on certain uses of *à* and *avec*).

# 9

# Infinitival clauses

## 9.1 Overview

The discussion in this chapter relies heavily on the concept of Case introduced in 1.5.6 and developed in subsequent chapters.

In 9.2, this concept is exploited as a means of accounting for the absence of an overt subject in most types of infinitival clauses and for some systematic differences between English and French. A distinction is drawn between constructions in which the subject of the infinitive is empty in the underlying structure and is interpreted in relation to some participant in the main clause and constructions in which the subject of an infinitive is moved into the main subject position to acquire Case.

In 9.3, there is an examination of the syntactic strategies for expressing the subject in constructions with *faire*, *laisser* and verbs of perception, whose properties are strikingly different from their English counterparts and which often pose problems for learners of French. This discussion continues in 9.4 with a detailed analysis of the apparently complicated behaviour of clitic pronouns in these constructions.

9.5.1 summarises generalisations proposed in earlier chapters concerning the distribution of infinitives with *de* and *à* and 'bare' infinitives. Finally, in 9.5.2, there is a review of some similarities and differences between infinitives and gerunds (verb-forms in *-ant*).

## 9.2 Infinitives without overt subjects

### 9.2.1 The Control phenomenon

As was shown in 1.3.2, infinitives typically lack an overt subject but they have an 'understood' subject which we can usually identify from the context. For example, in the following sentences, the understood subject of the infinitive is unambiguously identified with the subject of the main clause (e.g. (1a) means that Pierre wants Pierre to be elected, not somebody else):

(1)     a     Pierre veut être élu au conseil
        b     Marie espère gagner le concours
        c     Jean regrette d'avoir volé l'argent

With other verbs in the main clause, the subject of the infinitive may be identified with the direct or indirect object (*Luc* in (2)):

(2)    a   Marie a imploré Luc d'acheter une voiture
       b   Marie a demandé à Luc de préparer le dîner

This relation of identity is often referred to by the term **Control**. Thus, in (1a), *Pierre* controls the subject of the infinitive, whereas in (2) the Controller is *Luc*. In essence, this is similar to the relation which holds between a pronoun and its antecedent, except that it is more tightly constrained. For example, in (3), the pronoun *elle* can refer back to *Marie*, but it could also refer to some other person who is identified in the wider context, a possibility which is excluded in (1b):

(3)    Marie espère qu'elle gagnera le concours

A standard way of representing the Control relation is to assume that the subject position in the infinitival clause is occupied by an abstract element, conventionally represented by the symbol 'PRO', which is coindexed with its Controller.[1] Thus examples (1b) and (2b) have the structures in (4):

(4)    a   [Marie$_m$ espère [PRO$_m$ gagner le concours]]
       b   [Marie a demandé à Luc$_1$ de [PRO$_1$ préparer le dîner]]

In cases like (2), where the main clause contains more than one NP, the choice of Controller seems to be determined by the semantic properties of the main verb. For example, if we substitute *menacer* and *promettre* for the verbs in (2), we must interpret the subject *Marie* as the Controller, as shown in (5):

(5)    a   [Marie$_m$ a menacé Luc de [PRO$_m$ acheter une voiture]]
       b   [Marie$_m$ a promis à Luc de [PRO$_m$ préparer le dîner]]

No attempt will be made here to define these semantic properties since, on the whole, they appear to be the same in English, though in some cases the syntactic properties of certain verbs may limit the range of infinitival constructions which are possible. For example, *threaten* cannot take both a direct object and an infinitival complement, so English does not have constructions analogous to (5a) (**Mary threatened Luke to buy a car*) – for some speakers this is also true of *promise* (*%Mary promised Luke to cook the dinner*). Another point to bear in mind is that some English verbs require a gerund (-*ing* form) corresponding to the infinitive in French: e.g. *regret* in *John regrets stealing the money / *to steal the money* (cf. (1c)).

---

[1] In earlier versions of transformational grammar, the Control relation was described in terms of a deletion rule (called 'Equi NP deletion', or simply 'Equi'). Thus a sentence like (1b) was derived from the underlying structure below by deletion of the second occurrence of *Marie*:
[Marie espère [Marie gagner le concours]]

This is more a problem for learners of English than for English students of French and, for the most part, we can take infinitival complements in French as the equivalents of both infinitival and gerundive complements in English. Nevertheless, there are some cases where English infinitives and gerunds express different meanings, only one of which can be expressed by the infinitive in French. For example, with *try*, the infinitive denotes the 'objective' of the action whereas the gerund denotes the 'means', but *essayer* with the infinitive can only have the former interpretation:

(6)  a  Paul tried to start the car      Paul a essayé de démarrer la voiture
     b  Paul tried pushing the car  ≠  Paul a essayé de pousser la voiture

Conversely, *se souvenir* with the infinitive can only express the meaning of *remember* with the gerund:

(7)  a  Paul remembered to shut the door  *Paul s'est souvenu de fermer
                                            la porte
     b  Paul remembers shutting the door  Paul se souvient d'avoir fermé
                                            la porte

Except in a few marginal cases, gerunds in French (*-ant* forms) cannot be used as complements of verbs or indeed of any other categories except the preposition *en* but function only as modifiers with a circumstantial interpretation (see 9.5.2).

The Control phenomenon is not restricted to complements of verbs. The same effects are found with infinitival complements of adjectives, prepositions and nouns:

(8)     a  [Marie$_m$ est [$_{AP}$ fière de [PRO$_m$ avoir gagné le concours]]]
        b  [Jules$_j$ nous a téléphoné [$_{PP}$ avant de [PRO$_j$ partir]]]
        c  [Charles regrette [$_{NP}$ sa$_i$ décision de [PRO$_i$ quitter Paris]]]

Note that in (8c), PRO is controlled by the possessive *sa*, which may or may not refer back to *Charles*.

### 9.2.2 Infinitives with 'cognitive' verbs
In French, many verbs which express belief or communication of a belief can take infinitival complements of the Control type:

(9)     a  [Marie$_m$ croit [PRO$_m$ être malade]]
        b  [Sophie$_s$ estime [PRO$_s$ avoir résolu le problème]]
        c  [Jules$_j$ confirme [PRO$_j$ avoir envoyé le document]]

In English, most verbs of this type do not allow Control constructions:

(10)     a   *Mary believes to be ill

         b   *Sophie considers to have solved the problem

         c   *Jules confirms to have sent the document

To express the propositions in (9) in English, a finite complement must be used with an appropriate pronoun as subject (e.g. *Mary believes that she is ill*), a possibility which is of course also available in French: *Marie croit qu'elle est malade, Sophie estime qu'elle a résolu le problème, Jules confirme qu'il a envoyé le document*.

Conversely, in English, many verbs of this type (and others) can take infinitival complements with an overt subject (the **Accusative + infinitive** construction), a construction which is not possible in French:

(11)     a   John believes [Paul to have stolen the money]

         b   Mary considers [Sue to be intelligent]

         c   Luke confirmed [Peter to be the winner]

(12)     a   *Jean croit [Paul avoir volé l'argent]

         b   *Marie estime [Suzy être intelligente]

         c   *Luc a confirmé [Pierre être le gagnant]

In French, a finite complement must be used (but see also 2.5.4 for alternative constructions in cases like (12a)): *Jean croit que Paul a volé l'argent*, etc.

As was suggested in 1.5.6, the absence of overt subjects of infinitives in French can be attributed to the 'Case Principle', which requires every overt NP to bear a Case feature (Nominative, Accusative or Dative). If Case features are assigned only to subjects of finite clauses and objects of verbs and prepositions, it follows that the subject position of an infinitival clause can never be occupied by an overt NP and thus must be represented by the abstract element PRO. To accommodate English examples like (11), it was suggested that some verbs assign Accusative Case to the subject of the infinitival complement, treating it as if it were the direct object of the verb, thus allowing (and indeed requiring) this position to be occupied by an overt NP to the exclusion of the abstract element PRO. To account for the French facts, it can simply be assumed that this 'exceptional' Case-marking process is not available in French, at least not with verbs of this type.[2] In 9.3.4 some

---

[2] A problem with this account is that French does allow sentences analogous to the English examples in (11) when the subject of the infinitive is questioned or relativised:

    (i) Quel homme crois-tu avoir volé l'argent?

    (ii) l'homme que je crois avoir volé l'argent

These examples suggest that infinitival complements of cognitive verbs can have an overt subject provided that this subject is moved to another position at the surface level. Note, however, that removal of this subject by cliticisation to the main verb does not give a grammatical output:

    (iii) *Je le crois avoir volé l'argent

infinitival constructions (with *laisser* and verbs of perception) which perhaps manifest this process will be considered, but for the moment the following generalisation can be postulated:

*French has no means of assigning Case to the subject of an infinitive*
*(consequently the subject cannot be an overt NP).*

In both French and English, the infinitive complements of 'cognitive' verbs usually denote current situations or past events, whereas with many other verbs the infinitive often has a future orientation. For example, *J'espère gagner la course demain* can be paraphrased as *J'espère que je gagnerai la course demain*, but *\*Je crois gagner la course demain* and *\*I believe John to win the race tomorrow* are ungrammatical (see 4.6 for further discussion).

A further generalisation for French is that 'cognitive' verbs always take 'bare' infinitives. To be more precise, they do not allow the complementisers *de* or *à*. An apparent counter example is (13), where *se rendre compte* expresses a cognitive relation ('realise'):

(13)     Je me rends compte d'avoir fait une faute

However, in this case, *de* is clearly a preposition which introduces the indirect object, as in *Je me rends compte de cela*, not an infinitival complementiser (see 2.3.5 for discussion of this distinction). This generalisation is also borne out by the following contrast:

(14)     a   Pierre dit avoir lu ce livre
         b   Pierre nous a dit de lire ce livre

In (14a), *dire* has a purely cognitive interpretation ('Pierre says that he has read this book'), but when used with *de*, as in (14b), it assumes a 'manipulative' sense similar to that of *ordonner* – note that these examples also conform to the generalisation proposed above concerning the temporal orientation of the infinitive.

The possibility of Control constructions with cognitive verbs also extends to impersonal verbs of 'belief' such as *sembler*. Sentence (15) can mean 'It seems to me that I have seen you somewhere before' where the indirect object *me* controls the subject of the infinitive (it could also have the interpretation where *il* refers to a person who is the understood subject of the infinitive: 'He seems to me to have seen you before' – see 9.2.4):

(15)     Il me semble vous avoir déjà vu quelque part

### 9.2.3   *'Arbitrary PRO' and implicit Control*

It has been assumed so far that the implicit subject of an infinitive must be controlled by an NP in the higher clause. However, in French as in English, there are some cases where there is no actual NP which can act as the Controller. Typical examples are impersonal constructions with infinitival complements, as in (16):

(16)    a    Il est intéressant de [PRO lire les autobiographies]

        b    Il est douloureux de [PRO punir les enfants]

        c    Il faut [PRO travailler]

        d    Il s'agit de [PRO réparer cette voiture]

        e    Il est temps de [PRO changer les pneus]

        f    Il est cruel de [PRO punir les enfants]

        g    Il est dangereux de [PRO conduire une moto sur le trottoir]

In such cases, PRO is said to have 'arbitrary reference', which may range from a generic interpretation ('people in general') to one where the intended referent is identified as some contextually determined entity (typically including the speaker and/or the addressee). For example, (16a) seems to favour a generic reading, whereas (16d) favours a more specific interpretation ('je', 'vous' or 'nous') and (16c) is natural with either interpretation according to context (e.g. as a general statement about the trials of life or as an exhortation to a lazy student). The semantic and pragmatic factors which influence the interpretation of PRO are too complex to discuss here but include things like tense, and the aspectual and referential properties of other elements in the complement – e.g. compare (16a) with *Il a été intéressant de discuter cette question avec vous*, where the punctual tense of the main clause and the reference to the addressee contrive to impose a 'first-person' interpretation for PRO.

   In some of these cases, it might be argued that the main clause contains an implicit Controller. For example, *douloureux* in (16b) involves an Experiencer argument (the 'sufferer') which can be specified as in (17) by a Dative clitic which controls the subject of the infinitive:

(17)    Il lui$_i$ est douloureux de [PRO$_i$ punir les enfants]

Consequently one could argue that in (16b) it is not the item PRO which is arbitrary in reference, but the unspecified Experiencer which controls this PRO – note that (16b) cannot mean that it is painful for someone else to punish children. However, some of the other examples in (16) are less amenable to such an analysis. For example, *cruel* in (16f) also involves an implicit 'sufferer' but this entity does not correspond to the subject of the infinitive, whereas (16g) is ambiguous, or indeterminate, in this respect, according to whether the persons at risk are the motorcyclists or other people (e.g. pedestrians). In the light of these observations, let us assume that an arbitrary interpretation for PRO can be due either to Control by an argument which is itself implicit or to the absence of any Control relation. The dividing line between these two cases is sometimes difficult to draw, but as we saw in 7.4.1 this distinction is relevant to the possibility of 'object-gap' constructions: *Les enfants sont {douloureux / *cruels} à punir.*

Examples of the type in (16) are characteristic of English as well as French. However, the phenomenon of implicit control is more widespread in French. With many communicative–manipulative verbs, the receiver of the message can be left unspecified while still controlling the subject of the infinitive:

(18)    a  Les pompiers ont ordonné d'évacuer l'immeuble
        b  Le professeur a permis de photocopier les notes
        c  La police a recommandé d'éviter le quartier latin
        d  Les médecins conseillent de ne pas fumer

Such constructions are not generally possible with the infinitive in English (cf. *The firemen ordered to evacuate the building*), though some are acceptable with the gerund (e.g. *The police recommended avoiding the Latin Quarter*). This difference may be partly due to the fact that the verbs in (18) take an indirect (dative) object whereas their counterparts in English take a direct object – indirect objects being generally more readily omissible than direct objects. Indeed, with expressions which take an indirect object in English, the Controller can be implicit just as in French: e.g. *The General gave the order to retreat, The teacher said to hand the work in on Monday*, corresponding to *Le général a donné l'ordre de battre la retraite, Le professeur a dit de rendre le devoir lundi.*

With the English counterparts of some verbs of the type in (18) it is often difficult to tell whether the following NP is the object of the main clause (denoting the 'Receiver' of the order, permission, etc.) or simply the subject of the infinitive. When this NP is human, as in (19), the former analysis seems the most plausible:

(19)    a  The firemen ordered the inhabitants to evacuate the building
        b  The teacher allowed the students to photocopy the notes

However, examples like (20) favour the second analysis – it would be absurd to treat the inanimate NPs as denoting 'Receivers', even figuratively:

(20)    a  The firemen ordered the building to be evacuated
        b  The teacher allowed the notes to be photocopied

Thus, we may conclude that these verbs allow both Control constructions and Accusative + infinitive constructions of the type discussed in 9.2.2:

(21)    a  [the firemen ordered the inhabitants$_i$ [PRO$_i$ to evacuate the building]]
        b  [the firemen ordered [the building to be evacuated]]

Note now that the French counterparts of (20) are unacceptable, with or without *à*:

(22)     a  *Les pompiers ont ordonné (à) l'immeuble d'être évacué
         b  *Le professeur a permis {aux / les} notes d'être photocopiées

The versions of (22) with *à* can be ruled out on semantic grounds (the NPs are not appropriate 'Receivers') whereas the versions without *à* are ungrammatical because French does not allow Accusative + infinitive constructions. From this perspective the constructions in (18) may be seen as compensating for the ungrammaticality of the constructions in (22). Whereas English allows the Agent of the infinitive to be suppressed by using an Accusative + infinitive construction in which the complement is passivised, French achieves the same effect by simply omitting the phrase which controls the Agent.

A rather different range of cases where the understood subject of an infinitive may have arbitrary reference is illustrated in (23), where the main verb normally requires a direct object:

(23)     a  Le café empêche de dormir
         b  Ce roman incite à réfléchir sur la condition humaine
         c  Cette découverte oblige à réviser toute la théorie

In corresponding English examples, this direct object must be overtly realised: e.g. *Coffee prevents one from sleeping*. These constructions are subject to a number of restrictions which do not apply to the cases in (18). Typically the subject of the main verb is inanimate, as in (23), but even with a human subject the entity referred to is perceived as having a rather inactive role – e.g. in (24) the children do not deliberately prevent people from sleeping, rather it is the fact of having children, or some other circumstance involving children, which causes lack of sleep:

(24)     Les enfants empêchent de dormir

Also these constructions (unlike those in (18)) cannot describe specific events (*\*Ce café a empêché de dormir hier soir*) but can only be used to make general statements in which the understood subject of the infinitive must be interpreted as generic (referring to people in general or anyone who might be concerned) rather than as referring to specific individuals who can be identified by the context. Some examples of this type can be expressed in English, but not in French, by a passive version of the Accusative + infinitive construction:

(25)     a  This discovery requires the whole theory to be revised
         b  *Cette découverte oblige toute la théorie d'être révisée

The construction in (23) is also possible with many verbs which normally take an indirect object as well as the infinitive:

(26)        Ce système de sécurité permet de surveiller toute l'usine

For the constructions in (23) and (26), it is assumed that the subject of the infinitive is represented as a PRO which is not controlled (even by an implicit element) but is assigned generic reference: e.g. (23a) has the structure (27):

(27)        [le café empêche de [PRO dormir]]

### 9.2.4 Subject-raising

The Control analysis presented in 9.2.1 represents the clear intuition that in a sentence like (28), the person Marie has two theta-roles, the Experiencer of *espérer* and the Agent of *gagner*, represented respectively by *Marie* itself and the PRO which it Controls:

(28)        [Marie$_m$ espère [PRO$_m$ gagner beaucoup d'argent]]

However, this analysis seems implausible for the superficially similar sentence (29):

(29)        Marie semble gagner beaucoup d'argent

Here, *Marie* is clearly interpreted as the Agent of *gagner*, but there is no obvious semantic relation between *Marie* and *sembler*. This difference can be seen more clearly by comparing (28) and (29) with the examples in (30):

(30)        a   Marie$_m$ espère qu'elle$_m$ gagnera beaucoup d'argent
            b   Il semble que Marie gagne beaucoup d'argent

In (30a) as in (28) Marie is represented twice, but in (30b) she is represented only once, as the subject of *gagner*, the subject of *sembler* being the dummy pronoun *il*. Thus, an appropriate representation of the meaning of (29) would be a structure like (31), where *Marie* occurs only as the subject of *gagner* and the subject of *sembler* is left empty since it is not associated with a theta-role (see 3.4.1):

(31)        [∅ semble [Marie gagner beaucoup d'argent]]

The fact that (31) is not a possible sentence follows from the assumptions concerning Case which were presented in 9.2.1. As the subject of an infinitive, *Marie* cannot acquire a Case feature, so the sentence is ruled out by the Case Principle. However, in (31), there is also a vacant position (represented by ∅ which, as subject of a finite clause, receives Nominative Case. Consequently, *Marie* can acquire the Case feature which it needs by moving to this vacant position, giving the correct surface form:

(32)        [Marie semble [ __ gagner beaucoup d'argent]]

The process illustrated in (32) will be referred to as **Subject-raising**. This is essentially the same process as that which was proposed for passive sentences. In both cases, an NP cannot remain in the position relevant to its interpretation because no Case is assigned to this position, so it must move to a vacant position where it can receive a Case feature.

The theory of Case which has been presented allows two possibilities concerning the subject of an infinitive:

*I   The subject of an infinitive is represented as the abstract element* P R O, *which must be controlled by an element in the higher clause or be assigned arbitrary reference*
**or**
*II  The subject of an infinitive is represented by an overt NP which must move to a vacant position where it can acquire a Case feature.*

### 9.2.5   How to recognise Subject-raising constructions

The fundamental intuition that *Marie* in (29) is semantically a subject of *gagner* but not of *sembler* is supported by a number of empirical observations. Firstly, predicates typically impose semantic restrictions on their arguments. For example, by virtue of its meaning, *espérer* can normally only occur with a subject which denotes an animate being:

(33)      a   ??Cette table espère être ronde
          b   ??Cette idée espère passionner Paul

However, in infinitival constructions, *sembler* places no restrictions on its syntactic subject – any type of NP can occur in this position, provided that it is an appropriate subject of the infinitive:

(34)      a   Cette table semble être ronde
          b   Cette idée semble passionner Paul

The lack of restrictions on the subject of *sembler* extends to cases where this item forms part of an idiom, the rest of which is expressed by the infinitive complement:

(35)      a   Hommage semble avoir été rendu au roi
          b   La moutarde semble lui monter au nez

Generally, nouns like *hommage* in (35a) can only occur without a determiner in fixed expressions like *rendre hommage* (see 5.3.3) and as subjects of the passive forms of such expressions: e.g. *Hommage a été rendu au roi* (see 3.2.4). Example (35b) has an idiomatic interpretation, 'He seems to be losing his temper', where *la moutarde* represents (metaphorically) 'anger', an interpretation which is only available when it is the subject of *monter au nez*. In particular, *hommage* cannot occur without a determiner, nor *la moutarde* with the metaphorical sense, as subjects of other verbs: *\*Hommage flatte le roi, La moutarde l'a rendu fou* (literal meaning only – '{Mustard / \*Anger} drove him crazy'). The fact that these items can occur as subjects of *sembler* in (35) is explained under the Subject-raising analysis, since, at the underlying level, these items are not subjects of *sembler* but only of the idiomatic predicates:

(36)    a   [∅ semble [hommage avoir été rendu au roi]]
        b   [∅ semble [la moutarde lui monter au nez]]

For the same reason, the subject of *sembler* can be non-referential *il* (or *ça* with colloquial weather verbs such as *flotter*) if the verb or the construction in the complement requires such a subject:

(37)    a   Il semble être arrivé beaucoup de gens
        b   Il semble y avoir un problème
        c   Il semble pleuvoir
        d   Ça semble flotter

Evidence of the sort presented above can be used to distinguish cases of Subject-raising from Control constructions in the following way. Given a surface sentence of the form in (38):

(38)        NP $V_1$ $V_{2(INF)}$ $\cdots$

if the types of NP which can occur as subjects of $V_1$ are more restricted than those which can normally occur as subjects of $V_2$, the sentence is a Control construction – typically, in Control constructions the Controller is animate, so the possibility of an inanimate NP in this position suggests a Subject-raising analysis. If we can have any type of NP in this position (including idiomatic NPs and impersonal pronouns), as long as the NP is an appropriate subject of $V_2$, the sentence is a Subject-raising construction.

Another test of a rather different kind is provided by active/passive pairs like those in (39)–(40):

(39)    a   Marie semble avoir insulté Pierre
        b   Pierre semble avoir été insulté par Marie

(40)    a   Marie espère insulter Pierre
        b   Pierre espère être insulté par Marie

The sentences in (39) are synonymous to the extent that one cannot assert one and deny the other) in the same way as the simple sentences *Marie a insulté Pierre* and *Pierre a été insulté par Marie*, but those in (40) are clearly not synonymous – e.g. it is quite conceivable for (40a) to be true while (40b) is false. This difference is made clear in the underlying structures in (41)–(42):

(41)    a    [∅ semble [Marie avoir insulté Pierre]]
        b    [∅ semble [Pierre avoir été insulté par Marie]]

(42)    a    [Marie$_m$ espère [PRO$_m$ insulter Pierre]]
        b    [Pierre$_p$ espère [PRO$_p$ être insulté par Marie]]

The structures in (41) differ only with regard to the form of the complement (active or passive), but those in (42) differ also with respect to the person who is presented as desiring the realisation of the event denoted by the complement.

From this evidence, the following test can be deduced. If two sentences of the surface forms in (43) are synonymous, they are Subject-raising constructions, if not they are Control constructions:

(43)    a    $NP_1 \, V_1 \, V_{2(INF)} \, NP_2 \cdots$
        b    $NP_2 \, V_1$ être $V_{2(PAST\ PART.)} \cdots$ par $NP_1$

Most infinitival constructions are of the Control type. Verbs and other expressions which participate in the Subject-raising construction have a modal or aspectual meaning. For example, *sembler* can be assigned to the modal class since it attenuates the truth of the statement, presenting it as an apparent fact. This class also includes items such as *paraître, s'avérer* 'to turn out', *se trouver, faillir* 'to nearly do something', *être susceptible* 'be likely', *être censé* 'be supposed', and a few others which will be discussed in later sections. Within the aspectual class we have expressions such as *aller* (future use), *venir* (recent past use), *être en train, être sur le point, commencer, continuer, cesser*, etc. Some examples which suggest a Subject-raising analysis for these items are given below:

(44)    a    Il {paraît / s'avère} être arrivé beaucoup de monde
        b    Il {va / vient de} pleuvoir
        c    Il est censé y avoir une sortie de secours
        d    Hommage {est susceptible d' / a failli} être rendu à cet imposteur
        e    La moutarde {commence / continue} à lui monter au nez

The contrast between *espérer* and *sembler* is particularly clear, partly because the subject of *espérer* has an independent theta-role which is easy to identify and also these verbs take different constructions when the complement is finite (see examples in (30) in 9.2.4). In many cases, evidence of this sort is not available. For example, *faillir* and *essayer* cannot occur with a finite complement in either of the constructions in (30) and in an example like (45a) it is not clear whether *Jules* has

an independent theta-role (e.g. 'attempter') of the sort assigned to the subject of
*essayer*:

(45)     a   Jules a failli assassiner le roi
         b   Jules a essayé d'assassiner le roi

However, the tests proposed above reveal a clear difference between the two
cases: *faillir* can be substituted in all the examples in (44), but *essayer* cannot. Also,
(45a) is synonymous with (46a), but (45b) does not mean the same as the (slightly
odd) sentence (46b):

(46)     a   Le roi a failli être assassiné par Jules
         b   ?Le roi a essayé d'être assassiné par Jules

### 9.2.6   Some syntactic 'faux-amis'

It would be tempting to suppose that the sentences in (47) are equivalent:

(47)     a   Jules est certain de gagner la course
         b   Jules is certain to win the race

However, application of the tests proposed in 9.2.5 reveals a significant difference.
In English, the subject of *certain* can be any type of NP, but in French the subject
must be animate:

(48)     a   The building is certain to collapse
         b   It is certain to rain
         c   There is certain to be an inquiry
         d   Homage is certain to be paid to the king

(49)     a   *Le bâtiment est certain de s'écrouler
         b   *Il est certain de pleuvoir
         c   *Il est certain d'y avoir une enquête
         d   *Hommage est certain d'être rendu au roi

The conclusion should be clear. The French example (47a) is a Control construction meaning 'Jules is certain that he will win' whereas (47b) is a Subject-raising
construction corresponding to 'It is certain that Jules will win.' This is confirmed
by the facts in (50):

(50)     a   Paul est certain d'aimer Suzy   ≠   Suzy est certaine d'être
                                                 aimée par Paul
         b   Paul is certain to like Sue     =   Sue is certain to be liked by
                                                 Paul

The French construction with *certain* and the infinitive corresponds to the English
construction with the gerund (i.e. the examples in (49) are deviant in the same way

424

as *The building is certain of collapsing, *It is certain of raining, etc., and the examples in (50) correspond to *Paul is certain of liking Sue* vs *Sue is certain of being liked by Paul*).

A more subtle contrast can be observed in (51):

(51)      a   Marcel risquait de perdre son emploi
          b   Marcel risked losing his job

In English, *risk* requires an animate subject and tends to imply that this person is in some sense responsible for the situation, but French *risquer* simply expresses possibility (with the implication that the situation is unwelcome) and allows all types of subject:

(52)      a   Le bâtiment risquait de s'écrouler
          b   Il risque d'y avoir beaucoup de protestations
          c   La moutarde risque de lui monter au nez

In other words, *risk* behaves like a Control verb, but *risquer* is a Subject-raising verb.

### 9.2.7  Some ambiguous or indeterminate cases

In 9.2.1, *menacer* and *promettre* were classified as Control verbs. This seems justified in examples like *Pierre a {promis / menacé} de venir*, where the meaning is 'Pierre said that he would come' (the choice of verb depending on whether the event is perceived as welcome or not). However, the same verbs can be used with an inanimate or even non-referential subject to express likelihood of an event (with the same connotations of (un)welcomeness):

(53)      a   Les prix {promettent / menacent} d'augmenter
          b   Il {promet / menace} d'y avoir une révolution

With a human subject, the Control interpretation (issuing of a promise or threat) tends to predominate, but the probability interpretation is also possible:

(54)      a   Le patron menace de revenir à tout instant
          b   Ce jeune auteur promet de devenir célèbre

When the receiver of the promise or threat is specified, the probability interpretation is excluded and the subject must be animate:

(55)      a   Le patron nous {promet / menace} de revenir bientôt
          b   *Les prix nous {promettent / menacent} d'augmenter
          c   *Il nous {promet / menace} d'y avoir une révolution

Also, the probability interpretation seems to be possible only with non-punctual tense forms (e.g. the present or imperfect):

(56)     a   *Les prix ont {promis / menacé} d'augmenter
         b   *La situation {promettra / menacera} de changer

This restriction also holds for *risquer* (*\*Les prix ont risqué d'augmenter*) and for the purely temporal uses of *aller* and *venir*: *\*Les prix sont {allés / venus d'} augmenter* – see 2.7.5.

The properties of *promettre* and *menacer*, which are also found with English *promise* and *threaten*, can be characterised in terms of a clear ambiguity. With the meaning 'issue a promise/threat', they are three-place verbs involving an Agent (the 'utterer'), a Receiver and a Theme (represented by a clause describing a future event), where the Agent controls the subject of the infinitive. However, for examples like (53) and (54), a Subject-raising analysis is appropriate – the verbs select only a Theme argument (the infinitival clause) and express probability with regard to the situation which it describes:

(57)     [ ∅{menacent / promettent} de [les prix monter]]

There are other cases where the distinction between Control and Subject-raising is less clear. In 9.2.4 *commencer* and *continuer* were analysed as Subject-raising verbs on the grounds that they impose no restrictions on their surface subjects. However, their near-synonyms *se mettre* and *persister* normally require a subject whose referent (typically animate) is capable of deliberately instigating or protracting the situation described by the complement:

(58)     a   Pierre {se met / persiste} à travailler
         b   ?La linguistique {se met / persiste} à intéresser Luc
         c   ?Il {se met / persiste} à y avoir un problème

The examples in (58) are broadly consistent with a Control analysis – these verbs select a subject which is interpreted as an Agent. The problem is that when *commencer* and *continuer* have a human subject, this entity is typically interpreted as deliberately instigating or protracting the situation, just as in (58a):

(59)     Pierre {commence / continue} à travailler

A possible conclusion is that *commencer* and *continuer* can function as Control verbs (like *se mettre* and *persister*) as well as Subject-raising verbs, even though the semantic differences are much less clear than in the case of *promettre* and *menacer*. In essence, this is the same problem as was encountered with the English examples in (19) and (20) in 9.2.3 (*The firemen ordered the inhabitants to evacuate the building* vs *The firemen ordered the building to be evacuated*), where the animate NP *the inhabitants* appears to function as the direct object of *order* (denoting the Receiver) whereas the inanimate NP *the building* is interpreted only as the subject of the infinitive.

Further evidence of the 'blurring' between the two syntactic types is provided by the examples in (60):

(60)      a  Luc {a l'air d' / semble} avoir reçu une gifle

          b  Une gifle {?a l'air d' / semble} avoir été donnée à Luc

Both *sembler* and *avoir l'air* present a situation as being 'apparent', but *avoir l'air* tends also to portray the situation as a perceptible property of the subject entity – plausibly, one can tell by Luc's appearance that he has been slapped, but it is more difficult to deduce from the nature of the slap that it was inflicted on Luc, hence the oddness of *avoir l'air* in (60b) (cf. *Cette gifle avait l'air de faire très mal* which is fine). For this reason, *avoir l'air* is unnatural with idiomatic or impersonal subjects, though it occurs quite readily with 'weather' *il*:

(61)      a  ?Hommage a l'air d'avoir été rendu au roi

          b  ?Il a l'air d'être arrivé beaucoup de monde

          c  Il a l'air de pleuvoir

Also the active/passive pairs in (62) show a subtle difference in meaning – e.g. (62a) might suggest a smug attitude on the part of Marie as opposed to outrage or distress on Pierre's part in (62b), so that (62c) is not contradictory:

(62)      a  Marie a l'air d'avoir insulté Pierre

          b  Pierre a l'air d'avoir été insulté par Marie

          c  Marie a l'air d'avoir insulté Pierre, mais Pierre n'a pas l'air
             d'avoir été insulté par Marie

These differences between *sembler* and *avoir l'air* seem to be a matter of degree. Indeed, *paraître* seems to have an intermediate status, inviting a 'property of the subject' reading more strongly than *sembler*, but less strongly than *avoir l'air*. At a further point on the gradation, we find the expression *donner l'impression* which behaves fairly systematically like a Control expression – it requires a fully referential, non-idiomatic subject denoting an animate being or a physical object, often with an implication of deliberate pretence:

(63)      a  Jean donne l'impression d'admirer Marie

          b  Ce livre donne l'impression d'être intéressant

          c  *Hommage donne l'impression d'avoir été rendu au roi

          d  *Il donne l'impression d'être arrivé beaucoup de monde

          e  *Il donne l'impression de pleuvoir

It is not clear at what point on this continuum the distinction between Subject-raising and Control should be drawn: i.e. at what point a connotation associated with the surface subject should be construed as a theta-role assigned by the main verb. More generally, the examples discussed in this section show that it is not always easy to determine whether an NP in the main clause is an argument of the main verb or not.

### 9.2.8 The modal verbs 'pouvoir' and 'devoir'

Like their English counterparts *can/may* and *must*, the verbs *pouvoir* and *devoir* are potentially ambiguous according to whether they express notions of capacity, permission or obligation (as in (64)), or possibility or certainty (as in (65)):

(64)    a   Pierre peut résoudre ce problème
        b   Les enfants peuvent jouer dans la cour
        c   Ces étudiants doivent lire ce livre

(65)    a   Pierre peut arriver à tout instant
        b   Ces étudiants doivent être très intelligents

These examples are themselves potentially ambiguous, but on their preferred readings they may be distinguished by the approximate paraphrases in (66)–(67):

(66)    a   Pierre est capable de résoudre ce problème
        b   Les enfants ont le droit de jouer dans la cour
        c   Ces étudiants sont obligés de lire ce livre

(67)    a   Pierre risque d'arriver à tout instant
           Il {est possible / se peut} que Pierre arrive à tout instant
        b   Ces étudiants semblent être très intelligents
           Il est {probable / certain} que ces étudiants sont très intelligents

Linguists sometimes use the term **root** modality to describe the types of modality illustrated in (64) and (66) (capacity, permission, obligation) whereas the types illustrated in (65) and (67) (possibility, probability, certainty) are referred to as instances of **epistemic** modality.

Note that the root modal constructions in (66) are of the Control type – they require a referential (typically animate) subject and do not allow impersonal or idiomatic subjects (as readers may verify for themselves). On the other hand the epistemic modal expressions in (67) either take an impersonal subject (with a finite complement) or they belong to the Subject-raising class – i.e. in both cases, they fail to assign a theta-role to the subject position. By analogy, it is tempting to suppose, as some linguists have argued, that *pouvoir* and *devoir* are Control verbs in cases like (64) (assigning a 'Possessor of capacity' or 'Receiver of obligation/permission' role to the subject) but Subject-raising verbs in cases like (65), as shown in (68)–(69):

(68)     a  [Pierre$_p$ peut [PRO$_p$ résoudre ce problème]]
         b  [les enfants$_e$ peuvent [PRO$_e$ jouer dans la cour]]
         c  [ces étudiants$_e$ doivent [PRO$_e$ lire ce livre]]

(69)     a  [∅ peut [Pierre arriver à tout instant]]

         b  [∅ doit [ces étudiants être très intelligents]]

One piece of evidence which supports this approach is that, if the infinitival clause is replaced by the pronoun *le*, only a root reading is possible; e.g. the examples in (70) can correspond to (64a, c), but not to the sentences in (65) with the epistemic readings paraphrased in (67):

(70)     a  Pierre le peut
         b  Ces étudiants le doivent

Similarly, there is no *\*Le train le doit* corresponding to *Le train doit être en retard*. These observations follow directly from the analysis under discussion. If *le* replaces the entire complement clause in the underlying structure (e.g. [PRO résoudre ce problème] in (68a), but [Pierre arriver à tout instant] in (69a)), there is no source for the superficial subject under a Subject-raising analysis of the examples in (70). Thus, the pronominalisation facts confirm the hypothesis that an epistemic interpetation always correlates with a Subject-raising construction.

The converse hypothesis that a root interpretation with *pouvoir* and *devoir* is always associated with a Control structure does not hold systematically. For example, it is possible to construct sentences with an impersonal or idiomatic subject (hence, derived by Subject-raising) which allow a root (permission or obligation) interpretation:

(71)     a  Il {peut / doit} y avoir moins de dix étudiants dans chaque groupe
         b  Hommage {peut / doit} être rendu au roi

Note that the infinitival expression cannot be replaced by *le* in this case: *\*Hommage le doit.* This restriction is also found in some cases where the subject is an inanimate, non-idiomatic NP:

(72)     a  Ce livre doit être lu par tous les étudiants
         b  Ce livre peut être lu par un enfant de six ans
         c  \*Ce livre le peut

The examples in (71) and (72) differ from those in (64) and (70) in that the subject does not denote the entity who is endowed with the relevant ability or on whom permission or obligation is conferred, this entity being the object of *par* in (72a, b) and some unspecified person or persons in (71b). This observation suggests that a Control analysis for root uses of *pouvoir* and *devoir* is only appropriate when the subject denotes the person who has the capacity, permission or obligation in question. The availability of a root interpretation for constructions of the Subject-raising type is not restricted to these two verbs. For example, *être censé* 'be supposed to' expresses obligation, but its subject need not denote the person on whom the obligation is imposed and can be instantiated by the full range of NPs typical of Subject-raising constructions:

(73)  a  Les étudiants sont censés lire ce livre
      b  Ce livre est censé être lu par tous les étudiants
      c  Hommage est censé être rendu au roi
      d  Il est censé y avoir moins de dix étudiants dans chaque groupe

Nevertheless, most predicates which express root modality (e.g. those in (66)) function as two-place predicates and, with an infinitival complement, show the restrictions associated with Control: e.g. *\*Hommage a le droit d'être rendu au roi*, *\*Ce livre est obligé d'être lu par tous les étudiants*, *\*Ce livre est capable d'être lu par un enfant*, etc.).

### 9.3  Infinitival constructions with 'faire', 'laisser' and verbs of perception
#### 9.3.1  Expressing the subject

Infinitival constructions with *faire*, *laisser* and verbs of perception (principally *voir*, *regarder*, *écouter*, *sentir* and *apercevoir*) show strategies for expressing the understood subject of the infinitive which are different from the Control and Subject-raising types discussed in 9.2. In the following examples, *Marie* is the understood subject of the infinitive, but its position relative to the infinitive is that of a direct or indirect object:

(74)  a  Paul a {fait / laissé / regardé} danser Marie
      b  Paul a {fait / laissé / entendu} descendre Marie dans la cave
      c  Paul a {fait / laissé / vu} ouvrir la porte à Marie

The pattern observed in (74) can be summarised informally as follows:

*In constructions with 'faire', the subject of the infinitive is realised:*
*I  as a direct object if the infinitive has no direct object of its own (the 'accusative strategy')*
*II  as an indirect object introduced by* à *if the infinitive already has a direct object (the 'dative strategy')*

For the purposes of this generalisation, complement clauses count as direct objects, as shown in (75) where the *que* clause forces the dative strategy:

(75)    a  Paul a fait croire à Marie que la voiture était en panne

       b  *Paul a fait croire Marie que la voiture était en panne

On the other hand, complements of 'copular' verbs like *devenir* do not count as direct objects, even when they are of the category NP:

(76)    a  Paul a fait devenir Marie très célèbre

       b  Paul a fait devenir Marie une actrice très célèbre

Note, however, that *être* (in all of its uses) is excluded from these constructions, no matter what we try to do with the subject:

(77)    a  *Paul a fait être Marie en retard

       b  *Paul a fait être en retard (à) Marie

Also excluded are certain types of verb + infinitive constructions, notably those of the Subject-raising type and modal verbs followed by an infinitive:

(78)    a  *Paul a fait sembler Marie dormir

       b  *Paul a fait sembler dormir (à) Marie

(79)    a  *Paul a fait {devoir / pouvoir} Marie sortir

       b  *Paul a fait {devoir / pouvoir} sortir (à) Marie

Moreover, the infinitive cannot be negated:

(80)    *Paul a fait ne pas sortir (à) Marie

With *laisser* and the perception verbs, but not with *faire*, there are alternative constructions in which the subject occurs in its 'normal' position to the left of the infinitive:

(81)    a  Paul a {*fait / laissé / regardé} Marie danser

       b  Paul a {*fait / laissé / entendu} Marie descendre dans la cave

       c  Paul a {*fait / laissé / vu} Marie ouvrir la porte

The syntax of the constructions reviewed above will be analysed in detail in 9.3.4–9.3.5. For the moment let us provisionally assume that the constructions in (81) correspond to the underlying structures of the sentences in (74) and that the accusative and dative strategies for realising the subject of the infinitive are obligatory with *faire*, but optional for *laisser* and the perception verbs.

### 9.3.2   The 'par' strategy

When the infinitive takes a direct object, an alternative construction with *par* instead of *à* is often possible:

(82) a Paul a fait traduire la lettre par Marie

   b Paul a {laissé / vu} nettoyer le bureau par Marie

Despite superficial similarities, there are a number of syntactic and semantic differences between *par* in (82) and *à* in (74c) which suggest that examples like (82) should not be treated as variants of the dative strategy, but rather as analogues of the passive construction.

The semantic differences can be seen most clearly in examples with *faire*. Generally, sentences of the *faire . . . par* type can be rendered in English by *have* with the past participle, whereas the construction with *à* corresponds to *make* with the infinitive:

(83) a Paul a fait réparer les robinets par le plombier

    'Paul had the taps repaired by the plumber'

   b Paul a fait réparer les robinets au plombier

    'Paul made the plumber repair the taps'

In (83), the construction with *par* is the more natural way of describing a normal customer-tradesperson arrangement, whereas (83b) would imply some less usual circumstance beyond simply getting the job done (e.g. the plumber was responsible for the damage to the taps and is being made to put it right, or Paul is testing the plumber's skill or, perhaps, doing him a favour by offering him work). More generally, the construction with *à* presents this entity as being affected in some way by the event whereas *par* presents this entity as the means by which the state of affairs is accomplished. For this reason, there are many cases where the construction with *par* is inappropriate, as in (84) where it is difficult to construe 'taking a bath' as an objective for which the child is the means, but perfectly natural to take it as an event which affects the child:

(84) a ??Paul a fait prendre un bain par l'enfant

   b Paul a fait prendre un bain à l'enfant

The syntactic properties of the *par* construction show many similarities with passives. In 3.2.1 we saw that the *par* phrase can generally be omitted in passives (*Les robinets ont été réparés (par le plombier)*). The same is true of the *faire...par* construction:

(85) Paul a fait réparer les robinets

However, the *à* phrase cannot be omitted freely (but see 9.3.3):

(86)      ??Paul a fait prendre un bain

Moreover, just as the *par* phrase must be omitted in impersonal passives of the type *Il sera parlé de cette question* (see 3.4.11), it must be omitted in the corresponding causative construction:

(87)      Les journalistes feront parler de cette question (*par les lecteurs)

Also verbs which allow or favour *de* instead of *par* in passives show the same property in causatives (see 3.2.9):

(88)      a   Marie est détestée de tout le monde
          b   Son attitude fait détester Marie de tout le monde

Verbs and idiomatic expressions which do not allow the passive construction (see 3.2.3–3.2.4) do not allow the *faire... par* construction either, but they do allow the construction with *à*:

(89)      a   *Un jeune officier a été épousé par Marie
          b   Paul a fait épouser un jeune officier {à / *par} Marie

(90)      a   *Cinq kilos de moins seront pesés par Marie
          b   Ce régime fera peser cinq kilos de moins {à / *par} Marie

(91)      a   *La croûte a été cassée par l'enfant
          b   Paul a fait casser la croûte {à / *par} l'enfant

Further differences emerge in cases involving a relation between an expression and its antecedent, where we find that the *à* phrase can act as an antecedent, just like the subject of an active sentence, but the NP introduced by *par* cannot, as in (92) where the reflexive clitic *se* is to be taken as referring to *Marie*:

(92)      a   Marie s'achètera cette voiture
          b   Paul fera s'acheter cette voiture à Marie
          c   *Cette voiture se sera achetée par Marie
          d   *Paul fera s'acheter cette voiture par Marie

Similarly, in (93a, b), *la bouche* denotes a body-part which is most naturally interpreted as belonging to Marie, but in (93c, d) we can only have the rather odd interpretation where it belongs to someone else:

(93)      a   Marie a ouvert la bouche
          b   Paul a fait ouvrir la bouche à Marie
          c   ?La bouche a été ouverte par Marie
          d   ?Paul a fait ouvrir la bouche par Marie

The same difference is found in (94) where *son* can refer back to *Marie* in (94a, b) but must refer to somebody else in (94c, d):

(94)  a  Marie$_m$ apprendra son$_m$ rôle
      b  Le metteur en scène fera apprendre son$_m$ rôle à Marie$_m$
      c  *Son$_m$ rôle sera appris par Marie$_m$
      d  *Le metteur en scène fera apprendre son$_m$ rôle par Marie$_m$

The fundamental similarity between passives and the infinitives in cases like (83a) and (85) is that the 'logical subject' (the external argument) is either suppressed or is internalised (realised as the complement of *par* within the VP). The obvious differences are that the infinitive is active in form (*\*Paul a fait être réparés les robinets (par le plombier)*) and the direct object does not move into the subject position. These two differences are related. In 3.2.2 it was proposed that passive verb forms cannot assign a Case feature to their direct object, so the direct object must move to the vacant subject position in order to acquire Nominative Case, as shown in (95):

(95)  [ $\varnothing$ $_{NOM}$ a été réparé les robinets (par le plombier)]

However, in the infinitival construction, such movement would be futile since, as has been remarked repeatedly, no Case is assigned to the subject of an infinitive in French – indeed the whole of the discussion so far in this chapter has focused on strategies which avoid having an overt NP in the subject position of an infinitive at the surface level. Moreover, there is no need for the direct object to move if we assume that the infinitive, being active in form, can assign Accusative Case just like any other active transitive verb. Thus, for examples (83a) and (85) we can assume the structure (96) at both the underlying and surface levels:

(96)  [Paul a fait [$_S$ $\varnothing$ réparer les robinets$_{[ACC]}$ (par le plombier)]]

Note, however, that the empty subject position $\varnothing$ in (96) plays no role in the interpretation of the sentence (it does not receive a theta-role and, unlike the element PRO, is not controlled or assigned arbitrary reference) or in the syntactic derivation (nothing is moved into it or out of it). Consequently, the structure in (96) can be simplified by eliminating this subject position entirely, analysing the complement *réparer les robinets (par le plombier)* as simply a VP rather than a clause:

(97)  [Paul a fait [$_{VP}$ réparer les robinets (par le plombier)]]

The possibility of omitting the *par* phrase can lead to ambiguity when the infinitive is a verb which takes a direct object and an optional dative complement. For example, (98) can be analysed either as a passive-like construction in which the

Agent is suppressed ('Paul had the story read to the children') or as an instance of the dative strategy where the indirect object of *lire* is left unspecified ('Paul made the children read the story'):

(98)        Paul a fait lire l'histoire aux enfants

When the latter interpretation is intended, but not clear from the context, it may be preferable to use the construction with *par*: *Paul a fait lire l'histoire par les enfants*.

### 9.3.3    Other constructions with 'faire' and a missing subject

There are some *faire* constructions with a missing subject of the infinitive which cannot be analysed as reduced forms of the passive-like construction discussed in 9.3.2:

(99)        a    Ce médicament fait dormir (*par les enfants)
            b    Le vin fait danser (*par les ivrognes)

Not only do these examples disallow the *par* phrase, but the verbs in question do not allow passives of any sort: *\*Il a été {dormi / dansé}*.

   Examples of this type have a number of properties which distinguish them from cases like (85) or (87) in 9.3.2, and indeed from other infinitival constructions with *faire*. Firstly, the understood subject in (99) must have a generic interpretation, whereas the missing Agent in passive-like examples such as *Paul a fait réparer les robinets* can be a specific person. Similarly, the construction in (99) can only be used to make general statements, not to report specific events:

(100)       a    *Ce médicament a fait dormir hier soir à dix heures
            b    *Le vin a fait danser à minuit

Also the subject of *faire* is typically inanimate, involving a rather inert type of causation.

   These properties are exactly the same as those which were discerned in examples like *Le café empêche de dormir* in 9.2.3. It is proposed therefore that they be analysed in the same way: i.e. the subject of the infinitive is the abstract element PRO which, in the absence of a Controller, is assigned arbitrary, generic reference:

(101)       [Le vin fait [PRO dormir]]

### 9.3.4    Constructions with 'laisser' and verbs of perception

In 9.3.1 it was noted that *laisser* and the perception verbs differ from *faire* in that they allow the subject of the infinitive to precede it:

(102)       a    Paul a {laissé / regardé} Marie danser

    b   Paul a {laissé / entendu} Marie descendre dans la cave

    c   Paul a {laissé / vu} Marie ouvrir la porte

It is not immediately clear whether *Marie* in (102) should be analysed as simply the subject of the infinitive, as in (103a), or as the direct object of the main verb controlling a P R O in the complement as in (103b):

(103)    a   [Paul a {laissé / regardé} [$_S$ Marie danser]]

          b   [Paul a {laissé / regardé} Marie$_m$ [$_S$ P R O $_m$ danser]]

The possibility of examples like (104) with the idiomatic interpretation 'I let / saw him get angry' suggest that the structure (103a) is at least available (for the reasons discussed in connection with Subject-raising vs Control in 9.2.5), though it does not exclude structure (103b) for examples of the type in (102):

(104)      J'ai {laissé / vu} la moutarde lui monter au nez

For the sake of concreteness, the structure (103a) will be assumed for all cases.

    This means that there must be some relaxing of the generalisation proposed in 9.2.2 which prevents overt NPs from occurring as subjects of infinitives at the surface level in French. More specifically, it must be assumed that *laisser* and the perception verbs (like cognitive verbs in English) can assign Accusative Case to the subject of the dependent infinitive. Accordingly, examples like (102) will be referred to as 'Accusative + infinitive' constructions.

    The choice between this construction and the other constructions discussed above in relation to *faire* is largely a matter of style, depending partly on the relative length or importance of the infinitival VP and its subject. In cases like (105) where the verb has no complement of its own and its subject is short, the two constructions are more or less interchangeable, though (105a) tends to be preferred unless there is an implied contrast concerning the action described by the verb (e.g. 'dance' rather than 'sing'):

(105)    a   Paul a {laissé / vu} danser Marie

          b   Paul a {laissé / vu} Marie danser

This preference is stronger when the NP is significantly longer than the infinitive: e.g. (106a) is more natural than (106b), though both are possible:

(106)    a   Paul a {laissé / vu} danser la sœur de Marie

          b   Paul a {laissé / vu} la sœur de Marie danser

Conversely, when the infinitive has a complement of its own, the Accusative + infinitive construction is usually preferred, particularly when the complement is a direct object. In this case, the very fact that the Accusative + infinitive construction is available may favour its use as a form which is neutral with respect to the semantic connotations associated with à and *par* (see 9.3.2).

With perception verbs in English, the gerund is used instead of the infinitive to denote perception of an event which is in progress rather than a complete event: e.g. *Paul saw Mary writing a letter* vs *Paul saw Mary write a letter*. In French the infinitive is used in both cases. Similar gerundive constructions are possible in French, but they are much less widespread than in English:

(107)    Paul a vu Marie travaillant dans son bureau

Arguably, in cases like (107), *travaillant dans son bureau* does not form part of the complement of *voir* but constitutes a separate expression describing the circumstances in which Marie was seen (i.e. 'Paul saw Marie as she was working in her office') in rather the same way as *dans son bain* in *Paul a vu Marie dans son bain*. This analysis is consistent with the generalisation that gerunds do not normally occur as complements in French (see 9.5.2). A more usual alternative to the infinitive is the construction in (108), where the verb takes the finite form in what looks like a relative clause (see 10.7.1):

(108)    a    Paul a vu Marie qui travaillait
         b    J'ai entendu le vent qui soufflait dans les arbres

Like the English gerundive construction, this construction presents the perceived event as being in progress.

### 9.3.5   The accusative and dative strategies

As we saw in 9.3.4, structures like (109) are not possible as surface sentences, because *faire* (unlike *laisser* and the perception verbs) cannot assign a Case feature to the subject of the infinitive:

(109)    a    [Paul a fait [Marie danser]]
         b    [Paul a fait [Marie descendre dans la cave]]
         c    [Paul a fait [Marie ouvrir la porte]]

From this perspective, the accusative and dative strategies presented informally in 9.3.1 can be seen as ways of reorganising the structure so that Case can be assigned to the subject of the infinitive. There are various ways in which this idea might be implemented. The approach which will be adopted here, following Kayne (1975), is that the infinitive is raised into a position in the main clause creating a relation with its underlying subject which mimics the 'normal' relation between a verb and its complement and which allows the infinitive to assign a Case feature to its underlying subject. This phenomenon of **Infinitive-raising** can be seen as the converse of the Subject-raising phenomenon discussed in 9.2.4;

whereas in constructions with *sembler*, etc., the subject of the infinitive raises to a position where it can acquire Case, in *faire* constructions the infinitive raises to a position where it can assign Case to its subject.

Application of Infinitive-raising to the structure in (109a) gives the correct surface form, as shown in (110):

(110)    [Paul a fait danser [Marie __ ]]

At this point *Marie* is treated as if it were the direct object of *danser* (or perhaps of the combination *faire danser*) and is assigned Accusative Case. The same analysis gives the right results for (109b), where the infinitive is raised, leaving the complement PP behind in the lower clause:

(111)    [Paul a fait descendre [Marie __ dans la cave ]]

Example (109c) is a bit more complicated. Raising of the infinitive on its own gives an ungrammatical sentence:

(112)    *[Paul a fait ouvrir [Marie __ la porte]]

The complication here is that the infinitive *ouvrir* has a direct object of its own, so that if *Marie* were treated as a direct object of *faire ouvrir* for the purposes of Case assignment we would end up with a structure containing two direct objects of the same verb, a situation which is not generally possible in French (see the discussion of examples like *\*Paul a donné Marie un cadeau* vs *Paul a donné un cadeau à Marie* in 2.3.2). Moreover, it seems reasonable to suppose that the genuine direct object *la porte* has a prior claim on the Accusative Case feature, so *Marie* must be marked with a different Case feature. The correct surface form (113) can be derived by raising the direct object along with the infinitive, as shown in (114):

(113)    Paul a fait ouvrir la porte à Marie

(114)    [Paul a fait ouvrir la porte [Marie __ ]]

In (114), *la porte* acquires Accusative Case in the normal way, being the direct object of *ouvrir* and occurring straight after the verb, whereas *Marie* is treated in rather the same way as the 'second object' of verbs like *donner* and is assigned Dative Case, indicated on the surface by the preposition *à*

The subject of the infinitive must also be marked as Dative when the infinitive takes a complement clause which qualifies as a direct object (see 2.3.5):

(115)    Paul a fait croire à Marie que la voiture était en panne

Again this pattern is similar to that observed in simple sentences with verbs which take a clausal direct object: e.g. *Paul a dit à Marie que*... The order of elements in (115) conforms to the general tendency for complement clauses to follow all other complements (see 1.5.4), but it also indicates that the *que* clause is left behind when the infinitive is raised:

(116)    a    [Paul a fait [Marie croire [que la voiture était en panne]]]
         b   ⇒ [Paul a fait croire [Marie __ [que la voiture était en panne]]]
         c   ⇒ [Paul a fait croire [à Marie __ [que la voiture était en panne]]]

For the cases discussed above, the Infinitive-raising rule can be formulated as follows:

**Infinitive-raising (preliminary formulation):**
*in constructions with* faire *(optionally with* laisser *and perception verbs), the infinitive is raised into the main clause, along with its direct object NP if it has one.*

The assumptions regarding Case assignment in these constructions are, roughly, that *faire* + $V_{INF}$ can assign Accusative Case to the subject of the infinitive unless the infinitive takes a direct object (NP or clause), in which case the subject is marked as Dative.

An important feature of this analysis is that, despite appearances, the subject does not move – it remains in the subject position even when it is preceded by the preposition *à* and even when the whole of the remainder of the infinitival clause is removed by Infinitive-raising (as in (114)). In this respect, the *à* phrases in examples like (113) and (115) have a very different status from the *par* phrases in the constructions discussed in 9.3.2.

### 9.3.6   Extensions of the dative strategy

There are some examples where the dative strategy is available or required even though the infinitive does not take a direct object. With expressions of the type *changer de N* the subject can be Accusative or Dative:

(117)    a    [Paul a fait [Marie changer d'avis]]
         b    Paul a fait changer Marie d'avis
         c    Paul a fait changer d'avis à Marie

When the infinitive is modified by an adjective which functions like a manner adverb, only the Dative strategy is possible:

(118)    a    [Paul a fait [Marie voir clair]]
         b    *Paul a fait voir Marie clair
         c    Paul a fait voir clair à Marie

The order of elements in the (c) examples indicates that *d'avis* and *clair* have been raised along with the infinitive. Moreover, there appears to be a correlation between raising of this 'other element' and assignment of Dative Case to the subject (we cannot add *à* in the (b) examples or omit it in the (c) examples).

The facts in (117) and (118) may perhaps be regarded as peripheral exceptions to the rule proposed in 9.3.5, but they suggest a more flexible approach to Infinitive-raising which will be needed in the discussion below of some problems concerning clitic pronouns in these constructions. As a radical step, let us revise the Infinitive-raising rule as follows:

**Infinitive-raising (revised formulation):**
*in* faire *constructions the infinitive is raised into the main clause, optionally with any complements or modifiers, provided that the resulting structure allows Case to be assigned to all arguments of the infinitive.*

The effect of this revision is to make the structural properties of Infinitive-raising (i.e. whether anything is raised along with the infinitive) dependent on conditions on Case assignment, which can be stated as follows:

**Case assignment in 'faire' constructions:**
 *I* Faire+$V_{INF}$ *can assign Accusative Case to* $NP^x$ *unless:*
  *(a)* $V_{INF}$ *has a direct object distinct from* $NP^x$,
 *or* *(b)* $NP^x$ *is separated from* $V_{INF}$ *by another element*
 *II If* $NP^x$ *is the direct object of* $V_{INF}$ *it must receive Accusative Case.*
 *III If conditions (a) and (b) prevent assignment of Accusative Case to the subject of the infinitive, this subject is marked as Dative (as a last resort).*

The only new condition is (Ib), which forces Dative Case assignment in examples like (117c) and (118c) where the 'other element' is *d'avis* or *clair*. The caveat 'as a last resort' in (III) is an informal way of suggesting that the dative strategy is normally available only when there is no derivation which will allow assignment of Accusative Case to the subject of the infinitive.

In principle, the revised Infinitive-raising rule allows the direct object of the infinitive to be left behind, as in (119):

(119)     *[Paul a fait ouvrir [Marie __ la porte ]]

This structure is ruled out because condition (II) requires *la porte* to receive Accusative Case, but the presence of *Marie* prevents this (by condition (Ib)). Thus the only option is to raise *la porte* along with the infinitive and to mark *Marie* as Dative, as discussed in 9.3.5.

By the same token, the revised rule allows an indirect object to be raised with the infinitive, as in (120):

(120)    *[Paul a fait descendre dans la cave [Marie __ ]]

The presence of *dans la cave* prevents assignment of Accusative Case to *Marie*, but assignment of Dative to *Marie*, as in (121), would violate the 'last resort' caveat in (III), since there is an alternative derivation ((111) in 9.3.5) which allows *Marie* to receive Accusative Case:

(121)    *Paul a fait descendre dans la cave à Marie

For the examples in (118) above, it is tentatively suggested that *voir clair* is a fixed expression which cannot be easily split up – this is consistent with the unacceptability of (118b) where *voir* has been raised on its own. Thus the only option is to raise the two elements together and to mark *Marie* as Dative (since Accusative assignment is blocked by (Ib)), but since this is the only option, the 'last resort' caveat in (III) is satisfied. Expressions like *changer d'avis* seem to have an intermediate status. The acceptability of (117b) indicates that the two elements can be separated by Infinitive-raising, but intuitively *d'avis* is not a 'fully fledged' independent PP in the way that *dans la cave* is. From this perspective, the surface structures in (117) may be viewed as alternative solutions to a dilemma – the use of the Dative in (117c) is not strictly a 'last resort', since (117b) is possible, but it preserves the integrity of the expression *changer d'avis* which is sacrificed in (117b).

In most cases, the clearest ones, the approach outlined above gives the same results as the more stipulative rule proposed in 9.3.5: generally speaking, only direct object NPs can be raised along with the infinitive. The main difference is that this approach relates this restriction directly to conditions on Case assignment in these constructions.

### 9.3.7  Lexical and syntactic causatives
In 2.4.3 we saw that many verbs can be used transitively with a causative meaning, as in (122a), or intransitively to describe a change of state, as in (122b):

(122)    a  Jules a cuit le poulet
         b  Le poulet a cuit

Another way of expressing the proposition in (122a) is to use a construction with *faire*:

(123)    Jules a fait cuire le poulet

Examples like (122a) will be referred to as **lexical causatives** (since causation is part of the meaning of the verb itself) whereas examples like (123) will be called **syntactic causatives**.

441

Example (123) is actually ambiguous. Apart from the meaning expressed in (122a), it can also have an interpretation involving an intermediate Agent: 'Jules had the chicken cooked (by someone else).' These two meanings are associated with different syntactic structures: with the meaning of (122a), sentence (123) is an Infinitive-raising construction where *cuire* is used intransitively as in (122b) – i.e. 'Jules caused the meat to cook':

(124)     [Jules a fait  [le poulet cuire]]

On the second interpretation, (123) is a passive-like construction of the type discussed in 9.3.2, where *cuire* is used transitively but the Agent is suppressed (though it could be specified by a *par* phrase):

(125)     [Jules a fait [cuire le poulet (par la servante)]]

Note now that sentence (126) is not ambiguous in this way – it can only mean 'The terrorists blew up the plane':

(126)     Les terroristes ont fait sauter l'avion

This is due to the fact that *sauter* (unlike English *blow up*) can only be used intransitively with a 'change of state' meaning:

(127)     a   *Les terroristes ont sauté l'avion
          b   L'avion a sauté

Conversely, with verbs like *détruire* which cannot be used intransitively (see (128b)), only the 'intermediate Agent' reading is possible for the syntactic causative – i.e. (129) cannot mean (128a) but only 'The terrorists had the bridge destroyed':

(128)     a   Les terroristes ont détruit le pont
          b   *Le pont a détruit

(129)     Les terroristes ont fait détruire le pont

With verbs like *ouvrir* whose non-causative sense is expressed by a Neutral pronominal form (see 2.4.4, 3.3), there is a three-way semantic distinction:

(130)     a   Pierre a ouvert la porte
          b   Pierre a fait ouvrir la porte
          c   Pierre a fait s'ouvrir la porte

In (130a) Pierre opens the door in the normal way (e.g. by turning the handle), (130b) implies the intervention of an intermediate Agent ('Pierre had the door opened (by the caretaker)'), whereas (130c) means something like 'Pierre caused the door to open (of its own accord)' – i.e. the causal link between Pierre's action and the opening of the door is indirect but does not involve the intervention of a human Agent (e.g. Pierre opened the window which created a draught causing the door to open).

The difference between (130a) and (130c) can be discerned in some cases with verbs which are non-pronominal in their intransitive use, as in (131) where judgements are based on the assumption that the shopkeeper has direct control over the prices whereas consumers can only influence them indirectly through market forces:

(131)   a   Le marchand a {baissé / ?fait baisser} les prix
        b   Les consommateurs ont {?baissé / fait baisser} les prix

Similarly, the syntactic causative construction tends to be preferred when the causative element is a circumstance rather than a human Agent:

(132)       La situation économique a {?baissé / fait baisser} les prix

With movement verbs which can be used transitively or intransitively, we find a fairly sharp distinction between the two constructions:

(133)   a   Pierre a sorti le mouchoir de sa poche
        b   ??Pierre a sorti les invités du salon
        c   Pierre a fait sortir les invités du salon

When the Theme entity is animate (capable of autonomous movement), the syntactic causative construction is strongly favoured, as in (133c), while the lexical causative must be used with inert entities, as in (133a) – *Pierre a fait sortir le mouchoir de sa poche* is possible with an 'intermediate Agent' reading (*Pierre had the handkerchief taken out of his pocket*) or perhaps as a description of a conjuring trick in which the handkerchief emerges from the pocket of its own accord.

All things being equal, lexical causatives express a direct type of causation where the cause and the effect are presented as a single event and, typically, the Agent manipulates the Theme entity directly, whereas syntactic causatives express a much looser causal relation in which the change of state retains some degree of autonomy. In some cases, like (133), this difference is quite sharp while in others, like (122a) and (123), it is negligible. However, with verbs like *sauter* in (126) which cannot be used as lexical causatives, the construction with *faire* expresses direct causation. Further examples of this type are given in (134), where the verbs in question cannot be used transitively, but the constructions with *faire* express direct causation and can be translated by transitive verbs in English:

(134)   a   Luc a {*trébuché / fait trébucher} Paul   'Luc tripped Paul up'
        b   Jules a {*coulé / fait couler} le bateau   'Jules sank the boat'

The expression *laisser tomber* is rather interesting from this point of view. The Infinitive-raising construction (135) can be assimilated to the cases in (134), expressing direct causation in the same way as English *drop*:

(135)   Marie a laissé tomber le verre

However, the Accusative + infinitive construction in (136) implies a much looser causal relation 'allow to fall' (e.g. Marie saw the glass about to fall but did nothing to prevent it):

(136)   Marie a laissé le verre tomber

Note also that the Infinitive-raising construction with *laisser tomber* can be used with some nouns which do not occur naturally as subjects of *tomber* and cannot occur in the Accusative + infinitive construction:

(137)   a   Marie a laissé tomber la question
        b   *Marie a laissé la question tomber
        c   *La question tombe

## 9.4   Clitic pronouns in infinitival constructions

### 9.4.1   *Accusative and Dative clitics*

In most types of infinitival constructions, clitics which represent complements of the infinitive are attached to the infinitive, not to the verb in the higher clause:

(138)   a   Pierre veut le manger
        b   *Pierre le veut manger

(139)   a   Pierre semble les admirer
        b   *Pierre les semble admirer

However, in constructions with *faire, laisser* and verbs of perception, there is a mixed pattern – clitics must be attached to the infinitive in some cases, but to the higher verb in others.

In 6.2.2 it was proposed that the Clitic-placement rule always attaches clitics as far to the left as possible within the restrictions of the Specified Subject Condition (SSC), which prevents (certain types of) rules from applying across a subject position. This condition rules out the (b) examples in (138)–(139), since they could only be derived by moving the clitic across the PRO element in (138) or the position vacated by the raised subject in (139):

(140)     a [Pierre   veut [PRO   manger PRONOUN]]

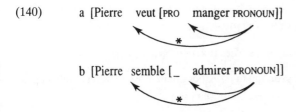

        b [Pierre  semble [_   admirer PRONOUN]]

The positions of Accusative and Dative non-reflexive clitics can be accounted for in terms of the same restrictions, bearing in mind the structures proposed in the preceding sections.

In Accusative + infinitive constructions, clitics representing complements of the infinitive must be attached to the infinitive, not to the higher verb:

(141)     a   Paul laissera Marie les manger
        b   Paul laissera Marie leur parler

(142)     a   *Paul les laissera Marie manger
        b   *Paul leur laissera Marie parler

However, clitics which represent the subject of the infinitive are attached to the higher verb:

(143)     Paul la laissera manger les frites

Given the underlying structures in (144), it should be clear that attachment of the pronouns in (144a, b) to *laissera* would involve crossing the subject *Marie*, but no violation of the SSC arises in (144c):

(144)     a   [Paul laissera [Marie manger PRONOUN$_{ACC}$ ]]
        b   [Paul laissera [Marie parler PRONOUN$_{DAT}$ ]]
        c   [Paul laissera [PRONOUN$_{ACC}$ manger les frites]]

The situation in constructions derived by Infinitive-raising is rather more complicated. Recall that in the normal case, direct objects are raised along with the infinitive. Thus, corresponding to (144a), we have the structure (145):

(145)     [Paul fera manger PRONOUN$_{ACC}$ [à Marie __ ]]

Attachment of the clitic to either verb in (145) is compatible with the SSC, since there is no intervening subject position, but only attachment to *fera* satisfies the requirement that clitics must be attached as far to the left as possible:

(146)     a   Paul les fera manger à Marie
        b   *Paul fera les manger à Marie

In the structure corresponding to (144c), where the subject of the infinitive is a pronoun, this pronoun must bear Dative Case:

(147)     [Paul fera manger les frites [PRONOUN$_{DAT}$ __ ]]

Again, cliticisation of the pronoun to *fera* does not involve crossing a subject position and satisfies the 'leftmost verb' requirement:

(148)     a   Paul lui fera manger les frites
          b   *Paul fera lui manger les frites

The case corresponding to (144b), where the indirect object of *parler* is pronominalised presents an apparent puzzle. If we try to replace *aux étudiants* in *Paul fera parler Marie aux étudiants* by a pronoun (*leur*), we find that it cannot be attached to either verb:

(149)     a   *Paul leur fera parler Marie
          b   *Paul fera leur parler Marie

The ungrammaticality of (149a) is particularly surprising since it looks essentially the same as (148a) – in both cases we have a Dative clitic attached to *fera* and an NP following the infinitive. This puzzle can be solved by looking at the structure which results from Infinitive-raising (assuming that indirect objects are not raised along with the infinitive):

(150)     [Paul fera parler [Marie __ PRONOUN$_{DAT}$ ]]

In this structure, the Dative pronoun cannot be attached to either verb without crossing the subject *Marie*, in contrast to (147) where the Dative pronoun is itself the subject of the infinitive.

The descriptive generalisation which emerges from the last example is that in sentences derived by Infinitive-raising, a Dative clitic can only represent the subject of the infinitive, not its indirect object. Thus, sentence (151) can only mean 'I made them give a present to Marie', not 'I made Marie give a present to them':

(151)     Je leur ai fait donner un cadeau à Marie

More precisely, (151) must be derived from (152a) not (152b):

(152)     a   [J'ai fait donner un cadeau [PRONOUN$_{DAT}$ __ à Marie]]
          b   [J'ai fait donner un cadeau [à Marie __ PRONOUN$_{DAT}$ ]]

In the above discussion, Infinitive-raising and Accusative + infinitive constructions have been dealt with separately, using *faire* and *laisser* to avoid confusion between the two. With *laisser* and the perception verbs, the two constructions are often indistinguishable when the subject of the infinitive is a clitic pronoun – e.g. *Je la laisserai danser* can correspond to either *Je laisserai Marie danser* or *Je laisserai danser Marie.* When the infinitive is transitive, the two constructions are distinguished only by the Case form of the clitic:

(153)    a   Paul la laissera manger les frites.   (Accusative + infinitive)
          b   Paul lui laissera manger les frites.   (Infinitive-raising)

However, the syntactic difference between these constructions shows up clearly if we replace *les frites* by a clitic pronoun:

(154)    a   Paul la laissera les manger.   (cf. (141a))
          b   Paul les lui laissera manger.   (cf. (146a))

Note that we cannot use *lui* to represent the subject of the infinitive and attach the direct object clitic to the infinitive:

(155)      *Paul lui laissera les manger

The reason for this should be clear. The use of *lui* to represent the subject indicates that the infinitive has been raised, but attachment of the object clitic to the infinitive occurs only when the infinitive is not raised.

> In 9.3.6 we saw that the dative strategy is sometimes employed even when the infinitive does not take a direct object (e.g. *Paul lui a fait changer d'avis*). This option is more widely available when the subject of the infinitive is represented by a clitic. Thus alongside the expected form (156a) we find the variant (156b):
>
> (156)  a  Paul la fera penser à cette question
>         b  Paul lui fera penser à cette question
>
> Examples like (156b) can be accommodated if we assume that the indirect object is raised along with the infinitive:
>
> (157)  [Paul fera penser à cette question [PRONOUN __ ]]
>
> Since *fera penser* is separated from PRONOUN, the only Case which can be assigned is Dative. However, in order to allow this, the 'last resort' condition (which permits Dative Case assignment only when the Accusative strategy is unavailable) must be relaxed since the variant (156a) is fully acceptable.
>
> Conversely, we occasionally find examples like (158b) where the subject of the infinitive is represented by an Accusative clitic even though the infinitive has a direct object (though this construction is generally regarded as archaic or Non-standard in comparison with the fully acceptable form (158a)):
>
> (158)  a  Paul lui fera manger le ragoût
>         b  %Paul la fera manger le ragoût

Example (158b) can be analysed as an Accusative + infinitive construction, normally available only with *laisser* and the perception verbs (cf. *Paul la laissera manger le ragoût*). Although *faire* cannot normally assign Accusative Case directly to the subject of the infinitive, it seems that this is marginally possible when this subject is realised as a clitic.

Both (156b) and (158b) can be derived by syntactic processes which operate in other constructions. Their exceptional status can be characterised in terms of a relaxation of the normal conditions on Case assignment when the element involved is realised as a clitic.

None of the above complications arise in the passive-like constructions discussed in 9.3.2 (with or without the *par* phrase). In these constructions, clitics corresponding to direct or indirect objects of the infinitive are always attached to the verb in the higher clause:

(159)    a    Paul le fera traduire (par Marie)
         b    Paul leur fera donner un cadeau (par Marie)

Given the proposal in 9.3.2 that the infinitive in such constructions is simply a VP, there is no intervening subject position to prevent attachment of the clitic to *faire*, while attachment to the infinitive (giving *\*Paul fera le traduire (par Marie)*, *\*Paul fera leur donner un cadeau (par Marie)*) is ruled out by the requirement that clitics should always be attached as far to the left as possible.

### 9.4.2    *Ordering of syntactic operations*

In 9.4.1, it was tacitly assumed that Clitic-placement applies after Infinitive-raising. Consider what would happen if we applied Clitic-placement directly to underlying structures like (160):

(160)    a    [Paul fera [Marie manger PRONOUN]]
         b    [Paul fera [Marie parler à PRONOUN]]

Cliticisation of the pronoun to *fera*, across the subject *Marie*, would be blocked by the SSC, but it ought to be possible to attach the pronoun to the infinitive. Raising of the infinitive (with the clitic attached to it) would then give the ungrammatical sentences *\*Paul fera les manger à Marie* and *\*Paul fera leur parler Marie*. Consequently, for the analysis to give the right results, we must ensure that Clitic-placement does not apply before Infinitive-raising.

In 1.5.6, it was pointed out that the Case features of pronouns must be assigned before pronouns are attached to the verb. However, in many instances, Case assignment is dependent on the prior application of Infinitive-raising. Putting these two observations together, it follows that Clitic-placement must apply to the output of Infinitive-raising, as required.

### 9.4.3  'En' and 'y' in causative constructions

When *en* functions as an indefinite pronoun (with or without a numeral or indefinite determiner) it occurs in the same positions as Accusative clitics (with the numeral or determiner left behind in the position from which the clitic is moved). In (161) *en* represents the direct object of the infinitive and triggers assignment of Dative Case to the subject when it is raised along with the verb, as in (161a):

(161)  a  Paul en fera manger (plusieurs)   'Paul will make Marie eat
         à Marie                                     several of them'
      b  Paul laissera Marie en manger   'Paul will let Marie eat many
         (beaucoup)                             of them'
      c  Paul en fera traduire trois     'Paul will have three of them
         (par Marie)                          translated (by Marie)'

In (162), *en* represents the subject of the infinitive:

(162)  a  Paul en fera danser (trois)        'Paul will make three of
                                         them dance'
      b  Paul en laissera (trois) boire le vin   'Paul will let three of
                                         them drink the wine'

When *en* and *y* function as indirect objects of the verb, they follow the same pattern as other object clitics in Accusative + infinitive constructions (attached to the infinitive) and the passive-like constructions (attached to the higher verb):

(163)  a  Paul laissera Marie en parler
      b  Paul laissera Marie y descendre

(164)  a  Paul en fera descendre les bagages (par le porteur)
         'Paul will have the bags brought down from there (by the porter)'
      b  Paul y fera mettre les bagages (par le porteur)
         'Paul will have the bags put there (by the porter)'

In Infinitive-raising constructions, *en* and *y* behave in a rather different way from other clitics. When *en* or *y* represents the only complement of the infinitive it is normally attached to the higher verb, in sharp contrast to Dative clitics (see 9.4.1):

(165)  a  Paul en fera parler Marie
      b  Paul y fera descendre Marie
      c  *Paul leur fera parler Marie

The underlying structure of (165a, b) can be represented as (166):

(166)    [Paul fera [Marie V$_{INF}$ pro-PP]]

If the infinitive is raised on its own, as in (167), subsequent cliticisation across *Marie* would violate the SSC:

(167)    [Paul fera V$_{INF}$ [Marie __ pro-PP]]

It cannot be claimed that the SSC does not apply to cliticisation of these items, since this condition is respected in other infinitival constructions (e.g. *Paul veut en parler* vs *\*Paul en veut parler*). To derive (165a, b) it must be assumed that the pro-PP is raised with the infinitive, as in (168), and then cliticised to *fera*:

(168)    [Paul fera V$_{INF}$ pro-PP [Marie __ ]]

In 9.3.6 it was argued that indirect objects cannot normally be raised with the infinitive because the intervening PP would prevent assignment of Accusative Case to the subject of the infinitive. However, this is not a problem if the pro-PP is moved out of the way (by cliticising to *fera*) before Case is assigned to *Marie*. Nevertheless, this proposal raises two questions: (i) why is this derivation not available for *leur* in (165c), and (ii) how can cliticisation of *en* and *y* apply before Case assignment? A possible answer to both questions is that *en* and *y*, unlike Accusative or Dative clitics, are not Case-marked pronouns but substitutes for PPs (see 6.4.6). If this is correct, the argument in 9.4.2 concerning the necessary ordering of Case assignment before Clitic-placement does not apply to *en* and *y*.

When *en* and *y* function as complements of verbs which also take a direct object, cliticisation to the higher verb is not normally possible in Infinitive-raising constructions (cf. (164) above with *par*):

(169)    a   *Paul en fera descendre les bagages à Marie
             'Paul will make Marie bring the bags down from there'
         b   *Paul y fera mettre les bagages à Marie
             'Paul will make Marie put the bags there'

In order to derive these examples in the manner proposed for (165a,b), it would have to be assumed that both the direct and indirect objects are raised along with the infinitive. Since the examples are ungrammatical we may conclude that this possibility is not available (i.e. no more than one complement can be raised with the infinitive).

Some speakers accept examples like (170)–(171) where *en* or or *y* is attached to the raised infinitive, though judgements are rather hesitant:

(170)    a   ?Paul fera en parler Marie
         b   ?Paul fera y descendre Marie

(171)    a  ?Paul fera en descendre les bagages à Marie

            b  ?Paul fera y mettre les bagages à Marie

This possibility is not entirely surprising. If cliticisation of *en* and *y* can apply before Case assignment (as proposed for (165a, b), there is no obvious reason (given the argument in 9.4.2) why cliticisation of these items should not also apply before Infinitive-raising. Suppose we cliticise the pro-PP in (166) to the infinitive and then raise the infinitive, the result will be sentences like those in (170) – examples like (171) can be derived in the same way from underlying structures like (172):

(172)      [Paul fera [Marie $V_{INF}$ les bagages pro-PP]]

### 9.4.4 Reflexive clitics in causative constructions

Reflexive clitics behave in a rather different way from other clitics, mainly because of the requirement that they must refer back to the subject NP. For the sake of clarity, examples with the form *se* will be used, but the observations here apply equally to *me, te, nous* and *vous* when they have a reflexive or reciprocal interpretation.

The basic generalisation concerning the position of these items can be stated informally as follows:

*In constructions with* faire, *etc., se is always cliticised to the verb whose subject is the antecedent.*

In the passive-like construction, se must refer back to the subject of the main verb (recall that the complement of *par* is not a possible antecedent, see 9.3.2) and is attached to the higher verb:

(173)    a  Paul s'est fait inviter à la fête (par Marie)

              'Paul got himself invited to the party (by Marie)'

            b  Paul s'est fait envoyer le colis (par la secrétaire)

              'Paul had a parcel sent to him (Paul) (by the secretary)'

As was pointed out in 3.2.11, constructions of this type do not necessarily have a literal causative interpretation but can be used as alternatives to ordinary passives (e.g. (173a) can mean 'Paul was invited to the party ...').

In Accusative + infinitive constructions, we find two basic patterns:

(174)      Les espions se sont vus voler des documents

(175)    a  Paul a laissé Marie se contredire

            b  Le professeur a laissé les étudiants se parler

In (174), *se* is the subject of the infinitive and refers back (reciprocally) to *les espions* ('the spies saw each other stealing documents'), whereas the examples in (175) involve coreference between an object of the infinitive (direct in (175a), indirect in (175b)) and the subject of the infinitive. When an object of the infinitive is coreferential with the subject of the main verb, a non-reflexive pronoun must be used (as in English, *Paul let Mary kiss him*):

(176)      Paul a laissé Marie l'embrasser

In Infinitive-raising constructions, *se* can also be used to represent the subject of the infinitive referring back to the subject of the main verb:

(177)      Les étudiants se faisaient boire du café
           'The students were making each other drink coffee'

In all of the above cases, *se* occupies the same position as a non-reflexive clitic would occupy in cases where no coreference is involved. Consequently, these examples can be derived in the same way as their non-reflexive counterparts, as discussed in the preceding sections.

The syntactic difference between reflexive and non-reflexive clitics emerges in Infinitive-raising constructions where *se* functions as an object of the infinitive. In (178), *se* refers back to the subject of the infinitive:

(178)      a   Paul a fait se critiquer Marie      'Paul made Marie criticise herself'
           b   Paul a fait se parler les enfants   'Paul made the children talk to each other'

Attachment of *se* to the infinitive conforms to the generalisation expressed at the beginning of this section. However, the examples in (178) cannot be derived in the same way as their non-reflexive counterparts – recall that (non-reflexive) direct object pronouns must be cliticised to the highest verb whereas Dative pronouns cannot be cliticised at all (see 9.4.1):

(179)      Paul les a fait critiquer à Marie.   'Paul made Marie criticise them'

(180)      a   *Paul leur a fait parler les enfants
           b   *Paul a fait leur parler les enfants
               'Paul made the children talk to them'

A further important difference is that *Marie* receives Accusative Case in (178a) (cf. *\*Paul a fait se critiquer à Marie*) but must be marked as Dative in (179).

The simplest way of accounting for the examples in (178) is to suppose that *se* is cliticised to the infinitive before it is raised, as shown below:

(181)     [Paul a fait [Marie critiquer PRONOUN]]
          ⇒ [Paul a fait [Marie se critiquer]]
          ⇒ [Paul a fait se critiquer [Marie __ ]]

(182)     [Paul a fait [les enfants parler PRONOUN$_{[DAT]}$]
          ⇒ [Paul a fait [les enfants se parler]]
          ⇒ [Paul a fait se parler [les enfants __ ]]

The basic idea behind this ordering of processes is that cliticisation of *se* must apply at a stage where its antecedent can be identified, in purely structural terms, as the immediate subject – i.e. before Infinitive-raising. For present purposes, let us simply assume that this requirement overrides the argument advanced in 9.4.2. The fact that *Marie* receives Accusative Case in (178a) is actually consistent with the conditions proposed in 9.3.6. The relevant condition is condition (I) repeated below, where NP$^x$ = *Marie*:

I  *Faire*+$V_{INF}$ can assign Accusative Case to NP$^x$ unless:
     (a) $V_{INF}$ has a direct object distinct from NP$^x$,
   or  (b) NP$^x$ is separated from $V_{INF}$ by another element

Condition (b) is satisfied since *se* is cliticised to the infinitive before it is raised and therefore does not separate *critiquer* from *Marie*. Moreover, although *se* functions as the direct object of *critiquer*, it is arguably not 'distinct' from *Marie* since the two expressions are coreferential.

As we might expect, pronominal verbs like *s'ouvrir* and *se réunir* behave like intransitive verbs in *faire* constructions, assigning Accusative Case:

(183)     a   Paul a fait s'ouvrir (*à) la porte
          b   Paul a fait se réunir (*à) l'équipe

With many Intrinsic pronominal verbs like *se taire* and *s'évanouir* (see 3.3.2), *se* is frequently omitted in Infinitive-raising constructions, though it must be retained in Accusative + infinitive constructions:

(184)     a   Le professeur a fait taire les étudiants
          b   La chaleur a fait évanouir Marie

(185)     a   Paul a vu Marie s'évanouir
          b   *Paul a vu Marie évanouir

A problem arises in examples where the object of the infinitive refers back to the subject of the higher verb, as in the underlying structure (186) to be interpreted as 'Paul will make Marie kiss him (=Paul)':

(186)     [Paul$_p$ fera [Marie embrasser PRONOUN$_p$]]

At this stage the pronoun cannot be cliticised as *se* to *embrasser* since it is not coreferential with the immediate subject (*Marie*), nor can it be cliticised to *fera* since this would violate the SSC. However, if the pronoun is raised with the infinitive, giving (187) with Dative marking of *Marie*, the conditions for cliticisation should be satisfied:

(187)     [Paul$_p$ fera embrasser PRONOUN$_p$ [à Marie __ ]]

Nevertheless, the resulting sentence is ungrammatical:

(188)     *Paul se fera embrasser à Marie

Note also that we cannot use a non-reflexive clitic to express this meaning (cf. the Accusative + infinitive construction (176): *Paul a laissé Marie l'embrasser*):

(189)     *Paul$_p$ le$_p$ fera embrasser à Marie

A further problem is that the construction in (188) is perfectly acceptable with certain other verbs instead of *embrasser*:

(190)     a    Paul se fera connaître à Marie
          b    Paul se fera voir à Marie

This construction appears to be possible only with verbs expressing awareness or perception, giving a Goal or Experiencer role to the *à* phrase, as opposed to the Agent role in (188). It may be relevant that this Goal/Experiencer role is the interpretation which is typically associated with *à* in simple sentences – e.g. in *Paul se présentera à Marie* or *Paul se montrera à Marie*, which are roughly synonymous with the examples in (190). Possibly, the examples in (190) are not instances of the Infinitive-raising construction at all, but *faire voir* and *faire connaître* are 'complex verbs' which take an indirect object in the same way as *montrer* and *présenter*. However, this is a complex matter and for the purposes of this book, the data in (188)–(190) will be left as an interesting but unresolved problem.

### 9.4.5 A note on agreement of the past participle

Agreement of the past participle in infinitival constructions with *faire*, etc., is often presented in traditional grammars as a problem for the 'rule of thumb' which requires past participles to agree in number and gender with a preceding direct object. To some extent, this problem may have arisen from efforts by grammarians to prescribe usage in ways which do not always have a rational basis. In practical terms this is a rather academic issue since in all of these constructions non-agreement of the participle is at least 'tolerated'. Nevertheless, it may be interesting to consider how far established or prescribed usage can be accounted for in terms of the structural analyses which we have presented

One point on which everyone agrees is that *faire* never shows past participle agreement in infinitival constructions, contrary to the 'rule of thumb':

(191)      a   Paul les a fait(*s) danser

             b   Paul les a fait(*s) traduire {à / par} Marie

However, in constructions like the following, agreement is possible with *laisser* and generally preferred with perception verbs:

(192)      a   Paul les a {laissé(s) / vu(s)} danser

             b   Paul les a {laissé(s) / entendu(s)} réciter des poèmes

In terms of the analyses presented in the preceding sections, the examples in (191) must be analysed as Infinitive-raising constructions or passive-like constructions in which the clitic gets Accusative Case from the infinitive, not from *faire*. However, the examples in (192) can be analysed as Accusative + infinitive constructions in which the higher verb (i.e. the past participle) assigns Accusative Case directly to the pronoun. Accordingly, we may reformulate the traditional 'rule of thumb' as follows:

*A past participle agrees with the preceding Accusative element provided that this element receives its Case feature directly from the participle.*

This revision is independently motivated by the lack of agreement in examples like (193), where *quels livres* is the direct object of *lire* and therefore gets its Case from *lire*, not from *essayer*:

(193)      Quels livres as-tu essayé(*s) de lire?

The rule proposed above predicts that *laisser* and the perception verbs should not show agreement with an Accusative clitic which represents the direct object of the infinitive in Infinitive-raising and passive-like constructions. This prediction corresponds to established usage, as prescribed by grammarians, at least with the perception verbs, though agreement of *laisser* is deemed permissible by some grammarians:

(194)      a   Paul les a laissé(?s) traduire par la secrétaire

             b   Paul les a laissé(?s) manger à Marie

             c   Paul les a entendu(*s) réciter par les enfants

Whether the possibility of agreement in (194a, b) represents an aberration on the part of traditional grammarians or whether it reflects a deficiency in the account above is a matter which will be left open.

## 9.5 Some further issues

### 9.5.1 Infinitival particles

One of the biggest practical difficulties relating to infinitival constructions is deciding whether an infinitive should be introduced by *à* or *de* or by nothing at all (a 'bare' infinitive). Various aspects of this problem have already been commented on elsewhere in this book. The main points are summarised below with brief examples and references to relevant sections.

- Where the infinitive functions as an indirect object of the verb (or adjective or noun), it is always introduced by *à* or *de*. Here *à* and *de* can be regarded as prepositions and the choice between them is usually (but not always) the same as we find with an NP which has the same semantic function (see 2.3.5 for criteria for determining whether an infinitive is an indirect object): *se souvenir de, être prêt à, inviter à, être content de* (counterexamples: *être {forcé / obligé} de*).

- Infinitives in the surface subject position are usually 'bare', but can be introduced by *de* in more formal style (see 3.4.2): *(De) voyager me plaît.*

- In derived impersonal constructions where the infinitive is the understood subject, the infinitive is always introduced by *de* (see 3.4.2): *Il me plaît de voyager, Il est difficile de choisir.*

- In Intrinsic impersonal constructions, where there is no paraphrase with the infinitive in subject position (see 3.4.1), no absolute generalisation can be made: *Il faut partir, Il est temps de rentrer, Il me reste à vous remercier.*

- In 'object gap' constructions (see 7.4.1) and infinitival relatives (see 10.5.9), the infinitive is always introduced by *à*: *Ce problème est difficile à résoudre, Je cherche quelque chose à lire.*

- Infinitives which function as direct objects of 'cognitive' verbs (see 9.2.2) are always bare (apparent exceptions are cases where the infinitive is an indirect object – e.g. *Pierre se rend compte d'avoir fait une faute*): *Je croyais être en retard, Elle affirme avoir envoyé la lettre.*

- *Faire, laisser* and verbs of perception always take a bare infinitive in the constructions discussed in 9.3 (but *laisser* takes *à* with the meaning 'leave it to someone to do something': *J'ai laissé aux étudiants à trouver des exemples*).

- Purposive clauses accompanying verbs of movement are expressed by the bare infinitive: *Je suis allé acheter du pain, Elle est venue me voir.* (*Pour* + infinitive is also possible, but indicates a purpose which is much less directly related to the movement itself, e.g. *Je suis parti pour te faire plaisir* vs *Je suis parti faire des courses.*)

- In cases not covered above, the choice between *à*, *de* and a bare infinitive is unpredictable and must be learnt as a property of the main verb. Some verbs allow more than one possibility (e.g. *aimer {Ø / à}, commencer {à / de}, souhaiter {Ø / de}*). Most direct object infinitives other than those mentioned above are introduced by *de*. Clear examples of direct object infinitives introduced by *à* are rare (the principal examples being *apprendre, enseigner* and *montrer*).

### 9.5.2 Gerundive constructions

Constructions with the gerund (or 'present participle') resemble infinitival constructions of the Control type.

When the gerund is introduced by *en* its subject is normally controlled by the subject of the main clause:

(195)      a   Pierre$_p$ a vu un renard en [PRO$_p$ traversant la forêt]]
            b   Le verre$_v$ s'est cassé en [PRO$_v$ tombant par terre]
            c   *Luc a cassé le verre$_v$ en [PRO$_v$ tombant par terre]
            d   *Ce film a amusé Pierre$_p$ en [PRO$_p$ le regardant]

However, in passive and Middle constructions, the Controller can also be the Agent of the main verb, even if the Agent is not specified (see 3.3.5 for further examples):

(196)      a   Le verre a été cassé (par Luc$_l$) en [PRO$_l$ faisant la vaiselle]
            b   Ce vin se boit en [PRO mangeant]

Examples of this type are potentially ambiguous, particularly when the surface subject is animate, as in (197) where PRO could refer either to *le voleur* or to *la police*:

(197)      Le voleur a été arrêté (par la police) en [PRO sortant de l'immeuble]

Gerunds introduced by *en* have a progressive interpretation, describing an event which is simultaneous with that described in the main clause.

When the gerund is introduced by *tout en*, it typically has a concessive function, similar to that of subjunctive clauses with *bien que* or *quoique*. In this use, the gerund is often stative and the Controller must be the syntactic subject of the main clause even in passive constructions:

(198)    a  Tout en [PRO$_j$ étant malade], Jules$_j$ est allé au travail

          b  *Tout en [PRO$_j$ étant malade], on a envoyé Jules$_j$ au travail

          c  Tout en [PRO$_j$ étant malade], Jules$_j$ a été envoyé au travail

          d  *Tout en [PRO$_l$ prenant du soin], le verre a été cassé (par Luc$_i$)

Without *en* the gerund describes a situation which is presented as a reason for the event described in the main clause and its subject must be controlled by the subject of the main clause:

(199)    a  [PRO$_g$ ayant faim], Gaston$_g$ est allé au restaurant

          b  *[PRO$_g$ ayant faim], on a envoyé Gaston$_g$ au restaurant

          c  [PRO$_v$ étant très fragiles], ces verres$_v$ ne se mettent pas dans le lave-vaisselle

          d  [PRO$_j$ ayant fini son travail], Jules$_j$ s'est couché

In rather formal style, the subject of the gerund can be an overt NP, particularly when the verb is *être* (including auxiliary uses):

(200)    a  [Jules étant malade], nous avons dû finir le travail nous-mêmes

          b  [Le train n'étant pas encore arrivé], Gaston est allé prendre un café

          c  [Ces verres étant très fragiles], il ne faut pas les mettre dans le lave-vaisselle

To accommodate such cases, we must assume that gerunds, unlike infinitives, can assign a Case feature to their subjects.

In all the constructions discussed above, the gerund acts as a modifier rather than as a complement of the verb. In constructions with perception verbs, like (204), the function of the gerundive clause is less clear:

(201)       J'ai vu Gaston sortant du restaurant

In 9.3.4, it was suggested that the gerund acts as a modifier, describing a circumstance concerning the direct object entity. If this view is correct, we must assume that the direct object controls the subject of the gerund, in contrast to all the other cases discussed above:

(202)       J'ai vu Gaston$_g$ [PRO$_g$ sortant du restaurant]

In constructions like (203) the gerund can perhaps be analysed as a complement of the verb:

(203)       L'inflation va croissant.   'Inflation is on the increase'

Given the similarity in meaning with *L'inflation est en train d'augmenter*, one might envisage a Subject-raising analysis for (203):

(204)      [∅ va [l'inflation croissant]]

However, the construction in (203) is rare in Modern French and is restricted to a few fixed expressions such as *aller diminuant, aller grandissant*. It would therefore be inaccurate to conclude that there is a productive Subject-raising process with gerunds in French.

### Exercises

1   Look up the following words in one or more good dictionaries (monolingual or bilingual):

> *certain, exiger, faillir, manquer, permettre, risquer, susceptible, tendre*

Do the entries provide adequate guidance on the ways in which these words can be used with an infinitival complement? If not, suggest ways of improving these entries.

2   In English, the subject of an infinitive can often be specified by using a construction with *for*:

(a)  It would be interesting for Marie to visit Paris
(b)  It would be interesting for these results to be published

From the meaning of these examples and the data below, try to determine whether *Marie* and *these results* are actual subjects of the infinitive or objects of the preposition *for* (controlling the understood subject of the infinitive):

(c)  For Marie to visit Paris would be interesting
(d)  For these results to be published would be interesting
(e)  To visit Paris would be interesting for Marie
(f)  *To be published would be interesting for these results

In the light of your conclusions, how can you account for the French examples below:

(a)  Il serait intéressant pour Marie de visiter Paris
(b)  *Il serait intéressant pour ces résultats d'être publiés
(c)  *Pour Marie de visiter Paris serait intéressant
(d)  *Pour ces résultats d'être publiés serait intéressant
(e)  Visiter Paris serait intéressant pour Marie
(f)  *Être publiés serait intéressant pour ces résultats

3    Ruwet (1972, ch. 2) observes that under certain conditions the clitic *en* attached to an infinitive can be interpreted as a complement of the subject of the main clause in constructions of the Subject-raising type (see 6.6.3 for discussion of this phenomenon in simple sentences):

(a)  L'auteur semble en être intelligent
     = L'auteur de ce livre semble être intelligent

However, this is not possible in Control constructions:

(b)  *L'auteur prétend en être intelligent

How can this difference be accounted for in terms of the analyses proposed in 9.2.1 and 9.2.4?

What conclusions can we draw from the following examples, where the phrases in parentheses indicate possible translations for the subject?

|     |                                                  |                                                |
| --- | ------------------------------------------------ | ---------------------------------------------- |
| (c) | La préface a l'air d'en être intéressante        | ('the preface of the book')                    |
| (d) | L'auteur commence à en être célèbre              | ('the author of the book')                     |
| (e) | Les résultats méritent d'en être publiés         | ('the results of the experiment')              |
| (f) | L'analyse ne prétend pas en être exhaustive      | ('the analysis of these facts')                |
| (g) | Les conclusions exigent d'en être prises au sérieux | ('the conclusions of the research')         |

4    Which of the following meanings can be expressed by the sentence: *Il me semble avoir compris*?

(a)  'He seems to me to have understood'
(b)  'It seems to me that I have understood'
(c)  'He seems to have understood me'

Explain your answer by giving appropriate structures and derivations.

5    Using examples of your own, discuss the correspondences between *pouvoir* (in various tenses, with and without auxiliaries) and English *can/could*, *may/might* and other expressions like *be able*. Does the distinction between 'epistemic' and 'root' modality offer any insight into this question?

6 In (a) *se* can be used to refer back to *Pierre*, but this is not possible in (b) (intended interpretation: 'It seems to Pierre that he (Pierre) has solved the problem'):

    (a) Pierre s'est permis d'interrompre le professeur

    (b) *Pierre se semble avoir résolu le problème

Explain this difference

7 Comment on the differences in meaning and/or acceptability (if any) between the following pairs of sentences:

    (a) Le patron a fait écrire une lettre à sa secrétaire
        Le patron a fait écrire une lettre par sa secrétaire
    (b) La marquise a fait nettoyer le tapis à la servante
        La marquise a fait nettoyer le tapis par la servante
    (c) J'ai entendu chanter cette aria par La Callas
        J'ai entendu La Callas chanter cette aria
    (d) Jules a laissé sortir le chien
        Jules a laissé le chien sortir
    (e) J'ai entendu dire des bêtises à Luc
        J'ai entendu Luc dire des bêtises

8 With the help of a native speaker, try to establish the differences in meaning and/or acceptability between lexical and syntactic causatives in the following examples:

    (a) Les voyous ont {brisé / fait briser} la vitrine
    (b) Le tremblement de terre a {brisé / fait briser} la vitrine
    (c) Jacques a {fondu / fait fondre} deux sucres dans son café
    (d) Marie a {descendu / fait descendre} les bagages du grenier
    (e) Le guide a {descendu / fait descendre} les touristes dans les catacombes
    (f) Les soldats ont {descendu / fait descendre} les terroristes
    (g) Le pilote a {atterri / fait atterrir} l'avion
    (h) Les aiguilleurs du ciel ont {atterri / fait atterrir} l'avion
    (i) Les terroristes ont {atterri / fait atterrir} l'avion
    (j) Une grosse vague a {renversé / fait renverser} le bateau
    (k) Luc a {mijoté / fait mijoter} le potage pendant une heure

How can these judgements be accounted for?

9 Some grammarians classify *faire* and *laisser* as auxiliary verbs (when they take an infinitive). To what extent and in what respects do these

verbs share the properties of auxiliary verbs discussed in 2.7?

10 Given that *faire* can occur with an indirect object (or perhaps a dative of interest, see 6.8.2) in sentences like *Pierre a fait quelque chose à Luc*, one might analyse sentences like *Pierre a fait boire le café à Luc* as straightforward Control constructions as below:

[Pierre a fait [PRO$_1$ boire le café] à Luc$_1$]

To what extent could this analysis account for the semantic and syntactic properties of such constructions?

**Further reading**

Sandfeld (1965b) provides a solid traditional description of infinitival constructions; see also Réquédat (1980). Within a distributional framework, M. Gross (1975) and Huot (1981) cover many aspects of infinitives.

On Subject-raising vs Control (with particular reference to the clitic *en*) see Ruwet (1972, ch. 2: 1982, ch. 1), and in a more cautionary vein Ruwet (1983a, 1983b); also Couquaux (1980), Rooryck (1990). Pollock (1978) discusses Subject-raising in relation to various other processes. The relevance of Case theory to the syntax of infinitives is developed in Pollock (1984). On the semantics of Control constructions, see Fauconnier (1974, 1976, 1980). For discussion of *pouvoir* and *devoir*, see Sueur (1977). On *sûr* and *certain*, see Casagrande (1974).

The analysis of infinitives with *faire*, etc., is adapted from Kayne (1975) who discusses these constructions extensively, particularly with respect to Clitic-placement; for other generative approaches see J.-Y. Morin (1978), Rouveret & Vergnaud (1980), Pijnenburg & Hulk (1989), Reed (1991, 1992), Authier & Reed (1991) and, from a cross-linguistic perspective, Aissen (1979), Radford (1978). On semantic properties of *faire* constructions see Cannings & Moody (1978) and, with regard to lexical vs syntactic causatives, Ruwet (1972, ch. 4). The passive-like construction with *se faire* is discussed in detail in Kupferman (1995), Tasmowski-De Ryck & van Oevelen (1987).

On infinitival particles, see Long (1976), Huot (1981).

# 10
# Inversion and QU-movement

## 10.1 Overview

**Inversion** is the traditional term for the process of reversing the normal order of the subject and the verb. **QU- movement** (sometimes called 'WH- movement' even in discussions of French) is the term which will be used here for movement of expressions such as *qui, quand, où, combien*, etc., to the beginning of the sentence in questions and other constructions. Although these two processes are independent of each other, in the sense that one can occur without the other, there are many constructions whose properties can be elucidated in terms of interaction between these processes. For this reason it makes sense to discuss them together.

The main thrust of the discussion in 10.2 is that there are two fundamentally different types of Inversion in French which are distinguished in terms of their structural properties and the types of sentence in which they occur. In 10.3, a closer look is taken at the structural properties of these two types of Inversion and the conditions under which they are used or avoided.

In 10.4, we will look in greater detail at the operation of Inversion and QU-movement in questions of various types, paying particular attention to the conditions which govern the use of the interrogative pronouns *qui, que* and *quoi* and the syntactic properties of other QU- items (notably *quel, pourquoi* and *combien*) which behave in rather different ways from their English counterparts.

In 10.5, we will investigate the role of QU- movement in the analysis of relative clauses, looking at the different types of relative clauses and the properties of certain relative pronouns (particularly *dont*) which pose problems for students of French. A dominant issue in this discussion concerns the status of *que* and *qui* – are they relative pronouns analogous to English *who* or *which* (as traditional grammarians tend to assume) or complementisers corresponding to English *that*? This issue is explored further in 10.6 where the distinction between complementisers and moved QU- items is used to account for some apparently puzzling differences between different types of exclamative constructions, and in 10.7, where we will consider a range of constructions which look like relative clauses but which actually have rather different properties.

In this chapter, the 'X-bar' analysis of clause structure outlined in 1.4.3 is adopted, where the Inflection element (I) is taken to be the head of S (now relabelled IP) and the Complementiser (C) is the head of S′ (now relabelled CP). The main reason for adopting this approach is that it enables the structural positions of moved elements (QU- expressions and 'inverted' verbs) to be defined more precisely. For readers who are confused by this 'new' notation, the important points to remember are that IP corresponds to S and that CP corresponds to S′.

### 10.2 Types of Inversion
#### 10.2.1 Inversion in questions
In French, as in English, yes/no questions can be formed by means of Inversion:

(1)  a  Il est arrivé          ⇒    Est-il arrivé?
     b  He has arrived        ⇒    Has he arrived?

However, the apparent similarity between the cases in (1) obscures two important differences between English and French, which have already been mentioned in earlier chapters.

In English, this Inversion process is possible only with certain 'light' verbs (auxiliaries and *be*), but it can apply with all types of verb in French:

(2)  a  Il arrivait  ⇒    Arrivait-il?
     b  He arrived ⇒    *Arrived he?

Conversely, in French this process can only apply when the subject is a clitic pronoun, not a full NP or a disjunctive pronoun such as *cela* (see 6.2.1), a restriction which does not hold in English:

(3)  a  Pierre est arrivé            ⇒    *Est Pierre arrivé?
     b  Les autres iront en taxi     ⇒    *Iront les autres en taxi?
     c  Cela est vrai               ⇒    *Est cela vrai?

(4)  a  Pierre has arrived           ⇒    Has Pierre arrived?
     b  The others will go by taxi   ⇒    Will the others go by taxi?
     c  That is true                ⇒    Is that true?

In cases like (3), in order to form a question by means of Inversion we must insert an appropriate subject clitic after the finite verb in addition to the existing subject:

(5)  a  Pierre est-il arrivé?
     b  Les autres iront-ils en taxi?
     c  Cela est-il possible?

Informally, if the subject is not a clitic pronoun, an appropriate subject clitic is added and inverted with the verb.

464

Given that the element which is placed after the verb in the French cases illustrated above is always a subject clitic, the term **Subject-clitic Inversion** (abbreviated to S U B J - C L - I N V) will be used to refer to the processes involved. Examples like (1a) and (2a) illustrate the **simple** form of S U B J - C L - I N V, whereas those in (5) involve a **complex** version of this process, where the clitic is used in addition to the normal NP subject.

The same types of Inversion are also found in **partial questions** (questions which request specific information rather than a yes/no answer):

(6)      a  Quand est-il arrivé?

          b  Pourquoi prendra-t-on le métro?

          c  Quand ton père est-t-il arrivé?

          d  Dans quelle voiture les autres iront-ils?

          e  Comment cela est-il possible?

However, in 'partial' questions a rather different type of Inversion is often possible:

(7)      a  Quand est arrivé ton père?

          b  Quel journal lisent les hommes d'affaires?

          c  Dans quelle voiture iront les autres?

The process illustrated in (7) differs from the S U B J - C L - I N V processes in (6) in a number of respects. Firstly, and most obviously, the subject which is inverted with the verb is a full NP, not a clitic pronoun. Secondly, in examples with a compound tense, the full NP is placed after the participle (as in (7a) – cf. *Quand est ton père arrivé?*) whereas in parallel cases like (6a, c) the subject clitic must occur after the first verb (the auxiliary) – cf. *Quand (ton père) est arrivé-t-il?*. Thirdly, the range of constructions in which the two types of Inversion can occur are not the same; for example, S U B J - C L - I N V can occur in yes/no questions but the process in (7) cannot: *Est arrivé ton père?* There are other differences which will be pointed out as the discussion proceeds, but the above observations consititute a prima facie case for treating the process in (7) as a separate phenomenon – this process will be referred to as **Stylistic-inversion** (abbreviated as S T Y L - I N V). The properties of these different types of Inversion can be summarised informally as follows:

**S U B J - C L - I N V:**

**(Simple)** *If the subject is a clitic pronoun, it is placed immediately after the first verb*

**(Complex)** *If the subject is a full NP or a disjunctive pronoun, it remains in the preverbal position and a corresponding subject clitic is placed immediately after the first verb.*

**STYL-INV:**

*The subject NP (not a clitic pronoun) is inverted with the whole of the verbal complex (the main verb and its accompanying auxiliaries).*

In indirect questions, we usually find the normal (subject – verb) order:

(8)        a   Je ne sais pas [quand ton père est arrivé]

            b   Je me demande [quel journal les hommes d'affaires lisent]

            c   Marie veut savoir [dans quelle voiture les autres iront]

Moreover, both forms of s u b j - c l - i n v are excluded in indirect questions, just as in (Standard) English we cannot invert the subject with the auxiliary (*\*I wonder when did your father arrive*):

(9)        a   *Je ne sais pas [quand (ton père) est-il arrivé]

            b   *Je me demande [quel journal les hommes d'affaires lisent-ils]

            c   *Marie veut savoir [dans quelle voiture ira-t-on]

However, s t y l - i n v can apply in indirect questions:

(10)       a   Je ne sais pas [quand est arrivé ton père]

           b   Je me demande [quel journal lisent les hommes d'affaires]

           c   Marie veut savoir [dans quelle voiture iront les autres]

The effect of s t y l - i n v in these cases is to achieve a more balanced sentence-structure in which the verb occupies a central position within its clause. This tendency is particularly strong when the subject is relatively long (as in (10b)). However, although style is a motivating factor, it is not the sole consideration. In particular, s t y l - i n v never applies in indirect questions of the yes/no type (introduced by *si*) even when the subject is fairly long, as in (11c):

(11)       a   *Je ne sais pas [si est arrivé ton père]

           b   *Je me demande [si dorment les petits]

           c   *Marie veut savoir [si viendront les personnes qu'elle a invitées]

In these cases, the normal subject – verb order must be retained:

(12)       a   Je ne sais pas [si ton père est arrivé]

           b   Je me demande [si les petits dorment]

           c   Marie veut savoir [si les personnes qu'elle a invitées viendront]

The pattern of Inversion in interrogative constructions can be summarised as follows: s u b j - c l - i n v (simple and complex) occurs in direct questions ('partial' and 'yes/no'); s t y l - i n v occurs in 'partial' questions with a preposed QU- item (direct and indirect).

The fact that both types of Inversion are possible in direct 'partial' questions (*Quand (ton père) est-il arrivé?*, *Quand est arrivé ton père?*) follows from the fact that these constructions satisfy both of the conditions given above.

> There is also a correspondence with English. As we have seen, in English, Inversion of the subject and the auxiliary (henceforth SUBJ-AUX-INV) occurs in direct questions; i.e. in the same constructions as SUBJ-CL-INV (*(When) did your father arrive?*). However, English also has an analogue of STYL-INV which can occur marginally in 'partial' questions (direct or indirect), in a rather literary style when the subject is indefinite and particularly long: *Where can be found a solution to all these problems?*, *I do not know where can be found a solution to all these problems.* This phenomenon is much less common and more severely restricted than STYL-INV in French, but it illustrates a cross-linguistic correspondence which we will find in other Inversion contexts.

### 10.2.2 Further cases of Stylistic-inversion

Relative clauses (like the bracketed sequences in (13)) resemble 'partial' indirect questions in that they allow STYL-INV, as in (14), but not SUBJ-CL-INV, as shown in (15):

(13)  a  le lit [dans lequel la cousine de la reine a dormi]
      b  le journal [que la plupart des téléspectateurs lisent]

(14)  a  le lit [dans lequel a dormi la cousine de la reine]
      b  le journal [que lisent la plupart des téléspectateurs]

(15)  a  *le lit [dans lequel (la cousine de la reine) a-t-elle dormi]
      b  *le journal [que (la plupart des téléspectateurs) lisent-ils]

A similar pattern is observed in exclamative constructions like those in (16):

(16)  a  Quel bruit les voisins ont     'What a noise the neighbours made!'
         fait!
      b  Quelle chance Pierre           'What luck Pierre had!'
         a eue!

Application of SUBJ-CL-INV to these examples yields well-formed sentences, but they must be interpreted as questions (e.g. 'What noise did the neighbours make?') not as exclamations ('What a noise the neighbours made!'):

(17)  a  Quel bruit (les voisins) ont-ils fait?
      b  Quelle chance (Pierre) a-t-il eue?

This observation bears out the correspondence between SUBJ-CL-INV and direct questions proposed in 10.2.1 – note that the English versions given above show the same pattern with regard to Inversion of the subject and the auxiliary. However, STYL-INV is possible in cases like (16):

(18)      a   Quel bruit ont fait les voisins!

           b   Quelle chance a eue Pierre!

A common property of relative clauses and the exclamatives illustrated above, which they share with 'partial' questions, is that they are derived by QU- movement. For example, the relative clause in (13a) and the exclamation (16a) can be derived from structures analogous to *La cousine de la reine a dormi dans ce lit* and *Les voisins ont fait tant de bruit*, roughly as in (19):

(19)      a   [la cousine de la reine a dormi [dans lequel]]

           b   [les voisins ont fait [quel bruit]]

Thus, the possibility of STYL-INV in (14) and (18) further illustrates the correlation between STYL-INV and QU- movement, with the effect of reestablishing a balanced sentence pattern with the verb in the middle.

This stylistic effect can also be seen in examples like (20)–(21):

(20)      a   Un magnétophone se trouvait sur la table

           b   La nouvelle autoroute passera près d'ici

           c   Le jour de la liberté arrivera bientôt

(21)      a   Sur la table se trouvait un magnétophone

           b   Près d'ici passera la nouvelle autoroute

           c   Bientôt arrivera le jour de la liberté

Although these examples do not involve QU- expressions, it seems reasonable to suppose that the examples in (21) are derived by moving the expressions of place or time to the beginning of the sentence with compensatory application of STYL-INV to reestablish the balance of the sentence.

None of the constructions reviewed above allow SUBJ-AUX-INV in English, but some of them do allow the analogue of STYL-INV: e.g. in relative clauses – *a magazine in which can be found many interesting articles* – and with a preposed expression of place – *On the table could be seen a tape-recorder.*

A further instance of STYL-INV which does not correlate with fronting of an element is found in certain types of complement clause, almost always in the subjunctive:

(22)  a   Le ministre exige que soient réalisées toutes les réformes qui avaient été promises avant les élections

      b   Cette campagne a été entreprise pour que renaisse cet esprit de solidarité nationale qui régnait pendant la guerre

This construction, which is confined to formal usage, is generally possible only when the verb in the complement is passive or expresses the existence of the subject entity (rather than describing an action performed by this entity). The function of Inversion in this case seems to be to place the most important or informative element in the clause (the subject NP) at the end of the sentence. Note also that this use of Inversion is especially favoured when the subject NP is particularly long or complex. These conditions are rather similar to those which govern the marginal cases of SUBJ-CL-INV in English.

### 10.2.3 Subject-clitic Inversion in 'peut-être' constructions

In formal registers, sentences introduced by certain 'modal' adverbs or 'sentence connectives' (see 7.5.5) such as *peut-être, sans doute, à peine, aussi* and *encore* (with the sense 'even so') normally undergo SUBJ-CL-INV (simple or complex):

(23)  a  Peut-être (Marie) reviendra-t-elle

      b  À peine (Gaston) était-il sorti que le bâtiment s'est écroulé

      c  C'est un problème difficile; encore faut-il le résoudre

In less formal registers, SUBJ-CL-INV is often avoided by using the complementiser *que* or by placing the adverb within the clause:

(24)  a  Peut-être que Marie reviendra bientôt

      b  Marie reviendra peut-être bientôt

However, STYL-INV does not occur with adverbs of this type:

(25)  a  *Peut-être reviendra ton père

      b  *À peine étaient sortis les habitants que le bâtiment s'est écroulé

It is assumed here that the items in (23) originate in the sentence-initial position, unlike the adverbial expressions in 10.2.2 (21) which are moved to this position. Thus, the impossibility of examples like (25) is consistent with the view that STYL-INV typically compensates for movement of some element to the beginning of the clause. In this connection, the adverb *ainsi* shows an interesting pattern. When it occurs after the verb, as in (26a), it has a manner interpretation ('like that'), but in sentence-initial position, as in (26b), it can function as a sentence connective ('and so ...'):

(26)  a  L'histoire s'est terminée ainsi   ('That is how the story ended')

      b  Ainsi, l'histoire s'est terminée   ('And so the story came to an end')

Note now that if *ainsi* in (26a) is preposed, it induces STYL-INV with the same meaning as (26a):

(27)     Ainsi s'est terminée l'histoire

However, as a sentence connective, it optionally triggers SUBJ-CL-INV (like *aussi* or *encore*) giving (28) with the same meaning as (26b):

(28)     Ainsi l'histoire s'est-elle terminée

The possibility of SUBJ-CL-INV in cases like (23) shows that this process is not restricted to direct questions. Nevertheless, at a very intuitive level, we may postulate a semantic similarity between direct questions and sentences like those in (23). Direct questions, by definition, are not statements of fact but they call on the addressee to provide a truth-value ('yes' or 'no') or specific information, corresponding to the QU- phrase, which will make the proposition true. In a similar vein, adverbs like *peut-être* and (rather paradoxically) *sans doute* express doubt concerning the truth of the proposition. Admittedly, it is less easy to see how this observation might apply to some of the other items listed above (e.g. *aussi* or *encore*) except in so far as they convey hints about the way in which the clause is to be interpreted (e.g. in terms of relevance to the immediate context).

Generally, the English counterparts of these items do not trigger Inversion (an exception being *hardly* (*à peine*): *Hardly had he left when . . .*). However, placement of negative adverbs at the beginning of the sentence induces SUBJ-AUX-INV: *Never had she seen such a thing.* As was noted in 7.6.5, Inversion does not occur in similar constructions in French: *Jamais elle n'avait vu une chose pareille.* Nevertheless, this evidence suggests an association between the Inversion processes found in direct questions (SUBJ-CL-INV and SUBJ-AUX-INV) and some concept of 'modality', though the relevant type of modality is different in the two languages: negation in English vs doubt or 'contextually dependent relevance' in French.

### 10.2.4  Subject-clitic Inversion in condition clauses

In literary French, a construction with SUBJ-CL-INV can be used instead of the more usual construction with *si* (cf. English *Had he arrived on time...*):

(29)     a   S'il était arrivé à l'heure, nous l'aurions vu
         b   {Fût-il / Serait-il} arrivé à l'heure, nous l'aurions vu

Note that the finite verb form in this construction occurs in the imperfect subjunctive or the conditional, as opposed to the imperfect indicative in the *si* construction (see 4.8.1). Parallel examples with the complex form of Inversion are rather rarer, but possible, as in the following example from Grévisse (1964):

(30)     Le danger {fût-il / serait-il} dix fois plus grand, je l'affronterais
         encore

In these constructions, the link between SUBJ-CL-INV and modality is clear – the condition clause expresses a hypothetical or counterfactual proposition.

### 10.2.5 Incises

In all the cases discussed so far, the simple and complex forms of SUBJ-CL-INV go hand-in-hand (they are permitted or excluded in the same range of constructions), but there is no significant correlation between either of these two types and STYL-INV. However, there is one case where we find both STYL-INV and the simple form of SUBJ-CL-INV, but the complex form of SUBJ-CL-INV is not possible. This is the case of phrases such as *demanda-t-elle, pensent-ils, semble-t-il*, sometimes referred to in French as **incises**, parenthetical expressions used to attribute direct quotations or opinions:

(31)  a «L'argent, disait ma mère, ne fait pas le bonheur»
    b «L'argent, disait-elle, ne fait pas le bonheur»
    c *«L'argent, ma mère disait-elle, ne fait pas le bonheur»

*Incises* do not share the properties which are typically associated with either type of Inversion – there is no movement of an element to the beginning of the sentence, nor do they have any distinctive modal properties of the sort found in other cases of SUBJ-CL-INV. They are also peculiar from a cross-linguistic viewpoint. English allows Inversion in these constructions, though less systematically than French: *'Money', said she, 'is the root of all evil', 'Money', said my mother, 'is the root of all evil.'* However, the type of Inversion involved here is clearly not SUBJ-AUX-INV, which would give *\*'Money', did {she / my mother} say, . . .*, nor does it resemble the variety of STYL-INV noted in other cases (it can occur with subjects which are pronouns or other 'short' NPs). Possibly the function of Inversion in these cases is to indicate that the *incise* is not part of the quotation, by placing the verb before the subject. If this suggestion is on the right track, the impossibility of complex SUBJ-CL-INV might be accounted for on the grounds that it does not yield a reversal of the order of the lexical subject and the verb, unlike STYL-INV and the simple form of SUBJ-CL-INV.

### 10.2.6 Inversion contexts: a summary

The observations concerning the constructions in which Inversion can occur and the types of Inversion involved are summarised in table 10.1 (see p. 472).

The distribution of ticks and crosses in table 10.1 clearly supports the view that the simple and complex forms of SUBJ-CL-INV are variants of the same process. This conclusion conflicts with the practice of many traditional grammarians, who subsume simple SUBJ-CL-INV and STYL-INV under a single category of 'simple inversion', as opposed to 'complex inversion', making a finer distinction within

Table 10.1. *Inversion contexts*

| Construction type | SUBJ-CL-INV Complex | Simple | STYL-INV |
|---|:---:|:---:|:---:|
| Direct yes/no questions | ✓ | ✓ | ✗ |
| Direct 'partial' questions | ✓ | ✓ | ✓ |
| Indirect 'partial' questions | ✗ | ✗ | ✓ |
| Exclamatives | ✗ | ✗ | ✓ |
| Relative clauses | ✗ | ✗ | ✓ |
| Sentences with preposed adverbials | ✗ | ✗ | ✓ |
| Existential complement clauses | ✗ | ✗ | ✓ |
| Sentences with modal adverbs (*peut-être*, etc.) | ✓ | ✓ | ✗ |
| Condition clauses without *si* | ✓ | ✓ | ✗ |
| *Incises* | ✗ | ✓ | ✓ |

'simple inversion' according to whether the subject is a pronoun or a full NP. In fact, the only case which systematically reflects the traditional dichotomy is that of *incises*, which, as we saw in 10.2.5, show other peculiarities and can reasonably be treated as a special case.

The constructions reviewed above do not exhaust the range of cases in which Inversion of the subject is possible, but they can be taken as representative of the typical cases. Although it is difficult to identify any single feature which defines the conditions appropriate to each type of Inversion, we have seen that SUBJ-CL-INV tends to be associated with certain modal properties of the sentence whereas STYL-INV, as its label suggests, is a stylistic process which is exploited to achieve a more balanced (verb-central) structure when some item has been fronted from the postverbal position or, in some cases (as in the examples in (22) in 10.2.2), to place a particularly heavy or informative subject NP in the final position of the clause.

### 10.3  The syntax of Inversion

#### 10.3.1  Simple Subject-clitic Inversion

In the simple case of SUBJ-CL-INV the clitic subject pronoun is placed after the first verb (i.e. the verb which bears the finite tense inflection) regardless of whether it is a main verb or an auxiliary. Like other clitics, the postverbal subject forms a close syntactic unit with the verb, which is reflected in pronunciation by obligatory liaison in cases like *Voit-il?* [vwatil] and by the insertion of [t] to avoid hiatus between vowels (*Viendra-t-il?*) and, in writing, by the obligatory use of a hyphen. Like other clitics, the inverted pronoun cannot be separated from the verb by any other element: *\*Ne viendra pas il?* vs *Ne viendra-t-il pas?*

For some reason, the first-person singular pronoun *je* does not readily undergo SUBJ-CL-INV, except with a few very common verbs; e.g. *?Cours-je?* is decidedly odd compared with *Courons-nous?, Court-il?,* etc. Moreover, where SUBJ-CL-INV does occur with *je,* there is sometimes a distinctive inflection on the verb. The clearest case of this is with the verb *pouvoir* where we have *Puis-je . . .* as opposed to *Je peux . . .* In highly formal styles, the final 'mute' *-e* of some finite verb forms is changed to *-é* (pronounced as an open [ɛ]) before *je*: e.g. *Je monte,* but *Monté-je?*

In principle, SUBJ-CL-INV could be effected either by moving the subject clitic rightwards across the verb or by moving the verb to the left. Among generative linguists, the latter view is generally favoured, though the issue is not particularly important for practical purposes. See 10.3.6 for some discussion.

### 10.3.2   A note on 'est-ce que'

It will be assumed here that the interrogative sentence (32a) is derived from the declarative sentence (32b) by application of SUBJ-CL-INV to *c'est*:

(32)    a  Est-ce que Pierre est malade?
        b  C'est que Pierre est malade

However, sentences like (32b) have certain discourse properties which are not shared by examples like (32a). Typically, the use of *c'est que . . .* implies that the sentence is offered as an explanation for some state of affairs – e.g. sentence (32b) might be appropriate as a reply to someone who has just remarked that the doctor's car is parked outside the house next door, but could not be used naturally to initiate a conversation. However, questions such as (32a) do not necessarily carry any such implications. Thus, in terms of its function within the discourse, (32a) corresponds to the simple sentence *Pierre est malade,* rather than to (32b). Note also that *est-ce que* can be combined with *c'est que* to form the question corresponding to (32b), as in (33a), even though its non-inverted counterpart (33b) is ungrammatical:

(33)    a  Est-ce que c'est que Pierre est malade?
        b  *C'est que c'est que Pierre est malade

A further difference between the two constructions in (32) is that the declarative construction (32b) can be used in a variety of tenses, but the interrogative construction (32a) can only be used in the present tense (e.g. *C'était que . . . , Ce sera que . . .* are possible but not *\*Était-ce que . . .* or *\*Sera-ce que . . .*). Similarly, *C'est que* in (32b) can be modified by adverbs such as *peut-être,* to indicate a tentative explanation for a state of affairs (as in (34b)), whereas *Est-ce que* cannot:

(34)    a  *Est-ce peut-être que Pierre est malade?
        b  C'est peut-être que Pierre est malade

These observations have led some linguists to suggest that *est-ce que* is not the inverted form of *c'est que*, but that it has acquired the status of an interrogative particle, perhaps a complementiser, /ɛsk/.

Nevertheless, there are other arguments which point in the opposite direction. In 'partial' questions where the questioned element is the subject, the final *que* changes to *qui* (as in relative clauses – see 10.5.7): *Qu'est-ce qui est arrivé?* vs *Qu'est-ce que tu fais?* This suggests that the final *que*, at least, functions as an independent element. Moreover, in colloquial speech the non-inverted form *c'est que* is often used in 'partial' questions without the connotations associated with cases like (32b) above: *Qui c'est qui est venu?*

### 10.3.3 Complex inversion and left-dislocation

Superficially, cases of complex inversion, like (35a), resemble left-dislocated constructions such as (35b) (see 1.5.5):

(35)      a    Marie parle-t-elle anglais?
           b    Marie, elle parle anglais

In both cases we have duplication of an NP (*Marie*), which is understood as the subject, by an appropriate subject pronoun. Thus, it might be supposed that the effect of complex inversion in (35) is merely the result of applying simple SUBJ-CL-INV to the dislocated sentence (35b). However, there are a number of considerations which invalidate this hypothesis.

Firstly, in left-dislocated constructions the initial NP is usually separated from the rest of the sentence by a pause or break in the intonation contour (indicated by the comma) which is absent in cases like (35a). Similarly, the dislocated NP in cases like (35b) is usually singled out as being particularly salient in the discourse, either to confirm the referent as a topic ('As for Marie, she speaks English') or for a contrastive effect (e.g. *Marie, elle parle anglais, mais pas les autres*), whereas the interrogative construction (35a) is neutral in this respect. More generally, left-dislocation occurs predominantly in colloquial speech whereas the use of complex SUBJ-CL-INV as in (35a) is largely confined to formal usage. Although these objections are not conclusive, they shed doubt on the idea that (35a) is simply the interrogative version of (35b).

These doubts are confirmed by more concrete syntactic evidence. In cases of complex inversion with *cela* as subject, the resumptive pronoun is always *il*:

(36)      a    Cela est-il important?
           b    Cela te gêne-t-il?

However, when *cela* is a left-dislocated subject, the resumptive pronoun is *ce* (with *être*) or *ça* (with other verbs), but never *il*:

(37)     a   Cela, c'est important
         b   Cela, ça me gêne

(38)     a   *Cela, il est important
         b   *Cela, il me gêne

Consequently, examples like (36) cannot be treated as inverted versions of dislocated constructions.

A similar point can be made for cases where the subject is a negative pronoun, where again the resumptive pronoun is *il* in inverted constructions:

(39)     a   Personne ne m'aidera-t-il?
         b   Rien ne vous amuse-t-il?

Items like *personne* and *rien* cannot be dislocated, presumably because they do not designate an entity which can be singled out as a topic. Consequently, there are no left-dislocated sentences which could provide a source for the examples in (39):

(40)     a   *Personne, il (ne) m'aidera
         b   *Rien, il (ne) m'amuse

A further syntactic distinction concerns the position of the NP relative to QU-expressions. In cases of complex inversion, the full NP subject occurs between the QU- expression and the verb:[1]

(41)     a   Pourquoi cela te gêne-t-il?
         b   *Cela pourquoi te gêne-t-il?

(42)     a   *Pourquoi cela ça te gêne?
         b   Cela, pourquoi ça te gêne?

This evidence points to two fundamental differences between complex inversion and left-dislocation. Firstly, left-dislocated NPs occupy a more peripheral structural position than the NP subject in cases of complex inversion. Secondly, in dislocated constructions, the resumptive pronoun is always the one that would be used if the dislocated NP were absent (e.g. *ce* or *ça* when referring to an idea or when pointing at something – see 6.4.2), whereas the clitic in cases of complex inversion appears to simply duplicate the grammatical features of the subject NP (i.e. number and gender, with masculine singular *il* as the default form for items like *cela, personne* and *rien* which have no grammatical gender).

[1] In (41) and (42) examples with *cela* have been used to make the distinction between complex inversion and left-dislocation clearer through the choice of resumptive pronoun. In (42), a non-inverted question form has been used since this is stylistically most compatible with left-dislocation.

Many English students of French appear to confuse complex inversion with left-dislocation. In many cases (like (35a)) this has no adverse effect since the resulting sequence is the same. However, this confusion may lead the student to produce deviant sentences like *??Marie, quand arrivera-t-elle?* (or, with right-dislocation, *??Quand arrivera-t-elle, Marie?*). From a purely syntactic viewpoint, these sentences may be deemed grammatical (as inverted versions of dislocated sentences), but they are stylistically incongruent in so far as dislocation is largely confined to colloquial registers whereas SUBJ-CL-INV is characteristic of formal style. To avoid such stylistic conflict, one would either use complex inversion (*Quand Marie arrivera-t-elle?*) in a formal style or, in colloquial speech, dislocation with *est-ce que* (*Marie, quand est-ce qu'elle arrivera?*, *Quand est-ce qu'elle arrivera, Marie?*) or, still less formally, a non-inverted structure (*Marie, elle arrivera quand?*, *Elle arrivera quand, Marie?*).

### 10.3.4  Stylistic-inversion
In certain respects, Stylistic-inversion resembles the NP-postposing process which was suggested tentatively in the earlier discussion of derived impersonal constructions (see 3.4.3). In particular, it appears to involve movement of the subject to a position within the VP – more specifically, to the direct object position. This approach is problematic from a theoretical viewpoint in that it involves a lowering operation, but for descriptive purposes it provides an adequate basis for discussion.

As in the case of derived impersonals, the presence of certain complements such as direct objects blocks the application of STYL-INV (but not SUBJ-CL-INV). For instance, we can form a 'partial' question based on the proposition *Jean résoudra le problème* by means of either form of SUBJ-CL-INV, but not by means of STYL-INV:

(43)     a  Comment (Pierre) résoudra-t-il le problème?
         b  *Comment résoudra Pierre le problème?
         c  *Comment résoudra le problème Pierre?

The same restriction holds in relative clauses and other constructions which normally allow STYL-INV:

(44)     a  l'étudiant à qui le professeur a prêté un livre
         b  *l'étudiant à qui a prêté le professeur un livre
         c  *l'étudiant à qui a prêté un livre le professeur

(45)     a  Mes parents construiront une maison près d'ici
         b  *Près d'ici construiront mes parents une maison
         c  *Près d'ici construiront une maison mes parents

STYL-INV is also inapplicable in constructions with the verb *être* followed by a complement (e.g. an AP or PP):

(46)      a   *Dans quelle mesure est ce livre intéressant?

            b   *Dans quelle mesure est intéressant ce livre?

(47)      a   *Depuis combien de temps est ton frère à Paris?

            b   *Depuis combien de temps est à Paris ton frère?

However, these restrictions do not apply when the element which normally blocks STYL-INV undergoes QU- movement. For example, the underlying structure (48a) contains a direct object (*quel problème*) which would normally prevent STYL-INV (as in (43b, c) above), but when the direct object is preposed, as in (48b) STYL-INV can apply to give sentence (48c):

(48)      a   [Pierre résoudra quel problème]

            b   quel problème [Pierre résoudra __ ]

            c   Quel problème résoudra Pierre?

Similarly, in (49) the QU- element corresponds to the complement of *être* which blocked STYL-INV in (46)–(47):

(49)      a   Comment est ce livre?

            b   Où est ton frère?

Note that in cases like (48) the combined effect of QU- movement and STYL-INV is to reverse the position of the subject and direct object in relation to the verb, giving a mirror-image of the normal subject–verb–object order. Generally, constructions of this type are possible only when there is no risk of confusion over the roles of the two NPs. Thus, in (48), we can readily interpret *quel problème* as the object and *Pierre* as the subject since it is quite normal for a person to solve a problem but not for a problem to solve a person. Where both NPs are potential subjects or objects of the verb, as in (50), the mirror-image interpretation is excluded: i.e. (50) cannot have the reading 'Which tiger did the hunter kill?', derived by application of QU- movement and STYL-INV to the structure [le chasseur a tué quel tigre], but can only mean 'Which tiger killed the hunter?':

(50)      Quel tigre a tué le chasseur?

The presence of other types of complements (indirect objects, finite or infinitival complement clauses) inhibits STYL-INV to a greater or lesser extent according to a variety of factors, one of which is style. STYL-INV is used (or, according to some grammarians, abused) much more freely in literary style than in 'ordinary' discourse, to the extent that it is possible to find attested literary examples which violate some of the restrictions proposed below. Consequently, the judgements presented in the following discussion should not be taken as absolute.

As a prelude to this discussion, a distinction must be drawn between postverbal expressions which are complements of the verb and those which which modify the verb or the sentence:

(51)     a   *Quand a voté votre père pour le candidat communiste?
         b   Quand a voté votre père pour la première fois?

In (51a), the phrase *pour le candidat communiste* functions as a complement (indirect object) of the verb and cannot be separated from the verb by an inverted subject, but STYL-INV can apply in (51b) where *pour la première fois* acts as a modifying adverbial expression. However, it would be inaccurate to claim that the presence of an indirect object always blocks STYL-INV. In both of the following examples *à ses parents* has the status of a complement, yet (52b) is perfectly acceptable, in contrast to (52a) which is deviant in the same way as (51a):

(52)     a   *Quand téléphonera cette fille à ses parents?
         b   Que dira cette fille à ses parents?

The difference between these two examples is that in (52b) the interrogative pronoun *que* is a direct object which has been moved from a position between the verb and the indirect object, whereas in (52a) *quand* is an interrogative adverb which has been moved from a more peripheral position after the indirect object, as we can see from the corresponding statements in (53):

(53)     a   Cette fille téléphonera à ses parents demain
         b   Cette fille dira ceci à ses parents

It seems then that the gap left by the QU- item in (52b) allows STYL-INV to place the subject in this position, but, in the absence of a gap, the indirect object blocks STYL-INV, as shown in (54):

(54)     a   [quand cette fille téléphonera à ses parents ___ ]
                                    *

         b   [que cette fille dira ___ à ses parents]

In some cases, STYL-INV can place the subject after the indirect object, provided that the subject is a particularly 'heavy' NP – let us call this 'long' STYL-INV, as opposed to 'short' STYL-INV where the subject is placed immediately after the verb:

(55)     a   Quand téléphonera à ses parents cette jeune fille que la police cherche depuis six mois?
         b   *Quand téléphonera à ses parents cette jeune fille?

However, 'long' STYL-INV is blocked by a direct object or complement of *être*, even when the subject is 'heavy':

(56)    a  *Comment résoudra ce problème le nouveau chef de service qui vient d'être nommé?

        b  *Quand était malade cet étudiant qui n'a pas assisté à un seul cours pendant toute l'année?

Complements of copular verbs other than *être* allow 'long' STYL-INV but not 'short' STYL-INV (i.e. they behave like indirect objects in this respect):

(57)    a  Quand deviendra célèbre ce jeune auteur qui n'a pas publié un seul roman?

        b  *Quand deviendra ce jeune homme célèbre?

Finite complement clauses generally block both 'long' and 'short' STYL-INV:

(58)    a  *Quand veut que tu partes le monsieur qui vient d'acheter ton appartement?

        b  *Quand veut le nouveau propriétaire que tu partes?

Infinitival complements also inhibit 'short' STYL-INV, but allow 'long' STYL-INV within certain limits (e.g. the infinitive must not be followed by a direct object):

(59)    a  *Quand commenceront ces étudiants à travailler

        b  Quand commenceront à travailler ces étudiants qui n'ont rien fait pendant toute l'année?

        c  *Quand commenceront a faire leurs devoirs ces étudiants qui n'ont rien fait pendant toute l'année?

With modal verbs which take a bare infinitive (e.g. *pouvoir, devoir, vouloir, aller,...*), even relatively short subjects can be placed after the infinitive:

(60)    a  Quand va partir le train?

        b  Que voulait dire le professeur?

        c  Comment peuvent s'évader les prisonniers?

However, this process is blocked with these verbs when the infinitive is followed by a complement of the sort which normally inhibits STYL-INV:

(61)    a  *Comment pourront résoudre ce problème les étudiants?

        b  *Quand va parler à son patron ton mari?

        c  *Quand va parler ton mari à son patron?

In this respect, modal verbs followed by an infinitive behave in the same way as auxiliary verbs followed by a past participle (see 2.7.4 for some discussion).

    Within the limits outlined above, the semantic importance of the subject relative to that of the verb plays a role in determining the applicability of STYL-INV. For example, items like *quelqu'un* or *cela* which have a fairly low information content do not readily undergo STYL-INV even when the syntactic conditions are satisfied:

(62)      a  ?Comment m'aidera quelqu'un?

           b  ?Quand s'est passé cela?

Conversely, STYL-INV is highly favoured with semantically 'weak' verbs, particularly *être*, as can be seen in (63) where the alternative question forms are decidedly odd, though they are syntactically well formed:

(63)      a  Où est la salle de bains?

           b  ??Où est-ce que la salle de bains est?

           c  ??Où la salle de bains est-elle?

The same preference can be seen in indirect questions, where STYL-INV is usually optional:

(64)      a  Je ne sais pas où est la salle de bains

           b  ?Je ne sais pas où la salle de bains est

The facts illustrated in (62)–(64) can be seen as part of a general tendency to place the most informative elements at the end of the sentence (see 1.5.5).

### 10.3.5  *Avoidance of Inversion*

On the whole, Inversion (of all types) is characteristic of fairly formal styles. The strategies for avoiding Inversion in less formal registers depend on the type of construction, the type of Inversion involved and the degree of informality of the discourse.

In informal speech, STYL-INV tends to be reserved for cases like *Où est la salle de bains?* or *Sur la table se trouvait un magnétophone*, where there is a strong need to place an informative element in final position. Nevertheless, other constructions which achieve the same effect are often preferred at the more colloquial end of the spectrum: e.g. right-dislocation in *Je ne sais pas où elle est, la salle de bains* or an impersonal construction with *il y a* in *Sur la table il y avait un magnétophone*. In most other cases, STYL-INV can be avoided simply by using the normal subject–verb order.

The simple form of SUBJ-CL-INV occurs more readily than the complex form in informal styles. In order to avoid SUBJ-CL-INV, it is usually necessary to make certain readjustments to the syntax of the sentence or to use an alternative construction.

In direct questions, Inversion can be avoided by means of the periphrastic construction with *est-ce que*. This construction is used over a wide range of registers and is not perceived as being particularly colloquial. In casual conversation, we can use normal declarative word order without *est-ce que* (and, in 'partial' questions, without fronting of the QU- item):

(65)  a  Tu aimes le poisson?
      b  Pierre est allé où?

In very colloquial speech, it is also possible to front the QU- item without Inversion when the subject is a clitic pronoun or *ça*:

(66)  a  Où tu vas?
      b  Comment elle s'appelle?
      c  A quoi ça sert?

Note, however, that we cannot use Inversion or *est-ce que* without fronting of the QU- item: *\*Est-il allé où?*, *\*Est-ce qu'elle s'appelle comment?* Another highly colloquial variant of the construction in (66) is to place *que* after the QU- item:

(67)  a  Où que tu vas?
      b  Pourquoi que tu as fait ça?

The use of *que* to avoid SUBJ-CL-INV can also be seen in *incises* and in constructions with modal adverbs:

(68)  «L'argent, qu'elle disait, ne fait pas le bonheur»

(69)  a  Peut-être que Pierre reviendra plus tard
      b  Sans doute qu'elle va amener sa mère

An alternative strategy in cases like (69) is to place the modal adverb within the sentence:

(70)  Pierre reviendra peut-être plus tard

Note that the strategies in (67)–(70) are incompatible with SUBJ-CL-INV:

(71)  a  *Où que vas-tu?
      b  *«L'argent, que disait-elle, ne fait pas le bonheur»
      c  *Peut-être que (Pierre) reviendra-t-il plus tard
      d  *Pierre reviendra-t-il peut-être plus tard

The use of SUBJ-CL-INV to form condition clauses (*Fût-il arrivé à l'heure, nous l'aurions vu* – see 10.2.4) is confined to highly formal style, and is avoided simply by using the construction with *si*: *S'il était arrivé . . .* As in the corresponding English construction, we cannot have *si* and Inversion: *\*Si fût-il / était-il arrivé . . .* (cf. *If he had arrived . . .*, *Had he arrived . . .*, *\*If had he arrived . . .*).

### 10.3.6 *Subject-clitic Inversion and QU- movement*

Among generative linguists, it is widely assumed that SUBJ-CL-INV (and English SUBJ-AUX-INV) involves movement of the verb to the position normally occupied by a complementiser (the C position). In 'partial' questions, it is also assumed that QU- expressions are moved to a position to the left of C. This can be seen clearly in colloquial examples like *Où que tu vas?* where the QU- item *où* precedes the complementiser *que*. In the standard construction *Où vas-tu?*, there is no overt complementiser, but the verb raises to the C position.

These assumptions can be made more precise in terms of the analysis of clause structure envisaged in 1.4.3, where the 'core' sentence (S) is regarded as a projection of the I (inflection) category and S' is a projection of the C category, as shown in (72):

(72)

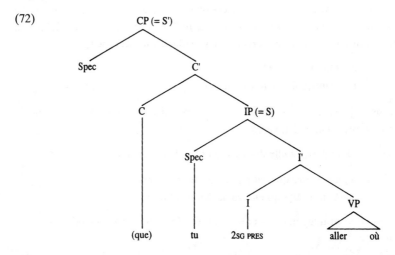

In all cases, the verb must raise to the I position to pick up its tense and agreement features (as discussed in 1.4.3). If nothing else happens, this produces the sentence *Tu vas où?* (similarly, ordinary declaratives like *Pierre va à Paris*, etc.). The general X-bar framework provides a position to the left of C to which the QU- item can be moved – namely the Spec position in CP. Thus, the QU- movement rule can be stated as follows:

**QU- movement:**

$[_{CP}[_{SPEC}\ ]\ C\ [_{IP}\ldots QU\text{-}\ldots]]$

This process gives the (Non-standard) colloquial constructions *Où (que) tu vas?* To derive the standard construction *Où vas-tu?*, the verb previously raised to I is raised one stage further to the C position. In French, this last process is only possible when the subject (in the Spec of IP) is an element which can be cliticised to the verb, a restriction which will simply be stipulated here. These processes are shown in (73):

(73)     $[_{CP}$ où $[_C$ vas$]$ $[_{IP}$ tu I $[_{VP}$ __ __ $]]]$

The idea that S U B J - C L - I N V is movement of the verb to the C position explains the fact, noted in 10.3.5, that, although *que* can often be inserted as an alternative to S U B J - C L - I N V, we cannot have *que* as well as S U B J - C L - I N V. The reason for this is simple: if *que* occupies the C position, the verb cannot move into it. The same explanation applies to the incompatibility between *si* (or English *if*) and Inversion in conditional constructions if conditional *si* is analysed as a complementiser, as many linguists argue (though see 8.3.3–8.3.4).

How complex inversion can be accommodated within this approach is a more contentious issue. For the sake of concreteness, let us assume that a sentence like *Comment cela est-il possible?* is derived from the structure (74):

(74)     $[_{CP}$ Spec C $[_{IP}$ cela I $[_{VP}$ être possible comment$]]]$

As in the case of simple inversion, the QU- item moves to the Spec of CP and the finite verb raises to C via I, giving the structure (75):

(75)     $[_{CP}$ comment est $[_{IP}$ cela I $[_{VP}$ __ possible __ $]]]$

As it stands, this structure is ill-formed because *cela* is not an element which can be cliticised to the verb, contrary to the restriction stipulated above. In order to satisfy this restriction, let us suppose that *cela* moves to a position between the QU- item and the verb in C (e.g. it is adjoined to the C′ node) leaving an appropriate clitic pronoun behind, as shown in (76):

(76)     $[_{CP}$ comment $[_{C'}$ cela $[_{C'}$ est $[_{IP}$ il I $[_{VP}$ __ possible __ $]]]]]$

This analysis raises some theoretical problems, but it captures the idea that the NP subject (*cela*) is the 'real' subject whereas the clitic is simply a copy which encodes its grammatical features (number, person and gender). In a corresponding dislocated construction (e.g. *Cela, comment c'est possible?*), no movement is involved. Rather, the clitic *ce* is the underlying subject and is interpreted as coreferential with the dislocated element *cela* which is inserted independently in a presentential position (perhaps adjoined to CP) to identify the topic of the sentence, as shown in (77):

(77)    $[_{CP}$ cela$_i$ $[_{CP}$ $[_{SPEC}$ $]$ C $[_{IP}$ ce$_i$ I $[_{VP}$ être possible comment]]]]

### 10.4  Interrogative constructions

#### 10.4.1  Interrogative pronouns ('qui', 'que' and 'quoi')

The item *qui* is used to question the identity of a human participant regardless of its grammatical function (subject, object, complement of a preposition):

(78)    a  Qui a volé mon stylo?

        b  Qui as-tu vu?

        c  Pour qui votera Jean?

The same forms are used in 'partial' questions without QU- movement as in (79):

(79)    a  Tu as vu qui?

        b  Jean votera pour qui?

In (78a) we assume that *qui* has been moved into the Spec position in CP, just as in (78b, c), even though this does not affect the linear order of elements. Thus the sentences in (78) are derived as follows, with subsequent Inversion of the subject in the (b) and (c) cases as described in the previous sections:

(80)    a  $[_{CP}$ qui $[_{IP}$ ___ a volé mon stylo]]

        b  $[_{CP}$ qui $[_{IP}$ tu as vu ___ ]]

        c  $[_{CP}$ pour qui $[_{IP}$ Jean votera ___ ]]

The inanimate counterparts to *qui* are *que* and *quoi*, but analysis of these forms is rather less straightforward. When the interrogative pronoun is the complement of a preposition, it assumes the form *quoi* regardless of whether QU- movement is applied:

(81)    a  Vous parlez de quoi?

        b  De quoi parlez-vous?

When the interrogative pronoun is a direct object, it is realised as *quoi* if it remains in the direct object position, but as *que* if it is moved into Spec of CP:

(82)    a  Vous faites quoi?

        b  Que faites-vous?

Neither *que* nor *quoi* can be used to question a subject entity, as in (83):

(83)    a  *Que tracasse Pierre?

        b  *Quoi tracasse Pierre?

In such cases we must use the construction with *qu'est-ce qui*:

(84)      Qu'est-ce qui tracasse Pierre?

The examples in (81) and (82) can be accounted for by postulating *quoi* as the underlying form of the inanimate interrogative pronoun in all cases, with an obligatory rule which changes *quoi* to *que* when it appears alone within CP:

(85)      $[_{CP}$ quoi IP$] \Rightarrow [_{CP}$ que IP$]$

Thus, (82b) is derived from (82a) via an intermediate stage (86) which obligatorily undergoes the rule in (85) yielding the final form (82b):

(86)      $[_{CP}$ quoi faites-vous __ ]

The rule in (85) will not apply to examples such as (81a) and (82a) where *quoi* has not been preposed, nor to (81b) where *quoi* is governed by a preposition and is, therefore, not alone in CP.

It is not clear why examples like those in (83) should be ungrammatical. For present purposes, let us simply assume that *quoi* (and therefore its derivative *que*) cannot be inserted in the subject position. A consequence of this assumption is that in cases like (84) the initial *que* cannot originate as the subject of *tracasser*, but must be analysed as the object of *être*, as in the colloquial example (87):

(87)      C'est quoi qui tracasse Pierre?

This in turn means that, in these constructions at least, *est-ce que* must be analysed as the inverted form of *c'est que*, not as a fossilised interrogative particle (see 10.3.2). Note that in constructions of the type *qu'est-ce qui*, the choice between *qui* and *que* as the first QU- item is determined by the human versus non-human nature of the questioned element whereas the form of the second QU- item indicates its grammatical function (subject versus direct object) as in relative clauses (see 10.5.6–10.5.7):

(88)      a   Qu'est-ce qui tracasse Pierre?      (non-human, subject)
          b   Qui est-ce qui a vu Marie?         (human, subject)
          c   Qu'est-ce que je dois faire?       (non-human, direct object)
          d   Qui est-ce que Luc a rencontré?    (human, direct object)

A further peculiarity of interrogative *que* is that, unlike most other QU- items, it does not allow the complex form of S U B J - C L - I N V in direct questions, though it does permit the simple form and S T Y L - I N V:

(89)      a   *Que Jean fera-t-il?
          b   Que fera-t-il?
          c   Que fera Jean?

This is somewhat surprising in view of the conclusions reached in 10.2.6. However, the restriction illustrated in (89) results from a particular condition on interrogative *que* which is independent of the Inversion processes themselves – namely that *que*, unlike other QU- items, cannot be separated from the verb by any item other than *ne* or a clitic pronoun:

(90)   a   *Que, d'après toi, fera Pierre?
      b   Où, d'après toi, partira Pierre?
      c   Quand, d'après toi, arrivera Pierre?

Clearly this condition is sufficient to rule out examples like (89a) without need to revise the earlier conclusions about the types of sentences in which complex SUBJ-CL-INV can apply.

This adjacency condition may be related to the rule proposed in (85). If we consider *que* to be the clitic form of *quoi*, just as *me* and *te* are clitic forms of *moi* and *toi*, the restriction illustrated in (89a) and (90a) reduces to the generalisation that clitic forms associated with the verb (e.g. clitic pronouns and the negative particle *ne*) cannot be separated from the verb by anything other than another clitic form.

### 10.4.2   The item 'quel'

The item *quel* (and its feminine and plural variants) can be used in two ways: either as an interrogative determiner accompanied by a common noun (e.g. *Quelle réponse a-t-il donnée?*) or on its own (e.g. *Quelle est la réponse?*). The first use of *quel* presents no particular problems in that *quel* + noun can be used in all grammatical functions, regardless of whether QU- movement applies, and allows all types of Inversion:

(91)   a   Quelle équipe a gagné le championnat?
      b   Quel journal lisent les intellectuels?
      c   Dans quel tiroir (la secrétaire) a-t-elle mis les dossiers?
      d   Les intellectuels lisent quel journal?
      e   Elle a mis les dossiers dans quel tiroir?

Unlike English *which*, *quel* does not allow the following noun to be omitted freely when the class of entities referred to is evident from context; e.g., even if the topic of conversation is football teams or newspapers, we cannot formulate the questions in (92) corresponding to English *Which will win the championship?* or *Which do intellectuals read?*:

(92)   a   *Quelle va gagner le championnat?
      b   *Quel lisent les intellectuels?

In such cases, we must use the appropriate form of *lequel*:

(93)    a    Laquelle va gagner le championnat?

         b    Lequel lisent les intellectuels?

*Lequel* can also be used with a definite NP introduced by *de* to question an element from a specific set:

(94)    a    Laquelle de ces trois équipes va gagner le championnat?

         b    Lequel de ces journaux lisent les intellectuels?

The use of *quel* without a following noun is restricted to sentences with *être* as the main verb, as in (95)

(95)    Quel est le problème?

At first sight, *quel* looks like the subject of *être*. However, there is strong evidence to suggest that *quel* is actually the complement of *être* (preposed by QU- movement) while the subject in (95) is *le problème*, placed after the verb by STYL-INV, as shown in (96):

(96)    $[_{CP}$    $[_{IP}$ le problème est quel]]

    ⇒    $[_{CP}$ quel $[_{IP}$ le problème est __ ]]    (QU- movement)

    ⇒    $[_{CP}$ quel $[_{IP}$ __ est le problème]]    (STYL-INV)

Firstly it may be noted that the restriction on the use of *quel* without a following noun goes beyond the choice of *être* as main verb – the phrase which follows *être* at the surface level must be an NP, normally definite:

(97)    a    Quel est le professeur de français?

         b    *Quel est un professeur de français?

         c    *Quel est professeur de français?

         d    *Quel est intelligent?

         e    *Quel est dans la salle de bains?

If *quel* were the subject of *être*, we would have to impose special conditions on the types of complement which can co-occur with *quel*, since the expressions in (97) can readily occur as complements of *être* with other subjects such as *Pierre* or indeed the interrogative pronoun *qui*:

(98)    $\begin{Bmatrix} \text{Pierre} \\ \text{Qui} \end{Bmatrix}$ est $\begin{Bmatrix} \text{le professeur de français} \\ \text{un professeur de français} \\ \text{professeur de français} \\ \text{intelligent} \\ \text{dans la salle de bains} \end{Bmatrix}$

487

On the other hand, the types of expressions which can follow *quel est . . .* correspond to those which can occur as subjects of *être* when the complement is a definite NP:

(99)     a   Le professeur de français est Pierre
         b   *Un professeur de français est Pierre
         c   *Professeur de français est Pierre
         d   *Intelligent est Pierre
         e   *Dans la salle de bains est Pierre

If *quel* is the complement of *être*, corresponding to *Pierre* in (99), the restrictions in (97) follow directly from those in (99).

A second argument is based on pronominalisation of the complement of *être*. Normally a definite NP complement of *être* can be replaced by the clitic *le*, as in (100):

(100)     a   Pierre est le meilleur ami de Paul
          b   Pierre l'est

If the definite NP which occurs in sentences with *quel* were the complement of *être*, we would expect it to be pronominalised in the same way, but it cannot:

(101)     a   Quel est le meilleur ami de Paul?
          b   *Quel l'est?

If we wish to pronominalise this NP, we must use a subject pronoun, as we would expect if this NP is the underlying subject:

(102)     Quel est-il?

A more subtle argument in favour of the analysis proposed in (96) is based on concessive constructions of the type illustrated in (103):

(103)     a   Qui que tu sois, tu ne rentreras pas      ('Whoever you are, . . .')
          b   Quoi que tu fasses, tu auras tort        ('Whatever you do, . . .')
          c   Où que tu ailles, les agents te chercheront ('Wherever you go, . . .')

It is assumed that the concessive clauses in (103) are derived by means of QU-movement, as in (104):

(104)           $[_{CP}$ que $[_{IP}$ tu sois qui$]]$
          $\Rightarrow$   $[_{CP}$ qui que $[_{IP}$ tu sois __ $]]$

An important restriction on this construction is that the QU- item cannot function as the subject of the concessive clause:

(105)    a    *Qui qui gagne le championnat,    ('Whoever wins the cup, . . .')
              je serai heureux

         b    *Quoi qui arrive, je m'en fous    ('Whatever happens, . . .')

However, such constructions are possible with *quel*, thus corroborating the hypothesis that *quel* functions as a complement of *être* rather than as a subject:

(106)    Quelle que soit ta réponse, je l'accepterai

A possible problem with this account is that if *le problème* is the subject in (95), we would expect it to undergo complex inversion as an alternative to STYL-INV. However, this is not the case:

(107)    *Quel le problème est-il?

The ungrammaticality of (107) can be accounted for by a condition, similar to that proposed for *que* in 10.4.1, which requires *quel* to be adjacent to the verb. Indeed, *quel*, like *que*, cannot be separated from the verb by a parenthetical expression:

(108)    *Quel, d'après toi, est le problème?

Examples like (107) can also be ruled out by the stylistic principle evoked in 10.3.4 to explain the contrast between *Où est la salle de bains?* and *??Où la salle de bains est-elle?*

### 10.4.3 'Pourquoi'

*Pourquoi* has a number of peculiar properties which distinguish it from other QU-items. Firstly, unlike all other QU- items, it does not allow STYL-INV in direct or indirect questions, though it allows both forms of SUBJ-CL-INV (compare similar examples with *comment*):

(109)    a    Pourquoi (les étudiants) sont-il partis?

         b    *Pourquoi sont partis les étudiants?

         c    *Je ne sais pas pourquoi sont partis les étudiants

Secondly, in colloquial constructions without Inversion, *pourquoi* cannot be 'left behind' at the end of the sentence (cf. *Il a répondu comment?*):

(110)    *Il a répondu pourquoi?

(This example is only acceptable if it is interpreted as two separate utterances – a statement followed by an elliptical question: *Il a répondu. Pourquoi?*)

Possibly these two observations are related. The deviance of (110) might be taken as evidence that *pourquoi*, unlike other QU- adverbs, does not originate in a postverbal position but is inserted directly in the sentence-initial position (e.g.

under CP), perhaps in the same way as modal adverbs such as *peut-être*. If so, the examples in (109) are not derived by QU- movement. This would explain the ungrammaticality of (109b, c) in so far as STYL-INV usually correlates with left-ward movement of some other element (see 10.2.6).

A further peculiarity, which *pourquoi* shares with English *why*, is that it cannot be used in indirect infinitival questions (cf. *I do not know how/*why to do it*):

(111)     a   *Je ne sais pas pourquoi le faire
          b    Je ne sais pas comment le faire

The reason for this difference is unclear. See 10.4.7 for discussion of indirect infinitival questions and for further examples involving direct infinitival questions where *pourquoi* and *why* differ from other QU- items in more subtle ways.

### 10.4.4 *'Combien'*

It is assumed that *combien* is a determiner, similar to *beaucoup*, which occurs in quantitative and partitive constructions of the form [*combien de* N'] or [*combien de* NP] (see 5.3.6–5.3.7).

As with English *how much* or *how many*, the whole NP (or PP) containing *combien* can be preposed:

(112)     a   Combien de livres as-tu lu?
          b   Dans combien de maisons es-tu entré?

However, when the *combien* phrase functions as a direct object it is possible to separate *combien* from the element which it quantifies:

(113)     a   Combien as-tu lu de livres?
          b   Combien as-tu emprunté de mes livres?

In English, this separation is possible in partitive constructions analogous to (113b) (*How many did you borrow of my books?*) but not in quantitative constructions corresponding to (113a) (**How many did you read books?*). Nevertheless, it is reasonable to suppose that the condition on 'separation' is essentially the same in both languages: the determiner can be separated from the element which it quantifies provided that the quantified element is introduced by *de* or *of*. The difference observed above can thus be attributed to the fact that *combien* requires *de* in both quantitative and partitive constructions whereas the corresponding English forms take *of* only in the latter case. The same pattern can be seen with the interrogative determiners *quel, lequel* and English *which*:

(114)     a   *Quel as-tu lu livre?          (Quel livre as-tu lu?)
          b   *Which did you read book?      (Which book did you read?)

(115)   a   Lequel as-tu lu de ces livres?        (Lequel de ces livres as-tu lu?)
        b   Which did you read of those books? (Which of those books did you
                                                read?)

We also find cases where *combien* has been separated from the rest of the
subject NP, which occurs after the verb:

(116)       a   Combien sont arrivés d'invités?
            b   Combien se sont évadés de prisonniers?
            c   Combien ont été mangées de tartes?

This phenomenon appears to be limited to passive constructions, certain pronominal verbs and other verbs which can plausibly be classified as 'unaccusative'
(i.e. principally verbs which take *être* as their auxiliary – see 2.8.2 for discussion).
It does not occur with transitive verbs or intransitive verbs which describe
actions:

(117)       a   *Combien ont vu de personnes cette émission?
            b   *Combien ont vu cette émission de personnes?
            c   *Combien ont dormi d'étudiants pendant la conférence?
            d   *Combien ont rouspété d'amis?

Given the analysis of passives proposed in 3.2.2 and the more tentative suggestions concerning 'unaccusative' verbs in 2.8.2, the *combien* phrases in (116) can be
analysed as underlying objects of the verb whereas those in (117) are subjects in
the underlying structure. If this is correct, the cases in (116) can be assimilated to
those in (113) – both involve separation of *combien* from the underlying direct
object – thus avoiding the need for a special rule which moves the *de* phrase rightwards from the subject position in (116).

*Combien* can also be used as a degree modifier of verbs:

(118)       Combien m'aimes-tu?

Note that French has no interrogative degree item which can modify adjectives or
adverbs in the manner of *how* in English (*How old is he?*, *How fast was he going?*,
*How heavy is it?*). In such cases, the question must be formulated in such a way
that the questioned element is presented as a noun (with *quel*) or by choosing a
verb which can take a measure phrase as its complement (represented by
*combien*):

(119)       a   Quel âge a-t-il?
            b   À quelle vitesse roulait-il?
            c   Combien pèse-t-il?

However, in certain types of indirect questions, *combien* can be used to modify an adjective or adverb, but it must occur alone in CP, with the adjective or adverb 'left behind':

(120)      a   Je sais combien elle est intelligente

             b   Je sais combien il roulait vite

Possibly this is an extension of the construction in (118) – i.e. *combien* actually modifies the VP rather than the adjective or adverb. Also, constructions like (120) seem to be restricted to cases where the complement clause is interpreted as a relative clause (paraphrasable as 'I know the extent to which she is intelligent', 'I know the speed at which he was travelling') rather than as reports of genuine questions: *?Je lui ai demandé combien elle est intelligente*. For discussion of other cases where the distinction between indirect questions and relative clauses is somewhat blurred, see 10.4.6. See also the discussion of exclamative constructions with *combien* in 10.6.2.

In English the expressions *how much* and *how many* can be used without a following noun when the quantified element is clear from the context (e.g. *How many (of them) did you buy?*, *How much (of it) did you eat?* ). With *combien* (as with *beaucoup*, etc., see 5.3.7 and 6.6.4), the quantified element must be expressed by *en* when it functions as a direct object:

(121)      a   Combien en as-tu acheté?     (= 'combien de livres')

             b   Combien en as-tu mangé?    (= 'combien de viande')

However, *combien* is used without *en* when the quantified phrase is interpreted as a unit of measurement (such as 'weight' in (119c) above, or 'money' (122)), rather than as a particular substance or class of things:

(122)      Combien gagne-t-il?   (= 'combien d'argent')

*Combien* is also used without *en* when the quantified phrase functions as a subject or as an object of a preposition (i.e. in those cases where cliticisation of *en* from within an NP is ruled out for syntactic reasons – see 6.6.4):

(123)      a   Combien sont arrivés?         (= 'combien d'invités')

             b   À combien avez-vous téléphoné?   (= 'combien de clients')

As a final point, the colloquial French construction in (124) may be noted:

(124)      Qu'est-ce que tu as lu comme livres?

Such sentences typically question the identity of the direct object (= *Quels livres as-tu lus?*) but a quantitative interpretation is also possible (= *Combien de livres as-tu lu?*) though it is more natural in exclamations than in genuine questions (see 10.6.5).

The *comme* phrase is taken to be a modifier of the interrogative pronoun *quoi* in the underlying structure, as in (125), which is also permissible as a surface structure:

(125)     Tu as lu quoi comme livres?

### 10.4.5   Indirect questions

The term 'indirect question' is something of a misnomer in so far as it is used to refer not only to sentences which report a question as in (126), but also to syntactically similar constructions which express uncertainty or ignorance about a situation (as in (127)) or even, though more rarely, sentences which assert a person's knowledge about a situation (as in (128)):

(126)     a   Pierre a demandé si la réunion aura lieu à l'heure prévue
          b   Pierre a demandé quand la réunion aura lieu

(127)     a   Paul ne sait pas s'il pourra venir
          b   Jules se demande quand le train arrivera
          c   Je ne comprends pas pourquoi la voiture ne marche pas

(128)     Je sais comment on pourra résoudre ce problème

Note that the mood of indirect questions is always the indicative, in spite of the tendency to use the subjunctive in other types of complement clauses which involve some element of doubt (see 4.9).

The basic syntax of indirect questions is similar to that of direct questions, with the following provisos:

- *Indirect questions of the yes/no type are introduced by the complementiser si.*
- *QU- movement is obligatory in indirect 'partial' questions.*
- *Indirect questions do not allow SUBJ-CL-INV (simple or complex).*
- *Indirect 'partial' questions allow STYL-INV under the same conditions as direct questions.*

With regard to the last point, recall in particular that STYL-INV is impossible with *pourquoi* (see 10.4.3), obligatory with *quel* (see 10.4.2) and highly preferred in other cases where *être* would otherwise occur as the last element in the clause:

(129)     a   Je me demande pourquoi ce milliardaire travaille
          b   *Je me demande pourquoi travaille ce milliardaire

(130)     a   *Je ne sais pas quelle la réponse est
          b   Je ne sais pas quelle est la réponse

(131)     a   ?Je ne sais pas où la salle de bains est
          b   Je ne sais pas où est la salle de bains

### 10.4.6 *'Que', 'qui' and 'quoi' in indirect questions*

As in direct questions, *qui* can be used with human reference as a subject, direct object or complement of a preposition:

(132)    a  Je ne sais pas qui arrivera demain
          b  Pierre veut savoir qui Marie a rencontré
          c  Luc se demande pour qui il va voter

When the questioned element is non-human and occurs as the object of a preposition, *quoi* is used, just as in direct questions:

(133)    a  Je ne sais pas à quoi tu penses
          b  Je me demande de quoi il parle

However, if the questioned element is a subject or a direct object, neither *quoi* nor *que* can be used:

(134)    a  *Je ne sais pas {quoi / que} tracasse Pierre.
          b  *Je me demande {quoi / que} Pierre dira

In order to express the intended meaning of the examples in (134) a construction is used in which the interrogative clause is introduced by *ce*, as in (135):

(135)    a  Je ne sais pas ce qui tracasse Pierre
          b  Je me demande ce que Pierre dira

In (135b) STYL-INV can apply to give the variant (136):

(136)    Je me demande ce que dira Pierre

Note that in this construction the choice between *qui* and *que* is determined by the grammatical function (subject and direct object respectively) of the questioned element, not according to whether it is animate or inanimate. Indeed, the construction with *ce* is only possible when the questioned element is inanimate. Thus, when the questioned element is a subject, the distinction between inanimate and animate reference is signalled by the presence or absence of *ce*, not by the form of the QU- item, as shown in (137):

(137)    a  Je me demande qui arrivera    'I wonder who will arrive'
          b  Je me demande ce qui arrivera   'I wonder what will happen'

Note also that *ce* cannot precede indirect questions introduced by other QU-expressions:

(138)    a  *Je ne sais pas ce à quoi vous pensez

b   *Je me demande ce où vous êtes allé

c   *J'ai oublié ce comment Marie a résolu le problème

Although the constructions in (135) and (136) are interpreted as indirect questions they show a striking resemblance to relative clause constructions in which *ce* acts as the modified nominal elèment (see 10.5.10 below). In particular, the functions of *que* and *qui* described above are the same as in relative clauses (*la chose qui est arrivée* vs *la chose que j'ai vue*). Moreover, as we can see in (135b), *que* is not subject to the adjacency condition which holds for *que* in direct questions (see 10.4.1) – note that this condition does not hold for *que* in relative clauses: *le livre que Pierre a écrit*.

A further similarity with relative clause constructions is revealed in cases where the indirect question complements an item which is not a verb. For some reason, indirect questions do not occur readily as complements of adjectives, but examples like the following are accepted by some speakers:

(139)      a   ?Je ne suis pas sûr comment cette machine fonctionne

           b   ?Je ne suis pas sûr quand le patron rentrera

           c   ?Je ne suis pas sûr où Pierre a mis les dossiers

However, indirect questions of the *ce que/qui* type are completely impossible in this context:

(140)      a   *Je ne suis pas sûr ce que Pierre fera

           b   *Je ne suis pas sûr ce qui plairait à Marie

It is not clear why examples like (139) are odd (since *sûr* can take a declarative complement clause – *Je suis sûr que Pierre fera cela*), but the ungrammaticality of (140) can be related to that of examples like *Je suis sûr la chose que Pierre fera*, where *sûr* is followed by an NP containing a relative clause. More precisely, (140) can be excluded if we assume that the complement is an NP with a structure like that in (141), given that adjectives can never take an NP as their direct complement,[2] whereas indirect questions like those in (132) and (133) and the cases discussed in 10.4.5 are CPs like the corresponding direct questions:

(141)      $[_{NP}$ ce $[_{CP}$ que/qui IP]]

This is the structure which will be proposed in 10.5.10 for 'free' relatives such as *Pierre fera ce que je lui demanderai*.

---

[2] When an NP functions as a complement of an adjective, it must be introduced by a preposition, typically *de*: *Je suis sûr de ce fait*. By the same token, the examples in (140) are significantly improved by the addition of *de*: *Je ne suis pas sûr de ce que Pierre fera*, *?Je ne suis pas sûr de ce qui plairait à Marie*.

To summarise, in the general case, indirect 'partial' questions are derived in the same way as direct questions by movement of the QU- expression into the Spec of CP. However, to compensate for the ungrammaticality of examples like (136), where we would expect to find *que* or *quoi* as the QU- item (and only in these cases, see (138)), French resorts to a construction involving a 'free' relative which masquerades as an indirect question – for further discussion see 10.5.10.

The deviance noted in (139) is sharper still when an indirect question is used as a complement of a noun:

(142)  a  ??la question (de) si Jean partira
       b  ??la question (de) pourquoi ces expressions sont inacceptables

In such cases, the construction is reformulated in such a way that the interrogative clause occurs as the complement of a verb:

(143)  a  la question de savoir si Jean partira
       b  la question de savoir pourquoi ces expressions sont inacceptables

### 10.4.7 *Infinitival questions*

In French, as in English, some types of indirect questions can be expressed by means of the infinitive:

(144)  a  Je ne sais pas où aller
       b  Le contre-maître nous expliquera comment faire ce travail
       c  L'étudiant m'a demandé à qui s'adresser

The working assumption adopted here is that these interrogative infinitives are CPs whose subject position is empty (as in the case of the non-interrogative infinitives discussed in 9.2.1) and that the QU- expression is moved into the Spec of CP (as in the case of finite interrogatives):

(145)  Je ne sais pas $[_{CP}$ où $[_{IP}$ PRO aller __ $]]$

The empty subject of the infinitive is typically understood as referring back to either the subject or the object of the main verb depending on which of these two entities is construed as the receiver of the information (e.g. the subject in (144a, c), the indirect object in (144b)).

The infinitival construction is not possible with indirect yes/no questions (compare with English where the infinitival construction is possible with *whether* but not with *if*: *I do not know {whether / *if} to leave}*):

(146)  *Je ne sais pas si partir

Also, indirect infinitival questions are not possible with *pourquoi*, a restriction which also applies to English *why* (**I do not know why to study linguistics*):

(147)      *Je ne sais pas pourquoi étudier la linguistique

The infinitival construction cannot be used to question the subject, presumably because the subject of the infinitive must be an empty element whose reference is contextually dependent – e.g. we cannot say (148) with the meaning 'I wonder who may arrive':

(148)      *Je me demande qui arriver

A human direct object can be questioned by *qui* in the infinitival construction:

(149)      Je ne sais pas qui embaucher

When the questioned element is a non-human direct object, the normal form of the QU- item is *quoi*:

(150)      Je ne sais pas quoi donner à Marie

Note that to accommodate this example we must assume that the QUOI ⇒ QUE rule proposed in 10.4.1, which applies obligatorily in finite interrogatives, does not apply in this case. However, *que* does occur in more formal registers after *savoir* when negated without *pas*:

(151)      Je ne savais que faire

Infinitival interrogatives can also be used as direct questions, as in (152):

(152)      a   Comment répondre à cette question?
           b   Où aller?
           c   A qui s'adresser?

Such constructions can be used as genuine questions in French, unlike parallel constructions in English which can only be used as titles or headings (e.g. *How to make friends and influence people* or *Where to send your application*). In this construction, the empty subject of the infinitive is usually understood as referring to the speaker, or a set of people which includes the speaker, though it can also have generic reference corresponding to 'one' or 'anyone'. Also, questions of this type have a modal value which would be expressed in English by a modal verb (e.g. 'How can I answer this question?', 'Where shall I go?', 'Who must I contact?').

Infinitives cannot be used as direct yes/no questions, except perhaps as a rhetorical device: *Fumer? Moi, jamais!* However, contrary to what was observed in the case of infinitival indirect questions, *pourquoi* can be used in infinitival direct questions:

(153)      Pourquoi apprendre le japonais?

The construction with *pourquoi* differs slightly from those with other QU-items (as in (152)) in that the empty subject tends to be interpreted as referring

497

to the hearer rather than the speaker (or has generic reference) and the sentence as a whole is typically construed as a challenge or reproach rather than as a genuine question, like its English counterpart *Why learn Japanese?* (Curiously, *why* is the only interrogative element which can introduce direct infinitival questions in English; also, with *why* the infinitive is not introduced by *to*, in contrast to the 'title' use of infinitives with other interrogative items mentioned above.)

In direct infinitival interrogatives where the questioned element is a non-human direct object, the usual form of the QU- item is *que* (though *quoi* is sometimes used in colloquial speech):

(154)     a   Que faire?
          b   Que répondre à cette question?

This is the opposite situation to that which we observed in indirect infinitival questions (see (150) above). This observation suggests that the QUOI ⇒ QUE rule proposed in 10.4.1 normally applies only in direct questions.

### 10.5   Relative clauses
#### 10.5.1   *The functions of relative clauses*

A relative clause is a clause which is appended to an NP and which describes a property of the entity to which the NP refers. Typical examples are the bracketted expressions in (155):

(155)     a   le problème [qui me tracasse]
          b   le vin [que je préfère]
          c   le tiroir [dans lequel j'ai mis les bijoux]

Usually relative clauses provide information which serves to define the intended referent of the NP in a way which distinguishes it from other potential referents. Thus, in (156a), the clause *qui a écrit cela* picks out a particular individual from the class of individuals who might be referred to by the noun *homme*, and in (158b) *qui travaillent bien* indicates that the claim being made does not apply to all students, but only to those who have this property:

(156)     a   L'homme qui a écrit cela doit être fou
          b   Les étudiants qui travaillent bien trouveront de bons emplois

Relative clauses of this type, which are known as **restrictive relatives**, cannot be used to modify proper nouns or disjunctive pronouns:

(157)     a   *Jules qui a écrit cela doit être fou
          b   *Je pensais à lui dont tu m'avais parlé

There is a second type of relative clause (known as **non-restrictive relatives** or 'appositive' relatives) whose function is not to restrict reference to the individual(s) in question but rather to convey additional information about the referent, in passing as it were. Relative clauses of this type are usually separated from the rest of the sentence by commas:

(158)        Mon voisin, qui est très intelligent, m'a parlé de cette question

The relative clause in (158) does not serve to distinguish the person in question from other neighbours who are not particularly intelligent, but adds relevant information which could be conveyed equivalently (though less elegantly) by means of a conjoined clause: *Mon voisin m'a parlé de cette question et il est très intelligent.* Similarly, the statement in (159) (compare (156b)) is not confined to a subclass of the set referred to by *les étudiants* but includes the information that all members of this set work well:

(159)        Les étudiants, qui d'ailleurs travaillent bien, trouveront de bons
             emplois

The use of expressions like *d'ailleurs* in (159), which help to underline the parenthetical nature of the clause, is quite common in non-restrictive relatives but does not occur in restrictive relative clauses. Unlike restrictive relatives, non-restrictive relative clauses can be used with proper nouns and disjunctive pronouns:

(160)     a   Chantal, qui vient de passer six mois en Afrique, va nous faire
              une conférence sur ses expériences
          b   Je ne voterai jamais pour lui, qui d'ailleurs ne voterait pas pour
              moi non plus

Non-restrictive relatives can also be used to make comments on sentences, in which case they are introduced by *ce*, as in (161a, b), unless the QU- item is governed by a preposition as in (161c):

(161)     a   Solange arrive toujours en retard, ce qui m'énerve beaucoup
          b   Jules a raconté des mensonges sur Marie, ce qu'elle n'a pas du
              tout apprécié
          c   Ma voiture est tombée en panne, sans quoi je serais arrivé à
              l'heure

Relative clauses usually occur in the indicative mood. However, the subjunctive can be used (and tends to be preferred in more formal styles) in restrictive clauses which define an entity whose existence is hypothetical (see 4.9.11):

(162)     a  Je n'ai pas trouvé un seul fauteuil qui soit confortable

             b  Juliette cherche une personne à qui elle puisse se confier

Also, in some cases an infinitival relative clause construction can be used (see 10.5.9):

(163)     a  Je cherche un sac dans lequel mettre mes affaires

             b  Pierre a trouvé quelque chose à lire

### 10.5.2 Structural properties of relative clauses

It is assumed that restrictive relative clauses belong to the category CP and are adjoined to the N′ node in the same way as other modifiers of the noun, as in (164):

(166)     $[_{NP} \, D \, [_{N'} \, N' \, CP]]$

The structural position of non-restrictive relative clauses is less clear. For present purposes let us simply assume that they occur outside the NP to which they relate since they are separated from the NP by a comma (or pause) and, on the semantic level, they do not make any contribution to the way in which the reference of the NP is established.

With regard to their internal structure, restrictive and non-restrictive relatives have essentially the same syntactic properties, apart from a few minor differences which will be discussed in 10.5.11. In the underlying structure, the modified noun is represented by a **relative pronoun** (a QU- item) occupying the position which corresponds to its grammatical function within the relative clause. To derive the surface structure, the relative pronoun or a phrase containing it is moved (obligatorily) to the Spec of CP, as in the case of interrogative sentences – this is shown in the general schema (165), where the subscripts on N′ and QU- indicate that the QU- item is identified with the modified noun:

(165)     $[_{NP} \, D \, [_{N'} \, N'_i \, [_{CP} \, [_{SPEC} \quad ] \, C \, [_{IP} \cdots QU_{-i} \cdots ]]]]$

Thus, the phrase *le tiroir dans lequel j'ai mis les bijoux* is derived as in (166):

(166)     $[_{NP} \, le \, tiroir_t \, [_{CP} \, [_{SPEC} \quad ] \, C \, [_{IP} \, j'ai \, mis \, les \, bijoux \, [_{PP} \, dans \, lequel_t \, ]]]]$

Here, *lequel* occurs as the object of a preposition, indicating that it is the indirect object of *mettre* and the whole PP undergoes QU- movement because of the general restriction which prevents items from being extracted from PPs in French.

### 10.5.3 Relative clauses in English

Relative clauses in English show a complication which has repercussions for the analysis of certain types of relative clauses in French. In English, it is often possible to use *that* instead of a relative pronoun *which* or *who*, as long as the relative pronoun is not governed by a preposition in the surface structure:

(167)     a   the book {which / that} I read
          b   the person {who / that} wrote the book
          c   the book in {which / *that} I found the information

A standard generative approach to such cases is to analyse *that* not as a relative pronoun but as the complementiser which typically introduces finite subordinate clauses. If we assume that this complementiser is present in the underlying structure of relative clauses, example (167a) can be derived from the structure (168):

(168)     $[_{NP}$ the book$_b$ $[_{CP}$ Spec that $[_{IP}$ I read which$_b$ ]]]

Movement of *which* to Spec of CP will give the sequence **the book which that I read*, which is not possible in Modern English (though such constructions are attested in earlier stages of the language). However, the surface forms in (167a) can be derived by a rule which deletes either the relative pronoun or the complementiser (or indeed both, giving *the book I read*). The cases in (167b) can be derived in the same way except that we cannot delete both elements when the relative pronoun functions as a subject (e.g. **the person wrote the book* is not possible as a relative clause construction, though it is fine as a complete sentence). In example (167c), the PP containing the relative pronoun is moved, giving the intermediate structure (169):

(169)     $[_{NP}$ the book$_b$ $[_{CP}$ $[_{PP}$ in which] that $[_{IP}$ I found the information __ ]]]

Here, the option of deleting *which* is not available, plausibly because it is contained in a larger phrase (the PP), so *that* must be deleted.

The assumptions behind this analysis are summarised below.

  *I   The complementiser is present in the underlying structure of relative clauses*
  *II  Either the relative pronoun or the complementiser must be deleted*
  *III The relative pronoun cannot be deleted if it is contained in a larger phrase*

The relevance of these observations to French is that this analysis extends naturally, with some refinements, to *que* in cases like *le livre que j'ai lu* (i.e. *que* is a complementiser corresponding to *that* rather than a relative pronoun). Rather less obviously, there is strong evidence that *qui* in *la personne qui a écrit ce livre* and *le livre qui m'intéresse* is also a complementiser. These issues will be explored in 10.5.6 and 10.5.7. Pending this discussion, the notion of a 'relative pronoun' in French will be restricted to those items which must be translated as *which* or *who(m)* (and which cannot be translated as *that*) in syntactically parallel constructions in English – in practice, the items which occur as complements of prepositions.

### 10.5.4 Relative pronouns

The relative pronouns which can occur as objects of prepositions are *qui, lequel* (and its feminine/plural variants) and *quoi*. The use of these items is similar to that which has been observed in interrogative constructions.

When introduced by a preposition, the relative pronoun *qui* is used exclusively to refer to human beings (or sometimes to animals), like interrogative *qui*:

(170)     l'homme à qui j'ai parlé

The non-human relative pronoun used after prepositions is *lequel* (which must agree in number and gender with the modified noun: *laquelle, lesquels, lesquelles*):

(171)     la chaise sur laquelle je suis assis

*Lequel* and its variants can also be used with human reference, as an alternative to *qui*, particularly in plural cases; indeed *qui* cannot be used after prepositions such as *parmi* which require a plural complement:

(172)     a   le candidat pour {lequel / qui} je voterai
          b   les étudiants parmi {lesquels / *qui} on doit choisir le meilleur

Finally, the invariable form *quoi* is used after prepositions as a neuter relative pronoun to modify items such as *ce, rien* or *quelque chose* which are inanimate and do not contain a head noun which can determine the gender of the relative pronoun (see 10.5.10), also in non-restrictive relatives which modify a clause (see 10.5.1 example (161c)):

(173)     a   ce à quoi je pensais
          b   Il n y a rien sur quoi je puisse m'asseoir
          c   quelque chose sur quoi je puisse m'asseoir

The pattern observed in (171)–(173) reflects that found in questions, where *lequel* invites the addressee to select a particular member (or members) of a specific set previously identified by a noun which provides the appropriate gender (e.g. *Lequel veux-tu voir?* = *lequel de ces films* or *lequel de ces hommes*), whereas *quoi* (and its clitic variant *que*, see 10.4.1) invites selection from an open-ended class which is not associated with any particular noun which can provide a gender feature (e.g. *À quoi penses-tu?, Que manges-tu?*).

On the basis of the above data, we can classify relative pronouns as in table 10.2 (see p. 503).

### 10.5.5 Relative 'adverbs'

The items discussed in 10.5.4 act as substitutes for NPs. Accordingly, it will be assumed that they have the syntactic status of NPs. However, the QU- item in a

Table 10.2. *Classification of French relative pronouns*
*(after prepositions)*

| | |
|---|---|
| *qui* | [+ human] |
| *lequel*, etc. | [± animate], gender supplied by modified noun |
| *quoi* | [– animate], neuter |

relative clause can also consist of a single word which acts as a substitute for a PP. For example, to modify nouns denoting a place, we can use *où* (instead of a preposition followed by a relative pronoun – e.g. *dans lequel*) when the exact spatial relation is not important:

(174)      l'endroit où j'ai mis les bijoux

In (174) *où* corresponds to the identical interrogative 'adverb' (as in *Où as-tu mis les bijoux?*) and to the 'adverb' of place *là* or the 'adverbial' clitic *y* in declarative sentences.[3] Note, however, that the relative 'adverb' *où* has a more extensive use than these other items. In particular, it can be used to denote a time relation – conversely, *quand* cannot be used as a relative adverb:

(175)      le jour {où / *quand} Kennedy a été assassiné

*Pourquoi* can also be used as a relative adverb:

(176)      la raison pourquoi je suis parti

Other interrogative adverbs cannot be used in this way. For example, corresponding to the interrogative manner adverb *comment*, we find the form *dont* in relative clauses:

(177)      la façon dont il a résolu le problème

In English, the relative clauses in (175)–(177) can be introduced by *that* (or nothing at all): *the day (that) Kennedy was assassinated, the reason (that) I left, the way (that) he solved the problem.* Similar examples with *que* are occasionally attested, but this usage is no longer standard except in ordinal time expressions with the noun *fois*, where the relative adverb *où* is excluded: *la première fois {que / *où} je l'ai vu.*

The item *dont*, illustrated in (177), generally acts as a substitute for phrases of the type *de* + NP in rather the same way as the adverbial clitic *en* (though with some important differences). This item is discussed in detail in 10.5.8. Note that

---

[3] The terms 'adverb' and 'adverbial' are used here (as in many traditional accounts) in a very loose mnemonic sense. A more exact, but cumbersome, term would be 'pro-PP'; see 6.4.6.

*dont* cannot be used as an interrogative adverb: *\*Dont te souviens-tu?* (cf. *De quoi te souviens-tu?*).

### 10.5.6 'Que' in relative clauses

The item *que* in cases like (178) is traditionally classified as a relative pronoun, presumably on the grounds that it introduces a relative clause.

(178)    a  le livre que j'ai lu

         b  l'homme que j'ai rencontré

         c  ce que je préfère

However, in the light of the remarks in 10.5.3, we could also analyse it as a complementiser like *that* in English. Indeed, the assumption that a complementiser is present in the underlying structure of relative clauses is more plausible for French than for English, since *que* is obligatory in almost all types of subordinate clause including cases where it is optional or excluded in English (e.g. *Je crois qu'il est là* vs *I think (that) he is here*, *avant qu'il parte* vs *before \*(that) he leaves*).

Let us briefly consider how the traditional view might be integrated with the formal analysis sketched in 10.5.3. If *que* were a relative pronoun, we would have to stipulate that it can only function as the direct object of a verb (not for instance as the object of a preposition: *\*le livre à que je pense*) and that it is neutral with respect to the factors which distinguish between *qui*, *lequel* and *quoi* as objects of prepositions. Conversely, we would have to ensure that *qui*, *lequel* and *quoi* cannot occur as direct objects, to exclude examples like (179):

(179)    a  *le livre lequel j'ai lu

         b  *l'homme qui j'ai rencontré

         c  *ce quoi je préfère

This leads to a rather complicated classification of relative pronouns based partly on properties of the modified item and partly on the grammatical function of the pronoun within the relative clause. Neverthless, this classification will ensure that *que*, but not *lequel*, can be inserted as the object of *lire* in the underlying structure (180), thus excluding any source for the ungrammatical example (179a):

(180)    [$_{NP}$ le livre [$_{CP}$ Spec que [$_{IP}$ j'ai lu {que / *lequel} ]]]

Movement of the relative pronoun will give an intermediate structure in which the relative clause is introduced by two items *que* (one corresponding to *which*, the other to *that*):

(181)    [$_{NP}$ le livre [$_{CP}$ que que [$_{IP}$ j'ai lu __ ]]]

Deletion of either *que* will yield the surface form (179a).

This analysis works, but it is rather suspect. The effect of stipulating that *que* (and only *que*) can be used as a direct object relative pronoun is that the item which introduces the relative clause on the surface is identical to the complementiser *que* which, it has been assumed, was in this position in the underlying structure. The same effect can be achieved by supposing that in French, the relative pronoun (whatever its form might be) is always deleted leaving the complementiser *que* to appear on the surface. More concretely, let us suppose that *lequel, qui* and *quoi* can occur in the direct object position as well as after prepositions under the conditions summarised in table 10.2 in 10.5.4, giving the underlying structure (182a) and, after QU- movement, the intermediate structure (182b):

(182)      a     [NP le livre [$_{CP}$ Spec que [$_{IP}$ j'ai lu lequel ]]]
           b  ⇒ [$_{NP}$ le livre [$_{CP}$ lequel que [$_{IP}$ j'ai lu __ ]]]

In order to derive the grammatical (178a) while excluding (179a), we must ensure that *lequel* is deleted rather than *que*, in contrast to English where both options are available. This can be achieved by stipulating that relative pronouns (but not relative 'adverbs' like *où* or *dont*) are obligatorily deleted in French unless they are contained in a larger phrase, e.g. a PP as in *le livre dans lequel j'ai trouvé cette information*.

In fact, this restriction can be subsumed under a wider generalisation. Consider the examples in (183):

(183)      a  l'homme à la femme de qui j'ai téléphoné
           b  *l'homme la femme de qui j'ai insultée

Example (183a) is grammatical, if somewhat clumsy, but (183b) is impossible (the grammatical version is *l'homme dont j'ai insulté la femme* – see 10.5.8). According to the general approach above, these examples would be derived from the following underlying structures by QU- movement of the PP in (184a) and of the NP in (184b), with deletion of the complementiser *que*:

(184)      a  [$_{NP}$ l' homme [$_{CP}$ Spec que [$_{IP}$ j'ai téléphoné [$_{PP}$ à la femme de qui ]]]]
           b  [$_{NP}$ l' homme [$_{CP}$ Spec que [$_{IP}$ j'ai insulté [$_{NP}$ la femme de qui ]]]]

To exclude examples like (183b), the following condition is prepared:

**The 'Relativised NP' condition:**
*in French restrictive relative clauses, the Spec of CP cannot be occupied by an NP*

Assuming that relative pronouns like *lequel, qui* and *quoi* are NPs, this condition will force deletion of the relative pronoun in cases like (182b), thus ruling out examples like those in (179). Note that this condition does not apply in English (cf.

*the man the wife of whom I met* or, more naturally, *the man whose wife I met*), hence the possibility of retaining the relative pronouns in the English counterparts of (179).

The above arguments do not prove conclusively that *que* is not a relative pronoun. However, they do show that in all cases where this item occurs, it can be analysed as a complementiser. An advantage of this analysis is that we do not need to restrict *lequel, qui* and *quoi* to occurring as objects of prepositions – the fact that they only occur in this environment at the surface level can be attributed to the independent condition stated above, which entails deletion of these items unless they are 'protected' by a preposition. See 10.5.9 and 10.5.11 for further evidence which supports this analysis.

### 10.5.7 *'Qui' in subject relatives*

In this section, the focus of concern is the use of *qui* in cases like (185), where the modified noun corresponds to the subject of the relative clause:

(185)     a   le livre qui m'intéresse
           b   l'homme qui a écrit ce livre
           c   ce qui m'intéresse

In traditional grammar, *qui* in such cases is analysed as a subject relative pronoun. However, this analysis raises a number of problems. Firstly, unlike interrogative *qui* and the relative pronoun *qui* which occurs as the object of a preposition, this item is not restricted to human reference. Secondly, this analysis is inconsistent with the 'Relativised NP' condition proposed at the end of 10.5.6 if *qui* is a pronoun (i.e. an NP) which has been moved into the Spec of CP. Other difficulties will be presented below.

However, if *qui* in (185) is not a relative pronoun, what is it?

According to the conclusions reached in 10.5.6, example (185a) and its English counterparts *the book which interests me* or *the book that interests me* should be derived from the structures in (186), where *que* and *that* are complementisers and *lequel* and *which* are the relative pronouns which correspond to inanimate nouns:

(186)     a   $[_{NP}$ le livre   $[_{CP}$ Spec que $[_{IP}$ lequel m'intéresse]]]
           b   $[_{NP}$ the book $[_{CP}$ Spec that $[_{IP}$ which interests me]]]

QU- movement gives the intermediate structures in (187):

(187)     a   $[_{NP}$ le livre   $[_{CP}$ lequel que $[_{IP}$ ___ m'intéresse]]]
           b   $[_{NP}$ the book $[_{CP}$ which that $[_{IP}$ ___ interests me]]]

In (187b) deletion of either *which* or *that* gives the correct surface forms. In (187a) deletion of *que* yields the ungrammatical (188a), but this is independently explained by the 'Relativised NP' condition; however, the result of deleting *lequel*, as in (188b) is also ungrammatical:

(188)    a    *[$_{NP}$ le livre [$_{CP}$ lequel [$_{IP}$ ___ m'intéresse]]]
         b    *[$_{NP}$ le livre [$_{CP}$ que    [$_{IP}$ ___ m'intéresse]]]

Thus, neither of the 'normal' options gives the correct form (185a).

To overcome this problem, let us postulate that *qui* in (185) is a variant of the complementiser *que* which is derived by a rule along the following lines:

**The QUE ⇒ QUI rule:**
*the complementiser* que *is changed to* qui *whenever there is a gap in the subject position of the immediately following IP.*

In (188b) the conditions for this rule are satisfied, so *que* is converted to *qui*, giving the correct surface form (185a).

The advantages of this approach over one which treats *qui* in (185) as a relative pronoun may appear slight, particularly in cases like (185b) where it seems reasonable to suppose that the underlying relative pronoun is *qui*, since it refers to a human being. However, this account requires us to assume that the *qui* which appears on the surface is actually the reflex of the complementiser *que* (derived by the QUE ⇒ QUI rule), since if it were the relative pronoun the 'Relativised NP' condition would be violated. To justify the account outlined above, it must be shown that the QUE ⇒ QUI rule is independently motivated, by cases where *qui* precedes a subject gap but cannot be analysed as a relative (or interrogative) pronoun.

In this light consider the underlying structure (189), where the questioned element is the subject of a complement clause, corresponding to the English sentence: *Which student do you think is ill?*.

(189)    [$_{CP}$ Spec C [$_{IP}$ tu crois [$_{CP}$ que [$_{IP}$ quel étudiant est malade]]]]

Application of QU- movement, moving *quel étudiant* to the Spec of the highest CP, and of SUBJ-CL-INV gives the structure (190):

(190)    [$_{CP}$ quel étudiant crois [$_{IP}$ tu ___ [$_{CP}$ que [$_{IP}$ ___ est malade]]]]

However, in the correct surface form of this sentence, the complement clause is introduced by *qui* not *que*:

(191)    Quel étudiant crois-tu {qui / *qu'} est malade?

There is no obvious source for a relative or interrogative pronoun *qui* in this position, but the facts in (191) follow directly from the QUE ⇒ QUI rule, since *que* is followed by the gap left by movement of *quel étudiant* in (190).

This approach also gives a straightforward account of the otherwise puzzling data in (192), where *qui* appears to be in the 'wrong' position, compared with *who* in the English version:

(192)  a l'étudiant que je crois qui est malade
     b *l'étudiant qui je crois qu'est malade
     c the student who I think is ill

If *qui* were the relative pronoun corresponding to the subject of *être malade*, we would expect it to move to the beginning of the whole relative clause, like *who* in (192c) or *où* in *l'endroit où je crois qu'il a caché les bijoux*, but in (192a) it appears to remain within the lowest clause. This mystery is solved if we assume that the *qui* which appears on the surface is not the underlying relative pronoun, but the reflex of the complementiser which introduces the embedded complement clause. To clarify, the derivation of (192a) is summarised in (193):

(193) a $[_{NP}$ l'étudiant $[_{CP}$ Spec que $[_{IP}$ je crois $[_{CP}$ que $[_{IP}$ qui est malade]]]]]
   b $\Rightarrow [_{NP}$ l'étudiant $[_{CP}$ qui que $[_{IP}$ je crois $[_{CP}$ que $[_{IP}$ __ est malade]]]]]
   c $\Rightarrow [_{NP}$ l'étudiant $[_{CP}$ $\varnothing$ que $[_{IP}$ je crois $[_{CP}$ qui $[_{IP}$ __ est malade]]]]]

In the underlying structure (193a), the subject of *est malade* is the relative pronoun *qui* referring back to the noun *étudiant*. This pronoun is moved to the Spec of the higher CP, like *who* in (192c), as shown in (193b). However, in order to satisfy the 'Relativised NP' condition, *qui* must be deleted, leaving the complementiser *que* in the higher CP, as shown in (193c). As a result of QU- movement, the complementiser in the embedded clause is immediately followed by a gap in the subject position and is thus converted to *qui* by the QUE $\Rightarrow$ QUI rule.

The important point about this example (and indeed (191)) is that *qui* occurs not in the position to which a relative pronoun is moved but immediately before the position from which a QU- item has been moved. This is exactly what is predicted by the hypothesis that *qui* in subject relatives is a variant of the complementiser, not a relative pronoun. For further constructions which support this hypothesis, see 10.7.1 and 10.7.2.

### 10.5.8 The item 'dont'

*Dont* can be characterised as a relative 'adverb' which corresponds to phrases introduced by *de* in much the same way as the clitic *en* functions as a pronominal substitute for such phrases (see 6.6), though there are some significant differences which will be pointed out as the discussion proceeds.

Like *en*, *dont* is used to replace complements of verbs or adjectives which normally take the preposition *de*:

(194)    a    l'incident dont je me souviens
         b    la femme dont Jules est amoureux
         c    ce dont il s'agit

In cases like (194a, b), *duquel* or *de qui* can be used instead of *dont*, though *dont* is generally preferred, but in neuter cases like (194c), *de quoi* is not possible as an alternative:

(195)    a    l'incident duquel je me souviens
         b    la femme de qui Jules est amoureux
         c    *ce de quoi il s'agit

As a working hypothesis, let us assume that *duquel, de qui* and *de quoi* are the underlying forms of *dont* and that they are converted to *dont* at some stage in the derivation by a rule of the form *de* + QU- $\Rightarrow$ *dont* whose application is obligatory when QU- is *quoi* but optional (though preferred) in other cases. Thus the constructions in (194) and (195) are derived from the same underlying structures, given in (196):

(196)    a    [$_{NP}$ l'incident [$_{CP}$ que [$_{IP}$ je me souviens [$_{PP}$ de lequel]]]]
         b    [$_{NP}$ la femme [$_{CP}$ que [$_{IP}$ Jules est amoureux [$_{PP}$ de qui]]]]
         c    [$_{NP}$ ce [$_{CP}$ que [$_{IP}$ il s'agit [$_{PP}$ de quoi]]]]

One case where *dont* cannot be used to correspond to a complement of the type *de* + NP is where *de* expresses movement from a Source – in such cases *d'où* is normally used:

(197)    a    *la chambre dont Pierre est sorti
         b    la chambre d'où Pierre est sorti

Note that in this respect *dont* differs from *en*:

(198)    Marie est entrée dans la chambre au moment où Pierre en sortait

*Dont* can also be used in cases where the relativised element is the complement of a direct object or subject NP:

(199)    a    le livre dont j'ai lu la préface
         b    un homme dont j'ai insulté la femme

(200)    a    le livre dont la préface m'intéresse
         b    un homme dont la femme m'a insulté

However, *dont* cannot correspond to the complement of an NP which is introduced by a preposition:

(201)     a   *le livre dont j'ai réfléchi à la préface
          b   *un homme dont j'ai parlé à la femme

Given underlying structures of the form in (202), the ungrammaticality of the examples in (201) follows from the PP-Island Constraint, which prevents extraction of any element from within a PP (see 1.5.7):

(202)     ... [$_{CP}$ [$_{SPEC}$     ] que [$_{IP}$ j'ai réfléchi [$_{PP}$ à la préface [$_{PP}$ de QU-]]]]

In the case of (199)–(200), *dont* is not subject to the various restrictions which apply in similar constructions with *en*. Firstly, *dont* can be used readily with human reference as possessor or complement of a noun, as in (199b), (200b), whereas the corresponding use of *en* is generally avoided by using a possessive determiner (e.g. *J'ai insulté sa femme* vs *\*J'en ai insulté la femme*, see 6.6.2). Secondly, extraction of *dont* from a subject NP, as in (200), is not constrained by the nature of the verb, unlike cliticisation of *en* from a subject NP which is possible only with a restricted class of verbs (principally *être*, see 6.6.3): *La préface en est intéressante* vs *\*La préface m'en intéresse*.

Like *en*, *dont* can represent an expression quantified by an indefinite quantifier such as *beaucoup*, *plusieurs*, *certains*, etc., but there is a striking asymmetry between *en* and *dont* in this case. Whereas *en* can only represent a quantified direct object (*J'en ai acheté beaucoup* vs *\*Beaucoup en sont difficiles*), this use of *dont* is restricted to subjects:

(203)     a   *ces pommes dont j'ai acheté beaucoup
          b   ces questions dont beaucoup sont difficiles

Neither *dont* nor *en* can represent a quantified phrase which is part of a PP, by virtue of the PP-Island Constraint invoked above in connection with (201):

(204)     a   *ces questions dont j'ai répondu à beaucoup
          b   *J'en ai répondu à beaucoup

In cases like (204a) and (201) above, a grammatical (though rather clumsy) surface construction can be derived by moving the whole of the indirect object to the Spec of CP. Taking (201b) and (204a) as illustrative examples, the following underlying structures are postulated:

(205)     a   [$_{NP}$ un homme [$_{CP}$ Spec que [$_{IP}$ j'ai parlé [$_{PP}$ à la femme de qui]]]]
          b   [$_{NP}$ ces questions [$_{CP}$ Spec que [$_{IP}$ j'ai répondu [$_{PP}$ à beaucoup de lesquelles]]]]

QU- movement of the PP (followed by deletion of *que*) gives the following surface structures:

(206)　a　[$_{NP}$ un homme [$_{CP}$ [$_{PP}$ à la femme de qui] [$_{IP}$ j'ai parlé __ ]]]

　　　b　[$_{NP}$ ces questions [$_{CP}$ [$_{PP}$ à beaucoup de lesquelles] [$_{IP}$ j'ai répondu __ ]]]

In these cases, sequences of the type *de* + QU- cannot be converted to *dont*: in these cases:

(207)　　　a　*un homme à la femme dont j'ai parlé

　　　　　b　*ces questions à beaucoup dont j'ai répondu

The crucial difference between these cases and the earlier examples where the use of *dont* is obligatory is that in (206) *de* + QU- is embedded within a larger phrase. Thus, the rule which converts *de* + QU- to *dont* is restricted (in a manner similar to the QUOI ⇒ QUE rule proposed for interrogatives in 10.4.1) to cases where *de*+QU- occurs alone in the Spec of CP:

de+ *QU-* ⇒ dont *in the context:*

*[$_{NP}$ ... [$_{CP}$ de + QU- C IP]]*

There are some cases, involving verbs of saying or believing, where the connection between *dont* and phrases introduced by *de* is rather tenuous:

(208)　　　a　un homme dont je pense que je l'ai vu quelque part

　　　　　b　un homme dont j'ai dit qu'il ne réussira pas

　　　　　c　un homme dont il me semblait qu'il avait mauvaise mine

For the cases in (208a, b) it might be argued that *dont* corresponds to a complement of *penser* or *dire* (cf. *[Je pense / J'ai dit] de cet homme que ...*), but *sembler* in (208c) does not allow such a complement (**Il me semble de cet homme que ...*). Possibly, these examples represent a different use of *dont* which does not involve QU- movement. Informally, *dont* appears to present the modified element as the topic of a reported belief or assertion which serves to identify the individual concerned. Note that in this construction the modified element is represented by a personal pronoun (*il* or *le*) – see 10.5.12 for other relative clause constructions which make use of a personal pronoun rather than a relative pronoun.

A final construction with *dont*, which will simply be mentioned here, is the elliptical construction illustrated in (209), where the phrase introduced by *dont* designates a part of the set referred to by an earlier quantified NP:

(209)　　　a　Marie a sept enfants, dont trois filles

　　　　　b　Je voudrais cinq cafés, dont deux décaféinés

　　　　　c　Il y avait beaucoup de gens sur la plage, dont plusieurs anglais

　　　　　d　Dans la classe il y avait trois garçons, dont moi

As an alternative to *dont, parmi lesquels* can often be used: *Marie a sept enfants, parmi lesquels deux filles.* This construction can be characterised as a type of non-restrictive relative clause which specifies a part of the set denoted by the antecedent NP. A rather similar elliptical construction is found with *d'où*:

(210)   Le parlement a voté contre le gouvernement, d'où la crise actuelle

In such cases, *d'où* introduces a consequence of the situation described in the preceding sentence.

### 10.5.9   *Infinitival relatives*

Infinitival relatives, illustrated by the bracketed expressions in (211), typically modify indefinite NPs which describe hypothetical entities, usually defined in terms of a 'purpose':

(211)      a   Je cherche un sac [dans lequel mettre mes affaires]
           b   Je cherche un prêtre [à qui me confesser]
           c   Je cherche un livre [à lire]
           d   Je cherche une fille [à inviter à la fête]

Like most other infinitival constructions, infinitival relatives do not allow an overt subject, but the 'understood' subject is equated with an appropriate participant in the main clause (e.g. (211a) means *Je cherche un sac dans lequel je puisse mettre mes affaires*).

As in the case of finite relatives, overt relative pronouns can only occur when they are governed by a preposition (e.g. *dans* in (211a), *à* in (211b)). Thus we cannot use a relative pronoun (or indeed *que*) to denote the direct object in cases like (211c, d):

(212)      a   *Je cherche un livre [{lequel / que} lire]
           b   *Je cherche une fille [{qui / que} inviter à la fête]

This follows from the 'Relativised NP' condition proposed in 10.5.6 (though note that in infinitival relatives this condition applies to English as well: *I am looking for a book (*which) to read*).

In the absence of an overt QU- phrase (as in (211c, d)), the infinitival relative is introduced by *à*, which is taken to be a complementiser (see 9.5.1). However, this complementiser cannot co-occur with a QU- phrase:

(213)      *Je cherche un sac [dans lequel à mettre mes affaires]

To account for these restrictions, underlying structures of the type in (214) are postulated:

(214)      a   [$_{NP}$ un sac [$_{CP}$ Spec à [$_{IP}$ PRO mettre mes affaires [$_{PP}$ dans lequel]]]]
           b   [$_{NP}$ un livre [$_{CP}$ Spec à [$_{IP}$ PRO lire [$_{NP}$ lequel]]]]

In both cases the PP or NP containing *lequel* is moved to the Spec of CP, and in both cases either *lequel* or the complementiser *à* must be deleted. In (214a) the first option is precluded because *lequel* is contained in a larger phrase, so *à* is deleted giving (211a), but in (214b) *lequel* must be deleted to satisfy the 'Relativised NP' condition and *à* is retained, giving (211c). Note that this is exactly the same situation as was observed in 10.5.6 for *que* in finite relatives. This parallel between *à* and *que* thus provides indirect support for the claim that *que* is a complementiser, since it is fairly clear that *à* is not a relative pronoun. The observation that *que* cannot introduce infinitival relatives follows from the fact that the complementiser *que* only introduces finite clauses. Note that this exclusion of *que* would be more difficult to explain according to the 'traditional' view whereby *que* is the direct object relative pronoun while *qui* and *lequel* are restricted to occurring after prepositions.

### 10.5.10  Free relatives

**Free relatives** are constructions in which a relative clause modifies an NP which lacks a lexical head noun. For this reason, they are sometimes called 'headless' relatives. Typical examples are relative clauses introduced by the item *ce*, as in (215):

(215)     a   J'ai mangé ce que vous aviez laissé sur la table
          b   Luc regrette ce qui s'est passé
          c   Je ne comprends pas ce à quoi vous faites allusion
          d   Jean a pris ce dont il a besoin

For the sake of concreteness, it is assumed that *ce* is a determiner which governs an empty noun (or N') in the head position, as in (216), though this assumption is not crucial to the present discussion:

(216)     $[_{NP}$ ce $[_{N'} \varnothing ] [_{CP} \ldots]]$

The internal syntax of the relative clause (the CP) is essentially the same as for other relative clauses. The underlying form of the relative pronoun is assumed to be *quoi* since this is the form which always surfaces when governed by a preposition, as in (215c) (see 10.5.4). However, when the preposition is *de*, *de* + *quoi* is always converted to *dont*, as in (215d) (see 10.5.8).

Free relatives introduced by *ce* can only be used to denote inanimate entities whose grammatical gender has not been established. In this respect the use of these constructions is similar to that of the pronoun *cela*. When referring to humans or to inanimate entities whose gender has been established (e.g. by previous use of an appropriate noun), the relative clause is introduced by *celui*, *celle*, etc.:

(217)  a  Celui qui a volé mon stylo doit être puni
       b  Quel train prenez-vous? Je prends celui qui arrive à midi
       c  Ces pommes sont magnifiques, mais celles que j'ai achetées sont pourries

This use reflects that of *celui-là*, *celui-ci*, etc. Finally, when referring to places the free relative is preceded by the adverb *là*:

(218)  J'ai rangé ces documents là où se trouvaient les autres

As was noted in 10.4.6, free relatives of the type *ce qui*... and *ce que*... can be used as indirect questions, as in (219):

(219)  a  Je me suis demandé ce que vous aviez laissé sur la table
       b  Je me demande ce qui s'est passé

The distinction between genuine free relatives and free relatives which masquerade as indirect questions can be seen more clearly by reformulating the constructions using an appropriate noun:

(220)  a  J'ai mangé la chose que vous aviez laissée sur la table
       b  *J'ai mangé quelle chose vous aviez laissée sur la table

(221)  a  *Je me suis demandé la chose que vous aviez laissée sur la table
       b  Je me suis demandé quelle chose vous aviez laissée sur la table

Ultimately, the interpretation of a free relative depends on the properties of the verb in the main clause: *manger* is a verb which takes an NP complement (denoting a physical object) whereas *se demander* (with the meaning 'wonder'[4]) normally takes an interrogative CP. Thus in (215a) and (220a) we can substitute an NP such as *ce morceau de fromage*, while in (219a) and (221b) we can substitute a clause introduced by *si*, e.g. *si vous aviez laissé un morceau de fromage sur la table*. Similarly, (215b) can be paraphrased by *Luc regrette cet incident* or *Luc regrette la chose qu'il a fait*, but *regretter* cannot take an interrogative complement: *\*Je regrette si cela s'est passé*.

With verbs which allow both possibilities, potential ambiguities may arise:

(222)  J'ai demandé ce qu'elle avait envie de manger

With the sense of 'request' or 'ask for', *demander* takes an NP, giving the interpretation 'I ordered the particular dish which she wanted', but with the sense of 'ask a question', we get the reading 'I asked (her to tell me) which dish she

---

[4] Example (221a) is just about acceptable with the rather contrived meaning 'I requested for myself the thing which you left on the table.'

wanted.' Again these interpretations can be distinguished by the procedure illustrated in (220)–(221):

(223)    a  J'ai demandé le plat qu'elle avait envie de manger
         b  J'ai demandé quel plat elle avait envie de manger

### 10.5.11  Non-restrictive relatives

The basic properties of non-restrictive relative clauses were outlined in 10.5.1. Recall that non-restrictive relatives do not serve to define the entity being referred to but make a 'passing comment' on the entity which is already identified by the NP. For this reason, non-restrictive relatives can modify proper nouns and other expressions (e.g. pronouns like *cela*) which directly identify a unique referent. On the other hand, free relatives do not allow a non-restrictive interpretation, presumably because the element *ce* is not sufficient to identify a particular entity independently of the information provided by the clause. Also, subjunctive and infinitival relatives do not allow a non-restrictive interpretation – as was noted in 10.5.1 and 10.5.9, these types of relative clause typically define an entity whose existence is hypothetical, whereas non-restrictive relatives presuppose the existence of the entity about which the passing comment is made.

The internal syntax of non-restrictive relatives is essentially the same as that presented above for restrictive relatives, with one minor, but interesting difference. In 10.5.4 it was noted that the 'true' relative pronouns, *lequel* and its variants, can only occur on the surface when they are governed by a preposition – in other cases, the construction with a complementiser *que* or *qui* (corresponding to English *that*) must be used: *le livre {*lequel / que} j'ai lu, le livre {*lequel / qui} m'intéresse*. However, this restriction does not apply systematically in non-restrictive relatives:

(224)    a  Nous avons entendu quatre témoins, lesquels affirment avoir vu l'accusé le jour du meurtre
         b  Le ministre a fait un résumé de l'enquête, lequel sera publié dans le «Journal officiel»

We also find non-restrictive relative clauses introduced by an NP containing a relative pronoun (cf. *\*l'homme la femme de qui j'ai insultée*):

(225)    a  Ce poème, [$_{NP}$ l'auteur duquel] est inconnu, est un chef d'œuvre
         b  Ces pommes, [$_{NP}$ beaucoup desquelles] sont pourries, sont dégoûtantes

However, examples of the type in (224) and (225) appear to be possible only when the QU- expression is the subject of the relative clause:

(226)    a  *Le ministre a fait un résumé de l'enquête, lequel on publiera dans le «Journal officiel»

          b  *Ce poème, l'auteur duquel je ne connais pas, est un chef d'œuvre

Within the approach presented in 10.5.6, the data in (224) and (225) might be taken as evidence that the condition which prevents NPs (including relative pronouns) from occurring in the Spec of CP of a restrictive relative (the 'Relativised NP' condition) is relaxed in the case of non-restrictive relatives. Alternatively, we might conclude that the 'Relativised NP' condition does hold for non-restrictive relatives, but QU- movement of subjects is optional in non-restrictive relatives – i.e. the relative pronouns in (224) and the NPs in (225) are not moved into Spec of CP, but remain in the subject position, so the 'Relativised NP' condition does not come into play. This would explain why apparent violations of this condition are possible only with subjects.

Under either approach, the examples in (224) show clearly that *lequel* and its variants are not restricted to occurring as objects of prepositions. This undermines the 'traditional' view whereby *lequel, que* and *qui* are all relative pronouns distinguished according to their grammatical function within the relative clause (i.e. *lequel* = object of preposition, *que* = direct object, *qui* = subject), but it is entirely consistent with the hypothesis proposed in 10.5.6 that the surface distribution of genuine relative pronouns such as *lequel* (as opposed to the complementisers *que* and *qui*) is determined by conditions on the occurrence of NPs in the Spec position of relative clauses.

Examples like (224) and (225) are characteristic of formal style and occur predominantly in legal or administrative texts. In all registers we can use the complementisers *que* and *qui* to introduce non-restrictive relatives:

(227)    a  Nous avons entendu quatre témoins, qui affirment avoir vu l'accusé le jour du meurtre

          b  Le ministre a fait un résumé de l'enquête, qui sera publié dans le «Journal officiel»

(228)    Le ministre a fait un résumé de l'enquête, qu'on publiera dans le «Journal officiel»

Similarly in cases like (225) and (226b) we can use the construction with *dont* with a non-restrictive interpretation:

(229)    a  Ce poème, dont l'auteur est inconnu, est un chef d'œuvre

          b  Ces pommes, dont beaucoup sont pourries, sont dégoûtantes

          c  Ce poème, dont je ne connais pas l'auteur, est un chef d'œuvre

### *10.5.12 Relative clauses with resumptive pronouns*

Alongside regular relative clause constructions like (230), derived by QU- movement, in colloquial speech we often find constructions like (231), involving a
'resumptive' pronoun, though they tend to be regarded as substandard:

(230)    a  le professeur à qui j'ai parlé
          b  le livre dont j'ai besoin
          c  l'homme dont j'ai oublié le nom
          d  la fille à côté de qui je me suis assis

(231)    a  le prof que je lui ai parlé
          b  le bouquin que j'en ai besoin
          c  le type que j'ai oublié son nom
          d  la fille que je me suis assis à côté d'elle

The constructions in (231) can be assigned essentially the same underlying structures as regular relatives except that in place of a QU- item (relative pronoun)
they have an appropriate personal pronoun, realised as a clitic in (231a, b), a possessive in (231c) and a disjunctive form in (231d). Thus, whereas (230a) is derived
from (232) by movement of *à qui* to Spec of CP, (231a) is derived from (233) by
cliticisation of the item represented as PRONOUN to the verb:

(232)    $[_{NP}$ le professeur $[_{CP}$ que $[_S$ j'ai parlé à qui]]]

(233)    $[_{NP}$ le professeur $[_{CP}$ que $[_S$ j'ai parlé à PRONOUN]]]

Constructions of the type in (231) lend further support to the hypothesis that relative clauses are introduced by the complementiser *que* in underlying structure – in
these cases, this complementiser appears in the surface structure since no other
item is moved into Spec of CP.

### *10.5.13 Apparent cases of preposition stranding*

Another relative clause construction encountered in colloquial speech is illustrated in (234):

(234)    a  la fille que je suis sorti avec
          b  une valise que je ne peux pas voyager sans
          c  la maison que je suis passé devant

At first sight, these examples appear to be parallel to English cases such as *the girl
{who / that} I went out with* derived as in (235) by extracting the complement of a
preposition:

(235)     [$_{NP}$ the girl [$_{CP}$ that [$_S$ I went out with who]]]

If this analysis were correct for the examples in (234), the PP-Island Constraint would have to be weakened. However, there is evidence that the constructions in (234) are not derived by QU- movement of the complement of the preposition, but are analogous to the resumptive pronoun cases in 10.5.12.

Firstly, this construction is possible only with a highly restricted set of prepositions; for instance it is not possible with *à* or *de*, unlike English *to* or *of* which can be stranded quite readily:

(236)     a  *l'homme que j'ai parlé à      (cf. 'the man who I talked to')
          b  *la chose que j'ai rêvé de     (cf. 'the thing which I dreamt of')

Secondly, some prepositions must assume a different form when used in this construction (e.g. *dessus, dedans*, as opposed to *sur, dans*):

(237)     a  une affaire que je sauterais {dessus / *sur}
          b  la maison que je suis entré {dedans / *dans}

The preposition forms which allow the construction in (234) are the same as those which can be used in simple sentences without an overt complement (see 8.3.6):

(238)     a  Je connais cette fille, mais je ne suis jamais sorti avec
          b  Cette maison m'intrigue; je suis souvent passé devant mais je ne
             suis jamais entré dedans
          c  Si on me proposait une affaire comme ça, je sauterais dessus

As can be seen from the examples in (238), although these prepositions lack an overt complement, they have an understood complement which can be construed as referring back to a previous NP in much the same way as a pronoun (compare (238a) with English *I know that girl, but I have never gone out with her*). Thus, in so far as these prepositions have the same function as phrases of the type preposition + pronoun, examples like those in (234) and (237) can be regarded as relative clauses of the resumptive pronoun type, on a par with (231), the only difference being that the resumptive pronominal element is implicit, incorporated as it were in the preposition.

## 10.6   QU- exclamatives
### 10.6.1   *Types of QU- exclamatives*
We have already looked at exclamative constructions like (239) derived by QU-movement and (optionally) STYL-INV:

(239)    a    Quel bruit les manifestants faisaient!

        b    Quel bruit faisaient les manifestants!

Here, *quel* corresponds to English *what a* and makes an exclamative comment on the quality or intensity of the thing referred to. As in English, the QU- expression can be used as an exclamation in its own right, perhaps through ellipsis of the rest of the clause:

(240)    a    Quel bruit!

        b    Quel sale temps!

English also has exclamatives analogous to (239) where *how* qualifies an adjective or adverb:

(241)    a    How pretty she is!

        b    How fast it goes!

In French, exclamations like (241) can be expressed in a variety of ways, ranging from the highly literary (and now archaic) construction with *combien* in (242a) and (243a) to the highly colloquial construction with *qu'est-ce que* in (242e) and (243e):

(242)    a    †Combien elle est jolie!

        b    Comme elle est jolie!

        c    Qu'elle est jolie!

        d    Ce qu'elle est jolie!

        e    Qu'est-ce qu'elle est jolie!

(243)    a    †Combien il roule vite!

        b    Comme il roule vite!

        c    Qu'il roule vite!

        d    Ce qu'il roule vite!

        e    Qu'est-ce qu'il roule vite!

The same items can be used in examples like (244), where the intensifying effect relates to the verb (cf. *How I love you!*):

(244)    a    †Combien je t'aime!

        b    Comme je t'aime!

        c    Que je t'aime!

        d    Ce que je t'aime!

        e    Qu'est-ce que je t'aime!

The examples in (242)–(244) are similar to declarative sentences in which an adjective or adverb is modified by *si* or the verb is modified by *tant*:

(245)     a   Elle est si jolie
          b   Il roule si vite
          c   Je t'aime tant

Thus, we might take the initial expressions in (242)–(244) to be QU- equivalents of the degree adverbs *si* and *tant*, which are preposed by QU- movement, leaving the adjective or adverb behind in (242)–(243). This approach seems justified for the English examples with *how*, except that in (241) QU- movement must apply to the whole AP or AdvP. An alternative view is that these expressions are simply items which can be put in front of a sentence to turn it into an exclamation, rather like *boy* in (246) except that this item triggers S U B J - A U X - I N V which has no analogue in the French cases:

(246)     a   Boy is she pretty!
          b   Boy does it go fast!
          c   Boy do I love you!

### 10.6.2   Exclamatives with 'combien'

The item for which the QU- movement analysis seems most plausible is *combien*. As in questions, this item can quantify a noun in exclamative constructions (cf. *What a lot of books you have read!*):

(247)     †Combien de livres vous avez lu!

Here it is clear that the NP containing *combien* has undergone QU- movement. There are also attested literary examples[5] where *combien* immediately precedes an adjective or adverb, either in elliptical constructions analogous to (240) or via QU- movement:

(248)     a   †Le joli système d'éducation et combien pratique!   (Prévost)
          b   †Combien souvent j'eus à l'entendre répéter!       (Gide)

Such examples are rare, even compared with the constructions in (242a) and (243a), but they show that *combien* can function as a degree modifier of adjectives and adverbs and thus support the view that cases like (242a) and (243a) are derived by QU- movement of *combien* from a position within the AP or AdvP – e.g. as in (249):

(249)     $[_{CP} [_{SPEC}$   $] C [_{IP}$ elle est $[_{AP}$ combien jolie]]]

---

[5] The literary examples in (248) and others in this section are taken from Gérard (1980). References in parentheses indicate the author, where known, or the grammar in which the examples are cited.

Further evidence in support of the QU- movement analysis is provided by cases involving STYL-INV[6] (recall that STYL-INV typically correlates with leftward movement of some other element):

(250)  a  †Combien de crimes a commis ce triste sire!     (R. Le Bidois 1952)
       b  †Combien vive est ma joie!                            (R. Le Bidois 1952)
       c  †Combien est étroit le chemin qui mène à la vie! (R. Bossuet)

### 10.6.3  Exclamatives with 'comme'

Turning now to *comme*, we find a rather different picture. Firstly, *comme* never occurs within an AP or AdvP (cf. (248)):

(251)        a  *Comme jolie elle est!
            b  *Comme vite il roulait!

Nor can it occur as a determiner within an NP (cf. (247)):

(252)        *Comme de livres il a lu!

In (253a), *comme* seems to focus on the quantity of meat involved, suggesting perhaps that *comme* is the underlying determiner of the direct object, like *combien* in questions of the type in (253b) (see 10.4.4):

(253)        a  Comme il mangait de la viande!
            b  Combien a-t-il mangé de viande?

Note, however, that the definite article is obligatory in (253a), though it does not occur in the construction with *combien* unless a partitive interpretation is intended:

(254)        *Comme il mangeait de viande!

Also, with *comme* the NP can be quantified independently, a possibility which is excluded with *combien*:

(255)        a  Comme il mangeait beaucoup de viande!
            b  *Combien mangeait-il beaucoup de viande?

Similarly, in cases of the type in (244) *comme* can occur with a degree adverb modifying the verb, but *combien* cannot:

(256)        a  Comme je t'aime beaucoup!
            b  *Combien je t'aime beacoup!

---

[6] Note that (250c) violates the condition which normally prevents STYL-INV from operating across *être* with an AP complement (see 10.3.4). This may be symptomatic of the generally more 'liberal' use of STYL-INV in literary style.

Finally, exclamative constructions with *comme* never allow S T Y L - I N V :

(257)     a     Comme les enfants chantaient!
          b     *Comme chantaient les enfants!

This evidence strongly suggests that *comme* is not a QU- item (determiner or degree adverb) which is moved from some position within the clause, but is simply an exclamative particle inserted at the beginning of the sentence. To be more precise, let us assume that exclamative *comme* is a complementiser. Thus, example (242b) has the structure (258) (compare (249) for (242a)):

(258)     $[_{CP} [_C$ comme] $[_{IP}$ elle est jolie]]

### 10.6.4   Exclamatives with 'que'

The case of exclamative *que* is more complicated. In literary French, *que* can occur within an NP as a determiner expressing quantity, like *combien*:

(259)     †Que de trésors on perd dans sa jeunesse!     (Musset)

In such cases, *que* can be separated from the NP which it quantifies, in the manner of *combien* in questions:

(260)     a     †Que vous me faites de peine!     (Zola)
          b     †Qu'il a d'esprit!     (Molière)

Similar constructions occur in more 'normal' registers, but with the definite article before the quantified noun:

(261)     a     Que vous me faites de la peine!
          b     Qu'il a de l'esprit!

Also, the NP can be quantified independently:

(262)     Qu'il a beaucoup d'esprit!

In view of the comments on *comme* and *combien* in (253)–(256), this evidence suggests that exclamative *que* has undergone a change in status, from a determiner like *combien* in Classical French to a complementiser like *comme* in Modern (non-literary) French. However, the older usage persists in elliptical exclamatives like (263):

(263)     a     Que de travail pour pas grand'chose!
          b     Que de larmes!

This dual status of exclamative *que* makes it difficult to ascertain the syntax of cases like (242c), (243c) and (244c), but outside literary usage *que* seems to function like a complementiser (i.e. like *comme*), disallowing STYL-INV but allowing degree modifiers of the verb:

(264)  a  *Que travaillent les étudiants de première année!
       b  Que je t'aime beaucoup!

### 10.6.5 *Exclamatives with 'ce que' and 'qu'est-ce que'*

The colloquial constructions with *ce que* and *qu'est-ce que* look like free relatives and 'partial' questions respectively, except that there is no gap in the direct object position (but see discussion of examples (268) below). For this reason, it is unclear what the syntactic source of *ce* and the other components of *qu'est-ce que* might be. In terms of the patterns discerned above, these items behave like the complementiser *comme*. They do not allow STYL-INV:

(265)  a  *Qu'est-ce que travaillent les étudiants de première année!
       b  *Ce que travaillent les étudiants de première année!

They can occur with other degree modifiers:

(266)  a  Qu'est-ce que tu parles beaucoup!
       b  Ce que tu parles beaucoup!

When the exclamation is focused on an NP, with a quantitative interpretation, this NP has a determiner of its own:

(267)  a  Qu'est-ce qu'il a dépensé du fric!
       b  Ce qu'il a dépensé du fric!

Although it may be implausible to argue that *ce que* and *qu'est-ce que* constitute complementisers, the above evidence suggests that the constructions in question do not involve QU- movement of a determiner or degree item. Nevertheless, there is one range of cases for which a QU- movement analysis seems well motivated. Alongside examples like (267) and (239), where the exclamatory force is focused on a direct object NP, we have the alternative constructions in (268), where the nominal element is introduced by *comme*:

(268)  a  {Qu'est-ce qu' / Ce qu'} il a dépensé comme fric!
       b  {Qu'est-ce qu' / Ce qu'} ils faisaient comme boucan!

These examples are identical in form to genuine questions and free relatives:

(269)  a  Qu'est-ce qu'il a dépensé comme fric?
       b  J'ai calculé ce qu'il a dépensé comme fric

Note that we do not have analogous examples introduced by the complementisers *que* and *comme*:

(270)     a   *Qu'il a dépensé comme fric!

          b   *Comme ils faisaient comme boucan!

For the cases in (268)–(269), it is reasonable to postulate an underlying pronoun *quoi* (modified in some way by the *comme* phrase) which undergoes QU- movement in the normal way:

(271)     a   [$_{CP}$ [$_{SPEC}$    ]C [$_{IP}$ c'est [$_{CP}$ que [$_{IP}$ il a dépensé quoi comme fric]]]]

          b   [$_{NP}$ ce [$_{CP}$ [$_{SPEC}$    ] que [$_{IP}$ il a dépensé quoi comme fric]]]

In (271a) S U B J - C L - I N V applies, raising *est* to C, and *quoi* is converted to the clitic form *que*, while in (271b) *quoi* must be deleted to satisfy the 'Relativised NP' condition. The fact that examples like (268) can be derived by means of independently motivated processes suggests that these constructions may represent the model from which the constructions in (242d, e), (243d, e), (244d, e), (266) and (267) evolved. Just as the determiner/degree modifier *que* of Classical French has been reanalysed as an exclamative complementiser, we may postulate that *qu'est-ce que* and *ce que*, derived by QU- movement in (268), have extended their use to become general exclamation markers largely supplanting *que* and *comme* in colloquial speech.

## 10.7   Other QU- constructions

### 10.7.1   *Pseudo-relatives*

The bracketted sequences in (272) look like relative clauses:

(272)     a   J'ai vu Pierre [qui embrassait Marie]
          b   J'entends le vent [qui souffle dans les arbres]
          c   Voilà le facteur [qui arrive]

However, they do not conform to either of the types of relative clauses which have been discussed in the preceding sections. They cannot be analysed as restrictive relatives since in (272a) the clause accompanies a proper noun and in (272b, c) the clause does not identify the particular wind or postman which the speaker is referring to (as opposed to other winds or postmen). Note also that this NP can be realised as a clitic pronoun, a possibility not available with normal relative clauses (e.g. we cannot say *Je les ai mangées qui étaient pourries* to mean something like 'I ate those (apples) which were rotten'):

(273)     Je l'ai vu qui embrassait Marie

In (272a) we can replace *Pierre* by an NP containing a relative clause:

(274)      J'ai vu l'homme dont tu es amoureuse qui embrassait Marie

However, it is not possible to have two genuine restrictive relatives modifying the same noun, unless they are conjoined by *et*:

(275)      a  *L'homme dont tu es amoureuse qui habite à côté de moi est
              entré
           b  L'homme dont tu es amoureuse et qui habite à côté de moi est
              entré

This evidence strongly suggests that the *qui* clauses in (272)–(274) have a very different syntactic function from the restrictive relative *qui* clause in (275).

The constructions in (272)–(274) do not have the interpretation normally associated with non-restrictive relatives – e.g. the *qui* clause does not make a 'passing comment' about Pierre (as in *J'ai vu Pierre, qui (d'ailleurs) est mon meilleur ami*) but represents part of the description of the event which was witnessed (as in English *I saw Pierre kissing Marie*). Also, we cannot replace *qui* by *lequel* or insert a parenthetical expression such as *d'ailleurs*. More significantly, this construction does not allow the full range of relative clause types:

(276)      a  *J'ai vu Pierre que Marie embrassait
           b  *J'ai vu Pierre à qui Marie donnait des bisous
           c  *J'ai vu Pierre que je crois qui embrassait Marie

Pursuing the idea that the *qui* clauses in (272)–(274) represent the event which was witnessed, we can derive (272a) from the underlying structure in (277), where the clause is the complement of *voir*, by a rule which moves the subject *Pierre* to the left of the complementiser (its exact position is not very important here):

(277)      [$_{IP}$ j'ai vu [$_{CP}$ que [$_{IP}$ Pierre embrassait Marie]]]

A slight problem with this analysis is that the underlying structure (277) also corresponds to the surface sentence (278), which has a different meaning from (272a):

(278)      J'ai vu que Pierre embrassait Marie

The essential difference is that the *que* clause in (278) represents the fact of Pierre's kissing Marie (giving a meaning 'understand' or 'realise' for *voir*) whereas the clause in (272a) denotes the event itself. Thus we might postulate that movement of the subject in (277) occurs if, and only if, the clause has an event interpretation.

Alternatively, we might take the view that *Pierre* is semantically a complement of *voir* as well as the understood subject of *embrasser* – after all, (272a) entails that

I saw Pierre as well as his action. This interpretation can be represented by the structure (279), where *voir* takes a direct object (*Pierre*) and a complement clause whose subject is null (controlled by *Pierre* in much the same manner as subjects of infinitives, see 9.2.1):

(279) $[_{IP}$ j'ai vu $[_{NP}$ Pierre$_p$ $]$ $[_{CP}$ que $[_{IP}$ P R O $_p$ embrassait Marie]]]

Conceptually, these two analyses are quite different, but no attempt will be made here to choose between them (cf. the similar dilemma concerning infinitival constructions like *J'ai {vu / laissé} Pierre embrasser Marie* discussed in 9.3.4). They can be seen as different ways of representing the intuition that the *qui* clause in (272)–(274) is a complement of the verb, not a modifier of the NP (i.e. not a relative clause). The reason why these constructions look like relative clauses is that they are introduced by *qui* rather than the normal complementiser *que*. However, this can be accounted for, under either analysis, by the rule proposed in 10.5.7 which converts *que* to *qui* whenever it is followed by a gap in the subject position. Moreover, the fact that this rule operates in clauses which are not interpreted as relative clauses and are not derived by QU- movement provides further support for the argument that the *qui* which introduces genuine relative clauses is a form of the complementiser rather than a relative pronoun.

### 10.7.2  Cleft constructions

A common means of focusing on a particular constituent of a sentence is to present it as a complement of *c'est* as in (280):

(280)   a   C'est Luc qui a volé mon stylo
         b   C'est mon stylo que Luc a volé

This construction, which will be referred to as the **cleft** construction, raises questions similar to those discussed in the previous section. In (280a), the *qui* clause does not make a passing comment about Luc, and the *que* clause in (280b) does not serve to identify the particular pen in question (at least not under the most natural interpretation of these sentences). In other words, the clauses introduced by *que* or *qui* do not function as relative clauses. The typical effect of clefting is to give a contrastive emphasis to the element which is presented as the object of *c'est* – e.g. contrasting Luc with another potential culprit (whom the addressee perhaps suspected) or emphasising that the stolen object was my pen (rather than, say, my watch).

The constructions in (280) can be derived from underlying structures where *c'est* takes a complement clause from which the focused item is raised to become the object of *c'est*, as in (281):

(281)     a  [$_{IP}$ c'est   [$_{CP}$ que Luc a volé mon stylo]]

      b  [$_{IP}$ c'est   [$_{CP}$ que Luc a volé mon stylo]]

In example (281a), movement of *Luc* leaves a gap in the subject position of the embedded clause, thus triggering the QUE ⇒ QUI rule, to give the surface form in (281a).

An alternative approach which we might envisage is to assume that the clefted expression is the complement of *c'est* in the underlying structure and that it is represented within the embedded clause by a QU- item, as shown in (282) for example (280b):

(282)     [$_{IP}$ c'est mon stylo [$_{CP}$ [$_{SPEC}$  ] que [$_{IP}$ Luc a volé lequel]]]

QU- movement and subsequent deletion of the pronoun (as in relative clauses) will give the surface form (280b). The essence of this approach is that the embedded clause has the same internal syntax as a relative clause even though its function is different.

Both of these approaches give the same result for cases like those in (280), but they make different predictions in cases where the focused expression is an indirect object: e.g. *Marie* in *J'ai parlé à Marie*. According to the first approach, we have the underlying structure (283):

(283)     [$_{IP}$ c'est   [$_{CP}$ que [$_{IP}$ j'ai parlé [$_{PP}$ à Marie]]]]

Since no element can be moved out of a PP, the whole PP *à Marie* must be moved into the complement position of *c'est*, giving (284):

(284)     C'est à Marie que j'ai parlé

This is the normal cleft construction in such cases.

According to the second approach, *Marie* can be introduced directly as the complement of *c'est* (without a preposition) but the QU- item in the embedded clause must be introduced by *à* to indicate that it is an indirect object:

(285)     [$_{IP}$ c'est Marie [$_{CP}$ Spec que [$_{IP}$ j'ai parlé [$_{PP}$ à qui]]]]

QU- movement of *à qui* will give the sentence (286):

(286)     C'est Marie à qui j'ai parlé

This construction is much less widespread than the construction in (284) and is perceived as rather archaic, but it is used occasionally in more formal styles. Thus, it seems that both of the analyses envisaged above are valid, but the first one represents the norm in Modern French.

The availability of these two derivations may shed some light on the question of agreement of the verb in cases where the focused item is a plural NP. In colloquial speech *c'est* can retain the singular form even when the following NP is plural, but in more formal registers there is a strong tendency to use the plural form *ce sont*, which is generally regarded as the 'correct' form:

(287)  a  C'est les roses que je préfère
      b  Ce sont les roses que je préfère

This difference can be accounted for if we assume that *c'est* agrees in number with its underlying complement. In the colloquial construction (287a) the underlying complement is a clause, which is treated as singular for purposes of agreement, but if we consider the formal construction (287b) to be an instance of the derivation illustrated in (282) above, the underlying complement of *c'est* is the plural NP *les roses*.

On the question of agreement, it may be noted that when the focused item is a first- or second-person subject pronoun, *c'est* always assumes the third-person singular form, but the verb in the subordinate clause agrees in number and person with the understood subject:

(289)  a  C'est nous qui avons raison
      b  C'est toi qui as volé mon stylo

### 10.7.3  *'Pseudo-cleft' constructions*

Another way of giving contrastive emphasis to a phrase is to use the construction illustrated in (289), sometimes called the **pseudo-cleft** construction:

(289)  a  Celui qui a volé mon stylo, c'est Luc
      b  Ce que Luc a volé, c'est mon stylo

These can be analysed as left-dislocated constructions, where the dislocated expression is a free relative (see 10.5.10) and the 'core' sentence is an identificational construction (see 2.5.1). Thus, apart from the form of the dislocated expression, the examples in (289) are parallel to *Le voleur, c'est Luc* and *L'objet du vol, c'est mon stylo*.

Where the focused element is the object of a preposition, this preposition occurs within the free relative (giving *dont* corresponding to *de*):

(290)  a  Celui à qui j'ai parlé, c'est Marie
      b  Ce dont je suis fier, c'est mon travail

However, in some cases (particularly with *de*) there is a tendency to repeat the preposition after *c'est*:

(291)  Ce dont je suis fier, c'est de mon travail

The use of a preposition after *c'est* is obligatory when the focused expression describes a place and the free relative has the form *là où* ...:

(292)     Là où j'ai mis les bijoux, c'est dans le tiroir

**Exercises**

1   The following is an imaginary exercise on Inversion completed by an imaginary (and rather weak) student; his answers are given in italics. Your task is to mark this exercise and to provide constructive comments on his mistakes. (N.B. not all the answers are completely wrong.)

Rewrite the following sentences applying Inversion to the sequence in bold type. Where more than one type of Inversion is possible, list all the possibilities. If no Inversion is possible, write 'NONE'.

(a) Par quel chemin **Pierre est arrivé**?
*Par quel chemin est Pierre arrivé?*
*Par quel chemin Pierre est-il arrivé?*

(b) **Cela est vraisemblable**?
*Est cela vraisemblable?*

(c) Le candidat que **la plupart des électeurs favorisaient** était Mitterand
*NONE*

(d) Quel bruit **les manifestants ont fait**!
*Quel bruit les manifestants ont-ils fait!*
*Quel bruit ont les manifestants fait!*

(e) Pourquoi **Jaurès a été tué**?
*Pourquoi a été tué Jaurès?*

(f) Peut-être **Robert a gagné**
*Peut-être a Robert gagné*

(g) «La femme, **Aragon a dit**, est l'avenir de l'homme»
*«La femme, Aragon a-t-il dit, est l'avenir de l'homme»*

(h) Dans trois jours **Marcel achetera une nouvelle voiture**
*Dans trois jours Marcel achètera-t-il une nouvelle voiture*

(i) Je ne sais pas comment **ils sont sortis**
*Je ne sais pas comment sont-ils sortis*

(j) Quand **Charles a rencontré Diane**?
*Quand a Charles rencontré Diane?*
*Quand Charles a-t-il rencontré Diane?*

(k)   Je me demande pourquoi **Jules a démissionné**
      *Je me demande pourquoi Jules a-t-il démissionné*

(l)   **Pierre est fou**?
      *Est Pierre fou?*

(m)   L'endroit où **Luc cachera les bijoux** est difficile à trouver
      *L'endroit où cachera Luc les bijoux est difficile à trouver*

(n)   Demain **nous partirons en vacances**
      *Demain partirons-nous en vacances*

2   Project: Study the use and avoidance of Inversion in a corpus of texts and/or recordings of speech from a variety of registers. Classify each example of Inversion according to its type and the construction in which it occurs; also make a note of each instance where Inversion would have been possible but is not actually used. Try to ascertain whether certain types of Inversion are exploited or avoided more than others in different registers.

3   Discuss the following 'concessive' constructions with particular reference to the problem of Inversion.

    (a)   Si bons que soient vos arguments, vous n'arriverez pas à me convaincre

    (b)   Cette demande, si raisonnable soit-elle, sera refusée

    (c)   Cette demande, si raisonnable qu'elle soit, sera refusée

    (d)   Cette plaisanterie, fût-elle innocente, m'a choqué beaucoup

    (e)   Cette plaisanterie, qu'elle fût innocente où méchante, m'a choqué beaucoup

    (f)   Quelles que soient vos explications, je ne veux pas les entendre

    (g)   Je ne veux pas entendre vos explications, quelles qu'elles soient

4   To what extent to the following formulae conform to the more productive patterns of Inversion presented in this chapter?

    (a)   Vive la France!

    (b)   Soit un triangle ABC

    (c)   Puisse-t-il arriver à temps!

    (d)   Vienne le printemps, nous partirons

5   Account for the judgements of the following examples in the light of the comparison between dislocation and complex SUBJ-CL-INV presented in 10.3.3. The examples are given without internal

punctuation (i.e. without the comma/pause which separates dislocated items from the core part of the sentence).

(a) Cela est-il nécessaire?
(b) ?Cela est-ce nécessaire?
(c) Pourquoi cela est-il nécessaire?
(d) ?Cela pourquoi est-ce nécessaire?
(e) *Cela pourquoi est-il nécessaire?
(f) Comment rien ne vous intéresse-t-il?
(g) *Rien comment ne vous intéresse-t-il?
(h) Pourquoi quelqu'un vous insulterait-il?
(i) *Quelqu'un pourquoi vous insulterait-il?

6  In the discussion of *quel* in 10.4.2, it was assumed that there were
underlying structures in which *être* takes a subject NP and a complement phrase. How could the properties of *quel* be accounted for
within the more abstract 'small clause' analysis envisaged in 2.5.2?

7  There are two basic ways in which examples like *Combien as-tu lu de
livres* might be derived:

APPROACH A
*Combien* is extracted directly from the direct object NP leaving
the *de* phrase behind (with subsequent application of SUBJ-CL-
INV):

$$[_{CP} \text{ combien C } [_{IP} \text{ tu } [_{VP} \text{ as lu } [_{NP} \_\_ [_{N'} \text{ de livres}]]]]]$$

APPROACH B
The *de* phrase is first extracted from the direct object NP by the
Extraposition process:

$$[_{CP} \text{ Spec C } [_{IP} \text{ tu } [_{VP} \text{ as lu } [_{NP} \text{ combien } \_\_ ] [_{N'} \text{ de livres}]]]]$$

Subsequently, the whole direct object NP (including the trace of
the extraposed *de* phrase) undergoes QU- movement:

$$[_{CP} [_{NP} \text{ combien } \_\_ ] C [_{IP} \text{ tu } [_{VP} \text{ as lu } \_\_ [_{N'} \text{ de livres}]]]]$$

Discuss the possible derivations of examples like *Combien ont été
publiés de livres?* within these two approaches.

According to Obenauer (1976), examples like *?À combien as-tu* *parlé d'étudiants?* are marginally acceptable for some speakers. How does this observation bear on the choice between the two approaches sketched above?

8   Comment on the contrast between the following sets of examples:

  a  (i)  Jules nous expliquera comment on peut réparer la machine
    (ii)  Jules nous expliquera ce qu'il faut faire
  b  (i)  ?Jules nous informera comment on peut réparer la machine
    (ii)  *Jules nous informera ce qu'il faut faire

9   The following examples illustrate the correspondence between *en*, *dont* and phrases introduced by *de*:

    (i)   Pierre se souvient de cet incident
    (ii)  Pierre s'en souvient
    (iii) un incident dont Pierre se souvient

Construct examples parallel to (ii) and (iii) on the basis of the following sentences and discuss the similarities and differences which emerge from your examples:

    (a)  Marie est partie du restaurant sans payer
    (b)  Max a visité la maison de ce ministre
    (c)  J'ai cassé le pied de la table
    (d)  Le parlement a voté contre l'introduction de cette loi
    (e)  Les implications de cette mesure ne sont pas évidentes
    (f)  Solange a lu trois de ces articles
    (g)  Plusieurs de ces livres sont intéressants
    (h)  Sophie a téléphoné à beaucoup de ces garçons

10  In casual speech one sometimes encounters examples like *l'homme dont j'ai insulté sa femme* where *dont* acts as a complement of a noun which is also introduced by a possessive. This use is generally condemned by traditional grammarians. Thus, Grévisse (1964, p. 479) states:

Le nom sujet, attribut ou objet direct ayant *dont* pour complément ne reçoit pas, en principe, l'adjectif possessif qui ferait pléonasme avec *dont*. On ne dira pas: *L'homme dont sa maison brûle*; *une catastrophe dont nous sommes ses victimes*; *c'est un livre dont j'ignore son auteur*; – mais: . . . *dont* LA *maison brûle*; . . . *dont nous sommes* LES *victimes*; . . . *dont j'ignore* L'*auteur.*

However, later in the section, Grévisse continues:

La règle n'est pas absolue et, dans certains cas, le possessif peut aider à la clarté de la phrase: *Cette malheureuse créature,* DONT *la mort prématurée attriste aujourd'hui* SES *parents. – Un puits rempli de cadavres de petites filles* DONT LEURS *parents se sont débarassées. – Venu à Thonon voir ma mère toujours malade, mais* DONT *la maladie n'a pas interrompu* SON *activité.*

How do the acceptable examples quoted in the second paragraph differ from the 'incorrect' cases presented in the first? Give the underlying structure for the relative clause in each example to make the differences clear.

11  Comment on the interpretations of the expressions introduced by *ce que* or *ce qui* in the following sentences:

   (a)  Je n'ai pas vu ce que vous avez mis dans ma pôche
   (b)  Je ne sais pas ce qui se passe
   (c)  J'ai lu ce que vous m'avez envoyé
   (d)  Je ne peux pas dire ce que Luc a proposé
   (e)  J'ai oublié ce qu'il fallait apporter
   (f)  Je n'ai pas compris ce que vous avez dit

12  Comment on the status and function of *qui* in the following constructions. Is it reasonable to treat the clauses introduced by *qui* as relative clauses?

   (a)  Voilà le train qui arrive
   (b)  Il y a Jules qui est malade
   (c)  J'ai vu Marie qui partait
   (d)  Avec les enfants qui font du bruit, je ne peux pas travailler

**Further reading**

The analysis of Inversion presented in 10.2 is based on Spang-Hanssen (1971) and Kayne (1972); see also Langacker (1972) which appears in the same volume and Atkinson (1973). Traditional accounts of Inversion can be found in Blinkenberg (1969) and Le Bidois (1952). More technical and theoretical discussion of both types of Inversion can be found in various parts of Kayne (1984), especially chapters 1, 3 and 10. Korzen (1983) gives an informal but lucid account of Stylistic-inversion; for more technical discussion, see Kayne & Pollock (1978) and Obenauer (1984). The analysis of complex inversion envisaged in 10.3.6 is based on Rizzi & Roberts (1989); this analysis is criticised on theoretical grounds by Wind (1994).

The general descriptive framework adopted in the discussion of partial questions and relative clauses is based on the proposals of Chomsky (1977) for English; see Radford (1981, chs. 5, 7 and 9) for a rather simpler presentation. Obenauer (1976) presents a detailed account of French interrogatives within this framework, though his treatment of interrogative *que* is rather different from that given in 10.4.1; see also Obenauer (1974) for discussion of constructions with *combien*. The arguments concerning the status of *quel* presented in 10.4.2 are taken from Ruwet (1982, ch. 6). Cornulier (1974a) and Korzen (1985) discuss some of the peculiarities of *pourquoi* in the context of STYL-INV in interrogatives. On the syntax of indirect questions, see Borillo (1976). For a brief survey of the frequency of use of different types of interrogative constructions, see Désirat & Hordé (1976, 5.6) and, from a sociolinguistic perspective, Coveney (1990). On the use of *comme* mentioned in 10.4.4 and 10.6.5 (*Qu'est-ce que vous avez lu comme livres?*), see Delabre (1984).

Relative clauses are studied in detail by Godard (1988). The analysis in this chapter, particularly regarding the status of *que* and *qui*, is based on Kayne (1976), but see Moreau (1971) for an earlier analysis along similar lines. The syntax of *dont* is discussed within a generative framework by Godard (1984), Kupferman (1985) and, briefly, in Couquaux (1981), though all of these papers are fairly technical. For a discussion of non-restrictive relatives, see Huot (1978).

The analysis of exclamative constructions is based largely on Gérard (1980); for further discussion of exclamatives, see Culioli (1974), Milner (1974, 1977), Vinet (1991).

Cleft constructions are discussed in Fradin (1978). For discussion of the syntax and/or pragmatics of some of the other constructions discussed in this chapter see Barnes (1985), Dupont (1985), Fradin (1988), Lambrecht (1988), Larsson (1979), Zaring (1992).

A brief synopsis of the history of many of the constructions discussed in this chapter is given in Harris (1978).

# BIBLIOGRAPHY

Ager, D. E. (1990) *Sociolinguistics and Contemporary French*, Cambridge University Press.

Aissen, J. L. (1979) *The Syntax of Causative Constructions*, New York, Garland.

Andersson, S. (1954) *Études sur la syntaxe et la sémantique du mot français 'tout'*, Lund, CWK Gleerup.

(1960) *Nouvelles études sur la syntaxe et la sémantique du mot français 'tout'*, Lund, CWK Gleerup.

Anscombre, J.-C. (1991a) 'L'article zéro sous préposition', *Langue française* 91: 24–39.

(ed.) (1991b) *Absence de déterminant et déterminant zéro* (*Langages* 102).

Ashby, W. J. (1976) 'The loss of the negative morpheme, *ne*, in Parisian French', *Lingua* 39: 119–37.

(1981) 'The loss of the negative particle *ne* in French: a syntactic change in progress', *Language* 57: 647–87.

(1991) 'When does variation indicate linguistic change in progress?', *Journal of French Language Studies* 1.1: 1–19.

Atkinson, J. C. (1973) *The Two Forms of Subject Inversion in Modern French*, The Hague, Mouton.

Attal, P. (1976) 'À propos de l'indéfini *des*: problèmes de représentation sémantique', *Le français moderne* 44.2: 126–42.

Authier, J.-M. (1992) 'Is French a null subject language in the DP?', *Probus* 4.1: 1–16.

Authier, J.-M., and L. Reed (1991) 'Ergative predicates and dative cliticisation in French causatives', *Linguistic Inquiry* 22: 197–205.

(1992) 'On the syntactic status of French affected datives', *The Linguistic Review* 9.4: 295–311.

Azoulay, A. (1978) 'Article défini et relations anaphoriques en français', *Recherches linguistiques de Vincennes* 7: 5–46.

Azoulay-Vicente, A. (1985) *Les tours comportant l'expression DE + adjectif*, Geneva, Droz.

(1989) 'Cas partitif et quantification à distance', *Recherches linguistiques de Vincennes* 18: 81–100.

Barbaud, P. (1974) 'Constructions superlatives et structures apparentées', *Linguistic Analysis* 2.2: 125–74.

*Bibliography*

(1992) 'Recycling words' in Lauefer & Morgan (1992).

Barnes, B. (1980) 'The notion of "dative" in linguistic theory and the grammar of French', *Linguisticae Investigationes* 4.2: 245–92.

(1985) *The Pragmatics of Left Detachment in Spoken French*, Amsterdam, John Benjamins.

Bartning, I. (1980) *Syntaxe et sémantique des pseudo-adjectifs français*, Stockholm, Almquist and Wiksell International.

Battye, A. (1991) 'Partitive and pseudo-partitive revisited: reflections on the status of *de* in French', *Journal of French Language Studies* 1.1: 21–43.

Battye, A., and A.-M. Hintze (1992) *The French Language Today*, London, Routledge.

Benveniste, E. (1966) *Problèmes de linguistique générale I*, Paris, Gallimard.

Berthonneau, A. M., and P. Cadiot (eds.) (1991) *Prépositions, représentations, référence* (*Langue française* 91).

(eds.) (1993) *Les prépositions: méthodes d'analyse*, Presses Universitaires de Lille.

Blinkenberg, A. (1960) *Le problème de la transitivité en français moderne*, Copenhagen, Munksgaard.

(1969) *L'ordre des mots en français moderne*, Copenhagen, Munksgaard.

Boons, J.-P. (1974) 'Acceptabilité, interprétation et connaissance du monde. A propos du verbe *planter*' in Rohrer & Ruwet (1974), vol. II.

(1984) 'Sceller un piton dans le mur; desceller un piton du mur', *Langue française* 62: 95–128.

(1987) 'La notion sémantique de déplacement dans une classification syntaxique des verbes locatifs', *Langue française* 76: 5–40.

Boons, J.-P., A. Guillet and C. Leclère (1976) *La structure des phrases simples en français*, Geneva, Droz.

Borillo, A. (1976) 'Remarques sur l'interrogation indirecte en français' in Chevalier & Gross (1976).

Borillo, A., J. Tamine and F. Soublin (1974) *Exercices de syntaxe transformationnelle du français*, Paris, Armand Colin.

Burzio, L. (1986) *Italian Syntax*, Dordrecht, Kluwer.

Byrne, L. S. R. and E. L. Churchill (1986) *A Comprehensive French Grammar* (3rd edn revised by G. Price), Oxford, Basil Blackwell.

Bysen, G. (1971) *Subjonctif et hiérarchie*, Odense University Press.

Cadiot, P. (1991a) '*À la hache* ou *avec la hache*? Représentation mentale, expérience située et donation du référent', *Langue française* 91: 7–23.

(1991b) 'De la grammaire à la cognition, la préposition *pour*', *Cahiers de la lexicologie* 58: 63–79.

Cadiot, P., and A. Zribi-Hertz (eds.) (1990) *Aux confins de la grammaire: l'anaphore* (*Langages* 97).

Callebaut, B. (ed.) (1992) *Les négations* (*Langue française* 94).

Cannings, P., and M. Moody (1978) 'A semantic approach to causation in French', *Linguisticae Investigationes* 2.2: 331–62.

Casagrande, J. (1974) '*Sûr* et *certain* en français et en anglais', *Le français moderne* 42: 121–32.

Casagrande, J., and B. Saciuk (eds.) (1972) *Generative Studies in Romance Languages*, Rowley, Mass., Newbury House.

Cellard, J. (1978) *Le subjonctif: comment l'écrire? Quand l'employer?*, Gembloux, Duculot.

Chevalier, J.-C., C. Blanche Benveniste, C. Arrivé and J. Peytard (1964) *Grammaire Larousse du français contemporain*, Paris, Larousse.

Chevalier, J.-C., and M. Gross (eds.) (1976) *Méthodes en grammaire française*, Paris, Klincksieck.

Chomsky, N. (1977) 'On WH-Movement' in P. W. Culicover, T. Wasow and A. Akmajian (eds.) *Formal Syntax*, New York, Academic Press.

(1981) *Lectures on Government and Binding*, Dordrecht, Foris.

Cohen, M. (1965) *Le subjonctif en français contemporain*, Paris, Société d'Édition d'enseignement supérieur.

Comrie, B. (1976) *Aspect*, Cambridge University Press.

(1985) *Tense*, Cambridge University Press.

Connors, K. (1978) 'The meaning of the French subjunctive', *Linguistics* 211: 45–56.

Corblin, F. (1983) 'Défini et démonstratif dans la reprise immédiate', *Le français moderne* 2: 118–34.

(1987) *Indéfini, défini et démonstratif*, Geneva, Droz.

Cornish, F. (1986) *Anaphoric Relations in English and French*, London, Croom Helm.

Cornulier, B. de (1973) 'Sur une règle de déplacement de négation', *Le français moderne* 1: 43–57.

(1974a) '*Pourquoi* et l'inversion du sujet non-clitique' in Rohrer & Ruwet (1974), vol. I.

(1974b) 'Remarques à propos de la négation anticipée', *Le français moderne* 3: 206–16.

Couquaux, D. (1976) 'Une règle de réanalyse en français', *Recherches linguistiques de Vincennes* 4: 32–74.

(1980) 'Place de la transformation MONTÉE dans la syntaxe du français moderne', *Le français moderne* 48.3: 193–218.

(1981) 'French predication and linguistic theory' in May & Koster (1981).

Coveney, A. (1990) 'Variation in interrogatives in spoken French: a preliminary report' in J. N. Green and W. Ayres-Bennett (eds.) *Variation and Change in French. Essays presented to Rebecca Posner on the occasion of her sixtieth birthday*, London, Routledge.

Culioli, A. (1974) 'À propos des énoncés exclamatifs', *Langue française* 22: 6–15.

Danlos, L. (1992) 'Support verb constructions: linguistic properties, representation, translation', *Journal of French Language Studies* 2.1: 1–32.

Dannell, K. J. (1973) *L'emploi des formes fortes des pronoms personnels pour désigner des choses en français moderne*, Acta Universitatis Uppsaliensis, Uppsala, Sweden.

Darmesteter, A. (1922) *A Historical French Grammar*, London, Macmillan.

David, J., and G. Kleiber (eds.) (1989) *Termes massifs et termes comptables*, Paris, Klincksieck.

David, J., and R. Martin (eds.) (1980) *La notion d'aspect*, Paris, Klincksieck.

Delabre, M. (1984) '*Comme* opérateur d'inclusion référentielle', *Linguisticae Investigationes* 8.1: 21–36.

Désirat, C., and T. Hordé (1976) *La langue française au 20e siècle*, Paris, Bordas.

# Bibliography

Dobrovie-Sorin, C. (1986) 'À propos du contraste entre le passif morphologique et *se* moyen dans les tours impersonnels', *Linguisticae Investigationes* 10.2: 289–312.

Dubois, J. (1965) *Grammaire structurale du français: nom et pronom*, Paris, Larousse.

—— (1967) *Grammaire structurale du français: verbe*, Paris, Larousse.

—— (1969) *Grammaire structurale du français: la phrase et les transformations*, Paris, Larousse.

Dubois, J., and F. Dubois-Charlier (1970) *Éléments de linguistique française: syntaxe*, Paris, Larousse.

Ducrot, O. (1970) *La preuve et le dire*, Paris, Mame.

—— (1972) *Dire et ne pas dire*, Paris, Hermann.

—— (1979) 'L'imparfait en français', *Linguistische Berichte* 60: 1–24.

Dupont, N. (1985) *Linguistique du détachement en français*, Berne, P. Lang.

Emonds, J. (1975) 'A transformational analysis of French clitics without positive output constraints', *Linguistic Analysis* 1: 3–24.

—— (1976) *A Transformational Approach to English Syntax*, New York, Academic Press.

—— (1978) 'The verbal complex V'-V in French', *Linguistic Inquiry* 9: 151–75.

Engel, D. M. (1990) *Tense and Text. A Study of French Past Tenses*, London, Routledge.

Eriksson, O. (1979) 'Remarques sur le type *avec un livre à la main*', *Revue romane* 14.2: 217–41.

—— (1994) 'Les prépositions *à* et *avec*', *Revue romane* 29.2: 163–72.

Fauconnier, G. (1974) *La coréférence: syntaxe ou sémantique?*, Paris, Seuil.

—— (1975) 'Polarité syntaxique et sémantique', *Linguisticae Investigationes* 1: 1–37.

—— (1976) 'Complement subject deletion and the analysis of *menacer*' in Hensey & Luján (1976).

—— (1980) *Étude de certains aspects logiques et grammaticaux de la quantification et de l'anaphore en français et en anglais*, Paris, Champion.

Feigenbaum, S. (1992) 'Verbes causants et verbes causatifs dans la formation des verbes pronominaux français: la nouvelle valence ou *se mourir d'ennui*', *Journal of French Language Studies* 2.1: 33–60.

Ferrar, H. (1981) *A French Reference Grammar* (2nd edn), London, Oxford University Press.

Fiengo, R., and M. R. Gitterman (1978) 'Remarks on French clitic order', *Linguistic Analysis* 4: 115–48.

Fradin, B. (1978) 'Les phrases clivées en français: propositions pour une réanalyse', *Recherches linguistiques de Vincennes* 7: 89–132.

—— (1988) 'Approche des constructions à détachement: la reprise interne', *Langue française* 78: 26–56.

Franckel, J.-J. (1989) *Étude de quelques marqueurs aspectuels en français*, Geneva, Droz.

Fuchs, C. (1978) 'De quelques phénomènes syntaxiques et lexicaux d'aspect', *Recherches linguistiques de Vincennes* 5–6: 93–102.

—— (1979) *Vers une théorie des aspects: les systèmes du français et de l'anglais*, Paris, Mouton.

Gaatone, D. (1970) 'La transformation impersonnelle en français', *Le français moderne* 38.4: 389–411.

(1971a) 'Articles et négations', *Revue romane* 6.1: 1–16.

(1971b) *Étude descriptive du système de la négation en français contemporain*, Geneva, Droz.

(1971c) 'Éléments pour une description de *bien* quantifieur', *Revue de linguistique romane* 54: 211–30.

(1975) 'Réflexions sur les verbes pronominaux réfléchis et réciproques', *Folia Linguistica* 8: 199–222.

(1991) 'Un calembour syntaxique en français', *Journal of French Language Studies* 1.1: 45–53.

(1992) '*De* négatif entre la syntaxe et la sémantique', *Langue française* 94: 93–102.

Gaiffe, F., E. Maille, E. Breuil, S. Jahan, R. Wagner and M. Marijon (1936) *Grammaire Larousse du XXe siècle*, Paris, Larousse.

Galmiche, M. (1989) 'À propos de la définitude', *Langages* 94: 7–37.

Gary-Prieur, M.-N. (1994) *Grammaire du nom propre*, Paris, Presses Universitaires de France.

Gérard, J. (1980) *L'exclamation en français: la syntaxe des phrases et des expressions exclamatives*, Tübingen, Max Niemeyer.

Giorgi, A., and G. Longobardi (1991) *The Syntax of Noun Phrases*, Cambridge University Press.

Giry-Schneider, J. (1978) *Les nominalisations en français: l'opérateur 'faire' dans le lexique*, Geneva, Droz.

(1987) *Les prédicats nominaux en français: les phrases simples à verbe support*, Geneva, Droz.

Godard, D. (1984) 'French relative clauses with *dont*; A′ chains and binding principles' in Guéron, Obenauer & Pollock (1984).

(1988) *La syntaxe des relatives en français*, Paris, Éditions du CNRS.

(1992) 'Extraction out of NP in French', *Natural Language and Linguistic Theory* 10: 233–78.

Grévisse, M. (1964) *Le bon usage* (8th edn), Gembloux, Duculot.

(1993) *Le bon usage* (13th edn, revised by A. Goose), Paris/Louvain-la-Neuve, Duculot.

Gross, G. (1989) *Les constructions converses du français*, Geneva, Droz.

(ed.) (1993) *Sur le passif* (*Langages* 109).

Gross, M. (1967) 'Sur une règle de cacophonie', *Langages* 7: 105–19.

(1968) *Grammaire transformationnelle du français. Syntaxe du verbe*, Paris, Larousse.

(1975) *Méthodes en syntaxe*, Paris, Hermann.

(1977) *Grammaire transformationnelle du français. Syntaxe du nom*, Paris, Larousse.

(1978) 'Correspondance entre forme et sens à propos du subjonctif', *Langue française* 39: 49–65.

(1983) 'Sur quelques types de coréférence contrainte', in Herslund, Mørdrup & Sørensen (1983).

Guéron, J. (1983) 'L'emploi "possessif" de l'article défini en français', *Langue française* 39: 66–75.

(1984) 'Inalienable possession, PRO-inclusion and lexical chains', in Guéron et al. (1984).

## Bibliography

(1986) 'Le verbe *avoir*', *Recherches linguistiques de Vincennes* 14–15: 155–88.

Guéron, J, H.-G. Obenauer and J.-Y. Pollock (eds.) (1984) *Grammatical Representation*, Foris, Dordrecht.

Guillaume, G. (1919) *Le problème de l'article et sa solution dans la langue française*, Paris, Hachette.

(1929) *Temps et verbe. Théorie des aspects, des modes et des temps*, Paris, Champion.

Guillemin-Flescher, J. (1981) *Syntaxe comparée du français et de l'anglais: problèmes de traduction*, Paris, Ophrys.

Guillet, A., and C. Leclère (1992) *La structure des phrases simples en français. II, Constructions transitives locatives*, Geneva, Droz.

Haegeman, L. (1991), *Introduction to Government and Binding Theory* (2nd edn), Oxford, Basil Blackwell.

Haff, M. H. (1990) 'Quelques hypothèses sur les constructions hypothétiques', *Revue romane* 25: 35–45.

Harmer, L. C. (1954) *The French Language Today*, London, Hutchinson.

(1979) *Uncertainties in French Grammar* (ed. P. Rickard and T. G. S. Combe), Cambridge University Press.

Harris, M. (1978) *The Evolution of French Syntax: A comparative approach*, London, Longman.

Heldner, C. (1992) 'Sur la quantification négative', *Langue française* 94: 80–92.

Hensey, F. and M. Luján (eds.) (1976) *Current Studies in Romance Linguistics*, Washington D.C., Georgetown University Press.

Herschensohn, J. (1979) 'The French presentational as a base-generated structure', *Studies in Language* 6.2: 193–219.

(1980) 'On clitic placement in French', *Linguistic Analysis* 6.2: 187–219.

(1992a) 'Case marking and French psych-verbs', *Linguisticae Investigationes* 16: 21–40.

(1992b) 'French inalienable binding' in Lauefer & Morgan (1992).

(1993) 'A postfunctionalist perspective on French psych unaccusatives', in W. J. Ashby, M. Mithun, G. Perissinotto and E. Raposo (eds.) *Linguistic Perspectives on the Romance Languages*, Amsterdam, John Benjamins.

Herslund, M. (1983) 'Le datif de la possession inaliénable en français', in Herslund et al. (1983).

(1990) 'Les verbes inaccusatifs comme problème lexicographique', *Cahiers de la lexicologie* 56–7: 35–44.

Herslund, M., O. Mørdrup and F. Sørensen (eds.) (1983) *Analyses grammaticales du français. Études publiées à l'occasion du 50ᵉ anniversaire de Carl Vikner* (*Revue romane numéro spécial 24*), Institut d'Études Romanes, University of Copenhagen.

Horrocks, G. (1987) *Generative Grammar*, London, Longman.

Huot, H. (1978) 'Appositions et relatives appositives', *Recherches linguistiques de Vincennes* 5–6: 103–42.

(1981) *Constructions infinitives du français; le subordonnant 'de'*, Droz, Geneva.

Hurford, J. R. (1994) *Grammar: A student's guide*, Cambridge University Press.

Imbs, P. (1968) *Emploi des temps verbaux en français moderne*, Klincksieck, Paris.

Jones, M. A. (1983) 'Speculations on the expression of movement in French' in J. Durand (ed.) *A Festschrift for Peter Wexler* (University of Essex, Department of Language and Linguistics, Occasional Papers 23), Colchester, University of Essex.

Judge, A., and F. G. Healey (1983) *A Reference Grammar of Modern French*, London, Edward Arnold.

Kampers-Manhe, B., and C. Vet (eds.) (1987) *Etudes de linguistique française offertes à Robert de Dardel par ses amis et collègues*, Amsterdam, Rodopi.

Karolak, S. (1989) *L'article et la valeur du syntagme nominal*, Paris, Presses Universitaires de France.

Kayne, R. S. (1972) 'Subject inversion in French interrogatives', in Casagrande & Saciuk (1972).

(1975) *French Syntax: The transformational cycle*, Cambridge, Mass., MIT Press (French trans: Kayne (1977)).

(1976) 'French relative *que*' in Hensey & Luján (1976).

(1977) *Syntaxe du français*, Paris, Seuil (tr. of Kayne (1975) by P. Attal).

(1979) 'Rightward NP movement in French and English', *Linguistic Inquiry* 10: 710–19.

(1983) 'Le datif en français et en anglais' in Herslund et al. (1983) (English version in Kayne (1984)).

(1984) *Connectedness and Binary Branching*, Foris, Dordrecht.

(1985) 'L'accord du participe passé en français et en italien', *Modèles linguistiques* 7: 73–91.

(1993) 'Toward a modular theory of auxiliary selection', *Studia Linguistica* 47: 3–31.

Kayne, R. S., and J.-Y. Pollock (1978) 'Stylistic Inversion, successive cyclicity and Move-NP in French', *Linguistic Inquiry* 9: 595–621.

Keyser, S. J. (ed.) (1978) *Recent Transformational Studies in European Languages*, Cambridge, Mass., MIT Press.

Kleiber, G. (1981) *Problèmes de référence: descriptions définies et noms propres*, Paris, Klincksieck.

(1984) 'Sur la sémantique des descriptions démonstratives', *Linguisticae Investigationes* 8.1: 63–86.

(1990) *L'article 'le' générique. La généricité sur le mode massif*, Geneva, Droz.

(1992a) 'Article défini, unicité et permanence', *Revue romane* 27: 60–89.

(1992b) 'Quand le nom propre prend l'article: le cas des noms propres métonymiques', *Journal of French Language Studies* 2.2: 185–205.

Korzen, H. (1983) 'La position du sujet dans les propositions interrogatives en français' in Herslund et al. (1983).

(1985) *'Pourquoi' et l'inversion finale en français: étude sur le statut de l'adverbial de cause et l'anatomie de la construction tripartite* (*Revue romane*, numéro spécial 30), Copenhagen, Munksgaards.

Korzen, H., and C. Vikner (1980) 'La structure profonde des temps verbaux en français moderne', *Linguisticae Investigationes* 4.1: 103–30.

Kupferman, L. (1979a) 'L'article partitif existe-t-il?', *Le français moderne* 47: 11–16.

(1979b) 'Les constructions *il est médecin* / *c'est un médecin*: essai de solution', *Cahiers de linguistique* 9: 131–64.

(1980) '«Il y a une place de libre»: study of a construction', *Linguistics* 18: 821–48.

(1985) 'Note sur *dont, de qui/de quoi/duquel*', *Recherches linguistiques de Vincennes* 13: 5–32.

(1991) 'L'aspect du group nominal et l'extraction de *en*', *Le français moderne* 59: 113–47.

(1995) 'La construction passive en *se faire*', *Journal of French Language Studies* 5.1: 57–83.

Labelle, M. (1990) 'Unaccusatives and pseudo-unaccusatives in French', *Proceedings of the Northeastern Linguistics Society (NELS)* 20: 303–17.

(1992) 'Change of state and valency', *Journal of Linguistics* 28: 375–414

Lagae, V. (1990) 'Les caractéristiques aspectuelles de la construction réflexive ergative', *Travaux de linguistique* 20: 23–42.

Lambrecht, K. (1981) *Topic, Antitopic and Verb Agreement in Non-standard French*, Amsterdam, John Benjamins.

(1988) 'Presentational cleft constructions in spoken French' in J. Haiman and S. A. Thompson (eds.) *Clause Combining in Grammar and Discourse*, Amsterdam, John Benjamins.

Langacker, R. W. (1972) 'French interrogatives revisited' in Casagrande & Saciuk (1972).

Larsson, E. (1979) *La dislocation en français: étude de syntaxe générative*, Lund, CWK Gleerup.

Lasnik, H., and J. Uriagerika (1988) *A Course in GB Syntax: Lectures on Binding and Empty Categories*, Cambridge, Mass., MIT Press.

Lauefer, C., and T. E. Morgan (eds.) (1992) *Theoretical Analyses in Romance Languages*, Amsterdam, John Benjamins.

Le Bidois, G., and R. Le Bidois (1971) *Syntaxe du français moderne*, 2 vols (2nd edn), Paris, Éditions A. et J. Picard.

Le Bidois, R. (1952) *L'inversion du sujet dans la prose contemporain*, Paris, Éditions d'Artrey.

Leclère, C. (1976) 'Datifs syntaxiques et datif éthique', in Chevalier & Gross (1976).

(1978) 'Sur une classe de verbes datifs', *Langue française* 39: 66–75.

Leeman, D. (ed.) (1990) *Sur les compléments circonstantiels* (*Langue française* 86).

Legendre, G. (1989) 'Unaccusativity in French', *Lingua* 79: 95–164.

Lodge, R. A. (1993) *French: From dialect to standard*, London, Routledge.

Long, M. E. (1976) 'French infinitival complementizers and their place in a generative grammar', in Hensey & Luján (1976).

Lyons, C. (1982) 'Pronominal voice in French' in Vincent & Harris (1982).

Mansion, J. E. (1952) *A Grammar of Present-day French*, London, Harrap.

Martin, R. (1970) 'La transformation impersonnelle en français', *Revue de linguistique romane* 34: 377–94.

(1971) *Temps et aspect*, Paris, Klincksieck.

Martinon, P. (1927) *Comment on parle en français*, Paris, Larousse.

Mauger, G. (1968) *Grammaire pratique du français d'aujourd'hui* (7th edn), Paris, Hachette.

May, R. and J. Koster (eds.) (1981) *Levels of Syntactic Representation*, Dordrecht, Foris.

Milner, J.-C. (1973) *Arguments linguistiques*, Paris, Mame.

(1974) 'Les exclamatifs et le Complementizer', in Rohrer & Ruwet (1974), vol. I.

(1977) 'De l'interprétation exclamative comme valeur sémantique résiduelle' in M. Ronat (ed.) *Langue: théorie générative étendue*, Paris, Hermann.

(1978) *De la syntaxe à l'interprétation*, Seuil, Paris.

(1979) 'Le système de la négation en français et l'opacité du sujet', *Langue française* 44: 80–105 (also in Milner (1982)).

(1982) *Ordres et raisons de langue*, Paris, Seuil.

Moeschler, J. (ed.) (1993) *Temps, référence et inférence* (*Langages* 112).

Molendijk, A. (1985) 'Point référentielle et imparfait', *Langue française* 67: 78–94.

(1987) 'Point référentielle et implication temporelle: le passé simple et l'imparfait du français' in Kampers-Manhe & Vet (1987).

(1990) *Le passé simple et l'imparfait: une approche reichenbachienne*, Amsterdam, Rodopi.

Moreau, M-L. (1971) '«L'homme que je crois qui est venu»; *qui, que*: relatifs et conjonctions', *Langue française* 11: 77–90.

(1976) *C'est. Études transformationnelles*, Presses Universitaires de Mons.

Morin, J.-Y. (1978) 'Une théorie interprétative des causatives en français', *Linguisticae Investigationes* 2: 363–417.

Morin, Y.-C. (1974) 'En-avant, en arrière' in M. W. Lagaly, R. A. Fox and A. Bruck (eds.) *Papers from the Tenth Regional Meeting*, Chicago Linguistics Society.

(1976) '*De ces*: the lexicalisation of a syntactic expression', *Linguistic Inquiry* 7: 706–7.

Moritz, L., and D. Valois (1994) 'Pied-piping and Specifier–head agreement', *Linguistic Inquiry* 25.4: 667–707.

Mouchaweh, L. (1984) 'En faveur des "small clauses"', *Recherches linguistiques de Vincennes* 12: 92–124.

Muller, C. (1975) 'Remarques syntactico-sémantiques sur certains adverbes de temps', *Le français moderne* 43.1: 12–38.

(1977) 'À propos de *de* partitif', *Linguisticae Investigationes* 1: 167–95.

(1978) 'La négation explétive dans les constructions complétives', *Langue française* 39: 76–103.

(1983) 'Les comparatives du français et la négation', *Linguisticae Investigationes* 7.2: 271–316.

(1984) 'L'association négative', *Langue française* 62: 59–94.

(1991) *La négation en français. Syntaxe, sémantique et éléments de comparaison avec les autres langues romanes*, Geneva, Droz.

Nique, C. (1974) *Initiation méthodique à la grammaire générative*, Paris, Armand Colin.

Noailly, M. (1990) *Le substantif épithète*, Paris, Presses Universitaires de France.

Nølke, H. (1983) *Les adverbes paradigmatisants: fonction et analyse* (*Revue romane numéro spécial* 23), Copenhagen, Akademisk Forlag.

## Bibliography

Nordahl, H. (1969) *Les systèmes du subjonctif corrélatif: étude sur l'emploi des modes dans la complétive en français moderne*, Bergen/Oslo, Universitetsverlaget.

Obenauer, H.-G. (1974) 'Combien je suppose qu'il faut de règles pour isoler *combien*' in Rohrer & Ruwet (1974), vol. I.

(1976) *Études de syntaxe interrogative du français*, Tübingen, Max Niemeyer.

(1983) 'Une quantification non canonique: la "quantification à distance"', *Langue française* 58: 66–88.

(1984) 'Connectedness, variables and stylistic inversion in French' in Guéron et al. (1984).

Offord, M. (1990) *Varieties of Contemporary French*, Basingstoke, Macmillan.

Olié, A. (1984) 'L'hypothèse de l'inaccusatif en français', *Linguisticae Investigationes* 8: 363–401.

Ouhalla, J. (1994) *Introducing Transformational Grammar*, London, Edward Arnold.

Péry-Woodley, M.-P. (1991) 'French and English passives in the construction of text', *Journal of French Language Studies* 1.1: 55–70.

Pica, P. (1984) 'Subject, tense and truth: towards a modular approach to binding', in Guéron *et al.* (1984).

Picabia, L. (1975) *Éléments de grammaire générative: applications au français*, Paris, Armand Colin.

(1976) 'En marge de Tough-Movement' in Chevalier & Gross (1976).

(1978a) *Les constructions adjectivales en français. Systématique transformationnelle*, Geneva, Droz.

(1978b), 'Sur une règle non-transformationnelle des prédicats adjectivaux', *Recherches linguistiques de Vincennes* 7: 133–45.

(ed.) (1986) *Déterminants et détermination* (*Langue française* 72).

Picabia, L., and A. Zribi-Hertz (1981) *Découvrir la grammaire française*, Paris, CEDIC.

Picone, M. D. (1992) 'Compound word formation in French: one hundred years later' in Lauefer & Morgan (1992).

Pijnenburg, H., and A. Hulk (1989) 'Datives in French causatives', *Probus* 1.3: 259–82.

Pinchon, J. (1972) *Les pronoms adverbiaux 'en' et 'y'*, Geneva, Droz.

Pinkham, J. E. (1985) *The formation of comparative clauses in French and English*, New York, Garland.

Pollock, J.-Y. (1978) 'Trace theory and French syntax', in Keyser (1978).

(1979) 'Réanalyse et constructions impersonelles', *Recherches linguistiques de Vincennes* 8: 72–130.

(1981) 'On Case and impersonal constructions' in May & Koster (1981).

(1982) 'Accord, chaînes impersonnelles et variables', *Linguisticae Investigationes* 7: 131–81.

(1983) 'Sur quelques propriétés des phrases copulatives en français', *Langue française* 58: 89–125.

(1984) 'On Case and the syntax of infinitives in French' in Guéron et al. (1984).

(1989) 'Verb movement, Universal Grammar and the structure of IP', *Linguistic Inquiry* 20: 365–424.

Poplack, S. (1992) 'Inherent variability of the French subjunctive' in Lauefer & Morgan (1992).

Posner, R. (1985) 'Post-verbal negation in Non-Standard French: a historical and comparative view', *Romance Philology* 39: 170–97.

Price, G. (1971) *The French Language: Present and past*, London, Edward Arnold.

Price, S. (1990) *Comparative Constructions in Spanish and French Syntax*, London, Routledge.

Quicoli, A. C. (1976) 'Conditions on quantifier movement in French', *Linguistic Inquiry* 7: 583–607.

Radford, A. (1978) 'Agentive causatives in Romance: accessibility versus passivisation', *Journal of Linguistics* 14: 35–58.

(1981) *Transformational Syntax: A student's guide to Chomsky's Extended Standard Theory*, Cambridge University Press.

(1988) *Transformational Grammar: A first course*, Cambridge University Press.

Reed, L. (1991) 'The thematic and syntactic structure of French causatives', *Probus* 3: 317–60.

(1992) 'Remarks on word order in causative constructions', *Linguistic Inquiry* 23: 164–72.

Reichenbach, H. (1947) *Elements of Symbolic Logic*, New York, The Free Press.

Réquédat, F. (1980) *Les constructions verbales avec l'infinitif*, Paris, Hachette.

Rickard, P. (1989) *A History of the French Language* (2nd edn), London, Unwin Hyman.

Riegel, M. (1985) *L'adjectif attribut*, Paris, Presses Universitaires de France.

Rivière, N. (1981) *La construction impersonnelle en français contemporain*, Paris, Éditions Jean-Favard.

Rizzi, L., and I. Roberts (1989) 'Complex Inversion in French', *Probus* 1: 1–30.

Rohrer, C., and N. Ruwet (eds.) (1974) *Actes du colloque franco-allemand de grammaire transformationnelle*, 2 vols., Tübingen, Max Niemeyer.

Ronat, M. (1979) 'Pronoms topiques et pronoms distinctifs', *Langue française* 44: 105–27.

Rooryck, J. (1990) 'Montée et contrôle: une nouvelle analyse', *Le français moderne* 58.1: 1–27.

Rosenberg, S. N. (1970) *Modern French 'ce'*, The Hague/Paris, Mouton.

Rouveret, A. (1977) 'Les consécutives: forme et interprétation', *Linguisticae Investigationes* 1.1: 197–234.

(1978) 'Result clauses and conditions on rules' in Keyser (1978).

(1980) 'Sur la notion de proposition finie. Gouvernement et inversion', *Recherches linguistiques de Vincennes* 9: 76–140.

Rouveret, A., and J.-R. Vergnaud (1980) 'Specifying reference to the subject: French causatives and conditions on representations', *Linguistic Inquiry* 11.1: 97–202.

Rowlett, P. (1993) 'On the syntactic derivation of negative sentence adverbials', *Journal of French Language Studies* 3.1: 36–69.

Ruwet, N. (1967) *Introduction à la grammaire générative*, Paris, Plon.

(1969) *À propos des prépositions de lieu en français* in C. Hyart (ed.) *Mélanges Fohalle*, Gembloux, Duculot (also in Ruwet (1982)).

Bibliography

(1972) *Théorie syntaxique et syntaxe du français*, Paris, Seuil.

(1975) 'Montée du sujet et extraposition', *Le français moderne*, 43.2: 97–134 (also in Ruwet (1982); English version Ruwet (1976)).

(1976) 'Subject raising and extraposition' in Hensey & Luján (1976). (tr. of Ruwet (1975)).

(1982) *Grammaire des insultes et autres études*, Paris, Seuil.

(1983a) 'Montée et contrôle: une question à revoir', in Herslund et al. (1983).

(1983b) 'Du bon usage des expressions idiomatiques dans l'argumentation en syntaxe générative', *Recherches linguistiques de Vincennes* 11: 6–84.

(1989) 'Weather verbs and the unaccusative hypothesis' in J. DeCesaris and C. Kirschner (eds.) *Studies in Romance Linguistics*, Amsterdam, John Benjamins.

(1990) '*En* et *y*: deux clitiques pronominaux antilogophoriques', *Langages* 97: 51–81.

(1991) *Syntax and Human Experience*, Chicago University Press.

Sanders, C. (ed.) (1992) *French Today: Language in its social context*, Cambridge University Press.

Sandfeld, K. (1965a) *Syntaxe du français contemporain: les propositions subordonnées*, Paris, Champion (first published 1936).

(1965b) *Syntaxe du français contemporain: l'infinitif*, Geneva, Droz (first published 1943).

(1970) *Syntaxe du français contemporain: les pronoms*, Paris, Champion (first published 1928).

Schlyter, S. (1974) 'Une hiérarchie d'adverbes et leurs distributions – par quelles transformations?' in Rohrer & Ruwet (1974), vol. II.

Schwarze, C. (ed.) (1981) *Analyse des prépositions*, Tübingen, Max Niemeyer.

Sells, P. (1987) *Lectures on Contemporary Syntactic Theories*, Stanford, Center for the Study of Language and Information.

Skårup, P. (1994) 'La place de *de* en français contemporain: devant ou dans le syntagme nominal?' *Revue romane* 29.2: 195–211.

Sorace, A. (1993) 'Unaccusativity and auxiliary choice in non-native grammars of Italian and French: asymmetries and predictable indeterminacy', *Journal of French Language Studies* 3.1: 71–93.

Spang-Hanssen, E. (1963) *Les prépositions incolores du français*, Copenhagen, Gad.

(1971) 'Le classement des formes de l'inversion du sujet en français moderne', *Revue romane* 6.1: 63–73.

(1983) 'La notion de verbe auxiliaire' in Herslund et al. (1983).

(1993) 'De la structure des syntagmes à celle de l'espace', *Langages* 110: 12–25.

Sportiche, D. (1988) 'A theory of floating quantifiers and its corollaries for constituent structure', *Linguistic Inquiry* 19: 425–49.

Stati, S. (1973) 'Autour du système des adjectives', *Revue romane* 8: 286–93.

Sten, H. (1952) *Les temps du verbe fini (indicatif) en français moderne*, Copenhagen, Munksgaard.

Sueur, J.-P. (1977) 'À propos de restrictions de sélection: les infinitifs *devoir* et *pouvoir*', *Linguisticae Investigationes* 1.2: 375–410.

(1978) 'Adverbes de modalité et verbes modaux épistémiques', *Recherches linguistiques de Vincennes* 5–6: 235–72.

Tasmowski-De Ryck, L. (1985) 'L'imparfait avec et sans rupture', *Langue française*, 67: 59–77.

(1990) '...*en semble*... ou ...*semble en*...', *Le français moderne* 58.1: 28–42.

Tasmowski-De Ryck, L., and H. van Oevelen (1987) 'Le causatif pronominal', *Revue romane* 22.1: 40–58.

Tucker, G. R., W. E. Lambert and A. A. Rigault (1977) *The French Speaker's Skill with Grammatical Gender*, The Hague, Mouton.

Van de Velde, D. (1994) 'Le défini et l'indéfini', *Le français moderne* 62.1: 11–35.

Vandeloise, C. (1986) *L'espace en français*, Paris, Seuil.

(ed.) (1993) *La couleur des prépositions* (*Langages* 110).

Verheugd-Daatzelaar, E. (1990) *Subject Arguments and Predicate Nominals. A Study of French Copular Sentences with Two NPs*, Amsterdam, Rodopi.

Verleuten, S. P. (1979) 'The semantic interpretation of French verb tenses in adverbial clauses', *Linguisticae Investigationes* 3.2: 355–74.

Vet, C. (1980) *Temps, aspects et adverbes de temps: essai de sémantique formelle*, Droz, Geneva.

(ed.) (1985) *La pragmatique des temps verbaux* (*Langue française* 67), Larousse, Paris.

Vet, C., and A. Molendijk (1986) 'The discourse functions of the past tenses of French' in V. Lo Cascio and C. Vet (eds.) *Temporal Structure in Sentence and Discourse*, Foris, Dordrecht.

Vetters, C. (1989) 'Grammaticalité au passé récent', *Linguisticae Investigationes* 13: 369–86.

(ed.) (1993) *Le temps, de la phrase au texte*, Presses Universitaires de Lille.

Vinay, J. P., and J. Darbelnet (1958) *Stylistique comparée du français et de l'anglais*, Paris, Didier.

Vincent, N. (1982) 'The development of the auxiliaries HABERE and ESSERE in Romance' in Vincent & Harris (1982).

Vincent, N., and M. Harris (eds.) (1982) *Studies in the Romance Verb*, London, Croom Helm.

Vinet, M.-T. (1991) 'French non-verbal exclamative constructions', *Probus* 3: 77–100.

Wagner, R., and J. Pinchon (1962) *Grammaire du français classique et moderne*, Paris, Hachette.

Walter, H. (1988) *Le français dans tous les sens*, Paris, Robert Laffont.

(1994) *French Inside Out*, London, Routledge (tr. of Walter (1988), by P. Fawcett).

Wartburg, W. von, and P. Zumthor (1973) *Précis de syntaxe du français moderne*, Berne, Francke.

Wehrli, E. (1986) 'On some properties of French clitic *se*' in H. Borer (ed.) *The Syntax of Pronominal Clitics*, Syntax and Semantics 19, New York, Academic Press.

Williams, E. (1994) 'A reinterpretation of evidence for verb movement in French' in D. Lightfoot and N. Hornstein (eds.) (1994) *Verb Movement*, Cambridge University Press.

*Bibliography*

Wilmet, M. (1976) *Études de morpho-syntaxe verbale*, Paris, Klincksieck.

(1986) *La détermination nominale*, Paris, Presses Universitaires de France.

(1991) 'L'aspect en français: essai de synthèse', *Journal of French Language Studies* 1.2: 209–22

Wind, M. de (1994) 'Against V-to-C in French complex inversion' in M. L. Mazzola (ed.) *Issues and Theory in Romance Linguistics*, Washington D.C., Georgetown University Press.

Zaring, L. (1992) 'Extensions of R-binding' in Lauefer & Morgan (1992).

Zribi-Hertz, A. (1978) '*Economisons-nous*: à propos d'une classe de formes réflexives métonymiques en français', *Langue française* 39: 104–28.

(1980) 'Coréférence et pronoms réfléchis: notes sur le contraste *lui/lui-même* en français' *Linguisticae Investigationes* 4.1: 131–79.

(1982) 'La construction "se-moyen" du français et son statut dans le triangle: moyen – passif – réfléchi', *Linguisticae Investigationes* 6: 345–401.

(1983) 'Orphan prepositions in French', Indiana University Linguistics Club.

(1987) 'La réflexivité ergative en français', *Le français moderne* 55: 23–54.

# INDEX

549